Springer Proceedings in Business and Economics

Springer Proceedings in Business and Economics brings the most current research presented at conferences and workshops to a global readership. The series features volumes (in electronic and print formats) of selected contributions from conferences in all areas of economics, business, management, and finance. In addition to an overall evaluation by the publisher of the topical interest, scientific quality, and timeliness of each volume, each contribution is refereed to standards comparable to those of leading journals, resulting in authoritative contributions to the respective fields. Springer's production and distribution infrastructure ensures rapid publication and wide circulation of the latest developments in the most compelling and promising areas of research today.

The editorial development of volumes may be managed using Springer Nature's innovative EquinOCS, a proven online conference proceedings submission, management and review system. This system is designed to ensure an efficient timeline for your publication, making Springer Proceedings in Business and Economics the premier series to publish your workshop or conference volume.

This book series is indexed in SCOPUS.

Timothy Jung · M. Claudia tom Dieck ·
Seok Chan Jeong · Sung-Hee Kim · Daniel Sahl ·
S. J. Kim
Editors

XR and Metaverse

Proceedings of the 9th International XR-Metaverse Conference 2024, Busan, South Korea

Springer

Editors
Timothy Jung
Faculty of Business and Law
Manchester Metropolitan University
Manchester, UK

M. Claudia tom Dieck
Faculty of Business and Law
Manchester Metropolitan University
Manchester, UK

Seok Chan Jeong
Faculty of Artificial Intelligence
Dong-Eui University
Busan, Korea (Republic of)

Sung-Hee Kim
Faculty of Artificial Intelligence
Dong-Eui University
Busan, Korea (Republic of)

Daniel Sahl
University of Nevada Las Vegas
Las Vegas, NV, USA

S. J. Kim
University of Nevada Las Vegas
Las Vegas, NV, USA

ISSN 2198-7246 ISSN 2198-7254 (electronic)
Springer Proceedings in Business and Economics
ISBN 978-3-031-77974-9 ISBN 978-3-031-77975-6 (eBook)
https://doi.org/10.1007/978-3-031-77975-6

This Springer imprint is published by the registered company Springer Nature Switzerland AG
The registered company address is: Gewerbestrasse 11, 6330 Cham, Switzerland

Scientific Committee

David Finken, ETH Zurich
Carlos Flavian, University of Zaragoza
Alba García-Milon, University of La Rioja
Naji Gharibi, Victoria University of Wellington
Ricard Gras, Captic.io
João Guerreiro, ISCTE-IUL
Shashi Gupta, Eudoxia Research University
Ramy Hammady, University of Essex
Danny Han, Zuyd University of Applied Sciences
Tilo Hartmann, Vrije Universiteit (VU) Amsterdam
Ronald Haynes, University of Cambridge
Jonas Heller, University of Maastricht
Tim Hilken, University of Maastricht
Linda Hirsch, Fraunhofer FIThan
Dominik O. W. Hirschberg, University of the Bundeswehr Munich
Katherine Hoolahan, VR Healthy
Sergio Ibáñez-Sánchez, University of Zaragoza
Ryan Johnston, Ulster University
Timothy Jung, Manchester Metropolitan University
Tuulikki Keskitalo, Lapland University of Applied Sciences
Alexander Kies, RWTH Aachen University
Sunghak Kim, National Cancer Center, Korea
Byung-Gyu Kim, Sookmyung Women's University
Sung-Hee Kim, Dong-Eui University
Maksym Koghut, Manchester Metropolitan University
Anthony Kong, The Hong Kong Polytechnic University
Nina Krey, Rowan University
Anna Krispin, Zuyd University of Applied Sciences
Harish Kumar, Great Lakes Institute of Management
Vladimir Kuts, Tallinn University of Technology
Ján Lacko, Pan-European University Bratislava
Chun-I Lee, National Taiwan University of Arts
Jaein Lee, Dong-Eui University
Gunnar Liestøl, University of Oslo
Maria Alesanco Llorente, University of La Rioja
Adele Magnelli, ETT S.p.A.
Dominik Mahr, University of Maastricht
Ryan Mathew, University of Leeds
Tj Matthews, i3 Simulations
Natalia Medrano, University of La Rioja
Cynthia Mejia, University of Central Florida
Andy Miah, Salford University
Deepanjali Mishra, Kalinga Institute of Industrial Technology
Ash Murphy, Manchester Metropolitan University
Raziye Nevzat, Eastern Mediterranean University

Preface

The year 2024 marked a significant milestone for the International XR-Metaverse Conference as it ventured beyond its traditional Western European and North American settings to the vibrant city of Busan, South Korea. This inaugural Asian edition served as a testament to the global reach and growing influence of immersive technologies.

As an annual flagship event of the International Association of Immersive Technology Innovation (IAITI), the conference continues to serve as a pivotal platform for industry leaders, researchers, and innovators to converge, share insights, and drive the advancement of the immersive technology landscape. The theme of "Metaverse: Where Reality Meets Imagination" aptly encapsulated the conference's focus on exploring the intersection of physical and digital worlds.

This volume, a collection of papers presented at the 9th International XR-Metaverse Conference, offers a comprehensive overview of the latest research, trends, and innovations in the field. The contributions from esteemed experts provide valuable insights into the challenges, opportunities, and potential applications of immersive technologies. We hope that this compilation will serve as a valuable resource for researchers, industry professionals, and policymakers seeking to navigate the exciting and rapidly evolving landscape of the metaverse.

As we look to the future, the potential of immersive technologies is boundless. By fostering collaboration, innovation, and ethical considerations, we can harness the power of the metaverse to create more immersive, engaging, and inclusive experiences for individuals and societies worldwide.

Manchester, UK	Timothy Jung
Manchester, UK	M. Claudia tom Dieck
Busan, Korea (Republic of)	Seok Chan Jeong
Busan, Korea (Republic of)	Sung-Hee Kim
Las Vegas, USA	Daniel Sahl
Las Vegas, USA	S. J. Kim

Contents

XR in Sports and Entertainment

The Added Value of Virtual Reality Headsets on Esport Viewing Experience

Karsten Beeker, Miruna Doicaru, and Marnix S. van Gisbergen

Abstract With a growing interest in immersive technologies to elevate digital spectating experiences, Virtual Reality (VR) is viewed by many academics and industry actors as the future of esport spectatorship. The majority of the esport fans are the same group that show interest in immersive technologies as VR. This group is, therefore, expected to accept the technology and adopt it in their spectating experience. However, given the fact that this target group is mostly used to utilize interactive VR for gaming purposes, it is not clear how they would experience a passive non-interactive VR experience, and to what extent the technology could contribute to enhancing their viewing experience. This study compared two versions of the same summary recording of the livestream of an esport competition: a 2D version and a VR version: 92 participants watched the esport competition either on a 2D screen or in VR, then they had to answer questions regarding their experience. Compared to 2D, the VR experience scored higher on immersion, presence, social presence, emotional contagion, and enjoyment. This paper confirms the potential of VR to efficiently enhance the digital spectating experiences of esports, while highlighting the need for more research in how to produce the content to best fit VR and increase VR adoption intention.

Keywords Virtual reality · Esport · Spectatorship · Experience

1 Introduction

As the number of consumers engaging in live video game streaming and esports continues to climb into the millions (Migliore 2021; Sahin 2023; Yao 2022), there is a growing interest in exploring immersive technologies to elevate digital spectator experiences, especially in the application of VR in esports (Cacho-Elizondo et al. 2020; Cranmer et al. 2021; Miah et al. 2020; Sahin 2023). VR has the potential to provide a sense of presence, embodiment and physicality to digital sports, changing

K. Beeker · M. Doicaru · M. S. van Gisbergen (✉)
BUAS—Breda University of Applied Sciences, Breda, The Netherlands
e-mail: Gisbergen.m@buas.nl

T. Jung et al. (eds.), *XR and Metaverse*, Springer Proceedings in Business and Economics, https://doi.org/10.1007/978-3-031-77975-6_1

a passive viewing experience into a more dynamic experience that could attract more diverse audiences. In addition, there seems to be an overlap between the audiences of esports and the users of VR. Both seem technology enthusiasts and show interest in videogames (Cacho-Elizondo et al. 2020), suggesting that esports spectators are open to embed VR in their viewing experiences. However, many producers lack VR (e)sports experience and are still experimenting with different strategies to make reach and engage audiences. Moreover, VR investments come at slow pace (Mainelli 2023), due to the small size of the audience owning a VR headset and even a decreasing growth in sales (Alsop 2023, 2024). To overcome these hurdles a priority is to gain more information about the added value of VR over 2D screen viewing. This study is focused on the comparison between VR and 2D screen viewings of a recorded streaming of a major esports tournament. There are many reasons why VR can increase a spectating experience of esports. VR can offer a higher level of interactivity than a 2D screen through its capacity to be more immersive, by simply allowing the audience the freedom to watch the game from different perspectives, and changing points of view, giving more freedom to look around. VR creates proximity, participation (interactivity), and thus presence; a feeling of being closer to and inside the esports world (Kriglstein et al. 2020; Pallavicini et al. 2019; van Gisbergen 2016; Vincent and Frewen 2023). This is especially important for fans viewing (e)sports events (Lai et al. 2022). This feeling of presence links with a key reason to visit real life events: sharing social experiences (Stander and Beer 2016; Kim and Mao 2021; Lai et al. 2022; Smith and Smith-Ditizio 2021; Sjöblom et al. 2020; Pu et al. 2022). On the other hand, gamers are used to interact with other players and move within VR environments. A passive VR experience might be disappointing and even confusing, not knowing where or how to look at the content provided. However, no study investigated the impact VR may have on social presence and emotional contagion when viewing esports tournaments. The goal of this research is to compare 2D screen and VR headset viewing experiences around streamed esports events, focusing on differences in immersion, presence, social presence, emotional contagion, and enjoyment.

2 Literature Review

Research that focuses on the comparison between 2D and VR productions usually reveal positive effects of VR compared to 2D. Multiple studies revealed the capacity of VR to produce presence in the environments it creates, and at higher levels than 2D images and videos (e.g., Taufik et al. 2021; Xu et al. 2021; Ambika et al. 2023), showing high capacity of persuasion and leading to behavioural change through its content. Also, within the domain of sport, the added value of VR has been demonstrated. For instance, a study around the viewing of basketball sport games, showed the added value in presence, vividness, and flow of VR over traditional 2D viewing (Kim and Ko 2019; Vincent and Frewen 2023). Other studies revealed different brain activity for VR and 2D screens when watching sport (Kweon et al. 2018), often showing a stronger emotional arousal for VR compared to 2D (Tian and Zhang 2021). VR increased immersion, presence and positive feelings when playing games (Cummings and Bailenson 2016; Pallavicini and Pepe 2019; Roettl and Terlutter 2018; Smith and Neff 2018), even when VR did not allow for interactions, but just imagined interactions (Regenbrecht and Schubert 2002). However, it remains unclear how a group of people that are used to the most interactive forms of VR for gaming are affected by the streaming of esports tournaments in VR, produced as non-interactive videos. It is important to understand if in this context and for this specific target group VR can enhance the spectatorship experience by increasing *presence*, *immersion* and *enjoyment*, important markers of a positive spectating experience (e.g., Pavic et al. 2023). Another important marker of sports viewership experience is social presence (Short et al. 1976), which is the sense of being and interacting with another in a virtual or mediated environment. Social presence is particularly important when digitally viewing sports events, including esport, as the socialization opportunities represent one of the biggest motivators of following sports events in general (e.g., Qian et al. 2020; Yu et al. 2022; Kim et al. 2019; Kim and Mao 2021). An elevated level of social presence could translate into a feeling of being in the tournament arena with the other fans, sharing the space, the experience, and their emotions through emotional contagion. Emotional contagion is highly relevant when spectating sports or any events together with a group, and it has a significant impact on the quality of the experience: emotional contagion was found to enhance enjoyment and emotional experiences when watching movies with a group (Cohen et al. 2016), and when being surrounded by a virtual audience during a sports event (Yin et al. 2013). Similarly, emotional contagion was found to promote engagement during live music events (Garrito and MacRitchie 2020).

Immersion. VR has been established as an immersive technology in many fields (White et al. 2015; Pallavicini and Pepe 2019; Yao and Kim 2019). Immersion refers to the feeling of being introduced, body and mind, in a different environment, this environment being produced by a technology. Unlike presence, immersion does not refer solely to a feeling of being present in an environment created by technology, but it also captures a mental involvement with what happens in that environment, a form of interaction with that environment (MacMahan 2003). The more senses a technology stimulates, the more immersive it is considered, placing VR on an elevated level of immersion (Ranasinghe et al. 2013). And the more encompassing a technology is, such as the larger the screen, the more immersive it is (Lombard et al. 2000; Thomson et al. 2012; Hou et al. 2012; Rigby et al. 2016; Ahn et al. 2014; Bruder et al. 2016). Research showed VR to exhibit higher levels of immersion than a 2D screen in domains such as games (Pallavicini and Pepe 2019; Pallavicini et al. 2019), while interactivity has been established as an important factor of immersion (Komarac and Ozretić Došen 2022; Mütterlein 2018). This means that interactive VR esports experiences are more likely to be immersive than non-interactive VR and 2D esports experiences. However, in certain contexts non-interactive VR experience, such as a 360° video also leads to more immersion compared to 2D screen experiences. Thoravi Kumaravel and Wilson (2022), compared three modes of spectating VR games competitions: one in VR and two different modes in 2D. The VR spectating experience was reported to be significantly more immersive. However, the spectating experience in that study had some level of interactivity: viewers could choose between various camera positions and different points of view. The VR spectating in our study does not give the audience the possibility to choose what they will see, instead it is pre-directed. Despite this lower level of interactivity, we argue based on previous findings that in the VR experience the audiences will feel more cognitively engaged with the game and more immersed. We therefore hypothesize that: **(H1)** *Spectating the streaming of an esports competition in VR will lead to more immersion than spectating it on a 2D screen.*

Presence. This paper views presence as spatial presence: the feeling of being relocated from one's real environment to an environment created by technology, and 'being there' in that environment (Steuer 1992). Some older studies failed to show a significant difference in presence between VR and desktop conditions, or showed even a higher presence in the desktop conditions (Tichon and Banks 2006). However, at that time the technological development of VR was more basic, and immersion might have been lower. Having the possibility of moving around, interacting, or just looking around in the mediated environment have been proven to lead to more presence (Riva et al. 2007; Regenbrecht and Schubert 2002). In general, the more immersive the media, the more presence the user experiences (Cummings and Bailenson 2016; Parong et al. 2020). Correlations between subjective immersion and presence have been consistently documented (Shu et al. 2019; Jeong and Oh 2020). Moreover, in recent studies VR has consistently been shown to lead to more presence than 2D videos or LCD, through its highly immersive capabilities (Cummings and Bailenson 2016; Baños et al. 2004) in applications such as therapy (Alsina-Jurnet et al. 2011); education (Shu et al. 2019; Buttussi and Chittaro 2017; Makransky et al. 2019), gaming (Pallavicini et al. 2019; Carroll et al. 2019), journalism (Pérez-Seijo et al. 2022; Sundar et al. 2017) and sport spectatorship (Wilson and Mayhorn 2020; Kim and Ko 2019). We expect the same result in the case of esports spectatorship: **(H2)** *Spectating an esports competition in VR will lead to more presence than spectating it on a 2D screen.*

Social presence. Research reveals that audiences follow esports competitions by similar motivations (such as the need for drama and entertainment) as with viewing traditional sports (Pizzo et al. 2018; Qian et al. 2020; Hamari and Sjöblom 2017; Rietz and Hallmann 2022; Rogers et al. 2022; Smith and Smith-Ditizio 2021; Yu et al. 2022). Skill improvement and vicarious sensation are motivations more unique to esports due to the gaming element and the easy way viewers can portray themselves as athletes due to the (sitting) context (Qian et al. 2020). The need for social contact shows contradictions when it comes to results regarding motivation to watch. From being a relevant motivation and part of viewing behaviour through social channels like Twitch (Qian et al. 2022; Yu et al. 2022; Neus and Neus 2020; Pu et al. 2021), to results showing esports fans to not strive for socialization, but prefer to stay away from it (Sjöblom et al. 2020). Social presence refers to the ability of a medium to connect the users with others (Rice 1993; Short et al. 1976). According to the media richness theory (Daft and Lengel 1986), involving more senses and providing multiple modes of communication leads to more social presence (de Greef and IJsselsteijn 2001; Bailenson and Yee 2006; Bailenson et al. 2004). Social presence is the subjective experience of connecting with and being with others through a medium. It is not only media richness that matters in determining social presence, but also the social dynamic and interaction between the actors (Kear 2010; Schultze and Brooks 2019; Kreijns et al. 2024). Social presence has three dimensions: co-presence, psychological involvement and behavioural engagement (Biocca et al. 2001, 2003). Co-presence refers to the feeling of sharing the mediated space with others. Psychological involvement refers to mutual awareness and attention to the others. Both these dimensions of social presence could be enhanced by a 360° video, even when actual interaction is missing due to the feeling of being in a place surrounded with people. Many VR recordings of music concerts and sport events capture the audience in that way. In several studies the capacity of 360° non-interactive video to enhance empathy and prosocial behaviour through social presence is explored (Pimentel et al. 2021; Steed et al. 2018), also in the context of pre-recorded music events (Shin et al. 2019). Moreover, research has revealed a strong positive correlation between spatial presence and social presence in VR (e.g., Bulu 2012). The more one feels located in the virtual environment, the more one perceives themselves as sharing this space with others. It is, therefore, expected that in the VR streaming of an esports event, the audience will feel present in the arena where the event takes place and surrounded by the other audience members, as if they would experience the event on location. This leads to the third hypothesis **(H3)**: *Spectating an esports competition in VR will increase social presence compared to 2D screen viewing.*

Emotional contagion. Once audiences are socially present in the esports arena through VR, then they can experience emotional contagion. Emotional contagion is the phenomenon of converging emotionally with others, mimicking sounds, postures, reactions, emotional expressions and the emotions themselves of other people in the surroundings (Hatfield et al. 1994). Emotional contagion in sport spectatorship has been linked to event enjoyment and satisfaction (Madrigal 2003; Biscaia et al. 2012; Moreno et al. 2015, 2016). Current VR streaming esports competition productions, such as those produced by the livestreaming service Sliver.tv, are 360° videos. These 360° videos recordings can capture images of the playing athletes, the arena, the cheering fans and the entire atmosphere of the event on location. It can also capture different 360° point of views from outside or within the game: from first person point of view of different players, to bird view of the entire game world, often also making visible the score board and game statistics either in the game world, or in the arena, on a 2D large screen (Kim et al. 2018a, b; Cacho-Elizondo et al. 2020). With the immersive capacities of VR, this technology could bring audiences closer to the game world and inside of it, contributing to the motivations of knowledge acquisition, vicarious sensations, and entertainment, as well as closer to the arena and the other fans. Visual aspects, such as seeing a crowd of fans and their emotional reactions, have a strong impact on emotional contagion (Qureshi et al. 2023). The

POV that VR creates of being in the middle of the fans will replicate better the real life experience compared to 2D, and this will stimulate emotional contagion more compared to a 2D experience. Therefore, the fourth hypothesis is: **(H4)** *Spectating an esports competition in VR will lead to more emotional contagion than spectating it on a 2D screen.*

Enjoyment. All the concepts addressed in this literature review, immersion, presence, social presence and emotional contagion are known to positively influence the enjoyment of an experience or of an event (Abernathy et al. 2017; Bulu 2012; Gonçalves et al. 2019; Hassanein and Head 2005; Tussyadiah et al. 2018), especially when the emotions are positive (Biscaia et al. 2012). In general, immersive technologies have been consistently associated with entertainment and the capacity to produce pleasant experiences (Wagler and Hanus 2018; Shelstad et al. 2017) and this is the case also in the context of digital sport spectatorship (Kim and Ko 2019). Therefore, it is hypothesized **(H5)**, that: *Spectating the streaming of an esports competition in VR will lead to more enjoyment than spectating it on a 2D screen.*

3 Methodology

Design. An online experiment that compared two groups was conducted. One group viewed the esports event using a 2D screen (e.g., laptop), while the other group viewed the same event in VR. After the viewing experience, both groups filled in an online questionnaire. The participants were randomly assigned to the 2D or VR condition and viewed the esports event in a place of their choice, using their own 2D screen or VR headset. The participants started by answering questions about demographics and familiarity with VR and esports. After these questions were answered, participants watched the assigned esports video and answered the questions that measured immersion, presence, social presence, emotional contagion, and enjoyment. The average duration was 15 min, and data was collected in May 2020.

Materials. The stimuli were based on a recorded live stream of the finale of the esports IEM Oakland tournament (2016). In the finale, two teams, SK Gaming and Ninjas in Pyjama, played Counterstrike Global Offensive, one of the most popular games in esports (Pannekeet 2019). Both the 2D and VR groups viewed the same event for a duration of approximately 9 min. The visual content, editing, commentator voices, sound effects and background music are the same in both versions. The 2D video showed the event from a point-of-view camera angle from the perspective of the players, switching from one player to another, when it showed images from inside the game. When the action in the arena is shown, the 2D video shows close-ups of the fans and players and a wide shot of the entire arena. The VR video showed the events inside the game from the perspective of moving 360° cameras placed inside the game world, offering the point of view of the player, and switching from player to player, as well as to a bird point of view over the entire game world (at this point a

POV of one of the players is also offered on a 2D screen inside the game world). The selection of scenes, cuts and POV were decided upon by the editors of the movie. When it comes to offering images from the arena, these were captured by a steady camera placed in the middle of the audience (Fig. 1).

Participants. A total of 112 European esports fans participated in the online survey and participants who did not own a VR headset or did not complete the questionnaire were excluded, leaving 92 participants for in the analysis. The reason to excluding people that did not own a VR headset was to be able to focus on esports fans that have experience with VR (games) and as such exclude the newness effect (Van Gisbergen 2016). The age of the participants ranged between 18–30 years ($M = 23$) and 65% was male. The participants were divided over 15 European countries, but the majority lived in Germany (52%) and the Netherlands (21%). The participants were familiar with esports ($M = 3.72$, $SD = 0.77$, 1 = '*not familiar*', 5 = '*very familiar*') and used their VR headsets frequently ($M = 3.22$, $SD = 0.67$). There was no effect of esports familiarity, VR frequency or age on presence, social presence, emotional contagion, or enjoyment. However, more esports familiarity seems to increase enjoyment.

Measures. The survey started with questions about the *background of the participants:* age, country of origin, VR use frequency, esports familiarity, esports viewing behavior, video game familiarity and esports teams and competition familiarity and fandom. The key dependent variables were immersion, presence, social presence, emotional contagion, and enjoyment, all measured using 5-point Likert scales (1 = '*strongly disagree*', 5 = '*strongly agree*'). *Presence* was measured using 12 items ($\alpha = 0.94$) from the ITC- SOPI scale (Lessiter et al. 2001). *Immersion* was measured

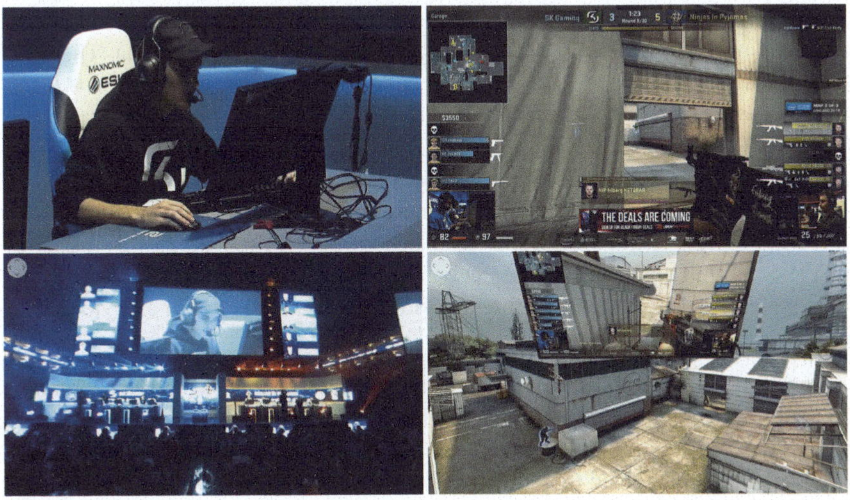

Fig. 1 Screenshots of the 2D (above) and VR (below) viewing experience (retrieved from Youtube and SLIVER.tv (2016)

using the Film Immersive Experience Questionnaire (Rigby et al. 2019) and Immersive Experience Questionnaire for video games (Jennett et al. 2008). The 24 items measured four dimensions: Captivation ($\alpha = 0.9$), real-world dissociation ($\alpha = 0.85$), comprehension ($\alpha = 0.86$) and transportation ($\alpha = 0.85$). To measure screen related *emotional contagion*, a 7-item scale ($\alpha = 0.91$) was created, inspired by the character identification scale (Cohen 2001) and empathy scale (Davis 1980). The scale used items like 'I could feel the emotions of the cheering crowd'; 'I felt I was a member of the crowd myself' and 'I found myself cheering together with the others'. *Social Presence* was measured using six out of seven items ($a = 0.89$) from the original scale (De Kort et al. 2007), based on the Networked Minds Social Presence questionnaire (Biocca et al. 2001). The *Enjoyment* measurement was based on the movie enjoyment scale which distinguishes between enjoyment as experience and enjoyment as appreciation (Doicaru 2016). Replacing story references with livestream references did not alter the high reliability of the scale ($\alpha = 0.76$).

4 Findings

Based on the obtained data, all five hypotheses were confirmed. The results show a positive impact of using VR headsets on all variables related to esports watching. The results reveal a positive impact of VR on ***Immersion*** ($M_{2d} = 3.37$, $M_{vr} = 3.94$, $t\ (89) = -4.45\ p <== 0.001$). The positive effect of VR is present in all subdimensions of immersions among which *Captivation* ($M_{2d} = 3.47$, $M_{vr} = 3.99$, $t(89) = -3.45$, $p <= 0.001$), real-world *Dissociation* ($M_{2d} = 3.19$, $M_{vr} = 3.8$, $t(89) = -3.19$, $p <= 0.001$), *Transportation* ($M_{2d} = 3.23$, $M_{vr} = 3.99$, $t(89) = -3.61$, $p <= 0.001$) and *Comprehension* ($M_{2d} = 3.57$, $M_{vr} = 3.99$, $t(89) = -3.95$, $p <= 0.001$). The level of ***Presence*** was high for both conditions, but higher for the VR condition ($M_{2d} = 3.35$, $M_{vr} = 4.01$, $t\ (92) = -4.19$, $p <= 0.001$). The results also show a positive effect of VR on ***Social Presence*** ($M_{2d} = 3.49$, $M_{vr} = 4.11$, $t\ (89) = -3.78$, $p <= 0.001$). In addition, a positive correlation between presence and social presence was found ($r = 0.84$, $p <= 0.001$). VR also increased ***Emotional Contagion*** ($M_{2d} = 3.51$, $M_{vr} = 4.11$, $t\ (86) = -3.9$; $p <= 0.001$). Finally, ***Enjoyment*** was higher in the VR condition compared to the 2D condition ($M_{2d} = 3.72$, $M_{vr} = 4.01$, $t\ (92) = -2.92\ p <= 0.001$), also revealing a positive correlation between enjoyment and presence ($r = 0.67$, $p <= 0.001$).

Background variables. Linear regression analysis showed that background variables had no significant influence on presence. All other dependent variables were affected by one or more background variables. Some noteworthy findings are: *Being a fan* of an esports team influenced the immersion dimension of *transportation.* The results indicated that fans of a losing team (SK Gaming) were less transported compared to those that were not fans ($t\ (0.86) = -2.1$, $\beta = -2.67$, $p = 0.038$). All immersion dimensions were also affected by background variables, except for comprehension. Team Familiarity with the winning team ($t\ (0.126) = -2.31$, $\beta = -0.38$, $p = 0.02$), and being fan of the losing team (t (0.662) = −2.07, β = −2.59, p = 0.04), also have a positive effect on social presence: Familiarity with the winning team makes it less likely for the participants to experience social presence, and fandom of the losing team makes it less likely to experience social presence. Familiarity with the winning team (t(0.083) = −2.52, β = −0.41, p = 0.014) and with the tournament (t (0.056) = −3.44; β = −0.52, p <= 0.001) both led to lower *enjoyment.* One-way ANCOVA analyses revealed a signifficant main effect of media on the immersion dimensions (*Captivation* (F(1,45) = 20.53, p <= 0.001; *Real World Dissociation* (F(14,44) = 2.22, p = 0.02), *Transportation* (F(1,81) = 6.78, p = 0.011)), *Social Presence* (F(1,68) = 5.15, p = 0.026), *Emotional Contagion* (F (1,63) = 4.18, p = 0.045) and *Enjoyment* F(1,69) = 8.3, p = 0.005).

5 Conclusion

This study shows a clear advantage of VR headsets over traditional 2D media when it comes to watching esports events. Five hypotheses were confirmed, showing that the use of VR headsets increases immersion (H1), presence (H2), social presence (H3,) emotional contagion (H4), and enjoyment (H5). These findings confirm findings from previous studies (e.g., Kim and Biocca 1997; Kim and Ko 2019; Riva et al. 2007; Regenbrecht and Schubert 2002; Roettl and Terlutter 2018; Schuemie et al. 2001; Smith and Neff 2018; Vora et al. 2002). This study positions for the first time non-interactive VR as an improvement to the spectating experience of esports events even for gamers with experience in using VR headsets: A non-interactive 360-degree video enhancing their experience rather than diminishing it. This study also adds to the body of research that reveal that 360° videos are able to induce social presence even without interaction with social actors (Pimentel et al. 2021; Steed et al. 2018; Shin et al. 2019; Biocca et al. 2001), by expanding this finding to (e)sports spectatorship. It also confirmed that VR can increase emotional contagion by giving the feeling of being surrounded by a crowd, which increases the effect of emotional reactions like cheering (Jutte and van der Wal 2016). As emotional contagion is key for good spectating experiences (Biscaia et al. 2012), it shows that VR might decrease the need of expensive interactive productions.

However, it is not clear if VR would have the same positive effects for esports fans that are not experienced with VR headsets. This study was also not aimed at trying to find out if this positive effect is strong enough to motivate people to purchase a VR headset. Further research should explore this target group. It would also be interesting to research a full (live) esport event instead of a summary and to expand towards different esports games and VR viewing options and strategies. Studies revealed different effects on immersion for different VR viewing strategies (Emmerich et al. 2021; Thoravi Kumaravel and Wilson 2022). We could not perfectly capture a realistic experience of spectating an esports competition (in VR), the study providing results for a selection of moments from a competition, without confering the knowledge of how long people are willing to watch an event in VR or if these recorded moments are the best moments to experience in VR (van Gisbergen 2016). In this study we also did not check for 2D screen size and VR headset type, which can have an impact on the audience's experience (Alamäki et al. 2021; Thompson et al. 2012; Rigby et al. 2016). Future research could also incorporate variables that have an effect on esports viewing, regardless of the used media, such as the relationship with the competing teams and the dynamics of the game, such as whether the preferred team wins or loses (Bryant et al. 1994). Finally, it is recommended to investigate the effect of types of esports spectators, and their motivations to follow esports events both on location and digitally, on 2D and VR recorded and live spectating experiences. Some of the participants of this study might have already known the results of the watched competition, and this might have affected their viewing experience, regardless of the used medium, which might have lowered experience in general, missing the suspense of the unknown (Haimson and Tang 2017; Bizzozero et al. 2016; Bryant et al. 1994). Nonetheless, the current study clearly shows the potential advantages of investing in VR (research) to reach and engage esports audiences.

References

Abernathy, M., Shaw, L. A., Lutteroth, C., Buckley, J., Corballis, P. M., & Wünsche, B. C. (2017, January). Enjoyment, immersion, and attentional focus in a Virtual Reality exergame with differing visual environments. In *ICAT-EGVE* (pp. 117–124).

Ahn, D., Seo, Y., Kim, M., Kwon, J. H., Jung, Y., Ahn, J., & Lee, D. (2014). The effects of actual human size display and stereoscopic presentation on users' sense of being together with and of psychological immersion in a virtual character. *Cyberpsychology, Behavior, and Social Networking, 17*(7), 483–487.

Alamäki, A., Dirin, A., Suomala, J., & Rhee, C. (2021). Students' experiences of 2D and 360° videos with or without a low-cost VR headset: An experimental study in higher education. *Journal of Information Technology Education: Research, 20,* 309–329.

Alsop, T. (2023, November 10th) *Virtual reality (VR) headset unit sales worldwide from 2019 to 2024* [infographic]. Statista. VR headset unit sales worldwide 2024 | Statista.

Alsop, T. (2024, February 9th) *Revenue growth of the VR headsets market worldwide from 2019 to 2028*. Statista. Global: VR headsets revenue growth 2019–2028 | Statista.

Alsina-Jurnet, I., Gutiérrez-Maldonado, J., & Rangel-Gómez, M. V. (2011). The role of presence in the level of anxiety experienced in clinical virtual environments. *Computers in Human Behavior, 27*(1), 504–512.

Ambika, A., Shin, H., & Jain, V. (2023). Immersive technologies and consumer behavior: A systematic review of two decades of research. *Australian Journal of Management,* 03128962231181429.

Bailenson, J. N., Beall, A. C., Loomis, J., Blascovich, J., & Turk, M. (2004). Transformed social interaction: Decoupling representation from behavior and form in collaborative virtual environments. *Presence: Teleoperators & Virtual Environments, 13*(4), 428–441.

Bailenson, J. N., & Yee, N. (2006). A longitudinal study of task performance, head movements, subjective report, simulator sickness, and transformed social interaction in collaborative virtual environments. *Presence: Teleoperators and Virtual Environments, 15*(6), 699–716.

Baños, R.M., Botella,C., Alcañiz, M.,Liaño, V.,Guerrero,B., & Rey, B. (2004). Immersion and emotion: Their impact on the sense of presence. *Cyber Psychology and Behavior, 7*(6), 734–741.

Biocca, F., Harms, C., & Gregg, J. (2001, May). The networked minds measure of social presence: Pilot test of the factor structure and concurrent validity. *In 4th annual international workshop on presence, Philadelphia, PA* (pp. 1–9).

Biocca, F., Harms, C., & Burgoon, J. K. (2003). Toward a more robust theory and measure of social presence: Review and suggested criteria. *Presence: Teleoperators & Virtual Environments, 12*(5), 456–480.

Biscaia, R., Correia, A., Rosado, A., Maroco, J., & Ross, S. (2012). The effects of emotions on football spectators' satisfaction and behavioural intentions. *European Sport Management Quarterly, 12*(3), 227–242.

Bizzozero, P., Flepp, R., & Franck, E. (2016). The importance of suspense and surprise in entertainment demand: Evidence from Wimbledon. *Journal of Economic Behavior & Organization, 130*, 47–63.

Bruder, G., Argelaguet, F., Olivier, A. H., & Lécuyer, A. (2016). Cave size matters: Effects of screen distance and paralax on distance estimation in large immersive display setups. *Presence, 25*(1), 1–16.

Bryant, J., Rockwell, S. C., & Owens, J. W. (1994). Buzzer beaters" and "barn burners": The effects on enjoyment of watching the game go "down to the wire. *Journal of Sport and Social Issues, 18*(4), 326–339.

Bulu, S. T. (2012). Place presence, social presence, co-presence, and satisfaction in virtual worlds. *Computers & Education, 58*(1), 154–161.

Buttussi, F., & Chittaro, L. (2017). Effects of different types of virtual reality display on presence and learning in a safety training scenario. *IEEE Transactions on Visualization and Computer Graphics, 24*(2), 1063–1076.

Cacho-Elizondo, S., Álvarez, J. D. L., & Garcia, V. E. (2020). The emerging esport market: Analyzing the impact of virtual and augmented reality. *Chinese Business Review, 19(2)*, 37–54.

Carroll, M., Osborne, E., & Yildirim, C. (2019, June). Effects of VR gaming and game genre on player experience. In *2019 IEEE Games, Entertainment, Media Conference (GEM)* (pp. 1–6). IEEE.

Cohen, E. L., Bowman, N. D., & Lancaster, A. L. (2016). RU with Some1? Using text message experience sampling to examine television coviewing as a moderator of emotional contagion effects on enjoyment. *Mass Communication and Society, 19*(2), 149–172.

Cohen, J. (2001). Defining identification: A theoretical look at the identification of audiences with media characters. *Mass Communication and Society, 4*(3), 245–264.

Cranmer, E. E., Han, D. I. D., van Gisbergen, M., & Jung, T. (2021). Esports matrix: Structuring the esports research agenda. *Computers in Human Behavior, 117*, 106671.

Cummings, J. J., & Bailenson, J. N. (2016). How immersive is enough? A meta-analysis of the effect of immersive technology on user presence. *Media Psychology, 19*(2), 272–309.

Daft, R. L., & Lengel, R. H. (1986). Organizational information requirements, media richness and structural design. *Management Science, 32*(5), 554–571.

Davis, M. H. (1980). A multidimensional approach to individual differences in empathy. In *JSAS Catalog of Selected Documents in Psychology, 10*, p. 85.

De Greef, P., & Ijsselsteijn, W. A. (2001). Social presence in a home tele-application. *CyberPsychology & Behavior, 4*(2), 307–315.

De Kort, Y. A., IJsselsteijn, W. A., & Poels, K. (2007). Digital games as social presence technology: Development of the Social Presence in Gaming Questionnaire (SPGQ). *Proceedings of PRESENCE, 195203*, 1–9.

Doicaru, M. M. (2016). *Gripped by movies: From story-world to artifact absorption.* [Doctoral dissertation: Universiteit van Amsterdam]. 169243_02_1_.pdf (uva.nl).

Emmerich, K., Krekhov, A., Cmentowski, S., & Krueger, J. (2021). Streaming VR games to the broad audience: A comparison of the first-person and third-person perspectives. In *Proceedings of the 2021 CHI Conference on Human Factors in Computing Systems* (1–14).

Garrido, S., & Macritchie, J. (2020). Audience engagement with community music performances: Emotional contagion in audiences of a 'pro-am' orchestra in suburban Sydney. *Musicae Scientiae, 24*(2), 155–167.

Goncalves, G., Coelho, H., Monteiro, P., Melo, M., & Bessa, M. (2019, November). Correlation between game experience and presence in immersive virtual reality games. In *2019 International Conference on Graphics and Interaction (ICGI)* (pp. 107–114). IEEE.

Haimson, O. L., & Tang, J. C. (2017, May). What makes live events engaging on Facebook Live, Periscope, and Snapchat. In *Proceedings of the 2017 CHI Conference on Human Factors in Computing Systems* (pp. 48–60).

Hamari, J., & Sjöblom, M. (2017). What is eSports and why do people watch it?. *Internet Research, 27*(2), 211–232.

Hassanein, K., & Head, M. (2005). The impact of infusing social presence in the web interface: An investigation across product types. *International Journal of Electronic Commerce, 10*(2), 31–55.

Hatfield, E., Cacioppo, J., & Rapson, R. L. (1994). *Emotional contagion.* New York: Cambridge University Press.

Hou, J., Nam, Y., Peng, W., & Lee, K. M. (2012). Effects of screen size, viewing angle, and players' immersion tendencies on game experience. *Computers in Human Behavior, 28*(2), 617–623.

Jennett, C., Cox, A. L., Cairns, P., Dhoparee, S., Epps, A., Tijs, T., & Walton, A. (2008). Measuring and defining the experience of immersion in games. *International Journal of Human-Computer Studies, 66(9)*, 641–661.

Jeong, W., & Oh, S. (2020, October). Correlation between the immersion and presence: Focused on virtual reality contents. In *2020 International Conference on Information and Communication Technology Convergence (ICTC)* (pp. 474–477). IEEE.

Jutte, B., & van der Wal, C. N. (2016). Cognitive modelling of emotion contagion in a crowd of soccer supporter agents. In *Computational Collective Intelligence: 8th International Conference, ICCCI 2016, Halkidiki, Greece, September 28–30, 2016, Proceedings, Part I 8* (pp. 40–52). Springer International Publishing.

Kear, K. (2010). Social presence in online learning communities. In *Proceedings of the 7th International Conference on Networked Learning 2010.*

Kim, T., & Biocca, F. (1997). Telepresence via television: Two dimensions of telepresence may have different connections to memory and persuasion. *Journal of Computer-Mediated Communication, 3(2)*, JCMC325.

Kim, H. W., Lee, J. S., & Yang, S. H. (2018a). Study of capturing real-time 360 VR 3D game video for 360 VR E-sports broadcast. *Journal of Broadcast Engineering, 23*(6), 876–885.

Kim, H., Yang, J., Choi, M., Lee, J., Yoon, S., Kim, Y., & Park, W. (2018b, June). Immersive 360 VR tiled streaming system for esports service. In *Proceedings of the 9th ACM Multimedia Systems Conference* (pp. 541–544).

Kim, D., & Ko, Y. J. (2019). The impact of virtual reality (VR) technology on sport spectators' flow experience and satisfaction. *Computers in Human Behavior, 93*, 346–356.

Kim, Y., Magnusen, M., Kim, M., & Lee, H. W. (2019). Meta-analytic review of sport consumption: Factors affecting attendance to sporting events. *Sport Marketing Quarterly, 28*(3).

Kim, M. J., & Mao, L. L. (2021). Sport consumers motivation for live attendance and mediated sports consumption: A qualitative analysis. *Sport in Society, 24*(4), 515–533.

Komarac, T., & Ozretić Došen, Đ. (2022). Discovering the determinants of museum visitors' immersion into experience: The impact of interactivity, expectations, and skepticism. *Current Issues in Tourism, 25*(22), 3675–3693.

Kreijns, K., Yau, J., Weidlich, J., & Weinberger, A. (2024, January). Towards a comprehensive framework of social presence for online, hybrid, and blended learning. *Frontiers in Education (8).*

Kriglstein, S., Wallner, G., Charleer, S., Gerling, K., Mirza-Babaei, P., Schirra, S., & Tscheligi, M. (2020, April). Be part of it: Spectator experience in gaming and esports. In *Extended Abstracts of the 2020 CHI Conference on Human Factors in Computing Systems* (pp. 1–7).

Kweon, S. H., Kweon, H. J., Kim, S. J., Li, X., Liu, X., & Kweon, H. L. (2018). A brain wave research on VR (virtual reality) usage: Comparison between VR and 2D video in EEG measurement. *In Advances in Human Factors and Systems Interaction: Proceedings of the AHFE 2017 International Conference on Human Factors and Systems Interaction, July 17– 21, 2017, USA 8 (pp. 194–203).* Springer International Publishing.

Lai, W., Wang, W., & Li, F. (2022). The impact of eSports performance and social interaction on eSports online viewership and viewer experience. In *Proceedings of the 2022 Wuhan International Conference on e-Business* (pp. 599–601).

Lessiter, J., Freeman, J., Keogh, E., & Davidoff, J. (2001). A cross-media presence questionnaire: The ITC-Sense of Presence Inventory. *Presence, 10*(3), 282–297.

Lombard, M., Reich, R. D., Grabe, M. E., Bracken, C. C., & Ditton, T. B. (2000). Presence and television. The role of screen size. *Human Communication Research, 26*(1), 75–98.

MacMahan, A. (2003). Immersion, engagement, and presence: A method for analysing 3-D video games. In M. J. P. Wolf & B. Perron (Eds.), *The video game theory reader* (pp. 67–86). New York: Routledge.

Madrigal, R. (2003). Investigating an evolving leisure experience: Antecedents and consequences of spectator affect during a live sporting event. *Journal of Leisure Research, 35*(1), 23–48.

Mainelli, T. (2023). Market analysis perspective: Worldwide augmented reality and virtual reality, 2023 [PowerPoint slides]. IDC's Consumer and Device Research. Market Analysis Perspective: Worldwide Augmented Reality and Virtual Reality, 2023 (idc.com).

Makransky, G., Terkildsen, T. S., & Mayer, R. E. (2019). Adding immersive virtual reality to a science lab simulation causes more presence but less learning. *Learning and Instruction,* 60, 225–236.

Miah, A., Fenton, A., & Chadwick, S. (2020). Virtual reality and sports: The rise of mixed, augmented, immersive, and esports experiences. *21st Century Sports: How Technologies Will Change Sports in The Digital Age, 249–262.*

Migliore, L. (2021). What is esports? The past, present, and future of competitive gaming. In *Handbook of Esports Medicine: Clinical Aspects of Competitive Video Gaming* (pp. 1–16). Cham: Springer International Publishing.

Moreno, F. C., Prado-Gascó, V., Hervás, J. C., Núñez-Pomar, J., & Sanz, V. A. (2015). Spectator emotions: Effects on quality, satisfaction, value, and future intentions. *Journal of Business Research, 68*(7), 1445–1449.

Moreno, F. C., Prado-Gascó, V., Hervás, J. C., Núñez-Pomar, J., & Sanz, V. A. (2016). Predicting future intentions of basketball spectators using SEM and fsQCA. *Journal of Business Research, 69*(4), 1396–1400.

Mütterlein, J. (2018). The three pillars of virtual reality? Investigating the roles of immersion, presence, and interactivity. In *Proceedings of the 51st Hawaii International Conference on System Sciences.*

Neus, F., & Neus, F. (2020). Differences and similarities in motivation for offline and online eSports event consumption. *Event Marketing in The Context of Higher Education Marketing and Digital Environments,* 79–99.

Pallavicini, F., & Pepe, A. (2019). Comparing player experience in video games played in virtual reality or on desktop displays: Immersion, flow, and positive emotions. *In Extended abstracts of the annual symposium on computer-human interaction in play companion extended abstracts* (pp. 195–210).

Pallavicini, F., Pepe, A., & Minissi, M. E. (2019). Gaming in virtual reality: What changes in terms of usability, emotional response and sense of presence compared to non-immersive video games?. *Simulation & Gaming, 50*(2), 136–159.

Pannekeet, J. (2019). *Global esports market report.* Newzoo. Retrieved from Newzoo-Global-Esports-Market-Report-2019.pdf (strivesponsorship.com)

Parong, J., Pollard, K. A., Files, B. T., Oiknine, A. H., Sinatra, A. M., Moss, J. D., ... & Khooshabeh, P. (2020). The mediating role of presence differs across types of spatial learning in immersive technologies. *Computers in Human Behavior, 107*, 106290.

Pavic, K., Chaby, L., Gricourt, T., & Vergilino-Perez, D. (2023). Feeling virtually present makes me happier: The influence of immersion, sense of presence, and video contents on positive emotion induction. *Cyberpsychology, Behavior, and Social Networking, 26*(4), 238–245.

Pérez-Seijo, S., Vicente, P. N., & López-García, X. (2022). Immersive journalism: The effect of system immersion on place illusion and co-presence in 360-degree video *Reporting. Systems, 11*(1), 1.

Pimentel, D., Kalyanaraman, S., Lee, Y. H., & Halan, S. (2021). Voices of the unsung: The role of social presence and interactivity in building empathy in 360 video. *New Media & Society, 23*(8), 2230–2254.

Pizzo, A., Baker, B., Na, S., Lee, M., Kim, D., & Funk, D. (2018). eSport vs sport: A comparison of spectator motives. *Sport Marketing Quarterly, 27,* 108–123.

Pu, H., Kim, J., & Daprano, C. (2021). Can esports substitute traditional sports? The convergence of sports and video gaming during the pandemic and beyond. *Societies, 11*(4), 129.

Pu, H., Xiao, S., & Kota, R. W. (2022). Virtual games meet physical playground: Exploring and measuring motivations for live esports event attendance. *Sport in Society, 25*(10), 1886–1908.

Qian, T. Y., Wang, J. J., Zhang, J. J., & Lu, L. Z. (2020). It is in the game: Dimensions of esports online spectator motivation and development of a scale. *European Sport Management Quarterly, 20*(4), 458–479.

Qian, T. Y., Matz, R., Luo, L., & Xu, C. (2022). Gamification for value creation and viewer engagement in gamified livestreaming services: The moderating role of gender in esports. *Journal of Business Research, 145*, 482–494.

Qureshi, A. W., Monk, R. L., Quinn, S., Gannon, B., McNally, K., & Heim, D. (2023). Catching a smile from individuals and crowds: Evidence for distinct emotional contagion processes. *Journal of Personality and Social Psychology.*

Ranasinghe, N., Cheok, A., Nakatsu, R., & Do, E. Y. L. (2013, October). Simulating the sensation of taste for immersive experiences. In *Proceedings of the 2013 ACM international workshop on Immersive media experiences* (pp. 29–34).

Regenbrecht, H., & Schubert, T. (2002). Real and illusory interactions enhance presence in virtual environments. *Presence: Teleoperators and Virtual Environments, 11*(4), 425–434.

Rice, R. E. (1993). Media appropriateness: Using social presence theory to compare traditional and new organizational media. *Human Communication Research, 19*(4), 451–484.

Rietz, J., & Hallmann, K. (2022). A systematic review on spectator behavior in esports: Why do people watch? *International Journal of Sports Marketing and Sponsorship, 24*(1), 38–55.

Rigby, J. M., Brumby, D. P., Cox, A. L., & Gould, S. J. (2016, September). Watching movies on netflix: Investigating the effect of screen size on viewer immersion. *In Proceedings of the 18th international conference on human-computer interaction with mobile devices and services adjunct* (pp. 714–721).

Rigby, J. M., Brumby, D. P., Gould, S. J., & Cox, A. L. (2019, June). Development of a questionnaire to measure immersion in video media: The film IEQ. In *Proceedings of the 2019 ACM International Conference on Interactive Experiences for TV and Online Video* (pp. 35–46).

Riva, G., Mantovani, F., Capideville, C. S., Preziosa, A., Morganti, F., Villani, D., & Alcañiz, M. (2007). Affective interactions using VR: The link between presence and emotions. *Cyber Psychology & Behavior, 10*(1), 45–56.

Roettl, J., & Terlutter, R. (2018). The same video game in 2D, 3D or VR–How does technology impact game evaluation and brand placements?. *PloS one, 13*(7).

Rogers, R., Farquhar, L., & Mummert, J. (2022). Motivational differences among viewers of traditional sports, esports, and NBA 2K league. *Communication & Sport, 10(2)*, 175–194.

Sahin, A. (2023). E-sports: An analysis on global growth, revenue streams, and threats. *Journal of ROL Sport Sciences*, 514–529.

Schuemie, M. J., van Der Straaten, P., Krijn, M., & van Der Mast, C. A. (2001). Research on presence in VR: A survey. *CyberPsychology & Behavior, 4*(2), 183–201.

Schultze, U., & Brooks, J. A. M. (2019). An interactional view of social presence: Making the virtual other "real". *Information Systems Journal, 29*(3), 707–737.

Shelstad, W. J., Smith, D. C., & Chaparro, B. S. (2017, September). Gaming on the rift: How virtual reality affects game user satisfaction. In *Proceedings of the human factors and ergonomics society annual meeting* (Vol. 61, No. 1, pp. 2072–2076). Sage CA: Los Angeles, CA: SAGE Publications.

Shin, M., Song, S. W., Kim, S. J., & Biocca, F. (2019). The effects of 3D sound in a 360-degree live concert video on social presence, parasocial interaction, enjoyment, and intent of financial supportive action. *International Journal of Human-Computer Studies, 126*, 81–93.

Short, J., Williams, E., & Christie, B. (1976). *The social psychology of telecommunications*. London.: John Wiley & Sons, Ltd.

Shu, Y., Huang, Y. Z., Chang, S. H., & Chen, M. Y. (2019). Do virtual reality head-mounted displays make a difference? A comparison of presence and self-efficacy between head-mounted displays and desktop computer-facilitated virtual environments. *Virtual Reality, 23*, 437–446.

Sjöblom, M., Macey, J., & Hamari, J. (2020). Digital athletics in analogue stadiums: Comparing gratifications for engagement between live attendance and online esports spectating. *Internet Research, 30*(3), 713–735.

Smith, H. J., & Neff, M. (2018). Communication behavior in embodied VR. *In Proceedings of the 2018 CHI Conference on Human Factors in Computing Systems* (pp. 1–12).

Smith, A. D., & Smith-Ditizio, A. A. (2021). eSports: A new era of spectator games from a consumer's viewpoint. International *Journal of Business Information Systems, 36*(3), 406–431.

Stander, F. W., & De Beer, L. T. (2016). Towards engagement: A comparison of fan groups in the context of a major South African football club. *SA Journal of Industrial Psychology, 42*(1), 1–10.

Steed, A., Pan, Y., Watson, Z., & Slater, M. (2018). "We wait"—the impact of character responsiveness and self embodiment on presence and interest in an immersive news experience. *Frontiers in Robotics and AI, 5*, 112.

Steuer, J.S. (1992). Defining virtual reality: Dimensions determining telepresence. *Journal of Communication, 42*(4), 73–93.

Sundar, S. S., Kang, J., & Oprean, D. (2017). Being there in the midst of the story: How immersive journalism affects our perceptions and cognitions. *Cyberpsychology, Behavior, and Social Networking, 20*(11), 672–682.

Taufik, D., Kunz, M. C., & Onwezen, M. C. (2021). Changing consumer behaviour in virtual reality: A systematic literature review. *Computers in Human Behavior Reports, 3*, 100093.

Thompson, M., Nordin, A. I., & Cairns, P. (2012, September). Effect of touch–screen size on game immersion. In *The 26th BCS Conference on Human Computer Interaction. BCS Learning & Development.*

Thoravi Kumaravel, B., & Wilson, A. D. (2022). DreamStream: Immersive and interactive spectating in VR. In *Proceedings of the 2022 CHI Conference on Human Factors in Computing Systems* (pp. 1–17).

Tian, F., & Zhang, W. (2021). The difference of emotional arousal between traditional 2D and VR movies: A comparative study based on EEG signals. *In 2021 6th International Conference on Intelligent Computing and Signal Processing (ICSP)* (pp. 734–737).

Tichon, J., & Banks, J. (2006). Virtual reality exposure therapy: 150-degree screen to desktop PC. *CyberPsychology & Behavior, 9*(4), 480–489.

Tussyadiah, I. P., Wang, D., Jung, T. H., & Tom Dieck, M. C. (2018). Virtual reality, presence, and attitude change: Empirical evidence from tourism. *Tourism Management, 66*, 140–154.

Van Gisbergen, M. S. (2016). Contextual connected media: How rearranging a media puzzle brings virtual reality into being. Breda: NHTV.

Vincent, A., & Frewen, P. (2023). Being where, with whom, and when it happens: Spatial, interpersonal, and temporal presence while viewing live streaming of collegiate sports in virtual reality. *Frontiers in Virtual Reality, 4*, 1167051.

Vora, J., Nair, S., Gramopadhye, A. K., Duchowski, A. T., Melloy, B. J., & Kanki, B. (2002). Using VR technology for aircraft visual inspection training: Presence and comparison studies. *Applied Ergonomics, 33*(6), 559–570.

Wagler, A., & Hanus, M. D. (2018). Comparing virtual reality tourism to real-life experience: Effects of presence and engagement on attitude and enjoyment. *Communication Research Reports, 35(*5), 456–464.

White, P. J., Byagowi, A., & Moussavi, Z. (2015, August). Effect of viewing mode on pathfinding in immersive virtual reality. In *2015 37th Annual International Conference of the IEEE Engineering in Medicine and Biology Society (EMBC)* (pp. 4619–4622). IEEE.

Wilson, R., & Mayhorn, C. B. (2020, December). On the field: Examining differences in video format in sports media viewing. In *Proceedings of the Human Factors and Ergonomics Society Annual Meeting (Vol. 64*, No. 1, pp. 781–785). Sage CA: Los Angeles, CA: SAGE Publications.

Xu, C., Siegrist, M., & Hartmann, C. (2021). The application of virtual reality in food consumer behavior research: A systematic review. *Trends in Food Science & Technology, 116,* 533–544.

Yao, L. (2022, March). Video game livestream trend analysis based on Twitch livestream data. In *2022 7th International Conference on Financial Innovation and Economic Development (ICFIED 2022)* (pp. 2890–2895). Atlantis Press.

Yao, S., & Kim, G. (2019). The effects of immersion in a virtual reality game: Presence and physical activity. In *HCI in Games: First International Conference, HCI-Games 2019, Held as Part of the 21st HCI International Conference, HCII 2019, Orlando, FL, USA, July 26–31, 2019, Proceedings 21* (pp. 234–242). Springer International Publishing.

Yin, Y. J., Tang, W. Q., & Wei-Qing, L. I. (2013). Emotion modeling of arena spectator based on emotional contagion. *Computer Engineering & Design, 34*(9), 3205–3209.

Yu, B., Brison, N. T., & Bennett, G. (2022). Why do women watch esports? A social role perspective on spectating motives and points of attachment. *Computers in Human Behavior, 127*, 107055.

A New Universal XR Metaverse Platform for Playing Virtual Sports Games with Multiple XR Devices

Jong-Sung Kim

Abstract XR metaverse has been regarded as a promising way for virtualizing real sports to play sports games with virtualized humanoid avatars on a virtual world without limitations of space and time. Many researchers expect that real sports will be trans-formed to virtual sports through XR metaverse techniques, such as XR devices, XR avatars, XR simulators and so on. However, it is still remained as a technically difficult problem to play virtual sports with XR metaverse techniques because it is not easy to apply various XR techniques developed by several companies into a unified XR metaverse platform. In this paper, we proposed a new universal XR metaverse platform to play virtual sports games with multiple XR devices in a XR metaverse world. The proposed plat-form was developed with the OpenVR and OpenXR modules for systematically supporting multiple XR devices. In addition, a full-body tracking system and a treadmill were combined with the proposed platform in order to synchronize the body motion and locomotion of user with his or her avatar. The usefulness of the proposed platform was demonstrated with three XR metaverse-based virtual sports games in practice.

Keywords Extended reality · Metaverse · Universal platform · Virtual sports

1 Introduction

Meta has developed its own XR metaverse platform, so-called the Meta platform, supporting its own XR headsets, such as Oculus Rift S, Oculus Quest 2 and Meta Quest 3, and XR metaverse worlds, titled as Horizon Worlds (Meta 2020). On the Meta platform, players can move and interact with each other in various events, games and social activities. The number of users for the Meta platform reached about 300,000 by October 2022, but the number of users did not increase any more due to various reasons, such as the environment of unenjoyable user experience,

J.-S. Kim (✉)
Creative Contents Research Division, Electronics and Telecommunications Research Institute, Daejeon, South Korea
e-mail: js.kim@etri.re.kr

T. Jung et al. (eds.), *XR and Metaverse*, Springer Proceedings in Business and Economics, https://doi.org/10.1007/978-3-031-77975-6_2

the access limitation of users having other XR devices, and so on. Technically, the Meta plat-form is developed with the Meta's software development kits (SDKs) and application program interfaces (APIs). Therefore, users having XR devices of other companies cannot access to the Meta platform. Vive has also developed its own metaverse plat-form, so-called the Vive platform, supporting metaverse worlds, tilted as Viverse with other mobile devices as well as Vive headsets, such as Vive Pro, Vive Focus, and Vive XR Elite (Vive 2022). On the Vive platform, users having mobile devices can play various activities as users having Vive devices, but users having mobile devices cannot experience XR metaverse worlds. In addition, users having other XR devices cannot ac-cess the Vive platform because the Vive platform is developed with the Vive's SDKs and APIs.

OpenVR was developed to support multiple XR devices on a single platform (ValveSoftware 2015) and then it was adopted to develop the SteamVR platform (Steam 2016), which supports multiple XR devices, including HTC Vive, Oculus Rift, and Microsoft MR Headsets. Therefore, OpenVR can be utilized to develop a universal XR metaverse platform supporting various XR devices. OpenXR was developed as the standard for supporting various XR devices as OpenVR does (Khronos 2019). In the recent year, most XR authoring tools, including Unity and Un-real, support the SDKs and APIs for both OpenVR and OpenXR. Appnori has developed a VR game for various virtual sports, titled by All-In-One Sports VR (Appnori 2021), which can play 13 sports in 1 game on the SteamVR platform. Although this game can support multiple virtual sports with multiple XR headsets, it is originally designed as a VR game, not a XR metaverse. Roblox, the biggest global metaverse platform, also have various sports games, called Roblox Sports (Roblox 2017), but Roblox is a mobile metaverse, not a XR metaverse. Recently, Metaverse has begun to be studied for the physical fitness for the enhancement of exercise capability of youth (Lee et al. 2023). However, a mobile, not XR, platform was also used in this work.

2 Methodology

The proposed platform is designed to support multiple XR devices, including XR headsets, XR trackers, e.g., Vive Trackers (Vive 2021), and XR treadmills, e.g., KAT VR Omnidirectional Treadmills (KAT VR 2023) for XR sports games. As shown in Fig. 1, the proposed platform has several XR metaverse modules, including the FinalIK module (Rootmotion 2023) for the inverse kinematics-based XR avatar animation using the motion data of XR trackers and the PhysX module (Nvidia 2023) for the physics-based XR metaverse simulation as well as the OpenVR and OpenXR module. In this way, the proposed platform supports multiple XR devices of several companies, including Vive, Meta, Pico, and so on. OpenVR-SpaceCalibrator (Li 2022) was used to calibrate the 3D coordinate systems of XR headsets and XR trackers.

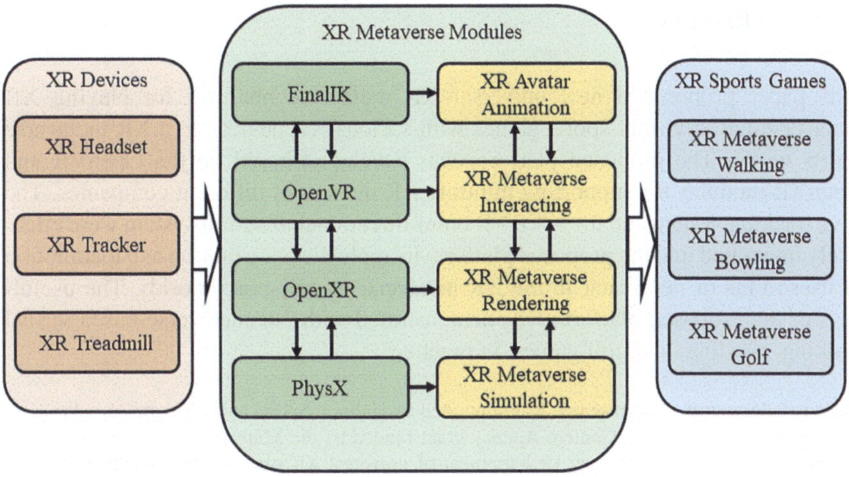

Fig. 1 Architecture of the proposed universal XR metaverse platform for virtual sports games

3 Findings

Contrary to the previous XR metaverse platforms, such as the Meta platform and the Vive platform, the proposed universal XR metaverse platform can systematically support multiple XR devices and XR sports games at the same time as shown in Fig. 2. Players can see their own walking or swing motion forms through his or her own XR avatar. In addition, players having XR headsets of other companies can enjoy XR metaverse sports games on the proposed universal XR metaverse platform.

Fig. 2 XR metaverse-based virtual walking, bowling, and golf games playing on the proposed universal XR metaverse platform

4 Conclusions

This paper proposed a new universal XR metaverse platform for playing XR metaverse-based virtual sports games with various XR devices in a XR metaverse sports world. The proposed platform was developed based on the OpenVR and OpenXR modules for supporting multiple XR devices of different companies. The Vive tracking system and the KAT VR omni-directional treadmill system were effectively integrated into the proposed platform to apply the body motion and locomotion of user to his or her avatar in the XR metaverse-based sports worlds. The usefulness of the proposed platform was demonstrated with XR metaverse-based virtual walking, bowling, and golf games, in practice.

Acknowledgements This research was supported by Culture, Sports and Tourism R&D Program through the Korea Creative Content Agency grant funded by the Ministry of Culture, Sports and Tourism in 2023 (Project Name: Development of universal XR platform technology to build a metaverse supporting digital cultural inclusion, Project Number: RS-2023-00270006, Contribution Rate: 100%).

References

Appnori (2021). *All-In-One Sports VR*, https://www.appnori.com/all-in-one-sports-vr.
KAT VR (2023). *Omni-directional Treadmills*, https://www.kat-vr.com.
Khronos (2019). *OpenXR Overview*, https://www.khronos.org/openxr.
Lee, J.-W., Yoon, H.-K., Kim, D.-H. (2023). Design of Metaverse-Based Physical Fitness Servces for the Enhancement of Exercise Capability for Youth, *Mobile Information Systems*, 2023(2):1–19.
Li, J. (2022). *OpenVR-SpaceCalibrator*, https://github.com/pushras/OpenVR-SpaceCalibrator.
Meta (2020). *Horizon Worlds on Meta Quest*, https://www.meta.com/experience.
Nvidia (2023). *PhysX*, https://developer.nvidia.com/physx-sdk.
Roblox (2017). *Roblox Sports*, https://www.roblox.com/game-pass/sport.
Rootmotion (2023). *FinalIK*, https://root-motion.com//final-ik.
Steam (2016). *SteamVR*, https://store.steampowered.com/app/SteamVR.
ValveSoftware (2015). *OpenVR*, https://github.com/ValveSoftware/openvr.
Vive (2021). *Vive Tracker 3.0*, https://www.vive.com/accessory/tracker3.
Vive (2022). *Viverse*, https://www.viverse.com.

Action Recognition in Sports Training: An Exploratory Study Using Machine Learning Algorithms for X-Reality

Anthony Kong, Zeping Feng, Newman Lau, Mengru Liu, Refati Rehe, and Kun-Pyo Lee

Abstract With the gradual penetration of artificial intelligence technology into the field of education, improving learning efficiency and learner experience better has gradually become a research direction of great interest, especially in the sports training part of the physical education field. The addition of AI brings deep potential for the innovative development of XR. For youth basketball training, researchers conducted a series of model training through machine learning algorithms of artificial intelligence. The player's action behaviour and the trajectory of the ball were captured through image recognition to provide timely feedback to the player. The study results showed that the algorithm stopped training in the 69th to 81st round, indicating that the action recognition model set by the study reached a better balance here. It can maintain high accuracy in recognizing player behaviours and actions and provides a research basis for the subsequent implementation of continuous tracking and analysing behaviors of each player and their actions on the basketball court from start to finish. Afterwards, we discuss the future use of action recognition and extended reality to personalise player profiles in sports training, including the possibility of drawing training advice from multiple stakeholders to make player training more efficient and to increase the immersion of players in sports training.

Keywords Basketball training · Physical education · Sports training · X-reality innovation · AI design · Machine learning

A. Kong (✉) · Z. Feng · N. Lau · M. Liu · R. Rehe · K. Lee
School of Design, The Hong Kong Polytechnic University, Hong Kong, China
e-mail: anthony-pui-keung.kong@polyu.edu.hk

Laboratory for Artificial Intelligence in Design, Hong Kong Science and Technology Park, Hong Kong, China

T. Jung et al. (eds.), *XR and Metaverse*, Springer Proceedings in Business and Economics, https://doi.org/10.1007/978-3-031-77975-6_3

1 Introduction

In the past few years, a variety of emerging educational technologies have been gradually applied in the field of education and have achieved milestones. This digital reinvention also deserves to be considered in physical education. Especially in the case of traditional face-to-face sports education, such as youth basketball training, the coach-centered approach, the lack of formal and professional teaching resources as well as the insufficient number of venues and the lack of customization of training methods have led to the increasing use of AI and mixed reality technologies in the development of sports training. However, few studies have been conducted on machine learning (ML) algorithms in the field of action recognition.

In this study, a 100-round training cycle was developed using the Yolo V8l model to investigate the impact of machine learning algorithms in basketball movement recognition in youth, to contribute to the development of systems that can automatically record and analyse the number of times a player performs a behaviour (e.g., shooting, dribbling, passing) on the court. The value of this study will not only help researchers and designers to design youth sports training more aptly but also help to generate innovative advances in XR by AI in the field of sports.

2 Literature Review

2.1 Artificial Intelligence-Based Coaching

Artificial Intelligence (AI) is a type of machine that is usually responsible for performing the cognitive functions associated with human beings (Rai et al. 2019), providing skills including learning, social interaction, problem solving and creativity. In practice, AI has made its way into the world of coaching, for example AI coaches promote attitudinal shifts in clients' performance (Theeboom et al. 2014), well-being and self-regulation, with particular emotional outcomes.

In sports training, coaches are often a key element in training youth players and helping them get ready for basketball games. Artificial intelligence-powered coaching robots have been shown to have a positive effect on the training of young players and give them positive feedback in appropriate scenarios. (Khandelwal and Upadhyay 2021). Unlike traditional face-to-face sports instruction, the addition of artificial intelligence brings a better scenario in that personalized and targeted training programs can be developed based on the individual abilities and needs of different youth players (Zhang 2022), at the same time, this targeted coaching is thoughtless and instantaneous, real-time coaching and feedback based on the players' past behaviour (Feng 2023).

In 2016, Li et al. debuted the concept of adding AI technology to basketball training instruction (Tingting n.d.). In this study, the AI's teaching system was significantly more effective than a control group of traditional instruction and could be adapted to form a personalized teaching model by tracking a player's historical performance. Zhuo Yang has shown that a system to build an AI sports coach should be linked to the Baum-Welch algorithm to collect players' sports data and centralize the collected data to explore the rules of players' sports behavior, and the addition of this technology has been proven to enhance the sports efficiency of basketball players and will stimulate their potential to a certain extent.

2.2 *Benefits of Artificial Intelligence-Based Coaching*

An AI-based coaching system is a virtual entity that not only has the capability to process information and provide feedback at a significantly faster rate compared to traditional face-to-face athletic training, but also mitigates human bias and inefficiency inherent in human-led coaching (Khandelwal and Upadhyay 2021). This system invokes advanced algorithms and machine learning techniques to analyse huge amounts of data in real time, thereby offering players immediate and precise statistics, actionable advice, and comprehensive performance reviews, which enhance the training experience for club participants (Mohan et al. 2020). Furthermore, the integration of AI into sports training shifts the focus from a coach-centred instructional format to a player-centred experience, empowering athletes to take a more active role in their development and learning process (Palumbo et al. 2020). By reducing the time spent on trial-and-error methods, AI-based coaching systems facilitate more efficient and effective training regimes, leading to significant improvements in athletic performance and adherence to training protocols. This evolution in coaching methodology represents a profound shift in how athletic training is conducted, offering a more personalised, data-driven, and interactive approach that aligns with the modern demands of sports and athlete development.

2.3 *Technologies for Basketball Motion Recognition*

In order to understand human motor behaviour, past researchers have tried various methods of action recognition, e.g. picture-based action recognition is the most common way. During the COVID-19 pandemic, people tended to rehabilitate their bodies and exercise training at home, People tended to rehabilitate their bodies and exercise training at home, which led to a deeper portion of pixel testing.

For visual recognition and capture of basketball training, OpenPose (Li et al. 2021), Mask R-CNN (Pobar and Ivasic-Kos 2018), YOLO (Rahati and Rahbar 2022), and C3D (Convolutional 3D) Networks (Rongved et al. 2021) are all methods for capturing and detecting motion targets. However, the first two methods are more complex and slower, so they may not be suitable for basketball training scenarios. Basketball training scenarios have high real-time requirements and need a simple and fast way to perform motion capture and subsequent analysis.

The YOLO algorithm (Guntuboina et al. 2021) is a single-stage target detection algorithm, which does not need to generate region proposals, but directly completes target detection and classification through a forward propagation. This end-to-end architecture greatly improves the computational efficiency and inference speed, which is very suitable for real-time applications.

Overall, YOLO has higher computational efficiency and real-time performance than other methods (Buric et al. 2019), which makes it very suitable for sports training analysis scenarios that require fast feedback. While OpenPose and Mask R-CNN can provide richer target information, they may be difficult to meet the real-time requirement. Therefore, the choice of algorithms needs to be weighed according to the needs of specific application scenarios.

3 Methods

3.1 Study Design

This section is used to describe the steps and methods we used to conduct the experiment. In order to be able to complete the study smoothly and produce good arithmetic results. The study uses a total of three steps, the first is data collection and pre-process, the second is the labelling of images and model training, and the third is the presentation of the predicted results. Continuous cycles and validation are carried out in this process to achieve optimal results. As shown in Fig. 1.

In this study, multiple angles of youth basketball training videos and images were sought from search engines to be used as input data to be imported into the models selected for the study. To perform action recognition on videos from youth basketball training, the Yolov8-l model was chosen as the basis for the basketball sports model and a 100-round training cycle was developed using the Yolov8-l model to ensure that the emphasis on model performance was minimised. Videos and images of basketball sports training were obtained from search engines and field photography. Validation testing of the machine learning algorithms was required before the experiments could begin. After testing and comparing different several algorithms, the study chose the Yolov8 model, which is highly adaptable to multidimensional and complex backgrounds. After data collection and processing, we performed image annotation and primary training of the model. Eventually a new training cycle was developed

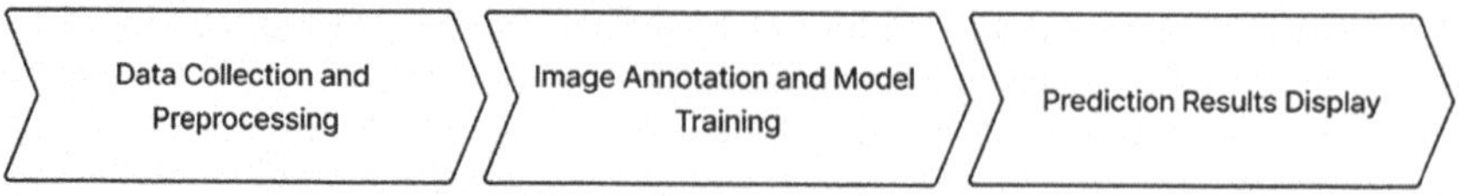

Fig. 1 Experimental procedure

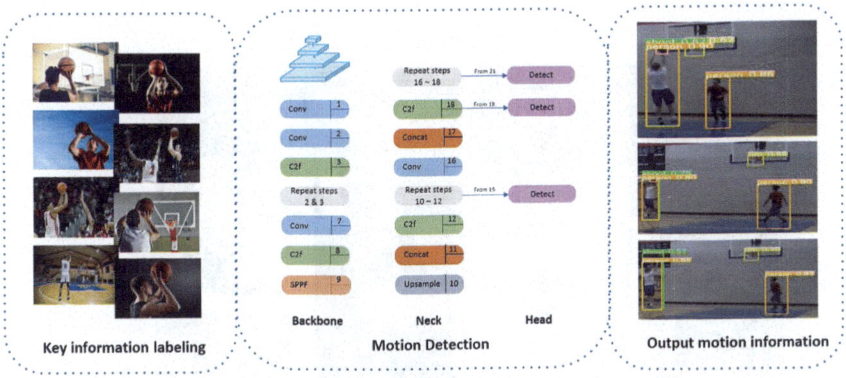

Fig. 2 Flow of motion recognition

based on the model to accommodate the analysis of players' movement data. The specific process is shown in Fig. 2.

3.2 Data Collection and Pre-processing

In order to carry out the machine learning research related to basketball training, we first collected a large amount of video and image data of basketball games and training from search engines and on-site shooting. These raw data cover a variety of complex environmental backgrounds, such as the court, locker room, gym, etc., which provide sufficient material for the subsequent algorithm validation and optimisation. During the pre-processing and annotation of these data, we need to address various challenges such as occlusion of viewpoints, dynamic backgrounds, etc. to ensure the integrity and reliability of the data. Through this series of work, we have laid a solid data foundation for the subsequent experiments. As shown in Fig. 3.

Before starting the experiments formally, we conducted extensive comparative testing and validation of multiple target detection and tracking algorithms. Firstly, we comprehensively evaluated the performance of each algorithm using a series of metrics such as precision, recall, processing speed, etc. for different scenarios and backgrounds. Through repeated debugging and optimisation, we finally chose the Yolov8 model as the core algorithm in this study. This model shows excellent adaptability and robustness in complex multi-dimensional background, which not only can accurately detect the position of the players, but also can achieve efficient real-time tracking, which meets our research needs. With the support of the reliable algorithm, we can further develop targeted player tracking and behavioural analysis solutions to provide intelligent support and optimization suggestions for basketball training. As shown in Fig. 4.

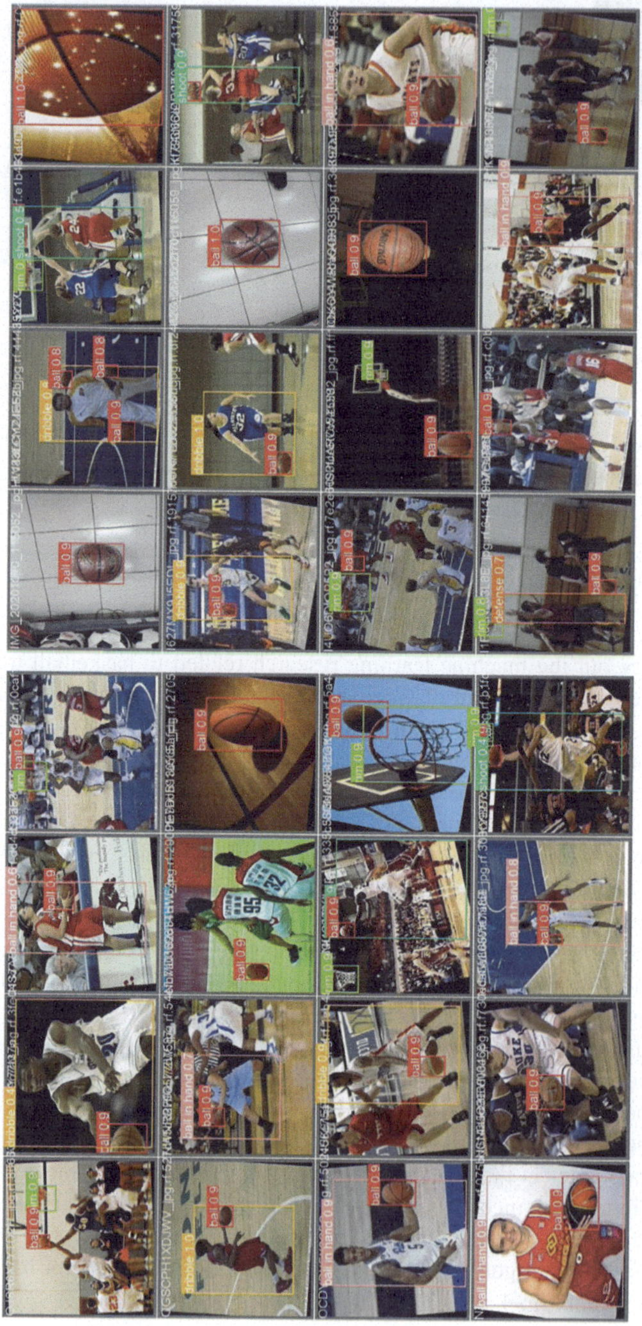

Fig. 3 Input pictures of basketballs, basketball courts

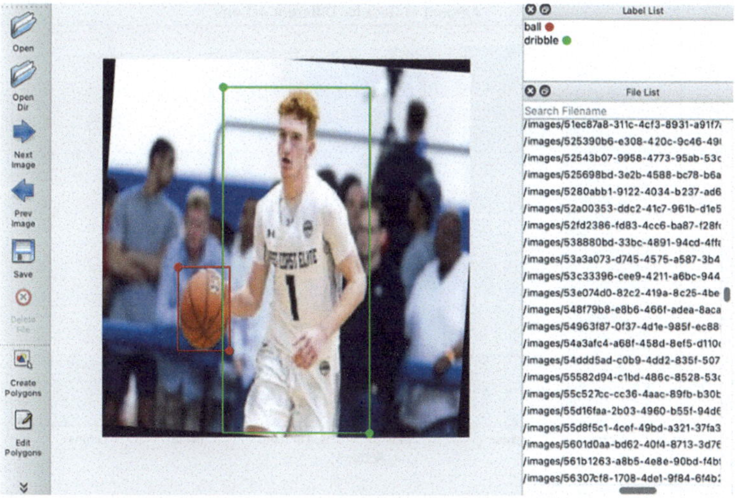

Fig. 4 Inside view of motion capture software

3.3 Image Annotation and Model Training

The process of basketball training produces different playing movements for players in solo and group exercise situations. Even in performing a coherent set of training movements, it can still be broken down into 4–5 movements. In order to make the experiment smooth and simple to perform, we decompose the basketball movements so that the AI can capture the key steps in the movements. For this purpose, we extracted 6 basic movements from a large number of movements that appear in almost every basketball player's training process and are necessary to perform basketball training. These 6 movements are: dribble, shoot, pass, ball in hand, made, defence.

During model training, nearly 6500 data were labelled with six different categories of basketball movements. The most labelled are dribble and shoot, with more than 1600, followed by pass, with more than 1500. The least labelled is the defensive action, with close to 400 labelled. This is shown in Fig. 5.

After the chart markers, we can see the side view of the motion capture range box for all the pictures, and all the captured motions are almost in the centre of the view, indicating that the camera is relatively accurate in capturing the motions. And the size of the action also affects the position of the picture recognition. As shown in Fig. 6.

At the end of the experiment, we wanted to come up with a more optimised model, so we added new images for capture analysis. The optimised iteration of the model was carried out from 69 to 81 rounds.

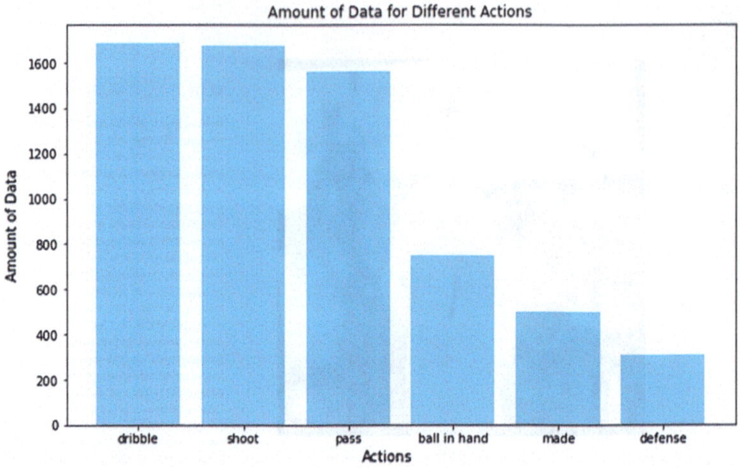

Fig. 5 Amount of data for different actions

Fig. 6 Side view of the captured image

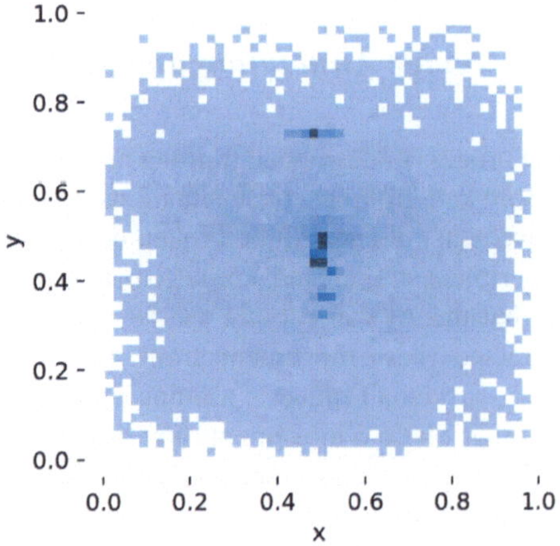

4 Findings

The study demonstrated the feasibility of capturing and analysing the movements of youth basketball players using advanced visual recognition algorithms combined with a high-quality dataset. The AI model significantly outperformed existing recognition algorithms, achieving an around 10% increase in accuracy and a 30% improvement in processing efficiency. The model reached a critical training milestone, achieving performance balance at the 81st iteration, as indicated by a stabilisation in the loss function and validation accuracy. Additionally, the AI system maintained a consistent frame rate of 30 FPS during real-time feedback on a personal computer, ensuring practical applicability in live training sessions. These findings underscore the potential of AI-driven solutions to enhance sports training through precise and efficient movement analysis.

4.1 *Training Epoch Analysis*

During the training of the AI visual recognition model on the annotated dataset, we closely monitored its performance, efficiency, and accuracy. To balance high precision with hardware limitations, we conducted multiple rounds of model derivation and optimisation across various models. Ultimately, we selected the Yolov8-l model for our basketball application due to its high accuracy and compatibility with our computational resources.

Subsequently, we developed a 100-epoch training cycle for the Yolov8-l model, aiming to maximise performance. Additionally, we performed multiple fine-tuning adjustments on parameters (such as learning rate and confidence threshold) to prevent overfitting, implementing early stopping if no significant improvement was observed over 10 consecutive epochs. Consequently, after observing no significant performance gains between epochs 71 and 81, we halted training at epoch 81. As illustrated

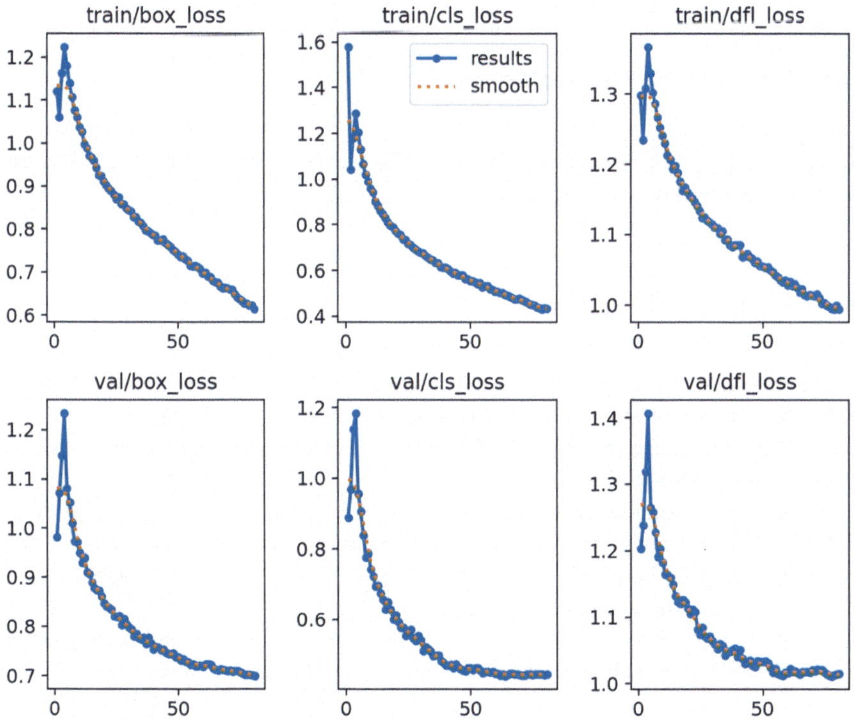

Fig. 7 The results of model training

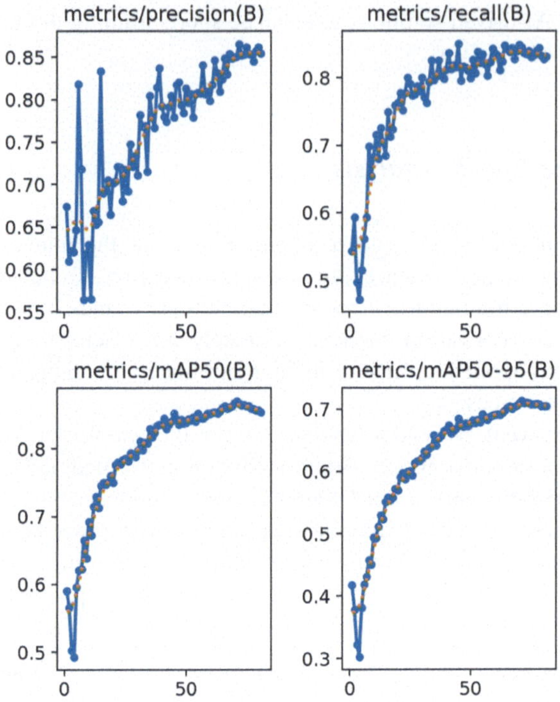

Fig. 8 The results of model training (Continue)

in Figs. 7 and 8, this indicates that our model achieved an optimal balance between high accuracy and robustness.

4.2 Model Performance

At the end of the training phase, we evaluated the performance of the basketball action recognition model trained by the YoloV8-l model by analysing the F1 scores at different confidence thresholds and providing a detailed summary of the model's classification performance.

Figure 9 F1-Confidence Curve shows the F1 confidence curves for various basketball-related categories, including "ball", "holding the ball", "defence", "dribbling", "making", "passing", "rebounding", and "shooting". The F1-Confidence Curve offers a comprehensive view of the model's precision and recall balance at different confidence levels. The thick blue line represents the overall performance across all categories, achieving an F1 score of 0.84 at a confidence threshold of 0.264. This indicates that the model performs optimally when the confidence threshold is set

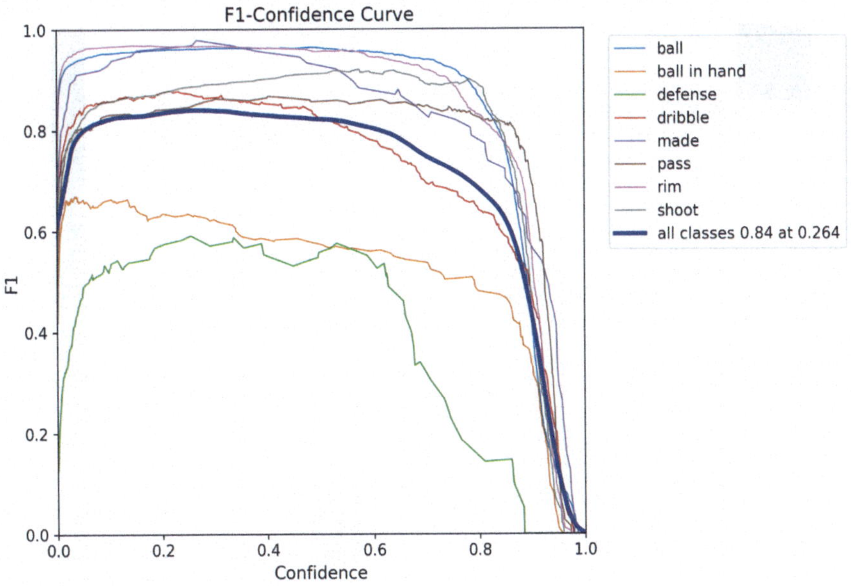

Fig. 9 F1-confidence curve

at 0.264, maintaining high accuracy and robustness across diverse basketball activities. Furthermore, considering the model's recognition accuracy for core basketball actions (e.g., shooting, dribbling), the recognition accuracy can be as high as approximately 0.9 when the confidence threshold is set to around 0.6.

Figure 10 Confusion Matrix provides a comprehensive view of the model's classification performance by comparing the predicted labels with the actual labels. In the matrix, each row corresponds to the predicted categories, and each column represents the actual categories. The diagonal elements represent the number of correct predictions for each category, while the off-diagonal elements indicate the number of misclassifications. The matrix reveals that the basketball action recognition model performs exceptionally well in the "ball" and "rim" categories, which are objects with larger data volumes and object categories, achieving 98% and 94% recognition accuracy, respectively. In the action categories such as dribbling, shooting, and passing, which also have relatively large data volumes, the model demonstrates commendable performance. Although the recognition rates in other categories are less impressive, the overall performance of the model underscores its great potential in the field of action recognition.

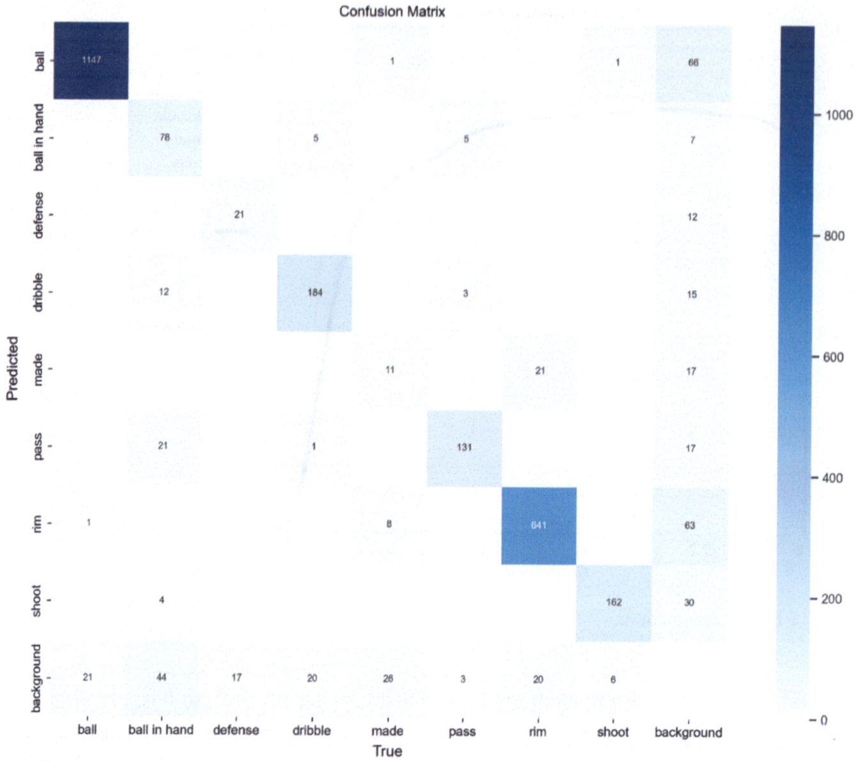

Fig. 10 Confusion matrix

5 Discussion and Conclusion

The results show that the machine learning algorithms can accurately identify the player's action behavior and the trajectory of the basketball. In order to achieve continuous tracking of each player and his movements on the basketball court from start to finish, we plan to add tracking algorithms to the current model. Therefore, it is recommended to conduct initial smart coaching for players accepted by the AI and XR technology. This will not only improve the efficiency of the players' movement, but also save the coach's resources and link labor costs. Future research can be extended to develop systems that can automatically record and analyze the number of times a player acts on the court (e.g., shooting, dribbling, passing) based on our model. This will provide coaches and players with valuable data to help them analyze game strategies and improve their skills. This research will incorporate a user-friendly interface with XR scenarios for multi-sensory design, such as training coaching to assist augmented reality.

In addition to real-time tracking and analysis of player movement and basketball trajectory, AI and XR technology can bring additional unique benefits to basketball training. With XR technology, coaches can provide personalised visual feedback and guidance to players in a virtual simulation environment. Players are able to immerse themselves in the coach's real-time comments and demonstrations, which helps them to better master and correct their own technical movements. This interactive training mode not only enhances the learning efficiency of players, but also reduces the workload for coaches. The automated analysis system based on artificial intelligence can record and evaluate all data indicators of players in the actual game. Coaches and players can analyse these data in depth, discover their own strengths and weaknesses, and develop more targeted training plans accordingly. This not only promotes the individual progress of players, but also helps to improve the tactical level of the whole team.

In addition, AI can also help coaches optimise the team's overall training strategy. Through the intelligent analysis of a large amount of historical data, the system can provide coaches with professional data support and decision-making advice, such as the best tactical solutions for different opponents. This will greatly improve the coach's coaching efficiency and bring better performance for the team. The application of AI and XR technology in basketball training is injecting new vitality and imagination into the sport. These technologies will bring more expected innovations, creating a more intelligent and personalised training experience for coaches and players.

6 Future Study

For the development of artificial intelligence in the field of sports training contains a vast research space. Based on the current research, we will continue to optimise the algorithmic models, hardware equipment and data analysis means in the subsequent research, to bring new support and intelligent training changes for coaches and players. Firstly, for the enhancement of player motion tracking technology, besides DeepSORT-based player tracking, more advanced computer vision algorithms, such as multi-target tracking and attitude estimation, can be explored in the future to further improve the tracking accuracy. Meanwhile, our research will consider combining sensors worn by players with visual tracking to obtain more comprehensive motion data. These data can not only be used for tactical analysis, but also provide the basis for player fitness monitoring and injury prevention. Secondly, the optimisation of the camera setup is particularly important when it comes to capturing players' training movements. In addition to optimising the number and layout of cameras, in the future, we can also try to introduce panoramic cameras or array cameras to further expand the monitoring range and reduce the dead space. At the same time, our research will consider the use of RGBD cameras, combined with depth information to achieve more accurate human posture recognition. In addition, real-time processing of large amounts of high-definition video data also puts higher demands on the hardware configuration, which requires optimising the efficiency of computing resources.

Finally, for the analysis of player behaviour, based on automated action recognition, our research expects to further develop deep learning-based behavioural analysis models, which can not only identify the type of action, but also evaluate the quality of the action, and provide more targeted feedback to the players. At the same time, these data can be combined with information such as game results and player attributes to explore influencing factors and provide a basis for coaches to formulate training plans. In addition, it is possible to explore the visualisation of the analysis results, so that coaches and players can understand the data insights intuitively.

Acknowledgements The work described in this paper was fully supported by a grant from the Hong Kong Polytechnic University (Project No. P0042738).

References

Buric, M., Ivasic-Kos, M., & Pobar, M. (2019). Player Tracking in Sports Videos. *2019 IEEE International Conference on Cloud Computing Technology and Science (CloudCom)*, 334–340. https://doi.org/10.1109/CloudCom.2019.00058.

Feng, J. (2023). Designing an Artificial Intelligence-based sport management system using big data. Soft Computing, 27(21), 16331–16352. https://doi.org/10.1007/s00500-023-09162-0.

Guntuboina, C., Porwal, A., Jain, P., & Shingrakhia, H. (2021). Deep Learning Based Automated Sports Video Summarization Using Yolo. *ELCVIA Electronic Letters on Computer Vision and Image Analysis, 20*(1), Article 1. https://doi.org/10.5565/rev/elcvia.1286.

Khandelwal, K., & Upadhyay, A. K. (2021). The advent of artificial intelligence-based coaching. Strategic HR Review, 20(4), 137–140. https://doi.org/10.1108/SHR-03-2021-0013.

Li, Y.-C., Chang, C.-T., Cheng, C.-C., & Huang, Y.-L. (2021). Baseball Swing Pose Estimation Using OpenPose. *2021 IEEE International Conference on Robotics, Automation and Artificial Intelligence (RAAI)*, 6–9. https://doi.org/10.1109/RAAI52226.2021.9507807.

Mohan, S., Venkatakrishnan, A., & Hartzler, A. L. (2020). Designing an AI Health Coach and Studying Its Utility in Promoting Regular Aerobic Exercise. ACM Transactions on Interactive Intelligent Systems, 10(2), 14:1–14:30. https://doi.org/10.1145/3366501.

Palumbo, F., Crivello, A., Furfari, F., Girolami, M., Mastropietro, A., Manferdelli, G., Röcke, C., Guye, S., Salvá Casanovas, A., Caon, M., Carrino, F., Abou Khaled, O., Mugellini, E., Denna, E., Mauri, M., Ward, D., Subías-Beltrán, P., Orte, S., Candea, C., … Rizzo, G. (2020). "Hi This Is NESTORE, Your Personal Assistant": Design of an Integrated IoT System for a Personalized Coach for Healthy Aging. Frontiers in Digital Health, 2. https://www.frontiersin.org/10.3389/fdgth.2020.545949.

Pobar, M., & Ivasic-Kos, M. (2018). Mask R-CNN and Optical Flow Based Method for Detection and Marking of Handball Actions. *2018 11th International Congress on Image and Signal Processing, BioMedical Engineering and Informatics (CISP-BMEI)*, 1–6. https://doi.org/10.1109/CISP-BMEI.2018.8633201.

Rahati, A., & Rahbar, K. (2022). Sports movements modification based on 2D joint position using YOLO to 3D skeletal model adaptation. *Journal of AI and Data Mining, 10*(4), 549–557. https://doi.org/10.22044/jadm.2022.11975.2344.

Rai, A., Constantinides, P., & Sarker, S. (2019). Next generation digital platforms: Toward human-AI hybrids. *MIS Quarterly, 43*(1), Article 1.

Rongved, O. A. N., Hicks, S. A., Thambawita, V., Stensland, H. K., Zouganeli, E., Johansen, D., Midoglu, C., Riegler, M. A., & Halvorsen, P. (2021). Using 3D Convolutional Neural Networks for Real-time Detection of Soccer Events. *International Journal of Semantic Computing, 15*(2), 161–187. Q4. https://doi.org/10.1142/S1793351X2140002X.

Theeboom, T., Beersma, B., & van Vianen, A. E. M. (2014). Does coaching work? A meta-analysis on the effects of coaching on individual level outcomes in an organizational context. *The Journal* of Positive Psychology, 9(1), 1–18. https://doi.org/10.1080/17439760.2013.837499.

Zhang, Y. (2022). The construction of college students' sports health management service platform based on artificial intelligence. International Journal of System Assurance Engineering and Management, 13(3), 1102–1110. https://doi.org/10.1007/s13198-021-01440-0.

The Potential of Volumetric Captured Humans in Augmented Reality to Enrich Music Event Experiences

Shima Rezaei Rashnoodi, Maren van der Burght, Tim van Ieperen, and Marnix S. van Gisbergen

Abstract New technologies to create very real virtual humans in XR enter the market, providing new opportunities and challenges for the music industry. An important stepping stone to efficiently implement technologies to create new or resemble existing music artists, is to understand the hurdles and potential of these new XR technologies. Eighteen interviews with experts, artists and event visitors familiar with AR, revealed important possibilities and barriers to use Virtual Humans created by means of Volumetric Capturing. Seeing the potential and need of realistic virtual beings, participants prioritized necessary improvements within three themes: (1) Ease of Use, deals with technological complexity, connection issues (distraction and obstruction) and the need of new business models and lower production costs. (2) Usefulness, deals with new opportunitics based on high realism digital twin opportunities and the changing perspective of 'live performance. (3) Content, stressed the need for successful examples, the value of proximity, and disruption due to the lack of awareness and creativity.

Keywords Augmented Reality · Virtual Humans · Music · Events · Volumetric Capturing · Needs

1 Introduction

With a revenue of more than 65 billion euros worldwide, the music events industry is constantly seeking innovations to enhance visitor experience and sustain revenue growth (Yeoman 2013). In 2019, the Netherlands hosted 1,117 music festivals and 28,862 shows, underlining the industry's significance (Statista 2021; VNPF 2019). The use of smartphones, averaging over three hours of daily usage per person, emphasizes the importance of exploring mobile-related innovations in improving music event experiences (Pop 2021). Technologies such as Augmented Reality (AR) and Volumetric Capturing, present opportunities and challenges for artisits and music

S. Rezaei Rashnoodi · M. van der Burght · T. van Ieperen · M. S. van Gisbergen (✉)
BUAS—Breda University of Applied Sciences, Breda, The Netherlands
e-mail: Gisbergen.m@buas.nl

T. Jung et al. (eds.), *XR and Metaverse*, Springer Proceedings in Business and Economics, https://doi.org/10.1007/978-3-031-77975-6_4

event organizers (Houston 2020). Volumetric Capturing (VolCap), also referred to as 3D free-viewpoint capturing, captures the movements of people using 3D construction techniques (Zerman et al. 2020). VolCap enables individuals to experience humans in a realistic and immersive way, that resembles the movements and looks of a real person. Moreover, it creates a 3D view from any angle and distance which makes it possible to walk around the virtual humans. VolCap content can be implemented in many applications, including 2D and 3D videos, 360° videos, and Virtual and Augmented Reality.

1.1 Advantages of VolCap AR

Volumetric Captured Augmented Reality (VolCap AR) offers distinct advantages over conventional AR or VR. It provides realistic content, cost-effectiveness, rapid deployment, and portability (Sterzentsenko et al. 2019). VolCap enables the creation of digital humans, defined as lifelike beings capable of conversing, communicating, and establishing emotional connections (Silva and Bonetti 2021). Silva and Bonetti (2021) stress the significance of human-like characteristics and natural interaction for optimal engagement. In live music events, using VolCap AR may *enhance visitor presence.* It offers a realistic AR experience with digital humans that fosters *immersion* and visual appeal. This, in turn, can contribute to a *richer overall experience* and the desired wow effect, crucial for attracting and retaining visitors (Ivanova 2018). Several music artists have been recorded in VolCap (see for instance www.4dviews.com), which stresses the importance of gaining insights into how to incorporate them to create enhanced or new types of music experiences before, during, or after music events (Fig. 1).

Although these examples show high realism, resemblance, production efficiency, and quality, it remains unclear how to utilize these in AR at festivals or in music venues. This is especially complex for starting artists, or artists with much smaller budgets compared to the successful and more well-known VolCap-created examples such as Coldplay, ABBA, or Elton John. Research indicated that content that reflects a high level of realism and resemblance enhances the sense of presence and the illusion of being there (Biocca 1996). Studies affirm that VolCap AR generates a heightened sense of presence compared to for instance 360° videos creating an experience akin to real-life events (Orús et al. 2021).

1.2 Challenges Around VolCap AR

However, more is needed besides high realism and immersion. Aligning with Pine and Gilmore's (2011) experience economy model, a successful VolCap AR application should balance aesthetics, education, entertainment, and escapism to engage visitors and enhance the overall event experience (Olya et al. 2020). Moreover, to create a

Fig. 1 Photos of VolCap recorded artists (on top: the band Clouseau from Belgium, below: the Dutch performer Chagall)

high experience, the audience needs to feel connected to a person (Pine and Gilmore 2011), in this case, a digital twin of that person. In addition, for a new technology to be adopted, several factors need to be taken into consideration, among which is the acceptance of the technology. Therefore, even though the technology seems promising concerning the creation of high realism and resemblance, questions remain on how to effectively implement the technology to create effective enhanced music experiences. The Technology Acceptance Model (TAM), suggests that the perceived usefulness and ease of use are pivotal for users, particularly in music events, to adopt and accept technology like VolCap AR. Ongoing experiments are actively exploring techniques for VolCap, emphasizing the urgency of understanding the capabilities and constraints in this field (McIlvenny 2020; Zell et al. 2021; Schreer et al. 2020; Huang et al. 2018). *Practical issues* include limitations of head-mounted displays (HMDs) and mobile phones with small field of view, resolution limitations, refresh rate constraints (Billinghurst 2021), but also the constraints in freedom of movement (the latter is an important reason to use but also improve AR glasses). *Interaction challenges* arise from the need for intuitive usage, proper position tracking for 3D objects, and potential distractions from the immersive event experience (Billinghurst 2021). *Content creation issues* also appear, that deal with challenges in aligning VolCap content with the narrative and aesthetics of music events to avoid cognitive dissonance and ensure a positive user experience (Dirin and Laine 2018). In addition, a high level of realism can also be perceived as eerie and experience as postulated in the *Uncanny Valley* theory (Seymour et al. 2021). *Quality content creation* issues around VolCap AR involve challenges in digital lighting, spatial awareness, and VolCap capture limitations such as challenges in capturing transparent or reflective elements (clothes). However, as technology is advancing, solutions are developed to optimize these technical obstacles (Billinghurst 2021). *Connectivity issues* arise often at live events for smartphones but seem to be more of a challenge around VolCap AR considering the size of the files and the delay that can cause interaction problems between an artist and VolCap application. The 5G network might be seen as a potential solution, but is still a technology in development. Another connection challenge deals with the fear of distraction. The use of the technology may *distract* from the live experience, the artist performing, when it is presented simultaneously (Billinghurst 2021; O'Dwyer et al. 2020; Dirin and Laine 2018; Scheffels 2020). *Legal challenges* associated with the realism of VolCap AR causes problems in what can and cannot be recorded, streamed and used and prompt the need for updated laws and clarity (Lemley and Volkokh 2018). In summary, understanding the practical constraints, and aligning potential solutions with visitor and artist needs are vital for a successful integration of VolCap AR in music events. This study aims to understand artists, visitor and expert needs and preferences, design considerations, and the challenges and benefits associated with VolCap AR in the context of music performances and events. In addition, it provides a better understanding of music artists' experiences and expert opinions on how to further develop and implement VolCap AR technology efficiently to enhance the visitor experience.

2 Methodology

2.1 Design

A qualitative approach was used to investigate the hurdles and potentials of using VolCap AR within music events. Semi-structured interviews were conducted with (a) musicians who had experience with Volcap and (b) music event visitors and AR experts. As such, perceptions around VolCap from different stakeholders in the music industry are discussed to provide insights and guidelines around creation and implementation.

2.2 Participants

Through purposeful sampling 18 participants were interviewed from July to September in 2022. Participants were divided into two groups. The first group included (early-career) music artists from different genres ranging from pop and metal to classic and experimental. In addition, the roles ranged from lead singers to live-DJ's often combining roles as producer, composer and manager. The age of the artists ranged between 20 and 60 years, and they were all already familiar with VolCap. Some artists released full (successful) VolCap based music videos in 2D or in VR (often capturing themselves as virtual humans), released AR apps for famous events or as enriched experiences on vinyl, and created 360° music videos. An example VolCap project of one of the artists, Coloray, can be downloaded or seen online as well as an interview with the artist on AIXR (van Happen 2022). Others where in the middle of testing the technology (see also https://www.effenaar.nl/nl/hybrid-music-vibes-english). The second group (aged between 18 and 34), included three visitors, three experts in AR technology and three music/ event managers. The visitors frequently visit music events and are familiar with AR (Table 1).

2.3 *Material*

The visitors and experts not familiar with VolCap, were shown a video illustrating VolCap technology at the start of the interview, created by 4D views who provides among others the software to make VolCap possible (Fig. 2). The video is called Dynamic Volumetric Capture technology and shows the process of how Volumetric Captured Augmented Reality is made along with examples of how the VolCap AR content is applied into an application. However, given that the artists were already familiar with the technology, they were not shown VolCap examples at the start of the interview. They instead talked about their own experience with VolCap and how this can be implemented within their music.

2.4 *Measures*

The interviews had an average duration of 30–50 min. The interviews started with background information about music event visits, expertise, artist engagement and phone usage (at events). The topic list was structured around conceptual frameworks such as the AR conceptual model that includes subtopics like Reality, Content, and Information Visualization (Klinker et al. 2003), the AR/VR adoption model that seals with channel, creation, content, costs, and connection (Van Gisbergen 2016), and topics related to the Technology Acceptance Model derived from previous research (Singh and Srivastava 2019). In addition, questions were asked about preferences, (expected) experiences, and expertise regarding the application and development of VolCap AR. Analysis revealed four main themes: Ease of Use, Usefulness, Reality (Live), and Content.

Table 1 Participant overview

NR	Occupation	Gender	Age	VolCap interest	VolCap Experience (in years)
R01	Artist, released AR app in 2019	F	30–40	Yes	4
R02	Artist rock & music manager	M	20–30	Maybe	1
R03	Artist, musician & composer	M	50–60	Yes	1
R04	Artist, released VolCap VR 2022	M	20–50	Yes	2
R05	Artist, released VolCap video 2023	F	30–40	Yes	3
R06	Artist, released 3D music animations	M	40–50	Maybe	1
R07	Artist, starting to work with VolCap	F	30–40	Yes	1
R08	Artist, released VolCap music clip	M	30–40	Yes	3
R09	Artist, released several VolCap clips	F	30–40	Yes	5
R10	Visitor music events	F	20–30	Yes	0
R11	Visitor music events	F	20–30	Yes	0
R12	Visitor music events	F	20–30	Yes	0
R13	VolCap creator	M	30–40	Yes	10
R14	Music digital manager	M	40–50	Yes	1
R15	XR (VR + AR) creator	M	30–40	Yes	2
R16	Music label manager	M	30–40	Yes	4
R17	Music research + Coordinator	F	30–40	Yes	1
R18	Music venue marketing prog	M	40–50	Yes	5

3 Results

Overall visitors, artists, and experts consider VolCap AR as a technology that can be used to enhance music experiences if improvements are made within the three themes: Ease of Use, Usefulness, and Content that are connected to the five topics around the main issues found in previous studies. For Ease of Use these concern high costs, complexity and the questions around connectivity (will it increase or decrease?). For usefulness the main issues were focused around the meaning of

Fig. 2 Screenshot of the instruction example video around VolCap. Retrieved from: https://www.youtube.com/watch?v=bsDtIpQQR5A

live performing, proximity, (technical) quality and realism, which next to practical examples and legal constrains, were also the main issues within the Content theme.

3.1 Ease of Use

Visitors, artists, and experts are aware of the advantages of VolCap AR to increase experiences. The key hurdle is concentrated around the implementation challenges when it comes to live performance. The key concerns are related to the practical dimension of (a) *high production costs* (b) *usage complexity* and the connectivity dimension (c) *unclear audience artist link.*

High costs. This point of concern was mainly raised by the artists. For them, the technology seems first and foremost promising for artists who can reach a large audience for their life performances in events and venues. Ease of use in this context also refers to the **complexity of business models** around VolCap AR and the rapid developments in the technology itself (***R1***: "*The first problem is the money…everything needs to go to the technology itself and nothing is left for marketing and creativity. The music Industry does not provide a good business model for technology innovation. The music Industry is so to say a bit broken*"). For artists it is unclear if the audience is **willing to pay extra** for VolCap AR. Early career artists are concerned about **raising enough money for production**, especially as there is (a) **no reach**, making it hard to obtain a sustainable (extra) audience (***R2***: " *we do not have enough reach, as it is already hard to attract a large audience as a starting artists, let alone if they also need to have AR glasses. Not for famous artists as Beyonce. Moreover, if they [famous artists] use this, it will also kill the newness effect for us and we will not be* *considered as original*"). The volumes for starting artists are considered too small to cover the costs or to have (enough) budget to experiment. This is connected with the second reason; (b) **no clarity** on how VolCap AR can **increase (durable) income** even when it considers artists that have already died, especially as they believe that there is already so much free content out there (***R4***: *Lack of budget is the most important bottleneck as it is too expensive as the physical experience, sound, light and so forth, has priority. This is problematic, especially as you cannot reach a lot of people. We had to change the original plan from reaching a large audience through online streaming to a few people in VR to a few people in smartphones as not all devices can play it and Apple store would not provide access*"). According to the experts there is currently **not a real business model** or business model ownership for VolCap productions within the music industry (***R16***: "*therefore it is mainly used as a promotional tool, which is often the case when it deals with innovations*"). On the other hand, the experts claim that VolCap can be a potential opportunity to deal with the new forms of competition of (music) entertainment consumption (***R14***: "*Why is it hard to fill a music venue? Where are these people and what are they doing instead? Maybe they are playing games and artists should be more in the games*").

Complexity. All participants agreed that in this phase, all technology lacks the quality and easiness to get the full potential of a VolCap production successful and viable (with a few exceptions of major productions like the Sphere or Abba production). In addition, the participants questioned whether it was clear enough for the artists and the audience how to use it, when suddenly confronted with the technology before, during, or even after the event (***R4***: "*Also, besides the artists and audience, all the people within the creation pipeline, do not understand the technology*"). The complexity first deals with a lack of knowledge, unfamiliarity with and hard to access AR volumetric capturing at all, and then also the lack of in-depth knowledge of how it can be applied in a live environment (***R8***: "*Only because I used it myself, it took away my prejudices such as that it would disconnect*"). Many participants mention the learning curve that is needed and that will take time to make VolCap, and technologies to access VolCap, mainstream. Another challenge is how to integrate the VolCap in the real world, taking into account the context and specific conditions as weather and light, as well as the difficulty to create a shared social VolCap AR experience at the same time (***R15***: "*It is very hard to translate VolCap, or any AR, to the real world, to create a natural transition between the digital and real which includes the visual as well as the audio*"). The unclarity also deals with practical usage of their own devices, the ease with how the app should function, and technical concerns such as if it would drain the batteries, overheat the phone as well as no being able to hear the sound from the speaker due to the noise (***R10***: "*maybe they should sell more powerbanks and facilitate more charging opportunities*"). It also concerns technological questions related to connection and access issues, even when 5G would be available (***R10***: "*very often the internet connection at events are horrible*"). Another challenge, according to the experts, is the technical deployment and the different devices and versions of software and legal constrains. Making it hard to create one VolCap experience that runs of all devices. Moreover, the lack of a universal framework or structure that can be used on all operating systems and devices is seen as a major bottleneck as also mentioned in previous research (Kounavis et al. 2012). ***R13***: "*It is a complex choice between choosing for reach and easy access using existing apps, or to create your own app with full control and less restrictions*". Moreover, new technologies arise fast and as such experts also expect much competition from other ways to capture artists digital, especially from the game engines, that either might compete with or enrich current VolCap technologies. For many of the experts the technology is not ready and too expensive to be used for small events and to connect to already successful streaming, cloud and easy to access technologies (***R14***: "*Over 80 percent of the artists do not have budgets like the big artists such as ABBA, and for them using VolCap to create crossovers with existing technologies and current ways how music is consumed and streamed, is too expensive, too difficult and unclear. But the technology will get more mainstream and adapted, especially when the big engines like unreal keep investing*"). In addition, it is hard for artists, especially those with no background in domains like games or design, to find and connect with different specialists that are needed, like programmers and designers (***R9***: "*I wanted a real time controlled avatar, but at that time the technology was not ready yet and certainly not seamless. People are afraid of the learning curve needed. But only by learning myself I also was able to reduce better the barriers between me, the artis, and the technology people like the programmers*").

Connection. The final barrier was related to how to use the technology to connect with the audience, and between the audience members, during a (live) performance, especially when VolCap is accessed via the smartphone. They consider on the one hand devices like phones as non-social and individualistic. On the other hand they also acknowledge that phones are already used during live performances (***R10***: "*I use my phone during a music event to make pictures, to film artists, to find locations, and schedules, share content on social media, have contact with friends and to pay*"). As such, phones and VolCap can provide new ways of interaction according to artists and experts, taking into account that many bands do not fully play live anymore using pre-recordings also due to the high demand for quality (***R2***: "*People are more critical at home compared to at an event in which the phone itself also becomes more of a shield between artists and audience, reducing intensity and interactivity*"). It is unclear how to use and view the VolCap while, at the same time, experiencing the life performance. This also fuses the fear of the visitors of being too much distracted (***R11***: "*If it is* via *the phone, it would be cool for a short moment, like during one song. Otherwise it's a pity of the real experience and it loses that feeling of reality, like when you are constantly filming…Hmm yes if it was* via *[headmounted] glasses it would be very cool and less of a problem*"). A major concern was whether the VolCap AR would hinder the live experience and as such reduce connection and engagement (***R4***: "*It is just a super big hurdle to have to put on AR glasses but also to get an idea into the App store for instance*"). In addition, there is a lack of (visible) creativity according to the artists themselves. Several artists and experts have not seen good examples that are considered innovative and inspirational. The experts add the complexity and hurdle of VolCap now mainly being a recording, making it limited in what you can change in the VolCap after production, which makes it difficult to integrate it with (live) performances. At the moment the participants consider VolCap AR more commercial driven, making it a cool and useful marketing and branding tool, instead of providing creative artistic value (***R6***: "*It is not yet creative enough but more a trick. To be able to place the artist [with VolCap AR] everywhere and make a picture of you with the artist, feels like the first movie without sound*"). As such, most experts look for possibilities for VolCap Ar within the whole customer journey, without a clear sales proposition, before, during and after a live visit, while artists first look for additions during the live performance.

3.2 Usefulness

All agreed that VolCAP AR will never replace a real live performance, despite the need for replacement due to pandemics like Corona and the desire to be more sustainable (to travel less). As such, experts and artists mainly look for the added value next to or on top of a real performance (***R7***: "*It will never replace live as you cannot feel and really see an artist behind a screen…but it opens up connections with people in a new way. It is hard to find the usefulness, as a really good artist or band does not need much extra, but on the other hand people want innovation*").

Duplication. Several artists stressed the potential of the technology to create virtual and augmented duplicates of themselves which creates potential new *connection* possibilities between artists and audience, between the audience itself (***R10***: "*A key reason for me to visit is to be with friends and to experience the music with other people*"), and between artists (***R4***: "*If that allows me to perform, for example with Björk…she's in Iceland with a full audience and I come there as a guest in an augmented reality. Yes. That's super cool*"). Some stressed the opportunities that AR and virtual humans offer to create more experience (***R3***: "*Fantastic, AR might explain my abstract music and reduce environment distraction as you can guide the audience*") and more proximity (***R2***: "*You can add more experience dimensions and you can get an artist much more up close and personal at home in front of TV but mainly during an event. Especially for famous artists that are often far away and this might increase the experience comparted to only using large 2D screens*"). Some experts stressed the need for artists to promote themselves as beings, which VolCap can provide, as a lot of songs are listened to in streaming services as Spotify (***R19***: "*while listing to songs at home, the audience often has no idea who the artist is or looks like. VolCap creates an engaging opportunity to get some of the attention back to the artis and their stories*").

Realness. An important value according to the participants is the high realism in appearance and movement created through VolCap. Some artists and experts, however, were more concerned about the uncanny valley (as being perceived as weird due to the very realistic nature of the VolCap which makes all incorrections feel creepy), the challenges around deep fakes, and losing the attention and engagement of the audience for the physical performance (***R9***: "*The VolCap can bring high quality and error free performance, but on the other hand the magic of live performance is also that it can go wrong*"). Also the visitors stressed the importance of realness or resemblance when it comes to the performers (***R10***: "*Yes viewing artists or dances, it really has to look and move like the real person. But the examples you showed me really did look real*"). The participants stressed their concern about a disconnected interaction with the audience. As such, especially for artists, 'place' becomes important (***R7***: "*the VolCap should only be visible between the artists on stage during the performance*"). This also means that the production of the VolCap, for instance the lighting used, should be congruent (real) with the context and place of the performance. Which according to the experts is very difficult to realize. Interestingly, the visitors and experts were less worried about the negative effects and stressed the engagement and connection VolCap is likely to create with the artists (***R13***: "*Users really felt a connection with the performers*"; ***R16***: "*We did some research and it showed that the VolCap experience came very close to the feeling of a live experience for the audience, except of course when the technology failed*"). They focused on the possibilities outside of the artist's performance, conceptualizing creative ways VolCap could be incorporated into the customer journey and for marketing purposes. Experts also mentioned that despite low user numbers for the VolCap productions they created, they could infer from the data that a lot of people like to share the content showing how artists perform in their home or during a social event on their table for instance (***R8***: "*In an afterparty, people go into a blackhole not seen by the artists. Now [with Volcap AR] I can enter myself or the after party can be filled with VolCap artist representations*").

3.3 Content

Several of the possibilities and issues mentioned in previous studies were recognized. The potential was recognized but the lack of successful commercial and creative examples was seen as the most important bottleneck related to content.

Live. All participants first and foremost concentrated on possibilities during *live performances*, stimulating a discussion on what live means for themselves (***R7***: "*If Volumetric can't be used in real-time, it doesn't make much sense for my shows*"), and for the audience (***R6***: "*I think it mainly means a shared experience, being there at the moment with some form of interaction, so not only streaming*"). However, at the same time, artists, experts and visitors had difficulties visualizing ideas in how to use AR VolCap during a real performance. The participants would like to understand better what the audience would perceive as live (***R9***: "*Is Karaoke live?*"), especially around new possibilities such as performing with remote or artists that have passed away (***R1***: "*It is about the human touch. About what live means, as with a virtual human it means you are present and you are not present especially if it lacks interactivity* *and when the technology comes between the artists and audience. Also I would still feel lonely interacting only with a fake band*"). The feeling of being present, with or without being acknowledge by other people, was also seen as a core aspect of whether or not something is considered as a live performance by the audience (***R10***: "*I think it means that I am really present in real time and that it happens on that moment*"). Some stressed that digital cannot include all senses like in live (yet) and that at least the audience should be physical present, but that the performance can be physical, digital or a mix (***R11***: "*My eyes and ears need to be there physically, I already live enough in my phone*"; ***R17***: "*When I am physically there with friends, it does not matter for me at all whether it is a projection or physical life performance. It is live*"). The experts distinguished between different levels of live, adding the importance of exclusivity in time or that it needs to be produced at that moment to be perceived as live (***R12***: "*Live seems to imply also that you can access it only once at a certain time, but that could be a pre-recording. But the highest level is being at the location when it is performed at that moment, giving a feeling of being unique, which for me can also be a digital location*"). The experts themselves also acknowledged that the technology changed their perception of the meaning of live (***R19***: "*It used to be a physical performance on a stage with a real audience connecting with the artists performing on stage. Now it mainly means for me that a connection through interactions has been realized*"). The experts added to that discussion that on demand and streaming experiences also stretch the feeling of what live time wise means (***R14***: "*Now people consider starting a show or news broadcast live, even when they start 5 min later, as it is still the latest broadcast*"). Finally, the participants stressed the importance of a recorded VolCap production or a life VolCap production (***R16***: "*life Volcap and recorded Volcap both offer ways to extend a life concert to more venues or places at the same time, but technology developments need to speed up to make it viable*").

Proximity. A key benefit mentioned was proximity; the possibility AR VolCap brings to get the artists closer to the audience as, especially for famous artists, as the stage is often far away making it hard to see the artists up close and certainly not in 3D (***R10***: "*Seeing your examples, I would think it would be super cool if it brings artists to the event, and see them in3D or even 4D, because they already have died or because they often only send their DJ and they now could add a dancer to the performance or something...I would pay extra for that*"). Some idea's mentioned within proximity also addressed the possibilities before or after the event (***R11***: "*It would be nice if an artist showed me the way or introduced the other artists*"). The proximity does not only refer to the physical distance, but also to the context of place, at home or at the festival (e.g., backstage, bathroom or waiting line performances), or bringing (physical and digital) audiences closer together (***R16***: "*What we tried with the VolCap of the band, was to get the artists as close as possible to the audience, not only making it able to look at the artists from up close from all directions, but also in the most close pace like their homes and kitchens*"). Finally, the participants stress that the proximity not only concerns the distance between the artis and audience, but also between artists.

Creativity. Despite finding it hard to come up with good concepts, artists, visitors and experts mentioned several ideas in how to use AR VolCap (***R9***: "*The key value is that it makes invisible things like feelings and emotions visible, right in front of you. Look, DJ movements are not inspiring to watch, it is just pressing buttons, and when they look at their instruments they also loose connection with the audience*"). However, the participants ale mention the lack of creativity and knowledge in how to integrate VolCap within a live performance (***R11***: "*I probably would not know where and when to watch and that would stress me out*"). Some pointed out the chances and opportunities based on the already existing implementation of digital 2D content within music performances. The experts also stress that it is important to understand the added value of VolCap to be able to make use of the creativity (***R15***: "*To make use of the potential of VolCap AR, we need ideas for instance on why you want to experience something in 3D, why you would want or need to walk around it for instance*"). Content related examples mentioned, concerned ideas like (a) enrichment: making lyrics visible, making the event theme more visible, making elements from the music clips or persons in them visible, creating different worlds and interpretations of the same song, (b) reaching the audience in new places for instance via a (live) VolCap performance at home or away from the physical context and into a game, painting or metaverse, (c) create digital twins from the artists and event, (d) create an alter ego an extended version of the artists (***R5***: "*You need to give it something I cannot do in real, give me wings or something*"), (e) to experience a performance while being between the band or on stage (***R15***: "*This for instance also requires a different kind of performance and understanding of the performers*"), (f) to capture the audience, and (g) changing the avatar in size and looks based on the song or audience interactions (***R10***: "*Would be cool that when I use my phone to find a next performance of an event and I look at the map on my phone, I would be able to see the artist perform in VolCap...makes it more human*"). The artists and experts also stressed the value of innovation VolCap could bring during the performance and stress to go for idea's that cannot be realized 'in the physical reality' (***R8***: (*[VolCap AR] needs to enrich the emotion or story of the performance... also as the old things like confetti or fire or light-effects are outdated and you cannot really do something new with those. Maybe if we use it really good, people will not have to use drugs anymore*"). However, despite the visitors claiming they would pay extra for VolCap, the artists and experts immediately raised the question about the business models behind these ideas, stressing the urge for commercial successful examples (***R4***: "*We need something the audience cannot ignore...with the least effort to use and that makes use of the context around the performance*").

4 Conclusion

Artists, Experts, and Visitors are aware of the potential of VolCap AR and articulate potential benefits as well as hurdles of which some are stipulated in previous studies. Although the visitors focused more on potential benefits while the artists and experts focused more on the challenges to overcome, both expect a role for VolCap AR in and around live music visits. Consistent with existing technology acceptance and user & gratification models, the use and acceptance of VolCap AR is according to the visitors, experts and artists depended on three factors: (**a**) the ease of use of the technology, (**b**) the expected usefulness of the technology, but also on the need for good (**c**) financial sustainable content.

'Ease of use' incorporates some of the same dimensions found in previous research and models but within the context of music and VolCap AR, such as: (**a1**) technological complexity, based on lack of knowledge, unfamiliarity, difficulty to access the technology and issues using smartphones like overheating and battery drainage, as found in previous research (Billinghurst 2021; Luxford and Dickinson 2015). The second being (**a2**) connection challenges, due to the fear the technology will produce too static non creative content that, due to the use of phones, will distract and hinder the live performance (see also Dirin and Laine 2018). This research added the challenges around the (**a3**) high costs and difficulties around making a profit. According to the artists and experts a clear business model and ownership is missing, which due to high production costs and no obvious new audience need or reach, makes the use of the technology very risky. This dilemma raises a clear need for more research and experiments around existing and new business models. As long as these are not in place, VolCap AR is mostly seen as a useful marketing tool to reach people before, during and after the live experience. This need for new technology to keep existing and new audience entertained and engaged before, during and after the event, is also stressed in previous research (Adema and Roehl 2010; Ivanova 2018).

The 'usefulness' factor mainly relates to (**b1**) duplication, creating an enriched and more immersive live performance based on virtual and augmented representation of artists (see also van Winkle et al. 2018) and (**b2**) realness and resemblance. The VolCap is able to create very realistic representations of artists and audiences, which creates innovative ways to engage the audience in new places next to the stage itself (such as between the audience or in waiting lines). This seems in line with previous research showing that VolCap creates more social presence compared to 2D or other forms of 3D representations (Cho et al. 2020; Young et al. 2023). However, some experts raised concerns about the uncanny feeling, making it due to the high realism creepy, and the need for good VolCap placement strategies.

The final factor, content consists out of three factors: (**c1**) live, (**c2**) proximity and (**c3**) creativity. This research stressed the changes in priority to first and foremost understand how to implement VolCap within a live performance, stressing follow-up research on what live entails and stressing the need for solutions in how to consume the VolCap content without distracting. It showed that VolCap AR changes the perception of live even more stressing new dimensions of what live nowadays entails such as presence, acknowledgement, exclusivity and real time shared experiences, that connect with the three dimensions time, place and social found in previous research (Hammelburg 2021), for which the content can be physical as well as digital Moreover, the high level of realism created by VolCap, pushes the boundaries of what visitors will accept as being a live performance. This creates new opportunities, despite technical challenges around creative complexity and real-time usage constraints. VolCap AR, in addition, has the potential to create more proximity, in which VolCap brings the artist closer to the audience and audience context (such as at home) and to other artists (distant live collaboration). More proximity means a better connection and higher engagement according to the experts and artists, and is needed and appreciated by music event visitors (Tom Dieck et al. 2018; Dieck et al. 2021; Pine and Gilmore 2011). However, more successful examples are needed and lack of creativity due to lack of experience and technology usage, hinder mainstream use of VolCap AR.

There seems less need to create higher levels of realism, but more on how to blend VolCap performance with live performance and remote collaborations. This outcome stresses the need for more creative strategies and at the same time urges the need for proven business models that cover the high investments. The outcomes presented provide new strategies to make use of the expected benefits and to realize the hurdles that need to be dealt with. While a lot of effort is being put into evolving the technology itself, this research indicates that there is more need for research and solutions around a successful implementation, advocating a change in (priority within) the VolCap AR R&D agenda.

Acknowledgements The authors would like to thank 4DR studios (especially Natasja Paulssen) and the Effenaar (especially Jos Feijen), for their valuable contributions that ranges from providing access to content and examples, to helping with recruitment of participants and access to technology and content. More specific we want to express the gratitude to be involved in two projects, Chronosphere (I and II) as well as Hybrid Music Vibes (I and II), that made this study possible.

References

Adema, K. L., & Roehl, W. S. (2010). Environmental scanning the future of event design. International Journal of Hospitality Management, 29(2), 199–207. https://doi.org/10.1016/j.ijhm.2009.10.017.

Billinghurst, M. (2021). Grand Challenges for Augmented Reality. Frontiers in Virtual Reality, 2. https://doi.org/10.3389/frvir.2021.578080.

Biocca, F. (1996). Can the engineering of presence tell us something about consciousness. In 2nd International Conference on the Science of Consciousness, Tuscon, AR.

Cho, S., Kim, S. W., Lee, J., Ahn, J., & Han, J. (2020, March). Effects of volumetric capture avatars on social presence in immersive virtual environments. In 2020 IEEE conference on virtual reality and 3D user interfaces (VR) (pp. 26–34). IEEE.

Dieck, M., Dieck, D. T., & Jung, T. (2021). Exploring usability and gratifications for virtual reality applications at festivals. Event Management, 25(6), 585–599.

Dirin, A., & Laine, T. H. (2018). User experience in mobile augmented reality: emotions, challenges, opportunities and best practices. *Computers*, *7*(2), 33.

Gisbergen, M. V. (2016). Contextual connected media: How rearranging a media puzzle, brings virtual reality into being.Global music industry revenue | Statista. (2023). Retrieved January 14, 2024, from https://www.statista.com/statistics/259979/global-music-industry-revenue/.

Hammelburg, E. (2021). Being there live: an ethnographic approach for studying social media use in mediatized live events. Social Media+ Society, 7(1), 2056305120984454.

Houston, B. (2020, May 28). What is augmented reality (AR)? A practical overview. Product Configurator and Product Visualization | Threekit. https://www.threekit.com/blog/what-is-augmented-reality.

Huang, Z., Li, T., Chen, W., Zhao, Y., Xing, J., LeGendre, C., ... & Li, H. (2018). Deep volumetric video from very sparse multi-view performance capture. In Proceedings of the European Conference on Computer Vision (ECCV) (pp. 336–354).

Ivanova, A. V. (2018). VR & AR technologies: Opportunities and application obstacles. Strategic decisions and risk management, (3), 88–107. https://doi.org/10.17747/2078-8886-2018-3-88-107.

Klinker, G., Stricker, D., & Reiners, D. (2003). Augmented Reality for Exterior Construction Applications. Augmented Reality and Wearable Computers.

Kounavis, C. D., Kasimati, A. E., & Zamani, E. D. (2012). Enhancing the tourism experience through mobile augmented reality: Challenges and prospects. International Journal of Engineering Business Management, 4, 10.

Lemley, M. A., & Volokh, E. (2018). Law, Virtual Reality and Augmented Reality. University of Pennsylvania Law Review, 166(5). https://doi.org/10.2139/ssrn.2933867.

Luxford, A., & Dickinson, J. E. (2015). The role of mobile applications in the consumer experience at music festivals. Event Management, 19(1), 33–46. https://doi.org/10.3727/152599515x14229071392909.

McIlvenny, P. (2020). The future of 'video' in video-based qualitative research is not 'dumb' flat pixels! Exploring volumetric performance capture and immersive performative replay. Qualitative Research, 20(6), 800–818. https://doi.org/10.1177/1468794120905460.

O'Dwyer, N., Young, G. W., Johnson, N., Zerman, E., & Smolic, A. (2020, July). Mixed Reality and Volumetric Video in Cultural Heritage: Expert Opinions on Augmented and Virtual Reality. In International conference on human-computer interaction (pp. 195–214). Springer, Cham.

Olya, H., Jung, T. H., Tom Dieck, M. C., & Ryu, K. (2020). Engaging visitors of science festivals using augmented reality: Asymmetrical modelling. International Journal of Contemporary Hospitality Management, 32(2), 769–796. https://doi.org/10.1108/ijchm-10-2018-0820.

Orús, C., Ibáñez-Sánchez, S., & Flavián, C. (2021). Enhancing the customer experience with virtual and augmented reality: The impact of content and device type. International Journal of Hospitality Management, 98, 103019. https://doi.org/10.1016/j.ijhm.2021.103019.

Pine, B. J., & Gilmore, J. H. (2011). The experience economy. Harvard Business Press.

Pop, D. (2021, June 15). The impact of mobile technology in our lives. Mobiversal. https://blog.mobiversal.com/the-impact-of-mobile-technology-in-our-daily-life.html.

Scheffels, H. (2020). Augmented Reality Marketing: An exploratory of ways AR face filters affect consumer experiences, attitudes and feelings towards a brand [Master's thesis]. https://www.buas.nl.

Schreer, O., Feldmann, I., Kauff, P., Eisert, P., Tatzelt, D., Hellge, C., ... & Ebner, T. (2020). Lessons learned during one year of commercial volumetric video production. *SMPTE Motion Imaging Journal*, *129*(9), 31–37.

Seymour, M., Yuan, L., Dennis, A. R., & Riemer, K. (2021). Have We Crossed the Uncanny Valley? Understanding Affinity, Trustworthiness, and Preference for Realistic Digital 59 Humans in Immersive Environments. Journal of the Association for Information Systems, 22(3), 591–617. https://doi.org/10.17705/1jais.00674.

Silva, E., & Bonetti, F. (2021). Digital humans in fashion: Will consumers interact? Journal of Retailing and Consumer Services. https://doi.org/10.1016/j.jretconser.2020.102430.

Singh, S., & Srivastava, P. (2019). Social media for outbound leisure travel: A framework based on technology acceptance model (TAM). Journal of Tourism Futures, 5(1), 43–61. https://doi.org/10.1108/jtf-10-2018-0058.

Statista. (2021). Music events - Netherlands | Statista market forecast. https://www.statista.com/outlook/dmo/eservices/event-tickets/music-events/netherlands#demographics.

Sterzentsenko, V., Karakottas, A., Papachristou, A., Zioulis, N., Doumanoglou, A., Zarpalas, D., & Daras, P. (2019). A Low-Cost, Flexible and Portable Volumetric Capturing System. https://doi.org/10.48550/arXiv.1909.01207.

Tom Dieck, M. C., Jung, T. H., & Rauschnabel, P. A. (2018). Determining visitor engagement through augmented reality at science festivals: An experience economy perspective. Computers in Human Behavior, 82, 44–53. https://doi.org/10.1016/j.chb.2017.12.043.

Van Happen (2022). Future Static: No Show Without an Artist. Insight case studies. AIXR. Retrevied from: https://aixr.org/insights/future-static-no-show-without-an-artist/.

van Winkle, C., MacKay, K., & Halpenny, E. (2018). Information and communication technology and the festival experience. In J. Mair (Ed.), The Routledge handbook of festivals (pp. 254–262). Routledge.

VNPF. (2019). 2019 Poppodia en Festivals in Cijfers.

Young, G. W., O'Dwyer, N., Vargas, M. F., Donnell, R. M., & Smolic, A. (2023, July). Feel the Music!—Audience Experiences of Audio–Tactile Feedback in a Novel Virtual Reality Volumetric Music Video. In Arts (Vol. 12, No. 4, p. 156). MDPI.

Yeoman, I. (2013). A futurist's thoughts on consumer trends shaping future festivals and events. International Journal of Event and Festival Management, 4(3), 249–260. https://doi.org/10.1108/ijefm-06-2013-0017.

Zell, E., Castan, F., Gasparini, S., Hilsmann, A., Kazhdan, M., Tagliasacchi, A. & Zioulis, N. (2021). Volumetric Video-Acquisition, Compression, Interaction and Perception. Eurographics Proceedings, The Eurographics Association.

Zerman, E., O'Dwyer, N., Young, G. W., & Smolic, A. (2020). A case study on the use of volumetric video in augmented reality for cultural heritage. Proceedings of the 11th Nordic Conference on Human-Computer Interaction: Shaping Experiences, Shaping Society. https://doi.org/10.1145/3419249.3420115.

XR for Training and Education

Review on the Use of Augmented Reality Technology on Computational Thinking Education

Jung-Soon Kim, YoungMi Choi, and Sung-Hee Kim

Abstract Augmented Reality (AR) in educational environments enables students to interact with the real world in a natural manner. Numerous studies have reported that AR can enhance students' learning motivation and commitment, foster problem-solving and inquiry skills, stimulate learning interest and enthusiasm, and significantly boost students' creativity. Meanwhile, Computational Thinking refers to the thought processes involved in planning, organizing, researching, interpreting, abstracting, decomposing, automating, simulating, and solving problems, as required by computer scientists when carrying out projects. It involves thinking about potential problems and utilizing the basics of computer science, which everyone should possess, to find solutions beyond just programming skills. Many papers have been published on Computational Thinking and STEM related to AR. This paper collects, classifies, and summarizes research on AR-based Computational Thinking and STEM education from 2018 to 2023 over the past five years. It measures learning and approaches using AR in each study, introduces the hardware, software, and interface methods used to create AR, and summarizes the various metrics used to evaluate these projects. We hope this paper serves as a valuable guide for conducting research related to AR and Computational Thinking.

Keywords Augmented reality · Computational thinking · AR · Education · Interaction · STEM

J.-S. Kim
Department of Artificial Intelligence, Dong-eui University, Busan, Republic of Korea

Y. Choi
Department of Computer Engineering, Dong-eui University, Busan, Republic of Korea

S.-H. Kim (✉)
Department of ICT Industrial Engineering, Dong-eui University, Busan, Republic of Korea
e-mail: sh.kim@deu.ac.kr

T. Jung et al. (eds.), *XR and Metaverse*, Springer Proceedings in Business and Economics, https://doi.org/10.1007/978-3-031-77975-6_5

1 Introduction

Augmented Reality (AR) integrates virtual information with real-world information, processing it in real-time. Through AR interfaces, users can control and visualize information according to their needs. Using AR in an educational environment allows for more natural interaction with information, objects, or 3D events. This enables users to interact with the real world in new ways, often through heightened realism. This technology can also create learning environments that combine virtual objects with real ones, such as using tangible interfaces to manipulate virtual objects. AR environments are composed of three elements: the combination of the real and virtual worlds, real-time interaction, and insertion in a 3D environment.

In augmented reality for heritage sites and educational activities, interaction with AR guide systems effectively enhanced the sense of presence and learning motivation (Alnajdi et al. 2020). Augmented reality game-based learning showed that students were more motivated and interested in reading activities, and it promoted problem-solving, exploration, and social behaviors (Tobar-Muñoz et al. 2014). In an internship program for postal services, students who used AR systems were able to save time and demonstrated significantly higher interest, enthusiasm, motivation, and creativity in learning compared to those using traditional learning methods (Radosavljevic et al. 2020). Various fields have shown that AR-based learning has the potential to enhance student motivation and willingness to learn through interaction and immersion.

Wing describes Computational Thinking as the way computer scientists think. It involves planning, structuring, researching, interpreting, abstracting, decomposing, automating, simulating, and problem-solving, just as computer scientists do when carrying out projects. Additionally, Wing emphasized that computational thinking skills are fundamental for everyone, akin to reading, writing, and arithmetic, and the importance of integrating computational ideas with other academic fields (Wing 2006). AR can be explored as a technology that provides a wide range of skills, such as problem-solving, abstraction, and creative manipulation, making it efficient for applying Computational Thinking (Saraiva et al. 2021). In this context, AR is an effective method for applying Computational Thinking.

Strategies and technologies are being used to introduce Computational Thinking (CT) skills and teach basic programming concepts (Gomes et al. 2018). Both subjects are part of STEM concepts and are essential skills that all 21st-century citizens should develop, thus garnering significant attention.

However, summarizing various papers on AR-related Computational Thinking and STEM education, and detailing the authoring tools used to develop AR and the evaluation metrics, remains limited. Therefore, this paper formulates the following research questions, summarizes various papers in Chap. 3 by addressing these questions, and interprets the research results in Chap. 4, discussing the limitations and suggestions for future research.

Research Questions

- RQ1. What are the metrics used to measure learning outcomes when utilizing AR?
- RQ2. What technologies and authoring tools (software, hardware) are used to create and/or develop AR systems?
- RQ3. What interaction methods are used to enhance educational effectiveness?

2 Selection of Related Research

We collected and categorized research on AR-based Computational Thinking education over the past five years, from 2018 to 2023. Maarten Van Mechelen et al. provided a comprehensive overview of state-of-the-art technology based on 107 HCI publications from 2010 to 2020. In this study, we specifically examine AR-related papers investigated by Van Mechelen et al. (2023) from the perspective of Computational Thinking, and summarize and outline 10 AR-related papers on Computational Thinking and STEM (Science, Technical, Engineering, and Mathematics) education published since 2021. Additionally, this chapter investigates and describes terms frequently mentioned in AR-related papers, such as Cognitive Load and Scaffolding.

Cognitive Load has primarily been discussed in the fields of human factors and ergonomics. Sweller (1988) applied it to the field of education, and van Merriënboer (2010) and Paas (1992) defined cognitive load as the load imposed on an individual's cognitive system when engaged in a specific task. They stated that the complexity of the material and the amount of mental effort required for learning activities are closely related to the occurrence of cognitive load. Additionally, Cognitive Load is a multidimensional concept resulting from the interaction between "mental load" and "mental effort" (Paas 1992).

Scaffolding refers to temporary structures used to support workers and materials during the construction, maintenance, and repair of buildings, bridges, and other man-made structures. In education, it means providing learners with appropriate cognitive support and guidance to facilitate learning. Developmental psychologist Lev Vygotsky and other social constructivists emphasized the scaffolding strategy, which provides effective instructional support within the learner's Zone of Proximal Development (ZPD). In general classroom instruction, competent peers, instructors, and experts directly provide appropriate scaffolding to learners. In e-learning environments, scaffolding includes providing learners with various aids or cues and encouraging cognitive checks (Naver Knowledge Encyclopedia, Scaffolding, HRD Dictionary, Sep. 6, 2010, Korean Society for Corporate Education). Wood et al. stated that scaffolding plays a crucial role in enhancing learners' problem-solving abilities (Wood et al. 1976). Reiser (2018) also emphasized the role of scaffolding as a cognitive tool necessary for performing complex learning tasks. Using AR, there is great potential to improve the teaching–learning process in all areas and content of STEM (Science, Technical, Engineering, and Mathematics) that require spatial intelligence (Del Cerro and Morales 2017).

3 Methods

In Chap. 3, based on the Research Questions in Chapt. 1, we organized the Tools, Target Group, and Measurement in a table (Table 1) when using AR-based Computational Thinking and STEM learning studies. Section 3 provides an overall overview, including the framework, system, and tools used in each paper, and Sect. 3.1 describes computational thinking methods for solving AR-based coding problems in each paper and indicators for measuring the effect of STEM learning and suggest areas that need to be added or supplemented in the future. Section 3.2 describes the technologies for producing and/or developing the AR systems of each paper, and presents using these technologies. Finally, Sect. 3.3 explains the interaction method to increase the educational effectiveness in each paper and additionally presents other interaction methods.

3.1 Analysis of Learning Effects and Measurement Indicators Using AR

In this section, each paper describes computational thinking methods for solving AR-based coding problems and indicators for measuring the effects of STEM learning, and suggests areas that should be added or supplemented in the future.

Computational Thinking Method for Solving Coding Problems: This study explores the impact of AR technology on Computational Thinking methods by analyzing five key papers that leverage AR to enhance learning experiences. The commonalities among these papers include the broad use of AR technology to enrich learning, setting goals to improve computational thinking, and incorporating game elements to make the learning experience engaging. We evaluated these projects based on their design, target demographics, educational objectives, the effectiveness of AR implementation, and the metrics used to measure learning outcomes.

AR-Maze Project: To track user progress, a video recorder was used. After the initial game introduction, children displayed joy, immersion, and strong curiosity about the game system. The conclusion was that the game effectively helps children learn computer programming concepts in a fun and enjoyable way. It is necessary to consider both the physical placement of location maps and spatial constraints (Jin et al. 2018).

Programming Toy Project: The application test involved 3 male students and was conducted in four stages: presentation, exploration, activity, and questionnaire completion. Three methods were used to verify behaviors related to Computational Thinking: collecting application usage data from mobile devices, observing activities via video, and evaluating usability using a 5-point Likert scale. Despite tracking loss issues due to low-performance devices, the application successfully stimulated

Table 1 Measuring indicators and related research on the impact of AR on education

Author (year)	Tools	Target group	Measurement
Computational thinking			
Jin et al. (2018)	AR-Maze	8 people (5–9 years old)	interesting and intuitive
da Silva Esteves (2019)	Self-developed application	People (9, 11, 12 years old)	Indicators related to computational thinking skills (Programming, run, refactoring)
Cleto et al. (2020)	CodeCubes	9 people (9–13 years old)	Interest and motivation, interaction difficulties with CodeCubes
Saraiva et al. (2021)	SHREWS	Nothing about the experiment	
Huang et al. (2023)	Coding ocean board game	51 people (26 experimental group, 25 control group)	Scratch programming skills, cognitive load, system satisfaction, scaffolding
STEM			
del Cerro Velázquez et al. (2018)	MasicBook application	56 students (2 ESO 3rd years)	Interest, memorization, understanding, difficulty
Sarkar et al. (2020)	ScholAR	21 people (7–8 years old)	Interest, immersion
Annalisa Liccardo (2021)	Remote laboratory framework	53 engineering students	Preference, usefulness, reliability, usability, tactility
Radu and Schneider (2022)	Interactive hardware system	112 people (with bachelor's degree, engineering student, under 40 years old)	Especially transfer, Impact knowledge exchange between collaborators
Nadeem et al. (2022)	AR4FSM	60 people (19–22 years old)	Understanding, immersion, Usability, Motivate, acceptability

computational thinking and maintained high user interest (da Silva Esteves et al. 2019).

CodeCubes Project: Conducted with 9 students aged 9–13 using a user-centered design approach. The study allowed students to collaborate on creating and testing the application, providing suggestions and feedback, resulting in multiple prototypes. The first prototype followed the game mechanics of code.org, Angry Birds, and Classic Maze. Prototype testing yielded results related to usability and technology usage motivation (Cleto et al. 2020).

SHREWS Project: Described the principles and architecture of the video game and presented a method for learning computational thinking skills through puzzle games. The game involves navigating obstacles on a map to reach a target point, using a scoring system based on various statistics such as time taken and tasks used. It helps learners with pattern recognition, problem decomposition, algorithm design, and abstraction (Saraiva et al. 2021).

Coding Ocean Game Project: Evaluated the learning effects of an AR board game on computational thinking and programming skills with 51 third-grade students. The experimental group used the AR board game, while the control group used traditional board games. Assessments included pre-and post-tests on computational thinking concepts and Scratch programming skills, and surveys to measure cognitive load and user satisfaction. Results showed significant improvements in learning effectiveness, programming skills, and reduced cognitive load for the AR board game group compared to the control group (Huang et al. 2023).

In AR-related papers on Computational Thinking, the most common measurement metrics are related to the interest and motivation of learning tools. Code-Cubes analyzed interaction difficulties and solutions through a user-centered design approach, while AR-Maze and Programming Toy observed students' learning activities via video. The Coding Ocean Game measured cognitive load. Video observation allows for a detailed analysis of students' behaviors and interactions, and excessive cognitive load can lead to confusion and reduced learning efficiency. Future research should propose more papers on video observation and cognitive load-related studies.

STEM (Science, Technical, Engineering, and Mathematics)

MagicBook Project: The study compared a group learning with AR (n = 29) and a group learning with traditional methods (n = 27) to evaluate the effectiveness of learning. Both groups took written tests and completed surveys, and a t-test model was used to compare the differences between the groups. Results showed that the AR group achieved higher performance and motivation than the traditional learning group. AR was particularly effective for students with below-average performance, providing more meaningful learning experiences (del Cerro Velázquez et al. 2018).

ScholAR Project: This project designed, implemented, and evaluated an AR-based module on lines and angles with 21 seventh and eighth-grade students. In the first study, a 20-min review session on lines and angles was followed by a pre-test, three learning activities using ScholAR, and a post-test. Surveys were also conducted to assess the usefulness and overall motivation of the AR application. The results indicated that learning activities in pairs increased motivation and understanding of concepts. In the second study, the learning patterns of collaborative activities were tracked, and the peer involvement and immersive experience with AR were validated through sequences. Both studies found that exploring the 3D house was the most engaging and immersive activity (Sarkar et al. 2020).

Remote Laboratory Framework Project: This project updated the IoT-supported technology of a laboratory to enable remote experiments for 53 engineering students, allowing multiple students to conduct experiments simultaneously. The experiments were conducted in groups of 4–5, and surveys were used to measure preferences. Most students positively evaluated AR, with about 95% expressing willingness to use this technology in the future. However, there were negative responses regarding individual access to experiments. Most students had positive reactions to the usability and reliability of the technology but suggested improvements for additional information, such as tactile feedback, and proposed enhancing interactions with 3D models (Liccardo et al. 2021).

Interactive Hardware System Project: This project involved 112 engineering students using Hololens AR devices to conduct electrical and electronic experiments. The students were divided into groups with and without AR devices, and differences in collaboration by learning level were observed. The study found that AR was generally beneficial for both learning and collaboration, but AR participants were not superior in all aspects. The use of non-visual content tools and kinesthetic information was more effective for non-AR participants. The project demonstrated that AR can enhance learning and collaboration, but it also indicated potential negative effects such as increased dependency on technology, misunderstandings, and fatigue. The study emphasized the importance of further research on how to support learning and mitigate negative impacts as AR education technology advances (Radu and Schneider 2022).

AR4FSM Project: This project developed an AR-based learning tool using FSM (Finite-State Machine) handouts for 60 students aged 19–22, allowing them to redesign diagrams and control an avatar's movement. To increase engagement and motivation, the study measured students' expectations and acceptance rates for future classes. A 5-point scale survey (Maruping et al. 2017) was used to capture participants' responses, measuring usability and expectations. More than 85% of the students responded positively to using the application, but only 70% supported its use in the classroom. Students provided open feedback, suggesting improvements to the avatar's appearance and display size (Nadeem et al. 2022).

The following is a summary of the common and various metrics used in AR-based studies. Projects that measured learning achievement include the MagicBook, Interactive Hardware System, and AR4FSM Projects. Projects that assessed immersion include the ScholAR, Interactive Hardware System, and AR4FSM Projects. Usability evaluation was measured in the MagicBook, Remote Laboratory Framework Project, and AR4FSM Projects. Interest and motivation were assessed in the MagicBook, ScholAR, and AR4FSM Projects. The AR4FSM Project comprehensively evaluated the effectiveness of AR-based educational tools, including learning achievement, immersion, usability, interest, and motivation. Additionally, the Remote Laboratory Framework Project defined metrics from various perspectives, such as preference, usefulness, reliability, and tactility, to draw balanced conclusions. These diverse metrics allowed each project to evaluate the effectiveness of AR-based educational tools from multiple angles. Notably, some studies emphasizing the importance of collaborative learning evaluated how AR tools facilitate interaction and knowledge exchange among students. The ScholAR Project found that collaborative learning activities increased motivation and concept understanding. In this study, only two out of ten papers evaluated the effectiveness of collaborative learning: the ScholAR Project and the Interactive Hardware System Project. Therefore, future research needs to propose more studies evaluating the effects of collaborative learning.

3.2 Technological Approaches

In this section, we describe the technologies used to create and develop AR systems in various studies, summarize the commonalities of these technologies, and introduce the inconveniences from a system perspective. There are two main real-time interface methods between users and virtual objects: Marker-based and Markerless. Both methods play a crucial role in integrating virtual objects with the physical world in AR applications to provide users with an immersive experience.

Marker-based Interface uses identifiable objects and markers, where a smartphone's built-in camera recognizes the object and location to augment digital information. However, it cannot be identified by other sensors like compasses or GPS (Park and Park 2010). Markerless Interface, also known as location-based AR, does not require predefined markers to overlay digital content on the real world. These applications use environmental features like surfaces, patterns, or objects, or technologies like GPS, accelerometer data, or computer vision to position AR content (Klein et al. 2007). While Markerless AR is more flexible and provides a more immersive experience compared to Marker-based AR, it may not be as accurate or stable in certain situations due to complex algorithms (Rauschnabel et al. 2017).

Out of the 10 papers, 4 used Marker-based Interface, 2 used Markerless Interface, and 4 did not specify the interface method. Projects using Marker-based Interface include AR-Maze, CodeCubes, AR4FSM, and Coding Ocean board game. These projects combined physical reality-based elements with digital content to overlay digital information in the real world. AR-Maze used TopCode for object identification, CodeCubes and AR4FSM detected objects with mobile device cameras, and Coding Ocean board game presumably used Marker-based Interface to identify physical boats created with 3D printing. Of the four papers using Marker-based Interface, three utilized Unity game engine and Vuforia for overlaying physical elements with digital content. The remaining project, AR4FSM, used JAVA and OpenCV to develop an Android application.

Projects using Markerless Interface include ScholAR and MagicBook Application. Both developed applications using Unity software, and ScholAR utilized Google's ARCore to overlay virtual 3D objects on the screen in real-time. MagicBook Application did not mention its development tools but designed digital content through a smartphone and connected pre-made worksheets using Markerless technology.

Among the remaining four papers, SHREWS project used Unity and Vuforia libraries, Self-developed Application project rendered physical cards using EasyAR and developed an Android application on the Unity3D platform. Remote Laboratory

Table 2 Combining the physical and digital worlds

Interface	DevTools	Interfaces between device and tools
Marker	Unity + Qualcomm Vuforia	Elements based on physical reality + Digital contents
Markerless	Unity + Google ARCore	Virtual 3D object + Application
Other	Unity + C# Unity + EasyAR	LabVIEW + IoT Device + MQTT Protocol + FARO Laser ScanArm

Framework adopted a reverse engineering approach by scanning and reconstructing lab device images in 3D. The shapes were then reconstructed from the point cloud into a 3D model, connected in the AR environment using Vuforia. This entire process was conducted using LabVIEW software, and user input-based image rendering and interaction were performed on the Unity 3D development platform. Interactive Hardware System project developed a system to simulate electrical and electronic experiments using advanced AR hardware like Hololens AR devices. This system replicated a physical audio speaker and displayed AR visualizations to build an interactive hardware system.

What the 10 papers have in common is that they used Unity for screen design, reorganized the AR library screen, and demonstrated educational effectiveness through various interface methods. However, the inconveniences on the system side are as follows. The CodeCubes project had a problem recognizing markers under certain lighting conditions, and the self-developed application project found it difficult for children to actively use it. ScholAR said that certain operations were not intuitive. In the end, it can be said that it is important to select the appropriate technology according to the usage environment and purpose (Table 2).

3.3 Interaction Method to Increase Educational Effectiveness

Learners can interact with all educational content in a manner similar to interacting with the real world through the intuitive interactions provided by Augmented Reality (AR) (Radu 2012). Augmented interactions with real objects offer a more intuitive interface than systems that rely solely on screens, providing a more immersive and efficient real-time feedback system (Heun et al. 2013). This section introduces the methods of interaction between computers and users in AR education as discussed in various studies and proposes the application of multimodal user interface design principles to AR education.

In the AR-Maze project, when players violated programming rules, they received error messages (text prompts) and music feedback. It was found that players tended to ignore the text feedback, highlighting a need for improved interaction design (Jin et al. 2018). The ScholAR project used drawing functionality as an AR interaction medium, but the overall usability score was slightly below the standard score of

68. This indicates that the system needs to be redesigned to address conceptual and interaction difficulties faced by students (Sarkar et al. 2020).

The CodeCubes project adopted a user-centered design methodology, involving collaboration in application creation, testing, and providing suggestions and feedback. This approach helps improve the system based on user feedback, making interactions more intuitive (Cleto et al. 2020). The AR Board Game project utilized a design-based research (DBR) method to investigate the impact of AR board games on learning motivation and reading comprehension. Results showed that students using AR games had higher learning motivation and interest in journaling, enhanced their ability to connect text, consider answers, explore options, and find clues. AR games were found to enhance problem-solving and exploration skills, enriching students' reading learning experiences (Huang et al. 2023).

In the AR4FSM project, students interacted with FSM diagrams drawn on physical handouts. After learning the concepts, they could understand the avatar's state and associated music based on real-time changes, fostering creative and engaging participation through interactive model visualization and manipulation (Nadeem et al. 2022). The Remote Laboratory Framework project highlighted the need for improvements in providing additional information such as tactile feedback and proposed enhancements for interaction with 3D models by incorporating tactile interfaces (Liccardo et al. 2021). In summary, AR technology combines physical objects and digital content to provide intuitive interactions, improve learning efficiency through real-time feedback, and enhance problem-solving and exploration skills through game-based AR technology. Applying multimodal user interface design principles to AR education on E-learning platforms is proposed. This includes incorporating video lectures for learners to view educational content from various angles, converting text to speech for simultaneous audiovisual material usage, and integrating features for real-time interaction with peers and tutors to provide immediate feedback. Enhancing these interaction methods will improve user experience and explore application possibilities in various fields.

4 Discussion and Conclusion

This study investigates the impact of Augmented Reality (AR) on Computational Thinking (CT) and STEM education over the past five years (2018–2023). It summarizes and analyzes ten related research papers, exploring the tools, target groups, measurement methods, and educational outcomes associated with AR-based CT and STEM learning.

Experts emphasize that STEM-based education positively influences *creative thinking, problem-solving skills, and critical thinking* (Kasza and Slater 2017; Asunda 2014). Additionally, games as educational tools help educators create engaging learning activities, evaluate understanding in complex and incorrect situations, promote critical thinking and problem-solving skills, and ensure active participation from all students throughout the learning process (Raupp 2018).

- AR-based STEM education and Computational Thinking focus on enhancing students' abilities to analyze and solve complex problems. Projects like Code-Cubes and the Coding Ocean Board game use AR to combine real-world and virtual elements, enabling students to simulate and resolve real-world issues.
- STEM education and Computational Thinking promote creative thinking. In the AR4FSM project, students interact with FSM diagrams drawn on physical handouts. After learning the concepts, they can understand the avatar's state and associated music based on real-time changes, fostering creative and engaging participation through interactive model visualization and manipulation (Nadeem et al. 2022).
- Projects like CodeCubes, SHREWS, and the Coding Ocean game demonstrated the effectiveness of games in enhancing Computational Thinking skills. These games facilitated critical thinking and problem-solving abilities in students through interactive gameplay.

Despite these advantages, several studies have identified technical challenges and usability issues associated with AR applications. For instance, the CodeCubes project faced difficulties with marker recognition under specific lighting conditions, while the Self-developed application project found it challenging for children to use actively. Additionally, the ScholAR project reported that some interactions were not intuitive for users (Cleto et al. 2020; Sarkar et al. 2020). These issues highlight the importance of selecting appropriate technologies based on the user environment and purpose.

Future research should address the technical and usability issues identified in this study. There is a need for more robust hardware and better user interfaces that promote intuitive interactions. Incorporating new technologies, such as Mixed Reality (MR), could provide fresh insights into the educational field.

In conclusion, AR has significant potential to enhance Computational Thinking and STEM education by making learning more interactive, engaging, and effective. However, to fully realize these benefits, it is essential to address current challenges and expand the scope of research. This study provides a foundation for the practical application of AR in educational environments and aims to serve as a useful guide for conducting research related to AR and computational thinking.

Acknowledgements This work was supported by innovative Human Resource Development for Local Intellectualization program through the Institute of Information & Communications Technology Planning & Evaluation (IITP) grant funded by the Korea government (MSIT) (IITP-2024-RS-2020-II201791).

References

AlNajdi, S. M., Alrashidi, M. Q., & Almohamadi, K. S. (2020). The effectiveness of using augmented reality (AR) on assembling and exploring educational mobile robot in pedagogical virtual machine (PVM). Interactive Learning Environments, 28(8), 964–990.

Asunda, P. A. (2014). A conceptual framework for STEM integration into curriculum through career and technical education. Journal of STEM Teacher Education, 49(1), 4.

Cleto, B., Sylla, C., Ferreira, L., & Moura, J. M. (2020). Codecubes: Coding with augmented reality. In First international computer programming education conference (ICPEC 2020). Schloss Dagstuhl-Leibniz-Zentrum für Informatik.

da Silva Esteves, A. M., Santana, A. L. M., & Lyra, R. (2019, October). Use of augmented reality for computational thinking stimulation through virtual. In 2019 21st Symposium on Virtual and Augmented Reality (SVR) (pp. 102–106). IEEE.

del Cerro Velázquez, F., & Morales Méndez, G. (2018). Augmented reality and mobile devices: A binominal methodological resource for inclusive education (SDG 4). An example in secondary education. Sustainability, 10(10), 3446.

Del Cerro, F., & Morales, G. (2017). Augmented Reality as a tool for improving spatial intelligence in secondary education students. Revista de Educación a Distancia, 54(5).

Gomes, T. C. S., Falcão, T. P., & Tedesco, P. C. D. A. R. (2018). Exploring an approach based on digital games for teaching programming concepts to young children. International journal of child-computer interaction, 16, 77–84.

Heun, V., Hobin, J., & Maes, P. (2013a, September). Reality editor: programming smarter objects. In Proceedings of the 2013 ACM conference on Pervasive and ubiquitous computing adjunct publication (pp. 307–310).

Heun, V., Kasahara, S., & Maes, P. (2013b). Smarter objects: using AR technology to program physical objects and their interactions. In CHI'13 Extended Abstracts on Human Factors in Computing Systems (pp. 961–966).

Huang, S. Y., Tarng, W., & Ou, K. L. (2023). Effectiveness of AR board game on computational thinking and programming skills for elementary school students. Systems, 11(1), 25.

Jin, Q., Wang, D., Deng, X., Zheng, N., & Chiu, S. (2018, June). AR-Maze: a tangible programming tool for children based on AR technology. In Proceedings of the 17th ACM Conference on Interaction Design and Children (pp. 611–616).

Kasza, P., & Slater, T. F. (2017). A survey of best practices and key learning objectives for successful secondary school STEM academy settings. Contemporary Issues in Education Research, 10(1), 53–66.

Klein, G., & Murray, D. (2007, November). Parallel tracking and mapping for small AR workspaces. In 2007 6th IEEE and ACM international symposium on mixed and augmented reality (pp. 225–234). IEEE.

Liccardo, A., Arpaia, P., Bonavolontà, F., Caputo, E., de Pandi, F., Gallicchio, V., ... & Moriello, R. S. L. (2021). An augmented reality approach to remote controlling measurement instruments for educational purposes during pandemic restrictions. IEEE Transactions on Instrumentation and Measurement, 70, 1–20.

Maruping, L. M., Bala, H., Venkatesh, V., & Brown, S. A. (2017). Going beyond intention: Integrating behavioral expectation into the unified theory of acceptance and use of technology. Journal of the Association for Information Science and Technology, 68(3), 623–637.

Nadeem, M., Lal, M., Cen, J., & Sharsheer, M. (2022). AR4FSM: Mobile Augmented Reality Application in Engineering Education for Finite-State Machine Understanding. Education Sciences, 12(8), 555.

Park, H., & Park, J. I. (2010). Invisible marker–based augmented reality. Intl. Journal of Human–Computer Interaction, 26(9), 829–848.

Paas, F. G. (1992). Training strategies for attaining transfer of problem-solving skill in statistics: a cognitive-load approach. Journal of Educational Psychology.

Radosavljevic, S., Radosavljevic, V., & Grgurovic, B. (2020). The potential of implementing augmented reality into vocational higher education through mobile learning. Interactive Learning Environments, 28(4), 404–418.

Radu, I. (2012, November). Why should my students use AR? A comparative review of the educational impacts of augmented-reality. In 2012 IEEE International Symposium on Mixed and Augmented Reality (ISMAR) (pp. 313–314). IEEE.

Radu, I., & Schneider, B. (2022). How Augmented Reality (AR) Can Help and Hinder Collaborative Learning: A Study of AR in Electromagnetism Education. IEEE transactions on visualization and computer graphics.Azuma, R. T. (1997). A survey of augmented reality. Presence: teleoperators & virtual environments, 6(4), 355–385.

Raupp, Andrew (2018, October 9). How Video Games Help Students Level Up STEM Learning. [Web log post]. Forbes. Retrieved from https://www.forbes.com/sites/forbestechcouncil/2018/10/09/how-video-games-help-students-level-up-stem-learning/#74086a631a78.

Rauschnabel, P. A., Rossmann, A., & tom Dieck, M. C. (2017). An adoption framework for mobile augmented reality games: The case of Pokémon Go. Computers in human behavior, 76, 276–286.

Reiser, B. J. (2018). Scaffolding complex learning: The mechanisms of structuring and problematizing student work. In Scaffolding (pp. 273–304). Psychology Press.

Saraiva, F., Lima, L. V., Araújo, C., Magalhães, L. G., & Henriques, P. R. (2021). SHREWS: A Game with Augmented Reality for Training Computational Thinking (Short Paper). In Second International Computer Programming Education Conference (ICPEC 2021). Schloss Dagstuhl-Leibniz-Zentrum für Informatik.

Sarkar, P., Kadam, K., & Pillai, J. S. (2020). Learners' approaches, motivation and patterns of problem-solving on lines and angles in geometry using augmented reality. Smart Learning Environments, 7, 1-23.

Sweller, J. (1988). Cognitive load during problem solving: Effects on learning. Cognitive Science, 12(2), 257–285.

Tobar-Muñoz, H., Baldiris, S., & Fabregat, R. (2014, July). Gremlings in my mirror: an inclusive AR-enriched videogame for logical math skills learning. In 2014 IEEE 14th international conference on advanced learning technologies (pp. 576–578).

Van Mechelen, M., Smith, R. C., Schaper, M. M., Tamashiro, M., Bilstrup, K. E., Lunding, M., ... & Sejer Iversen, O. (2023). Emerging technologies in K–12 education: A future HCI research agenda. ACM Transactions on Computer-Human Interaction, 30(3), 1–40.

Wing, J. M. (2006). Computational thinking. Communications of the ACM, 49(3), 33–35.

Wood, D., Bruner, J. S., & Ross, G. (1976). The role of tutoring in problem solving. Journal of Child Psychology and Psychiatry, 17, 89–100.

Exploring the Synergy of Words and Worlds in Immersive Learning

Jeonghyun Kang and Donghun Chung

Abstract This study explored the impact of virtual agents and textual enhancement techniques on English language learning. A 2 × 2 mixed-factorial design experiment ($N = 60$) was conducted using a specially developed VR English learning content, involving two within-subject factors: the roles of virtual agents (teacher vs. clerk) and two between-subject factors: types of textual enhancement techniques (vocabulary only vs. vocabulary with image). The findings revealed no significant interaction between agent types and textual enhancement techniques. However, significant main effects were observed: agent types influenced memory, attitude, and intention to use, while textual enhancements influenced presence. Further implications of the findings were discussed.

Keywords Virtual reality · Foreign language learning · Virtual agent · Textual enhancement · Memory

1 Introduction

The importance of English in today's world cannot be overstated. It is the primary language used in international diplomacy, dominates scientific and technological fields, and has a profound influence on global entertainment and media. However, for learners of English as a Foreign Language (EFL) in non-English speaking countries, mastering this language is fraught with difficulties. These students often face challenges such as limited opportunities for real-world practice and insufficient exposure to authentic English language contexts.

J. Kang
Graduate School of Metaverse Convergence, Kwangwoon University, Seoul, Republic of Korea
e-mail: jh.joyce.k@kw.ac.kr

D. Chung (✉)
School of Media and Communication, Kwangwoon University, Seoul, Republic of Korea
e-mail: donghunc@kw.ac.kr

T. Jung et al. (eds.), *XR and Metaverse*, Springer Proceedings in Business and Economics, https://doi.org/10.1007/978-3-031-77975-6_6

One of the significant issues in EFL education is the reliance on traditional teaching methods, which are often passive and disconnected from real-life applications. These methods do not adequately prepare students for practical use of the language, resulting in a gap between theoretical knowledge and practical skills (Jin and Yoo 2019). This gap is exacerbated by the fact that students rarely engage with English in contexts that reflect its use in everyday life. To address this, educators are increasingly looking towards contextual learning strategies that incorporate real-world materials like news articles and films. These strategies, while effective, demand considerable preparation from teachers, creating an additional workload that can be burdensome (Jin and Yoo 2019).

In response to these challenges, Virtual Reality (VR) technology is gaining traction as a novel solution. VR can create immersive, interactive environments that simulate real-life situations (Chung 2017), providing learners with opportunities to practice English in a context that mirrors actual usage. This technology can significantly enhance vocabulary learning and overall language proficiency by offering a dynamic and engaging learning experience that traditional methods lack. VR's ability to place learners in lifelike scenarios allows for more effective language practice and acquisition.

Integrating VR technology into EFL education represents a promising advancement in teaching methodologies. VR's capability to replicate realistic interactions provides a potential solution to the limitations of conventional EFL instruction, enhancing students' practical language skills and preparing them for effective communication in a globalized world.

By examining the effectiveness of VR in vocabulary acquisition and language proficiency, the study seeks to understand how this technology can overcome the limitations of traditional EFL instruction. The goal is to determine whether VR can offer a more practical and immersive learning experience, bridging the gap between classroom learning and real-world application.

2 Literature Review

2.1 Beyond Real World, Language Learning

VR, a cutting-edge digital tool, generates immersive 3D environments that can replicate real-world scenarios or create entirely fictional settings. The core attributes of VR—immersion, virtuality, and interactivity—are revolutionizing language learning paradigms. The immersive quality of VR, which deeply involves learners in the virtual environment, significantly enhances their focus, enthusiasm, and motivation (Chen 2016). The virtuality, defined as the degree to which users perceive the VR environment as real, provides highly realistic experiences, thereby enriching the learning process. These characteristics of VR are particularly effective for foreign language education, further amplified by its interactivity, which allows users to control and actively engage with their learning experiences.

The immersive nature of VR provides learners with a sense of presence, making them feel as though they are part of the virtual world (Lan 2015). This heightened sense of involvement can lead to increased engagement and motivation, crucial factors in successful language learning. Moreover, the realistic simulations offered by VR can expose learners to various linguistic and cultural contexts, helping them to develop practical language skills that are transferable to real-life situations (Kang et al. 2024a). The interactive elements of VR facilitate active learning, allowing learners to practice language skills in a hands-on manner. By navigating virtual environments, participating in simulated conversations, and completing interactive tasks, learners can enhance their language proficiency in a more dynamic and engaging way.

2.2 Beyond Words, Textual Enhancement

In educational contexts, the use of audiovisual input is crucial for providing learners with a more comprehensive and diverse understanding of information. According to Dual Coding Theory (Paivio 1990), incorporating both visual and auditory elements can significantly improve cognitive processing and retention of information. Captions in videos, which help convey spoken dialogue, play a pivotal role in language learning by aiding in vocabulary acquisition, pronunciation accuracy, and comprehension of context and meanings. Captioned videos significantly aid in understanding the content, providing learners with essential language cues such as pronunciation, context, and word meanings, thereby fostering a deeper and more systematic learning experience.

Despite the established benefits of captions, the question of which caption formats, such as bold, italics, and underline, are most effective for language acquisition remains unresolved. Previous studies have shown inconsistencies regarding the effectiveness of various textual enhancements (White 1998; Leow 2001). These results highlight the need for further investigation into the most effective caption enhancement techniques for language learning.

Building on prior research into the effects of images and captions, this study aims to delve deeper into how different types of textual enhancements in audiovisual materials can support language acquisition and memory retention. Here, textual enhancement encompasses more than simple formatting techniques like bolding or italicizing text; it includes various forms of captioning and their effectiveness in improving language comprehension and learning efficiency. By examining the specific impacts of varied captioning methods in multimedia learning environments, this research seeks to identify which types of textual enhancements are most beneficial for learners.

2.3 Learning Unleashed

Contextual learning posits that meaning arises from the interplay between content and context (Johnson 2002). According to Horz et al. (2009), the integration of knowledge and skills within settings that simulate their real-world applications is crucial, suggesting that cognitive skills are intrinsically tied to their practical uses. These studies demonstrate that authentic learning environments significantly enhance educational outcomes, highlighting the essential role of real-world context in effective learning.

This approach is particularly critical in foreign language instruction. Vocabulary acquisition is facilitated when learners engage with language experiences that aid in forming memories of new words and the situations in which they are encountered. Repeated exposure to new vocabulary in diverse, meaningful contexts helps build and reinforce its lexical and semantic framework through associations with familiar words (Landauer and Dumais 1997), leading to a more profound understanding of language usage and application.

Unlike traditional classroom environments, VR broadens the learning landscape, providing learners with immersive, practical experiences in diverse, and realistic contexts (Kang et al. 2024a). By situating vocabulary and expression acquisition within authentic settings, VR can promote not only memorization but also a deeper understanding of language usage and application.

By embedding language learning within these realistic scenarios, the study aims to demonstrate how contextualized learning, supported by VR technology, can enhance the acquisition and practical use of a foreign language.

2.4 Presence

Presence is a psychological phenomenon where users become so engrossed in a technological experience that they lose awareness of the technology itself (ISPR 2000). This concept is crucial in the field of interactive media, where achieving high levels of user engagement and immersion is paramount. Presence is often viewed as a multidimensional construct, incorporating factors such as enjoyment, emotional involvement, and the perceived realism of the virtual environment. These components are essential in shaping users' experiences within virtual reality and the extent to which they feel immersed (Chung 2017).

Witmer and Singer (1998) emphasize that the degree of attention a user maintains in a virtual setting is a key factor in determining the intensity of presence. Thus, optimizing memory and learning outcomes involves minimizing external distractions and enhancing presence in virtual environments. For instance, Lin et al. (2002) found that the use of head-mounted displays (HMDs) significantly boosts user attention, which in turn increases presence and memory retention. Their study specifically identified a positive correlation between heightened immersion through HMDs and enhanced presence and memory.

Beyond the technological aspects, the design of virtual environments also plays a crucial role in fostering presence. Environments that closely mimic real-world settings or that are highly interactive can enhance users' sense of immersion. This is particularly relevant in educational applications of VR, where realistic simulations can provide learners with practical, hands-on experiences that traditional learning environments cannot offer (Kang et al. 2024b).

Examining the concept of presence in virtual reality environments is crucial for understanding its impact on user engagement and immersion. By investigating presence, this study aims to uncover how deeply immersive experiences influence user interactions and learning outcomes. Such insights can guide the development of more effective VR applications, enhancing the overall quality and effectiveness of virtual reality experiences across different fields, particularly in education and interactive media.

2.5 *Flow*

Flow, derived from Csikszentmihalyi's (1975) theory, refers to the holistic sensation experienced when individuals are fully engaged and immersed in an activity. According to Csikszentmihalyi (1996), people in a state of flow recognize clear goals, have an awareness of their performance, and feel that their abilities are appropriately matched to the task. Additionally, they often lose track of time, and when these elements align, any activity can become enjoyable. This state makes tasks feel inherently pleasurable, driving individuals to seek such experiences instinctively (Lee and Chung 2012).

VR technology offers unique opportunities to design learning environments that naturally foster flow. For instance, adaptive VR systems can dynamically adjust the difficulty of tasks to match the learner's skill level, maintaining the balance between challenge and ability that is critical for achieving flow. Furthermore, VR can provide immediate feedback and immersive sensory experiences that enhance the learner's engagement and sense of presence, which are crucial components for facilitating flow.

Flow influences not only attitudes but also behavioural intentions. Chang and Wang (2008) found that as the experience of flow increases in the use of online communication tools, users develop more positive attitudes, which in turn strengthen their behavioural intentions. They argued that the more intense the flow, the stronger the behavioural intention.

Virtual environments are designed to maximize learner immersion and engagement. In such settings, flow plays a crucial role in the learning process. Considering the concepts and characteristics of flow, it is essential to explore how the experience of flow in virtual reality learning environments impacts learning outcomes. This deep exploration could uncover the potential benefits and applications of flow in enhancing educational experiences through virtual reality.

2.6 Memory

VR can enhance memory processing through its immersive capabilities, which align closely with established cognitive theories such as the Limited Capacity Model (LCM). The LCM posits that human cognitive resources are finite (Lang 2000), and efficient processing depends on the optimal allocation of these resources. VR's immersive nature, which blends visual and auditory stimuli, leverages these cognitive resources more effectively than traditional media, thereby facilitating deeper memory encoding, storage, and retrieval.

Memory processing can be examined through three primary mechanisms: recognition, cue-dependent recall, and free recall (Lang 2006). Recognition involves identifying previously encountered information, a process that VR enhances through rich, detailed virtual environments. These environments provide a context that makes information more recognizable and easier to retrieve. Cue-dependent recall is another area where VR excels. This type of recall depends on specific prompts or cues to retrieve stored information. VR environments are inherently rich in contextual cues, from visual elements to spatial layouts, that can trigger memory recall. Free recall, or the ability to retrieve information without explicit cues, is also enhanced by VR's immersive experiences. The active engagement required in VR, such as interacting with objects and navigating virtual spaces, leads to stronger memory traces.

These traces are formed through the active involvement of multiple sensory modalities, including visual, auditory, and kinesthetic inputs. This multimodal engagement results in more robust and easily retrievable memories. For example, a language learner using VR to navigate a virtual market and interact with clerks will form stronger, more vivid memories of vocabulary and phrases, aiding free recall later.

2.7 Attitude and Intention

Attitude defined as a unique emotional or evaluative reaction to specific entities such as behaviours, objects, or policies, transcends the mere aggregation of opinions (Davis 1989). It represents an individualized assessment for each subject, reflecting personal experiences, beliefs, and emotions. Attitude plays a pivotal role in the ongoing use of services, significantly influencing factors such as customer satisfaction and the likelihood of future purchases. Intention to use, on the other hand, denotes the forecasting or planning of future actions (Oliver 2014). It serves as a reflection of how one's beliefs and attitudes might translate into concrete behaviours.

In the context of VR-based learning, attitudes and intentions are critical for enhancing the effectiveness and long-term success of language learning programs.

Positive attitudes towards VR-based learning can foster greater engagement, motivation, and persistence among learners, thereby improving their overall language acquisition experience. Intention to use VR technology in learning reflects learners' readiness and willingness to adopt such innovative methods, which is essential for the successful implementation and sustainability of VR learning programs.

Attitudes and intentions are integral to the successful implementation of VR-based language learning programs. By acknowledging and addressing these psychological factors, educators can enhance the efficacy and sustainability of VR learning initiatives, ultimately contributing to improved language learning outcomes. This underscores the need for a deep understanding of attitudes and intentions to ensure the effective adoption and continuation of VR learning programs in educational contexts.

2.8 Research Question

Grounded in the discussions above, this study investigates the impact of VR-based language learning on key variables, focusing on agent roles and textual enhancement techniques. It aims to analyse their effects on learners' psychological responses and vocabulary retention, thereby identifying critical factors for developing VR language education content.

Research Question 1: Are there interaction effects between the roles of virtual agents and textual enhancement techniques on (1) presence, (2) flow, (3) memory, (4) attitude, and (5) intention to use?

3 Methods

3.1 Participants and Experimental Design

A total of 60 undergraduates (Male: 23, Female: 37) from a university in Seoul voluntarily participated in the experiment. The average age of the participants was 21.0 years ($SD = 1.79$). None of the participants had prior experience with learning in English-speaking countries or using virtual reality. All participants signed a consent form prior to participation.

A 2×2 mixed-factorial design was employed, incorporating both within-subject and between-subject factors. The within-subject factor involved exposing participants to two videos with varying agent roles (teacher vs. clerk). For the between-subject factor, participants were randomly assigned to one of two types of captions (vocabulary only vs. vocabulary with image), each varying in textual enhancement techniques. To control for potential order effects on the experimental results, counterbalancing was employed, involving the alteration of the video presentation order for individual participants.

3.2 Stimulus and Experiment

This study developed VR English learning content to investigate the impact of virtual agent roles and textual enhancement techniques on vocabulary retention and psychological effects in VR learning. Utilizing Unity Editor (2020.3.27), the VR environment simulated a grocery store with realistic 3D food items, leveraging assets from the Unity Asset Store. Two virtual agents, a teacher and a clerk, were distinctly dressed to reflect their roles, with attire choices based on research showing that it enhances perceived professionalism (Lee 2012; Song and Lee 2015).

Textual enhancement techniques were categorized into two types: Vocabulary Only (VO), which presents vocabulary and its meaning within a single line, and Vocabulary with Image (VI), which shows vocabulary, meaning, and a related image for enhanced comprehension. High-quality images for VI were obtained via Google search.

Stimuli were viewed on an Oculus Quest 2, showcasing videos of the agents for 2 min and 38 s, containing 284 words and introducing seven vocabulary items per video. Captions were displayed in a single line.

Visual representations of the agents and textual enhancement techniques are available in Figs. 1 and 2.

3.3 Procedures

The experiment, conducted in a controlled environment free from external light and noise, began with a pre-experimental vocabulary assessment to ensure participants were unfamiliar with the target vocabulary. After providing a brief explanation of the procedures and obtaining consent forms, as well as administering an initial survey, participants were fitted with HMDs adjusted for comfort. They then watched a video featuring virtual agents, captions, and target vocabulary twice: first in a passive viewing mode and subsequently engaging in a rehearsal task by reading along with the captions. After each viewing, participants were given a vocabulary memory test and a post-experiment survey. The entire experiment lasted approximately 20 min.

Fig. 1 Roles of agents: a teacher (left) and a clerk (right)

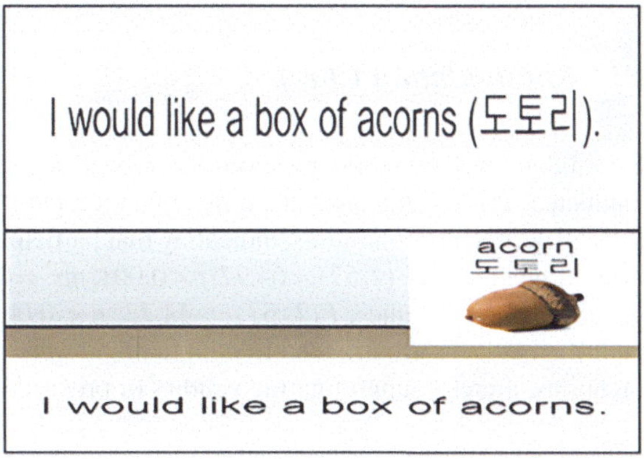

Fig. 2 Textual enhancement techniques: VO (top) and VI (bottom)

3.4 Measures

To assess the effectiveness of vocabulary memorization, a comprehensive evaluation was conducted. The evaluation consisted of three separate tests. In Test 1, free recall was measured by asking participants to list all the vocabulary words they remembered from the VR English learning content. Test 2 focused on cued recall, where participants indicated whether specific words appeared in the video content and provided the exact meanings of those words. Test 3 assessed recognition through four multiple-choice questions, where participants selected the correct meanings of the words.

This thorough assessment aimed to capture the nuances of vocabulary learning and offer a detailed understanding of the learners' vocabulary acquisition. The total score for memory assessment was 35, with 7 English words presented in the VR English learning content for each experimental condition. In Test 1, participants could earn up to 14 points by accurately recalling and defining all the English words and their meanings. Similarly, in Test 2, 14 points were available for correctly identifying the presence of the words and their meanings. Test 3 offered 7 points for selecting the correct definitions in the multiple-choice format.

To examine the psychological effects and overall engagement in the VR learning environment, four measures were utilized. Presence was measured using three five-point Likert scale items (Cronbach's $\alpha = 0.95$) adapted from the study by Lee and Chung (2019). Similarly, flow was assessed with three five-point Likert scale items (Cronbach's $\alpha = 0.74$) from Shin and Chung (2020). Attitude was evaluated using three five-point Likert scale items (Cronbach's $\alpha = 0.85$) from Chung (2009), and intention to use was measured with three five-point Likert scale items (Cronbach's $\alpha = 0.87$), also adapted from Chung (2009).

4 Results

4.1 *Manipulation Check*

To validate the research questions, a mixed repeated measures ANOVA was conducted. Prior to the analysis, a manipulation check confirmed the effectiveness of the experimental conditions, indicating that participants noticed significant differences in agent roles, $F(2, 57) = 64.72, p < 0.001, \eta p^2 = 0.69$, and in the types of textual enhancement techniques, $F(2, 57) = 44.72$, $p < 0.001$, $\eta p^2 = 0.61$. These results confirmed that the experimental manipulations were aligned with the researchers' intentions, thereby supporting the validity of proceeding with the study.

4.2 *Results*

The results indicated no statistically significant interaction effects between the roles of agents and textual enhancement techniques on the measures of presence, flow, memory, attitude, and intention to use. However, significant main effects were identified.

Regarding the role of the agent, the teacher role had a statistically significant positive impact on memory compared to the clerk role. The mean scores were 26.95 ($SD = 5.46$) for the teacher and 23.67 ($SD = 5.19$) for the clerk, $F(1, 58) = 23.77$, $p < 0.05$, $\eta p^2 = 0.29$. Attitudes towards the interaction were also significantly higher for the teacher role ($M = 4.31$, $SD = 0.62$) than for the clerk role ($M = 4.17$, $SD = 0.66$), $F(1, 58) = 4.27$, $p < 0.05$, $\eta p^2 = 0.06$. Similarly, the intention to use was marginally higher for the teacher role ($M = 4.05$, $SD = 0.81$) compared to the clerk role ($M = 3.92$, $SD = 0.78$), $F(1, 58) = 3.85$, $p < 0.1^*$, $\eta p^2 = 0.06$.

In terms of textual enhancement techniques, the VO technique was marginally more effective in influencing presence compared to the VI technique. The mean score for VO was 3.85 ($SD = 1.27$), whereas the mean score for the VI technique was 3.39 ($SD = 1.27$), $F(1, 58) = 3.79$, $p < 0.1^*$, $\eta p^2 = 0.06$.

5 Discussion

This study aimed to explore the potential interaction effects between the roles of virtual agents and textual enhancement techniques on several psychological and behavioural outcomes: presence, flow, memory, attitude, and intention to use. The results revealed no statistically significant interaction effects between the roles of agents and textual enhancement techniques on the examined outcomes. However, significant main effects were observed in relation to the roles of agents on memory, attitude, and intention to use, as well as the textual enhancement techniques on presence. These findings provide important insights into the isolated impacts of these variables on user experiences and suggest directions for future research and practical applications.

The teacher role had a significantly greater positive impact on memory compared to the clerk role. This finding aligns with previous studies on the educational impact of teacher figures, suggesting that users are more likely to retain information when presented by a perceived expert or authority figure in a learning context (Chen 2016; Cuddy et al. 2011). The teacher's role may inherently encourage deeper cognitive processing and engagement, thereby enhancing memory retention. Also, participants exhibited a more positive attitude towards the interaction when the agent played the role of a teacher versus a clerk. This result suggests that users may have a predisposition to trust and value interactions (Kang et al. 2024b) that appear educational rather than commercial. The teacher role likely conveys a sense of credibility and altruism, fostering a more favourable attitude (Cuddy et al. 2011). The teacher role also led to a higher intention to use the system compared to the clerk role. This finding indicates that users are more inclined to engage with and return to a system perceived as educational. The perceived utility and trust associated with the teacher role likely enhance users' willingness to continue using the system.

The study also revealed a significant main effect of textual enhancement techniques on presence, with VO techniques showing higher effectiveness compared to VI techniques. VO captions likely reduce cognitive load by integrating vocabulary and its meaning within the captions, making it easier for users to process and comprehend information without having to shift their attention away from the primary content (Witmer and Singer 1998; Lang 2006). This seamless integration helps users maintain focus and immersion within the virtual environment, thereby enhancing the sense of presence. Moreover, the presentation of VO captions within the primary visual field ensures that users do not miss critical information. In contrast, external images might require users to divert their attention, potentially disrupting the immersive experience (Mayer 2014). The continuous, integrated flow of information in VO captions supports sustained attention and presence.

The results of this study have several practical and theoretical implications. From a practical perspective, the findings suggest that virtual agents framed as teachers can significantly enhance memory retention, foster positive attitudes, and increase the intention to use virtual learning systems. Additionally, the use of vocabulary only captions as a textual enhancement technique can enhance users' sense of presence, thereby improving their overall experience and engagement. From a theoretical standpoint, the absence of significant interaction effects between the roles of agents and textual enhancement techniques indicates that these variables independently influence user outcomes. This insight can guide future research to further explore the isolated and combined effects of various virtual environment design elements on user experience and behaviour.

Future studies could benefit from examining a broader range of virtual contexts and agent roles to determine whether different settings or roles yield interaction effects. Additionally, increasing the sample size and employing more nuanced experimental manipulations may help uncover subtle interactions that were not detectable in the current study.

In conclusion, this study contributes to the understanding of how virtual agent roles and textual enhancement techniques independently influence user experiences in virtual environments. By leveraging these insights, developers and educators can design more effective and engaging virtual learning systems that enhance memory, attitude, intention to use, and presence.

Acknowledgements The present research has been conducted by the Excellent Researcher Support Project of Kwangwoon University in 2024.

References

Chang, H. H., & Wang, I. C. (2008). An investigation of user communication behavior in computer mediated environments. *Computers in Human Behavior, 24*(5), 2336–2356.

Chen, Y. L. (2016). The effects of virtual reality learning environment on student cognitive and linguistic development. *The Asia-Pacific Education Researcher, 25*, 637–646.

Chung, D. (2009). Influence of perceived gaming interactivity on various psychological states. *Journal of Korea Game Society, 9*(5), 3–11.

Chung, D. (2017). User-based theories and practices on virtual reality. *Informatization Policy, 24*(1), 3–29.

Csikszentmihalyi, M. (1975). *Beyond boredom and anxiety: The experience of play in work and games*. San Francisco: Jossey-Bass.

Csikszentmihalyi, M. (1996). *Creativity: Flow and the psychology of discovery and invention* (1st ed.). New York: HarperCollins Publishers.

Cuddy, A. J., Glick, P., & Beninger, A. (2011). The dynamics of warmth and competence judgments, and their outcomes in organizations. *Research in Organizational Behavior, 31*, 73–98.

Davis, F. D. (1989). Perceived usefulness, perceived ease of use, and user acceptance of information technology. *MIS Quarterly, 13*(3), 319–340.

Horz, H., Winter, C., & Fries, S. (2009). Differential benefits of situated instructional prompts. *Computers in Human Behavior, 25*(4), 818–828.

ISPR (International Society for Presence Research). (2000). *The concept of presence: Explication statement*. Retrieved from https://ispr.info/

Jin, Y. J., & Yoo, I. W. (2019). Why communicative language teaching has yet to work in Korea: Exploring teachers' viewpoints. *Journal of Asia TEFL, 16*(4), 1332–1347.

Johnson, E. B. (2002). *Contextual teaching and learning: What it is and why it's here to stay*. Thousand Oaks: Corwin Press.

Kang, J., Kwon, S., & Chung, D. (2024a). Effects of Linguistic Immersion Syntehsis on Foreign Language Learning Using Virtual Reality Agents. *Informatization Policy. 31*(1), 32–52.

Kang, J., Kwon, S., & Chung, D. (2024b). The Effectiveness of Foreign Language Learning in Virtual Environments and with Textual Enhancement Techniques in the Metaverse. *Knowledge Management Research, 25*(1), 155–172.

Lan, Y. J. (2015). Contextual EFL learning in a 3D virtual environment. *Language Learning & Technology, 19*(2), 16–31.

Landauer, T. K., & Dumais, S. T. (1997). A solution to Plato's problem: The latent semantic analysis theory of acquisition, induction, and representation of knowledge. *Psychological Review, 104*(2), 211–240.

Lang, A. (2000). The limited capacity model of mediated message processing. *Journal of Communication, 50*(1), 46–70.

Lang, A. (2006). Using the limited capacity model of motivated mediated message processing to design effective cancer communication messages. *Journal of Communication, 56*(1), 57–80.

Lee, H., & Chung, D. (2012). Difference in interactivity, flow, mood, attitude, and intention according to smartphone game sensor. *Korean Journal of Broadcasting and Telecommunication Studies, 26*(1), 126–166.

Lee, H., & Chung, D. (2019). Influence of virtual reality image depth on user's perceived characteristics, presence, and fatigue. *Korean Journal of Broadcasting and Telecommunication Studies, 33*(2), 184–216.

Lee, M. (2012). Influence of appearance decoration on women's professional image. *Journal of the Korea Fashion & Costume Design Association, 14*(4), 1–16.

Leow, R. P. (2001). Do learners notice enhanced forms while interacting with the L2?: An online and offline study of the role of written input enhancement in L2 reading. *Hispania, 84*(3), 496–509.

Lin, J. W., Duh, H. B. L., Parker, D. E., Abi-Rached, H., & Furness, T. A. (2002). Effects of field of view on presence, enjoyment, memory, and simulator sickness in a virtual environment. In *Proceedings IEEE Virtual Reality 2002* (pp. 164–171). Orlando, FL: IEEE.

Mayer, R. E. (2014). Principles based on social cues in multimedia learning: Personalization, voice, image, and embodiment principles. In R. E. Mayer (Ed.), *The Cambridge handbook of multimedia learning* (pp. 345–368). Cambridge, England: Cambridge University Press.

Oliver, R. L. (2014). *Satisfaction: A behavioral perspective on the consumer.* New York: Routledge.

Paivio, A. (1990). *Mental representations: A dual coding approach.* Oxford: Oxford University Press.

Shin, M., & Chung, D. (2020). An exploratory study examining users' psychological responses to screen speed in virtual reality exergame. *Journal of Korea Game Society, 20*(5), 41–51.

Song, W., & Lee, M. (2015). A study of impression formation according to men's accessories wearing and hairstyle. *Journal of the Korean Society of Costume, 65*(2), 17–32.

White, J. (1998). Getting the learners' attention: A typographical input enhancement study. In C. Doughty & J. Williams (Eds.), *Focus on form in classroom second language acquisition* (pp. 85–113). New York: Cambridge University Press.

Witmer, B. G., & Singer, M. J. (1998). Measuring presence in virtual environments: A presence questionnaire. *Presence, 7*(3), 225–240.

The Impact of VR-Based Safety Experience Education on Safety Awareness, Safety Behavior, and Accident Prevention: The Empirical Study of VR Application in Industrial Safety Education in Korea

Ok-seol Kim, Gil-sang Jang, and Seok-in Mun

Abstract This paper examines the impact of VR (Virtual Reality)-based safety training on safety awareness, safety behavior, and accident prevention. It also investigates the mediating effects of safety awareness and safety behavior in the relationship between VR-based safety training and accident prevention. To achieve the research objectives, responses from 957 safety managers and workers who participated in the 'Mobile VR Safety Experience Support' program, promoted by the Korea Occupational Safety and Health Agency, were analyzed using SPSS 24.0 and AMOS 20.0. The results showed that VR-based safety training has a significant positive (+) impact on safety awareness, safety behavior, and accident prevention. Additionally, safety awareness has a significant positive (+) impact on safety behavior and accident prevention, and safety behavior has a significant positive (+) impact on accident prevention. Furthermore, safety awareness and safety behavior were found to mediate the relationship between safety training and accident prevention. The findings also confirmed the existence of multiple mediating effects, as VR-based safety training enhances workers' safety awareness, improves safety behavior, and subsequently influences accident prevention. Based on these findings, the implications, limitations of the study, and directions for future research were discussed.

O. Kim
PhD candidate of College of Business Administration, University of Ulsan, Ulsan, Republic of Korea
e-mail: xlsk@hanmail.net

G. Jang (✉)
Professor of College of Business Administration, University of Ulsan, Ulsan, Republic of Korea
e-mail: gsjang@ulsan.ac.kr

S. Mun
Gangwon Regional Office, Korea Occupational Safety and Health Agency, Seongnam, Republic of Korea
e-mail: doordol@kosha.or.kr

T. Jung et al. (eds.), *XR and Metaverse*, Springer Proceedings in Business and Economics, https://doi.org/10.1007/978-3-031-77975-6_7

Keywords VR (Virtual reality) · Safety experience education · Safety awareness · Safety behaviour · Accident prevention · Multiple mediating effect

1 Introduction

Recently, VR, which is prominent in the gaming, entertainment, video, and medical fields, has also been attracting attention in the education field. VR technology, along with augmented reality (AR), provides virtual information to users through devices in today's media convergence environment. In particular, the importance of VR is increasing in the field of education, where experiential learning is required (Min and Kim 2018). VR can provide realistic educational experiences and repetitive training at a low cost in dangerous or difficult areas, so the demand for VR in the education field is expected to grow further. VR allows users to experience challenging or impossible situations in a virtual environment (Lee 2021).

Currently, the increase in the number of VR education participants and the expansion of VR's scope can be attributed to the high educational delivery power of VR technology, including immersion, realism, and interactivity, and its efficiency proven through various experiments and demonstrations around the world. Meanwhile, as industrial accidents and safety incidents have emerged as social problems in Korea, the importance of safety education as a preventive measure is being highlighted. In line with this, the Korea Occupational Safety and Health Agency (KOSHA) has been actively developing VR content for safety and health education since 2017. They have developed over 620 types of VR content to date and distributed them for free on a dedicated VR platform (360vr.kosha.or.kr). In particular, to lower the entry barrier to VR-based safety experience education, KOSHA has been focusing on producing VR content compatible with low- to mid-priced VR devices, such as HMD (Head Mounted Display)-centered videos and CG-based VR content, since 2019. Additionally, KOSHA has developed a content management system (CMS) that supports VR experiential education, allowing up to 100 workers to receive safety education simultaneously through a single tablet PC. The goal is to enable VR safety experience education to be used even in small- and medium-sized businesses with limited budgets and manpower (Mun 2021).

This study empirically examined the impact of VR-based safety experience education on workers' safety awareness and safety behavior, and furthermore, on accident prevention, targeting participants who received safety education using the VR-based safety experience education system developed and distributed by KOSHA.

2 Theoretical Background and Research Hypothesis

2.1 VR-Based Safety Experience Education

In industrial safety education, site-centered training is crucial and should utilize equipment or scenarios that might occur in actual sites. However, field education is costly and carries inherent risks due to direct training. Consequently, the need for VR-based safety and health education is growing, along with its demand (Min and Kim 2018).

2.2 Safety Awareness

Kim (2015) defined safety awareness as the consciousness of maintaining safety from risks in daily life and preventing accidents. Kim (2013) emphasized that safety awareness encompasses psychological aspects such as individuals' awareness and attitudes toward safety. Safety education that enhances both information and attitudes can improve safety awareness. To effectively boost safety awareness, education should be experience-centered rather than solely focused on knowledge transfer.

2.3 Safety Behavior

Neal and Griffin (2006) described safety behavior as practical actions taken to ensure safety, including complying with safety procedures and participating in safety activities to prevent accidents (Woo 2014). An (2017) defined it as actions aimed at preventing current and future risk factors from causing accidents. Woo (2014) further defined safety behavior as actions ensuring safe work performance.

2.4 Accident Prevention

Safety accidents can occur to anyone, at any time, and in any place, often when least expected (Suh 2019). Kwon et al. (2010) categorized safety accidents into public safety, transportation, school safety, life safety, product safety, and industrial safety. They argued that effective accident prevention requires integrating and utilizing accident data to develop optimal prevention measures based on trends, situations, and frequencies.

2.5 Relationship Between VR-Based Safety Experience Education, Safety Awareness, Safety Behavior, and Accident Prevention

VR safety experience education increases safety awareness by making trainees feel as if they are actually experiencing a dangerous situation. Studies have shown that people trained through VR have better risk awareness and increased safety awareness. This is because VR's highly immersive educational environment maximizes the effectiveness of safety education (Yoo et al. 2023; Shringi et al. 2022). Therefore, based on this theoretical background and the results of previous studies, the following research hypotheses are proposed.

H1: VR-based safety experience education will have a significantly positive impact on safety awareness.

VR safety experience education is very effective in improving safety behavior. Trainees become better able to perform actions in real situations through repeated practice in a virtual environment. This is because VR education induces not only theoretical knowledge but also practical behavioral changes (Toyoda et al. 2022). Therefore, based on this theoretical background and the results of previous studies, the following research hypotheses are proposed.

H2: VR-based safety experience education will have a significantly positive impact on safety behavior.

VR safety experience education plays an important role in accident prevention. Studies show that workers who receive VR training improve their ability to prevent accidents on the actual workplace. This is because by providing experiences similar to real situations in a virtual environment, trainees can recognize and respond to risks in advance (Yoo et al. 2023; Shringi et al. 2022). Therefore, based on this theoretical background and the results of previous studies, the following research hypotheses are proposed.

H3: VR-based safety experience education will have a significantly positive impact on safety accident prevention.

Wang et al. (2018) suggested that safety awareness significantly influences safety behavior. This study conducted in the Chinese construction industry found that a positive safety climate enhances the relationship between safety awareness and safety behavior. Workers with higher safety awareness are more likely to engage in safety behaviors, which include compliance with safety regulations and proactive safety participation. Uzuntarla et al. (2020) was shown that increased safety awareness leads to better safety behaviors, which in turn reduce the incidence of workplace accidents in occupational safety across various industries, including textile and metal sectors. This relationship highlights the importance of cultivating a safety awareness culture to promote safer work environments and minimize accident risks. Therefore, based on this theoretical background and the results of previous studies, the following research hypotheses are proposed.

H4: Safety awareness will have a significantly positive impact on safety behavior.
H5: Safety awareness will have a positive impact on safety accident prevention.

Li et al. (2020) suggested that safety behavior directly impacts accident prevention. For instance, in the railway industry, enhancing safety citizenship behavior (SCB) among employees leads to a reduction in accidents. Safety leadership and a positive safety attitude foster SCB, which involves voluntary actions by employees to ensure their own safety and that of their colleagues. This proactive behavior significantly reduces workplace accidents and fatalities (Lyu et al. 2018; Neal and Griffin 2006). Therefore, based on this theoretical background and the results of previous studies, the following research hypotheses are proposed.

H6: Safety behavior will have a positive impact on safety accident prevention.

In Kim's (2019) study, the impact of construction safety education utilizing virtual and augmented reality on safety behavior and accident prevention was examined among 400 construction site safety managers and process managers. The results indicated that, overall, VR and AR education had a significant impact on safety behavior, and safety behavior had a highly significant impact on accident prevention.

Summarizing the results of these previous studies, VR-based safety training has a significant impact on safety awareness and safety behavior. Safety awareness significantly affects safety behavior, and these antecedent factors ultimately have a significant impact on accident prevention. Therefore, based on this theoretical background and the results of previous studies, the following research hypotheses are proposed.

H7: Safety awareness will play a mediating role in the relationship between VR-based safety experience education and safety behavior.
H8: Safety awareness will play a mediating role in the relationship between VR-based safety experience education and safety accident prevention.
H9: Safety behavior will play a mediating role in the relationship between VR-based safety experience education and safety accident prevention.

2.6 Research Model

Based on previous studies, this research aims to examine the impact of VR-based safety experience education on safety awareness, safety behaviour, and accident prevention. Utilizing the experience model factors proposed by Pine and Gilmore (1998) in their Experience Economy Theory—educational experience, escapist experience, esthetic experience, and entertainment experience-, this study establishes the research model, as shown in the Fig. 1.

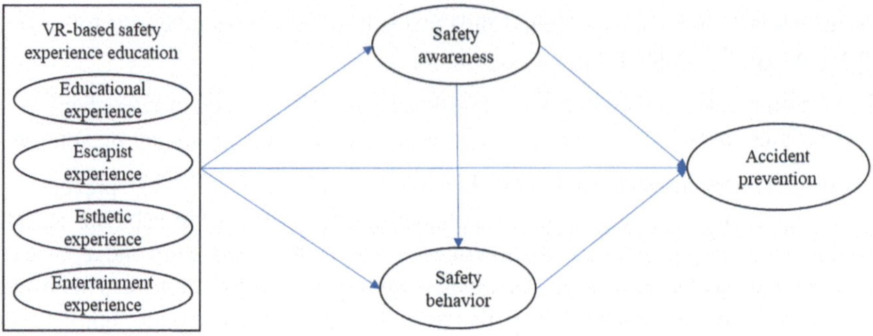

Fig. 1 Research model

3 Research Method

3.1 Sample and Data Collection Method

Data collection in this study was conducted on 1,025 people who received safety experience education through an HMD and CMS-based multi-person simultaneous VR-based safety education experience system over a period of approximately 45 days from September 23, 2023 to October 30, 2023. The sampling method used was the convenient sampling method, and the self-administration method was used for the questionnaire. The questionnaire was constructed using a 5-point Likert scale. After distributing the questionnaires, of the 1,025 returned questionnaires, 957 were used as final analysis data, excluding 68 questionnaires that had missing values unsuitable for analysis or were answered insincerely.

The characteristics of the sample are as follows: 95.8% were male and 4.2% were female. Age distribution was as follows: under 20 years old (8.0%), 30s (16.9%), 40s (20.4%), 50s (37.2%), and 60 years and older (17.5%). In terms of education, 55.6% had a high school diploma or less, 14.5% had an associate degree, 27.5% had a bachelor's degree, and 2.4% had a graduate degree or higher. Industry distribution was: manufacturing (6.0%), construction (69.1%), service (8.8%), and others (16.2%). Company size was distributed as follows: fewer than 5 employees (2.7%), 5–49 employees (37.1%), 50–99 employees (13.7%), 100–299 employees (28.4%), and 300 or more employees (5.1%). Job positions were distributed as follows: staff/assistant manager (74.7%), manager/assistant director (14.2%), director (6.1%), and executive or higher (5.0%). Job roles were: owner/management (1.0%), safety and health manager (4.8%), supervisor (13.4%), safety and health officer (1.3%), worker (77.2%), and others (2.3%). Length of service was distributed as follows: less than 5 years (37.9%), 5–10 years (26.1%), 10–15 years (13.2%), and more than 15 years (22.8%).

3.2 Operational Definition and Measurement of Variables

VR-based safety experience education refers to an educational program conducted using VR technology to prevent safety accidents. The measurement items were adapted from the previous study by Kim (2019) to fit the purpose and methodology of this study. The questionnaire included 20 items measuring four types of experiences: 5 items for educational experience, 5 items for escapist experience, 5 items for aesthetic experience, and 5 items for entertainment experience.

Safety awareness refers to the degree to which potential safety-related awareness and interest are expressed in safety behaviour. The measurement items tool, consisting of five items, were adapted from the previous studies by O (2015) and Min (2020) to fit the purpose and methodology of this study.

Safety behavior refers to a series of practical actions taken to ensure one's safety in hazardous or dangerous situations. The measurement tool, consisting of five items, was adapted from the previous studies by Griffin and Neal (2000), Kim (2019), and Suh (2019) to fit the purpose and methodology of this study.

Accident prevention is defined as all activities undertaken to eliminate the causes of safety accidents and prevent them beforehand. The measurement tool, consisting of five items, was adapted from the previous studies by Kim (2019) to fit the purpose and methodology of this study.

4 Empirical Analysis

4.1 Reliability and Validity Analysis

In order to test the hypotheses proposed in this study, the reliability and validity of the measurement instruments were examined. The Cronbach's alpha reliability coefficient was found to be above 0.6, meeting the criterion of 0.6 suggested by Nunnally (1978). For the factor analysis of the measurement instruments, the commonly used technique of principal component analysis with varimax rotation was employed for factor extraction.

In this study, the structural validity of the questionnaire was verified through Exploratory Factor Analysis (EFA) based on the collected data. Generally, before conducting EFA, it is essential to assess the feasibility of factor analysis. The KMO (Kaiser-Meyer-Olkin) measure was examined and found to be above 0.934, significantly higher than the commonly accepted minimum criterion of 0.6, indicating that the sample data is highly suitable for factor analysis.

First, for the VR-based safety experience education (independent variable), factor analysis results grouped items into single variables: educational experience (5 questions), escapist experience (2 questions, 3 removed), esthetic experience (4 questions, 1 removed), and entertainment experience (4 questions, 1 removed), with a cumulative variance ratio of 84.804%, indicating maintained validity. Cronbach's alpha coefficients were high: educational experience (0.959), escapist experience (0.867), aesthetic experience (0.932), and entertainment experience (0.922), indicating reliable measurement tools.

Next, for the mediating and dependent variables, factor analysis results grouped items into single variables: safety awareness (5 questions), safety behaviour (3 questions, 2 removed), and accident prevention (5 questions), and the cumulative variance ratio was 83.212%. Therefore, the validity of the factors is maintained. Additionally, the Cronbach's alpha reliability coefficients were all very high, with safety awareness at 0.933, safety behavior at 0.918, and accident prevention at 0.955, all exceeding 0.7. This indicates that the reliability of the measurement tools is not problematic.

4.2 Confirmatory Factor Analysis

In this study, following the Exploratory Factor Analysis (EFA), a Confirmatory Factor Analysis (CFA) was conducted for all factors. A second-order factor analysis was performed on the VR-based safety training, converting it into a single latent factor. The results of the CFA are shown in Table 1. Most of the indices met the fit evaluation criteria (GFI and CFI ≥ 0.9, RMR and SRMR ≤ 0.05), indicating an acceptable level of model fit. The Composite Reliability (CR) and Average Variance Extracted (AVE) were higher than the criteria suggested by Bagozzi and Yi (1988) (CR ≥ 0.7, AVE ≥ 0.5). The standardized factor loadings connecting the measurement items and constructs were statistically significant within the 95% confidence interval (C.R. > 1.96), demonstrating convergent validity (Anderson and Gerbing 1988).

Furthermore, this study examined the correlations between factors in addition to the validity and reliability analysis. Correlation coefficients range from -1 to 1, with larger absolute values indicating stronger correlations between variables. Discriminant validity analysis is used to verify whether there are statistically significant differences between different factors. Discriminant validity is established if the correlations between factors are low. If the correlation coefficient between variables does not exceed the square root of the AVE, discriminant validity is considered to be present (Fornell and Larcker 1981). Table 2 shows the correlation matrix of constructs. The numbers on the diagonal in Table 2 represent the square root of the AVE for each factor. The square root of the AVE for VR_SEE was found to be smaller than the correlation coefficient with SA, while the square roots of the AVE for the other factors were greater than the standardized correlation coefficients off the diagonal. Therefore, except for the AVE of VR_SEE being smaller than its correlation coefficient with SA, the AVE values for the remaining factors were larger than their correlation coefficients with other factors, confirming partial discriminant validity among the constructs.

Table 1 Results of confirmatory factor analysis

Variable/indicators	Standard estimate	S.E	C.R	P	AVE	CR	Fit index
VR-based safety experience education (VR_SEE)							$\chi^2 = 294.115$, df = 81, p = 0.000, χ^2/df = 3.631, RMR = 0.010, SRMR = 0.023, GFI = 0.960, AGFI = 0.941, NFI = 0.980, TLI = 0.981, CFI = 0.985, RMSEA = 0.052
ETE	0.794						
ESE	0.905	0.032	29.666	***	0.568	0.789	
ECE	0.505	0.051	17.143	***			
Safety awareness (SA)							
SA1	0.886						
SA2	0.823	0.030	33.917	***			
SA3	0.858	0.029	36.758	***	0.733	0.917	
SA4	0.856	0.029	36.571	***			
Safety behavior (SB)							
SB5	0.937						
SB4	0.943	0.019	54.332	***	0.807	0.926	
SB3	0.808	0.028	36.278	***			
Accident prevention (AP)							
AP1	0.846						
AP2	0.911	0.025	38.295	***			
AP3	0.927	0.025	39.632	***	0.806	0.954	
AP4	0.900	0.026	37.481	***			
AP5	0.903	0.026	37.68	***			

Table 2 Correlation matrix of constructs

	Mean	SD	VR_SEE	SA	SB	AP
VR_SEE	4.448	0.545	0.754			
SA	4.650	0.460	0.791***	0.856		
SB	4.629	0.506	0.741***	0.837***	0.898	
AP	4.568	0.515	0.867***	0.840***	0.795***	0.898

4.3 Hypothesis Testing

In order to examine the influence relationships among VR-based safety experience education, safety awareness, safety behavior, and accident prevention used in this study, the research model was tested using covariance structure analysis for the structural model. Reviewing the structural equation model, most values in the research model met the fit evaluation criteria: X2 = 294.115, df = 81, p = 0.000, X2/df = 3.631, RMR = 0.010, SRMR = 0.0232, GFI = 0.960, AGFI = 0.941, NFI = 0.980, TLI = 0.981, CFI = 0.985, RMSEA = 0.052, indicating an acceptable level

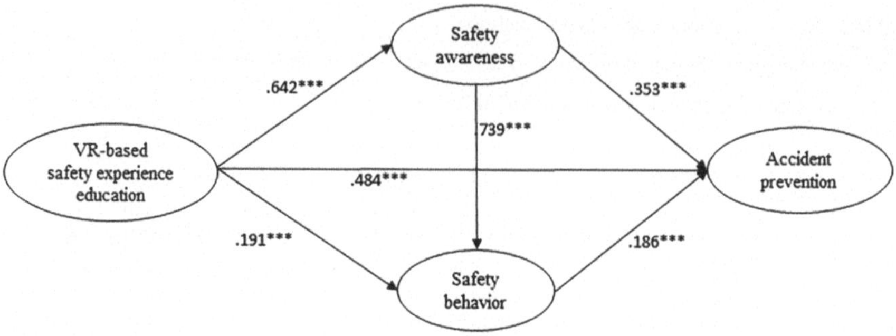

Fig. 2 Structural equation model

of overall model fit. The results of the validation of the model proposed in this study are presented in Fig. 2.

The results of the hypothesis testing for the research model are summarized in Table 3. The results indicate that all hypotheses were accepted. Specifically, VR-based safety experience education has a highly significant impact on safety awareness (H1), VR-based safety experience education has a highly significant impact on safety behavior (H2), and VR-based safety experience education has a highly significant impact on accident prevention (H3). Additionally, safety awareness has a highly significant impact on safety behavior (H4), safety awareness has a highly significant impact on accident prevention (H5), and furthermore, safety behavior has a highly significant impact on accident prevention (H6).

In this study, the mediating effects were tested using AMOS bootstrapping and phantom variables. Specifically, phantom variables are used in bootstrapping to verify the indirect effects of a multiple mediation model. Phantom variables are non-existent variables with a fixed variance of 0, created by fixing the path of the indirect effect

Table 3 Path analysis results of structural model

No	Hypothesis	Estimate	S.E	C.R	P	Result
H1	VR-based safety education → safety awareness	0.642	0.028	23.036	***	Accepted
H2	VR-based safety education → safety behavior	0.191	0.038	5.054	***	Accepted
H3	VR-based safety education → accident prevention	0.484	0.040	12.164	***	Accepted
H4	Safety awareness → safety behavior	0.739	0.047	15.621	***	Accepted
H5	Safety awareness → accident prevention	0.353	0.054	6.498	***	Accepted
H6	Safety behavior → accident prevention	0.186	0.041	4.531	***	Accepted

Table 4 Results of multiple mediation effect analysis

Path		Estimate	S.E	p	Result
Direct effects					
H3	VR-based safety education → accident prevention	0.484	0.064	0.002	Accept
Indirect effects					
H7	VR-based safety education → safety awareness → accident prevention	0.227	0.058	0.004	Accept
H8	VR-based safety education → safety behavior r → accident prevent ion	0.036	0.017	0.002	Accept
H9	VR-based safety education → safety awareness → safety behavior → accident prevention	0.089	0.033	0.001	Accept
	Sum	0.351	0.046	0.001	
Total effects		0.835	0.035	0.002	

to be measured to their factor loadings. Adding phantom variables does not affect the model fit as all parameters of the variables remain fixed (Loehlin 2004). The results of the multiple mediation analysis are summarized in Table 4. The analysis results indicate that safety awareness and safety behavior each have a mediating effect between VR-based safety experience education and accident prevention (H7, H8). Additionally, the results show that there is a multiple mediation effect where safety awareness and safety behavior sequentially mediate the relationship between VR-based safety experience education and accident prevention (H9).

5 Discussion and Conclusion

This study established a research model suggesting that VR-based safety experience education influences accident prevention, particularly through the mediating variables of safety awareness and safety behavior. The findings indicate that VR-based safety experience education plays a significant role in accident prevention by enhancing safety awareness and safety behavior, thereby strengthening accident prevention through these mediators. Therefore, the results suggest that, in order to prevent accidents, VR-based safety experience education should be implemented alongside educational programs aimed at simultaneously improving safety awareness and safety behavior. These findings are consistent with those of previous studies (Yoo et al. 2023; Shringi et al. 2022; Toyoda et al. 2022; Wang et al. 2018; Li et al. 2020; Uzuntarla et al. 2020).

The theoretical implications of this study are as follows: First, it is the first to propose a research model demonstrating the multiple mediating effects of safety awareness and safety behavior in the relationship between VR-based safety training and accident prevention. Second, it is the first to reveal that VR-based safety training influences safety awareness, which in turn affects safety behavior, ultimately leading to accident prevention through multiple mediating effects.

The practical implications of this study are as follows: First, VR-based safety experience education can realistically simulate high-risk situations, allowing learners to experience danger and learn safety behaviors, thereby preventing accidents. Second, without the need for physical equipment or dangerous experimental environments, VR can simulate various hazardous situations for training purposes, allowing for repeated experiences of risky scenarios, thus reducing the cost and time required in actual training settings. Third, VR enables the provision of the same level of safety training to large groups of people regardless of geographic constraints, ensuring consistent education anywhere. Fourth, the immersive nature of VR deeply engages learners emotionally with the educational content, promoting the formation of safety-related memories through experiences in realistic environments. This, in turn, enhances and internalizes safety behaviors in real situations.

This study has the following limitations. First, in the discriminant validity analysis among the constructs, the AVE value of VR-based safety experience education was found to be smaller than the squared correlation coefficient of safety awareness, indicating partial discriminant validity. The underlying cause of this needs to be investigated. Second, as approximately 69% of the study participants were construction workers, generalizing the study results might be challenging. Future empirical research should include various industries. Third, the collected data was based on a cross-sectional study at a single point in time, which limits the ability to draw definitive conclusions from the results. Future studies should employ longitudinal methods to explain the causal processes through which VR-based safety experience education influences safety awareness, safety behavior, and accident prevention. Finally, future research should conduct in-depth analyses of the sub-factors of VR-based safety experience education (educational experience, escapist experience, aesthetic experience, entertainment experience) and identify various mediators such as safety motivation, safety education, safety culture, and safety climate, in addition to safety awareness and safety behavior, in the relationship between VR-based safety experience education and accident prevention.

References

An, B. T. (2017), *A Study on the Safety Culture and Safety Behavior of Railway Workers: Focused on Seoul Transportation Corporation*, Master's thesis, Graduate School of Public Policy and Civic Engagement, Kyung Hee University.

Anderson, J.C. & Gerbing, D.W. (1988), Structural equation modeling in practice: A review and recommended two-step approach, Psychological bulletin, 103(3): 411–423.

Bagozzi, R. P. & Yi, Y. (1988). On the evaluation of structural equation models, *Journal of the Academy Marketing Science*, 16(1): 74–94.

Fornell, C. & Larcker, D.F. (1981), Evaluating structural equation models with unobservable variables and measurement error, Journal of Marketing Research, 18: 39–50.

Griffin, M. A., & Neal, A. (2000). Perceptions of Safety at Work: A Framework for Linking Safety Climate to Safety Performance, Knowledge, and Motivation, Journal of Occupational Health Psychology, 5(3), 347–358.

Kim, J. K. (2013). *A study on the Preventive Measures of Safety in accordance with the Safety Awareness of Taekwondo instructors*, Master's thesis, Graduate School of Sports Science, Yong In University.

Kim, S. Y. (2015). Safety Awareness and Safety Practice Behavior of College Students. Journal of Digital Convergence, 13(2): 279–289.

Kim, J. M. (2019). *An empirical study on the impact of construction safety education using virtual augmented reality on accident prevention*. Ph.D. dissertation, Graduate School, Myongji University.

Kwon, Y., Park, K., & Kim, C. (2010). A Study on the Classification System of Safety Accident. Korean Ergonomics Society Conference Proceedings, 2010(5): 152–155.

Lee, D. W. (2021). Trends in applying virtual augmented reality in the field of education. Weekly ICT Trends, (2000), 2–14.

Li, M., Zhai, H., Zhang, J. & Meng, X. (2020). Research on the Relationship Between Safety Leadership, Safety Attitude and Safety Citizenship Behavior of Railway Employees, *International Journal of Environmental Research and Public Health*, 17(1864): 1–17.

Loehlin, J. C. (2004), *Latent Variable Models: An Introduction to Factor, Path, and Structural Equation analysis*, 4th Edition, Mahwah, NJ: Lawrence Eribaum.

Lyu, S., Hon, C. K. H., Chan, A. P. C., Wong, F. K. W. & Javed, A. A. (2018). Relationships among Safety Climate, Safety Behavior, and Safety Outcomes for Ethnic Minority Construction Workers, *International Journal of Environmental Research and Public Health*, 15(484): 1–16.

Neal, A., & Griffin, M. A. (2006). A study of the lagged relationships among safety climate, safety motivation, safety behavior, and accidents at the individual and group levels. *Journal of applied psychology*, 91(4), 946–953.

Min, S. G., & Kim, S. H. (2018). A Study on Presence as a VR Content Activation Strategy—Focused on Safeline cases. Journal of Communication Design, 62, 60–70.

Min, K. R. (2020). A Study on the Effect of Self-Leadership on Safety Consciousness and Safety Culture, Master's thesis, Graduate School of Business Administration, University of Ulsan.

Mun, S. I. (2021). A study on the effect of safety experience education using virtual reality (VR) on the safety accident prevention and safety education satisfaction, Ph.D. dissertation, Graduate School, University of Ulsan.

Nunnally, J. C.(1978*), Psychometric Theory, 2d ed.*, New York: McGraw-Hill.

O, S.U. & Heo, C. (2015), The Influence of Qualitative and Quantitative Safety Management Activities and Employees' Safety Awareness on Safety Behavior in the Construction Company: Focusing on the Mediating Effects of Organizational Trust, *Asia-Pacific Journal of Business Venturing and Entrepreneurship*, 10(6): 203–213.

Pine, B. J., & Gilmore, J. H. (1998). Welcome to the Experience Economy. Harvard Business Review, 76(4), 97–105.

Shringi, A., Arashpour, M., Golafshani, E. M., Rajabifard, A., Dwyer, T. & Li, H. (2022). Efficiency of VR-Based Safety Training for Construction Equipment: Hazard Recognition in Heavy Machinery Operations, *Buildings*, 12(2084): 1–22.

Suh, H. S. (2019). The Effect of Safety Education on Safety Consciousness and Safety Behavior: Focusing on Farmer's village experience instructor.-. Graduate School, Myongji University, Doctoral dissertation. https://www.riss.kr/link?id=T15058084

Toyoda, R., Russo-Abegão, F. & Glassey, J. (2022). VR-based health and safety training in various high-risk engineering industries: a literature review, *International Journal of Educational Technology in Higher Education*, 19(42):2–22.

Uzuntarla, F., Kucukali, S. & Uzuntarla, Y. (2020). An analysis on the relationship between safety awareness and safety behaviors of healthcare professionals, Ankara/Turkey, *Journal of Occupational Health*, 62(1):e12129.

Wang, M., Sun, J., Du, H. & Wang, C. (2018). Relations between Safety Climate, Awareness, and Behavior in the Chinese Construction Industry: A Hierarchical Linear Investigation, *Advances in Civil Engineering; New York*, 2018:1–8.

Woo, S. C. (2014). The determinants of safety motivation and their relationships with the safety behaviors of Korean Air Force pilots. Graduate School, Sang Ji University, Doctoral dissertation. https://www.riss.kr/link?id=T13518230

Yoo, W. J., Park, J. S. & Park, H. J. (2023). Understanding VR-Based Construction Safety Training Effectiveness: The Role of Telepresence, Risk Perception, and Training Satisfaction, *Applied Sciences.* 13(2):1–15.

The Importance of Governance in Metaverse/Blockchain Technology in Education

Anju De Alwis, Anup Shrestha, and Tapan Sarker

Abstract

Purpose This study explores the governance frameworks necessary for the effective implementation of Blockchain and Metaverse technologies in the education sector, aiming to enhance transparency, data security, and equitable access to educational opportunities. **Methodology**: Adopting an interpretivist research philosophy, the study employs an inductive qualitative approach, combining data from document analysis and twenty semi-structured interviews to gather comprehensive insights from stakeholders in higher education. **Findings**: The research identifies significant cost reductions and efficiency improvements in certificate issuance and verification through blockchain technology. It also highlights the transformative potential of the Metaverse in democratizing education and promoting collaborative learning environments. **Originality/Value**: This study addresses a critical gap in the literature by focusing on the governance of emerging technologies in education. It also highlights the need for design principles necessary for a governance framework, providing valuable insights for policymakers and educational institutions to ensure the responsible and sustainable application of these innovations.

Keywords Governance · Blockchain · Web3 · Metaverse · Education · Certificate verification

1 Introduction

The United Nations' Sustainable Development Goals (SDGs) emphasize the critical role of education in nurturing healthier societies and sustainable development. Education not only raises awareness about the SDGs but also empowers individuals to take action towards achieving them (Saxena et al. 2021; Zagalaz et al. 2022). Despite progress in reducing global illiteracy, significant challenges remain. One

A. De Alwis (✉) · A. Shrestha · T. Sarker
School of Business, University of Southern Queensland, Springfield, Australia
e-mail: anju@ultimateaccess.net

T. Jung et al. (eds.), *XR and Metaverse*, Springer Proceedings in Business and Economics, https://doi.org/10.1007/978-3-031-77975-6_8

significant challenge is the compromised integrity of global education due to the prevalence of fraudulent academic certificates, which complicates the verification process for employers and strains academic-corporate relationships. Traditional verification methods are often cumbersome, costly, and outdated, leading to increased deception (Tahlil et al. 2022). Accessibility to education is another major issue, with 773 million people still lacking basic literacy skills, disproportionately affecting women (UN 2015; UNESCO 2022). As students increasingly seek learning experiences beyond traditional education in an interconnected world, the need for transparent and verifiable educational credentials becomes more pressing (Krishnamurthy 2020).

Academic accreditation is a formal procedure for assessing the standards and quality of education offered by higher education programs (Amirtharaj et al. 2022). Certification and accreditation serve as key methods for assessing a nation's educational quality (Chapman and Lindner 2016; de Paor 2016). Accreditation ensures educational integrity by confirming compliance with essential minimum standards, benefiting individuals, employers, and society as a whole (Rubinstein 1977).

Governance pertains to the management, regulation, and oversight mechanisms that guarantee decision-making, accountability, and the allocation of authority among stakeholders (Tan et al. 2023). This review establishes a basis for additional research on blockchain governance in education, promoting a more systematic approach to comprehending its mechanisms. The accreditation of certificates and validation will engage various stakeholders. Credential verification refers to the process of validating the authenticity of educational credentials, such as diplomas and transcripts, issued by academic institutions (Alnafrah and Mouselli 2021).

Decentralized technologies like blockchain power Web 3, the next generation of the World Wide Web. The decentralized architecture of blockchains, along with their immutable records and smart contract capabilities, distinguishes blockchain-based services from earlier internet innovations (El Koshiry et al. 2023; Narongsak and Nonsiri 2023). Blockchain systems enhance the security and reliability of the verification process by preventing single points of failure and providing detailed access control (Saleh et al. 2023). Web3 technologies envisions a decentralized and democratized digital landscape where users have full control over their data and online identities (Ray 2023). Emerging technologies such as blockchain within Metaverse environments offer new pathways for education, underpinning sustainability, mobility, and integrity, which can potentially revolutionise access to education and the validation of learning experiences (Joshi and P.J 2023; Mourtzis et al. 2023). Blockchain technology provides a secure and immutable platform for issuing verifiable academic certificates, ensuring the permanence and credibility of qualifications (Zhu and Cao 2021). Alongside blockchain technology, Stephenson's (2003) coined the phrase 'Metaverse'—a computer-generated virtual reality environment where users interact in real-time—is gaining popularity in education. This platform allows inclusive, collaborative learning communities that meet individual needs and preferences (Mourtzis et al. 2023). While current literature on blockchain and Metaverse in education primarily focuses on their functions and deployment, there is a significant research gap in building a governance framework to realize the benefits of these technologies in education.

This study addresses this gap by exploring how distributed ledger technology, such as blockchain and Metaverse, can be managed and governed in the educational sector. The findings highlight significant cost reductions and efficiency improvements in certificate issuance and verification through blockchain technology, as well as the transformative potential of the Metaverse in democratizing education and nurturing collaborative learning environments. By adopting an interpretivist research philosophy and an inductive qualitative method (Alshahrani et al. 2022; Choi 2020), this study combines data from document analysis and twenty semi-structured interviews to gather comprehensive insights from stakeholders in higher education (Son-Turan 2022).

The findings contribute to the literature by examining governance of emerging technologies in education, offering valuable insights for policymakers and educational institutions. The researchers underscore the need for design principles necessary for a governance framework, ensuring the responsible and sustainable application of these innovations (Liu et al. 2023).

The remainder of this paper is organized as follows: Sect. 2 details the literature review. Section 3 describes the research methodology. The findings are presented in Sect. 4, followed by discussions in Sect. 5. Finally, Sect. 6 concludes the study.

2 Literature Review Theory/Issues

2.1 Blockchain in Education Technology

In the evolving landscape of educational technology, blockchain is recognized as a pivotal force. Scholars have highlighted its multifarious benefits and enabling features, such as robust data security and the verifiable authenticity of academic qualifications. These characteristics mitigate fraud and counterfeit documents, as highlighted by Nousias et al. (2022), who detail blockchain's efficacy in enhancing data protection. The decentralisation aspect, highlighted by Razzaq (2023), enables stakeholders and third parties to access and verify credentials autonomously, without a central authoritative body. This independence from centralised verification systems marks a significant stride towards operational autonomy within educational institutions.

Further, blockchain's streamlining effect on administrative functions by reducing the physical documentation and intermediaries is recognised for ensuring cost-effectiveness and operational efficiency. The introduction of smart contracts automates and simplifies educational procedures, from enrolment to fee payments, enhancing the administrative experience for educational stakeholders (Reza et al. 2022).

While the operational benefits of blockchain in education are well-documented, there remains an opportunity to explore the governance structures necessary for effectively regulating and managing these technologies. Governance is a crucial element for the successful implementation and scalability of blockchain in the education sector, yet it has not been adequately addressed in existing studies.

2.1.1 Blockchain Business Model

A blockchain-based business model for higher education can promote equality and adapt to post-pandemic educational needs (Alsobhi et al. 2023). By leveraging blockchain, universities can establish a decentralized and transparent system for verifying and storing academic records, reducing fraud risk, and facilitating seamless credit transfers between institutions, thereby enhancing accessibility and flexibility for students (Sumithra et al. 2021). Additionally, this business model can facilitate partnerships between universities and industry, enabling students to gain real-world experience and enhance their employability upon graduation. The move away from just-in-case learning to just-in-time learning allows students to focus on acquiring practical skills and knowledge relevant to their chosen field, ensuring they are better prepared for the demands of the job market ("GPAI," 2023). Countries in Europe and India are now supporting educational reforms aimed at aligning education with industry needs and promoting employability. In Europe, apprenticeship programs and internships have bridged the gap between universities and industry, offering students hands-on training and real-world exposure for a competitive edge in the job market. Similarly, India has implemented skill development programs focused on industry-specific training, equipping students with the skills and knowledge employers require. These efforts reflect a growing recognition of the importance of practical education in preparing students for successful careers (Ministry of Education 2023). Launched in 2019 by the European Commission (EC) and various European governments and entities, including the European Court of Auditors, the European Blockchain Services Infrastructure (EBSI) stands as a significant blockchain initiative in Europe. It aims to facilitate cross-border government services and seeks to achieve interoperability with other governmental and commercial blockchain platforms. EBSI exemplifies policymakers' efforts to understand and regulate blockchain technology by actively engaging in its use (Grech et al. 2021).

2.2 *Metaverse in Education*

In tandem with blockchain, the concept of the 'Metaverse'—a term coined by Stephenson (2003) to describe a computer-generated virtual reality space where users interact in real-time is gaining traction in education. The Education Metaverse proposes a departure from the one-size-fits-all model of traditional education, offering personalised, context-rich learning environments (Mourtzis et al. 2023). It posits a platform for collaborative and inclusive learning communities, which cater to individual learning needs and preferences.

The transformative potential of the Education Metaverse extends to enhancing mobility in education. It enables students to participate in global classrooms without the need for physical relocation. Huynh-The et al. (2023) suggest that this feature could alleviate urban congestion and the ensuing neglect of rural regions, ensuring the growth of communities and preserving cultural authenticity.

The integration of the Education Metaverse and blockchain technology enhances the integrity of the educational process. By utilising distributed ledger technology, it ensures secure and verifiable tracking of educational credentials, thus curbing fraudulent activities and promoting inclusive educational communities.

In summary, the convergence of blockchain technology and the Education Metaverse embodies a promising frontier for the education sector. Together, they address enduring challenges, contribute to operational efficiency, advocate for equitable educational access, and strengthen the authenticity of educational credentials (Kaddoura and Al Husseiny 2023). Emerging research acknowledges the operational advantages of these technologies, while calling for an in-depth exploration of governance frameworks to oversee their integration and management within the educational ecosystem effectively. The absence of governance discourse within current literature signifies a pressing need for scholarly attention, aiming to establish comprehensive governance models that will ensure the responsible and sustainable application of these emergent technologies in educational settings.

3 Methods

By adopting an interpretivist research philosophy, this study acknowledges the importance of understanding the subjective experiences and meanings that individuals attribute to blockchain and Metaverse adoption in higher education (Dwivedi et al. 2022). The role of interpretivism in research philosophy and its implications for studying blockchain and Metaverse adoption in higher education is crucial for understanding the subtle and subjective experiences of stakeholders, thereby, providing deeper insights into the complex dynamics and potential impacts of these technologies in academic settings (Byrne 2022). This approach enables researchers to explore the complexities of individuals' perceptions, beliefs, and motivations, providing deeper insights into the factors influencing decisions about blockchain and metaverse adoption in higher education (Antonopoulou et al. 2023). Understanding the meanings and perceptions associated with these technologies among stakeholders is crucial for identifying the specific needs and preferences of students, faculty, and administrators. This understanding is necessary to tailor the implementation of blockchain and metaverse technologies to meet their requirements (Son-Turan 2022). By understanding their perspectives and expectations, educators can ensure that these technologies effectively support teaching, learning, and administrative processes, ultimately enhancing the overall educational experience for students (Schmoelz 2023).

The inductive qualitative method is well-suited for this research philosophy as it allows for the exploration and interpretation of participants' perspectives, experiences, and challenges (Son-Turan 2022). Additionally, the mixed-method research (Alshahrani et al. 2022; Choi 2020) approach provides a comprehensive and holistic overview by combining qualitative data from semi-structured interviews.

The governance of blockchain and metaverse technologies in higher education is a critical yet largely unexplored area (Liu et al. 2023). Understanding the governance frameworks and mechanisms for these technologies is essential for their effective and ethical use in educational settings. This study aims to investigate how to govern blockchain and metaverse technologies to generate value, enhance transparency, protect data privacy, and promote equitable access to educational opportunities. Exploratory case studies offer an ideal approach to examine governance complexities in real-life situations and uncover insights that can inform future policymaking and implementation strategies (Ajani et al. 2023; Bucea-Manea-Ţoniş et al. 2021). The qualitative phase of this study, which forms the basis for this example, involved conducting twenty semi-structured interviews, each lasting approximately 45–60 min. Participants included academics from multiple universities, employers, university students, students enrolled in professional accounting bodies, organizations that provide certificate validation, and technologists who have developed blockchain-based applications. These interviews were conducted online via Zoom and included participants from both developed and developing countries. All interviewees held an undergraduate degree and were proficient in English. The interviews aimed to explore participants' attitudes towards their experiences with education certificate s accreditation, validation, and the future of education. A flexible interview agenda was followed to ensure all key topics were covered. The questions comprised both open-ended and focused queries linking blockchain with certification, accreditation, and validation processes. A critical component of the data analysis involved case writing based on the information collected, covering the research objectives, questions, assumptions, results, and conclusions. Additionally, the data was extensively triangulated by corroborating findings from the interview data with observations from secondary sources, such as industry reports and academic journals. The study systematically scanned published reports by various organisations and academic journals from 2018 onwards. Studies by Alammary et al. (2019) and Loukil et al. (2021) indicate that blockchain research in the education sector is at a nascent stage. These studies collectively suggest that the period from 2018 onwards marks a significant phase of exploration and implementation of blockchain technology in education, making it a relevant and justifiable timeframe for the literature review.

4 Findings

Some prominent themes emerged as significant topics of interest in this research. A key issue that emerged from the interviews was widespread concern over increased fraudulent activities related to educational degrees. There was also significant emphasis on addressing inefficiencies in current validation and verification procedures, which stem from high costs and lengthy processes. Currently, traditional methods rely on the manual distribution of physical certificates without digitization or integration with blockchain technology. This leads to lengthy deadlines and costs when it comes to reissuing certificates. The use of blockchain certification results in a significant decrease in operating expenses, estimated to be about 70–80%, along with notable improvements in efficiency, speed of certificate retrieval, and accuracy of validation. The unchangeable characteristic of blockchain guarantees the absolute security of certificates, making them completely resistant to alteration and forging. In addition, companies sometimes rely on third-party background verification services, which may be costly, to authenticate certifications. This need could be eliminated by using blockchain certification.

In this context, a technology provider from company B who provides blockchain based certifications to universities stated the following: "*We have analysed the cost reduction before and after implementing our system, basically education institutions are likely to reduce 75–80% of the cost related to certificate insurance and verification process. If it is a bigger institute, it is highly likely to achieve 80% because the bigger the institute the more admin costs, verification and printing is required.*"

The adoption of the metaverse was praised for enhancing accessibility and democratizing the learning experience for a broad audience, while ensuring cooperation and creativity among students and educators. To ensure widespread implementation, it is crucial to establish a governance structure accepted by key stakeholders. Participants in the world's first metaverse education initiative, "Polyversity," emphasized the significant benefits derived from this distributed ledger technology.

A representative from company A stated the following: "*For the first time a student registered in one university is able to enroll for a course in another university in the metaverse, get the credits and include this as part of the 160 credits needed for the undergraduate degree. This is also transparent to the university and the education authority. With the new education system introduced in India it is important to have the technology to support it.*"

Immersive virtual reality improves language learning outcomes (Zeybek and Saygı 2023). Metaverse libraries emphasize the importance of cooperation, originality, flexibility, and user-focused design (Ajani et al. 2023). Blockchain technology has been explored for verifying diplomas and enhancing data security in higher education institutions. The proposed "Edu-metaverse," which combines metaverse and blockchain technology, aims to improve engagement and learning experiences in engineering education (Zhai et al. 2023). The Education Metaverse industry is expected to grow, indicating a shift towards immersive learning environments. However, challenges remain, including the digital divide and questions about the pedagogical efficacy of metaverse learning environments (Juncen et al. 2023). Challenges to be addressed also include privacy and data security concerns, ethical issues, addiction risks, and complexities related to digital identity and social interaction (Dwivedi et al. 2022). The Education Metaverse has the potential to promote integrity in educational achievements through blockchain technology. The disparity in education quality between developed and developing regions remains an issue. The Education Metaverse is still a work in progress, presenting both benefits and obstacles. Efforts are needed to bridge the digital divide and fully realize its potential as an inclusive educational tool. Despite progress, significant challenges remain, such as improving access to digital resources and ensuring effective teaching methods in these new learning environments (Brown 2022; Fawns 2022). Establishing a robust governance framework to address these challenges in the Education Metaverse industry is a priority.

5 Discussions

The findings from both interviews and the document analysis underscore the necessity for a governance framework that encompasses a diverse array of stakeholders, including education regulators, awarding bodies (such as universities), students/employees, employers, and technology providers. It is imperative that the framework remains responsive to their evolving needs.

A critical component of this framework is the process of certificate accreditation and subsequent verification. As highlighted by an interviewee, the system must exhibit agility to adapt to changes within the ecosystem. Additionally, it must address the sensitivity of data and the extent of content disclosure, which should be configurable based on the type of data and individual preferences. This consideration is vital for ensuring data integrity and security within the system.

For successful adoption by individuals and institutions, the system must prioritize data governance and security. Furthermore, the cost-effectiveness and sustainability of the system, from design and build to operational phases, are crucial factors. Given the dynamic nature of rules and regulations, particularly within the education sector, the system must also be adaptable to these changes.

In light of these considerations, it is evident that prior to designing a governance framework, it is essential to establish key design principles. These principles will guide the optimal design, construction, and operation of the system.

6 Conclusions

This study explores the governance frameworks necessary for the successful integration of blockchain and metaverse technologies in the education sector, aiming to enhance transparency, ensure data security, and promote equitable access to educational opportunities. The examination of the Education Metaverse reveals a complex yet promising digital landscape where education and technology intersect. The United Nations' commitment to the SDGs underscores the importance of education as a catalyst for social advancement and sustainability. By implementing blockchain technology in education, we enter a new era marked by transparency and integrity, which could help mitigate the widespread issue of fraudulent qualifications in the academic and business spheres (Saleh et al. 2021).

The metaverse inherently presents a revolutionary concept of educational mobility, surpassing physical limitations to provide high-quality education worldwide. The advancement in digital technology aims to more equitably divide educational resources, promoting sustainability in urban and rural areas, thus, supporting the achievement of SDGs 4.b and 11 (Zhai et al. 2023). Nevertheless, the contrast between the idealistic concept of the Education Metaverse and the practical challenges it faces is apparent.

The Education Metaverse has the capacity to improve the reliability of education and promote inclusive communities (Kim et al. 2024), aligning with SDG 16. This may be achieved by utilizing blockchain technology to provide safe tracking of credentials (El Koshiry et al. 2023; Halder et al. 2022). However, the pursuit of high-quality education for everyone, regardless of location, necessitates continuous and collaborative endeavours to overcome the remaining obstacles.

As we consider the future, it is evident that the Education Metaverse is not only an imaginative idea but a powerful and influential emerging phenomenon (Othman et al. 2024). To fully utilize its capabilities, key stakeholders must focus on developing the operational and leadership skills necessary for efficient governance (Sia 2023). To ensure that the Education Metaverse functions as a fair and efficient educational instrument, it is essential to focus not only on technology advancements but also on governance. A robust governance framework, grounded in strong design principles, will be crucial for upholding the fundamental principles of education.

This study focuses on higher education, providing insights into the specific challenges faced by universities and colleges. Future research on the intersection of distributed ledger technology and education can explore areas such as lifelong learning, global collaboration, personalized learning experiences, enhanced partnerships with corporate entities and the underlying design principles for governance framework.

References

Ajani, Y. A., Enakrire, R. T., Oladokun, B. D., & Bashorun, M. T. (2023). Reincarnation of libraries via metaverse: A pathway for a sustainable knowledge system in the digital age. *Business Information Review, 40*(4), 191–197. https://doi.org/10.1177/02663821231208044.

Alammary, A., Alhazmi, S., Almasri, M., & Gillani, S. (2019). Blockchain-Based Applications in Education: A Systematic Review. 9(12), 2400. https://doi.org/10.3390/app9122400

Alnafrah, I., & Mouselli, S. (2021). Revitalizing blockchain technology potentials for smooth academic records management and verification in low-income countries. *International Journal of Educational Development, 85*. https://doi.org/10.1016/j.ijedudev.2021.102460.

Alshahrani, M., Beloff, N., & White, M. (2022). Towards a Blockchain-based Smart Certification System for Higher Education: An Empirical Study. *International Journal of Computing and Digital Systems, 11*, 553–571. https://doi.org/10.12785/ijcds/110145.

Alsobhi, H. A., Alakhtar, R. A., Ubaid, A., Hussain, O. K., & Hussain, F. K. (2023). Blockchain-based micro-credentialing system in higher education institutions: Systematic literature review. *Knowledge-Based Systems, 265*, 110238. https://doi.org/10.1016/j.knosys.2022.110238.

Amirtharaj, S., Chandrasekaran, G., Thirumoorthy, K., & Muneeswaran, K. (2022). A Systematic Approach for Assessment of Attainment in Outcome-based Education. *9*(1), 8–29. https://doi.org/10.1177/23476311211017744.

Antonopoulou, K., Begkos, C., & Zhu, Z. (2023). Staying afloat amidst extreme uncertainty: A case study of digital transformation in Higher Education. *Technological Forecasting and Social Change, 192*, 122603. https://doi.org/10.1016/j.techfore.2023.122603.

Brown, B. A. (2022). Blockchain Technology in Teaching, Learning, and Academic Administration as a Long-term Solution to Emergencies in Higher Education. In B. A. Brown & A. Irons (Eds.), The Emerald Handbook of Higher Education in a Post-Covid World: New Approaches and Technologies for Teaching and Learning (pp. 173–194). Emerald Publishing Limited. https://doi.org/10.1108/978-1-80382-193-120221008

Bucea-Manea-Țoniş, R., Martins, O. M. D., Bucea-Manea-Țoniş, R., Gheorghiță, C., Kuleto, V., Ilić, M. P., & Simion, V.-E. (2021). Blockchain Technology Enhances Sustainable Higher Education. *13*(22), 12347. https://www.mdpi.com/2071-1050/13/22/12347.

Byrne, D. (2022). A worked example of Braun and Clarke's approach to reflexive thematic analysis. *Quality & Quantity, 56*(3), 1391–1412. https://doi.org/10.1007/s11135-021-01182-y.

Chapman, D. W., & Lindner, S. (2016). Degrees of integrity: the threat of corruption in higher education. *Studies in higher education (Dorchester-on-Thames), 41*(2), 247–268. https://doi.org/10.1080/03075079.2014.927854.

Choi, P. K. (2020). A Need for Co-Evolution between Technological Innovations and Social Innovations. *Journal of Open Innovation: Technology, Market, and Complexity, 6*(3), 54. https://doi.org/10.3390/joitmc6030054.

de Paor, C. (2016). The contribution of professional accreditation to quality assurance in higher education. *Quality in Higher Education, 22*(3), 228–241. https://doi.org/10.1080/13538322.2016.1263925.

Dwivedi, Y. K., Hughes, L., Baabdullah, A. M., Ribeiro-Navarrete, S., Giannakis, M., Al-Debei, M. M., . . . Wamba, S. F. (2022). Metaverse beyond the hype: Multidisciplinary perspectives on emerging challenges, opportunities, and agenda for research, practice and policy. *International Journal of Information Management, 66*, 102542. https://doi.org/10.1016/j.ijinfomgt.2022.102542.

El Koshiry, A., Eliwa, E., & Hameed, H. A. (2023). The Effectiveness of Using Blockchain Technology in Building High-Quality Educational Content Based on A Participatory Learning Environment and Its Impact on Increasing Student Achievement. *International Journal of Intelligent Systems and Applications in Engineering, 11*(1), 50–62. https://www.scopus.com/inward/record.uri?eid=2-s2.0-85160405930&partnerID=40&md5=7440f3f4f3ada48359103264f7840c2e.

Fawns, T. (2022). An Entangled Pedagogy: Looking Beyond the Pedagogy—Technology Dichotomy. Postdigital Science and Education, 4(3), 711–728. https://doi.org/10.1007/s42438-022-00302-7

Global Parnership on Artificial Intelligence. (2023, 12-14 December 2023). Global Parnership on Artificial Intelligence, India.

Grech, A., Sood, I., & Ariño, L. (2021). Blockchain, Self-Sovereign Identity and Digital Credentials: Promise Versus Praxis in Education [Perspective]. *4*. https://doi.org/10.3389/fbloc.2021.616779.

Halder, S., Kumar, H. A., Lavu, S., & Reeja, S. R. (2022). Digital Degree Issuing and Verification Using Blockchain. 2022 4th International Conference on Cognitive Computing and Information Processing, CCIP 2022.

Huynh-The, T., Gadekallu, T. R., Wang, W., Yenduri, G., Ranaweera, P., Pham, Q.-V., da Costa, D., Liyanage, M. (2023). Blockchain for the metaverse: A Review. Future Generation Computer Systems, 143, 401–419. https://doi.org/10.1016/j.future.2023.02.008

Joshi, S., & P.J, P. (2023). A Collaborative Metaverse based A-La-Carte Framework for Tertiary Education (CO-MATE). *Heliyon*, *9*(2), e13424. https://doi.org/10.1016/j.heliyon.2023.e13424.

Juncen, Z. H. U., Jiannong, C. A. O., Divya, S., Shan, J., & Houda, F. (2023). Blockchain-empowered Federated Learning: Challenges, Solutions, and Future Directions [Article]. *ACM computing surveys*, *55*(11), 1–31. https://doi.org/10.1145/3570953.

Kaddoura, S., & Al Husseiny, F. (2023). The rising trend of Metaverse in education: challenges, opportunities, and ethical considerations. *PeerJ Computer Science*, *9*, e1252. https://doi.org/10.7717/peerj-cs.1252.

Kim, S., Jung, T., Sohn, D. K., Suh, M., & Chang, Y. J. (2024). Factors Associated With Continuous Use of a Cancer Education Metaverse Platform: Mixed Methods Study. *J Med Internet Res*, *26*, e57762. https://doi.org/10.2196/57762.

Krishnamurthy, S. (2020). The future of business education: A commentary in the shadow of the Covid-19 pandemic. *Journal of Business Research*, *117*, 1–5. https://doi.org/10.1016/j.jbusres.2020.05.034.

Liu, Y., Lu, Q., Zhu, L., Paik, H.-Y., & Staples, M. (2023). A systematic literature review on blockchain governance. *Journal of Systems and Software*, *197*, 111576. https://doi.org/10.1016/j.jss.2022.111576.

Loukil, F., Abed, M., & Boukadi, K. (2021). Blockchain adoption in education: a systematic literature review [Article]. Education and Information Technologies. https://doi.org/10.1007/s10639-021-10481-8

Ministry of Education, I. (2023). *National Digital Education Architecture*. Ministry of Education India. Retrieved V9 from https://netf.aicte-india.org/major-initiatives.html.

Mourtzis, D., Angelopoulos, J., & Panopoulos, N. (2023). Metaverse and Blockchain in Education for collaborative Product-Service System (PSS) Design towards University 5.0. *Procedia CIRP*, *119*, 456–461. https://doi.org/10.1016/j.procir.2023.01.008.

Narongsak, S., & Nonsiri, S. (2023, 18–19 May 2023). Digital Token: Token-Based Degree Certificates with Credit Transfer System. 2023 8th International Conference on Business and Industrial Research (ICBIR).

Nousias, N., Tsakalidis, G., Michoulis, G., Petridou, S., & Vergidis, K. (2022). A process-aware approach for blockchain-based verification of academic qualifications. Simulation Modelling Practice & Theory, 121(1). https://doi.org/10.1016/j.simpat.2022.102642

Othman, A., Chemnad, K., Hassanien, A. E., Tlili, A., Zhang, C. Y., Al-Thani, D., . . . Altınay, Z. (2024). Accessible Metaverse: A Theoretical Framework for Accessibility and Inclusion in the Metaverse. *Multimodal technologies and interaction*, *8*(3), 21. https://doi.org/10.3390/mti8030021.

Ray, P. P. (2023). Web3: A comprehensive review on background, technologies, applications, zero-trust architectures, challenges and future directions. *Internet of Things and Cyber-Physical Systems*, *3*, 213–248. https://doi.org/10.1016/j.iotcps.2023.05.003.

Razzaq, A. (2023). A Web3 secure platform for assessments and educational resources based on blockchain. Computer Applications in Engineering Education. https://doi.org/10.1002/cae.22677

Reza, A. W., Islam, K., Muntaha, S., Abdur Rahman, O. B., Islam, R., & Arefin, M. S. (2022). Education Certification and Verified Documents Sharing System by Blockchain. *International Journal of Intelligent Engineering & Systems*, *15*(6). https://doi.org/10.22266/ijies2022.1231.60.

Rubinstein, E. (1977). Education: Accreditation: A debatable issue: Key officers of IEEE express diverging views on the role the Institute should play in accrediting electrical engineering programs. *IEEE Spectrum*, *14*(3), 84–88. https://doi.org/10.1109/MSPEC.1977.6369357.

Saleh, O. S., Ghazali, O., & Idris, N. B. (2021). A New Decentralized Certification Verification Privacy Control Protocol. 2021 3rd International Cyber Resilience Conference, CRC 2021.

Saleh, O. S., Ghazali, O., & Idris, N. B. (2023). A New Privacy-Preserving Protocol for Academic Certificates on Hyperledger Fabric. *International Journal of Advanced Computer Science and Applications*, *14*(2). https://doi.org/10.14569/IJACSA.2023.0140271.

Saxena, A., Ramaswamy, M., Beale, J., Marciniuk, D., & Smith, P. J. D. S. (2021). Striving for the United Nations (UN) sustainable development goals (SDGs): what will it take?, *2*, 1–14.

Schmoelz, A. (2023). Digital Humanism, Progressive Neoliberalism and the European Digital Governance System for Vocational and Adult Education. *29*(2). https://doi.org/10.1177/14779714231161449.

Sia, C. C. (2023). The Role of Legal Governance Framework in the Metaverse World. In *Strategies and Opportunities for Technology in the Metaverse World* (pp. 321–330). IGI Global. https://doi.org/10.4018/978-1-6684-5732-0.ch017.

Son-Turan, S. (2022). Fostering Equality in Education: The Blockchain Business Model for Higher Education (BBM-HE). *Sustainability (Switzerland)*, *14*(5), 2955. https://doi.org/10.3390/su14052955.

Stephenson, N. (2003). Snow crash: A novel. Spectra.

Sumithra, V., Shashidhara, R., Mukhopadhyay, D., & Gupta, S. K. (2021). Decentralized Accreditation of Educational Attainments using Blockchain. 2021 6th International Conference for Convergence in Technology, I2CT 2021.

Tahlil, T., Gomasta, S. S., & Ali, A. S. (2022). AlgoCert: Adopt Non-transferable NFT for the Issuance and Verification of Educational Certificates using Algorand Blockchain. 2022 IEEE Asia-Pacific Conference on Computer Science and Data Engineering (CSDE).

Tan E, Lerouge E, Du Caju J, Du Seuil D. Verification of Education Credentials on European Blockchain Services Infrastructure (EBSI): Action Research in a Cross-Border Use Case between Belgium and Italy. Big Data and Cognitive Computing. 2023; 7(2):79. https://doi.org/10.3390/bdcc7020079

UN. (2015). *Transforming our world: the 2030 Agenda for Sustainable Development*.

UNESCO. (2022). The Right to Education in the 21st Century: findings from the International Seminar on the Evolving Right to Education. In.

Zagalaz, J., Zafra, M., & Moreno, D. J. M. S. M. (2022). Active displacement and sustainable development objectives applied to education. *5*(4), 95–100.

Zeybek, N., & Saygı, E. (2023). Gamification in Education: Why, Where, When, and How?—A Systematic Review. *0*(0). https://doi.org/10.1177/15554120231158625.

Zhai, X. S., Chu, X. Y., Chen, M., Shen, J., & Lou, F. L. (2023). Can Edu-Metaverse Reshape Virtual Teaching Community (VTC) to Promote Educational Equity? An Exploratory Study. *IEEE Transactions on Learning Technologies*, *16*(6), 1130–1140. https://doi.org/10.1109/TLT.2023.3276876.

Zhu, X., & Cao, C. (2021). Secure Online Examination with Biometric Authentication and Blockchain-Based Framework [Article]. *Mathematical Problems in Engineering*, 1–12. https://doi.org/10.1155/2021/5058780.

Exploring Stakeholder Positions in AI-Powered Culture and Arts Education

Hanjin Lee, Seoyoung Byun, Yeeun Lee, and Gaeun Son

Abstract As AI technology and cultural arts are being fused in various ways, the design industry is opening new horizons for creativity and innovation. It is now possible to write scenario plans with ChatGPT, create and visualize numerous demonstration images with Midjourney, and conduct virtual world showcases that combine VR and AR technologies with Metaverse. In this paper, we aimed to analyze the positions of each stakeholder according to the main research agenda in the field of AI-based culture and arts education derived from previous studies. In addition, we explored how AI technology is fused in the fields of art design and culture to lead to innovation through case studies in order to enhance students' creativity and convergent thinking skills within the curriculum. The results of the study demonstrated the possibility of maximizing creativity and efficiency simultaneously by utilizing generative AI. With the support of AI, designers can not only create more innovative and original works, but also effectively reduce costs and time in the production process. In addition, it is expected that the AI technology that converges culture and arts will play a role in providing personalized services to consumers and suggesting a strategic approach for a sustainable design industry.

Keywords AI literacy · Artistic experience · Generative AI · Cultural engagement · Stakeholders

---

H. Lee (✉)
School of Creative Convergence Education, Handong Global University, Pohang, Republic of Korea
e-mail: cus@handong.edu

S. Byun · Y. Lee · G. Son
School of GE and ICT, Handong Global University, Pohang, Republic of Korea
e-mail: 22100346@handong.ac.kr

Y. Lee
e-mail: 22000545@handong.ac.kr

G. Son
e-mail: irreplaceable@handong.ac.kr

T. Jung et al. (eds.), *XR and Metaverse*, Springer Proceedings in Business and Economics, https://doi.org/10.1007/978-3-031-77975-6_9

1 Introduction

1.1 Research Objective

Artificial Intelligence (AI) is driving revolutionary changes in many industries. Among these, the emergence of generative AI is increasingly being applied and making an impact in the cultural sector (Feuerriegel et al. 2024). AI can support the creative process and provide people with easier and more efficient access to artistic creativity as a service (Xiao et al. 2024). It also provides artists with new tools, leading to richer and more diverse creative activities (Civit et al. 2022). Recently, these advances in AI technology in the field of culture and arts have been actively reflected in education, with tech convergence curricula being designed to encourage learners to express their creativity artistically.

In 2023, a new course titled 'AI, Culture and Arts' was launched at a four-year mission-oriented global university in the Republic of Korea, with about 80 students participating as part of the liberal arts curriculum. The course aims to improve students' AI literacy skills so they do not rely unconditionally on generative AI when using it, while simultaneously increasing their understanding and interest in the arts. While previous studies and classes have been conducted with similar objectives, this course places greater emphasis on learners' active use of AI, structuring the curriculum in terms of career exploration and vision design (Altares-López et al. 2024; Kim 2023). As AI technology rapidly develops, new approaches will be needed to organise the practice and content of specific topics.

As noted, the purpose of this curriculum is to equip students with an understanding of AI technologies and the ability to use them creatively in the arts and cultural sector. This will enable learners to cross the boundaries between art and tech, and strengthen their capabilities as future cultural creators (Tang et al. 2022). It is crucial to recognise AI as a new source of artistic inspiration and creativity, not just as an auxiliary tool, and to help participants experience the convergence of AI and arts through various cross-disciplinary approaches (Habib et al. 2024). Therefore, this research aims to enhance AI literacy in the field of culture and arts by proposing a use case of expressing creativity through generative AI in the virtual convergence space.

1.2 AI, Culture and Arts Curriculum

As part of the Advanced Convergence Course, the 'AI, Culture and Arts' class is organised into essentially four multimodal modules. Students will be introduced to key concepts, understanding, applications, examples, and exercises in the fields of text, image, audio, and video to enhance their creativity. The first module, Text Generative AI-Powered Storytelling, involves learners using AI technology to create creative stories. In this module, participants experience the creative possibilities of AI firsthand, using sentence-generative AI to construct original narratives and incorporate artistic flair. Then, in the Image and Audio Generative AI Comparison lab module, students use a variety of AI tools to compare the strengths and weaknesses of each. This will help learners understand the characteristics and possibilities of AI tools and improve their AI literacy and tool utilisation skills. In the real world, participants can digitally display the results of creating their own characters, generating NFTs, and creating AI music playlists, which naturally promotes cultural engagement.

Moreover, in the Video Generative AI module, students use cinematic storytelling AI tools to create a film based on a story they have previously created. In this course, learners can gain practical experience by submitting their work to a real film festival. To build on and integrate the previous foundational courses and develop an understanding of the extended reality (XR) world, the course will also include hands-on experiences in virtual reality (VR), augmented reality (AR), and mixed reality (MR). The AR Docent Field Trip will allow participants to experience first-hand how AR technology can transform the art exhibition and viewing involvement. This hands-on experience gives learners the opportunity to understand the impact of AR tech on the arts and culture sector, and explore creative applications. Finally, in the 3D motion capture lab module, students will learn how the technology can be applied to various fields based on the fusion of motion suits' movements and generative AI (Kim et al. 2023). Through these hands-on labs, students will be able to feel the practical impact of AI tech on artistic creation.

2 Literature Review

2.1 Generative AI & Art Application

Artificial Intelligence (AI) is becoming much more familiar to people in the form of services than in the past. Whereas AI tech was once associated with complex algorithms and specialised knowledge, it is now readily available to the average user through a variety of applications and platforms that are easily accessible in everyday life. For example, as voice-activated assistants, recommendation systems, and image generation technologies become more commonplace, people are naturally engaging with AI. This shift is contributing to a greater understanding and acceptance of AI technology (Lee and Lee 2024). Also it means that it is no longer the preserve of experts, but rather a tool that everyone can easily access and utilise in their daily lives. As a result, AI is making people's lives more convenient through user-friendly interfaces and intuitive features, which has played an important role in the development and popularisation of AI tech.

As such, AI services are now being utilised by people from diverse backgrounds and cultures as a tool for creative productivity (Xiao et al. 2024). At the centre of this development is generative AI, represented by ChatGPT. Generative AI refers to computing techniques that can generate new meaningful content based on training data (Feuerriegel et al. 2024). Various types of generative AI services have been developed in recent years, including text, images, audio, and video, and their applications are becoming more diverse (Dash and Agres 2024; Civit et al. 2022). Prior to ChatGPT, AI-generated outputs for human use were considered to be difficult to understand or of low quality on a human level. Surprisingly, nowadays quite satisfactory outputs are being produced that are appropriate to the cultural background and people's intentions (Bandi et al. 2023).

In other words, many studies have concluded that the era of customised generative AI that considers the characteristics of various artistic fields has arrived. This is because techniques such as prompt engineering, fine-tuning, and RAG plug-in are being developed together to further improve the level of generative AI (Ramdurai and Adhithya 2023). As such, generative AI is recognised as a tool to maximise human creativity, and empirical studies have shown that it has significantly increased human creative productivity (Zhou and Lee 2024). Furthermore, innovative attempts are being made in many fields, including art and entertainment, design, and scientific research, which contribute to breaking down boundaries and exploring new possibilities (Kouslis et al. 2024). In particular, the use of generative AI in the artistic field is noteworthy. For professional artists, AI can fully support their creativity in terms of identifying and searching for inspiration and new trends (Hernandez-Olivan et al. 2022).

2.2 Generative AI & Education

Meanwhile, generative AI has been increasingly explored as an exciting learning tool in education (Kim 2023). Educational applications of AI have the advantage of providing an engaging and immersive experience in the field of study, tailored to the needs of the individual (Altares-López et al. 2024). However, there are also concerns that early AI-enabled education may be more confusing for learners, both technically and ethically, than it is effective in the classroom (Murugesan and Cherukuri 2023). Therefore, the importance of introducing students to generative AI and how to use it as a tool, along with an in-depth understanding of its ethical and technical dimensions, is increasing (Ali et al. 2024).

Additionally, research on the impact of AI use on learners' creativity has been reported, with data showing pedagogies that best utilise AI to support learning and creativity (Habib et al. 2024; Lee 2023). Furthermore, in AI and arts and culture classes, participants use AI as a tool with discernment rather than indiscriminate acceptance, and generative AI can be used to express creativity in the field of artistic creation (Lee and Lee 2024; Kim et al. 2023). Based on these previous studies, the purpose of this research is to support the use of generative AI as a tool for learners' creative activities. In particular, we will explore how the various features provided by generative AI can contribute to enhancing participants' problem-solving and critical thinking.

3 Stakeholder Analysis

This research describes the process of developing students' understanding of AI technology and their ability to use it creatively in the field of culture and arts curriculum structure. In this study, we focus on the application of generative AI to express creativity in the field of fashion design, which is representative of the virtual convergence space. To this end, we first synthesised previous research through desk research on academic information platforms such as Google Scholar, Scholar GPT, and Elsevier from 10 to 25 May 2024. After that we divided the main stakeholders into five roles: designers, consumers, critics, retailers, and environmental and sustainability experts who propose policies.

Then, from 1 to 14 June 2024, the course randomly assigned learners to each of the five roles and asked them to use Google Slides collaboration to discuss what was important to them. We presented a unified standard for how to explore, collect, and analyse data, record the proposal process, and organise roles by stakeholder. To help students see the results of the discussion together and develop a broader understanding, we comprehensively analysed the roles of major stakeholders (Table 1) and proposed a final proposal on how to apply AI to the arts and culture (Table 2). This is expected to provide examples of applying new creative perspectives in the arts and culture field in a more concrete and practical way.

Table 1 Analyse key stakeholders' major concerns

Stakeholders	Major concerns	Differences	Common points
Designer (Artist)	Creative expression	Emphasis on artistic creativity and originality of the designer	Reflect trends and aesthetic elements
Consumer (Customer)	Practicality and price	Mainly interested in practicality, style, and price, reflecting personal preferences	Feel the appeal of the work and choose it
Critic & journalist	Evaluation and analysis	Evaluate the creativity and innovation of collections, assess social messages	Analyse designs and trends
Distributor (Retailer)	Commercial value	Concerned with market response and sales potential, including inventory and related management	Consider consumer reactions & demands
Environmental & sustainability expert	Sustainability and Eco	Emphasis on the eco-friendly materials and sustainability of production processes, includes policy proposals	Think about the future of the industry

Table 2 AI utilization methods by stakeholder

Stakeholder	AI utilization methods	Relevance
Designer (Artist)	Design software, pattern and style generation	Enhances creativity and efficiency, provides customized design
Consumer (Customer)	Recommendation system, personalized style suggestions	Provides personalised service, enhances satisfaction
Critic & journalist	Trend analysis, review and popularity assessment	Data-driven analysis for in-depth reviews
Distributor (Retailer)	Inventory management, demand prediction algorithm	Data-driven decisions for commercial success
Environmental & sustainability expert	Lifecycle monitoring, environmental impact analysis	Process optimisation and policy proposals for sustainability

3.1 Main Stakeholders as a Role-Playing

(1) **Designers**: Designers are at the forefront of key stakeholders, responsible for creating apparel and accessories, and driving the trends and artistic direction of fashion. They focus on creative expression and originality, aiming for artistic and innovative designs. They are the ones who directly carry out the original intention and concept of the piece, from market research, user interview, and sketches in the planning stage to the finished product. They have the best understanding of the work and place high value on completeness and artistic merit.

(2) **Consumers**: Customers or Consumers are the people who buy and use fashion design products and services, shaping trends and consumption patterns. Their feedback and tastes have a huge impact on the style industry. They value practicality and price, and evaluate whether an item fits their personal taste. Like other stakeholders, they recognise an attractive design and decide if it suits their style. In recent years, growing interest in eco-friendly materials and methods, social values, and ethical consumption have also become important.

(3) **Critics and Journalists**: Critics and journalists analyse fashion design and collections and communicate them to the public through reviews, assessing the current trends in the world. They evaluate the creativity and innovation of a piece in many ways, weighing in on style and cultural implications. They analyse and present the message of a collection and its place in fashion history. As the important stakeholder, they value design and trends and recognise the uniqueness of a piece.

(4) **Distributors**: Distributors are active in retail outlets (shops), showcases, flagship stores, galleries, exhibitions, etc. They are concerned with sales potential and market response, and plan inventory and sales strategies based on consumer needs. Commercial success, including revenue and sales excellence, operating margins, and low return rates, are important to them. However, like

other production-side stakeholders, they also consider consumer response and anticipate the demand and popularity of their work.

(5) **Environmental and Sustainability Experts**: Environmental and sustainability experts analyse the macro impact of the industry and promote sustainable fashion practices. They assess the environmental power and sustainability of production processes based on international promote disclosure and compliance. Like others in the standards (ISO) and ecosystem, they consider the sustainable future of the fashion industry and evaluate the design and production process of their work.

3.2 Examples of AI Utilisation by Stakeholder

(1) **Leveraging AI-based design software**: AI-based design software provides fashion designers with new creative tools. For example, designers can use GANs to experiment with new patterns and colour combinations, and text-generative AI to find inspiration for design concepts (Habib et al. 2024). For instance, Designer 'A' used Adobe Express and Firefly Creative Suites AI software to design a new collection every season, saving more than 30 percent of his work time, which provided him with more opportunities for creative exploration (Li et al., 2019).

(2) **AI recommendation systems for consumers**: AI-based recommendation systems can analyse customers' tastes and preferences to suggest personalised fashion items. For example, AI-powered and AR/VR-assisted systems on online fashion platforms make it easier for users to find clothing that matches their style. It increases shoppers' satisfaction, which can lead to higher conversion rates (Kouslis et al. 2024). This system will enhance the consumer experience and maximise the efficiency of shopping.

(3) **AI trend analysis tools for critics**: Fashion critics can use AI trend analysis tools to monitor and analyse the latest trends and public reactions in real-time (Habib et al. 2024). Journalists can analyse data collected from multiple social media (SNS) to assess the public's reaction to the latest collections, which will help them write more accurate and in-depth reviews and critiques. AI will be able to systematically analyse vast amounts of data to predict fashion trends and enable critics to provide more sophisticated analysis.

(4) **Optimized AI inventory management systems**: AI-powered inventory management systems can help retailers manage their products efficiently (Li et al. 2019). They can analyse sales data to predict demand and replenish inventory at the right time. In particular, historical sales data can be used to predict changes in demand due to seasonal factors or special promotions, allowing retailers to manage inventory more strategically. This increases operational efficiency and the ability to respond quickly to customer demand. In addition, such a system would provide transparency across the supply chain, enabling retailers

to better collaborate with suppliers and increase inventory turnover. This ultimately plays a key role in increasing sales, improving customer satisfaction, and enhancing competitiveness.

(5) **AI-powered sustainable production**: Sustainability experts are using AI technology to analyse the lifecycle of fashion products and develop strategies to minimise their environmental impact. For example, AI-based environmental impact analysis tools are used to monitor the products life cycle and identify approaches to reduce waste in production (Kouslis et al. 2024). Furthermore, in proposing policies, the product lifecycle of brands in each category can be analysed and linked to specific action plans based on the average carbon footprint reduction figures and projections. This would be an important step towards sustainable fashion production within the design ecosystem.

3.3 Analytics and Insights

As the stakeholder analysis above shows, AI technology benefits each stakeholder in different ways, increasing creativity and efficiency across the industry. Fashion designers can create more original pieces with the help of AI in the creative process, while consumers enjoy a personalised shopping experience with tailored recommendations. Fashion critics are able to use data analytics to provide accurate trend commentary, and retailers adopt AI to maximise the efficiency of inventory management. Moreover, sustainability experts utilise AI to make important contributions to reduce the environmental impact of the fashion industry and suggest policies to drive change.

These results highlight the important role that the convergence of AI and fashion will play in enhancing the creativity and sustainability of the industry in the future. The comparative analysis clearly demonstrates the value and possibilities that AI technology brings to different aspects of the fashion industry. This aligns with the goals of the curriculum and emphasises the importance of creative innovation through the collaboration of AI, arts and culture.

4 AI Technology Applications

Based on the above analysis of the roles of each stakeholder and the potential applications of AI, we would like to go a step further and propose key activities and interfaces within a practical curriculum, i.e., how each image-generating AI can be used in fashion design and how 3D motion capture technology can revolutionise the industry. To this end, we will introduce the main image-generating AI technologies and propose examples of their application in practice, which can be incorporated into future curricula. We focus on the top four services (75.4%) that were most frequently suggested by students in the curriculum. As shown in Table 3, Stable Diffusion, Midjourney, hotpot.ai, and openart.ai were selected for this study due to their popularity among students, ease of use, and ability to generate high-quality, diverse designs. These tools were evaluated as the most effective for fostering creativity and practical skills in the curriculum (Fig. 1). The enhancement of efficiency in creative work (time savings, cost reduction) and the possibility of experimenting with various visual styles are expected (Zhou and Lee 2024). It is anticipated that this will maximize the advantages of designing and simulating the development process of creative cultural and artistic design in a virtual convergence space (Habib et al. 2024).

(1) **Stable Diffusion** is a deep learning, text-to-image model released in 2022 and is a representative image application based on Python (Zhou and Lee 2024). It is capable of generating high-resolution images, which is advantageous for detailed design work, and since it is open source, it is highly customisable. Therefore, it is suitable for creating various styles of artworks such as in-painting and out-painting. On the other hand, it does have its limitations: it requires high computing resources, which can limit its accessibility, and it can be complicated to set up and use. Fashion designers will be able to use Stable Diffusion to create high-resolution patterns and textures for high-end product designs where detail is important.

(2) **Midjourney** is another AI software that was released in open beta in 2022 and is a text-to-image model where you prompt and the AI generates an image (Habib et al. 2024). Along with Stable Diffusion, it is the most widely used AI

Table 3 Key features of applicable generative AI

Image-generative AI	Advantages	Disadvantages	Utilisation methods
Stable diffusion	High-resolution image generation, various styles, open source	Requires high computing resources, complicated to use	Creation of high-resolution patterns and textures, high-end fashion product design
Midjourney	Provides various AI tools and templates, supports artistic style transformations	Subscription model (commercial use not possible with free version), operates on Discord app after sign-up	Artistic style transformation, creation of new patterns and collections
getimg.ai	Simple interface, quick results, various options	Image quality may be lower, limited for complex design work	Generation of various design samples, visualisation of initial ideas
openart.ai	AI-based art community integration, supports various art styles	Unpredictable results, limited for specific styles and complex design work	Generative images in many styles, incorporation of collection ideas and collaboration

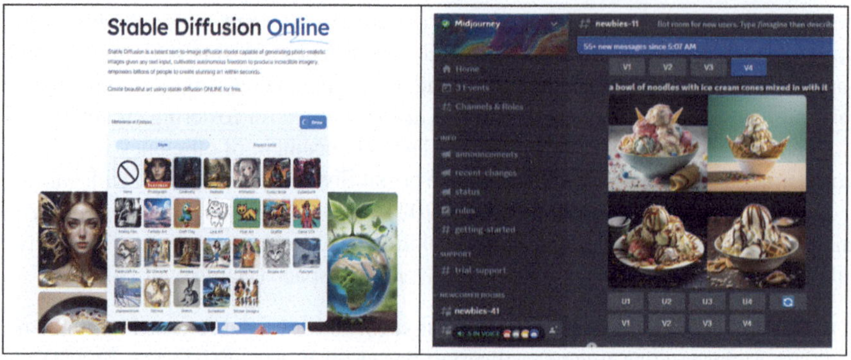

Fig. 1 AI technology application examples (Image generative AI focused)

image generation service globally, and the images produced are of high quality. All operations from sign-up to image creation/editing are performed on the Discord app server, which is an open community, and can be used as a paid subscription model after the free trial ends. As a result, it is not possible to use the free images for commercial purposes, and copyright attribution should be approached carefully. This allows fashion designers to apply different artistic styles to existing designs to create new patterns or collections virtually.

(3) **Getimg.ai** has a simple interface and usability that allows for quick results, and it offers a variety of image generation options to allow for creative experimentation (Kim et al. 2023). The wide range of AI tools and templates makes it easy for beginners to use, and the ease of switching between artistic styles leads users to experiment with different visual effects. However, there may be limitations in working with high-resolution images, and there may be copyright issues with uploaded images. Fashion designers can use getimg.ai to quickly generate a variety of design samples, visualise initial ideas, and develop concepts.

(4) **openart.ai** is an AI-based art community that allows users to share and collaborate on various creative ideas, with a user-friendly interface and support for a variety of art styles (Kim et al. 2023). Though, the unpredictability of the generated images can sometimes lead to unsatisfactory results, and there are limitations in generating images optimised for a particular style. This means that it is somewhat limited for sophisticated and complex design work. With openart.ai, fashion designers are able to work on collaborative projects by generating images of different styles and incorporating them into collection ideas.

5 Conclusion

5.1 Research Summary

At the intersection of AI technology and culture, the fashion industry is opening up new horizons for innovation. AI has shown that creativity and efficiency can be maximised simultaneously. Not only can designers create more innovative and original pieces, but they can also reduce costs and time in the production process. AI can provide personalised services to consumers and strategies for a sustainable creative industry. This study analysed the stakeholders' positions in relation to the research questions derived from previous studies and explored how AI tech is converging and innovating in arts design. Using the content from Google Arts & Culture, we analysed various stakeholders' perspectives and specific AI use cases. In particular, we explained how AI-based image generation tools even 3D motion capture technology can maximise inspiration and productivity in the fashion sector.

AI has the potential to revolutionise the entire cultural and design industry. It can help designers to be more creative and original in their work and expand the scope of their designs by discovering new trends and styles. AI-powered design software and inventory management systems can also increase work efficiency and save time and money in the production process. Additionally, AI is beneficial because it can analyse consumer data to provide personalised recommendations, virtual fitting experiences, and suggest strategies to make the design industry more sustainable.

5.2 Key Implications and Significance

The adoption of AI technology is revolutionising and transforming the arts and culture sector. This study extends AI tech to various areas of artistic creation so that learners can deeply explore and experience the potential of AI through various creative activities. In particular, the AI-based arts and culture curriculum is expected to enhance students' creative thinking skills, in-depth understanding of the principles of AI service, and exploratory applications (Lee 2023). Through these courses, participants will have the opportunity to cross the boundaries between AI and arts, and develop their capabilities as pioneers of a new era of creativity. The convergence of AI and arts will contribute to the creation of richer and more diverse artworks through the combination of creativity and technology, which will ultimately serve as an important factor in promoting the development of culture area.

This shift will also enable new forms of artistic expression through collaboration between artists and technologists. Besides it open up the possibility for AI to move beyond its role as a tool in the artistic process and become a creative partner. Of course, this is not just about enhancing individual creativity, but also has important policy implications. Governments and related organisations should develop educational programmes and support policies to foster the convergence of AI and the arts. As a good example, by developing curricula for arts education using AI technologies and supporting projects that encourage collaboration between artists and technologists, thereby creating an ecosystem for nurturing creative talent. Such policies will also accelerate the digital transformation of the arts and culture sector and contribute to the creation of new industry ecosystems. Policymakers will need to reflect these changes and formulate strategies to build a sustainable, technology-based cultural ecosystem.

In addition, it is necessary to discuss the ethical issues and social responsibilities of the convergence of AI and arts. The expanding role of AI in the artistic process will require new standards for copyright, creator's rights, and the value of AI-generated works. Researchers need to create a legal framework to address these issues and establish regulations that ensure fair collaboration between stakeholders. It is also important to study the impact of AI technologies on artistic creation and develop policies for sustainable development based on the results. This approach will contribute to ensuring that the convergence of AI and the arts is more than just a technological innovation, but has a positive impact on society as a whole.

5.3 Recommendations for Future Research

The methodology designed and implemented in this study should be valuable as a case study to bridge the gap between learning and practice in the rapidly evolving field of AI. Nevertheless, the development of AI technology continues to progress rapidly, and it is important to keep track of it. Therefore, to foster networking between practitioners and learners, it is proposed to organize trend seminars and hands-on sharing sessions. These sessions would provide opportunities for learners to share their content and exchange trends through social network services or communities, thereby identifying the latest tech trends and exploring the possibilities of AI applications in the cultural sector (Kim et al. 2024; Bristol 2020). It is also crucial to investigate consumer perceptions of AI-powered cultural services to improve personalised strategies and develop products that meet consumer demand. It will also be important to systematically assess the impact of AI technologies on the sustainability of the arts and culture industry. It will come up with concrete measures that can contribute to building a greener arts industry.

On the educational side, we need to continue to improve engaging programmes that address the convergence of AI and the arts. It will provide a variety of hands-on opportunities to help students develop both creative and technical skills. Finally, it needs to strengthen collaboration between the cultural industry and AI technology companies to jointly develop innovative solutions and increase the number of real-world applications. Such cooperation will improve the overall competitiveness of the arts and culture industry and unlock the full potential of AI tech. We hope that this study will serve as a stepping stone for these academic, technological, and policy implications to be implemented.

References

Ali, S., Ravi, P., Williams, R., DiPaola, D., & Breazeal, C. (2024). Constructing Dreams Using Generative AI. *Proceedings of the AAAI Conference on Artificial Intelligence*, 38(21): 23268–23275. https://doi.org/10.1609/aaai.v38i21.30374.

Altares-López, S., Bengochea-Guevara, J. M., Ranz, C., Montes, H., & Ribeiro, A. (2024). Generative AI: The Power of the New Education. arXiv:2405.13487. https://doi.org/10.48550/arXiv.2405.13487

Bandi, A., Adapa, P. V. S. R., & Kuchi, Y. E. V. P. (2023). The Power of Generative AI: A Review of Requirements, Models, Input–Output Formats, Evaluation Metrics, and Challenges. *Future Internet*, 15(8), 260. https://doi.org/10.3390/fi15080260.

Bristol, J. (2020, August). Google Arts & Culture. Retrieved from Common Sense Education: www.commonsense.org/education/website/google-arts-culture.

Civit, M.; Civit-Masot, J.; Cuadrado, F.; Escalona, M. J. (2022). A Systematic Review of Artificial Intelligence-based Music Generation: Scope, Applications, and Future Trends. *Expert Systems with Applications*, 209, 118190. https://doi.org/10.1016/j.eswa.2022.118190.

Dash, A., & Agres, K. (2024). AI-Based Affective Music Generation Systems: A Review of Methods and Challenges. *ACM Computing Surveys*, 56(11), Article 287, 34. https://doi.org/10.1145/3672554.

Feuerriegel, S., Hartmann, J., Janiesch, C., et al. (2024). Generative AI. *Business & Information Systems Engineering*, 66, 111–126. https://doi.org/10.1007/s12599-023-00834-7.

Google Arts & Culture. Retrieved from https://artsandculture.google.com.

Hernandez-Olivan, C.; Hernandez-Olivan, J.; Beltran, J. R. (2022). A Survey on Artificial Intelligence for Music Generation: Agents, Domains and Perspectives. arXiv:2210.13944. https://doi.org/10.48550/arXiv.2210.13944.

Habib, S., Vogel, T., Anli, X., & Thorne, E. (2024). How Does Generative Artificial Intelligence Impact Student Creativity?. *Journal of Creativity*, 34(1), 100072. https://doi.org/10.1016/j.yjoc.2023.100072.

Kim, S. (2023). Exploring the Possibilities of Using Generative Artificial Intelligence for Programming Education: Focusing on ChatGPT. *Proceedings of the Korean Computer Education Society Conference*, 151–154.

Kim, Y., Kim, J., Ahn, H. (2023). A Study on AI Literacy of University Students in Language and Language Education, *Journal of the Korea Contents Association*, 23(1): 165–174.

Kim, H., Kim, Y., Yun, D., & Lee, H. (2024). Empirical Research on the Interaction between Visual Art Creation and Artificial Intelligence Collaboration. *The Journal of the Convergence on Culture Technology*, 10(1): 517–524. https://doi.org/10.17703/jcct.2024.10.1.517.

Kouslis, E., Papachristou, E., Stavropoulos, T. G., et al. (2024). AI in Fashion: A Literature Review, *Electronic Commerce Research*. https://doi.org/10.1007/s10660-024-09872-z.

Lee, Y. (2023). A Study on the Effectiveness Analysis of Liberal Arts Education for the Improvement of Artificial Intelligence Literacy of Pre-service Teachers. *The Journal of Korean Association of Computer Education*, 26(1): 73–81. https://doi.org/10.32431/kace.2023.26.1.007.

Lee, H., & Lee, Y. (2024). Audio Generative AI Usage Pattern Analysis by the Exploratory Study on the Participatory Assessment Process. *Journal of the Korea Society of Computer and Information*, 29(4), 47–54. https://doi.org/10.9708/jksci.2024.29.04.047.

Li, Y., G. Wang, Z. Zhang, Y. Xu, X. Yin (2019). Artificial Intelligence in Fashion: Generative Models for Fashion Design, *IEEE Access*. https://doi.org/10.1109/ACCESS.2019.2936975.

Murugesan, S., & Cherukuri, A.K. (2023). The Rise of Generative Artificial Intelligence and Its Impact on Education: The Promises and Perils, *IEEE*. 56(5): 116–121.

Ramdurai, B., & Adhithya, P. (2023). The Impact, Advancements, and Applications of Generative AI. *International Journal of Computer Science and Engineering*, 10(6): 1–8. https://doi.org/10.14445/23488387/IJCSE-V10I6P101.

Tang, H.; Gu, Y.; Yang, X. (2022). Music Generation with AI technology: Is It Possible?. *2022 IEEE 5th International Conference on Electronics Technology (ICET)*, Chengdu, China, 1265–1272. https://doi.org/10.1109/ICET55676.2022.9824149.

Xiao, G., Xu, C., Misaki, D., Markus, H. R., & Tsai, J. L. (2024). How Culture Shapes What People Want From AI. *In Proceedings of the CHI Conference on Human Factors in Computing Systems (CHI '24)*, Association for Computing Machinery, New York, NY, USA, Article 95, 1–15. https://doi.org/10.1145/3613904.3642660.

Zhou, E., & Lee, D. (2024). Generative Artificial Intelligence, Human Creativity, and Art. *PNAS Nexus*, 3(3), Article page 52. https://doi.org/10.1093/pnasnexus/pgae052.

Study on Development and Effectiveness of Convergence Education Program

Eunee Park

Abstract The advancement of ICT has led to a rapid transformation of media platforms and elementary school students have developed a habit of easily selecting and creating content through smartphones. With the progression of wireless networks and smartphones, media is evolving into immersive media, garnering attention for its convergence with various industries. Consequently, there is a growing need for students to experience new media, emphasizing the importance of immersive media education programs. Researches on convergence education programs for preschool, elementary, and middle school students are increasing. This study aims to develop immersive media education using a floating hologram, targeting elementary students and analyze its effectiveness.

Keywords Convergence education · Floating hologram · Immersive media · Legacy media · Video education · Chroma key shooting · Compositing

1 Introduction

The spread of digital displays such as PCs, smartphones, and smart pads and the development of new media platforms have created an environment in which video content can be easily accessed anytime, anywhere (Yoon 2013). As the demand for various types of video content grows through the diversification and diversification of platforms, people who consume content are changing into producers who directly produce contents (Lee and Lee). As the influence of video content is growing in a rapidly changing media environment, the age at which video is consumed is getting younger. The proportion of students with smartphones increased as grades increased, and the smartphone ownership rate for sixth graders in elementary school was 92.6%, with 9 out of 10 using smartphones in South Korea. The smartphone function most used by elementary school students was 'watching YouTube', and the reason for watching YouTube was 'To get the information easily' (Lee 2022). In addition,

E. Park (✉)
Division of Media Arts, Baekseok Arts University, Seoul, Republic of Korea
e-mail: euneepark@bau.ac.kr

T. Jung et al. (eds.), *XR and Metaverse*, Springer Proceedings in Business and Economics, https://doi.org/10.1007/978-3-031-77975-6_10

platforms like YouTube are perceived as spaces where students can experiment with their identity, upload videos to their channels, and undergo trial and error to express themselves as creators, contributing to the formation of peer culture and cultural identity among elementary school students (Kim 2020).

As the digital media environment evolves into an immersive media environment, there is significant interest and investment from South Korean government agencies in the field of immersive media, which is expected to have a substantial impact on the education sector (Ministry of Science & ICT 2022). A meta-analysis by Kim and Won (2014) on creativity effects of elementary school STEAM (Science, Technology, Engineering, Arts, and Mathematics) education confirmed positive effects on creative thinking skills and tendencies. According to a 2019 report by the South Korean Ministry of Education, students showed increased interest in mathematics, consideration, and scientific self-efficacy through STEAM classes (Hyun and Park 2020). While there is a growing number of cases of developing immersive media for elementary students for smart education, most have been limited to VR/AR, with recent studies exploring the application of the metaverse (Jeon et al. 2022; Youn et al. 2021). Therefore, this research aims to diversify immersive media education by focusing on the development and application of a convergence program for creating immersive video content based on holograms. The study emphasizes the need for learner-centered immersive media creation through converged education.

This study developed an internal assessment tool to verify the effectiveness of the convergence education program and conducted statistical tests using SPSS Win 23.0. Among the 176 participants, 83 responded to the pre-survey, and 93 responded to the post-survey. The study measures educational effects through independent sample t-tests and regression analysis.

2 Literature Review

2.1 Changes in the Media

The term "Legacy media" combines "legacy," meaning heritage or artifact, with media, referring to traditional media such as newspapers, radio, terrestrial broadcasting, cable TV, and IPTV that has been present in the past and is still in use today. The development of 5G mobile communication networks and information technology through the Fourth Industrial Revolution has brought about the information industry revolution. "New media," as the second generation of media, is a term denoting emerging media excluding traditional ones like newspapers, magazines, radio, and TV, and it has emerged alongside technological advancements. The emergence of internet streaming-based new media, such as social media, portals, and YouTube, has transformed the structure of the media market into a multi-platform market. The market, which was previously dominated by legacy media focusing on monopolizing the production, delivery, and transmission of information, has now begun to be overwhelmed within a structure where information production, consumption, and access have become highly liberated. Ordinary individuals can selectively obtain information through various channels beyond what legacy media provides. Furthermore, people have moved beyond the position of receiving and consuming information, gaining the ability to directly produce and convey information (Park 2022).

Immersive media maximizes realism and immersion by delivering sensory information to users, enhancing their satisfaction. As a third-generation media, immersive media combines various media-based realistic effects and synchronized reproduction. It encompasses not only contents such as 3D stereoscopic images, virtual reality (VR), augmented reality (AR), and holograms but also integrates with computer graphics, display technologies, and the gaming industry to create new forms of immersive media. It refers to a medium that enhances the sense of presence and immersion by maximizing sensory and emotional expression in a mixed reality three-dimensional space, conveying all sensory information to the user and thus elevating user satisfaction (Chung 2017). Intelligent media, also known as B.I.G. media, encompasses technologies such as artificial intelligence, big data, IoT, and cloud computing. It refers to media that is massive (Big), intelligent (Intelligent), and self-growing (self-Glowing), integrating these technologies. It possesses characteristics of autonomous growth, fulfilling viewers' media consumption desires through interactive user-media interactions (Kim 2017).

2.2 Types of Immersive Media

Virtual Reality (VR) is an artificially created environment by humans, providing an experience similar to reality. It primarily utilizes Head Mounted Display (HMD) to stimulate the user's senses, enabling spatial experiences with interaction in a setting similar to the real world (Steuer 1992). Since the 2000s, advancements in graphic processing technology, hardware, and the widespread adoption of game engines have gradually secured VR technology. In 2012, Palmer Luckey introduced the modern concept of VR HMD with the development kit for 'Oculus Rift.' Following the release of Oculus Rift, various VR HMD products, such as HTC Vive through collaboration between Valve Corporation and HTC, Samsung's Gear VR, and Sony's PS VR, were introduced. The emergence of 2nd and 3rd generation products has brought us to the current state (Llamas 2023; Dreunen et al. 2018). Augmented Reality (AR) provides an interactive experience that enhances the real world using computer-generated perceptual information. Through technologies such as AR glasses, software, apps, and hardware, AR overlays digital content onto the actual environment and objects (Park et al. 2017). In augmented reality, multiple users can access a shared space filled with virtual objects while remaining grounded in the real world. This technology plays a significant role in educational settings, where users can be present in the same environment and engage in natural communication using language, gestures, and other means. Therefore, augmented reality can be considered as a technology to be explored for educational purposes (Kaufmann 2003).

In 2014, the Ministry of Science, ICT, and Future Planning announced the 'Hologram Industry Development Strategy' to activate the hologram industry within the information and communication sector (Ministry of Science, ICT & Future Planning 2022). This led to increased interest from industry, academia, and research institutions in holographic technology. Holography refers to the technology of recording three-dimensional information about objects using the interference phenomenon of light and reproducing images based on the principles of holography, providing a sense of depth and reproducing three-dimensional images similar to reality. Holograms use laser light to record the light emanating from an object by directing it to intersect with another laser beam on photosensitive film. When these two beams meet, an interference pattern consisting of bright and dark lines is created based on the phase difference of the reflected object waves from different parts of the object. Within this interference pattern, the amplitude and phase of the object are recorded. As shown in Fig. 1, this is the principle of holography, where the image of the object is recorded in the form of these interference patterns.

Using this holographic technology, it can be classified into analog hologram, floating hologram, and digital hologram (Lee 2019). Analog hologram is similar in principle to photography, which is an optical phenomenon through light, but use a laser light source and holographic film to record and reproduce the interference pattern of the target object on recording material. It is mainly used in exhibitions of artifacts in museums. A digital hologram is a form in which 3D digital data captured by an image sensor such as a CCD camera or CMOS sensor can be acquired to create a hologram, and then stored, processed, and edited. A high-resolution spatial light modulator (SLM) is required to reproduce digital holograms.

Floating hologram began in 1862 as a theater stage device called 'Pepper's Ghost' designed by British inventor Henry Dirk. The principle of the floating hologram technology currently being commercialized is shown in Fig. 2 (Englischlehrer.de 2023).

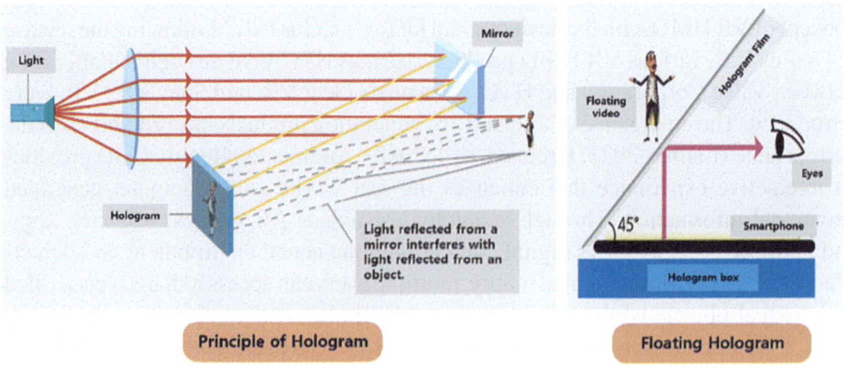

Fig. 1 Principle of hologram

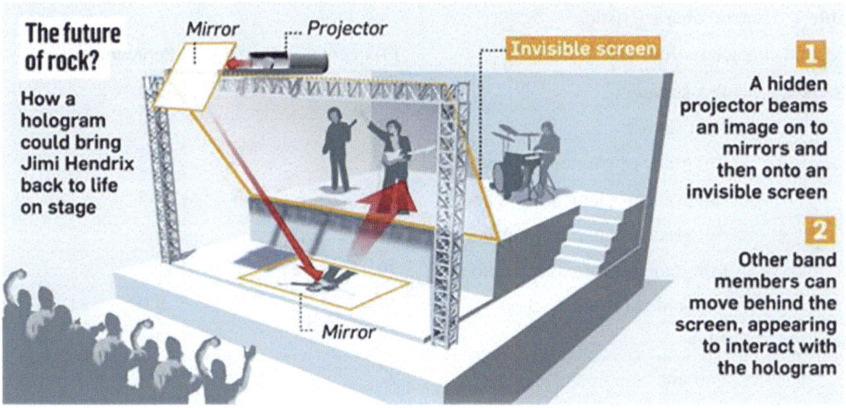

Fig. 2 Principle of floating hologram

A pre-filmed image is projected onto the floor through a projector installed at the top, and the image is reflected by a transparent foil tilted at 45°. It is a video technology that creates a three-dimensional effect for the audience watching from the front, as if the video is floating in the air. Because it can create an optical illusion close to a 'completely stereoscopic video', in the media field, hologram concerts by famous singers at home and abroad, including the Michael Jackson memorial performance in 2014, are being screened, and the service field is expanding to exhibitions, advertisements, theme parks, etc.

3 Methodology

3.1 Research Subject

To examine the general characteristics of the research participants in this educational program, frequency analysis was conducted as shown in Table 1.

3.2 Research Procedure

The process of this study regarding the impact of an immersive media-based convergence education program on learners, including the development of the program and the administration of pre and post surveys, is illustrated in Fig. 3.

Table 1 General characteristics

General characteristics		Frequency analysis	Percentage(%)
Pre/post	Pre-survey	83	47.2
	Post survey	93	52.8
Grade	3rd grade of elementary school	4	2.3
	4th grade of elementary school	66	37.5
	5th grade of elementary school	63	35.8
	6th grade of elementary school	29	16.5
	1st grade of middle school	14	8.0
Sex	Male	84	47.7
	Female	92	52.3

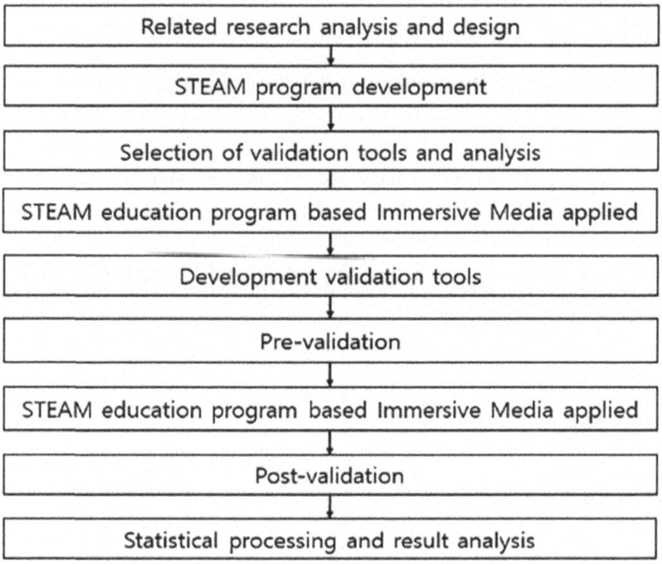

Fig. 3 Research procedure

3.3 Develpment of Convergence Education Program

The program involves students engaging in theatrical activities through play, where they construct their own situational dramas and express them directly in front of the camera. Students then edit and composite the recorded footage to produce video content, which they implement as floating holograms. The program is comprised a total of 8 sessions and each lasting 3 h. Through this program, students will produce three types of video content: pyramid hologram footage, AR face recognition hologram footage, and floating hologram footage. Additionally, they will manufacture

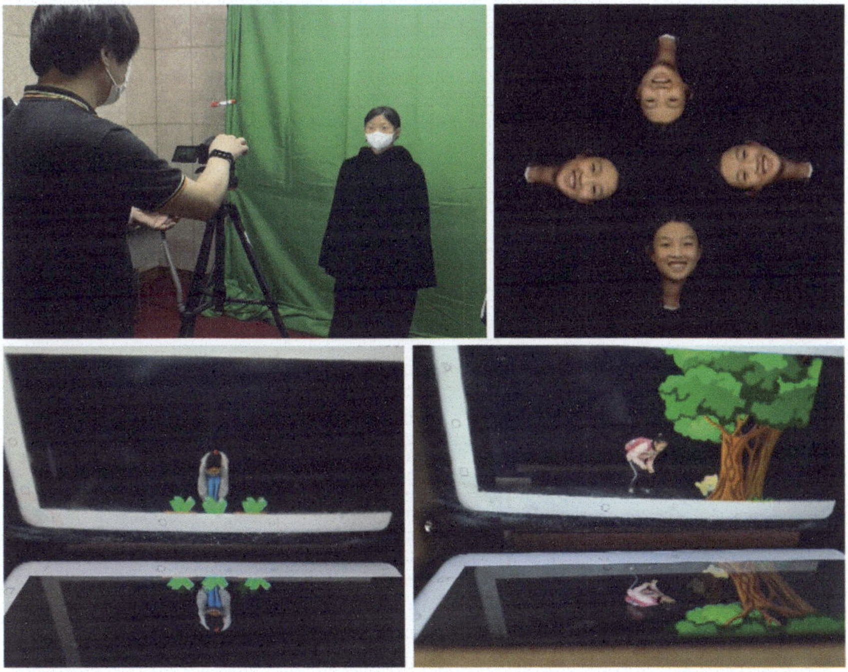

Fig. 4 Educational activities for floating hologram

one pyramid hologram box and one floating hologram box. The Fig. 4 shows the program activities appying to students.

3.4 Measurements

Based on the survey contents of the pre- and post surveys, data were collected and subjected to statistical analysis using SPSS Win 23.0. Frequency analysis was conducted to assess learner satisfaction based on the survey questionnaires administered before and after the application of the developed program. Additionally, an independent-samples t-test was performed to examine the educational impact of the program on learners. Regression analysis was conducted to investigate the influence of all program participation activities within the convergence education program on 'Acquisition of knowledge information', 'Convergence ability', 'Curiosity', 'Consideration and cooperation', 'Leadership', and 'Improvement of creativity'.

The internally developed assessment tool consists of a total of 11 evaluation scales, including 'Creative ideas,' 'Understanding of acting,' 'Understanding of lenticular and hologram technology,' 'Ability to convey ideas,' 'Acceptance,' 'Acquisition

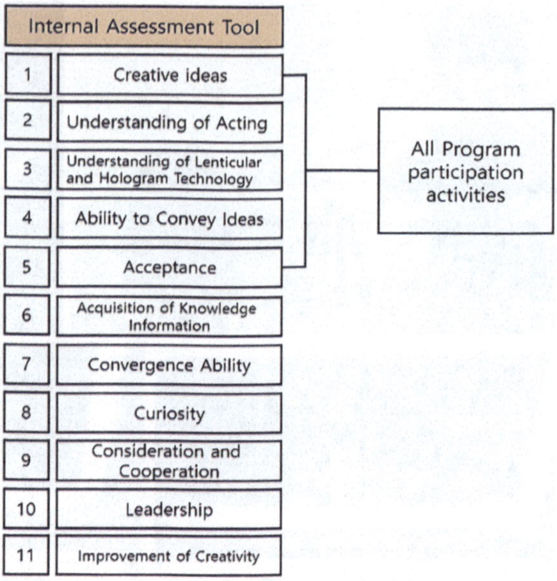

Fig. 5 Internal assessment tool

of knowledge information,' 'Convergence ability,' 'Curiosity,' 'Consideration and cooperation,' 'Leadership,' and 'Improvement of creativity' as shown in Fig. 5. It comprises a pre-survey with 15 items and a post survey with 25 items. To assess the effects before and after the program, five Likert scales were employed, and two open-ended questions were added to gather students' subjective opinions.

3.5 *Evaluation Scale Reliability Analysis*

In order to validate the reliability of the scales used, an analysis method utilizing Cronbach's α coefficient for assessing Internal Consistency Reliability was employed. Internal consistency is evaluated as the correlation among items, with higher correlations indicating greater internal consistency. In this study, Cronbach's α coefficient was adopted with a commonly conservative threshold of 0.6 or higher. As shown in Table 2, the Cronbach's α coefficient was notably high, with a value of 0.82 before and 0.87 after the intervention.

4 Results

An independent-sample t-test was conducted to examine the differences between pre- and post survey responses regarding the educational activities of this convergence education program, including 'All program participation activities (creative ideas,

Table 2 Internal consistency relability

Survey	Item	Number	Average	Standard deviation	Cronbach's α
Pre	Creative ideas	83	3.18	1.061	0.823
Pre	Understanding of acting	83	2.53	1.468	0.823
Pre	Understanding of lenticular and hologram technology	83	2.37	1.341	0.823
Pre	Abillity to convey ideas	83	3.34	0.966	0.823
Pre	Acceptance	83	3.53	0.888	0.823
Pre	Acquisition of knowledge information	83	3.57	0.990	0.823
Pre	Covergence ability	83	2.65	0.968	0.823
Pre	Curiosity	83	3.61	0.998	0.823
Pre	Consideration and cooperation	83	3.48	0.846	0.823
Pre	Leadership	83	3.16	0.981	0.823
Post	Creative ideas	93	4.16	0.959	0.873
Post	Understanding of acting	93	4.40	0.724	0.873
Post	Understanding of lenticular and hologram technology	93	4.34	0.787	0.873
Post	Abillity to convey ideas	93	4.27	0.724	0.873
Post	Acceptance	93	4.30	0.749	0.873
Post	Acquisition of knowledge information	93	4.60	0.574	0.873
Post	Covergence ability	93	4.27	0.754	0.873
Post	Curiosity	93	4.34	0.744	0.873
Post	Consideration and cooperation	93	4.22	0.750	0.873
Post	Leadership	93	4.18	0.846	0.873

understanding of acting, understanding of lenticular and hologram technology, ability to convey idea, acceptance)'. As shown in Table 3, the test results revealed statistically significant differences in 'Creative ideas' ($t = -6.441$, $p < 0.001$), 'Understanding of acting' ($t = 10.507$, $p < 0.001$), 'Understanding of lenticular and hologram technology' ($t = -11.710$, $p < 0.001$), 'Ability to convey ideas' ($t = -7.167$, $p < 0.001$), 'Acceptance' ($t = -6.186$, $p < 0.001$), and 'All program participation activities' ($t = 12.164$, $p < 0.001$). Specifically, examining further, the mean score for 'Creative ideas' increased from 3.18 in the pre-test to 4.16 in the post-test, 'Understanding of acting' increased from 2.53 to 4.40, 'Understanding of lenticular and hologram technology' increased from 2.37 to 4.34, 'Ability to convey ideas' increased from 3.34 to 4.27, 'Acceptance' increased from 3.53 to 4.30, and 'All program participation

Table 3 Differences between pre and post tests in convergence education programs

Item	Pre (n = 83)		Post (n = 93)		t	p-value
	Average	Standard deviation	Average	Standard deviation		
Creative ideas	3.18	1.0609	4.16	0.9588	−6.441	0.000***
Understanding of acting	2.53	1.4678	4.40	0.7244	−10.507	0.000***
Understanding of lenticular and hologram technology	2.37	1.3408	4.34	0.7871	−11.710	0.000***
Abillity to convey ideas	3.34	0.9662	4.27	0.7244	−7.167	0.000***
Acceptance	3.53	0.8881	4.30	0.7487	−6.186	0.000***
All program participation activities	2.99	0.8174	4.29	0.5661	−12.164	0.000***
Acquisition of knowledge information	3.57	0.9901	4.60	0.5737	−8.361	0.000***
Covergence ability	2.65	0.9682	4.27	0.7538	−12.266	0.000***
Curiosity	3.61	0.9979	4.34	0.7445	−5.445	0.000***
Consideration and cooperation	3.48	0.8462	4.22	0.7496	−6.095	0.000***
Leadership	3.16	0.9813	4.18	0.8463	−7.448	0.000***

* $p < 0.05$, ** $p < 0.01$ *** $p < 0.001$

activities' increased from 2.99 to 4.29 in the post-test compared to the pre-test. The statistical analysis of pre and post survey assessments for 'Acquisition of knowledge information' revealed a significant difference in 'Acquisition of knowledge information' (t = −8.361, p < 0.001) increased from 3.57 to 4.60. 'Convergence ability' was higher in the post survey at 4.27 compared to 2.65 in the pre-survey. 'Curiosity' revealed a significant difference in 'Curiosity' (t = −5.445, p < 0.001). It increased from 3.61 to 4.34. 'Consideration and cooperation' (t = −6.095, p < 0.001) increased from 3.48 in the pre-survey to 4.22 in the post survey. The statistical analysis of pre and post survey assessments for 'Leadership' revealed a significant difference in 'Leadership' (t = −7.448, p < 0.001). the mean score for 'Leadership' increased from 3.16 to 4.18.

5 Conclusions

As the importance of smart education increases, there is a perceived need for diversification in immersive media education. The aim is to design, develop, and apply a convergence program for creating immersive video content based on floating hologram technology and to investigate the educational effectiveness of the program on students through statistical data analysis. To investigate the differences between pre and post survey responses, an independent samples t-test was conducted on variables.

The analysis revealed that post program effectiveness was higher in the following order: 'Understanding of lenticular and hologram technology', 'Understanding of acting', 'Convergence ability', 'All program participation Activities (Creative ideas, Understanding of acting, Understanding of lenticular and hologram technology, Ability to convey ideas, Acceptance)', 'Acquisition of knowledge and information', 'Leadership', 'Creative ideas', 'Ability to convey ideas', 'Acceptance', 'Consideration and Cooperation', and 'Curiosity'. Through this analysis, it was observed that although students had limited prior experience with education on 'Lenticular and Hologram' technology, they developed an interest in it and expressed satisfaction with the results through this program. Additionally, while students had some experience with theatrical play, their experience with building stories and creating situational dramas through acting education and conducting chroma key set shootings was limited. Therefore, the post survey showed higher scores in 'Understanding of acting', indicating the program's distinctive educational effectiveness compared to traditional theatrical play activities. Furthermore, students who did not accurately understand the concept of 'Convergence' in the pre-survey significantly improved in 'Convergence ability' in the post survey, suggesting educational effectiveness in learning to integrate various fields to create outcomes and in the creative process through this program. Recent studies on the educational impact of immersive content are increasing. While initially focused mainly on AR/VR, recent research has been actively analyzing the educational effects of immersive content such as metaverse (Chang et al. 2023). Studies have shown that immersive content enhances learners' sense of presence, interactivity, motivation for learning, and immersion (Kim 2021). With advancements in video technology such as game engines, meta humans, and the emergence of generative AI, the conditions are set for producing diverse and creative outcomes in the field of video. In this context, it is essential for educational settings, both within and outside schools, to provide various convergence education programs and educational opportunities to students. Based on the educational effects observed in this study, it is possible to expand the immersive video education program to not only elementary school students but also middle and high school students.

Acknowledgements This paper was written with support from the internal academic research funds provided by Baekseok Arts University.

References

Chung, D. H. (2017). User-based theories and practices on virtual reality. *Information Policy*, 24(1), 3–29. https://doi.org/10.22693/NIAIP.2017.24.1.003.

Chang, J. W., Kim, E. H., & Kim, H. K. (2023). A case study of elementary experiential education converging the real world metaverse : For 6th graders in elementary school. *The Korean Society of Science & Art,41(2), 277–288.* https://doi.org/10.17548/ksaf.2023.03.30.277.

Englischlehrer.de. (2023). Hey Joe—Jimi's alive. Retrieved from http://englischlehrer.de/texts/hendrix.php (accessed August 2, 2023).

Hyun, S. S., & Park, C. J. (2020). Research analysis on STEAM education with digital technology in Korea to prepare for post-corona era education. *International Journal of Contents*, 16(3), 101–110.

Jeon, J. C., Jang, J. H., & Jung, S. K. (2022). analysis of learner's attitude and satisfaction through development and application of metaverse environment STEAM educational program. *Journal of The Korean Association of Information Education*, 26(3), 187–195.

Kaufmann, H. (2003). Collaborative augmented reality in education. I*nstitute of Software Technology and Interactive Systems*, Vienna University of Technology.

Kim, J. W., & Won, H. H. (2014). The effect of creativity in STEAM education by meta-analysis in elementary school. *Journal of Educational Evaluation*, 27(4), 965–985.

Kim, J. G. (2017). The media and 4th industrial revolution. *IITP*, Daejeon, South Korea, ICT Ref, 2017–10.

Kim, A. M. (2020). An exploratory study on children's YouTube culture: Focusing on children's experiences and perceptions. The Journal of Education, 40(3), 341–358. https://doi.org/10.25020/je.2020.40.3.341.

Kim, K. Y. (2021). A study on the effect of VR contents characteristics on educational effects: Focusing on the perceived characteristics of VR content. *Korea Service Management Society, 22(3), 369–390.* https://doi.org/10.15706/jksms.2021.22.3.016.

Lee, G. G. (2019). Understanding of Hologram Technology and Examples of services. *National IT Industry Promotion Agency,* Issue. Rep. 2019–24. Retrieved from https://url.kr/qu3isg.

Lee, S. M., & Lee, S. K. Changes in new media content production and distribution structure. Retrieved from https://url.kr/hixy8v (accessed November 21, 2022).

Lee, Y. J. Investigation of children's media use: Between 4 and 6 in elementary school, 9 out of 10 students use smartphones. Retrieved from https://url.kr/cw6nzh (accessed November 21, 2022).

Llamas, R. T. (2023). Worldwide augmented and virtual reality hardware forecast update, 2023–2027 : CY4Q23. *IDC*. Retrieved from https://url.kr/8bhhz8 (accessed Nov, 2023).

Ministry of Science & ICT. (2022). Digital New Deal 2.0 action plan 2022. Retrieved from https://url.kr/2mtk34 (accessed November 03, 2022).

Ministry of Science, ICT & Future Planning. (2022). Hologram industry development strategy. Retrieved from https://url.kr/x7jwuh (accessed January 19, 2022).

Park, I. W., Ryu, J. H., Cho, Y. S., Shon, M. H., & Jang, J. H. (2017). How to Understand Augmented Reality(AR) and Virtual Reality(VR) Contents and Use for Education. T*he Korea Education and Research Information Service(KERIS),* Issue Rep. 2017–8. Retrieved from https://url.kr/8q4bah.

Park, K. W. (2022). The media revolution and the upheaval of the media industry. Retrieved from https://url.kr/eja3um (accessed December 31, 2022).

Steuer, J. (1992). Defining virtual reality: Dimensions determing telepresence. *Journal of Communication*, 42(4), 73–93.

Van Dreunen, J., Llamas, S., & Sanmiguel, C. (2018). Nowhere to go but up : The future of XR (Virtual Reality, Mixed Reality, Augmented Reality). *Super Data Research*, New York.

Yoon, J. W. (2013). The advent of the smart media era and development direction. *Korea Society Broadcast Engineers Magazine*, 18(1), 10–20.

Youn, J. Y., Kim, Y. H., & Lee, C. W. (2021). A study on development of creative-based convergence education program using metaverse. T*he Korean Society of Science and Art,* 39(5), 273–283.

XR/AI/Metaverse in Tourism and Cultural Heritage

Exploring the Impact of Information Characteristics on Perceived Value, Attitude, and Behavioural Intention for Travel Information Provided by GAI (Generative Artificial Intelligence)

Saerom Wang and Tae-Hwan Yoon

Abstract As more people seek travel information through search engines, websites, and social media, the sheer volume of data can be overwhelming and impersonal. Generative Artificial Intelligence (GAI) technologies are revolutionizing travel information retrieval by offering personalized recommendations based on user preferences, past experiences, and real-time data. However, challenges such as data biases and trust issues persist. This study explores how GAI, specifically ChatGPT, affects users' perceived value, attitudes, and behavioural intentions to enhance GAI adoption and effectiveness in travel planning. Results indicate that completeness, usefulness and easiness of the information information boosts functional benefits, relevancy and usefulness enhance user enjoyment. Usefulness of the information is vital for both utility and enjoyment, while some other factors do not significantly impact perceived value, suggesting only certain information characteristics influence user perceptions.

Keywords Generative artificial intelligence (GAI) · ChatGPT · Travel information · Information characteristics · Perceived value · Attitude

1 Introduction

Individuals today search for travel information with the guidance of various online mediums including search engines, websites, and social media platforms. While offering a wealth of information, the sheer volume of travel data available online presents a double-edged sword as it can be perceived to be overwhelming and impersonal. Amidst this digital deluge, the travel-information retrieval landscape is witnessing a seismic shift with the advent of Generative Artificial Intelligence (GAI)

S. Wang · T.-H. Yoon (✉)
Hotel and Convention Management, Dong-Eui University, Busan, Republic of Korea
e-mail: thyoon@deu.ac.kr

S. Wang
e-mail: saeromw@deu.ac.kr

T. Jung et al. (eds.), *XR and Metaverse*, Springer Proceedings in Business and Economics, https://doi.org/10.1007/978-3-031-77975-6_11

technologies (Dwivedi et al. 2024). GAI, a subset of artificial intelligence, excels at harnessing online data, utilising user preferences, past travel experiences, and real-time information to curate highly personalised travel recommendations (Cooper 2023). The GAI travel agent constantly learns from interactions with individuals, crafting itineraries that perfectly match their interests and budget, and constantly refining its suggestions as their plans evolve (Wong et al. 2023). Moreover, GAI is equipped with plugins for other travel applications that allow users to book travel-related services including hotels, transportation, and tickets, eliminating the burden of having to spend time and make effort in visiting multiple websites to plan one's trip (Wong et al. 2023). This level of personalisation and convenience promises to transform travel planning from a chore into a collaborative and dynamic experience.

Despite its vast potential and benefits, GAI in travel information search is not without its challenges. Biases within data can lead to skewed recommendations and the question of trust remains paramount. While GAI can offer vast knowledge and personalised suggestions, travellers still value human expertise and emotional connection (Nadeem 2024). Also, adoption of GAI is still in its infancy and individuals are not accustomed to searching for information using GAI. In this sense, the mere presence of GAI may not be attractive to individuals for obtaining travel information for trip planning purposes. It is important to understand how the information provided by GAI should be curated to enhance users' attitudes and behavioural intentions. Past studies have explored various factors that impact individuals' intention to adopt GAI in information search including trust, creepiness, perceived usefulness, confirmation, perceived innovativeness, and privacy concerns (Baek and Kim 2023; Nan et al. 2024).

The characteristics of information provided by services tend to influence one's attitudinal or evaluative responses, which in turn influence one's behavioural intention to use the service is developed (Alotaibi et al. 2022). Perceived value and attitude towards information provided by GAI can be possible factors that impact individuals' behavioural intentions. Perceived value of using AI technology services has been found to play an important role in shaping individuals' behavioural responses such as intention to use the service, perceived service quality, and intention to spread the word of mouth (Yin and Qiu 2021). The notion of attitude has been known to be shaped by individuals' perceived value (Um and Yoon 2021) and thus, individuals' attitude could be another factor that shapes one's behavioural intention to use GAI.

While it is important to understand the triggers of individuals' adoption of GAI, limited knowledge regarding this issue has been explored in the existing tourism literature. Few studies have been conducted regarding usage of GAI in travel decision-making, but most of them have been in the form of commentary or conceptual research that reviewed existing literature and practices (Dwivedi et al. 2024; Wong et al. 2023). These forms of studies failed to empirically verify actual behavioural intentions of individuals and the factors that influence such behaviours. Thus, this exploratory research intends to investigate the role of characteristics of information offered by GAI in shaping users' perceived value, attitude, and their behavioural intention to use GAI for travel information search, specifically in the context of ChatGPT. By investigating this crucial relationship, we aim to unlock the true potential of GAI as a travel information tool, shaping a more informed, personalised, and ultimately, transformative travel experience for users in the digital age.

2 Literature Review

2.1 Generative Artificial Intelligence (GAI) and Travel Information Search

Generative Artificial Intelligence (GAI) refers to a category of AI systems designed to generate content, responses, or outputs that are not explicitly programmed (Baidoo-Anu and Ansah 2023). The core capability of GAI lies in its ability to understand and mimic patterns within datasets, allowing it to produce human-like responses or content (Ooi et al. 2023). In travel information search, traditional search engines operate on keywords, often resulting in a deluge of unfiltered information that can overwhelm travellers. GAI, however, takes a different approach. GAI engages in natural, conversational dialogues with users, understanding the nuances of their queries and tailoring responses accordingly (Cooper 2023). GAI systems can generate personalised recommendations as they analyse user preferences, past travel history, and contextual information, which could increase user engagement and booking conversions (Baidoo-Anu and Ansah 2023). GAI can also assist users in planning their trips dynamically by considering real-time factors such as weather, local events, and user preferences (Samara et al. 2020). It can provide up-to-date information on attractions, local transportation, and dining options, contributing to a more fluid and adaptable travel experience. Despite its importance, research on GAI and travel information search has been very limited in the existing literature.

In line with the abundance of research conducted regarding the intention to use or adopt new technology in general, studies on GAI have mostly explored individuals' intention to use GAI (Baek and Kim 2023; Jackson et al. 2024; Nan et al. 2024). Different antecedents to individuals' usage of GAI have been identified in the existing literature, and the importance of understanding intention is emphasised as the intention to use GAI ultimately leads to the actual usage of GAI (Jackson et al. 2024). The work of Nan et al. (2024) concluded that satisfaction plays an important role in enhancing the continuous intention to use as well as the intention to recommend ChatGPT, with satisfaction shaping these responses as influenced by perceived usefulness, confirmation, perceived innovativeness, and privacy concerns. Baek and Kim (2023) found that creepiness and trust towards ChatGPT, which are shaped by task efficiency, personalisation, and social interaction, positively influence individuals' continuance intention to use ChatGPT.

Several studies have been conducted in the context of service robots and services that are enabled by AI technologies in the hospitality industry (de Kervenoael et al. 2020; Kwak et al. 2021). The majority of these studies examined individuals' intention to use the robot or technology, and different antecedents have been identified. In exploring individuals' intention to use social robots for hospitality services, it was found that empathy, perceived value, and information sharing impact their intention to use the service (de Kervenoael 2020). In using service robots at restaurants, Alotaibi et al. (2022) found that perceived value, which is influenced by perceived service newness, hedonic benefits, and service quality, shapes individuals' willingness to visit the restaurant. Melián-González et al. (2021) concluded that several factors impact the intention to use travel chatbots, including expected chatbot performance, familiarity with using chatbots, enjoyment in using them, willingness to use self-service technologies, social influences, and whether the chatbot behaves in a human-like manner. As such, diverse factors that shape individuals' behavioural intention to use AI-powered or related services have been explored, but relatively limited research has examined the antecedents to the usage intention of GAI in the hospitality and tourism industry.

2.2 *Travel Information Characteristics*

Information characteristics refer to the qualitative attributes that define the nature and quality of information (Weathers et al. 2015). These characteristics include dimensions such as clarity, relevance, novelty, and credibility, collectively influencing user perceptions and interactions with the information (Chen and Dhillon 2003). Previous studies on travel information search highlight the importance of various aspects of information characteristics, including information quality, clarity, and personalisation in shaping user behaviour (Jung and Hwang 2023). For instance, Seo and Park (2018) classified airline social media information characteristics into quantity and quality, while Jung and Hwang (2023) adopted dimensions of usefulness and fun in measuring information characteristics of YouTube tourism content. As such, various aspects of information characteristics have been explored in regard to travel information characteristics, and no general consensus has been reached as to which dimensions are dominant constituents of information characteristics in delivering travel-related messages.

Research by Xiang and Gretzel (2010) emphasises the link between perceived website information quality and traveller satisfaction, while Yang et al. (2024) demonstrate how personalised travel recommendations impact user experience. Information characteristics could also lead to a more positive attitude towards the information. Kim and Lee (2022) found that the reliability, informativeness, and utility of in-flight safety information positively influence customers' attitudes towards the message. Information characteristics have also been identified as playing a vital role in shaping users' exposure to information on social media, as attested by the findings from the work of Seo and Park (2018) that information characteristics have a positive impact on online word-of-mouth intention in the context of airline social media content. Information characteristics have been found to be important not only in written form but also when delivered via video. Jung and Hwang (2023) concluded that the information characteristics of YouTube tourism content positively influence user satisfaction, which in turn impacts the intention to visit the destination as well as the intention to share information.

As attested by the findings outlined above, the information characteristics of messages induce individuals to formulate positive attitudinal and behavioural responses towards the messages delivered across various contexts. However, these studies largely focus on static websites and online travel agencies, overlooking the dynamic and conversational nature of GAI-based information search. While a few studies have been conducted regarding the role of specific information provided by GAI, such as the work of Kim et al. (2023) which found that inaccurate information provided by ChatGPT discourages individuals from travelling, barely any research has examined the comprehensive nature of the characteristics of information provided by GAI.

2.3 *Perceived Value*

Perceived value denotes the balance between the perceived benefits of using a service and the perceived costs, such as time and money spent while using the service (Sánchez-Fernández and Iniesta-Bonillo 2007). While the most widely recognised definition of perceived value includes what consumers gain in comparison to the costs they pay to purchase the service, different perspectives exist. Some emphasise the monetary value of services, such as those that treat high-quality services with low prices as representing high perceived value (Pihlström and Brush 2008), and the view that the perceived value of a service is high when a low price is paid using coupons or discounts compared to the regular price (Dodds 1991). Others argue that besides monetary transactions, additional costs such as the amount of time spent and costs associated with information gathering in comparison to the benefits individuals gain from the service determine their perceived value (Morar 2013). In some cases, the underlying meaning of obtaining the service within one's community, such as social status, determines the perceived value of the service (Sheth et al. 1991).

As how perceived value is defined tends to differ across studies, different measurement scales have been adopted to measure perceived value, with existing research measuring perceived value as either a unidimensional or multidimensional construct (Zauner et al. 2015). When examining perceived value as a unidimensional construct, the majority of the studies adopted the view that perceived value refers to how much greater the benefits are compared to the costs in terms of monetary value and service attributes (Tuncer et al. 2021). While such an approach bears valuable implications, applying a multidimensional construct to measure perceived value allows for a more nuanced understanding of which specific aspects of a service individuals perceive to be high in value in their attitudinal and behavioural response towards using the service. For instance, the work of Molinillo et al. (2023) classified perceived value into quality, price, emotional, and social value in examining the perceived value of using voice assistants, while Li et al. (2022) examined hedonic value and the value of perceived control in using AI contactless services. One approach through which the perceived value of hospitality services can be measured includes dissecting it into hedonic and utilitarian value (Vayghan et al. 2023). While some studies identified both types of value to have a positive impact on behavioural responses (Kim et al. 2023; Li et al. 2023), further research is warranted as some revealed specific value to be more important in shaping consumer response than others.

In general, perceived value plays an important role in shaping individuals' pre-purchase decisions as well as post-purchase related attitudinal and behavioural responses (Choi and Lee 2012). For instance, individuals' perceived value of the service robots in the restaurant setting was found to have a positive impact on their willingness to select the restaurant, indicating that perceived value of service prior to actual purchase could influence their purchase intention (Alotaibi et al. 2022). Perceived value also influences individuals' evaluation of the service after usage, as attested in the study by Cao et al. (2022), where individuals using live streaming commerce exhibited higher customer engagement when they perceived the service to be of high value.

Several studies conducted in the context of robot or AI technology services found that users' perceived value of the service induces individuals to develop a higher intention to use the service. The study by de Kervenoael (2020), which examined human-robot interaction in the context of hospitality services, identified that enhanced perceived value of the social robot service led to a higher intention to use the robot. Similar findings were revealed with senior consumers using robot service restaurants, showing that the higher the perceived value of using the robot service, the more positive attitude and enhanced intention to use the service they formed (Kwak et al. 2021). With the increased usage of AI-enabled technological services, studies have been conducted on the perceived value of these types of services, finding that enhanced perceived value of AI-enabled services also leads to positive responses from users, such as higher perceived service quality (Hui et al. 2023) and word-of-mouth intentions as well as actual usage of the service (Molinillo et al. 2023). Thus, it can be concluded that perceived value plays a vital role in shaping the experience of individuals using AI technology-enabled services. However, barely any research has been conducted regarding the role of different types of perceived value in the context of using GAI in tourism information search.

3 Research Method

3.1 Research Model

Based on the theoretical background discussed in the previous section, this research proposes a research model with hypotheses as illustrated below and in Fig. 1.

H1-1. Relevancy has positive effect on hedonic value.
H1-2. Timeliness has positive effect on hedonic value.

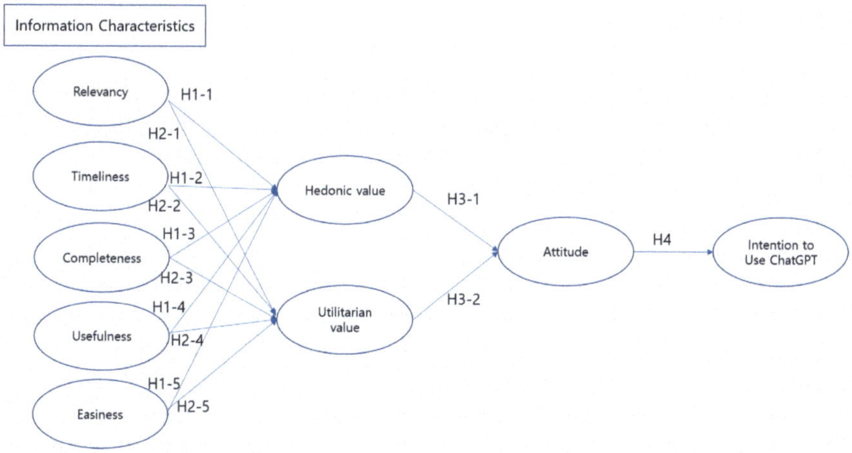

Fig. 1 Research model

H1-3. Completeness has positive effect on hedonic value.
H1-4. Usefulness has positive effect on hedonic value.
H1-5. Easiness has positive effect on hedonic value.
H2-1. Relevancy has positive effect on utility value.
H2-2. Timeliness has positive effect on utility value.
H2-3. Completeness has positive effect on utility value.
H2-4. Usefulness has positive effect on utility value.
H2-5. Easiness has positive effect on utility value.
H3-1. Hedonic value has positive effect on attitude.
H3-2. Utility value has positive effect on attitude.
H4. Attitude has positive effect on behavioural intention.

3.2 Measurements

Variables of information characteristics, hedonic value, utilitarian value, attitude, and intention to use ChatGPT were examined in this research. To measure information characteristics, five dimensions of relevancy, timeliness, completeness, usefulness, and easiness were used as adopted from previous studies (Chen and Dhillon 2003; Zhang 2022). Each dimension was measured using 3 items respectively. In measuring each hedonic and utilitarian value, measurement items were adopted from the work of and 3 items were used respectively. Attitude was measured using 3 items as adopted from the work of Lin et al. (2020) and intention to use ChatGPT with 2 items as adopted from the work of Rahman et al. (2017). All measurement items were measured using 5-point likert-type scale.

3.3 Data Collection

To collect data, an online professional research agency was commissioned to recruit survey respondents using convenience sampling. Given that ChatGPT usage is still in its early stages, the survey was conducted over approximately two weeks in September 2023. Prior to answering the survey questions, respondents were briefed about ChatGPT and instructed to freely explore the ChatGPT website, inquiring about their preferred travel plans and reviewing the responses. To ensure that they had searched for travel information reviewed them, they were prompted to copy and paste the information collected from ChatGPT and where asked questions regarding the information received. Then, they were asked questions about importance of travel information characteristics provided by ChatGPT, perceived value, attitude and intention to use ChatGPT for travel information search. After the surveys were collected, 10 insincere responses were excluded, resulting in 318 valid responses (a 97% validity rate) being used for the final analysis. For the demographic profile of the sample, 65% were male. As for age of the sample, 31% were in their 20 s, 38% were in their 30s, 25% were in their 40s, 6% were in their 50s or more.

3.4 Data Analysis

Data analysis was carried out using Partial Least Squares (PLS)-SEM with Smart PLS 4.0 software. PLS-SEM integrates principal components analysis with regression-based path analysis to estimate the parameters of a structural equation model (Ringle et al. 2020). This method has gained popularity recently due to its flexibility and capability to handle complex models, becoming a standard practice in marketing and management research (Hair et al. 2017).

4 Results

4.1 Measurement Model

We adopted a two-stage analytical procedure for PLS-SEM in accordance with recommendations by Hair et al. (2017), first testing the measurement model and then examining the structural model.

The measurement model was assessed for the reliability and validity of the constructs. Reliability was assessed through Cronbach's Alphas and Composite Reliability (CR). Both Cronbach's Alphas and composite reliability of all factors were greater than 0.8 whereas all rho-a values were greater than 0.7 showing high internal consistency for all constructs (see Table 1). Convergent validity of the scale was assessed through Average Variance Extracted (AVE) and factor loadings. AVE values were greater than accepted threshold of 0.5 varying between 0.677 and 0.936 and all the items have a loading above the threshold of 0.7 (see Table 1). Consequently, convergent validity of the model was confirmed (Hair et al. 2017).

Discriminant validity was tested using Heterotrait-Monotrait ratio of correlation (HTMT) (see Table 2). It is recommended the HTMT value should be lower than 0.85 or 0.9 (Rasoolimanesh 2022; Franke and Sarstedt 2021). Results show that all HTMT values were lower than 0.85 except one (Attitude/Behavior intention: 0.898) which was lower than the marginal threshold of 0.9. These results confirm acceptable level of the discriminant validity of the model (Rasoolimanesh 2022).

4.2 *Structural Model*

Before the examination of the structural model, we checked the collinearity of the structural model through variance inflation factor (VIF) as suggested by Hair et al. (2017). All VIF values were less than the threshold of 5 varying between 1 and 3.130, suggesting that the structural model showed no collinearity issue.

To test hypotheses (H1–H4), the proposed structural model was assessed using 5,000 bootstrap resamples (see Table 3). The results showed that among the five dimensions of information characteristics of ChatGPT, relevancy ($\beta = 0.202$, $p < 0.05$) and usefulness ($\beta = 0.258$, $p < 0.01$) have positive and significant effects on hedonic value. Meanwhile, completeness ($\beta = 0.255$, $p < 0.001$), usefulness ($\beta = 0.286$, $p < 0.001$), and easiness ($\beta = 0.218$, $p < 0.05$) have positive and significant effects on utility value. Usefulness was found to have the greatest influence on both hedonic and utility values. Furthermore, both hedonic value ($\beta = 0.397$, $p < 0.001$) and utility value ($\beta = 0.440$, $p < 0.0001$) positively and significantly influenced attitude. Finally, attitude was shown to have a positive and significant influence on behavioral intention ($\beta = 0.833$, $p < 0.0001$). Therefore, hypotheses H1-1, H1-4, H2-3, H2-4, H2-5, H3-1, H3-2, and H4 were supported, while H1-2, H1-3, H1-5, H2-1, and H2-2 were rejected.

We also examined the R^2 values of the endogenous variables to assess the explanatory power of the model. The results showed that the five information characteristic factors explain 39.3% of the hedonic value ($R^2 = 0.393$) and 61.2% of the utility value ($R^2 = 0.612$). Additionally, hedonic value and utility value together explain 58% of the attitude ($R^2 = 0.580$). Finally, attitude explains 69.4% of behavioral intention ($R^2 = 0.694$). According to Hair et al. (2017), R^2 values of 0.75, 0.50, and 0.20 can be considered substantial, moderate, and weak, respectively. Therefore, the suggested model demonstrates moderate to weak explanatory power.

Table 1 Validity and reliability of the scale

Constructs	Items	Loadings	CR	Rho_a	AVE	Alpha
Relevancy	ChatGPT provides information that I need	0.907	0.943	0.911	0.847	0.909
	Information that are provided by ChatGPT is pertinent to be used for travel information	0.944				
	Information that are provided by ChatGPT can be utilized as travel information	0.909				
Timeliness	ChatGPT provides up-to-date information for trip planning	0.924	0.942	0.908	0.843	0.907
	ChatGPT continuously provides new information for trip planning	0.912				
	ChatGPT promptly updates new information for trip planning	0.919				
Complete-ness	ChatGPT provides specific information for trip planning	0.919	0.940	0.905	0.840	0.904
	ChatGPT provides sufficient information for trip planning	0.927				
	ChatGPT provides accurate information for trip planning	0.902				
Usefulness	ChatGPT effectively provides information that I need	0.837	0.862	0.765	0.677	0.763
	ChatGPT is efficient in obtaining information	0.850				
	Information that ChatGPT provides is useful to me	0.779				
Easiness	ChatGPT is easy to use	0.917	0.924	0.845	0.859	0.836
	ChatGPT is easy to learn	0.936				
Hedonic value	It is fun to search travel information using ChatGPT	0.937	0.936	0.914	0.829	0.896

(continued)

Table 1 (continued)

Constructs	Items	Loadings	CR	Rho_a	AVE	Alpha
	It is enjoyable to search travel information using ChatGPT	0.946				
	Travel information search using ChatGPT a fun activity rather than being a burden	0.845				
Utility value	ChatGPT allows me to quickly search for travel information	0.894	0.929	0.886	0.813	0.885
	ChatGPT allows me to collect vast amount of travel information	0.891				
	ChatGPT allows me to collect travel information easily	0.920				
Attitude	Travel information search via ChatGPT allows me to obtain information conveniently	0.937	0.951	0.923	0.866	0.923
	I have a positive attitude towards using ChatGPT to obtain travel infromation	0.927				
	It is a good idea to use ChatGPT to search for travel information	0.928				
Behavioral intention	I will use ChatGPT to search for travel information in the future	0.969	0.967	0.933	0.936	0.931
	I will continuously use ChatGPT to search for travel information	0.966				

5 Conclusion and Discussion

With the advancement of generative artificial intelligence technology, the ways in which individuals search for information today are becoming more diverse and are no longer limited to traditional search engines. Accordingly, this study analysed the impact of information characteristics of GAI on attitudes and behavioural intentions, mediated by perceived value. The results show that the information characteristics of GAI significantly impact users' attitudes and behavioural intentions through perceived value. In particular, among the five dimensions of information characteristics, 'relevancy' and 'usefulness' were found to have a significant impact on

Table 2 HTMT (Heterorait-monotrait) analysis

Constructs	1	2	3	4	5	6	7	8	9
Attitude									
Behavioral Intention	0.898								
Completeness	0.634	0.576							
Easiness	0.755	0.684	0.709						
Hedonic value	0.747	0.742	0.479	0.636					
Relevancy	0.678	0.616	0.849	0.761	0.572				
Timeliness	0.632	0.620	0.824	0.665	0.498	0.785			
Usefulness	0.636	0.602	0.448	0.837	0.629	0.561	0.424		
Utility value	0.773	0.712	0.719	0.804	0.730	0.727	0.634	0.746	

Table 3 Results of hypotheses testing

Hypotheses		Beta	t-value	p-value	support	VIF
H1-1	Relevancy → Hedonic value	0.202	2.222	0.026	Yes	3.124
H1-2	Timeliness → Hedonic value	0.132	1.279	0.201	No	2.571
H1-3	Completeness → Hedonic value	-0.036	380	0.704	No	3.130
H1-4	Usefulness → Hedonic value	0.258	3.332	0.001	Yes	2.004
H1-5	Easiness → Hedonic value	0.190	1.791	0.073	No	2.853
H2-1	Relevancy → Utility value	0.136	1.808	0.071	No	3.124
H2-2	Timeliness → Utility value	0.048	0.931	0.352	No	2.571
H2-3	Completeness → Utility value	0.255	3.550	0.000	Yes	2.843
H2-4	Usefulness → Utility value	0.286	4.793	0.000	Yes	3.130
H2-5	Easiness → Utility value	0.218	2.196	0.028	Yes	2.004
H3-1	Hedonic value → Attitude	0.397	7.023	0.000	Yes	1.743
H3-2	Utility value → Attitude	0.440	7.984	0.000	Yes	1.743
H4	Attitude → Behavioral intention	0.833	42.718	0.000	Yes	1.000

'hedonic value'. Regarding 'utility value', 'easiness', 'completeness', and 'usefulness' were found to have a significant impact. Lastly, 'timeliness' among information characteristics does not have a significant effect on either hedonic value or utility value, indicating that only certain elements of information characteristics affect users' perceived value. In regards to the role of perceived value, both hedonic and utility value were found to have positive impact on attitude, which in turn were found to have positive influence on intention to use ChatGPT.

The theoretical implications of this study are multifaceted. Firstly, the findings underscore the importance of specific information characteristics of generative artificial intelligence (GAI) in shaping users' attitudes and behavioural intentions through perceived value. As limited studies examined attribute of the information provided by GAI system, this research is a pioneering attempt in identifying the characteristics of information that impact users' responses towards usage of GAI for travel information search.

The significant impact of 'relevancy' and 'usefulness' on hedonic value suggests that users derive enjoyment and pleasure from information that is both pertinent and practical. This aligns with theories of information processing which posit that content relevance and usefulness are critical for user engagement and satisfaction (Soane et al. 2015). Moreover, the influence of 'easiness', 'completeness', and 'usefulness' on utility value highlights the necessity for information to be accessible, thorough, and beneficial for users to perceive it as functionally valuable. Such a finding is partly in line with the findings of existing studies which identified these three factors to play an important role in sharing individuals' perceived value (Kim and Niehm 2009; Machdar 2016).

The finding that 'timeliness' does not significantly affect either hedonic or utility value suggests a nuanced understanding of user priorities. While timeliness might be presumed important, its lack of significant impact indicates that users may prioritise other information characteristics over updated information. This challenges the conventional emphasis on timeliness in information quality (Saha et al. 2012) and suggests that future models should consider the relative importance of different information characteristics.

Furthermore, this research expanded the finding of existing studies regarding the role of perceived value as a mediator (Alotaibi et al. 2022) in the context of using GAI in travel information search. Both hedonic and utility value positively influence users' attitudes, which in turn positively affect their intention to use ChatGPT. It suggests that enhancing both the enjoyment and functional benefits of GAI can lead to more favourable user attitudes and higher intention to adopt such technologies when searching for travel information.

The results of this study provide practitioners valuable insights regarding utilization of GAI in the tourism industry, including Tripadvisor that are incorporating GAI to their system to facilitate potential travellers in planning their trip. Practitioners should focus on ensuring that the information provided by GAI is highly relevant and useful to users. This can be achieved by refining algorithms to better understand and anticipate user needs and contexts, thereby delivering content that users find directly applicable and beneficial. In addition, to improve utility value, it is crucial to make information easily accessible and understandable. This involves simplifying user interfaces, improving navigation, and ensuring that information is presented in a clear and concise manner. Training GAI systems to provide straightforward explanations and actionable insights can significantly enhance user satisfaction and engagement. Moreover, providing comprehensive information that covers all necessary aspects of a query can significantly enhance the perceived utility of the GAI. Practitioners should work on expanding the knowledge base of the GAI and ensuring that it can deliver thorough and detailed responses. Last, while enhancing the functional benefits of the information (utility value), it is also important to focus on the enjoyment aspect (hedonic value). This can be achieved by making interactions with

GAI more engaging and enjoyable, perhaps through conversational tone, interactive elements, and personalisation features that resonate with users on an emotional level.

References

Alotaibi, S., Shafieizadeh, K., & Alsumait, K. (2022). Customers' perceptions toward service robots at restaurants: The moderating role of consumer innovativeness and the mediating role of perceived hedonic benefits. *Journal of Quality Assurance in Hospitality & Tourism*, 1–23.

Baek, T. H., & Kim, M. (2023). Is ChatGPT scary good? How user motivations affect creepiness and trust in generative artificial intelligence. *Telematics and Informatics*, *83*, 102030.

Baidoo-Anu, D., & Ansah, L. O. (2023). Education in the era of generative artificial intelligence (AI): Understanding the potential benefits of ChatGPT in promoting teaching and learning. *Journal of AI*, *7*(1), 52–62.

Cao, J., Zhang, G., Liu, D., & Shang, M. (2022). Influencing factors of users' shift to buying expensive virtual gifts in live streaming: empirical evidence from China. *Frontiers in Psychology*, *13*, 997651.

Chen, S. C., & Dhillon, G. S. (2003). Interpreting dimensions of consumer trust in e-commerce. *Information technology and management*, *4*, 303–318.

Choi, W. S., & Lee, S. B. (2012). The effect of servicescape of an eco-friendly restaurant on customer perceived value, attitude and behavior intention. *Culinary science and hospitality research*, *18*(5), 45–62.

Cooper, G. (2023). Examining science education in ChatGPT: An exploratory study of generative artificial intelligence. *Journal of Science Education and Technology*, *32*(3), 444–452.

de Kervenoael, R., Hasan, R., Schwob, A., & Goh, E. (2020). Leveraging human robot interaction in hospitality services: Incorporating the role of perceived value, empathy, and information sharing into visitors' intentions to use social robots. *Tourism Management*, *78*, 104042.

Dodds, W. B., Monroe, K. B., & Grewal, D. (1991). Effects of price, brand, and store information on buyers' product evaluations. *Journal of marketing research*, *28*(3), 307–319.

Dwivedi, Y. K., Pandey, N., Currie, W., & Micu, A. (2024). Leveraging ChatGPT and other generative artificial intelligence (AI)-based applications in the hospitality and tourism industry: practices, challenges and research agenda. *International Journal of Contemporary Hospitality Management*, *36*(1), 1–12.

Franke, G. R., Sarstedt, M., & Danks, N. P. (2021). Assessing measure congruence in nomological networks. *Journal of Business Research*, *130*, 318–334.

Hair Jr, J. F., Matthews, L. M., Matthews, R. L., & Sarstedt, M. (2017). PLS-SEM or CB-SEM: updated guidelines on which method to use. *International Journal of Multivariate Data Analysis*, *1*(2), 107–123.

Hui, Z., Khan, A. N., Chenglong, Z., & Khan, N. A. (2023). When service quality is enhanced by human–artificial intelligence interaction: an examination of anthropomorphism, responsiveness from the perspectives of employees and customers. *International Journal of Human–Computer Interaction*, 1–16.

Jackson, I., Ivanov, D., Dolgui, A., & Namdar, J. (2024). Generative artificial intelligence in supply chain and operations management: a capability-based framework for analysis and implementation. *International Journal of Production Research*, 1–26.

Jung, H., & Hwang, J. (2023). The information characteristics of YouTube tourism content and their impacts on user satisfaction and intention to visit and share information: the moderating role of word-of-mouth information acceptance. *Asia Pacific Journal of Tourism Research*, *28*(2), 143–156.

Kim, H., & Lee, N. (2022). The Effects of the in-flight safety information characteristics on the safety behavioral intention of airline passengers. *Sustainability*, *14*(5), 2819.

Kim, H., & Niehm, L. S. (2009). The impact of website quality on information quality, value, and loyalty intentions in apparel retailing. *Journal of interactive marketing, 23*(3), 221–233.

Kim, J., Kim, S. S., Jhang, J., Doust, N. A. S., Chan, R. Y., & Badu-Baiden, F.(2023). Preference for utilitarian or hedonic value options during a pandemic crisis: The moderation effects of childhood socioeconomic status and sensation-seeking. *International Journal of Hospitality Management*, 110, 103427.

Kwak, M. K., Lee, J., & Cha, S. S. (2021). Senior consumer motivations and perceived value of robot service restaurants in Korea. *Sustainability, 13*(5), 2755.

Li, H., Zhang, J., Wan, Q., Wang, Q., & Xu, J. (2023). Customers' hotel staycation experiences: implications from the pandemic. *Current Issues in Tourism*, 1–18.

Lin, S. Y., Juan, P. J., & Lin, S. W. (2020). A tam framework to evaluate the effect of smartphone application on tourism information search behavior of foreign independent travelers. *Sustainability, 12*(22), 9366.

Machdar, N. M. (2016). The effect of information quality on perceived usefulness and perceived ease of use. *Business and Entrepreneurial Review, 15*(2), 131–146.

Melián-González, S., Gutiérrez-Taño, D., & Bulchand-Gidumal, J. (2021). Predicting the intentions to use chatbots for travel and tourism. *Current Issues in Tourism, 24*(2), 192–210.

Molinillo, S., Rejón-Guardia, F., Anaya-Sánchez, R., & Liébana-Cabanillas, F. (2023). Impact of perceived value on intention to use voice assistants: The moderating effects of personal innovativeness and experience. *Psychology & Marketing, 40*(11), 2272–2290.

Morar, D. D. (2013). An overview of the consumer value literature–perceived value, desired value. *Marketing from information to decision*, (6), 169–186.

Nadeem, M. (2024). Generative Artificial Intelligence [GAI]: Enhancing Future Marketing Strategies with Emotional Intelligence [EI], and Social Skills?. *British Journal of Education, 12*(1), 1–15.

Nan, D., Sun, S., Zhang, S., Zhao, X., & Kim, J. H. (2024). Analyzing behavioral intentions toward Generative Artificial Intelligence: the case of ChatGPT. *Universal Access in the Information Society*, 1–11.

Ooi, K. B., Tan, G. W. H., Al-Emran, M., Al-Sharafi, M. A., Capatina, A., Chakraborty, A., ... & Wong, L. W. (2023). The potential of generative artificial intelligence across disciplines: Perspectives and future directions. *Journal of Computer Information Systems*, 1–32.

Pihlström, M., & Brush, G. J. (2008). Comparing the perceived value of information and entertainment mobile services. *Psychology & Marketing, 25*(8), 732–755.

Rahman, M. M., Lesch, M. F., Horrey, W. J., & Strawderman, L. (2017). Assessing the utility of TAM, TPB, and UTAUT for advanced driver assistance systems. *Accident Analysis & Prevention, 108*, 361–373.

Rasoolimanesh, S. M. (2022). Discriminant validity assessment in PLS-SEM: A comprehensive composite-based approach. *Data Analysis Perspectives Journal, 3*(2), 1–8.

Ringle, C. M., Sarstedt, M., Mitchell, R., & Gudergan, S. P. (2020). Partial least squares structural equation modeling in HRM research. *The international journal of human resource management, 31*(12), 1617–1643.

Saha, P., Nath, A. K., & Salehi-Sangari, E. (2012). Evaluation of government e-tax websites: an information quality and system quality approach. *Transforming Government: People, Process and Policy, 6*(3), 300–321.

Samara, D., Magnisalis, I., & Peristeras, V. (2020). Artificial intelligence and big data in tourism: a systematic literature review. *Journal of Hospitality and Tourism Technology, 11*(2), 343–367.

Sánchez-Fernández, R., & Iniesta-Bonillo, M. Á. (2007). The concept of perceived value: a systematic review of the research. *Marketing theory, 7*(4), 427–451.

Sheth, J. N., Newman, B. I., & Gross, B. L. (1991). Why we buy what we buy: A theory of consumption values. *Journal of business research, 22*(2), 159–170.

Soane, E., Schubert, I., Lunn, R., & Pollard, S. (2015). The relationship between information processing style and information seeking, and its moderation by affect and perceived usefulness: Analysis vs. procrastination. *Personality and Individual Differences, 72*, 72–78.

Tuncer, I., Unusan, C., & Cobanoglu, C. (2021). Service quality, perceived value and customer satisfaction on behavioral intention in restaurants: An integrated structural model. *Journal of quality assurance in hospitality & tourism*, *22*(4), 447–475.

Um, J., & Yoon, S. (2021). Evaluating the relationship between perceived value regarding tourism gentrification experience, attitude, and responsible tourism intention. *Journal of Tourism and Cultural Change*, *19*(3), 345–361.

Vayghan, S., Baloglu, D., & Baloglu, S. (2023). The impact of utilitarian, social and hedonic values on hotel booking mobile app engagement and loyalty: a comparison of generational cohorts. *Journal of Hospitality and Tourism Insights*, *6*(5), 1990–2011.

Weathers, D., Swain, S. D., & Grover, V. (2015). Can online product reviews be more helpful? Examining characteristics of information content by product type. *Decision Support Systems*, *79*, 12–23.

Wong, I. A., Lian, Q. L., & Sun, D. (2023). Autonomous travel decision-making: An early glimpse into ChatGPT and generative AI. *Journal of Hospitality and Tourism Management*, *56*, 253–263.

Xiang, Z., & Gretzel, U. (2010). Role of social media in online travel information search. *Tourism management*, *31*(2), 179–188.

Yang, X., Zhang, L., & Feng, Z. (2024). Personalized tourism recommendations and the E-tourism user experience. *Journal of Travel Research*, *63*(5), 1183–1200.

Yin, J., & Qiu, X. (2021). AI technology and online purchase intention: Structural equation model based on perceived value. *Sustainability*, *13*(10), 5671.

Zauner, A., Koller, M., & Hatak, I. (2015). Customer perceived value—Conceptualization and avenues for future research. *Cogent psychology*, *2*(1), 1061782.

Revolutionizing Cultural Heritage Engagement Through the Metaverse: A Study on Virtual Interactivity and Perception

Ahmad Alsuwaidi and Amal Almazrooei

Abstract This research investigates the impact of virtual environments on user engagement and perception of cultural heritage within the Metaverse, using a quantitative approach to examine responses from 200 participants. By conducting correlation and regression analyses, it scrutinizes the dynamics between technology use in the Metaverse, the authenticity of its virtual representations, inclusivity efforts, the fidelity of its environments, interactive elements, and overall user satisfaction. Results highlight a notable positive correlation between engagement levels and the use of Metaverse technology, emphasizing the critical role of intuitive and accessible Metaverse platforms in boosting user interaction. While the study underscores the vast opportunities for immersive experiences in cultural heritage, it also identifies ongoing challenges in ensuring inclusivity and maintaining authenticity. This paper enriches our understanding of virtual environment's role in enhancing cultural heritage engagement and suggests in employing Metaverse technologies to foster inclusive and genuine representations of cultural heritage.

Keywords Digital interaction · Cultural heritage · Metaverse · Virtual interactivity · User experience

1 Introduction

The Metaverse, combining virtual reality (VR), augmented reality (AR), and blockchain technologies, ushers in a new era in cultural heritage engagement. It offers a revolutionary platform for interactive and immersive exploration of cultural narratives across time (Vital and Sylaiou 2022). According to Dirin et al. (2023),

A. Alsuwaidi (✉)
Department of Digital Innovation, University of Nicosia, Nicosia, Cyprus
e-mail: alsuwaidi.a@live.unic.ac.cy

A. Almazrooei
Future Foresight Center, Dubai Police, Dubai, UAE
e-mail: a.almazrooei@dubaipolice.gov.ae

T. Jung et al. (eds.), *XR and Metaverse*, Springer Proceedings in Business and Economics, https://doi.org/10.1007/978-3-031-77975-6_12

the Metaverse transcends its role as a technological marvel, becoming a pivotal tool for cultural preservation and global connection. This shift aligns with broader trends in digital urbanism and smart cities, suggesting significant impacts on education, preservation, and cultural exchange (Allam et al. 2022).

Central to this study is the application of User Experience (UX) Design Theory, emphasizing clarity, usability, and emotional resonance as essential components for engaging virtual experiences (Berni and Borgianni 2021). The integration of these principles is crucial in the Metaverse, where user interaction quality deeply influences engagement with and appreciation of cultural heritage. This research aims to bridge the theoretical and empirical gap in understanding how UX design can enhance cultural heritage experiences in the Metaverse, drawing inspiration from the educational potential of virtual worlds (Mystakidis 2022).

Utilizing a quantitative approach, this study analyses responses from 200 participants to examine how technology adoption, authenticity, inclusivity, and environmental fidelity affect user engagement within the Metaverse. The primary objective is to identify factors that support user engagement and ensure inclusive and authentic representations of cultural heritage. This inquiry is underscored by advancements in blockchain for digital ownership (French et al. 2020) and the exploration of authenticity in digital cultural artifacts (Chandra 2022).

2 Literature Review

2.1 The Metaverse: A New Frontier for Cultural Heritage

The Metaverse offers immersive experiences that extend beyond traditional physical and temporal constraints, democratizing access to cultural narratives worldwide. Its potential as an educational, preservation, and exchange tool is significant, merging digital innovation with cultural preservation in ways previously unimagined (Dirin et al. 2023; Zhang et al. 2022). User Experience (UX) design principles, emphasizing clarity, usability, and emotional resonance, play a crucial role in this transformative space (Berni and Borgianni 2021). Moreover, blockchain technology addresses issues of digital ownership and authenticity, ensuring the integrity of virtual artifacts and increasing their trustworthiness and educational value (Lyu 2022; Al-Ghaili et al. 2022).

Access to cultural heritage (CH) is recognized as a fundamental human right, yet tangible artifacts often face limitations due to their cultural and historical significance. Organizations such as archives, libraries, and museums have developed digital repositories to house content like videos, images, text, audio, and GIS data, safeguarding and presenting CH in accessible formats (Rahmani and Tienken 2022). This initiative lays the groundwork for the Metaverse's role in further enhancing access to and engagement with cultural heritage.

2.2 Empirical Insights from Metaverse Applications

Empirical evidence highlights the Metaverse's potential for innovative cultural heritage engagement, despite facing challenges.

Innovative Practices: Projects such as LOCUS in Amiais, Portugal, and preservation efforts in Guangxi, China, demonstrate the Metaverse's role as an educational and engagement platform. These projects leverage gaming elements, advanced technologies, and sustainable methods for deeper cultural exploration (Ferreira 2012; Fan et al. 2022; Martins et al. 2022). Additionally, the digital reconstruction of the Palmyra theatre in Syria using 3D and VR technologies aims to preserve this ancient monument despite extensive war damage (Alkhatib et al. 2023).

Challenges: The digitization process, including creating detailed 3D models, presents technical challenges requiring collaboration between technologists and cultural experts to ensure authenticity (Song et al. 2023). Virtual worlds also face difficulties in accurately representing and conveying the cultural significance of artifacts (Paganopoulos 2022). Platforms like Decentraland.org and Meta Horizon Worlds highlight the challenges in maintaining user engagement, underscoring the need for more accessible and intuitive platforms (Cruz Franco et al. 2022).

These insights indicate the necessity of a balanced approach to interactivity, authenticity, and accessibility for meaningful cultural heritage connections in the Metaverse.

2.3 Factors Influencing User Engagement and Perception

- **Technology Utilization**: Using technology effectively enhances the realism and interactivity of virtual environments, which is crucial for engaging users with cultural heritage content. This relationship is foundational for creating accessible and intuitive Metaverse platforms (Dirin et al. 2023).
- **Authenticity**: Accurate virtual representations are essential for meaningful engagement, fostering deeper appreciation and trust within virtual environments. Authenticity also enhances the educational impact of cultural heritage experiences in the Metaverse (Lyu 2022; Al-Ghaili et al. 2022).
- **Inclusivity**: Ensuring diverse audience accessibility to virtual cultural heritage experiences is imperative for equitable engagement in the Metaverse. Addressing physical, technological, and cultural barriers is key to enhancing user satisfaction and fostering an inclusive virtual heritage space (Pouryousefzadeh and Akbarzadeh 2019).
- **Environmental Fidelity**: The quality and realism of virtual environments influence user perception and engagement, with high-fidelity environments offering more compelling experiences (Song et al. 2023).

2.4 Best Practices and Innovative Approaches

The Metaverse's integration into business models, especially within the tourism industry, demonstrates its extensive impact across various sectors, including marketing, education, healthcare, and social networking. This transformation facilitates a seamless transition between real and virtual experiences, highlighting its potential to redefine brand engagement and social interactions in digital spaces (Martí-Testón et al. 2023). Research into how VR influences tourist perceptions and attitudes towards destinations further emphasizes the Metaverse's role in reshaping tourism experiences (Buhalis et al. 2023; Koo et al. 2023). To maximize the Metaverse's potential in cultural heritage engagement, it is crucial to adopt strategies centred around interactivity, authenticity, and inclusivity:

- **Interactivity and Storytelling**: Engaging users through interactive narratives and gamification enriches the connection to cultural heritage, making learning enjoyable and impactful (Ferreira 2012).
- **Digital Replicas and Authenticity**: Technological advancements allow for the creation of accurate digital replicas of cultural artifacts and sites, offering immersive explorations while preserving authenticity (Fan et al. 2022; Lyu 2022).
- **Accessibility**: Developing user-friendly Metaverse environments accessible to all, including those with disabilities, is essential for an inclusive and equitable virtual heritage space (Cruz Franco et al. 2022).
- **Advanced Technologies**: Leveraging high-fidelity 3D models and immersive VR/AR experiences increases the realism and engagement of virtual cultural heritage, showcasing the potential for digital platforms to revitalize interest in cultural heritage (Longo and Faraci 2023; Pouryousefzadeh and Akbarzadeh 2019).

This literature review highlights the importance of creating immersive, authentic, and accessible virtual experiences. Addressing challenges and leveraging best practices can help cultural heritage professionals and technologists design Metaverse environments that foster meaningful cultural experiences.

3 Methodology

This research employs a quantitative research methodology to explore the impact of virtual environments on user engagement and perception of cultural heritage within the Metaverse, with a particular emphasis on the application of User Experience (UX) Design Theory. An online survey was administered to 200 participants familiar with Metaverse platforms, utilizing Likert scale questions to gauge the depth of their experiences and views on engaging with cultural heritage in these virtual spaces. Participants were fully informed about the study's aims, their rights to anonymity and confidentiality, and the voluntary nature of their participation. Informed consent was obtained from all individuals, ensuring ethical standards were upheld throughout the research process.

3.1 Data Analysis

To comprehensively understand the impact of various factors on user engagement and satisfaction, a range of independent variables were analysed. These included technology utilization, authenticity, inclusivity, environmental fidelity, and interactivity within the Metaverse. Utilizing SPSS for data analysis, Pearson correlation and multiple regression analyses were conducted to explore the relationships between these variables. Particular focus was given to the impact of Metaverse technology utilization on user engagement, as well as the role of inclusivity measures, to identify both strengths and potential areas for improvement. Additionally, ANOVA tests were performed to identify significant differences among groups, focusing on how specific Metaverse features influence user satisfaction and engagement.

3.2 Application of UX Design Theory in Research Methodology

The survey instrument was developed and refined through principles of UX design theory, emphasizing clarity, ease of use, and emotional resonance, to ensure the collection of meaningful data on user experiences within the Metaverse (Dirin et al., 2023; Berni & Borgianni, 2021).

- **Survey Design and Information Architecture**: Iterative user research, including pilot testing, informed the survey design to optimize question clarity and logical flow, minimizing respondent cognitive load and enhancing response accuracy.
- **Usability Testing for Survey Refinement**: Prior to broad distribution, the survey underwent usability testing to identify and address potential completion barriers, based on feedback regarding question clarity and the overall user experience of the survey.
- **Evaluating Inclusivity Measures**: Special attention was given to designing questions that assess the inclusivity of Metaverse platforms, ensuring that the survey could capture data on how inclusivity measures impact user engagement and satisfaction.
- **Analysing UX Factors**: The interpretation of survey data will consider UX design principles to analyse how Metaverse usability, information clarity, and emotional engagement impact user perceptions and engagement with cultural heritage.

4 Findings and Discussion

Employing Pearson correlation, multiple regression analyses, and ANOVA tests within SPSS, we explored how various factors, including technology utilization, authenticity, inclusivity, and interactivity, influence user engagement and satisfaction. The findings highlight the pivotal role of technology utilization and authenticity in enhancing user engagement within the Metaverse, while inclusivity measures indicate a potential disconnect between technology implementation and inclusivity objectives.

This research reveals how technology utilization and the authenticity of virtual representations significantly enhance user interaction. Our quantitative analysis, involving 200 participants, highlights a crucial consensus: 75% believe the Metaverse will fundamentally change digital communication, with notable impacts expected on education (78.6% agreement) and the economy (66.8% agreement).

Key insights include:

- Metaverse Technology Utilization and User Engagement: A strong positive correlation ($r = 0.248$, $p < 0.01$), underscoring the vital role of accessible platforms in deepening cultural connections.
- Authenticity of Virtual Depictions and Engagement: A positive correlation ($r = 0.251$, $p < 0.01$), emphasizing the need for accurate cultural representations.
- Fidelity of Virtual Environments and Cultural Heritage Engagement: Although sought after, high environmental fidelity (coefficient = 0.063, p-value > 0.05) may not be paramount in enhancing user interaction.
- Inclusivity Measures and Engagement: A negative correlation ($r = -0.156$, $p < 0.05$), indicating the need for solutions to ensure accessibility for diverse audiences.

4.1 *Interpreting Complex Relationships*

The positive correlation between technology utilization and user engagement underscores the importance of accessible and intuitive Metaverse platforms, aligning with Dirin et al. (2023). However, the negative correlation with inclusivity measures signals a critical challenge: as Metaverse platforms become technologically advanced, they must also become more inclusive to ensure broad accessibility (Pouryousefzadeh and Akbarzadeh 2019).

The analysis in Fig. 1 highlights several critical relationships:

- User Engagement and Metaverse Technology Use: There is a positive correlation ($r = 0.248$, $p < 0.01$), indicating that increased use of Metaverse technology is associated with higher user engagement.
- User Engagement and Authenticity of Virtual Representations: A positive correlation ($r = 0.251$, $p < 0.01$) suggests that more authentic virtual representations enhance user engagement.

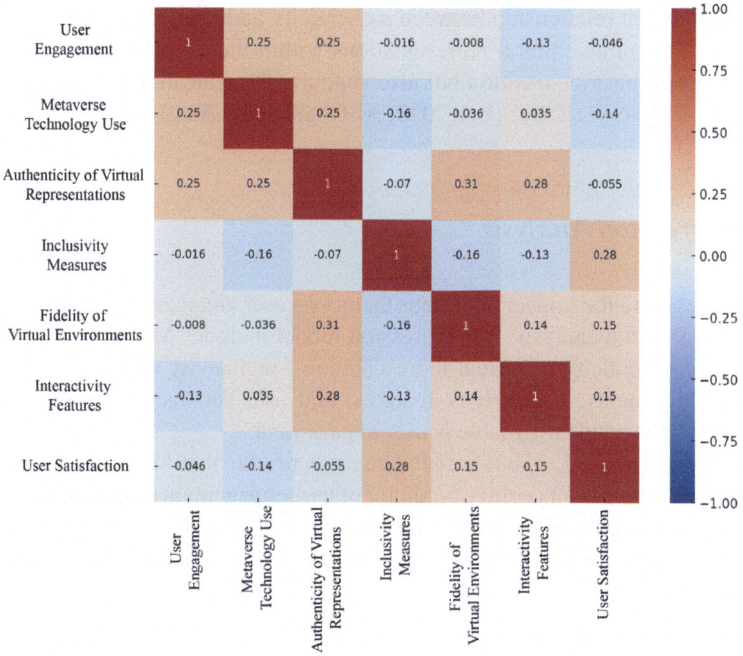

Fig. 1 Correlation matrix heatmap

- Metaverse Technology Use and Authenticity of Virtual Representations: There is a strong positive relationship ($r = 0.307$, $p < 0.01$), showing that users who value authentic cultural heritage representations are more likely to engage with Metaverse technology.
- Metaverse Technology Use and Inclusivity Measures: There is a negative correlation ($r = -–0.16$), indicating potential challenges in ensuring inclusivity as Metaverse technology usage increases.
- Authenticity of Virtual Representations and Fidelity of Virtual Environments: There is a positive correlation ($r = 0.31$), suggesting that high fidelity in virtual environments is often associated with more authentic representations.
- Inclusivity Measures and User Satisfaction: There is a positive correlation ($r = 0.28$), indicating that effective inclusivity measures are associated with higher user satisfaction.
- Interactivity Features and User Engagement: There is a slightly negative correlation ($r = -–0.13$), suggesting that current interactivity features may not be significantly enhancing user engagement.
- User Engagement and User Satisfaction: There is a slightly negative correlation ($r = -0.046$), indicating that user satisfaction alone does not directly drive engagement in the Metaverse.

The significant relationship between authenticity and user engagement reaffirms the need for accurate cultural representations within the Metaverse. This not only fosters a deeper user connection but also supports the educational value of virtual cultural heritage experiences (Lyu 2022; Al-Ghaili et al. 2022).

4.2 Regression Analysis

To further explore the impact of various factors on user engagement, we employed a multiple regression analysis. The regression model includes Metaverse technology utilization, authenticity of virtual representations, inclusivity measures, fidelity of virtual environments, interactivity features, and user satisfaction as independent variables. The dependent variable is user engagement.

As shown in Table 1, The regression analysis reveals that Metaverse technology utilization is a significant positive predictor of user engagement (coefficient = 0.360, $t = 3.932$, $p < 0.001$). This finding underscores the critical role of advanced and accessible Metaverse technologies in enhancing user interaction and engagement with cultural heritage.

Theoretical Implications: These findings contribute to UX design theory by illustrating the importance of designing Metaverse environments that balance technological sophistication with user-centric principles. This extends the work of Berni and Borgianni (2021), emphasizing the need for environments that prioritize clarity, ease of use, and emotional resonance.

Practical Applications: For Metaverse developers, this research underlines the necessity of incorporating advanced technologies and ensuring content authenticity while also focusing on making platforms accessible to diverse audiences. These insights are invaluable for cultural institutions seeking to engage users effectively in virtual heritage spaces.

Table 1 Regression coefficients

Model	Unstandardized coefficients	Standardized coefficients	t	Sig.
	B	Std. error	Beta	
(Constant)	3.191	0.617		5.170
Metaverse technology utilization	0.360	0.092	0.285	3.932

4.3 Recommendations for Future Research

The findings of this study suggest several promising avenues for future research that can deepen our understanding of cultural heritage engagement within the Metaverse. One important area to investigate further is the role of social interactions and community features in the Metaverse. By examining how these social components affect user engagement with cultural heritage, future studies could utilize longitudinal methods or experimental designs to capture the evolving dynamics of user interactions over time.

Another critical area for exploration is the long-term impact of Metaverse experiences on users' knowledge, attitudes, and behaviors towards cultural heritage preservation. This could involve employing both qualitative and quantitative research methods to understand not just the immediate effects, but also how sustained exposure to virtual cultural heritage environments influences users' perceptions and actions in the long run.

Inclusivity measures within Metaverse platforms also demand more attention. Developing and testing new inclusivity strategies is essential to ensure that virtual environments are accessible to a diverse audience, including people with disabilities and those from various cultural backgrounds. For instance, future research could involve user testing with diverse demographic groups to identify specific inclusivity needs and design solutions that address these challenges effectively.

Moreover, the rapid advancement of technology presents opportunities to enhance the fidelity and interactivity of virtual environments. Future studies could explore how emerging technologies, such as haptic feedback and AI-driven personalization, can improve user experiences and engagement. Investigating these technological advancements can provide insights into how to create more immersive and engaging virtual cultural heritage spaces.

By focusing on social interactions, long-term impacts, inclusivity measures, and technological advancements can provide a comprehensive understanding of how to enhance cultural heritage engagement in the Metaverse. These research directions not only address the current gaps identified in this study but also pave the way for creating more inclusive, engaging, and educational virtual environments.

5 Conclusion

This study investigated the Metaverse's capacity as a platform for cultural heritage engagement. By analyzing survey responses from 200 participants, it advocates for leveraging Metaverse technology to foster immersive and authentic experiences. The findings highlight the critical role of advancements in virtual environments that emphasize accessibility and user-centric design, promoting inclusive and authentic interactions with cultural heritage.

The study underscores the necessity of ensuring that these virtual platforms remain accessible to a diverse audience. The positive correlation between technology utilization and user engagement illustrates the importance of intuitive and advanced Metaverse technologies. Authentic virtual representations play a vital role in enhancing user engagement, emphasizing the need for accuracy in digital cultural depictions.

This research supports the strategic use of Metaverse technology to create enriching cultural heritage experiences. By addressing the identified challenges and focusing on user-centric design, cultural heritage professionals and technologists can develop Metaverse environments that foster meaningful and impactful cultural interactions.

Acknowledgements The authors acknowledge Dubai Police and Dubai Culture for their collaboration and support in this research project. We acknowledge the invaluable assistance provided by both entities. Their support has been instrumental in shaping the outcome of this research.

References

Al-Ghaili, A. M., Kasim, H., Al-Hada, N. M., Hassan, Z., Othman, M., Hussain, T. J., Kasmani, R. M., & Shayea, I. (2022). A review of metaverse's definitions, architecture, applications, challenges, issues, solutions, and future trends. IEEE Access.

Alkhatib, Y. J., Forte, A., Bitelli, G., Pierdicca, R., & Malinverni, E. (2023). Bringing Back Lost Heritage into Life by 3D Reconstruction in Metaverse and Virtual Environments: The Case Study of Palmyra, Syria. International Conference on Extended Reality.

Allam, Z., Sharifi, A., Bibri, S. E., Jones, D. S., & Krogstie, J. (2022). The metaverse as a virtual form of smart cities: Opportunities and challenges for environmental, economic, and social sustainability in urban futures. Smart Cities, 5(3), 771–801.

Berni, A., & Borgianni, Y. (2021). From the definition of user experience to a framework to classify its applications in design. Proceedings of the Design Society, 1, 1627–1636.

Buhalis, D., Leung, D., & Lin, M. (2023). Metaverse as a disruptive technology revolutionising tourism management and marketing. Tourism Management, 97, 104724.

Chandra, Y. (2022). Non-fungible token-enabled entrepreneurship: A conceptual framework. Journal of Business Venturing Insights, 18, e00323.

Cruz Franco, P. A., Rueda Márquez de la Plata, A., & Gómez Bernal, E. (2022). Protocols for the graphic and constructive diffusion of digital twins of the architectural heritage that guarantee universal accessibility through AR and VR. Applied Sciences, 12(17), 8785.

Dirin, A., Nieminen, M., Laine, T.H. (2023). Feelings of being for mobile user experience design. International Journal of Human–Computer Interaction 39(20), 4059–4079.

Fan, Z., Chen, C., & Huang, H. (2022). Immersive cultural heritage digital documentation and information service for historical figure metaverse: a case of Zhu Xi, Song Dynasty, China. Heritage Science, 10(1), 148.

Ferreira, C. (2012). Memory and heritage in Second Life: Recreating Lisbon in a virtual world. Journal of Gaming & Virtual Worlds, 4(1), 63–79.

French, A. M., Risius, M., & Shim, J. P. (2020). The interaction of virtual reality, blockchain, and 5G new radio: disrupting business and society. Communications of the Association for Information Systems, 46(1), 25.

Koo, C., Kwon, J., Chung, N., & Kim, J. (2023). Metaverse tourism: conceptual framework and research propositions. Current Issues in Tourism, 26(20), 3268–3274.

Longo, M. C., & Faraci, R. (2023). Next-Generation Museum: A Metaverse Journey into the Culture. Sinergie Italian Journal of Management, 41(1), 147–176.
Lyu, J. (2022). Cultural Heritage Preservation in the Metaverse: A Digitalized Student Study Tour of the Heritage Corridor of Sanjiang, Guangxi, China University of Cincinnati].
Martí-Testón, A., Muñoz, A., Gracia, L., & Solanes, J. E. (2023). Using WebXR Metaverse Platforms to Create Touristic Services and Cultural Promotion. Applied Sciences, 13(14), 8544.
Martins, D., Oliveira, L., & Amaro, A. C. (2022). The Spread of Cultural Heritage in Second Life: Case Study Amiais. World Conference on Information Systems and Technologies.
Mystakidis, S. (2022). Metaverse. Encyclopedia, 2(1), 486–497.
Paganopoulos, M. (2022). The Evolution of Representation from cave painting to terraforming: Metaverse worlds and the New Dialectics of Space. Anthropology, AI and the Future of Human Society.
Pouryousefzadeh, S., & Akbarzadeh, R. (2019). Internet of Things (IoT) systems in future cultural heritage. 2019 3rd International Conference on Internet of Things and Applications (IoT).
Rahmani, R., & Tienken, S. (2022). Distributed Meta-Learning for Context Based on Culture Heritage Collection Data in an Immersive Reality System. Procedia Computer Science, 210, 70–77.
Song, Y., Cao, J., Wu, K., Yu, P. L. H., & Lee, J. C.-K. (2023). Developing 'Learningverse'-a 3D Metaverse Platform to Support Teaching, Social and Cognitive Presences. IEEE Transactions on Learning Technologies.
Vital, R., & Sylaiou, S. (2022). Digital survey: How it can change the way we perceive and understand heritage sites. Digital Applications in Archaeology and Cultural Heritage, 24, e00212.
Zhang, X., Yang, D., Yow, C. H., Huang, L., Wu, X., Huang, X., Guo, J., Zhou, S., & Cai, Y. (2022). Metaverse for cultural heritages. Electronics, 11(22), 3730.

Development of AI Digital Human Based the Emperor Qin Shi Huang Terracotta Warriors XR Contents

Rebecca Jiyun Lee, Limao Yanchi, and Jin Ho Park

Abstract Digital restoration of traditional cultural heritage has been ongoing for some time. After experiencing the pandemic, the demand for contactless digital content increased significantly in countries around the world, especially in China. The protection of traditional cultural heritage has also been strengthened through policy measures. This study analyzes the political and social environment factors in China in the twenty-first century and examines a case where the Terracotta Army of Qin Shi Huang was developed into digital content. By analyzing China's political and social environment factors and aligning with the revival of smart tourism, digitalization should be industrially developed to meet the demands of the era. Lastly, the study discusses the development and utilization plans for such content.

Keywords Traditional Cultural Heritage · China culture industry · Digital contents · Digital Human · The Emperor Qinshihuang's Mausoleum

1 Introduction

The Emperor Qinshihuang's Mausoleum(秦始皇陵兵马俑) is located in Xi'an, Shanxi province, China. It was designated as the first national cultural heritage reserve by the Chinese City Council on March 4, 1961, and was listed as a World Heritage Site by UNESCO on December 7, 1987. Representing China, it is a UNESCO World Heritage Site and stands as one of the premier tourist attractions, drawing approximately 15 million visitors annually. However, there is a limitation as visitors can

R. J. Lee (✉)
Faculty of Technology Management, Kyung Hee University, Suwon, South Korea
e-mail: rebeccajiyunlee@khu.ac.kr

L. Yanchi
ByteDance Executive Producer, Beijing, China
e-mail: yclmmm@126.com

J. H. Park
Faculty of Korea University, Sejong, South Korea
e-mail: arkology@naver.com

T. Jung et al. (eds.), *XR and Metaverse*, Springer Proceedings in Business and Economics, https://doi.org/10.1007/978-3-031-77975-6_13

only view it by visiting The Emperor Qinshihuang's Mausoleum site Museum on the west coast of China. Simultaneously, efforts have been made to replicate the Qinshihuang's Terracotta Warriors anywhere in the world through digital media.

Over the past decade, contents of the Qinshihuang's Terracotta Warrior has been produced using VR (Virtual Reality) or AR (Augmented Reality). These methods prioritize the advantage of providing an experience without physically visiting the site, although no technology has yet replicated the true experience of being there in person. The Emperor Qinshihuang's Mausoleum is building that combines cultural technology technology through ICT (Information and Communication Technologies), and has built a VR experience center during COVID-19, which is currently in service. The purpose of this paper is to propose a more comprehensive digital experience of cultural heritage through artificial convergence technology, utilizing Extended Reality (XR) and Artificial Intelligence (AI). Through this, we aim to achieve a digital virtual travel experience that closely resembles the historical site through XR and AI.

2 Literature Review

The 1974 discovery of Terracotta army, built for China's first emperor, is regarded as one of the greatest archaeological finds of twenty-first century (Yunang Hu et al., 2022). The first Qin Emperor had his burial complex built in preparation for his death. In accordance with The ancient Chinese view that the human soul is immortal, the emperor needed objects and structures to enjoy in his afterlife (Xianqu Fan, 2019). The most astonishing thing in the terracotta army is the vividly crafted terracotta figures themselves. They are actually the ancient Qin people. These figures, made from fine clay of the Loess Plateau, are fired uniformly at temperatures exceeding 1,100 °C to achieve their completion. Judging by the optimistic expressions on their surfaces, these figures, completed over 20 years by approximately 80 specialized craftsmen and numerous laborers confirmed so far, serve as milestones of ancient handicraft history. + They are products that could only emerge under the powerful authority like Emperor Qin, not just anyone's achievement.

These terracotta figures varied in body size, armor, and ceremonial attire according to their ranks and positions. Even individuals holding the same rank exhibited diverse features such as facial hair, hairstyles, shoes, and belt buckles. They provided groundbreaking data across various fields of study including ancient military history, costume history, daily life, and science, resembling a sort of archaeological encyclopedia. What's even more intriguing is recent research revealing that originally, all these terracotta figures were painted, once again astonishing observers with their authenticity.

As I have already mentioned, it is a UNESCO World Heritage Site and stands as one of the premier tourist attractions, drawing approximately 15 million visitors annually. However, there is a limitation as visitors can only view it by visiting The Emperor Qinshihuang's Mausoleum site Museum on the west coast of China. After the COVID-19 pandemic, the digital cultural industry grew rapidly, and the combination of cultural heritage, science and technology, and creativity opened up infinite possibilities (毕颖华, 2021).

The rapid advancement of early technologies has redirected the focus of the service industry. Over the past decade, the People's Republic of China has unquestionably emerged as a leading force in global digital marketing (Nikola Zivlak et al., 2022). Consumers have now embraced digital consumption (Yenni Tima et al., 2020).

Utilizing information technology to develop the Terracotta Warriors as a historical and cultural heritage resource, and expanding the market for historical and cultural heritage consumption, not only promotes local economic growth but also meets the needs of the cultural industry. This approach realizes the close integration of culture and technology, comprehensively enhancing the innovative capabilities of the cultural and arts industry through high-tech advancements.

3 Digital Restoration About the Emperor Qinshihuang's Terracotta Warriors

3.1 Organizing the Primary Data for Digital Restoration: 3D Modelling

The Mausoleum of the First Qin Emperor Museum is located in Xi'an, Shaanxi province, China. Shaanxi is rich in historical and cultural heritage resources, with Xi'an, the provincial capital, serving as the political and economic center for thirteen dynasties and the starting point of the ancient Silk Road (Youngzhen Zou, 2021). As a World Heritage Site, it stands as one of the premier tourist attractions, but it can only be viewed by visiting The Emperor Qinshihuang's Mausoleum site Museum on the west coast of China. Simultaneously, efforts have been made to replicate the Qinshihuang's Terracotta Warriors anywhere in the world through digital media.

Besides the vast cultural scenes like the Mausoleum of the First Qin Emperor, there are also modern cultural landmarks such as the Tang Paradise, making it home to numerous internationally renowned cultural IPs and world-class cultural tourism sites. These cultural resources are invaluable assets in the fields of human culture, history, society, and economic development. They also serve as important content and sources of creativity for the national cultural industry (Fig. 1).

This involves a digital restoration process based on historical records such as Sima Qian's historical text, 'Records of the Grand Historian (史記)', as there are no photographs or precise documents depicting the actual appearance of Emperor Qin Shi Huang's mausoleum and the Terracotta Warriors from that time. The digital restoration of the XR content for Emperor Qin Shi Huang's mausoleum and the Terracotta Warriors involves three main stages: ① 3D scanning work for terracotta soldiers excavated from the terracotta mine site and its original archiving data construction. ② Virtual digital restoration through 3D modelling based on the historical evidence

Fig. 1 Results of aerial archaeological analysis of Qinshihuang's terracotta warriors (The first Terracotta Warriors (第一个坑)

of scholars in Jin (秦) countries ③ The production stage is divided into content utilization applying virtual production display technology.

Meanwhile, various types of SCAN, 3D, 3D stereoscopic, VR, and AR content related to the Tomb of Emperor Qin Shi Huang have been produced. Earlier, the Laboratory of the Information Technology Research Center for Cultural Heritage Conservation at Tianjin University in China has been working on a project to build circular 3D data of the West Bank's Qin Shi Huangtung Terracotta Warrior through three-dimensional scanning for years (Felix Hou, 2006) (Fig. 2).

Fig. 2 The Laboratory of the Information Technology Research Center for Cultural Heritage Conservation at Tianjin University in China Circular 3D scanning jobs (left), A scene from MACRO GRAPN., corp's VR silk road

3.2 The Emperor Qinshihuang's Terracotta Warriors Contents

In the past, the Korean VFX company Macrograph also planned a global content project based on the legend of Emperor Qin Shi Huang's pursuit of the Elixir of Immortality. This narrative revolves around the story of dispatching numerous soldiers across Asia in search of the Elixir of Immortality. The project centre around the character 'Seobok (2021, actor Park Bo-gum),' a soldier buried in the mausoleum of Emperor Qin Shi Huang. The envisioned project takes the form of a Silk Road VR experience, with Seobok as the protagonist, traversing various locations throughout Asia.

Additionally, the Korean virtual reality company Lita Corporation released a VR experience called "Lost World," which operates within a VR environment. This groundbreaking content is the world's first virtual reality experience that allows users to explore both the exterior surroundings of Emperor Qin Shi Huang's mausoleum, where the Terracotta Warriors are located, and the interior of the mausoleum itself.

In China, for example, China Central Television (CCTV) Science and Education Channel's program "Chinese Memory《国家记忆》," which took over three months to produce, successfully implemented a fusion media technology that allows VR images to be played on large screens via mobile phones. The hosts and guests interacted with online audiences using iPads and presented the results of the web-based "Digital Dunhuang (敦煌)" project on large on-site screens. For the first time, VR filming technology was used in the program's creation. Over 100 min of footage of the Terracotta Warriors was filmed, and post-production resulted in a nearly three-minute video titled "The Terracotta Warriors in VR Perspective," which was released on the CCTV website and widely disseminated on iPads and mobile devices.

The technical feature of this innovation is its ability to capture a 360° panoramic view, covering the scenic area and the three exhibition halls of the Terracotta Warriors. This provides the audience with a visual experience different from traditional perspectives. The use of this new technology aims to achieve a new form of visual expression in cultural programs, injecting innovative highlights into the show. VR technology enables the audience to enter the perspective of cultural heritage excavation sites. With VR lenses, it simulates placing the audience amidst the array of Terracotta Warriors, allowing them to experience the feeling of being part of the soldier formation and standing shoulder to shoulder with the grand formations from over 2,000 years ago. This novel visual presentation is undoubtedly an exciting creative practice experience.

4 Changing the Emperor Qinshihuang's Terracotta Warriors Museum in Virtual Reality

The Emperor Qinshihuang's Mausoleum site Museum on the west coast of China. Museums today function as more than a repository of objects—they are institutions that create social and cultural experiences for their visitors. As technology continues to evolve and consumers' demands grow more sophisticated, museums are being compelled to explore methods to engage with the public. At the Qin Museum, the pressing need for societal relevancy is digital transformation: Actualizing techno-influence for identity revitalization, digital contents, data (Zhang et al., 2018) (Fig. 3).

Regarding the Qin armoured warriors (秦甲士), this is a cultural and creative digital IP collection based on Qin culture, jointly issued by the Museum of the First Emperor of Qin and the digital collection platform iBox (Fig. 4).

"There is a new demand from society put forward for museums. Museums are no longer a place solely for knowledge and history, they are also a place to provide entertainment and to engage and interact with visitors… we need to find an engaging and fun way to allow everyone to understand history, and eventually, achieve our

Fig. 3 The Emperor Qinshihuang's Mausoleum site Museum

Fig. 4 Museum souvenir-the Qin armored warriors (秦甲士)

goal of preserving the history, preserving the Chinese culture."–Curator Hou in a public interview.

Emerging technologies provide new opportunities to enhance the museum experience. An analysis of the Qin Museum reveals how it leveraged AR technologies, social media, and mobile platforms to revitalize its identity. First, the capabilities of AR technologies were harnessed to create ground breaking digital experiences in museums. As the custodian of a vast mausoleum site containing countless artifacts, the Qin Museum has faced challenges in developing interactive experiences for its visitors (Xilian Luo, 2021). For instance, to prevent weathering, around 5000 terracotta warriors remain entombed in several pits, while many excavated relics are stored away, awaiting restoration before they can be displayed to the public. To date, only around 2000 restored terracotta warriors are on display for public view. The museum professionals recognized the potential of AR technologies in overcoming this challenge.

Our analysis indicates that AR technologies provide several opportunities for enhancing interactive and immersive museum experience. For instance, AR enables the creation of an "augmented reality", where virtual objects are superimposed onto the physical environment, opening up new ways to present and communicate information. In our case study, we observe how exhibition experts at the Qin Museum have utilized this technology to bring history to life. An AR-enabled application has been developed, offering visitors an exceptionally close and detailed view of the museum site and its artifacts. The application integrates over a thousand high-definition photos taken from multiple angles, creating a 20-billion-pixel panoramic image with a 360° view of the museum. It highlights both excavation pits 1 and 3 and is accessible on both desktop and mobile devices, allowing visitors to explore the terracotta warriors' grandeur with remarkable detail (Fig. 5).

The Terracotta Warriors VR Experience Center project at the Museum of the Terracotta Warriors of Qin Shi Huang relies on 5G technology to build a dedicated cloud VR platform (Look at Fig. 4.) This platform researches real artifact restoration

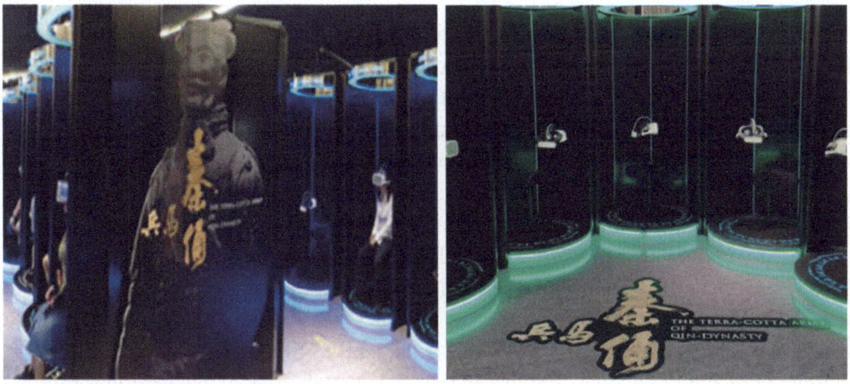

Fig. 5 The Terracotta Warriors VR Experience (秦始皇兵马俑VR沉浸式体验)

Fig. 6 The Museum of Terracotta Warriors hologram video experience

based on laser scanning and large-scale digital scene reproduction technology. On this foundation, dynamic digital interaction technology and a personalized recommendation system are applied to enhance the immersive experience. The project aims to develop a comprehensive virtual reality (VR) operation system for the Terracotta Warriors and implement a demonstration application. Ultimately, the goal is to create a replicable immersive VR experience solution customized for the cultural and museum industry IP. Based on the experience from the already operational "Terracotta Warriors VR Theater," the feasibility of a VR theater solution customized for the cultural and museum industry IP has been demonstrated. This initiative represents an innovative exploration where the cultural and museum industry actively participates in the integration of culture and technology, aiding in the reform of new cultural consumption (周珏. 2017) (Fig. 6).

5 Restoring the Original Color Using XR

In this paper, the intention is to propose the creation of content featuring Emperor Qin Shi Huang's mausoleum and the Terracotta Warriors using XR technology instead of traditional VR. The reconstruction of the mausoleum and the Terracotta Warriors, based on historical documents and authenticity, is more akin to a "reconstruction" rather than a mere representation. This endeavour aims to recreate the ancient appearance of the Qin(秦) Dynasty from over 2,200 years ago, emphasizing the significance of utilizing XR technology for a more immersive and authentic experience.

Qin Shi Huang dreamed of eternal life as the emperor who founded the Qin Dynasty, China's first centralized unified empire, but died during his tour at the age of 50. The Terracotta Army of Qin Shi Huang's Mausoleum was discovered by a farmer while digging to find a well, and is currently only partially excavated due to technical reasons. The most convincing theory is that the risk of excavation is high by creating water streams such as rivers and lakes with mercury in the tomb so that the

Fig. 7 The Terracotta Warriors

emperor can exercise great power in the afterlife. It was a great history, with 800,000 people mobilized to build the king's tomb, accounting for 4% of the 20 million people of the Qin Dynasty at the time. XR technology combines virtual reality (VR) and augmented reality (AR) and provides users with a higher sense of immersion. Through XR technology, users can freely explore the inside of the Terracotta Army and feel the history and culture of the Terracotta Army more vividly. Numerous digital contents have been created for the tomb of Qin Shi Huang and the Terracotta Army. However, no matter what content it was, it was a one-sided appreciation of flat displays, and there was no experience technology that achieved immersion into space at that time through a 360° environment (Fig. 7).

Qin Shi Huang dreamed of eternal life as the emperor who founded the Qin Dynasty, China's first centralized unified empire, but died during his tour at the age of 50. The Terracotta Army of Qin Shi Huang's Mausoleum was discovered by a farmer while digging to find a well, and is currently only partially excavated due to technical reasons. The most convincing theory is that the risk of excavation is high by creating water streams such as rivers and lakes with mercury in the tomb so that the emperor can exercise great power in the afterlife. It was a great history, with 800,000 people mobilized to build the king's tomb, accounting for 4% of the 20 million people of the Qin Dynasty at the time. XR technology combines virtual reality (VR) and augmented reality (AR) and provides users with a higher sense of immersion. Through XR technology, users can freely explore the inside of the Terracotta Army and feel the history and culture of the Terracotta Army more vividly. Numerous digital contents have been created for the tomb of Qin Shi Huang and the Terracotta Army. However, no matter what content it was, it was a one-sided appreciation of flat displays, and there was no experience technology that achieved immersion into space at that time through a 360-degree environment.

XR technology stands out among other media for its unparalleled immersion and on-site experience, allowing users to feel as if they have traveled back to the actual past during the Qin Dynasty or experience the sensation of facing a 1:1 Terracotta Warrior. In terms of providing realism and a sense of being on-site, XR technology excels, offering a superior level of engagement compared to other media. By implementing

Fig. 8 Restoring the original color using XR

terracotta warriors with XR technology, you can feel as if the terracotta warriors' cultural assets are at the site (Fig. 8).

A more interesting fact is that recent research has revealed that all of these figures were originally painted when they were first created, which has once again astonished us with their realism. Figure 4 is XR content that reproduces these colors. It allows visitors to experience the same thing even if they don't go to Xi'an China, where The Emperor Qinshihuang's Mausoleum exists. Currently, the digital experience of cultural heritage is mainly limited to the experience of restored ruins and buildings. There is very little that shows people of the time by reproducing them as VR-type characters (digital humans). If real-life visitors can experience not only past building experiences but also AI-type technology to reproduce Qin Shi Huang, the original owner of Qin Shi Huang tombs, as an AI digital human being, freely communicate with visitors, and furthermore, enjoy life (生活相) in the city center of Jin Dynasty in the past, it will be a true "artificial fusion type extended reality (XR)" experience.

6 Development of Qinshihuang Digital Human

6.1 Artificial Intelligence (AI) Digital Human Overview

Digital Human refers to a virtual character created with computer graphics (CG) that can express appearances and actions almost similar to real living humans. This digital human technology is a game. It is used to produce CG contents such as movie special effects, 3D animation, and VFX. Recently, digital human technology has been used to produce video content that restores late artists, famous actors, and historical figures.

6.2 Artificial Intelligence Digital Human Production Process

3D Digital Human technology is employed to recreate historical figures from the past, enhanced with AI capabilities. This digital human restoration project revives individuals who once lived but no longer exist. By integrating artificial intelligence, these digital recreations bring to life characters that previously only existed in portraits, allowing for the creation of interactive content that engages audiences with figures from history.

As a China domestic case, when Digital Heritage is combined with Artificial Intelligence (AI), AI-driven content provides explanations of the heritage site. While AI technology has a wide range of applications, at this stage, a practical solution is the use of interactive AI content for cultural heritage guidance, offering dynamic and personalized experiences for visitors. The "Qin Warriors" is a series of IPs created by the "Qin Warriors Dream Factory," an IP creation team from the Museum of the Mausoleum of the First Qin Emperor. Based on Qin culture and incorporating cultural elements extracted from artifacts unearthed at the Mausoleum, the "Qin Warriors" series uses interpretive thinking to design elements. Through the three chapters of Qin's division, alliances, and rise, the IP elements are refined to embody the invincibility of the Qin army. The Qin Warriors, like newborn calves clad in Armor, dream fearlessly, embodying the core spirit of Qin culture.

"Qin Warriors" is based on the culture of the Qin Dynasty and incorporates cultural elements extracted from artifacts unearthed at the Mausoleum of the First Qin Emperor. Through interpretive thinking and design, the project depicts the division, alliances, and rise of the Qin Dynasty across three chapters. It refines the IP elements to showcase the invincibility of the Qin army. The newly-born Qin warriors, clad in armor and full of dreams, fearlessly embody the core spirit of Qin culture.

6.3 Artificial Intelligence Digital Human Production Process

Technical Elements Explanation: First, we use the Unreal Engine 4 real-time engine to restore representative Terracotta Warriors characters. Then, we bring this restored Terracotta Warrior to life, adding movement and a storyline. At this point, we use 2D animation in the intro section to convey an overall worldview, allowing the audience to understand our creative intent. Finally, we use the Unreal Engine 4 real-time engine again to create 360° VR content, providing an immersive first-person perspective experience of the legendary journey of this restored Terracotta Warrior character. Of course, with the progressive development of AI technology, we will also conduct dialogue and interaction tests with this restored Terracotta Warrior character using large AI models. Additionally, we will employ generative AI methods from Testto Video to produce more video content. During the AI production process using Test to Video, we will ultimately use the Sora creation tool released by OpenAI to create historical biographies of Terracotta Warrior characters. These videos will be automatically generated in the Test to Video format. Before Sora is officially launched, we will first use the Image to Video and Video to Video methods for AI video production. After setting up virtual camera positions with Unreal Engine 4, we will create video scenes based on 3D digital models of the Terracotta Warriors. The backgrounds, character transformations, and FX within the video scenes will be automatically generated using Stability AI's Comfy UI.

7 Conclusion

The Emperor the Qin Shi Huang's Mausoleum is a cultural heritage site that has been excavated since 1974, but the excavation work has not yet been completed. However, there is a limit to seeing The Emperor the Qin Shi Huang's Mausoleum only if one visits The Emperor the Qin Shi Huang's Mausoleum site Museum. In response, this paper proposed "eXtendid Reality(XR)" technology for the UNESCO World Heritage experience. Previously, the Terracotta Army at the Mausoleum of Qinshihuang was limited to a VR cultural heritage experience. Currently, there is a focus on watching videos, but using the XR content, in the case of Terracotta Warriors at the Tomb of Qinshihuang, the scope is expanded to allow viewers to freely experience the target cultural property by giving them autonomy. In this way, by combining the XR technology with the artificial intelligence digital human technology, the effect of a more realistic experience can be increased for the users. For example, in the process of exploring the inside of the Terracotta Warriors, an artificial intelligence digital human can provide the functions such as explaining the history and culture of the Terracotta Warriors to the user or having a conversation with the user. In addition, by combining artificial intelligence digital human technology, customized Q&A services can be provided to the XR Terracotta Warriors experiencers. For example, it is possible to provide customized content based on the viewer's cultural tastes during the Qin Dynasty or interests in the Qin Empire. In addition, 'Qinshihuang AI Digital Human' can provide customized answers according to the level of questions asked by the audience. This is a kind of the XR Interactive (XR User Interface). The Qin Shi Huang Terracotta Warriors XR contents could be used as a stage for the relevant performances or musicals, and 'AI Qin Shi Huang' made of AI digital humans might make their appearances. This kind of XR contents could be used for various marketing purposes. In a situation where artificial intelligence is developing day by day, it goes beyond the offline VR/AR contents and is combined with the online artificial intelligence to experience the Qin Shi Huang Terracotta Warriors at home and compile the audience DIY-typed discussions and imaginations to facilitate the future generations learn about their cultural heritage, thereby heightening their interest and allowing for the free digital experiences.

In conclusion, based on the 'artificial fusion' technology which combines the XR and AI, one could visit the inside of the Terracotta Warriors, which is impossible to enter, and also see Emperor Qin Shi Huang, a figure from the Qin Dynasty 2,500 years ago. Given which, this technology may also be applied to other historic sites in the future. Ultimately, the XR technology would become a digital cultural heritage platform where one could experience the world cultural heritage.

References

Felix, H. (2006). Virtual color reconstruction performed on the 3D model of a selected figure from the Terracotta Army, Virtual Reality : colour reconstruction, *Final Report*, 55~90.

Nikola, Z., Shiyuan, Zhang., Yueqi, Shi. Digital Marketing in China - Weibo and Fan Economy.

Xianqu, F. (2019). What should we interpret first in an archaeological site: A value based identification of character defining features in first Qin emperor's mausoleum, Columbia University, Master of Science in Historic Preservation, 1~101

Xilian, L., Yuexi, D., Chuck, W. Yu., Zhaolin, G. (2021). The practice of local environment control for the funerary pits of Emperor Qin's Mausoleum Site museum, *Indoor and built environment*, Vol 30(3), 293–297.

Yongzhen, Zou. (2021) A Case Study on Service and Management of the Emperor Qinshihuang's Mausoleum Site Museum, *Scientific Research Publishing 14*, 576–584.

Yenni, Tima., Taohua, Ouyang., Delin Zengc. (2020). Back to the future: Actualizing technology affordances to transform Emperor Qin's terracotta warriors Museum> ScienceDirect. Volume 57, Issue 8, 103271

Yungang Hu, Desheng Lan, Jingyang Wang, Miaole Hou, Songnian Li, Xiuzhen Li, Lei Zhu, (2022). Measurement and analysis of facial features of terracotta warriors based on high-precision 3D point clouds, Heritage Science, 10–40.

Zhang, L., Weiying, Q., Zhao, K., Wang, L. (2018). VR Games and the Dissemination of Cultural Heritage, *Springer International Publishing*, 439~451.

毕颖华. (2021). 基于文博行业IP定制的沉浸式VR体验技术研发与应用研究:以秦始皇帝陵博物馆兵马俑VR体验中心为例,Seience Technology and Industry,jk 21(5)

周珏. (2017) . 当兵马俑遇到上VR–回顾《中国记忆》特别节目完成史上首次秦始皇兵马俑VR拍摄以及融媒体技术的实施, Arts & Teclnology, 119–122.

XR-Mediated Cultural Experiences: Enhancing Visitor Engagement

Jiaxin Liu

Abstract The utilisation of digital technologies for enhancing experiences has been on the rise in various industries. Lately, there has been a growing interest in the cultural and tourism sectors regarding the adoption of emerging technologies, specifically extended reality (XR). XR technologies facilitate interactive and immersive experiences that go beyond traditional exhibitions, catering to the diverse needs of various audiences. This study examines six XR exhibits; data were analysed using thematic analysis to reveal the potential of XR on engagement and provide guidance for future implementation. The findings reveal four key themes, (1) XR-based information contextualisation, (2) XR-enhanced interaction, (3) XR-enhanced immersion, and (4) XR-induced emotional connection. This study emphasises the potential of XR technologies in offering immersive and interactive cultural experiences. It also provides future research areas.

Keywords Extended reality · Interaction · Immersion · Cultural experience

1 Introduction

The utilisation of various media formats promotes a multimodal strategy for the dissemination, communication, and interpretation of art and cultural heritage within cultural institutions (Bekele et al., 2018; Silva & Teixeira, 2022). Digital technologies facilitate novel forms of interaction with cultural content (Bekele et al., 2018; Cameron & Kenderdine, 2010; Silva & Teixeira, 2022). Several cultural institutions have adopted innovative digital methods to offer their visitors immersive and interactive experiences that cannot be achieved in traditional exhibitions (Bekele et al., 2018; Silva & Teixeira, 2022). Extended Reality (XR) is a new concept that is becoming increasingly important in the cultural heritage context within the field of digital technology (Bekele et al., 2018; Carulli et al., 2023; Han et al., 2018; Jung et al., 2016; Trunfio et al., 2020a).

J. Liu (✉)
Department of Media and Culture Studies, Utrecht University, Utrecht, Netherlands
e-mail: j.liu1@uu.nl

T. Jung et al. (eds.), *XR and Metaverse*, Springer Proceedings in Business and Economics, https://doi.org/10.1007/978-3-031-77975-6_14

The integration of XR technology enables museums and cultural spaces to offer more immersive, interactive, and meaningful experiences (Bekele et al., 2018; Komianos, 2022; Silva & Teixeira, 2022; Zhou et al., 2022), while also reaching a broader range of audiences with diverse needs and expectations. Although many empirical (Hammady et al., 2021; Tussyadiah et al., 2018; Verhulst et al., 2021), explorative (Petrelli & Roberts, 2023), and review (Bekele et al., 2018) studies have investigated the implementation of XR technologies in cultural institutions, XR is still growing and cultural institutions are constantly optimising visitor experience strategies. It is necessary to review recent exhibits to understand key factors influencing XR-mediated cultural experiences in engaging visitors, in this evolving field. This article provides an analysis of XR approaches within the cultural heritage domain, examining previous practices of XR-mediated cultural experiences and offering valuable perspectives for future implementations.

2 Literature Review

2.1 Extended Reality (XR) and Its Implementation in Cultural Heritage Contexts

Extended reality (XR) is a broad term that includes augmented reality (AR), mixed reality (MR), and virtual reality (VR). These technologies combine the real and virtual worlds to create sensory experiences through different ways (Bekele et al., 2018). Cultural institutions utilise extended reality to offer alternative visitation options, allowing visitors to perceive art and cultural heritage in a new dimension. An interactive and immersive environment not only provides access to art and cultural knowledge but also enhances the overall experience of art and cultural heritage (Bekele et al., 2018; Liu, 2023).

Augmented reality (AR) overlays virtual information onto our view of the real world. Its purpose is to improve our understanding and perception of the real world (Bekele et al., 2018). Augmented reality offers several benefits that appeal to cultural institutions, including enhanced museum navigation and supplementary information for museum artefacts; additionally, augmented reality empowers cultural institutions to revive historical objects and events by means of reinterpretations and representations (Han et al., 2019a, b; Kenderdine et al., 2014; Marto et al., 2019). AR highlights the importance of obtaining context-specific information for visitors. Visitors can use a mobile device to activate the superimposition by scanning a physical object or a printed version. This action allows them to receive the content. Technological advancements have enhanced the efficiency and user-friendliness of augmented reality. Several studies suggest that augmented reality can improve the museum experience by creating an interactive and enjoyable environment for visitors; it also helps facilitate visitors' learning experience, offers digital reconstructions, and provides an additional information platform (Bekele et al., 2018; Tom Dieck & Jung, 2017).

Mixed reality (MR) creates a real-virtual environment that enhances our perception of both (Bekele & Champion, 2019). An interaction and relation space between users, virtual elements, and the real world co-exists in this environment (Bekele & Champion, 2019). In contrast to AR, where the real environment dominates, MR allows both environments to benefit from each other (Bekele & Champion, 2019). MR integrates virtual and real-world elements (Bekele & Champion, 2019) to help users understand the two worlds by letting them interact with them. Microsoft's aggressive HoloLens promotion has spread MR to museums, music performances, art education, and more (Sun, 2021). However, understanding MR can still be a bit confusing. Simply put, the MR experience, allows digital elements to be overlaid onto real-world environments like AR and also allows them to interact; it receives input from the environment and adjusts accordingly (Tremosa, 2023), such as spatial mapping for HoloLens (Hammady et al., 2019).

Virtual reality (VR) aims to enhance our immersion and engagement with a computer-generated environment, while excluding any visual or physical interaction with the real world (Bekele et al., 2018). VR is used in cultural institutions because of its ability to help museums and heritage sites offer visitors interactive and enhanced experiences; VR enables visitors to have educational, entertaining, escapist, and esthetic experiences (Lee et al., 2020). VR amplifies the feeling of actually being present in a given environment, thereby intensifying the pleasure derived from the experience for users (Verhulst et al., 2021). According to previous studies, VR may pose a challenge to physical museum visits; this is because VR can address problems associated with physical visits, such as inconvenience, which may lead visitors to believe that a real visit is no longer essential (Lee et al., 2020). Nevertheless, evidence has indicated that visitors hold the belief that a virtual tour or virtual experience cannot adequately replace an actual visit, as visitors still desire a genuine connection with the original work, however, virtual experiences could be a valuable tool in facilitating a genuine visit, whether it occurs onsite or offsite (Lee et al., 2020). Virtual reality provides visitors with an immersive environment that allows them to experience virtual artefacts or historical scenes as if they were real, while also gaining information in an interactive and engaging way.

2.2 *XR for Enhancing Interaction and Immersion*

The advent of digital transformation has fundamentally changed the way cultural institutions communicate and has enhanced visitors' engagement with the information they receive. According to Bekele et al. (2018), XR technologies have been employed to enhance museum experiences by incorporating narrative elements and interactive features, thereby making them more meaningful. XR digital interventions facilitate a seamless connection between the visitor's immersive experience and their virtual interaction with museum collections. The incorporation of educational elements and entertainment has broadened the possibilities for museums to enhance visitor engagement with their collections and the physical environment. XR revolutionises the way content is presented in museums and heritage sites, providing visitors with a new and innovative way to engage and interact. This leads to an improved museum experience and higher levels of satisfaction (Trunfio et al., 2020b). The interaction offers a diverse range of visitor experiences, enabling alternative methods of learning various forms of art and cultural heritage (Trunfio et al., 2022). Traditional museum facilities, such as descriptive panels, offer limited interactivity despite providing information and knowledge (Bekele et al., 2018). Several studies have found that interaction is a strong indicator of cognitive engagement, which is a key factor in promoting learning within an immersive environment (Bekele et al., 2018; Trunfio et al., 2022).

XR technology can also facilitate immersive experiences. Lately, immersive experiences have been defined as "the acceptance of one's involvement in the moment that is conceived through multiple senses, creating fluent and uninterrupted physical, mental, and/or emotional engagements with a present experience, with the ability to attain a lasting mental and emotional effect on the user post-experience" (Han et al., 2024). XR technologies enhance visitors' experiences in museums, heritage sites, and other cultural spaces by seamlessly combining elements from the real and virtual worlds (Bec et al., 2019). Immersion refers to the technical characteristic of a device that offers individuals with real-world sensorimotor experiences for perception and action. It measures the ability of a device to provide computer-generated input that enables the brain to construct a comprehensive and convincing representation of its environment through a perceptual fill-in mechanism (Verhulst et al., 2021). The immersion environment facilitates visitors' active exploration and understanding of intricate cultural objects (Kenderdine et al., 2014). An optimal immersion experience also replicates the auditory, tactile, kinetic, olfactory, and gustatory sensations. Immersive experiences aim to intensify the sensation of being present in a virtual environment (Bekele et al., 2018). Telepresence comprises two fundamental elements: seamless interaction and immersion within a virtual environment (Bekele et al., 2018). Compared to augmented reality, achieving a fully immersive experience is easier with mixed reality and virtual reality (Bekele et al., 2018).

3 Methodology

3.1 Sample and Data Collection

This study used a qualitative exploratory multiple case study method (Allal-Chérif, 2022) that examined six exhibits involving AR, MR, and VR (Table 1). Although the six cases under examination share certain similarities, they also exhibit significant differences. All chosen cases must pertain to the experience of cultural heritage and have been produced/exhibited in or after 2018. The data collection for each case encompassed a range of sources, including institutional and personal websites, museum media reports, and interview recordings. The size of the sample was

Table 1 Summary of the analysed studies

	Designation	Year	Displayed content	Context
AR	Hacking the Heist	2018	Painting	Art museum
	The Met Unframed	2020	Painting/Gallery	Art museum
MR	The Ghent Altarpiece Tour	2021	Painting/Architecture	Cathedral
	Revealing Krishna	2021	Sculpture	Art museum
VR	Mona Lisa: Beyond the Glass	2019	Painting	Art museum
	Eternal Notre-Dame	2022	Art/Architecture	Cathedral

determined by prior research conducted in a similar context (Allal-Chérif, 2022; Arrigoni & Galani, 2021).

3.2 Data Analysis

The case study method is particularly suitable for analysing contemporary, intricate, and complex topics, such as the application of XR and AI to improve the visitor experience (Allal-Chérif, 2022) or to comprehend digital interactive displays for dialogic remembering (Arrigoni & Galani, 2021). In the current study, case studies can be employed to study how XR technologies can be used to enhance visitor engagement; first through a single case study to gain an in-depth understanding of each case, and then through a cross-case analysis to understand how different types of XR engage visitors. The qualitative approach aims to offer a detailed, explanatory, and analytical description of the current and future applications of XR technology in the cultural and tourism sectors. The data analysis was conducted using thematic analysis (Allal-Chérif, 2022; Han et al., 2019a, b). The thematic analysis aims to identify the key themes of XR in relation to experiencing cultural heritage and engagement.

4 Case Studies

This section briefly introduces each analysed case. Space constraints prevent the author from providing more than a brief summary of each case; content sourced from institutional websites, museum media reports, and interview recordings.

- *Hacking the Heist* (2018) is an AR experience inspired by the 28th anniversary of the theft in the Isabella Stewart Gardner Museum. Users can scan empty frames to uncover stolen paintings and restore them to their original frames using the app (Hacking the Heist, 2018).

- *The Met Unframed* (2020) is a WebAR experience that enables audiences to use it anytime, anywhere, to visit virtual galleries, interact with The Met's art, and learn about art history. It is an effort by The Metropolitan Museum of Art to engage with live audiences in a safe and meaningful manner during the 2020 pandemic (UNIT9, n.d.).
- *The Ghent Altarpiece Tour* (2021) is an MR experience used during the visit to St Bavo's Cathedral. The cathedral is a place of worship, and the cable-free technology will keep it from getting damaged by putting in electric cables. A personal digital assistant leads the visitor from chapel to chapel through the cathedral, adding virtual layers of experience to the real environment of the cathedral (Alfavision, n.d.).
- *Revealing Krishna* (2021) is an MR experience offered by the Cleveland Museum of Art. In the background of an ancient sculpture of the Hindu god Krishna lifting a mountain lies a complicated story of upheaval, loss, and change. This guided experience was timed to bring six people together, and it brought the story of Krishna to life, offering visitors a new way to look at the enduring tale that has been told for thousands of years (Microsoft Unlocked, n.d.).
- *Mona Lisa: Beyond the Glass* (2019) is the first VR project by the Louvre, which makes use of the most recent scientific findings regarding Leonardo da Vinci's painting techniques and creative processes. With the help of virtual reality, the museum hopes that visitors to the Mona Lisa can get closer to this work of art, break through the barriers of fame, and uncover its hidden mysteries (Louvre Museum, 2021).
- *Eternal Notre-Dame* (2022) is a VR experience that enables visitors to travel through time, uncover the hidden secrets, and encounter the iconic figures of the Parisian cathedral, while admiring its magnificent architectural masterpieces. Visitors can immerse in the depths of Notre-Dame for 45 min, exploring the historical journey spanning from the 13th to the twenty-first century, and encountering the past (Eternelle Notre-Dame, n.d.).

5 Findings

5.1 XR-Based Information Contextualisation

XR technologies can provide information in different ways, and the type of information displayed in XR also varies. Different types of XR technologies can overlay, remix, or embed digital information. Access to previously inaccessible and difficult-to-understand information may benefit visitor learning and help museums achieve educational goals. Some museums noted they face physical restrictions and challenges in presenting or displaying contents, such as COVID-19, fragility of collections, prohibitions on installation of description panels, or theft of artworks; XR allows their visitors to "experience the eventful history" and "see what is no longer there". Virtual digital assistants were used in MR for wayfinding and guidance, "guarantees a smooth wayfinding and extra explanation for certain object". Museums recognised that the stories associated with collections are many, complex, difficult to tell through traditional formats, and limited description cannot unlock the story behind the artwork. MR allowed them to engage visitors in these complex stories, "see high-resolution 3-D holographic projections of sculptural pieces accompanied by spatial audio and narration as they experience the myth of Krishna lifting Mount Govardhan and come to understand the sculpture's history" and "presents the story, context, and new restoration of a masterwork in the museum's collection". Combining spatial audio and narration may further enhance the storytelling. Museums also noted that they are concerned with the information delivered through XR, so the content in XR was mostly based on scientific research, such as "the latest scientific research on Leonardo da Vinci" and "based on the knowledge compiled by exhibition curators Louis Frank and Vincent Delieuvin after a decade of research". A similar principle applied to another VR case, "Thanks to scientific surveys, and precise historical data, the cathedral and its surroundings have been precisely reproduced".

5.2 XR-Enhanced Interaction

XR experiences allow for interactivity. AR and VR cases enabled visitors to explore, "digitally placed the stolen art pieces back in their frames", "explore virtual galleries", "freely move around, interact with the art", "discover the secrets of an artwork", "discover the secrets and the emblematic characters of the Parisian Cathedral", "visitors will be able to move freely in a 500 sqm space in Virtual Reality", and providing users with the opportunity to "play", "solve puzzles, and take your favourite art home—in AR", it is "part AR, part game, part virtual tour". Interactions may also help users "learn about art history", or inspire them to learn or spark their interest and curiosity, "Users who proved to be worthy competitors were able to qualify as art loaners, unlocking the ability to receive a digital version of selected artworks to be loaned and displayed on their own private walls in AR, but only for a limited amount of time"; similar evidence includes "Visitors were put to the test in order to complete educational challenges and mini-games". MR may be used to support social interaction, for example, "This guided experience was timed to bring new groups of six visitors through the tour every two minutes, allowing for up to 36 visitors at a time".

5.3 XR-Enhanced Immersion

XR technologies can provide an immersive environment, but the level of immersion can vary with each type of XR. Art museum incorporated MR into their exhibition, "An immersive exhibit from the Cleveland Museum of Art brought this story to life, offering a fresh look at the enduring tale of Krishna passed down over millennia"; MR was also used in cathedrals to let users "experience the eventful history of the

Ghent Altarpiece as if you were there yourself". In AR, for instance, "a faithful true to scale replica of iconic spaces within the Met and created a newly imagined space within which fans could freely move around" can be recreated through WebAR and immersive 360 environments, and allowed users and art enthusiasts "to be transported into the heart of the Met and explore it as if they were truly there". Therefore, it is important to ensure the fidelity and realism of the environment. Furthermore, VR can offer a fully immersive experience due to the technology's unique characteristics, "This immersive VR experience, part of the Leonardo da Vinci exhibition in 2020, is also available on smartphone", and other evidence includes "a unique immersive virtual reality experience of this iconic landmark".

5.4 XR-Induced Emotional Connection

XR experiences were created to evoke emotional experiences and it may generate different types of emotions; when emotional connections were built, it may help visitors to "understand and memorise better". A famous painting, such as Mona Lisa, is known to almost everyone, but almost most people cannot get close to it on a "personal level". VR is "a way to create a strong emotional connection with the character". An AR case aimed to instil "feelings of wonder, hope, and inspiration", and the museum recognised the need to blur the lines between the physical and the digital and focus on the emotional impact through AR participation. The designer's ambition was to design VR experiences and create emotional connections within them. Furthermore, museums pointed out that "emotion" is one of the expectations of visitors, "In museums like everywhere else, people are seeking emotions". The cathedral's VR case also aimed to provide "a wonderful and emotional exploration". Additionally, in one case, visitors had a "wow" moment during their visit to the cathedral through MR.

6 Discussion

As technology progresses, visitors to museums and cultural institutions are increasingly looking for experiences that are interactive, immersive, personal, unique, and memorable. This requires these institutions to explore new ways of fostering a deeper level of engagement (Cranmer et al., 2020). Implementing the technological XR approach has the potential to greatly improve the traditional museum visit and enhance visitor engagement (Hammady et al., 2020). This study reveals the potential of XR-mediated experiences to engage visitors with cultural heritage and provides design implications (Fig. 1).

In order to enhance engagement, museums require supplementary mediation techniques to facilitate further learning (Hammady et al., 2020) through information contextualisation. XR experiences increase accessibility to previously inaccessible

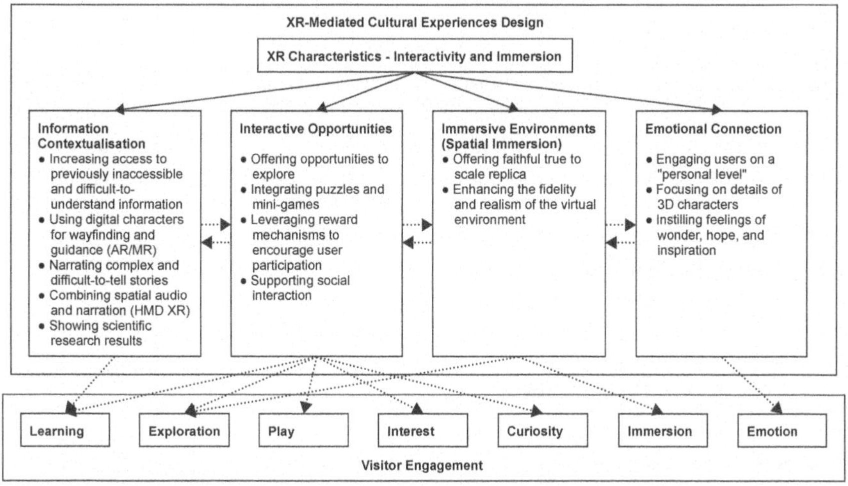

Fig. 1 Design implications for XR-mediated cultural experiences

information and facilitate narrate complex and difficult stories and display of scientific research results. Digital avatars can be used for wayfinding and guidance, and virtual characters can also be used to increase engagement with visitors through emotional communication (Hammady et al., 2020).

AR enables visitors to obtain interactive and informative information about artworks, making it a potential engagement tool (Cranmer et al., 2020; Moorhouse et al., 2019). Wearable MR is a non-intrusive approach that encourages engagement (Tom Dieck et al., 2018). MR improves the traditional museum visit by introducing new ways to enrich and amplify visitors' experiences, such as grabbing attention, increasing interest, and increasing engagement during their visits; it not only provides regular visitors with a new way to experience the museum, but it also appeals to new audiences and fosters cultural heritage and social memory (Trunfio et al., 2022). According to Bec et al. (2021) and Allal-Chérif (2022), VR has grown in popularity in recent years for improving engagement through an immersive virtual environment and visitor experience when combined with cultural exhibits. The emotional connection is believed to have a substantial impact on enhancing the memorability and lasting impression of an experience.

6.1 Theoretical Contributions

This study contributes to ongoing research topics on XR in the cultural sector, particularly its potential for visitor engagement. By examining six XR-mediated cultural experiences, four themes/strategies of XR's potential for visitor engagement are revealed, namely, XR-based information contextualisation, XR-enhanced interaction, XR-enhanced immersion, and XR-induced emotional connection. It highlights these potential areas within XR experiences to enhance onsite or offsite visitor experience and engagement. The key characteristics of XR, that is, allowing interaction and providing an immersive environment, were also emphasised again in the current study. In addition, due to the continuous development of new applications and new design choices, XR-mediated experiences have been explored by many researchers; this research brings new insights to this ongoing discussion through the use of a qualitative multiple case study method.

6.2 Practical Contributions

This research provides some practical contributions to the implementation of XR-mediated experiences in cultural institutions and XR experience design. The four themes/strategies revealed for enhancing visitor engagement through XR technology can help museum practitioners and designers conceptualise their future exhibits and applications. Cultural institutions can leverage the potential of XR to provide contextual information about their collections, provide enhanced interaction and immersion, and evoke emotions to enrich visitor experiences both onsite and offsite. This study also demonstrates how these strategies can be used in XR experiences through six examples. Cultural institutions may be inspired by the findings to upgrade their XR experiences or consider using them in future exhibitions. This research highlights the potential for XR applications in the cultural sector, where design studios and agencies can expand their portfolios to provide more engaging experiences for cultural heritage, and cultural institutions may reconsider how to integrate innovative technologies with their current digital strategies.

6.3 Limitation and Future Work

Although this study reveals several potential areas for using XR to enhance visitor engagement with cultural heritage. The current work has some limitations and some potential research areas are recommended. Due to the nature of the qualitative approach, which was not designed to generate numerical data and the sample size of the current work, these may limit a comprehensive understanding of the impact of XR on visitor engagement. However, qualitative methods and carefully selected cases allow for a more in-depth assessment of each case and reveal details and their peculiarities. The XR-displayed contents (art, virtual gallery, architecture, sculpture) and application contexts (art museums, cathedrals) in the selected cases are limited to specific scenarios and contexts. Future research can examine the implementation of XR in other scenarios, for example, difficult history, intangible cultural heritage, etc., and/or other types of museums and cultural institutions, such as heritage sites, house museums, archaeological parks, visitor centres, etc. Furthermore, the selected cases were produced/exhibited in the United States, Belgium, and France, it is recommended that future research examine exhibits/works in other geographical locations. It is also recommended that future studies adopt other methodological approaches to explore similar research questions. Empirical research should investigate the extent to which XR influences visitor engagement. To understand the impact of XR on engagement, it is also recommended to evaluate the experience of different types of user groups.

Even though XR is gradually being used for cultural heritage, traditional media formats are still quite common in these institutions (e.g., audio guides, apps), and some visitors may have never used XR (such as Microsoft HoloLens 2 or HTC VIVE XR Elite devices). It may be helpful to explore visitor attitudes towards XR and other media formats. Furthermore, researchers and studies are most focused on revealing the potential of emerging technologies, exploring the drawbacks/pitfalls/challenges of using new technologies may help us make the best use of the technology and its unique capabilities. Meanwhile, as interactivity and immersion are revealed and confirmed by many researchers and practitioners (including the current study), it is also important to consider the extent to which interactivity and immersion characteristics can be leveraged to create XR experiences in order to avoid disrupting the visitor experience, that is, too much interaction or immersion may bring negative effects. Most importantly, as XR technologies are still evolving and transforming, and are constantly being embedded in cultural institutions and tourism sectors or considered for use in the future, more research in this area is necessary to investigate continued advancements and diverse design concepts/strategies/methods/techniques and functionalities/esthetics of the designed-XR-experiences.

7 Conclusion

XR-mediated experiences provide museums and cultural institutions opportunities to actively engage visitors. Museum visitors have a desire for interactive, immersive, personalised, and emotionally engaging experiences. In order to fulfil these requirements and anticipations, XR technologies provide novel methods to enhance conventional museum visits. Enhancing visitor engagement can be achieved by leveraging the potential of XR, including XR-based information contextualisation, XR-enhanced interaction, XR-enhanced immersion, and XR-induced emotional connection. This article offers valuable insights for researchers and practitioners as they navigate the evolving landscape of cultural institutions. This article also suggests several future research areas.

Acknowledgements This project was funded by the China Scholarship Council. The author would like to thank Dr. Stefan Werning and Prof. Dr. Joost Raessens for their knowledge and insights.

References

Alfavision. (n.d.). The Ghent Altarpiece AR. *Alfavision*. Retrieved from https://alfavision.be/project/ghent-altarpiece-ar

Allal-Chérif, O. (2022). Intelligent cathedrals: Using augmented reality, virtual reality, and artificial intelligence to provide an intense cultural, historical, and religious visitor experience. *Technological Forecasting and Social Change*, *178*, 121604.

Arrigoni, G., & Galani, A. (2021). Recasting witnessing in museums: Digital interactive displays for dialogic remembering. *International Journal of Heritage Studies*, *27*(2), 250–264.

Bec, A., Moyle, B., Schaffer, V., & Timms, K. (2021). Virtual reality and mixed reality for second chance tourism. *Tourism Management*, *83*, 104256.

Bec, A., Moyle, B., Timms, K., Schaffer, V., Skavronskaya, L., & Little, C. (2019). Management of immersive heritage tourism experiences: A conceptual model. *Tourism Management*, *72*, 117–120.

Bekele, M. K., & Champion, E. (2019). Redefining Mixed Reality: User-Reality-Virtuality and Virtual Heritage Perspectives (pp. 675–684). Presented at the CAADRIA 2019: Intelligent & Informed, Wellington, New Zealand. Retrieved from http://papers.cumincad.org/cgi-bin/works/paper/caadria2019_196

Bekele, M. K., Pierdicca, R., Frontoni, E., Malinverni, E. S., & Gain, J. (2018). A Survey of Augmented, Virtual, and Mixed Reality for Cultural Heritage. *Journal on Computing and Cultural Heritage*, *11*(2), 1–36.

Cameron, F., & Kenderdine, S. (Eds.). (2010). *Theorizing digital cultural heritage: A critical discourse*. Media in transition. Cambridge, Mass. London: MIT Press.

Carulli, M., Generosi, A., Bordegoni, M., & Mengoni, M. (2023). Design of XR Applications for Museums, Including Technology Maximising Visitors' Experience. In S. Gerbino, A. Lanzotti, M. Martorelli, R. Mirálbes Buil, C. Rizzi, & L. Roucoules (Eds.), *Advances on Mechanics, Design Engineering and Manufacturing IV*, Lecture Notes in Mechanical Engineering (pp. 1460–1470). Cham: Springer International Publishing. Retrieved from https://link.springer.com/https://doi.org/10.1007/978-3-031-15928-2_127

Cranmer, E. E., Tom Dieck, M. C., & Fountoulaki, P. (2020). Exploring the value of augmented reality for tourism. *Tourism Management Perspectives*, *35*, 100672.

tom Dieck, M. C., & Jung, T. H. (2017). Value of augmented reality at cultural heritage sites: A stakeholder approach. *Journal of Destination Marketing & Management*, *6*(2), 110–117.

Eternelle Notre-Dame. (n.d.). Experience – Eternal Notre-Dame. *Eternelle Notre-Dame*. Retrieved from https://www.eternellenotredame.com/en/experience

Hacking the Heist. (2018). Hacking the Heist. *Hacking the Heist*. Retrieved from https://www.hackingtheheist.com

Hammady, R., Ma, M., AL-Kalha, Z., & Strathearn, C. (2021). A framework for constructing and evaluating the role of MR as a holographic virtual guide in museums. *Virtual Reality*, *25*(4), 895–918.

Hammady, R., Ma, M., & Strathearn, C. (2019). User experience design for mixed reality: A case study of HoloLens in museum. *International Journal of Technology Marketing*, *13*(3/4), 354.

Hammady, R., Ma, M., & Strathearn, C. (2020). Ambient Information Visualisation and Visitors' Technology Acceptance of Mixed Reality in Museums. *Journal on Computing and Cultural Heritage*, *13*(2), 1–22.

Han, D.-I. D., Jung, T., & Tom Dieck, M. C. (2019a). Translating Tourist Requirements into Mobile AR Application Engineering Through QFD. *International Journal of Human–Computer Interaction*, *35*(19), 1842–1858.

Han, D.-I. D., Melissen, F., & Haggis-Burridge, M. (2024). Immersive experience framework: A Delphi approach. *Behaviour & Information Technology*, *43*(4), 623–639.

Han, D.-I. D., Tom Dieck, M. C., & Jung, T. (2019b). Augmented Reality Smart Glasses (ARSG) visitor adoption in cultural tourism. *Leisure Studies*, *38*(5), 618–633.

Han, D.-I., Tom Dieck, M. C., & Jung, T. (2018). User experience model for augmented reality applications in urban heritage tourism. *Journal of Heritage Tourism, 13*(1), 46–61.

Jung, T., Tom Dieck, M. C., Lee, H., & Chung, N. (2016). Effects of Virtual Reality and Augmented Reality on Visitor Experiences in Museum. In A. Inversini & R. Schegg (Eds.), *Information and Communication Technologies in Tourism 2016* (pp. 621–635). Cham: Springer International Publishing. Retrieved from http://link.springer.com/https://doi.org/10.1007/978-3-319-28231-2_45

Kenderdine, S., Chan, L. K. Y., & Shaw, J. (2014). Pure Land: Futures for Embodied Museography. *Journal on Computing and Cultural Heritage, 7*(2), 1–15.

Komianos, V. (2022). Immersive Applications in Museums: An Analysis of the Use of XR Technologies and the Provided Functionality Based on Systematic Literature Review. *JOIV : International Journal on Informatics Visualization, 6*(1), 60.

Lee, H., Jung, T. H., tom Dieck, M. C., & Chung, N. (2020). Experiencing immersive virtual reality in museums. *Information & Management, 57*(5), 103229.

Liu, J. (2023). A Critical Review of Digital Experiences in Cultural Institutions: Is Digital Experience a Traction or Distraction Strategy? *Proceedings of the 11th International Conference on Digital and Interactive Arts* (pp. 1–6). Presented at the ARTECH 2023: 11th International Conference on Digital and Interactive Arts, Faro Portugal: ACM. Retrieved from https://dl.acm.org/doi/https://doi.org/10.1145/3632776.3632784

Louvre Museum. (2021). The Mona Lisa in virtual reality in your own home. *Louvre Museum*. Retrieved from https://www.louvre.fr/en/what-s-on/life-at-the-museum/the-mona-lisa-in-virtual-reality-in-your-own-home

Marto, A., Gonçalves, A., & De Sousa, A. A. (2019). DinofelisAR: Users' Perspective About a Mobile AR Application in Cultural Heritage. In M. Duguleană, M. Carrozzino, M. Gams, & I. Tanea (Eds.), *VR Technologies in Cultural Heritage*, Communications in Computer and Information Science (Vol. 904, pp. 79–92). Cham: Springer International Publishing. Retrieved April 29, 2024, from http://link.springer.com/https://doi.org/10.1007/978-3-030-05819-7_7

Microsoft Unlocked. (n.d.). Reconstructing Krishna. *Microsoft Unlocked*. Retrieved from https://unlocked.microsoft.com/reconstructing-krishna/

Moorhouse, N., Tom Dieck, M. C., & Jung, T. (2019). An experiential view to children learning in museums with Augmented Reality. *Museum Management and Curatorship, 34*(4), 402–418.

Petrelli, D., & Roberts, A. J. (2023). Exploring Digital Means to Engage Visitors with Roman Culture: Virtual Reality vs. Tangible Interaction. *Journal on Computing and Cultural Heritage, 16*(4), 1–18.

Silva, M., & Teixeira, L. (2022). eXtended Reality (XR) Experiences in Museums for Cultural Heritage: A Systematic Review. In Z. Lv & H. Song (Eds.), *Intelligent Technologies for Interactive Entertainment*, Lecture Notes of the Institute for Computer Sciences, Social Informatics and Telecommunications Engineering (Vol. 429, pp. 58–79). Cham: Springer International Publishing. Retrieved from https://link.springer.com/https://doi.org/10.1007/978-3-030-99188-3_5

Sun, J. (2021, October 19). What is MR and How Does it Create Exceptionally Immersive Experiences? *AMT Lab @ CMU*. Retrieved from https://amt-lab.org/blog/2021/10/what-is-mr-and-how-does-it-create-exceptionally-immersive-experiences

Tom Dieck, M. C., Jung, T. H., & Tom Dieck, D. (2018). Enhancing art gallery visitors' learning experience using wearable augmented reality: Generic learning outcomes perspective. *Current Issues in Tourism, 21*(17), 2014–2034.

Tremosa, L. (2023, July 25). Beyond AR vs. VR: What is the Difference between AR vs. MR vs. VR vs. XR? *The Interaction Design Foundation*. Retrieved from https://www.interaction-design.org/literature/article/beyond-ar-vs-vr-what-is-the-difference-between-ar-vs-mr-vs-vr-vs-xr

Trunfio, M., Campana, S., & Magnelli, A. (2020a). The Impact of Mixed Reality on Visitors' Experience in Museum. 'The Ara As It Was' Project in Rome. In T. Jung, M. C. tom Dieck, & P. A. Rauschnabel (Eds.), *Augmented Reality and Virtual Reality*, Progress in IS (pp. 313–322).

Cham: Springer International Publishing. Retrieved from https://link.springer.com/https://doi.org/10.1007/978-3-030-37869-1_25

Trunfio, M., Campana, S., & Magnelli, A. (2020b). Measuring the impact of functional and experiential mixed reality elements on a museum visit. *Current Issues in Tourism, 23*(16), 1990–2008.

Trunfio, M., Jung, T., & Campana, S. (2022). Mixed reality experiences in museums: Exploring the impact of functional elements of the devices on visitors' immersive experiences and post-experience behaviours. *Information & Management, 59*(8), 103698.

Tussyadiah, I. P., Wang, D., Jung, T. H., & Tom Dieck, M. C. (2018). Virtual reality, presence, and attitude change: Empirical evidence from tourism. *Tourism Management, 66*, 140–154.

UNIT9. (n.d.). The Met Unframed. *UNIT9*. Retrieved from https://www.unit9.com/project/the-met-unframed

Verhulst, I., Woods, A., Whittaker, L., Bennett, J., & Dalton, P. (2021). Do VR and AR versions of an immersive cultural experience engender different user experiences? *Computers in Human Behavior, 125*, 106951.

Zhou, Y., Chen, J., & Wang, M. (2022). A meta-analytic review on incorporating virtual and augmented reality in museum learning. *Educational Research Review, 36*, 100454.

Virtual Museum and XR Content Creation for Takht-I-Bahi World Cultural Heritage Site

Muhammad Tufail, Jinho Park, Hyunyim Park, and Deukyoum Cheon

Abstract Takht-i-Bahi is a globally significant world heritage site because of its artistic representation of Greco-Buddhism and deep connection to ancient Korea's cultural heritage. In addition to its cultural and historical significance, the site is at risk of extinction due to human-induced threats, including negligence, unsustainable tourism practices, and natural disasters such as earthquakes, floods, and landslides. In the realm of digital heritage, the most effective way to preserve a cultural heritage site is to digitally reconstruct and maintain it to ensure its easy transmission to future generations and clear representation to a wider audience. In light of this trend, our research team decided to digitally document the site and develop its extended reality (XR) content, enabling digital reconstruction and dissemination. This would allow for an accurate representation and experience of the site in a three-dimensional virtual environment, as well as expand its global audience. We first digitally captured the entire site and then used virtual reality (VR) technology in conjunction with XR content creation to turn the site into a museum's immersive content experience. First, we employed a drone camera to digitally record the entire site. Subsequently, we combined VR technology with XR content creation to transform the Takht-i-Bahi heritage site's digital data into an immersive virtual museum content experience. We hope that this will enable potential visitors to actively engage in a VR environment, providing them with the chance to fully immerse themselves in a realistic experience of time and space travel, with the visual representation accurately portraying real-world scenarios of the Takht-i-Bahi heritage site. The Takht-i-Bahi Heritage Site's virtual museum will effectively overcome the typical challenges faced during physical visits by incorporating XR content creation. The Takht-i-Bahi virtual museum's immersive content experience can lead to sustainable outcomes, such as reducing the

M. Tufail · H. Park
School of Design, The Hong Kong Polytechnic University, Hong Kong SAR, China
e-mail: hyunyim.park@polyu.edu.hk

J. Park (✉)
Sejong Campus Virtual Smart City Visualization System Convergence Education and Research Cluster, Korea University, Seoul, Republic of Korea
e-mail: arkology@naver.com

D. Cheon
Chonnam National University, Gwangju, Republic of Korea

T. Jung et al. (eds.), *XR and Metaverse*, Springer Proceedings in Business and Economics, https://doi.org/10.1007/978-3-031-77975-6_15

number of tourists visiting the physical site and increasing its cultural and historical value on a global scale.

Keywords Virtual Reality · XR content · Virtual Museum · Takht-i-Bahi ruins · Gandhara Art · Cultural heritage

1 Introduction

In 1980, UNESCO declared Takht-i-Bahi a World Heritage Site. The site offers a glimpse of a Buddhist monastery of great historical importance with its roots in ancient Korean cultural heritage, such as Greco-Buddhist art in the Seokguram Grotto World Heritage Site. In Pakistan's Khyber Pakhtunkhwa province, the Takht-i-Bahi heritage site is located 80 km from Peshawar City and 16 km northwest of Mardan City. The site lies on the northern slope of a remote spur near Takht-i-Bahi village. It comprises the largest Buddhist remains in the ancient kingdom of Gandhara. The Monastery of Kanishka also bears the name of the great Kushan King, who ruled Gandhara in the second century CE and was renowned for his military, political, and spiritual achievements (Loeschner, 2012).

Takht-i-Bahi is the Gandhara civilization's magnificent religious and ceremonial complex. These glorious endowments evoke a subtle experience that takes one back to the times when hundreds of Buddhists would gather to offer their religious services in the most serene environment. The majority of people believe that 'Takht' means the throne and 'Bahi' means water or spring in the Persian language. The combined meanings of 'Takht' and 'Bahi' suggest that the monastery's name, Takht-i-Bahi, originates from its location at the summit of a mountain, adjacent to a stream. The Buddhist monastic complex of Takht-i-Bahi was founded in the early first century (Cornish, 1995). Takht-i-Bahi was in continual use until the seventh century A.D. The construction of Takht-i-Bahi, an assemblage of buildings, followed Gandhara patterns, using locally dressed and semi-dressed stone blocks set in a lime and mud mortar. Today, the ruins comprise a main stupa court, a votive stupa court, a group of three stupas, the monastic quadrangle with meditation cells, conference halls, covered stepped passageways and other material buildings.

Besides its cultural and historical significance, the site is in danger of extinction from natural forces and human-induced threats, such as earthquakes, unsustainable tourism, and negligence (Tufail et al., 2022; Park et al., 2014). Therefore, it is crucial to digitally reconstruct the site, preserve it digitally, and develop its XR content to enhance its 3D representation in a virtual environment. Moreover, the Takht-i-Bahi heritage site is a significant world heritage, and its association with an ancient Korean cultural heritage is another crucial motive for its digital preservation and dissemination. XR encompasses a variety of new media technologies, including augmented reality (AR), virtual reality (VR), and mixed reality (MR). These technologies enable us to create more engaging and significant experiences, as well as interact with diverse audiences with different needs and expectations (Silva and Teixeira, 2021). The XR content thus includes both the physical and virtual spaces, fostering enhanced cultural experiences and enabling wide audiences to virtually explore significant cultural assets and deeply engage with their historical and cultural importance (Margetis et al., 2020).

The present study aimed to develop a virtual museum and XR content for the Takht-i-Bahi heritage site to create a detailed experiential space that bridges the gap between the physical world and virtual reality. First, we chose the stupa in the Takht-i-Bahi heritage site, amidst the Gandhara ruins, as the primary site for digital restoration because of its pioneering role in merging Eastern and Western traditions. Furthermore, the Gandhara stupas in present-day Pakistan demonstrate the evolution of Asian stupas before they spread to India, China, and Korea. Therefore, we chose the Takht-i-Bahi heritage site and its stupa as the focal point for digital restoration, given its inclusion in the Asia Stupa Road, a concept based on the belief that all Asian countries possess stupas (See Fig. 1). Second, we transformed the data acquired from scanning the Takht-i-Bahi heritage site into virtual reality content and replicated its original architecture in a virtual space. The VR content in the Takht-i-Bahi heritage site's virtual museum aimed to allow visitors to learn about one of the Asian stupas' historical origins and development process. Additionally, visitors can engage in a virtual reconstruction of the lost Takht-i-Bahi stupa.

Fig. 1 Asia Stupa concept road from India to Korea and Japan

2 Literature Review

The Buddhist ruins at Takht-i-Bahi exemplify the evolution of monastic and urban societies in the Gandhara region from the 1st to the seventh centuries AD (Cornish, 1996). These ruins are notable for their architectural form, design, and concentration techniques. Takht-i-Bahi remains in its original hilltop site, preserving its highly authentic environment. Takht-i-Bahi has maintained the originality of its form and design, and the arrangement of the monastic complex and structures accurately represents the genuineness of the materials, traditions, and construction methods used in Gandhara patterns. The Peshawar Museum acquired the stone sculptures, while the Lahore Museum in Pakistan conserved the Gondophares' stone inscription. The Takht-i-Bahi monastery is thought to have originated in the second and third century CE, under the rule of Parthian King Godophares (Cornish, 1995). In 1836, the initial excavation occurred, resulting in the discovery of a multitude of artifacts, including coins from different historical eras and 270 statues made from clay, stucco, and terracotta. The majority of the statues are currently shown at the Peshawar Museum, which houses the most extensive assortment of artifacts from the old Buddhist civilization. Xuanzang, a Chinese monk-pilgrim who lived from 602 to 646, discovered the remarkable archeological site by studying the existing trip records on his tour through greater India in pursuit of Buddhist texts (Wriggins, 2020). Nevertheless, the primary stupa of the site, which was the largest and most impressive he had ever witnessed, seems to have already experienced deterioration even during Xuanzang's day.

The first recorded reference to the place in contemporary times was made by General Court, a French officer serving Maharaja Ranjit Singh (1780–1839), in 1836, as previously stated. Dr. Henry Walter Bellew undertook an archaeological study of the Takht-i-Bahi heritage site in 1864 (Michon, 2015). This survey resulted in a series of excavations. Harold Hargreaves later researched the site from 1910 to 1911 (Guha, 2010). Sir John Marshall, the director-general of the Archaeological Survey of India from 1902 to 1931, posited that the emergence of high-walled monasteries in the Gandhara region can be traced back to the first century CE (Lidu, 2019)). The Department of Archaeology and Museums in Peshawar has conducted recent studies indicating that the site evolved into a Buddhist monastery complex during the first century BCE and this development began under the rule of Gondophares I, a Parthian ruler who reigned from approximately 20 BCE to 10 BCE (Morris, 2020). The site's transformation continued during the reigns of Kanishka I, an emperor of the Kushan Empire who ruled from 127 to 51, as well as Kanishka III and Vasudeva II, who were later kings of the Kushan Empire (Benjamin, 2020). The department has categorized the construction into four discrete periods based on its structure. The stupa court, consisting of a group of stupas located in a central courtyard, as well as the monastery, kitchen, and refectory, were built between the first century BCE and the second century CE (Kim, 2011). The second phase, occurring during the 3rd–fourth century, is thought to encompass the primary stupa court and assembly hall. The third phase, which corresponds to the fourth and fifth centuries, is believed to encompass the presence of a triad of stupas in the court. The fourth phase, which took place around the 6th–seventh century, is associated with the tantric complex. Guand-da et al. (1996) stated that the Hephthalites or White Huns (408–670) from Central Asia were mostly responsible for the destruction of Buddhist monasteries in Gandhara, notably Takht-i-Bahi. The design of the monastery complex is quite remarkable, particularly the arrangement of minor shrines encircling the main stupa court, which is particularly noteworthy.

Augmented reality (AR), virtual reality (VR), and mixed reality (MR) are among the new media technologies that are included in XR technology. In addition to facilitating interaction with a wide range of audiences with varying expectations and requirements, these technologies also allow us to develop more engaging and significant experiences (Silva and Teixeira, 2021). The XR content encompasses both the physical and virtual spaces, thereby facilitating the exploration of significant cultural assets and the profound engagement with their historical and cultural significance by a wide audience (Margetis et al., 2020).

3 Methods

3.1 Site Visit and Observation

Our research team conducted a one-week visit to the Takht-i-Bahi Cultural Heritage Site in April 2019, to examine and analyze its cultural and historical significance. The presence of multiple archaeological layers at the Takht-i-Bahi Heritage Site indicates the intricate history of its development and growth. The aforementioned structures, along with numerous more single and double-story material buildings discovered during excavation, are constructed from local or semi-dressed stone blocks with flakes, following the Gandharan diaper-masonry style. These stones are put in lime and mud mortar. The site serves as an excellent repository of historical knowledge for Buddhists. The archaeological evidence at the site is exceptionally abundant. A multitude of Gandharan sculptural artifacts have been unearthed, comprising both complete statues and broken pieces made of unfired clay, plaster, and terracotta. A significant number of the figures feature miniature cavities designed for attaching and providing support for the clay bodies and heads. Stucco figures retrieved from the site are also on display in other European museums. The history of the Gandhara civilization can be observed in several archaeological sites located in Taxila, Swat, and other regions of the current Khyber Pakhtunkhwa Province in Pakistan. What sets Takht-i-Bahi apart from other sites is its varied architecture and peaceful mountain location. The main Stupa is surrounded by minor shrines that are characterized by a distinctive design and arrangement, making them the most notable feature. The aesthetic magnificence and grandeur of this extraordinary edifice are unrivaled among Buddhist historical landmarks.

Fig. 2 Takht-i-Bahi main temple site with its archeological layers and its stone construction

The Gandhara civilization served as both a focal point for Buddhism and a center for the renowned Gandhara art and culture. Buddhist arts and culture originated in that area and spread as a religious influence throughout the Far East, including Japan, Korea, China, Java, and other regions. Therefore, the history of Buddhism represents a bygone era of great significance, which will never be repeated. However, its influence remains a significant milestone in the development of human civilization and culture, and its contributions are immeasurable. Buddhist civilization will continue to preserve its beauty for everybody, like a guiding light, at the archeological site of Gandhara, which still retains its historical significance. Figure 2 illustrates the multitude of archaeological layers associated with the development and growth of the site.

3.2 Digital Documentation

Upon investigating the digital documentation scenario, we discovered that the site's elevated position on the mountains presented challenges in effectively capturing it using 3D scanners (See Fig. 3). Hence, we employed a drone fitted with 4K UHD cameras to get detailed images of the delicate features of the Takht-i-Bahi ruins. We employed digital recording techniques to capture the present state of the ruins and endeavored to reconstruct their original appearance, which has been lost, within a

Fig. 3 Aerial view of the Takht-i-Bahi ruins

virtual setting. Initially, we conducted a comprehensive 3D recording of the current state of the Takht-i-Bahi cultural site in order to obtain the essential data for the 3D digital restoration and generation of XR content. The data-collecting approach employed was highly efficient in digitizing the Takht-i-Bahi ruins. The utilization of this data collection method demonstrated a high level of efficiency in the process of digitizing the Takht-i-Bahi ruins.

3.3 Digital Reconstruction

We conducted digital reconstruction on the stupa located in the central courtyard of the Takht-i-Bahi cultural site. More precisely, we restored the parts of the stupa that were previously absent by utilizing the data provided by local experts in archaeology and the extensive research conducted by international scholars on Takht-i-Bahi stupas and their origins (Marshall, 2000; Silva and Teixeira, 2021). Based on the data collected from excavations at the Gandharan monastery site, Tissot (1985) concluded that the main stupa at the Takht-i-Bahi site is likely similar to the Loriyan Tangai stupa but significantly taller, standing three floors high (See Fig. 4).

Following the completion of the initial phase of scenario planning, digital restoration, and scanning, the subsequent step entailed the creation of 3D models utilizing computer graphic technologies. In order to accomplish this goal, we utilized the advanced technology of Pixologic Zbrush to enhance the image to a superior degree

Fig. 4 The main stupa in the court of the Takht-i-Bahi heritage site from the illustration of Tissot (1985)

of quality by increasing the polygon count. In addition, we employed a substance to generate a surface quality that conforms to the principles of physically based rendering (PBR). The temple and Stupa were enhanced using visual effects (VFX) to achieve a lifelike depiction (See Fig. 5).

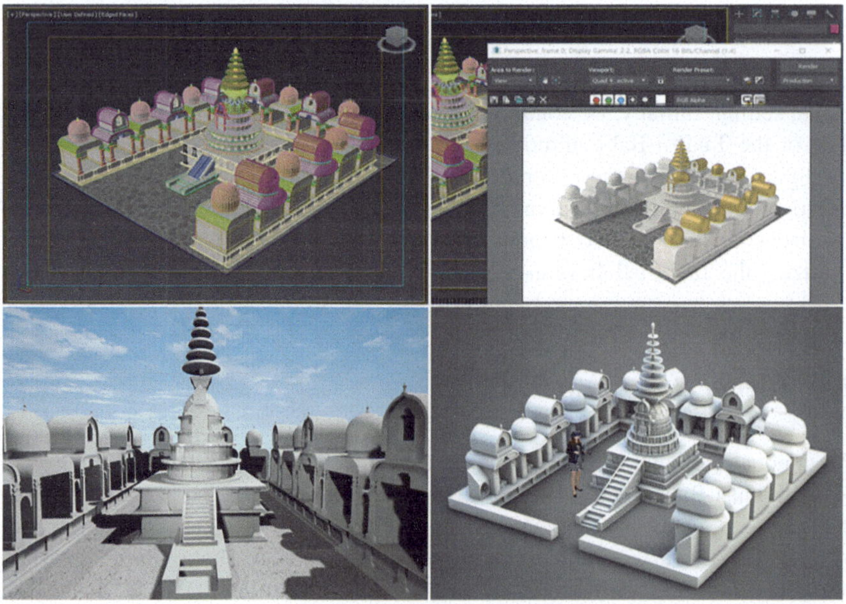

Fig. 5 Digital reconstruction and 3D modeling of the main stupa in the court of Takht-i-Bahi Heritage site

4 Results and Conclusions

We utilized XR technology to facilitate the immersive exploration of historical Buddhist stupas development from India to Korea. We designed a room dedicated to providing a VR/XR experience in Gwangju, Korea. This technology utilizes room-scale virtual reality to accurately replicate the setting of the Takht-i-Bahi temple and create an immersive VR experience (See Fig. 6). We integrated AI digital avatars into this VR environment. We postulated that Hyecho, a Buddhist monk hailing from the Silla dynasty who was actively engaged in the eighth century AD, visited the Takht-i-Bahi heritage site. Through our presence as an AI digital human in VR space, the VR space of the Takht-i-Bahi temple transcends the limitations of time and place. Visitors can experience the Hyecho digital avatar at the Takht-i-Bahi Temple, and it can also provide guided VR/XR-based digital tours to the Takht-i-Bahi Temple.

Virtual reality (VR) and extended reality (XR) are the two types of display technology that express the digital restoration of the Takht-i-Bahi Temple. The VR case allows visitors to immerse themselves in the Takht-i-Bahi Temple using a Head-Mounted Display (HMD). On the other hand, the XR case integrates the Takht-i-Bahi Temple into a virtual production system that includes a media wall. Visitors get the opportunity to not only see the Takht-i-Bahi Temple but also to learn about the historical evolution of stupas from India to Korea through the XR Experience (See Fig. 7). In the current immersive VR experience, VR is a fully engaging experience designed for one individual, but XR is a display that can be shared and experienced by numerous individuals at the same time.

The purpose of the present study was to exhibit the Takht-i-Bahi cultural heritage site in a museum's immersive content experience using VR technology. Visitors can fully engage in the VR environment, allowing them to feel as if they have been transported to different times and faraway places, while accurately depicting their original condition. Artificial intelligence-powered digital human technology replicates certain individuals from historical periods. The system can produce hybrid information that combines historical locations and historical individuals. AI technology facilitates the precise reproduction of historical space, creating the perception that it exists in the current moment. As a result, VR technology can accurately recreate

Fig. 6 Room-scale VR-Experience of the Takht-i-Bahi temple

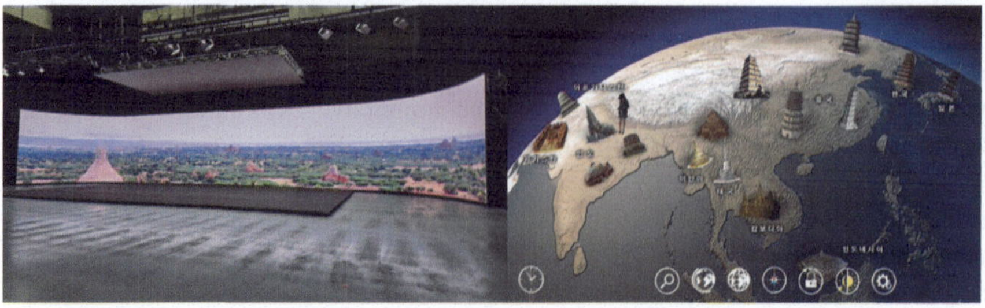

Fig. 7 XR-Experience of the Takht-i-Bahi temple and the historical evolution of stupas from India to Korea

any place from any point in human history, while AI can accurately replicate any person from the past. These components can be employed in different museums and exhibition halls globally. AI technology is anticipated to transform the museum experience, resulting in a more dynamic and interactive exhibition format. Our goal was to develop VR and XR material for the Takht-i-Bahi virtual museum, intending to create an immersive environment that combines the physical world with virtual reality.

Currently, digital technologies, such as virtual reality (VR), generally concentrate on delivering information and digitally reconstructing experiences. XR content technology encompasses a range of developing technologies, including VR, AR, simulations, holograms, and other digital tools and applications. These technologies can change our perception of the real world in different ways, distinguishing them from standard VR. These technologies stimulate our visual, auditory, and tactile senses, leading to a condition of full immersion in our digital environment. This is achievable through the utilization of digital avatars within the virtual Takht-i-Bahi museum. The virtual reality experience offers a first-person perspective by utilizing a head-mounted display and showing various scenarios within a virtual reality environment. Nevertheless, XR surpasses virtual reality in terms of breadth as it enables users to interact with others employing avatars. Thus, by utilizing the XR virtual environment, the virtual museum dedicated to the Takht-i-Bahi cultural site will effectively overcome the challenges associated with physically visiting the site.

The future outlook for 3D reconstruction of cultural heritage sites is extremely promising, as the application of this approach in the cultural heritage sector is currently undergoing a substantial increase. Many advanced and emerging countries have adopted these methods. As holographic displays, head-mounted displays, ubiquitous displays with AI, and immersive XR content technologies advance, we anticipate a growth in the utilization of digital representation and 3D rendering in cultural heritage for sustainable tourism development.

References

Benjamin, C. (2020). The Kushan Empire. The Oxford World History of Empire: Volume Two: The History of Empires, 325.

Cornish, S. (1995). A study of Takht-i-Bahi (A Gandharan Buddhist Site in the North West Pakistan).

Cornish, S. (1996). A Study of Takht-i-Bahi (A Gandharan Buddhist Site in the North West Pakistan) Part II.

Guand-da, Z., Litvinsky, B., & Shabani Samghabadi, R. (1996). History of civilizations of Central Asia: The Crossroads of Civilization: AD 250 to 750 (Vol. 3). UNESCO Publishing.

Guha, S. (2010). Archaeology, photography, histories. The Marshall Albums: Photography and Archaeology, 10–67.

Kim, Y. J. (2011). Evolution, Transformation, and Representation in Buddhist Architecture: The Square Shrines of Buddhist Monasteries in Central Asia after the fourth century. Architectural research, 13(4), 31–42.

Lidu, J. Y. (2019, March). Cross-cultural Buddhist monastery ruins on the Silk Road and beyond: the layout and function of Buddhist monasteries reconsidered. In The Global Connections of Gandhāran Art: Proceedings of the Third International Workshop of the Gandhāra Connections Project, University of Oxford, 18th (p. 207).

Loeschner, H. (2012). Kanishka in Context with the Historical Buddha and Kushan Chronology. Glory of the Kushans–Recent Discoveries and Interpretations, 137–194.

Margetis, G., Apostolakis, K. C., Ntoa, S., Papagiannakis, G., & Stephanidis, C. (2020). X-reality museums: unifying the virtual and real world towards realistic virtual museums. Applied Sciences, 11(1), 338.

Marshall, J. (2000). The Buddhist art of Gandhara: The story of the early school; its birth, growth and decline.

Michon, D. (2015). Archaeology and religion in early Northwest India: history, theory, practice. Routledge India.

Morris, L. (2020). Central Asian Empires. Handbook of ancient Afro-Eurasian economies, 1, 53–93.

Park, J. H., Muhammad, T., & Jae-Hong, A. (2014, December). The 3d reconstruction and visualization of seokguram grotto world heritage site. In 2014 International Conference on Virtual Systems & Multimedia (VSMM) (pp. 180–183). IEEE.

Silva, M., & Teixeira, L. (2021, December). eXtended Reality (XR) experiences in museums for cultural heritage: A systematic review. In International Conference on Intelligent Technologies for Interactive Entertainment (pp. 58–79). Cham: Springer International Publishing.

Tissot, F. (1985). Gandhara–La Vie Publique et privée dans l'Inde ancienne.

Tufail, M., Park, J., Kim, H., Kim, S., Kim, K., & Lee, J. H. (2022). How do visitors perceive the significance of tangible cultural heritage through a 3D reconstructed immersive visual experience at the Seokguram Grotto, South Korea?. Journal of Heritage Tourism, 17(4), 409–430.

Wriggins, S. (2020). Xuanzang: A Buddhist Pilgrim on the Silk Road. Routledge.

Motion Capture for Augmented Reality Storytelling in Archeology & Cultural Heritage Dissemination: Simulating an Animal Sacrifice at Ancient Phalasarna

Laura Bishop, Elpida Hadjidaki–Marder, Šarūnas Ledas, and Gunnar Liestøl

Abstract Augmented Reality (AR) employment in archaeological and cultural heritage settings are changing due to rapidly increase in computing power in mobile devices (smartphones, tablets and smartglasses). This has caused a transition from static only to richer and more dynamic environments including animation of human characters. This again opens for reconstructions and simulations of the intangible, particularly the significant context of human actions. Our chapter reports on an experiment with motion capture for AR simulation of an animal sacrifice at Ancient Phalasarna, Crete. The AR simulation was tested and evaluated by visitors on location. One conclusion is the importance of creating a balance between the fidelity of the human character's motions and their graphical appearance.

Keywords Motion Capture · Augmented reality · Digital cultural heritage · Computer animation · Situated simulation · Ancient Phalasarna

L. Bishop
RITMO Centre for Interdisciplinary Studies in Rhythm, Time and Motion, University of Oslo, Oslo, Norway

E. Hadjidaki–Marder
Association for Ancient Phalasarna, Crete, Greece

Š. Ledas
Tag of Joy, Vilnius, Lithuania

G. Liestøl (✉)
Department of Media and Communication, University of Oslo, Oslo, Norway
e-mail: gunnar.liestol@media.uio.no

T. Jung et al. (eds.), *XR and Metaverse*, Springer Proceedings in Business and Economics, https://doi.org/10.1007/978-3-031-77975-6_16

1 Introduction

Augmented Reality (AR) applications in archaeological simulations and cultural heritage settings are rapidly changing from static only to richer, more complex dynamic digital environments, made possible by the increased computing power in handheld devices (in this case primarily smartphones and tablets, but eventually also smartglasses). When creating reconstructions of archaeological sites, we are thus no longer limited to static terrain, buildings, artefacts and simple movements, but can also include more complex computer animations, hence adding the highly desired context of human actions and activities.

This chapter presents an experiment with motion capture for AR simulation of an animal sacrifice at the 5th c BC temple of goddess Demeter at Ancient Phalasarna, currently being excavated by Dr. Elpida Hadjidaki-Marder under supervision of the Greek Ministry of Culture. The reconstruction of the temple is based on drawings of architects A. and Th. Nakasis, while the form and content of the animated sacrifice are drawn from the archaeological evidence combined with Walter Burkert's structural analysis of Greek mythology and rituals.

In the following we describe the technical and the archaeological backgrounds, as well as the design and production process, from plotting the sacrifice scene, through motion capture and implementation, to testing and evaluation with visitors on location. Finally, we conclude with a discussion of findings and provide suggestions for future implementation and research questions, including a brief report from a more recent follow–up experiment.

2 State of the Art and Research Challenge

When AR first entered the domains of archaeology and cultural heritage dissemination, a quarter of a century ago (Höllerer et al. 1999; Vlahakis et al. 2002), the digital reconstructions were, for quite some time, limited to static structures and objects. A decade later elementary computer animations became more customary (Liestøl 2014). However, animation of human movement was still rudimentary, extremely time–consuming and difficult to create manually with a decent result. Libraries of generic human motions and animations also tend to be incomplete, especially when one needs specific character behavior, which is primarily the case in archaeological and cultural heritage contexts. In recent years motion capture in various forms has become more easily available to broader user groups, and consequently, animation of human characters have begun to surface in AR applications. However, so far, the uses of motion capture in AR for archaeological reconstruction and cultural heritage simulations have been limited (Doulamis et al. 2017; Barbara and Grech 2022).

Investments in intangible cultural heritage are often focused on documentation and conservation of current practices and activities, which do not leave physical traces. Intangible and immaterial heritage, however, also includes the intangible context of human behavior, that is the practices that provides meaning to the 'dead' artefacts and material remains we often encounter in museum exhibitions (Yang et al. 2006; Staubermann 2020). In the tangible artefact–dominated world of archaeological dissemination, whether in museum exhibitions or on site, there is a craving for the intangible context of human actions and practices. There is a need to show how ancient tools were produced and for which purpose they were used, to display social and cultural human behaviors, and to demonstrate how rituals and ceremonies were performed and practiced, including known historical events. Finding ways to bring this knowledge to life is thus a pertinent problem and challenge to solve.

In archaeological reconstruction and simulation, the combination of augmented reality and motion capture of human behavior could be the answer to this deficiency. Consequently, the primary challenge in the research, development and experimentation reported here has been to explore and answer the question: How may we best utilize motion capture for depicting human actions when employing AR to simulate intangible heritage practices in combination with archaeological and historical evidence?

3 The Archaeological Context

Phalasarna has been inhabited since prehistoric times and blossomed as an eighth century BC Dorian city-state, situated on top of a high promontory, at the far west end of the island of Crete facing the western Mediterranean Sea. The location of the town and its port gave the opportunity to the inhabitants to become skillful mariners, while Phalasarna's laws and social systems promoted excellence in military arts that led its citizens to offer themselves as mercenaries to Persian, Carthagenian, and Hellenistic kingdoms. Phalasarna was a naval power controlling the sea routes along the western Aegean Sea and maintaining watchtowers and naval bases along those sea lines. Ancient geographers took note of the artificial closed harbor, carved out of a lagoon, and ringed around with quays, walls, and towers (Müller 1855). The harbor and surrounding structures have been uncovered through research excavations ongoing since 1986 (Hadjidaki 1988, 2019a, b, 2020; Hadjidaki and Iniotakis 2000).

A temple dedicated to goddess Artemis is also reported (Dionysius Calliphontis 120) to have existed, but it has not yet been located. However, a temple dedicated to goddess Demeter, Greek goddess of agriculture, was located in 2022 and is currently being excavated (Hadjidaki 2022). It was built on top of the acropolis in the fifth century BC, at the same time as the Parthenon in Athens and the temple of Poseidon at Cape Sounion in Attica, with two Doric columns by the entrance covered with Corinthian rooftiles. Three lines of an elaborate staircase led to the paved interior (Cella) of the temple where dedicated offerings were found. Among them were elegant vessels of ceremonial importance such as jugs (hydria) with the name of the goddess inscribed on the shoulder of the vessels. The Cella had a door facing east that led to a sacrificial courtyard where layers of ashes and animal bones were uncovered (Fig. 1).

Fig. 1 The site of the fifth century BC temple dedicated to the goddess Demeter located on top of the ancient Phalasarna acropolis. The grand staircase facing south is clearly visible. The sacrificial area is to the left (east) of the temple, towards the boulders.

The sacrificial courtyard was the site where at least since Homeric times the process of Thesmophoria or animal sacrifice was carried out. A bull, pig, goat, or sheep was killed in ritual fashion, parts of it burned, and the entrails and meat then cooked and eaten on the spot within a holy circle by the women participants. The process is described in detail by (Burkert 1985, 55–57); see below.

4 Design and Direction

The terrain on the east side of the temple is not a flat regular plane. In particular, the circular ramp from where the procession moved towards the site of the sacrifice is uneven, first with a steep ascent then followed by a more modest descent entering the sacrificial area. The sacrificial area itself is less uneven but still not a level surface. Thus, it was necessary to identify a similar terrain for doing the motion capture since it was not possible to bring the recording equipment to the original site (Fig. 2).

Fig. 2 Left: Planning the procession sequence on the east side of the temple. Right: Intersecting photogrammetry models of the archaeological site and a substitute terrain at the University of Oslo campus.

To match the movement on the chosen substitute terrain with the original terrain, photogrammetry models of the two sites were compared and paths and positions were marked physically in the substitute terrain for the motion capture. One person acted as all the characters wearing the sensor suit, including members of the audience, while other individuals stepped in to mark the characters and positions that were not under recording.

The composition and order of the procession was drawn from Burkert's interpretation of 'the essence of the sacred act' in ancient Greek animal sacrifice (Burkert 1985). Burkert distinguish between various social groups and sizes of communities involved in the actual sacrificial rituals, where the family–based event may have the smallest number of participants. For practical purposes we had to choose a simplified version of Burkert's essential elements, however with key roles represented: the priestess, the sacrificer, the blameless maiden carrying the knife in a basket, one person guiding the sacrificial lamb, another carrying the incense burner, musicians, and finally an audience, a family or clan participating in and (hopefully) benefiting from the ritual.

5 Motion Capture

Motion capture recordings were collected using a Nansense Pro full-body suit, which contains 40 R2 sensors and is intended for use in animation. Each sensor contains a gyroscope, accelerometer, and magnetometer so that its orientation, rotation, and position relative to other sensors can be determined. The Nansense recording software uses a body solving algorithm to interpret motion of each body part. The suit includes detachable bands for the head and feet with one sensor each and detachable gloves with 12 sensors each. Data were streamed to a PC via cable connection and recorded in the Nansense software at a frame rate of 240 Hz. A height-tracking function was used so that changes in ground elevation were maintained in the recorded data. Although it was not possible to track the motion of objects in the environment, the subject wearing the suit grasped various props while acting out the different characters so that her hands would be in the correct position for objects to be added during animation.

The suit was determined to be the best option for motion capture because it can be used relatively easily in natural settings, unlike infrared-based optical systems. It also allows for detailed capture of the hands and fingers, even in cases where a person is grasping an object (as was the case in our data collection), which would lead to problems with occlusion for most camera-based systems that require a line-of-sight to maintain tracking. The main shortcoming of motion capture suits is that the sensors are susceptible to magnetometer interference, which leads to positional drift of individual sensors, disrupting their apparent spatial configuration. This was the main challenge that we encountered in our data capture. The fingers were especially affected since the sensors are close together and tend to interfere with each other. The outdoor setting also made it challenging to run a thorough calibration and monitor data quality while recording. Despite these challenges, the quality of data captured was generally satisfactory (Fig. 3).

6 3D–modelling and Animation

All the scene components were imported into the Unity engine, which is used to construct this type of interactive experiences. Then the terrain was assembled, which was generated using photogrammetry, the hand-modeled temple, the people models, as well as the aforementioned motion captured animations. The static 3D models and the motion capture were done independently, which means that discrepancies were expected. It is impossible to find an identical terrain off-site, and it's also very complicated to find even a similar terrain with only a 3D model at hand. This poses a challenge, to which one might consider multiple approaches: (1) after capturing and analyzing the animations in Unity, go back to motion capture and recapture them–this might also require one to look for a more precise terrain or even build one manually; (2) import the animations into 3D editing software and adapt them to the terrain; (3) import the animations straight into the Unity engine and use its Timeline feature to mix and match the animations to the 3D world. The first two approaches are time consuming and require excessive synchronization between different teams and need some very specific skills (either physical prop building or professional 3D rigging and animation). The third approach is much more rapid, but also much less flexible. One must understand that research in multi-disciplinary fields always involves a wide variety of tasks, which means that iterations at each stage are limited and often time restricted. With augmented reality projects, testing is also limited and must be carefully planned. This is why in the end the third approach made the

Fig. 3 The top two photos show motion capture of a person wearing the sensor suite to record movements for guiding the sacrificial lamb and the flute player, respectively. A small bicycle was used to keep the hand and bending of the body steady relative to the ground, and a wooden structure was applied to adequately position head and hands/fingers for the flute player. Suitable terrain at the University of Oslo campus was identified as sufficiently congruent with the actual terrain next to the temple of Demeter at Phalasarna. Middle screen shots show the exported motion capture files when displayed in FBX–Review and details of its implementation in the reconstructed AR–environment. Bottom photos depict the application in use on location with an iPhone 14 Pro Max, utilizing the Unity–based Sitsim AR platform. Note that both vertical and horizontal correspondence is not exact, due to the position and angle of the physical camera compared to the position and angle of the virtual camera. The lack of vertical alignment is deliberate since experience has proven that users prefer a 15% tilt offset to improve the visual relationship between the physical environment and the digital environment on the screen.

most sense in this project – having all the procession and motions in place was more important than making them perfect. The Timeline feature provided enough tools to quickly iterate and adapt the animations (cut, move, rotate, blend, loop, etc.) well enough for them to be informative and showcase the whole procession. It was very useful that the animated people had very limited interaction with each other or the environment, apart from the ground surface and one person holding a sheep by its neck, while another picked up a knife.

7 Methodologies: Media Design, Testing and Evaluation

The experiment–based research reported here was conducted as a media design project (Fagerjord 2012; Nyre 2014; Liestøl 2013, 2018) and informed by the key humanities disciplines: rhetoric and narratology, using theoretical–analytical concepts as topoi for synthesis and design for invention and experimental implementation of new rhetorical and storytelling techniques in AR mediation. In this project the adaptation of conventions from the documentary film genre has been a central source (topos) for many of the solutions in the narrative design. This overall approach was further supported by qualitative methodologies during the testing and evaluation with real user on location (user observation, written reply to questionnaires etc.).

For this type of qualitative and controlled testing on location where the focus is on a mix of UI elements and event/place related topics, valuable information and feedback can be drawn from even small numbers of testers if the questionnaire encourage qualitative and substantial answers. In usability studies, which is primarily focused on human–computer interactions, it is argued that five testers are sufficient (Nielsen 2012). With the site of the temple and the sacrificial area on top of a cliffy terrain access for and the availability of users were limited. For this research (related to a university course on 'media students as researchers' we had the chance to test with seven visitors during the limited time available. One would have preferred a somewhat larger number, but even single digit testers may provide valuable feedback and information. Testers were given a short introduction to the project and the general background, and supported throughout the testing if needed, but examined the application with as little interference as possible. Afterwards, they answered a written questionnaire (Fig. 4).

8 Results

Overall, the feedback from the visitors on location using and evaluating the app was very positive and encouraging. Here are some statements regarding the general experience of using the app:

> Excellent (female, 62).
>
> Really cool, brings it back to life, you can travel in time (female, 42).
>
> Easy to use, very informative (female, 52).
>
> It was like I really participated in this sacrifice (female, 33).

All participants except one answered that the AR simulation made them feel more connected to the ritual and when it took place in ancient times. The most important criticism was the lack of resolution regarding the character's body and clothing detail:

> Visualization of figures … quite blocky (male, 58).

Fig. 4 Photo of test application in use. The procession has arrived at the sacrificial area and the priestess is reciting her prayer in honouring the goddess Demeter.

> The models were of low quality (female, 34).

The characters movement, on the other hand, were more positively received:

> Very engaging (female, 52).

> Very smooth (female, 34).

Although the test/evaluation was limited it provided valuable feedback for an early iteration in a long–term design project like this. Based on the first round of testing with real users on location we can conclude that the prototype in general caused vivid and informative experiences for the users. They also seem to value the movement of the human characters in the animation sequence reconstructing the ritual of animal sacrifice. However, the graphical resolution of the characters involved was not impressive and even appeared 'dated'.

Consequently, it would be relevant in a follow–up production/case to improve the graphical quality of the characters in an animation, while using the same method for motion capture.

9 Follow–up Case: 'The Ides of March'

Since the same research and development team has conducted a new case study which can be seen as a follow–up to the Phalasarna case we would like to briefly mention some of its features and the feedback received from users. This time the topic was an historical event from ancient Rome, which has rather detailed classical descriptions: the assassination of Julius Caesar, which took place on the 'Ides of March' in 44 BC in Pompey's Curia. In some respect this is an easier site since it happened indoors so uneven terrain did not cause challenges for the motion capture and animation. However, the actions are more complex, involving more characters and much more interactions between characters. Following the conclusions from the Phalasarna case resolution, graphical quality and lighting of both characters and the environment were increased rather substantially (Liestøl et al. 2024) (Fig. 5).

The 'Ides of March' also includes significant improvements in reconstructing the senate chamber of Pompey's Curia as it may have looked with material surfaces as well as artificial and natural lighting and reflections (Fig. 6).

In the 'Ides of March' case the motion capture in principle followed the same procedure as in the Phalasarna case. However, to follow up on the much more complex actions of and interactions between characters, two Nansense Pro full-body suits were used simultaneously. Despite the increased investment in the motion capture process, the animation turned out to be immensely challenging and very time–consuming.

Three approaches to editing and iterating motion captured animation were described in an earlier section. For this project, it was decided to employ the process, where animation is imported into a 3D editing software and adjusted there. Due to the complexity of the actions and the number of animated characters in a small space, very delicate adjustments had to be applied, which would be impossible with either of the other approaches. The chosen process then required much more time dedication, but it was simply impossible to achieve a similar result otherwise. Finally, it was important to achieve a much higher level of realism not only in 3D models, but also in the movements and actions.

During the testing on location with invited guests and visiting tourists the relatively high resolution and quality of both movement and graphical solutions were

Fig. 5 Left: the character guiding the sacrificial lamb in the Phalasarna simulation displaying a 'blocky' mesh with a low triangle count. Right: The opening moment during the assassination of the dictator Julius Caesar. Casca is providing the first attack on Caesar from behind, while Cimber holds him down by the toga initially pretending to beg for his brother's pardon. The triangle count per character are multiple times higher.

Fig. 6 Left: The 'Ides of March' test application in use on location in Via di Torre Argentina in Rome, looking west across today's street level and towards the main entrance in the reconstruction of Pompey's Curia on the screen. Right: Detail from a screen shot of the application showing the high graphical quality of the environment and its inventory.

highly appreciated. Consequently, the criticism we saw directed towards the limited graphical quality of the models in the Phalasarna case is absent in the 'Ides of March' simulation. As the quality and detail obviously increased, the risk of the phenomenon known as the 'uncanny valley' effect (Bolter et al. 2021) grew. However, there was no direct feedback from users to indicate that they experienced the 'uncanny valley'. Almost all of the ten testers regarded the realism of the scene and the characters as convincing.

10 Conclusion

We started this chapter by pointing out the change in AR development from static environments to scenes with increasing use of animation and human characters that have been ongoing over the past decade. In the Phalasarna case feedback from users testing the system indicated that the animations for human characters provided by motion capture were adequate, while the graphical quality and detail of the same characters were too simple, 'blocky' and 'old'. With the 'Ides of March' case the graphical quality was improved as much as possible exploiting the best available hardware (iPad Pro M4). Overall, the testers of the latter case were satisfied and impressed by both the characters' movement and the quality of their graphical resolution and realism.

Acknowledgements Thanks to Angelos and Athanasious Nakasis for all the detailed information about the temple's architecture, and to Tag of Joy: Julius Gerulaitis, Laurynas Žuromskas-Kuolis, Eduardas Lukošiūnas, for their skillful contributions with 3D-modelling, –animation, implementation and programming. Thanks to the students at MEVIT3812 (V´23 & V´24) for valuable 3D contributions and editorial work. Thanks also to Nike Marder for photogrammetry documentation; and to Michael Marder for valuable input during the writing of this article. Finally, thanks to the Greek Ministry of Culture; the Dept. of Media & Communication, the C_2HO (Creative Computing) network, and the Norwegian Institute in Rome, all the University of Oslo, for continued support and funding. This work was also partially supported by the University of Oslo and the Research Council of Norway through its Centres of Excellence scheme (project 262762).

References

Barbara, J., & Grech, J. (2022, December). Motion Capture and Intangible Cultural Heritage Immersive Virtual Reality for Education. In *The Proceedings of the 4th International Conference on Virtual Reality* (Vol. 15, p. 94).

Bolter, J. D., Engberg, M., & MacIntyre, B. (2021). *Reality media: Augmented and virtual reality*. MIT Press.

Burkert, W. (1985). *Greek Religion*. (transl. by J. Raffan). Cambridge: Harvard University Press, 512 p.

Dionysius Calliphontis 120

Doulamis, N., Doulamis, A., Ioannidis, C., Klein, M., & Ioannides, M. (2017). Modelling of static and moving objects: digitizing tangible and intangible cultural heritage. *Mixed reality and gamification for cultural heritage*, 567–589.

Fagerjord, A. (2012). Design som medievitenskapelig metode. *Norsk medietidsskrift*, *19*(3), 198-215.

Hadjidaki, E. (1988) 'Preliminary Report of Excavations at the Harbor of Phalasarna in West Crete', American Journal of Archaeology, 92, pp. 463–479.

Hadjidaki, E. (2019a) 'Three Decades of Adventures with Honor Frost in Crete', in L. Blue (ed.) In the Footsteps of Honor Frost. The life and legacy of a pioneer in maritime archaeology. Leiden: Sidestone Press, pp. 165–182. Available at: https://www.ancientportsantiques.com/wp-content/uploads/Documents/PLACES/Crete-Cyprus/Phalasarna-Hadjidaki2019.pdf (Accessed: 30 December 2023).

Hadjidaki, E. (2019b). 'Three Decades of Adventures with Honor Frost in Crete.' In *In the Footsteps of Honor Frost. The Life and Legacy of a Pioneer in Maritime Archaeology*, edited by Lucy Blue, 165–82. Leiden: Sidestone Press. https://www.ancientportsantiques.com/wp-content/uploads/Documents/PLACES/Crete-Cyprus/Phalasarna-Hadjidaki2019.pdf.

Hadjidaki, E. (2020) '«... Κατά θάλασσαν οι Φαλασάρνιοι...»', in N.C. Stompolidis and M. Giannopoulou (eds) Eleutherna, Crete, and the Outside World. Rethymnon: University of Crete, pp. 384–394.

Hadjidaki, E. (2022) 'Report on Phalasarna excavations, the 2022 season', Archaeologikon Deltion, Forthcoming.

Hadjidaki, E. and Iniotakis, C. (2000) 'Hellenistic Ceramics from Phalasarna found from 1986-1990', The Ancient World, 31, pp. 54–73.

Höllerer, T., Feiner, S., & Pavlik, J. (1999, October). Situated documentaries: Embedding multimedia presentations in the real world. In *Digest of Papers. Third International Symposium on Wearable Computers* (pp. 79–86). IEEE.

Liestøl, G. (2013). Topics of innovation. *Towards a method of invention and innovation in digital media design. T. Storsul and A. Krumsvik (eds.) Media Innovations: A Multidisciplinary Study of Change*, 61–74.

Liestøl, G. (2014). Along the Appian Way. Storytelling and memory across time and space in mobile augmented reality. In *Digital Heritage. Progress in Cultural Heritage: Documentation, Preservation, and Protection: 5th International Conference, EuroMed 2014, Limassol, Cyprus, November 3–8, 2014. Proceedings 5* (pp. 248–257). Springer International Publishing.

Liestøl, G. (2018). Story and storage–narrative theory as a tool for creativity in augmented reality storytelling. *Virtual Creativity*, *8*(1), 75-89.

Liestøl, G., Ledas, Š., Ledas, Ž., Cruz, J., Carla, T., Antunes, V. (2024). Inside Out – Outside In. In: tom Dieck, M.C., Jung, T., Kim, YS. (eds) XR and Metaverse. XR 2023. Springer Proceedings in Business and Economics. Springer, Cham. https://doi.org/10.1007/978-3-031-50559-1_13

Müller, C., 1855. *Geographi Graeci Minores*. Paris: Editoire Abrosio Firmin Didot.

Nielsen, J. (2012). How Many Test Users in a Usability Study? Published on NN/g Nielsen Norman Group's web site. Visited on July 1st. 2024 https://www.nngroup.com/articles/how-many-test-users

Nyre, L. (2014). Media design method. *The Journal of Media Innovations*, *1*(1), 86-109.

Staubermann, K. (2020). Reconstructing the past: when intangible heritage meets scientific practice. *International Journal of Intangible Heritage, 15, pp. 30-38.*

Vlahakis, V., Ioannidis, M., Karigiannis, J., Tsotros, M., Gounaris, M., Stricker, D., ... & Almeida, L. (2002). Archeoguide: an augmented reality guide for archaeological sites. *IEEE Computer Graphics and Applications*, *22*(5), 52-60.

Yang, C., Peng, D., & Sun, S. (2006, november). Creating a virtual activity for the intangible culture heritage. In *16th International Conference on Artificial Reality and Telexistence--Workshops (ICAT'06)* (pp. 636–641). IEEE.

XR for Business and Marketing

A Study on the Impact of Metaverse Experience Factors on the Intention to Continue Use Based on the Experience Economy Theory

Sungbae Kang

Abstract In the era of digital transformation, as the real world and the virtual world merge, the metaverse is receiving attention as a new future value-added industry. The metaverse is not limited to a specific industry, but provides innovative spaces and differentiated value across various industries and society as a whole. This study aims to explore the relationships between metaverse experiences, perceptions, and behaviors using the theory of the experience economy. To achieve this, the study employed structural equation modeling to test hypotheses, and conducted surveys and statistical analyses with 191 participants. The results showed that entertainment, education, escapist, and esthetic experiences have a positive impact on perceived value, and perceived value significantly influences the intention to continue using. Therefore, the study identified the metaverse's experiential elements and found that valuing the metaverse experience positively influences continued usage intentions, offering relevant implications.

Keyword Experience economy theory · Metaverse · Perceived value · Intention to continue use

1 Introduction

The COVID-19 pandemic has globally underscored the importance of physical experiences and values, leading to an increase in services offering experiences akin to reality online. In particular, the metaverse is garnering attention as the next-generation platform succeeding social media in the post-COVID era. Transcending the boundaries between reality and virtual worlds, the metaverse is accelerating changes, evolving into a new future space, and thus, highlighting its central role in the new normal era. The term "metaverse" is a portmanteau of "meta," meaning beyond, and "universe," indicating a hyper-connected, ultra-realistic digital virtual

S. Kang (✉)
Dongguk University WISE, Gyeongju, Republic of Korea
e-mail: sbkang@dongguk.ac.kr

T. Jung et al. (eds.), *XR and Metaverse*, Springer Proceedings in Business and Economics, https://doi.org/10.1007/978-3-031-77975-6_18

world (Mystakidis, 2022). It refers to a digital virtual world that creates new value through the fusion of our real-world and the digital world (Buhalis et al., 2023; Lee et al., 2021; Kim et al., 2022).

The metaverse is creating new values distinct from the past as it is being applied across various sectors such as society, economy, culture, and education. In particular, the emergence of a new value-creating virtual convergence economy is being significantly propelled by the expansion of augmented reality (AR), virtual reality (VR), and the encompassing extended reality (XR) technologies (Daassi & Debbabi, 2021; Shin, 2022; Shen et al., 2021). In this era of the virtual convergence economy, a variety of content and services are being developed, capturing the attention of the new generation who seek to enjoy new experiences and values through seamless interaction and co-evolution between the real and virtual worlds (Lee & Han, 2021). The economic activity within the metaverse has generated over $120 billion globally in 2022, and it is projected to create a value of up to $5 trillion by 2030 (McKinsey, 2022).

As interest and application in the metaverse increase, being applied across various fields such as education, culture, and tourism, case studies, service development, and technology-related research are being conducted. A review of existing research related to the metaverse reveals that studies are largely conducted from technological and cognitive perspectives (Dieck et al., 2018; Ryu et al., 2019; Shen et al., 2021). However, a closer examination of existing studies on the metaverse indicates a gradual shift in research focus from technology-centered studies to service development and consumer perspectives. This shift is due to the ultimate goal of the metaverse, which is to maximize user experience. Recently, with this trend gaining momentum, the importance of experience is being emphasized than ever before. Yet, there is a lack of research presenting the structural relationship between experience perception, value, and behavioral intention among metaverse users.

Therefore, this study aims to clarify the influence relationship between experience, perception, and action in the metaverse by analyzing the intention to act according to various experiential elements based on the experience economy theory, thereby exploring metaverse content discovery and strategies for sustainable development. The research objectives are set as follows: First, to examine the value provided by the metaverse from the perspective of experience within the framework of the experience economy theory. Second, to empirically examine how the experiential value provided by various metaverses affects the intention to continue using the metaverse.

2 Literature Review and Hypotheses

2.1 Experience Economy Theory

Experience can be defined as a subjective perception that provides emotional, sensory, cognitive, and behavioral value through specific experiences one personally undergoes (Knutson & Beck, 2003). In other words, experience is a holistic experience that involves acquiring knowledge and skills through observing or participating in something (Radder & Xiliang, 2015). Recently, the focus has shifted from merely providing products and services to pursuing value through the experience of 'experiencing' across products and services. Meanwhile, the experience economy is an economic concept derived from the development of economic value. Experience is another product that creates economic value, and it must be endowed with memorable value in itself (Pine & Gilmore, 1998; Wang et al., 2023).

The concept of the experience economy is introduced by Pine and Gilmore (1998). They posited that an experience is not merely sensory but also encompasses entertainment, educational, escapist, and esthetic dimensions, defining it as a higher-order concept than goods and services. The entertainment experience element involves experiencing emotions that respond to elements that stimulate a pleasant mood state or arouse interest. Entertainment experiences are being highlighted as influencing factors for the intention to adopt new technologies, characterized by pleasurable emotions and playful joy. The educational experience element refers to acquiring new information or knowledge related to the experience and feeling an improvement in skills through direct or indirect experiences. This can encourage consumers' active participation in acquiring new information or knowledge related to the experience, aiding in personal capacity and curiosity enhancement. The escapist experience, compared to other experiential elements, tends to involve a stronger inclination towards immersion, leading to active participation once fully immersed. This element serves as a departure from everyday life, offering a novel aspect through immersion that provides a sense of detachment from the ordinary. The esthetic experience refers to the emotional perception an individual has towards the physical environment and facilities. Such esthetic experiences relate to perceiving the overall atmosphere or enjoyment and positive emotions provided by the experiential environment through visual, auditory, and olfactory cues (Pine & Gilmore, 1998; Dieck et al., 2018; Moon, 2023; Wang et al., 2023).

Buhalis et al. (2023) presented a vision of how the metaverse can revolutionize tourism experiences and transform tourism management and marketing. De Felice et al. (2023) analyzed the role of the metaverse as an educational tool, demonstrating its value as an innovative experiential tool. Wang et al. (2023) conducted an empirical study to analyze the influence relationship on the intention to use the metaverse exhibition platform based on the theory of the experience economy. They particularly emphasized the importance of entertainment and educational experiences. Shen et al. (2021) highlighted the importance of application design paradigms and factors influencing consumer behavior in virtual commerce through a literature review.

2.2 Value-Based Model (VAM)

Perceived value refers to the subjective experience and perception that a customer has while purchasing and using a product or service (Rokeach, 1973). It is not solely based on price or quality, but rather, it is the result of a comprehensive consideration of various factors such as the benefits, satisfaction, and usefulness that the customer gains from the product or service (Kim et al., 2007; Chun & Lee, 2022). The value-based theory (VAM) was first proposed by Kim et al. (2007). The value-based theory emphasizes the importance of customer value in individuals' acceptance of new information technologies and services. The theory distinguishes between perceived benefits and sacrifices as variables affecting perceived value and investigates the influence relationship between perceived value and intention to use.

Kim and Lee (2023) utilized an extended value-based acceptance model to investigate the impact of metaverse characteristics on user behavior. They proposed the characteristics of the metaverse as telepresence, interoperability, seamlessness, concurrence, and economy flow. As a result, the analysis indicated that perceived usefulness and enjoyment influence perceived value, and perceived value positively affects the intention to use. Cha et al. (2024) proposed the importance of perceived value (effectiveness, social gain and enjoyment) in explaining the influence relationship between gamification affordance of the metaverse and consumer engagement. Kim et al. (2019) integrated the value-based adoption model and the expectation-confirmation model to investigate the influence relationship between the continued intention to use accommodation apps. They suggested that perceived value is an important determinant that positively influences the intention to continue using. Therefore, the value perceived by customers through their experiences or consumption process becomes the basis for their decisions to revisit and recommend in the future (Cha et al., 2024; Kim & Lee, 2023).

2.3 Research Model and Hypotheses

The review of prior studies has confirmed that experiential elements have an impact on the intention to use, even in research applying the theory of the experience economy to technical aspects. Accordingly, this study aims to understand the relationship between experiential elements in the metaverse, perceived value, and the intention for continued use, by applying the theory of the experience economy (Pine & Gilmore, 1998; Kim et al., 2007; Venkatesh et al., 2003; Wang et al., 2023; Cha et al., 2024). Based on the experience economy theory, this research has established a research model as shown in Fig. 1 and set five hypotheses to examine the effect of metaverse experiential elements on perceived value and the intention to continue using.

Hypothesis 1 The entertainment experience of the metaverse will have a positive (+) impact on perceived value.

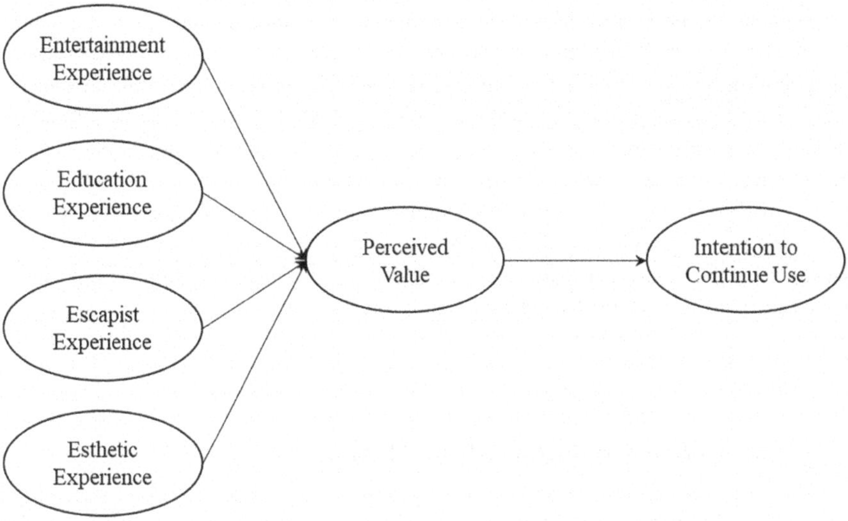

Fig. 1 Research model

Hypothesis 2 The educational experience of the metaverse will have a positive (+) impact on perceived value.

Hypothesis 3 The escapist experience of the metaverse will have a positive (+) impact on perceived value.

Hypothesis 4 The esthetic experience of the metaverse will have a positive (+) impact on perceived value.

Hypothesis 5 The perceived value of the metaverse will have a positive (+) impact on the intention to continue use.

3 Research Method

3.1 Operational Definition

The purpose of this study is to conduct an empirical study on the relationship between 4 factors of experience economy (entertainment, education, escapist, esthetic) and intention to continue use through perceived value of the Metaverse (Pine & Gilmore, 1998; Kim et al., 2007). Preexisting construct measures have been used in this study. According to previous studies of experience economy theory, this study developed the operational definition and measurement items of independent variables 4 factors of experience economy (4Es), perceived value and intention to continue use. Entertainment experience is defined as the mood enhancement and enjoyment gained through the metaverse experience. Education experience is defined as the extent to which one encounters new knowledge and information through the metaverse experience. Escapist experience is defined as the extent to which one feels a temporary escape from daily life through the metaverse experience. Esthetic experience is defined as the degree to which one discovers aesthetic aspects through the metaverse experience (Pine & Gilmore, 1998). Perceived value is defined as the degree to which one believes the metaverse experience to be valuable (Kim et al., 2007; Zeithaml, 1988). Intention to continue use is defined as the willingness or plan to continue using the metaverse in the future (Venkatesh et al., 2003). Some of questionnaire items were measured using a 5-Point Likert Scale ranging from 1 (very disagree) to 5 (very agree).

3.2 Data Collection and Analysis Methods

This study conducted a survey targeting metaverse users to elucidate the effects of metaverse experiences on perceived value and the intention to continue use. A total of 213 responses were collected, of which 22 insincere responses were excluded, leaving 191 responses for empirical analysis. The collected data were analyzed using SPSS 27.0 and SmartPLS 4.0 programs. The analysis methods included frequency analysis to understand the demographic characteristics of the sample. Additionally, reliability analysis (Cronbach's alpha), confirmatory factor analysis, and discriminant validity analysis were conducted to verify the reliability and validity of the measurement tools. Furthermore, structural equation modeling was utilized to test the hypotheses and verify the causal relationships between latent variables.

3.3 Sample Statistics

To understand the demographic characteristics of the sample, a frequency analysis was conducted. There were a total of 191 respondents, with 52.4% being male and 47.6% being female. The age distribution showed that the majority were in their 20 s, accounting for 81.7%, followed by those in their 40 s at 9.9%, and teenagers at 5.8%. Regarding education level, 82.7% were currently enrolled in a university, and the most common occupation was student, representing 88.0% of the sample.

3.4 The Measurement Model

This study utilized SmartPLS 4.0 software to analyze variance-based PLS-SEM for the assessment of the measurement and structural model. This study utilized Cronbach's alpha, composite reliability (CR), factor loadings, average variance extracted

Table 1 Sample description (n = 191)

Item	Classification	Frequency (n)	Percent (%)
Gender	Male	100	52.4
	Female	91	47.6
Age	~19	11	5.8
	20–29	156	81.7
	30–39	2	1.0
	40–49	19	9.9
	50~	3	1.6
Occupation	Students	168	88.0
	General occupation	11	5.8
	Housewife	5	2.6
	Professional occupation	7	3.6

(AVE), correlation coefficients, and the square root of AVE. The statistical analysis results for the measurement items are shown in Table 1. The factor loadings for the research variables ranged from 0.693 to 0.936, with all measurement items exceeding 0.7 cut off value. Additionally, Cronbach's alpha and composite reliability were found to be 0.763–0.931 and 0.861–0.951, exceeding the general criterion of 0.7, which indicates good reliability (Hair et al., 2014). The average variance extracted (AVE) values for the measurement model ranged from 0.634 to 0.829, indicating that they exceed the criterion value of 0.5. Therefore, the convergent validity of the measurement model was confirmed (Fornell & Larcker, 1981) (Table 2).

Next, to evaluate discriminant validity, the square roots of the AVE values were compared to the correlation coefficients among the constructs. Generally, if the square root of the AVE value is greater than the correlation coefficient of each latent variable, it is considered that discriminant validity has been secured (Fornell & larcker, 1981). The analysis confirmed that the square root of the AVE values (0.796–0.910) exceed the correlation coefficients (0.391–0.781), ensuring discriminant validity (Table 3).

3.5 *The Structural Model*

This study verified hypotheses based on a structural model, considering intention to continue use as the dependent variable and examining the influences of entertainment experience, education experience, escapist experience, and esthetic experience on the perceived value from the perspective of experience economy theory. The validation of the structural model is measured by the size of the path coefficient, statistical significance, and the explained (R^2) of the final dependent variable. Figure 2 shows the analysis results of the proposed structural model in this study, and Table 4 summarizes the detailed verification results for the proposed models.

Table 2 Validity and reliabilities

Constructs		Item loadings	Cronbach's alpha	Composite reliability	AVE
Entertainment experience	Ent1	0.907	0.931	0.951	0.829
	Ent2	0.912			
	Ent3	0.936			
	Ent4	0.886			
Education experience	Edu1	0.852	0.849	0.898	0.689
	Edu2	0.844			
	Edu3	0.781			
	Edu4	0.840			
Escapist experience	Esc1	0.868	0.763	0.861	0.674
	Esc2	0.791			
	Esc3	0.801			
Esthetic experience	Est1	0.693	0.806	0.873	0.634
	Est2	0.801			
	Est3	0.856			
	Est4	0.826			
Perceived value	Val1	0.866	0.890	0.919	0.695
	Val2	0.859			
	Val3	0.831			
	Val4	0.837			
	Val5	0.772			
Intention to continue use	Use1	0.924	0.920	0.943	0.806
	Use2	0.886			
	Use3	0.912			
	Use4	0.867			

First, entertainment experiences were found to have a significant positive (+) impact on the perceived value (b = 0.185, t = 2.121, $p < 0.05$). Education experiences were found to have a significant positive (+) impact on the perceived value (b = 0.262, t = 2.111, $p < 0.05$). Escapist experiences were found to have a significant positive (+) impact on the perceived value (b = 0.188, t = 2.652, $p < 0.01$). Esthetic experiences were found to have a significant positive (+) impact on the perceived value (b = 0.218, t = 2.333, $p < 0.05$). In particular, educational experience was found to have the greatest impact on perceived value. Therefore, Hypotheses H1, H2, H3, and H4 were accepted. Second, the perceived value was found to have a significant positive (+) impact on intention to continue use (b = 0.569, t = 9.397, $p < 0.01$). Therefore, Hypothesis H5 was accepted. Finally, the R^2 value for the perceived value and intention to continue use was shown to be 53.1% (0.531) and 32.3% (0.323), respectively.

Table 3 Discriminant validity

Variables	Education	Entertainment	Escapist	Esthetic	PV	ICU
Education experience	**0.830**					
Entertainment experience	0.724	**0.910**				
Escapist experience	0.530	0.391	**0.821**			
Esthetic experience	0.781	0.780	0.532	**0.796**		
Perceived value (PV)	0.666	0.618	0.515	0.667	**0.834**	
Intention to continue use (ICU)	0.531	0.744	0.415	0.679	0.569	**0.898**

Notes Square root of AVE is shown on the major diagonal (bold)

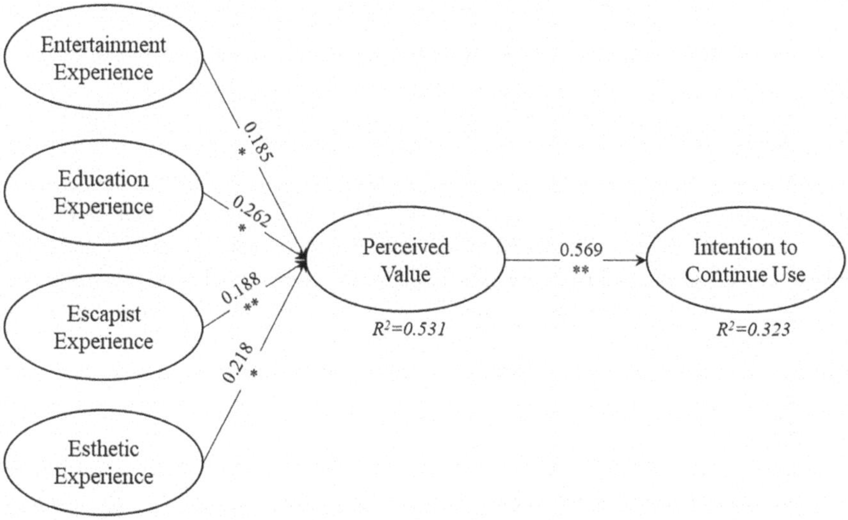

Fig. 2 Results for the research model. *Notes* * $p < 0.05$; ** $p < 0.01$

4 Discussion and Conclusion

In recent years, the potential of the metaverse as a tool to bridge the virtual and real worlds has been increasingly recognized. Particularly, the metaverse is expected to offer numerous opportunities across various sectors and applications (De Felice et al., 2023). The purpose of this study is to investigate and analyze the influence relationships among metaverse experiences, perceptions, and behaviors by utilizing

Table 4 Results of the research hypotheses

Paths			Path coefficient	t-value	Results
[H1] Entertainment experience	→	Perceived value	0.185*	2.121	Adopted
[H2] Education experience	→	Perceived value	0.262*	2.111	Adopted
[H3] Escapist experience	→	Perceived value	0.188**	2.652	Adopted
[H4] Esthetic experience	→	Perceived value	0.218*	2.333	Adopted
[H5] Perceived value	→	Intention to continue use	0.569**	9.397	Adopted

** t-value significant at $p < 0.01$
* t-value significant at $p < 0.05$

the theory of the experience economy. In particular, the study aims to understand the impacts of entertainment experience, education experience, escapist experience, and esthetic experience on perceived value, and whether perceived value affects the intention to continued use (Pine & Gilmore, 1998). To achieve these research objectives, this study constructs a structural equation model based on the theory of the experience economy and sets research hypotheses. The empirical study results are as follows.

First, it was found that entertainment, education, escapist, and esthetic experience have a significant impact on perceived value. This result indicates that metaverse users value entertainment experience, education experience, escapist experience, and esthetic experience importantly. Particularly, the educational experience showed the greatest impact on perceived value. This indicates the significant role of educational experiences in adding value, as they enable users to gain more knowledge and information in the metaverse. Additionally, the metaverse helps us better understand the benefits and potential of immersive and innovative learning experiences as a tool for education.

Second, perceived value was found to significantly affect the intention to continue use. The relationship between value and behavioral intention has been consistently proven in various fields. Unlike traditional experiential elements, the metaverse emphasizes the importance of experiential elements that combine entertainment, educational, escapist, and esthetic aspects. In this context, the value perceived by individuals is expected to positively influence their intention to continue using the metaverse. Therefore, high perceived value among metaverse users leads to positive behavioral intentions, aligning with existing research findings (Kim et al., 2007; Chun & Lee, 2022).

Based on these research findings, the academic and practical implications can be summarized as follows. First, this study emphasizes the importance of experiences by applying the theory of the experience economy to the metaverse environment, thereby broadening the understanding of its impact on consumer behavior. Additionally, it presented a model integrating perceived value into the experience economy theory, theoretically demonstrating the influence relationships between experience, value, and intention to use.

Second, the study highlights the significance of perceived value in driving the intention to continue using the metaverse. This is considered as the most influential variable on metaverse behavioral intentions, and as a critical factor and key measure for gaining competitive advantage. The metaverse, as a new industry of the future, has a wide range of applications and potential for development. By considering the characteristics of various fields and incorporating elements of entertainment, education, escapist, and esthetic experiences, the value and quality of innovation and services could be further enhanced. This approach will create new added value and spotlight the industry as a promising source of future sustenance.

Several limitations have been identified in this study, suggesting that future research should be conducted from various perspectives. Firstly, given the diverse fields where the metaverse is applied, it is impractical to generalize the results of this study to the entire metaverse environment. Future research should aim to explore differences across specific application areas and platforms through additional analysis. Second, as the respondents are predominantly individuals in their twenties, it would be meaningful for future studies to include a wider range of age groups to understand the differences among users.

References

Buhalis, D., Leung D. & Lin, M. (2023). Metaverse as a Disruptive Technology Revolutionising Tourism Management and Marketing, *Tourism Management*. 97:104724.

Cha, S., Kim C. Y. & Tang, Y. (2024). Gamification in the Metaverse: Affordance, Perceived Value, Flow State, and Engagement, *International Journal of Tourism Research*. 26(2):1–14.

Chun, S. & Lee, H. (2022). Metaverse Tourism Experiential Factors' Effect on Visitors' Perceived Value, Satisfaction, Action Intention: Focusing on Experience Economy Theory(4Es), *Korean Journal of Hospitality and Tourism*. 31(8):153–171.

Daassi, M. & Debbabi, S. (2021). Intention to reuse AR-based apps: The Combined role of the Sense of Immersion, Product Presence and Perceived Realism, *Information & Management*. 58(4):103453.

De Felice, F., Petrillo, A., Iovine, G., Salzano, C. & Baffo, I. (2023). How Does the Metaverse Shape Education? A Systematic Literature Review, *Applied Sciences*. 13:5682.

Dieck, M. C. T., Jung, T. H. & Rauschnabel, P. A. (2018). Determining Visitor Engagement through Augmented Reality at Science Festivals: An Experience Economy Perspective, *Computers in Human Behavior*. 82:44–53.

Hair, F., Jr, J., Sarstedt, M., Hopkins, L. & Kuppelwieser, V. (2014). Partial Least Squares Structural Equation Modeling (PLS-SEM), *European Business Review*. 26(2):106–121.

Fornell, C. & Larcker, D. F. (1981). Evaluating Structural Equation Models with Unobervable Variables and Measurement Error, *Journal of Marketing Research*. 18(1):39–50.

Kim, A., Kim Y. J. & Kim, S. S. (2022). A Comparative Study on User Perception by Metaverse Worldview using SPICE, *Knowledge Management Research*. 23(2):61–82.

Kim, S. B & Lee, H. (2023). Investigating the Impact of Metaverse Characteristics on User Behavior through the Combination of PLS-SEM and NCA within the Extended Value-Based Adoption Model, *Korean Management Review*. 52(5):1159–1195.

Kim, S. H., Bae, J. H. & Jeon, H. M. (2019). Continuous Intention on Accommodation Apps: Integrated Value-Based Adoption and Expectation–Confirmation Model Analysis, *Sustainability*. 11:1578.

Kim, H. W., Chan, H. C. & Gupta, S. (2007). Value-based Adoption of Mobile Internet: An Empirical Investigation, *Decision Support Systems*. 43(1):111–126.

Knutson, B. J. & Beck, J. A. (2003). Identifying the Dimensions of the Experience Construct: Development of the Model, *Journal of Quality Assurance in Hospitality and Tourism*. 4(3):23–35.

Lee, L., Braud, T., Zhou, P., Wnag, L., Xu, D., Lin, Z., Kumar, A., Bermejo, C. & Hui, P. (2021). All One Needs to Know about Metaverse: A Complete Survey on Technological Singularity, Virtual Ecosystem, and Research Agenda, *Journal of Latex Class Files*. 14(8):1–66.

Lee, S. & Han, S. (2021). Metaverse Begins: 5 Major Issues and Forecast. *Software Policy & Research Institute Issue Report*, 116.

McKinsey. (2022). Value Creation in the Metaverse. *McKinsey & Company*, 1–77.

Moon, Y. (2023). The Effect of Quality Factors of Augmented Reality Technology on User Experience: Based on Experience Economy Theory, *Journal of Korea Academia-Industrial Cooperation Society*. 24(11):758–766.

Mystakidis, S. (2022). Metaverse, *Encyclopedia*, 2(1):486–497.

Pine, B. J. & Gilmore, J. H. (1998), Welcome to the Experience Economy, *Harvard Business Review*. 76(4):97–105.

Radder, L. & Xiliang, H. (2015). An Examination of the Museum Experience Based on Pine and Gilmore's Experience Economy Realms, *The Journal of Applied Business Research*. 31(2):455–470.

Rokeach, M. (1973). *The Nature of Human Values*. Free Press.

Ryu, M., Lin, H. B. & Zhang, M. J. (2019). A Study on the Use Intention of the Unmanned Order Payment Service based on the Technology Acceptance Model and the Theory of Experience Economy: Focusing on the Moderating Effect of Time Pressure, Journal of Consumption Culture. 22(3):71–95.

Shen, B., Tan, W., Guo, J., Zhao, L. & Qin, P. (2021). How to Promote User Purchase in Metaverse? A Systematic Literature Review on Consumer Behavior Research and Virtual Commerce Application Design, *Applied Sciences*, 11:11087.

Shin, D. (2022). The Actualization of Meta Affordances: Conceptualizing Affordance Actualization in the Metaverse Game, *Computers in Human Behavior*. 133:107292.

Venkatesh, V., Morris, M. G., Davis, G. B. & Davis, F. D. (2003). User Acceptance of Information Technology: Toward a Unified View, *MIS Quarterly*. 27(3):425–478.

Wang M., Liu, S., Hu, L. & Lee, J. (2023). A Study of Metaverse Exhibition Sustainability on the Perspective of the Experience Economy, *Sustainability*. 15:9153.

Zeithaml, V. A. (1988). Consumer Perceptions of Price Quality, and Value: A Mean-end Model and Synthesis of Evidence, *Journal of Marketing*. 52(3):2–22.

Interactivity and Animation Effects in VR-Enhanced OOH Advertising

Minwoo Cho and Donghun Chung

Abstract The evolution of advertising has been closely linked to technological advancements, with virtual reality (VR) presenting new opportunities for creating immersive and interactive ad experiences. This study explores the impact of interactivity and animation effects on VR advertising effectiveness. In doing so, the level of interactivity (low vs. high) was manipulated and different animation effects (static, flickering, flowing) were tested to see how they impacted user attention, vividness, perceived intrusiveness, avoidance, and flow. The results show that there are significant differences in attention, vividness, and flow between high and low interactivity. All were higher when interactivity was high. The animation effect had no main effect on any of the variables. This suggests the importance of interactivity, and the possibility that interactivity may have made the animation less perceptible.

Keywords Advertising · Animation effect · Interactivity · OOH · VR

1 Introduction

The evolution of advertising has been closely linked to technological advancements. The proliferation of personal computers and the internet gave rise to banner advertising and short-form video ads. Furthermore, the enhancement of display technology and remote-control systems through networks has led to the expansion of digital signage advertising in public and commercial spaces. Recently, the rapid advancement in display technology has even introduced the emergence of 3D advertising utilizing anamorphic illusion techniques.

Within this technological evolution, virtual reality (VR) has garnered attention, experienced disappointment, and then regained positive prospects over the past few

M. Cho
Graduate School of Metaverse Convergence, Kwangwoon University, Seoul, Republic of Korea
e-mail: fpdltldzk30s@kw.ac.kr

D. Chung (✉)
School of Media and Communication, Kwangwoon University, Seoul, Republic of Korea
e-mail: donghunc@kw.ac.kr

T. Jung et al. (eds.), *XR and Metaverse*, Springer Proceedings in Business and Economics, https://doi.org/10.1007/978-3-031-77975-6_19

years. In 2021, the concept of the metaverse gained traction, with "Facebook" being renamed "Meta," and VR providing users with a near-realistic experience (Chung, 2017). However, the initial metaverse boom lacked consideration for user experience, leading to a gradual decline. The recent introduction of Apple's Vision Pro has reignited interest in VR. VR has the potential to yield new advertising effects when combined with outdoor advertising, which reaches a large audience in the places where people spend most of their time (Park, 2013). However, research on the utilization of VR in marketing has not yet established a sufficient theoretical foundation, and empirical studies in this area are scarce.

This study aims to address these gaps by experimentally examining the impact of the interactivity and animation effects of the combination of VR and outdoor advertising on advertising effectiveness. The goal is to provide a comprehensive understanding of VR advertising strategies and design, contribute to the theoretical development of this field, and offer practical implications for advertising practitioners.

2 Related Works

2.1 VR Advertising

VR has gained significant attention in the realm of advertising and marketing due to its unique characteristics, namely immersion, interactivity, and virtuality. These elements enable VR to provide users with near-realistic experiences that are distinct from the physical world (Brooks, 1999; Berg & Vance, 2017). The key strength of VR lies in its ability to trigger physical and emotional responses from users through interactivity, which enhances the level of immersion and optimizes the overall user experience (Chung, 2017). This interactivity, which allows users to engage with the virtual environment using multiple senses, is a critical aspect that sets VR apart from traditional advertising methods (Shin & Choi, 2015; Yi et al., 2007). The marketing potential of VR is well-documented, with research demonstrating its efficacy in offering immersive experiences, virtuality, and interactivity (Pantano & Servidio, 2012; Boyd & Koles, 2019).

Moreover, VR advertising has the potential to outperform traditional methods by offering novel visual experiences and fostering consumer-brand interaction (Kim & Chung, 2020). This is particularly advantageous in the context of out-of-home (OOH) advertising, where the transient exposure and various influencing factors have historically posed challenges in measuring the effectiveness of such campaigns (King & Tinkham, 1989; Fitts & Hewett, 1977). By presenting advertisements within a virtual environment through VR devices, the limitations of traditional OOH advertising can be overcome, as the virtual setting allows for controlled scenarios and enhanced measurability of advertising effectiveness.

In conclusion, the immersive, interactive, and virtual nature of VR has made it a compelling concept for advertisers and marketers, particularly in the evolving landscape of OOH advertising.

2.2 *Interactivity*

Interactivity is a multifaceted concept that encompasses the interactions between humans, and between humans and objects within a given environment (Lombard & Snyder-Duch, 2001). In the field of communication studies, interactivity is typically understood as the interaction between users and content, mediated through various channels (Um, 2013). This interactivity is achieved through speed, which is the rapidity of response, range, which is the degree of transformability, and mapping, which is the naturalness of the controls (Steuer, 1992).

Existing research has examined consumers' perceptions of interactivity, such as user control, responsiveness, personalization, and sense of presence, in various marketing and advertising contexts (Lee & Cho, 2011). In digital OOH advertising, studies have emphasized the core interactivity elements of perceived media realism, responsiveness to user needs, and understanding of the advertisement's narrative (Shin & Choi, 2015). Other literature has demonstrated the positive influence of interactivity on cognitive, affective, and behavioural outcomes in internet advertising (Yi et al., 2007).

Interactivity is a multifaceted concept that extends beyond merely capturing attention, as it can significantly impact user engagement, attitudes, and overall advertising effectiveness (Kim & Chung, 2019; Lee & Chung, 2012). Interactivity plays a crucial role in enhancing user experiences, strengthening the delivery of advertising messages, and fostering positive attitudes towards brands and products (Yi et al., 2007). Therefore, this study aims to determine through empirical research whether interactivity is sufficiently meaningful in VR advertising.

2.3 *Animation Effect*

Animation effects have been utilized as a design and advertising tool to enhance attention and emphasis (Diao & Sundar, 2004; Reeves & Nass, 1996), and are more effective than static advertising in terms of memory and attention (Yoo, Kim & Stout, 2004). Additionally, animation effects can influence immersion, aesthetics, and attitudes, which are critical factors in advertising effectiveness (Kim et al., 2013). In the VR context, the use of animation effects through lighting can be an appropriate approach because of the fact that all visual stimuli in VR are exposed as light cues, and also that light is a rapidly reactive visual element (Jeon & Hong, 2008).

Existing research has demonstrated the importance of lighting, illumination, and changes in light intensity in influencing attention and arousal (Park & Kim, 2020;

Kim & Hahn, 2009). These studies suggest that the quantity, colour, movement, shape, and speed of lighting can affect attention, comfort, aesthetics, negative warnings, and disturbance. Building on this, the comparison of flickering and flowing lighting effects could provide valuable insights, as they differ in rhythm despite similarities in speed and discontinuity (Baek et al., 2011). This study aims to explore the impact of lighting-based animation effects, as an example of virtuality, on advertising effectiveness.

2.4 Visual Attention

Visual attention, or selective attention, refers to the cognitive process by which the mind focuses on a specific object while diverting focus from other objects. It is considered the most crucial first step in the creative delivery process of an advertisement (Han, 2012), as information that fails to gain visual attention becomes challenging to process cognitively (Wedel & Pieters, 2000).

Among the various methods to enhance visual attention, the use of animation effects is widely employed as a key visual stimulus in advertising. Research has shown that animated banner advertisements elicit faster responses compared to their non-animated counterparts (Li & Bukovac, 1999). Furthermore, studies have found that higher levels of visual information or complexity leads to increased visual attention (Lu et al., 2011). Additionally, Kim et al. (2010) confirmed that greater interactivity results in heightened visual attention. However, excessive attempts to increase visual attention can lead to perceived intrusiveness and reactions such as avoidance or exceeding cognitive capacity (Ahn et al., 2009; Bang & Wojdynski, 2016).

Attention should be viewed as a starting point of advertising perception, and it is essential to adjust the level of visual attention accordingly, taking into account factors like the vividness of the stimulus, perceived intrusiveness, avoidance, and flow. Thus, attention is a crucial aspect to explore in the current study.

2.5 Vividness

Vividness refers to the ability provide sensory enrichment of the environment through new media or technologies (Jang et al., 2013; Steuer, 1992). The concept of vividness, significantly influenced by image aesthetics, is enhanced through high-resolution imagery, superior image quality, and the use of high-quality text (Vazquez et al., 2023).

These elements collectively contribute to markedly elevating the level of vividness perceived by users. Vividness is composed of two key dimensions: sensory depth and sensory breadth (Steuer, 1992). In the context of VR, interactivity with controllers engages the sense of touch, which likely to increases the sensory width and thus contributes to vividness (Hur et al., 2019). The animation effect is likely to affect sensory depth by increasing visual quality through the enhancement of movement and emotional factors.

Research has shown that information presentation with high vividness can stimulate users' sensory pathways and positively influence perceived shopping experience (van Noort et al., 2012). Importantly, vividness has been found to be closely related to the concept of flow, as both involve heightened engagement and immersion in the experience (Yoon et al., 2021). Therefore, vividness can be considered a key factor in enhancing the advertising experience in a VR environment.

2.6 *Perceived Intrusiveness and Avoidance*

Intrusiveness is defined as a phenomenon where an advertisement interferes with and disrupts the consumer's cognitive processes, thereby defeating its own purpose (Edwards et al., 2002). In this case, if the advertisement is perceived as intrusive or as a distraction, the consumer may feel that their cognitive processes are constantly interrupted by the ad. When an advertisement is perceived as intrusive, negative attitudes are formed toward it (Ying et al., 2009), which can subsequently lead to ad avoidance. Ad avoidance refers to the intentional behaviour of users ignoring or avoiding advertisements through a particular medium, encompassing all actions that reduce exposure to advertising messages (Yu & Kim, 2013).

A study by Jun (2020) found that the avoidance tendency tended to increase as the range of interactivity expanded. Avoidance is likely to increase as the level of interactivity increases, so it will be important to adjust to ensure that increased interactivity does not increase avoidance. In summary, perceived intrusiveness and avoidance have a negative impact on the overall ad experience and should be minimized. Therefore, this study investigates these dependent variables as part of its exploration.

2.7 *Flow*

The concept of flow, introduced by Csikszentmihalyi (1975, 1996), describes a state of complete engagement and satisfaction experienced during full participation in challenging activities. Flow is recognized as a multidimensional construct, encompassing elements such as challenge, control, attention, positive affect, mastery, curiosity, involvement, and intrinsic enjoyment (Trevino & Webster, 1992; Hsu & Lu, 2004). Csikszentmihalyi (1996) characterizes the flow state as involving clear goals, confidence, focused attention, minimized anxiety, a sense of unity, and altered time perception, all of which contribute to the activities becoming intrinsically enjoyable and sought after. In the advertising domain, this translates into an engaging, focused, and interesting ad viewing experience (Engel et al., 1986).

Research has supported the positive impact of flow on advertising effectiveness (Shin & Choi, 2014), highlighting the importance of examining flow in the context of VR OOH advertising. Given the high levels of immersion in VR, and the findings that interactivity and vividness can enhance flow (Rodríguez-Ardura & Meseguer-Artola, 2016; Yoon et al., 2021; Hoffman & Novak, 1996), these elements are crucial for inducing flow in VR advertising.

To summarize, flow is an important concept that is an indicator of whether an ad is interesting and engaging to viewers, also deeply connected to other important factors. This study aims to identify the link between flow, interactivity, and animation effect.

2.8 *Research Question*

This study aims to explore the basic considerations of ad design in the VR context by analyzing the impact of interactivity (low vs. high) and animation effect (static, flickering, flowing) on the mentioned factors when exposed to VR ads. Depending on the form of the ad, it is important to effectively capture attention and increase vividness and flow, while avoiding too much attention, as this can be perceived as intrusive and avoidable. Therefore, the research questions are as follows.

Research Question 1: Do interactivity and animation effects in virtual environment OOH advertisements have an interaction effect on (1) attention, (2) vividness, (3) perceived intrusiveness, (4) avoidance, and (5) flow?

3 Methodology

3.1 *Participants and Experimental Design*

The study involved 60 undergraduate students (26 males and 34 females) from a four-year university in northeastern Seoul. They were recruited through a public announcement, and the average age was 22.3 years old (SD = 2.01). None of the participants had previous experience with VR. All participants signed a consent form before participating in the experiment. Of the participants, 43.3% were without glasses, 36.7% wore glasses, and 20% wore contact lenses.

The study employed a 2 × 3 mixed factorial design, incorporating both a within-subject and a between-subject factor. The within-subject factor involved participants experiencing the virtual environment twice, each time with a different level of interactivity. For the between-subjects factor, participants were randomly assigned to one of three distinct ad formats, each with a different type of animation effect. To control for potential order effects, the researchers utilized counterbalancing, varying the order in which individual participants were presented with the virtual environment. The experiment was conducted with a total of 60 participants, who were evenly divided into three groups of 20.

3.2 Stimulus

This study developed a VR self-driving vehicle simulation to investigate the effects of interactivity and animation effect on VR advertising. The VR environment, created using the Unity Editor (2020.3.27f1), was condensed to a 90-s experience to prevent participant boredom. Participants interacted with the simulation using a Oculus Quest 2 HMD to maintain high precision and usability at interacting with VR content. The VR content was rendered at a resolution of 1832 × 1920, with a 90 Hz refresh rate and a field of view of 104° horizontally and 98° vertically.

Advertisement designs were standardized to optimize visibility, featuring light grey backgrounds and black text with concise messaging (Donthu et al., 1993). These advertisements used a high-involvement product, a notebook, with text incorporating the product, brand name and product features. By analysing 21 commercial advertisements from 2021 to 2023, the study included nine key product features in order of frequency: CPU, display, battery, design, weight, camera, connectivity, security, and speaker. Ad text exposure was controlled to prevent excessive familiarity, displaying each ad for 2.8 s with a 0.6-s interval (Leigh et al., 2006; MacInnis et al., 1991).

Interactivity levels were manipulated through the range and mapping of actions available with a levitating laptop model. High interactivity allowed participants to open/close, rotate, and on/off the laptop with 360° rotation using the controller's analogue stick (see Fig. 1a and b). In contrast, low interactivity restricted actions to horizontal laptop rotation using the controller buttons (see Fig. 1c).

In animation effect, three types of lighting animation effects were tested: static, flickering, and flowing. Static lighting remained constant (see Fig. 1a), flickering

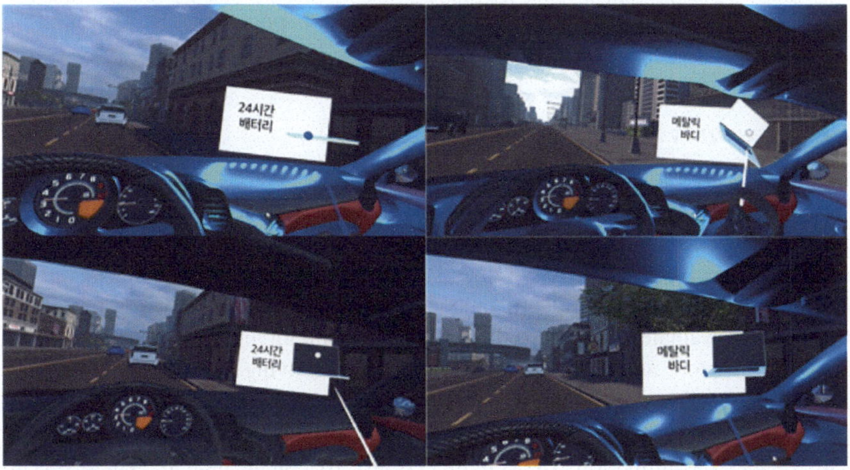

Fig. 1 Example of stimulus. From upper left to lower right, a, b, c, d. The text in the ad contains the product features of the laptop in Korean, and the text for each image is as follows in English a, c) 24 hour battery, b, d) metallic body(design).

lighting cycled on and off with a 0.4-s delay (see Fig. 1b and c), and flowing lighting moved along the edges of the advertisement (see Fig. 1d). All lighting conditions used a light range of 8 and an intensity of 1.7, with a blue-green colour (B4FF70) chosen for its soothing qualities and ability to attract attention (Kim & Hahn, 2009).

3.3 Procedures

The experimental setting was meticulously designed to ensure participants could fully engage with the experiment by isolating the space from external light and sound. Initially, participants received a detailed briefing on the experimental procedures, completed a consent form, and filled out a pre-survey. Subsequently, participants were fitted with a head-mounted display (HMD) adjusted for their comfort.

A preliminary tutorial was provided to help participants familiarize themselves with the various types of advertisements they would encounter in the virtual environment. Participants then experienced the self-driving vehicle simulation twice. Each session involved participants entering a virtual vehicle and observing a 30-s ad activation twice within a single drive. They were tasked with identifying both the type and the text of each ad. To maintain blinding and avoid bias, the conditions for each treatment were randomized. Participants encountered the virtual environment twice, each time with differing levels of interactivity, and one of the animation effects was randomly selected and applied to the ad in each session.

Post-exposure, participants were asked to evaluate the ad type they experienced based on several criteria: attention, vividness, perceived intrusiveness, avoidance, and flow. The entire experimental process, from instructions and tutorials to the VR experiences and subsequent survey completion, lasted approximately 30 min.

3.4 Measures

This study utilized and modified the survey items from the study by Lee and Chung (2012) to conduct a manipulation check. The questionnaire included four items to assess the perceived interactivity range, such as "I could manipulate this advertisement as I wanted" and "This advertisement is transformable." Additionally, four items were used to evaluate the perceived interactivity mapping, including "It was natural to move the laptop" and "It was natural to respond by moving the controller." In total, eight items were employed to measure the participants' perceived level of interactivity. The questionnaire included an item to verify whether participants correctly distinguished the animation effects in the VR advertisement, such as "There was no change in/was flickering/flowing animation effect on the advertisement background lighting."

The effectiveness of the level of interactivity and animation effects was measured using a 5-point Likert scale survey to evaluate participants' attention, vividness, perceived intrusiveness, avoidance, and flow. Attention is defined as 'the degree of how much an ad attracts attention and gaze' and was measured with 4 questions adapted from a questionnaire used by Chung (2015) ($\alpha = 0.816$). And vividness is defined as 'the degree of sensory richness of the ad type' and was measured with seven questions, which were adapted from a questionnaire by Chung and Yang (2012) ($\alpha = 0.880$). Perceived intrusiveness and ad type avoidance are defined as 'how much cognitive processing is interrupted by the ad type' and 'how much you want to intentionally avoid the ad type', and were measured using a questionnaire from Kim and Chung (2019), with 4 questions on perceived intrusiveness ($\alpha = 0.889$) and 3 questions on avoidance($\alpha = 0.860$), for a total of 7 questions. Lastly, flow is defined as 'the degree of engagement and high-quality experience with an ad type' and the questionnaire used to measure it is a seven-item questionnaire adapted from the Lee and Chung (2012) study ($\alpha = 0.873$).

4 Results

To verify the research question, a mixed repeated measures ANOVA was conducted. Prior to the analysis of the research question, we did a manipulation check to ensure that the experimental conditions and procedure were properly applied to the stimulus and performed to participants. Participants perceived significant differences among the three types of advertisements with different animation effects [$F(2, 57) = 491.145$, $p < 0.001$, $\eta p^2 = 0.945$], as well as significant differences between the two levels of interactivity applied to the advertisements [Overall interactivity: $F(1, 57) = 53.248$, $p < 0.001$, $\eta p^2 = 0.483$, Interactivity range: $F(1, 57) = 48.359$, $p < 0.001$, $\eta p^2 = 0.459$, Interactivity mapping: $F(1, 57) = 35.446$, $p < 0.001$, $\eta p^2 = 0.383$]. This confirmed that the experimental manipulations were applied as intended by the researcher, and the experimental stimuli could be used without any issues to conduct the research.

The results of the analysis for Research Question 1, which examined the differences in attention due to the interactivity and animation effects of advertisements in a virtual environment-based OOH setting, showed that the interaction effect was not statistically significant [$F(2, 57) = 1.342$, $p > 0.05$, $\eta p^2 = 0.045$]. The main effect of interactivity on attention was statistically significant [$F(1, 57) = 7.944$, $p < 0.01$, $\eta p^2 = 0.122$], with higher interactivity resulting in higher attention levels compared to lower interactivity [Low: $M = 3.917$, $SD = 0.685$, High: $M = 4.154$, $SD = 0.591$]. The main effect of animation effects on attention was not statistically significant [$F(2, 57) = 0.355$, $p > 0.05$, $\eta p^2 = 0.012$].

The results of the analysis for Research Question 2, which examined the differences in vividness due to the interactivity and animation effects of advertisements in a virtual environment-based OOH setting, showed that the interaction effect was not statistically significant [$F(2, 57) = 0.520$, $p > 0.05$, $\eta p^2 = 0.018$]. The main effect of interactivity on vividness was statistically significant [$F(1, 57) = 14.403$, $p < 0.001$, $\eta p^2 = 0.202$], with higher interactivity resulting in higher vividness compared to lower interactivity [Low: $M = 3.179$, $SD = 0.796$, High: $M = 3.560$, $SD = 0.764$].

The main effect of animation effects on vividness was not statistically significant [$F(2, 57) = 0.399$, $p > 0.05$, $\eta p^2 = 0.014$].

The results of the analysis for Research Question 3, which examined the differences in perceived intrusiveness due to the interactivity and animation effects of advertisements in a virtual environment-based OOH setting, showed that the interaction effect was not statistically significant [$F(2, 57) = 0.610$, $p > 0.05$, $\eta p^2 = 0.021$]. The main effect of interactivity on perceived intrusiveness was not statistically significant [$F(1, 57) = 0.731$, $p > 0.05$, $\eta p^2 = 0.013$]. The main effect of animation effects on perceived intrusiveness was also not statistically significant [$F(2, 57) = 0.324$, $p > 0.05$, $\eta p^2 = 0.011$].

The results of the analysis for Research Question 4, which examined the differences in avoidance due to the interactivity and animation effects of advertisements in a virtual environment-based OOH setting, showed that the interaction effect was not statistically significant [$F(2, 57) = 0.265$, $p > 0.05$, $\eta p^2 = 0.009$]. The main effect of interactivity on avoidance was not statistically significant [$F(1, 57) = 0.666$, $p > 0.05$, $\eta p^2 = 0.012$]. The main effect of animation effects on avoidance was also not statistically significant [$F(2, 57) = 0.011$, $p > 0.05$, $\eta p^2 = 0.000$].

The results of the analysis for Research Question 5, which examined the differences in flow due to the interactivity and animation effects of advertisements in a virtual environment-based OOH setting, showed that the interaction effect was not statistically significant [$F(2, 57) = 0.974$, $p > 0.05$, $\eta p^2 = 0.033$]. The main effect of interactivity on flow was statistically significant [$F(1, 57) = 12.145$, $p < 0.01$, $\eta p^2 = 0.176$], with higher interactivity resulting in higher flow compared to lower interactivity [Low: $M = 3.533$, $SD = 0.834$, High: $M = 3.919$, $SD = 0.791$]. The main effect of animation effects on flow was not statistically significant [$F(2, 57) = 0.636$, $p > 0.05$, $\eta p^2 = 0.022$].

5 Discussion

The present study examined the interaction effects of interactivity and animation effects in virtual environment advertisements on visual attention, vividness, perceived intrusiveness, avoidance, and flow. The results revealed no statistically significant interaction between interactivity and animation effects on any of the dependent variables. This finding suggests that the influence of interactivity and animation effects on consumer responses to virtual advertisements may be independent of each other.

One possible explanation for the lack of interaction effect is that the two design elements, interactivity and animation, may operate through distinct cognitive and perceptual processes. Interactivity, which allows users to actively engage with the advertisement content, may primarily influence attention, vividness, and flow by enhancing the user's sense of control and involvement. In contrast, animation effects may impact experience without necessarily interacting with the effects of interactivity.

The results showed that the high interactivity level had a significantly stronger positive effect on attention, vividness, and flow compared to the low interactivity level. This finding is consistent with previous research, which has suggested that interactivity can enhance user engagement and immersion in virtual environments (Hoffman & Novak, 1996; Steuer, 1992). When users are able to actively manipulate and interact with the advertisement content, they may become more attentive, experience a greater sense of vividness, and feel more immersed in the virtual experience, leading to increased flow.

Interestingly, despite the positive effects of interactivity on attention, vividness, and flow, the study found no significant differences in perceived intrusiveness and avoidance between the high and low interactivity conditions. This suggests that users may be able to maintain a level of control even in highly interactive virtual environments, mitigating any potential negative perceptions or avoidance behaviours.

The lack of a significant main effect of animation effects on any of the dependent variables was somewhat unexpected. This finding differs from the previous study (Cho & Chung, 2024), which found that the same form of lighting in virtual environment advertising can act as a visual attention-grabbing and influencing factor. In other words, it is possible that the specific animation effects used in this study (static, flickering and flowing light) were not sufficiently noticeable or engaging enough to elicit a significant difference in consumer response compared to interactivity.

Furthermore, the study found that the interactivity itself created a significant amount of visual complexity and load, which may have prevented attention to the animation effects and thus prevented cognitive processes from occurring properly (Lu et al., 2011; Ahn et al., 2009). These suggests that the interactivity may have been the dominant factor in shaping user perceptions, overshadowing the potential effects of the animation.

In conclusion, the present study provides valuable insights into the independent of interactivity and animation in virtual environment advertisements. While interactivity was found to have a positive influence on attention, vividness, and flow, the lack of interaction effects suggests that these design elements may operate through distinct mechanisms. Future research should analyse a broader range of perceived responses, such as ad memory effects, attitudes, and satisfaction, to determine actual ad effectiveness and expand the guidelines for advertising in VR.

Acknowledgements This work was supported by the Ministry of Education of the Republic of Korea and the National Research Foundation of Korea (NRF-2021S1A5A2A01062901).

References

Ahn, J., Byun, J., Lee, J., & Han, S. (2009). The Effect of Visual Stimuli in Internet Banner Ads: The Moderating Role of Task and Complexity of Visual Stimuli. *Korean Journal of Marketing, 24*(4), 67–86.

Baek, B.-N., Suk, H.-J., & Kim, M.-S. (2011). Visualizing Status Information Through Light Using LED. *Proceeding of 2011 Spring Conference from Korea Society of Color Studies*, 39–42.
Bang, H., & Wojdynski, B. W. (2016). Tracking users' visual attention and responses to personalized advertising based on task cognitive demand. *Computers in Human Behavior, 55*, 867–876.
Berg, L. P., & Vance, J. M. (2017). Industry use of virtual reality in product design and manufacturing: A survey. *Virtual Reality, 21*(1), 1–17.
Boyd, D. E., & Koles, B. (2019). Virtual reality and its impact on B2B marketing: A value-in-use perspective. *Journal of Business Research, 100*, 590–598.
Brooks, F. P. (1999). What's real about virtual reality? *IEEE Computer Graphics and Applications, 19*(6), 16–27.
Cho, M.-W., & Chung, D. (2024). The Effect of Depth Perception and Animation in Virtual Reality OOH Ad on Users' Cognitive Responses. *Journal of Information Technology Services, 23*(2), 117-133.
Chung, D. (2015). Eye tracking to select optimal advertising spots in Subway Cars. *The Korean Journal of Advertising and Public Relations, 17*(4), 146–172.
Chung, D. (2017). User-based theories and practices on virtual reality. *Informatization Policy, 024*(1), 3–29.
Chung, D., & Yang, H.-C. (2012). Reliability and validity assessment in 3D video measurement. *Journal of Broadcast Engineering, 17*(1), 49–59.
Csikszentmihalyi, M. (1996). *Creativity: Flow and the psychology of Discovery and invention.* New York: Harper/Collins.
Csikszentmihalyi, Mihaly. (1975). *Beyond boredom and anxiety: The experience of play in work and games.* San Francisco: Jossey-Bass Publishers.
Diao, F., & Sundar, S. S. (2004). Orienting response and memory for web advertisements: *Communication Research, 31*(5), 537–567.
Donthu, N., Cherian, J., & Bhargava, M. (1993). Factors influencing recall of outdoor advertising. *Journal of Advertising Research, 33*(3), 64–73.
Edwards, S. M., Li, H., & Lee, J.-H. (2002). Forced exposure and psychological reactance: Antecedents and consequences of the perceived intrusiveness of pop-up ads. *Journal of Advertising, 31*(3), 83–95.
Engel, J. F., Blackwell, R. D., & Miniard, P. W. (1986). *Consumer behavior*. Dryden Press.
Fitts, R. L., & Hewett, W. C. (1977). Utilizing the before after with control group experimental design to evaluate an outdoor advertising campaign. *Journal of Advertising, 6*(1), 26–39.
Han, K. (2012). An investigation on potential determinants of Social Network Service's promotional effects: Based on the analysis of Facebook users. *Journal of Public Relations, 16*(3), 132–168.
Hoffman, D. L., & Novak, T. P. (1996). Marketing in hypermedia computer-mediated environments: Conceptual Foundations. *Journal of Marketing, 60*(3), 50–68.
Hsu, C.-L., & Lu, H.-P. (2004). Why do people play on-line games? an extended Tam with social influences and flow experience. *Information & Management, 41*(7), 853–868.
Hur, H. J., Jang, J. Y., & Choo, H. J. (2019). The effect of VR fashion shopping channel characteristics and consumer's involvement in channel acceptance -focusing on the vividness, interactivity and fashion involvement-. *Journal of the Korean Society of Clothing and Textiles, 43*(05), 725–741.
Jang, S., Choi, J., & Lee, K. (2013). Evaluating the Sense of Presence for Mobile Augmented Reality Application Design. *Design convergence study, 12*(5), 335–350.
Jeon, S.-H., & Hong, J.-P. (2008). Considerations of automobile rear lamp design utilized LED light source. *KSDS Conference Proceeding*, 256–257.
Jun, J. (2020). Effects of immersion and empathy on college students' satisfaction of digital signage advertising. *Information Society & Media, 21*(2), 71–90.
Kim, J. S., & Chung, D. (2019). Influence of TrueView ad skip buttons on advertising effect. *Journal of Information Technology Service, 18*(1), 1–12.
Kim, K., Baek, S., Lee, H., & Chung, D. (2013). Effects of Visual Character Portal Site Advertising on Attention, Memory, Evaluation, and Intention. *Korean Journal of Broadcasting and Telecommunication Studies, 27*(6), 37–74.

Kim, M., & Hahn, M. (2009). Interactive LED light: A practical study of interactive design dimensions through an ambient information system for public. *Proceeding of HCI Korea 2009.*

Kim, W.-H., & Chung, H.-W. (2020). A conceptual study of application of digital technology to OOH advertising: Focused on extended reality technology. *Journal of Digital Contents Society, 21*(2), 301–310.

Kim, Y.-Y., Kwon, S.-H., & Kwon, Y.-J. (2010). Analysis of High School Students Visual Attention at Digital Contents on Biological Science. *Journal of Learner-Centrered Curriculum and Instruction, 15*(12), 91–110.

King, K. W., & Tinkham, S. F. (1989). The learning and retention of outdoor advertising. *Journal of Advertising Research, 29*(6), 47–57.

Lee, Hyunji, & Chung, D. (2012). Difference in Interactivity, Flow, Mood, Attitude, and Intention According to Smartphone Game Sensor. *Korean Journal of Broadcasting and Telecommunication Studies, 26*(1), 126–166.

Lee, S., & Cho, C. (2011). Influences of interactive ads‘ participation types on advertising effectiveness -Focusing on perceived interactivity of interactive film ads. *The Korean Journal of Advertising and Public Relations, 13*(4), 95–124.

Leigh, J. H., Zinkhan, G. M., & Swaminathan, V. (2006). Dimensional relationships of recall and recognition measures with selected cognitive and affective aspects of print ads. *Journal of Advertising, 35*(1), 105–122.

Li, H., & Bukovac, J. L. (1999). Cognitive impact of Banner Ad Characteristics: An experimental study. *Journalism & Mass Communication Quarterly, 76*(2), 341–353.

Lombard, M., & Snyder-Duch, J. (2001). Interactive advertising and presence : A framework. *Journal of Interactive Advertising, 1*(2), 56–65.

Lu, W., Li, M., Lu, S., Song, Y., Yin, J., & Zhong, N. (2011). Visual search strategy and information processing mode: An eye-tracking study on web pages under information overload. *Communications in Computer and Information Science*, 153–159.

MacInnis, D. J., Moorman, C., & Jaworski, B. J. (1991). Enhancing and measuring consumers' motivation, opportunity, and ability to process brand information from ADS. *Journal of Marketing, 55*(4), 32–53.

Pantano, E., & Servidio, R. (2012). Modeling innovative points of sales through virtual and immersive technologies. *Journal of Retailing and Consumer Services, 19*(3), 279–286.

Park, J. (2013). An exploratory study on redefining of role and status of OOH media. *Journal of Outdoor Advertising Research, 10*(2), 19–38.

Park, S.-J., & Kim, S.-W. (2020). Designing and fabricating of the high-visibility smart safety clothing. *Korean Society for Emotion and Sensibility, 23*(4), 105–116.

Reeves, B., & Nass, C. I. (1996). *The media equation: How people treat computers, television and new media like real people and places.* Stanford, CA: Centre for the Study of Language & Info.

Rodríguez-Ardura, I., & Meseguer-Artola, A. (2016). E-learning continuance: The impact of interactivity and the mediating role of imagery, presence and flow. *Information & Management, 53*(4), 504–516.

Shin, I., & Choi, Y. (2014). A study on the Effects of Storytelling Advertising. *Journal of Digital Convergence, 12*(10), 541–556.

Shin, I., & Choi, Y. (2015). A study on the acceptance of digital outdoor ad configuration factors : Focused on the type of difference. *Journal of Practical Research in Advertising and Public Relations, 8*(3), 73–104.

Steuer, J. (1992). Defining virtual reality: Dimensions determining telepresence. *Journal of Communication, 42*(4), 73–93.

Trevino, L. K., & Webster, J. (1992). Flow in computer-mediated communication. *Communication Research, 19*(5), 539–573.

Um, J. H. (2013). A study on the interaction types of interactive advertising based on the digital signage. *KOREA SCIENCE & ART FORUM, 14*, 271–284.

van Noort, G., Voorveld, H. A. M., & van Reijmersdal, E. A. (2012). Interactivity in brand web sites: Cognitive, affective, and behavioral responses explained by consumers' online flow experience. *Journal of Interactive Marketing, 26*(4), 223–234.

Vazquez, E. E., Patel, C., Alvidrez, S., & Siliceo, L. (2023). Images, reviews, and purchase intention on social commerce: The role of mental imagery vividness, cognitive and affective social presence. *Journal of Retailing and Consumer Services, 74*, 103415.

Wedel, M., & Pieters, R. (2000). Eye fixations on advertisements and memory for brands: A model and findings. *Marketing Science, 19*(4), 297–312.

Yi, K., Kim, W., & Kweon, S. (2007). A Study on the Effectiveness of Internet Ads : In terms of Interactivity and Context. *The Korean Journal of Advertising, 18*(1), 131–160.

Ying, L., Korneliussen, T., & Grønhaug, K. (2009). The effect of ad value, ad placement and ad execution on the perceived intrusiveness of web advertisements. *International Journal of Advertising, 28*(4), 623–638.

Yoo, C. Y., Kim, K., & Stout, P. A. (2004). Assessing the effects of animation in online banner advertising. *Journal of Interactive Advertising, 4*(2), 49–60.

Yoon, N., Lee, H., & Lee, Y. (2021). The Effect of VR Store Vividness on Immersion and User Satisfaction. *Journal of The Korean Society of Clothing and Textiles, 45*(3), 559–572.

Yu, S. Y., & Kim, J. H. (2013). The study on the ad avoidance factors affecting in Smartphones application display : Focus on advertising attitudes, perceived intrusion, medium dosage and media use motives. *The Korean Journal of Advertising, 24*(2), 125–143.

Factors Affecting Continuous Intention to Use of Unmanned Convenience Store TBSS in Korea: Focused on PPM Model

Haengnam Sung, Taeho Hong, and Jae-Ik Shin

Abstract After COVID-19, service contact points between humans and machines are expanding due to changes in the global economy and the development of the 4th Industrial Revolution technology. Additionally, the domestic minimum wage is rising, adding to the difficulties of operating convenience stores. With many convenience stores experimenting with unmanned convenience stores, the response from consumers can be said to be positive. This study investigates the factors that influence attitudes at unmanned convenience stores TBSS (technology-based self-service). The structural equation of AMOS 21.0 was used to test the hypotheses of this study. The results of the survey analysis of 587 respondents are as follows. First, it was found that authentication inconvenience has a negative effect on attitude. Second, usefulness and ease of use were found to affect attitude positively. Third, technology anxiety was found not to affect attitude at the 5% significance level. Fourth, social anxiety was found to have a positive effect on attitude. Fifth, the attitude affected the continuous intention to use positively. The conclusion presents the study's theoretical and practical implications and limitations based on these findings.

Keywords Unmanned convenience store · TBSS · Push-pull-mooring model · Attitude · Continuous intention to use

---

H. Sung
BK21 Digital Finance Education and Research Center, Pusan National University, Busan, South Korea
e-mail: haena@pusan.ac.kr

T. Hong
College of Business Administration, Pusan National University, Busan, South Korea
e-mail: hongth@pusan.ac.kr

J.-I. Shin (✉)
Department of Smart Distribution and Logistics, Gyeongsang National University, Jinju, South Korea
e-mail: sji15@gnu.ac.kr

T. Jung et al. (eds.), *XR and Metaverse*, Springer Proceedings in Business and Economics, https://doi.org/10.1007/978-3-031-77975-6_20

1 Introduction

Suppose the delivery method of services due to the development of technology has been made through the contacts between employees and customers in the past. In that case, it has recently been changing to service delivery through machines and human contacts. In particular, the prolonged coronavirus-19 has altered the world's economic order and the way people live and has been an opportunity to accelerate the growth of new retailers, such as unmanned stores (Kim & Kim, 2023). The increase in non-face-to-face consumption due to the impact of COVID-19, the burden of labor costs, and the development of information and communication technology (ICT), machine vision and electronic tags (RFID), the Internet of Things (IoT), and AI technology are combined to rapidly spread unmanned technology throughout the retail industry in Korea (Electronic newspaper, 2021). Unmanned convenience stores are becoming a new trend in retail. The TBSS of unmanned convenience stores is that digital experiences can provide novelty or joy to consumers. Still, on the other hand, they can also cause discomfort and fear due to unfamiliarity.

The unmanned distribution of traditional retail stores, such as convenience stores, hypermarkets, and supermarkets, where employees were considered essential, is rapidly becoming an irresistible change in consumers' lives. However, unlike the restaurant industry, using unmanned checkout counters in retail stores not only involves anxiety and risk for customers due to the difficulty of operating the machine and the absence of employees who can help but also may result in rejection of use due to negative user experiences. There is a high possibility that it will cause resistance to acceptance among non-inmates (Kim & Kim, 2023). Cheon (2018) suggested that while innovative, new services that have not been experienced before have the potential to cause negative attitudes due to their unfamiliarity. It is said that when an individual has doubts or negative feelings when facing a change, uncertainty or fear of newness is strengthened, and resistance occurs (Gelbrich & Sattler, 2014; Kim & Kim, 2023; Troisi et al., 2022). In Korea, unmanned stores rapidly expand due to changing working hours and pressure on labor costs. Although it is spreading, research on attitudinal factors such as consumers' refusal to accept or anxiety about unmanned stores is still lacking.

Studies on the acceptance of new technologies have been mainly based on the Technology Acceptance Model (TAM) (Gefen, 2003) and the TBSS quality evaluation model proposed by Davis (1989). Early studies of TBSS sought to identify important factors (e.g., convenience of use, enjoyment, etc.) of technology acceptance (Dabholkar & Bagozzi, 2002; Meuter et al., 2000). Research has been conducted to discuss consumers' satisfaction and acceptance attitudes toward innovative technologies introduced to reduce labor costs, such as bank ATMs and fast food kiosks, or to limit users' characteristics and interactivity about technology acceptance. However, many studies related to TBSS only address the positive aspects of motivation to accept technology through a technical and functional approach, such as perceived ease of use and usefulness and do not consider issues related to psychological factors, such as resistance or reluctance to accept technology (Kim & Kim, 2023).

In previous research on unmanned store TBSS, various studies have been conducted on attitude (Kim & Kim, 2023), loyalty (Kim & Jung, 2021), and success factors (Lee & Park, 2021). Consumers would have felt and evaluated the convenience and inconvenience of using the TBSS of an unmanned convenience store. In particular, consumers are being asked for a credit card when entering unmanned convenience stores in Korea and proving that they are adults. Switching behavior to a new system based on new information or innovative technology (Chang et al., 2017; Jeon et al., 2023) will help understand consumer behavior toward unmanned convenience stores. This switching behavior can be explained by the push-pull-mooring (PPM) theory (Park & Kim, 2018). In other words, meaningful implications can be derived if PPM theory is applied to explain why consumers use the TBSS of unmanned convenience stores.

The purpose of this study is to investigate the influence of push effects such as authentication inconvenience (entrance, adult), pull effects such as usefulness and ease of use, and mooring effects such as technological anxiety and social anxiety that affect the formation of consumer attitudes toward using TBSS at unmanned convenience stores. We also investigate the influence relationship between attitude and continuous intention to use and focus on presenting the implications and limitations of the research.

2 Literature Review

2.1 Push-Pull-Mooring

PPM comes from migration theory, which explains the factors that cause people to move from one region to another. Push factors are factors that cause people to leave their existing residences and are factors that have a negative impact (Moon, 1995). On the other hand, pull factors are attractive and positive factors that make potential migrants want to move to where they want to (Bansal & Taylor, 2002). However, even if all push-pull factors are reflected, migration may not occur due to individual circumstances or situations (Chung & Choi, 2019). Variables in the mooring concept that act as barriers to migration include switching costs, subjective norms, social influence, attitudes toward switching, past behavior, and the tendency to seek diversity (Bansal et al., 2005). Therefore, the push effect, pull effect, and mooring effect can be used as factors that can influence the attitudes formed by consumers while using unmanned convenience store TBSS.

The PPM theory can be seen as explaining feelings of anxiety, curiosity, excitement, and expectation of people's residential moving. This means that they have some fear, excitement, and anticipation of new environments and experiences that people are not familiar with. Similarly, changes in the retail industry's new environment include the fourth industrial revolution technology (artificial intelligence, big data, IoT, autonomous driving technology, robotics, 3D printing, etc.). It will also be meaningful to apply the PPM theory to how consumers' reactions to unmanned convenience stores are affected by the formation of attitudes and how they affect continuous use intentions.

Computers dominated initial studies related to technology acceptance. Attitude studies related to computers have developed into various fields according to different perspectives, such as social cognitive theory, technology acceptance model, and planning behavior theory. However, there needs to be more related studies that focus on personal-level variables, such as fear (Park et al., 2008). Innovation and the introduction of technology had a significant impact on the retail industry, and the rapid change in retail distribution has spread new types of stores, such as unmanned stores, by introducing self-service technology. The technology-based self-service used in banks, airports, and restaurants has expanded to retail business. TBSS means self-service technology such as ATMs, touch screens, kiosks, and self-scanning (Dabholkar, 1994). The importance of the unmanned store is emerging again. Companies can increase productivity by introducing TBSS and providing uniform service environments to reduce costs (Curran et al., 2003). TAM (Davis, 1989), a representative technology acceptance model, viewed ease of use and usefulness as a significant factor in the attitude toward technology acceptance. Dabholkar and Bagozzi (2002) used ease of use, performance, and fun as an effect of TBSS attitude. Ease of use and playfulness positively affect TBSS attitude (Min & Park, 2010). Perceived ease of use, performance, and pleasure positively affect TBSS attitude (Meng et al., 2017). TBSS motivation (ease of use, performance, and fun) affects TBSS attitude and use intention (Kim & Kim, 2023).

Concepts expressing users' fears related to the acceptance or use of technology include various terms such as technophobia, technology anxiety, computer anxiety, and computer phobia. With the growth of new technologies, it is essential to explore consumers' willingness and ability to use new technologies (Meuter et al., 2003). The spread of unmanned convenience stores depends on consumers' desire to use them. Technology anxiety leads to confusion about tasks to be performed, decreased motivation, and reduced ability awareness (Meuter et al., 2005). Technology anxiety also focuses on the user's psychological state related to technology tools. Technology anxiety is complex emotions such as nervousness, uncertainty, and fear related to technology use, how to use it, and learning (Troisi et al., 2022). Technology anxiety assesses an individual's emotional state regarding the acceptance and use of technology and is associated with fear of negative consequences such as mistakes. Consumers' familiarity with the technology used in unmanned convenience stores will determine the level of technology anxiety.

In addition, there are only studies on technical anxiety related to using kiosks in fast food stores or virtual unmanned clothing stores (Jeong & Park, 2020; Kim & Kim, 2023). Despite its importance, consumer attitudes toward complex technologies such as self-scanning at unmanned convenience stores were not entirely performed. Technology anxiety affects attitudes and experiences in using self-service (Meuter et al., 2003). Technology anxiety is an important decision factor for the attitude and behavior of intelligent city residents due to obstacles to accepting smart city technology (Troisi et al., 2022). It was confirmed that technical anxiety affects attitude (Jeong & Park, 2020). Ease of use and fun affect TBSS attitude through the moderating effect of technology anxiety (Kim & Kim, 2023).

Social anxiety is defined as an inconvenience of recognizing the perspective of others as a social object (Dabholkar & Bagozzi, 2002). The crowding of the retail environment can cause stress or lack of control (Hui & Bateson, 1991). In the retail industry, social anxiety is caused by the situational factors of on-site services, such as crowding of retail stores (Dabholkar & Bagozzi, 2002). If you can't use TBSS devices familiarly in the field of service, and if people on the side are watching it, tension may occur (Shim & Han, 2012). Perceived crowding has been shown to mediate the relationship between perceived ease of use, performance, and TBSS attitude (Meng et al., 2017). When ease of use and fun affect TBSS attitude, there is no moderating effect of social anxiety (Kim & Kim, 2023).

2.2 Attitude

Consumer attitude is an overall positive or negative evaluation of an object, and it is a significant phenomenon for researchers and marketing managers on consumer behavior because it influences consumers' actual purchasing behavior (Son et al., 2013). Attitudes strongly influence the final decision, especially when choosing a particular product or service and brand (Cherian & Jacob, 2012). The object of consumer attitude is a tendency that can be held toward a store, brand, or product and is maintained consistently (Jusoh & Ling, 2012). Consumer attitude can be divided into a cognitive component, which refers to the consumer's perception or belief about the consumer, and an affective component, which indicates the consumer's overall feeling about a specific object (Hawkins & Mothersbaugh, 2016). While the affective component is simply a combination of the consumer's feelings about exposure to a particular stimulus and the overall environment, the cognitive component can be said to be the experience of mental activities that involve not only exposure to stimuli but also acquiring new information and integrating it with existing knowledge (Van den Berg et al., 2006).

Attitude is a learned tendency to consistently react favorably or unfavorably toward a specific object, service, or product, through which customer behavior can be predicted (Engel et al., 2001). Attitudes are persistent because they are not significantly affected by time and have three components: affect, behavior, and cognition. Behavior refers to the consumer's intention to take action on the attitude object (Solomon, 2020). The principles of cognitive consistency, self-perception theory, and balance theory can explain attitude formation. Consumers value harmony between their cognition, affect, and behavior and seek to maintain the balance between these elements (Solomon, 2020). Morosan and DeFranco (2014) demonstrated that attitude impacts the customers' behaviors when using the latest mobile devices. Hence, the more favorable a consumer's attitude toward unmanned convenience store TBSS, the more likely they will rely on it in their purchasing decisions. A positive or optimistic attitude affects customer behavior (Molina & Saura, 2008). This is essential when customers first accept or adopt a new technology, whether they feel favorable or unfavorable (Adapa et al., 2020). This study used the PPM model to influence attitudes toward unmanned convenience store TBSS. This focuses on how PPM affects the attitude of unmanned convenience store TBSS.

Many previous studies have shown that attitudes toward TBSS positively affect intention to use (Dabholkar & Bagozzi, 2002; Kim & Kim, 2019; Meng et al., 2017). Lee et al. (2019) suggested that the perceived usefulness of the kiosk's relationship benefits had a positive effect on attitude, and attitude positively impacted the intention to continue using it. Kim (2021) argued that ease of use, usefulness, risk, and anxiety positively affect the attitude toward self-service technology. Jung and Cha (2020) suggested that show-rooming usage attributes (expectation confirmation, perceived usefulness) have a significant and positive effect on show-rooming attitude (cognitive, emotional). Showrooming attitude (cognitive, emotional) significantly and positively affects the continuance of showrooming intention.

Kim and Kim (2023) argued that the ease of use of unmanned store TBSS positively affects attitudes and that the degree of influence of ease of use on attitudes varies depending on the level of technological anxiety and social anxiety. Therefore, applying the PPM model as an influencing factor in consumers' attitudes when using unmanned convenience store TBSS seems possible.

2.3 Continuous Intention to Use

Consumers have varying degrees of loyalty to specific brands, stores, and companies. Loyalty has been defined as a deeply held commitment to rebuy or patronize a preferred product or service in the future despite situational influences and marketing efforts having the potential to cause switching behavior. More is needed to attract new customers; the company should also keep them and increase their business. Too many companies need more customer churn or defection. Adding customers here is like adding water to a leaking bucket (Kotler & Keller, 2016). The success of the unmanned convenience store TBSS will also depend on maintaining loyal customers. Loyal customers are more likely to continue using that store.

Consumer usage intentions are impacted by a variety of factors, such as pre-attachment (Shi et al., 2022), comfort (Hilken et al., 2020), informativeness, ease of use (Qin et al., 2021a, 2021b), perceived value (Oyman et al., 2022), and individual net benefits (Chiu et al., 2021). Though customers are interested in services with hedonic and utilitarian values, they form positive or negative attitudes about the services they experience. Once a positive attitude is formed, the continuous intention to use the service will increase. Unmanned convenience store TBSS can play a role in satisfying consumers' hedonic and utilitarian needs. The success of the store's TBSS will be influenced by continuous intention to use it.

Continuous intention to use is a crucial aspect of maintaining a constant relationship between service users and service providers, and the benefits formed based on past consumption experiences play a significant role in creating the intention (Yun et al., 2022). Park and Zhang (2022) suggested that attitudes toward unmanned convenience stores positively affect continuous intention to use. Lacap et al. (2023) argued that consumer attitude positively impacts loyalty in a chain of fast-food restaurants' innovative retailing technology. Continuous intention to use is a component of loyalty, and that attitude enhances loyalty. Khoa (2023) proved that attitude toward online advertising services positively influences continuous adoption intention. The fact that consumers are willing to continue using the TBSS of unmanned convenience stores will improve the store's sales and profitability.

Based on previous research, the following hypotheses were established to confirm the influence relationship between push-pull-mooring factors and attitudes according to the use of TBSS in unmanned convenience stores and the influence relationship between attitudes and continuous intention to use.

H1: Authentication inconvenience at unmanned convenience stores will significantly affect attitudes.
H2a: Usefulness at unmanned convenience stores will significantly affect attitudes.
H2b: Ease of use at unmanned convenience stores will significantly affect attitudes.
H3a: Technology anxiety at unmanned convenience stores will significantly affect attitudes.
H3b: Social anxiety at unmanned convenience stores will significantly affect attitudes.
H4: Attitude toward unmanned convenience stores will significantly affect continuous intention to use.

2.4 Methods

The purpose of this study is to focus on analyzing how push factors (authentication inconvenience), pull factors (usefulness and ease of use), and mooring factors (technology anxiety and social anxiety) affect attitudes among consumers who have experience using unmanned convenience stores, and how attitudes affect continuous usage intention. A research model, as shown in Fig. 1, is presented based on the theoretical background and hypothesis. Thus, Fig. 1 provides the conceptual model proposed in this study.

The survey included the push effect (authentication inconvenience), pull effect (usefulness and ease of use), mooring effect (technology and social anxiety), attitude, continuous intention to use, and demographic information. authentication inconvenience. Each variable borrowed items used in previous studies appropriately for this study. The operational definitions of the seven research variables used in this study were based on prior research and are shown in Table 1. Additionally, a 5-point Likert scale was used to measure the research variables.

An online survey was conducted to collect data targeting consumers who had experienced unmanned convenience stores in the western Gyeongnam region. Six hundred questionnaires were distributed, and 587 were used in the final analysis.

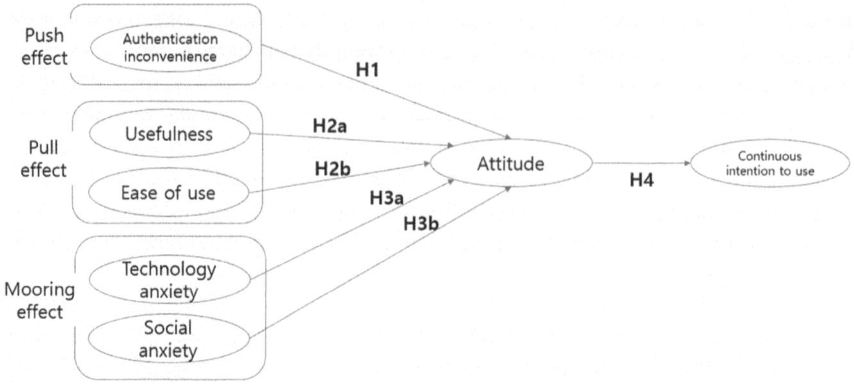

Fig. 1 Research model

Table 1 Operational definition of a variable

Latent variable (construct)		Operational definition	Researchers
Push effect	Authentication inconvenience	The inconvenience of authentication (credit card authentication, etc.) when entering an unmanned convenience store	Researchers themselves (2024)
Pull effect	Usefulness	The degree to which we believe that using unmanned convenience store TBSS will be helpful for visiting convenience stores (purchase speed, quality standardization, etc.)	Davis (1989), Pathasarathy and Bhattacherjee (1998)
	Ease of use	The degree to which you expect to be able to use TBSS of unmanned convenience stores without effort	Dabholkar and Bagozzi (2002), Karahanna et al. (1999), Davis (1989)
Mooring effect	Technology anxiety	Anxiety about the use of TBSS in unmanned convenience stores	Meuter et al. (2003), Troisi et al. (2022)
	Social anxiety	When using TBSS at an unmanned convenience store, discomfort with other people's gaze toward themselves	Dabholkar and Bagozzi (2002)
Attitude		The degree to which the use of unmanned convenience store TBSS is considered favorable or unfavorable	Dabholkar and Bagozzi (2002), Dabholkar (1994), Fishbein and Ajzen(1975)
Continuous intention to use		Intensity of continuous use of unmanned convenience store TBSS	Dabholkar and Bagozzi (2002), Gefen (1997), Davis (1989)

Table 2 Sample characteristics

Category		Freq	%
Gender	Male	131	22.3
	Female	456	77.7
Grade	1st grade	295	50.3
	2nd grade	202	34.4
	3rd grade	72	12.3
	4th grade or higher	18	3.1
Age	Teenagers (under 19)	11	1.87
	Early 20 s (20–24 years old)	559	95.23
	Late 20 s (over 25)	17	2.90

To the proposed relationships between the push effect, pull effect, mooring effect, attitude, and continuous intention to use, a structural equation modeling (SEM) was performed using analysis of moment structure (AMOS). SEM is an appropriate statistical method to examine hypothesized relationships among variables proposed in this study (Hair et al., 1998).

Please see the Table 1 for details of how to format headings.

3 Discussion and Conclusion

3.1 Sample Characteristics

Among 587 respondents, 77.7% are female, and 22.3% are male. The primary grade is 50.3% of the first grade. Early 20 s (20–24 years old) is 95.23%. Most of the users of the unmanned convenience store TBSS are young people, and the sample characteristics of this study can be considered suitable for this study (Table 2).

3.2 Validity and Reliability of Measurement Model

Confirmatory factor analysis (CFA) was conducted to evaluate the overall model fit of the measurement model (see Table 3). The model fit indices showed that $\chi^2 = 459.893$ (df = 168, χ^2/df = 2.737), GFI = 0.930, AGFI = 0.903, NFI = 0.955, IFI = 0.971, TLI = 0.963, CFI = 0.971, and RESEA = 0.053, which suggests that the measurement model reasonably fits the current data (Ha, 2012). Since Cronbach's alpha and composite reliability values exceed 0.7, the reliability of each variable is suitable (Hair et al., 1998; Nunnally & Bernstein, 1994). Since the factor loading value and AVE (average variance extracted) value exceeded 0.5, it can be said that convergent validity was secured (Anderson & Gerbing, 1988; Hair et al., 1998). A

Table 3 Confirmatory analysis

Latent variable	Indicator	Std. estimate	S.E	t-value	Cronbach's alpha	AVE	Composite reliability
Authentication inconvenience	AI1	0.826			0.895	0.743	0.897
	AI2	0.904	0.041	27.077***			
	AI3	0.859	0.042	25.13***			
Usefulness	Usef1	0.849			0.905	0.749	0.900
	Usef2	0.883	0.04	27.703***			
	Usef3	0.887	0.037	27.918***			
Ease of use	Eou1	0.851			0.910	0.765	0.907
	Eou2	0.899	0.039	28.498***			
	Eou3	0.888	0.04	27.968***			
Technology anxiety	TA1	0.864			0.891	0.714	0.882
	TA2	0.879	0.037	27.012***			
	TA3	0.822	0.037	24.449***			
Social anxiety	SA1	0.902			0.898	0.698	0.873
	SA2	0.933	0.03	34.25***			
	SA3	0.766	0.04	23.779***			
Attitude	Att1	0.886			0.838	0.551	0.784
	Att2	0.684	0.044	18.057***			
	Att3	0.832	0.042	23.035***			
Continuous intention to use	Ciu1	0.842			0.880	0.584	0.808
	Ciu2	0.845	0.046	22.858***			
	Ciu3	0.841	0.044	22.77***			

Model fit indices: $\chi^2 = 459.893$ (df = 168, χ^2/df = 2.737), GFI = 0.930, AGFI = 0.903, NFI = 0.955, IFI = 0.971, TLI = 0.963, CFI = 0.971, RESEA = 0.053

*** $p < 0.001$

more robust method of measuring discriminant validity is one in which a correlation between two constructs should be lower than the squared root of the AVE value for any of the two constructs (Fornell & Larcker, 1981). Thus, all variables have discriminant validity (Table 4).

3.3 Hypothesis Testing

A structural model was evaluated to test H1 through H4. The goodness-of-fit statistics of the proposed model showed that the model reasonably fits the current data ($\chi^2 =$ 492.098, df = 173, χ^2/df = 2.844, GFI = 0.925, AGFI = 0.900, NFI = 0.951, IFI =

Table 4 Discriminant validity

Variables	√AVE	Correlation					
		AI	Usef	Eou	TA	SA	Att
AI	0.862	1					
Usef	0.866	0.61	1				
Eou	0.874	0.537	0.592	1			
TA	0.845	0.569	0.595	0.574	1		
SA	0.835	0.625	0.614	0.569	0.596	1	
Att	0.742	0.508	0.622	0.563	0.567	0.632	1
Ciu	0.764	0.323	0.303	0.304	0.364	0.268	0.360

AI: Authentication inconvenience, Usef: Usefulness, Eou: Ease of use, TA: Technology anxiety, SA: Social anxiety, Att: Attitude, Ciu: Continuous intention to use

0.968, TLI = 0.961, CFI = 0.968, and RESEA = 0.056) (Ha, 2012). The results of testing the hypothesis using AMOS 21.0 are presented in Table 5.

Authentication inconvenience (entrance, adult) was found to have a negative effect on attitude (path coefficient = −0.212, t-value = −2.199), and hypothesis H1 was accepted at the significance level of 5%. Consumers who have used unmanned convenience stores feel uncomfortable with entrance and adult authentication and form negative attitudes. Usefulness was found to positively affect attitude (path coefficient = 0.179, t-value = 2.402), and hypothesis H2a was accepted at the significance level of 5%. The usefulness of unmanned convenience stores creates positive attitudes. Ease of use was found to positively affect attitude (path coefficient = 0.455, t-value = 4.764), and hypothesis H2b was accepted at the significance level of 1%.

Table 5 Hypothesis test results

Hypotheses: path		Std. estimate	S.E.	t-value	p-value	Results	R^2
H1: AI →	Att	−0.212	0.123	−2.199	0.025*	Supported	0.520
H2a: Usef →		Usef	0.092	2.402	0.016*	Supported	
H2b: Eou →		Eou	0.115	4.764	***	Supported	
H3a: TA →		TA	0.074	1.774	0.076	Not supported	
H3b: SA →		SA	0.067	3.976	***	Supported	
H4: Att →	Ciu	Att	0.049	7.177	***	Supported	0.110

Model fit indices: χ^2 = 492.098 (df = 173, χ^2/df = 2.844), GFI = 0.925, AGFI = 0.900, NFI = 0.951, IFI = 0.968, TLI = 0.961, CFI = 0.968, RESEA = 0.056

***$p < 0.001$, **$p < 0.01$, *$p < 0.05$

AI: Authentication inconvenience, Usef: Usefulness, Eou: Ease of use, TA: Technology anxiety, SA: Social anxiety, Att: Attitude, Ciu: Continuous intention to use

The ease of use of unmanned convenience stores creates positive attitudes. Technology anxiety does not affect attitude (path coefficient = 0.115, t-value = 1.774), and hypothesis H3a was rejected at the significance level of 5%. The fact that technological anxiety about unmanned convenience stores does not affect attitude formation shows that technological anxiety may not be high. Social anxiety appeared to positively affect attitude (path coefficient = 0.250, t-value = 3.976), and hypothesis H3b was accepted at the significance level of 1%. This shows that social anxiety plays a role in forming consumers' positive attitudes toward unmanned convenience stores. Attitude appears to positively affect the continuous intention to use (path coefficient = 0.332, t-value = 7.177), and hypothesis H4 was accepted at the significance level of 1%. It shows that a positive attitude toward unmanned convenience stores leads to continued intention to use them. Therefore, five hypotheses except hypothesis H3a were accepted as statistically significant.

3.4 Conclusion

This study applied the push-pull-mooring (PPM) model to consumers using unmanned convenience stores, which has recently become an issue. Based on the results of the empirical analysis, the research implications are presented as follows. First, authentication inconvenience (entrance, adult), which is a push effect, was found to have a negative effect on attitudes. Second, usability and ease of use, which are pull effects, were found to affect attitude positively. Third, technological anxiety, a mooring effect, was found not to influence attitude, and social anxiety was found to positively impact attitude. Fourth, it shows that the intention to continue using TBSS increases when the attitude toward the use of TBSS in unmanned convenience stores is favorable. Amid fundamental changes in retail formats and technology, it is essential to consider consumer attitudes and reactions. Consumers can experience the benefits of innovation and develop positive attitudes. At the same time, some consumers may fear incorrect identification and confusion when making transactions.

Based on the empirical analysis results of this study, theoretical and practical implications are presented as follows. In general, PPM theory is the leading paradigm of population migration research (Bansal et al., 2005). Although this theory has been applied to various areas of marketing (Handarkho & Harjoseputro, 2019; Lisana, 2023; Nugroho & Wang, 2023; Xu et al., 2021), it would be meaningful to apply it to unmanned convenience stores in this study. The attitude-continuous intention to use the model is also meaningful in distribution marketing. This study is meaningful in that it confirmed the influence of PPM on forming attitudes toward unmanned convenience stores. This study used technology and social anxiety to influence attitude factors. Unmanned convenience stores require technologies such as the Internet of Things, cameras, payment systems, entrance and adult authentication, artificial intelligence, and big data, and from the consumer's perspective, the experience of unmanned convenience stores arouses curiosity. Therefore, it was confirmed that the PPM-attitude-continuous use intention model was meaningful in unmanned convenience stores.

With the advent of the Fourth Industrial Revolution and rising labor costs, retailers began to show interest in unmanned stores. They are installing kiosks and self-checkout counters in stores and further introducing unmanned stores to monitor consumer reactions. Amid fundamental changes in retail formats and technology, it is important to consider consumer attitudes and reactions. Consumers experience the benefits of innovation and develop positive attitudes. At the same time, some consumers may fear incorrect identification and confusion when making transactions (Lee, 2019).

First, authentication inconvenience (entrance, adult), which is a push effect, was found to have a negative effect on attitudes. The sample in this study is 95.23% in their early 20 s, showing a negative perception of entering unmanned convenience stores and adult authentication. If they are the main target customers of convenience stores, they will need to change entrance and adult authentication in the direction they prefer.

Second, usefulness and ease of use, which are pull effects, were found to positively affect attitude. And ease of use appeared to have more influence on attitude than usefulness. The sample in this study can be said to be digital natives and may not find the digital experience of unmanned convenience stores very novel. Therefore, focusing on the strengths of unmanned convenience stores, such as ease of use rather than usefulness, may achieve better results.

Third, while technology anxiety, a mooring effect, was found not to affect attitude, social anxiety was found to have a positive impact on attitude. Troisi et al. (2022) suggested that technology anxiety is an essential determinant of attitude and behavioral intention. In the case of this study, the opposite result was obtained. This shows that consumers in their early 20 s do not experience technical difficulties in using unmanned convenience stores. On the other hand, it shows that social anxiety plays a role in forming positive attitudes toward unmanned convenience stores. This is because, in cases where TBSS devices cannot be used familiarly in the service provision field, tension may arise if people nearby are watching (Shim & Han, 2012).

Fourth, it shows that continuous intention to use TBSS increases when the attitude toward the use of TBSS in unmanned convenience stores is favorable. The theory of Reasoned Action (TRA) is the theory that attitudes influence behavioral intentions. It was empirically verified that attitude toward TBSS positively affects the intention to use (Dabholkar & Bagozzi, 2002). Therefore, it can be seen that forming a positive attitude toward unmanned convenience stores leads to continued intention to use them.

The limitations of this study and future research directions are presented as follows. First, it can be said that the gender ratio deviation is somewhat severe in the characteristics of the sample. Future research will require improvement in this area. Additionally, the sample's age is concentrated in those in their 20 s, and future research will need to investigate differences between various age groups. Second, it will be necessary to develop multiple research variables influencing attitudes toward unmanned convenience stores and continuous intention to use them. Third, because this study is a cross-sectional study that only investigated the survey period, there are limitations in tracking changes in attitudes toward and continuous intention to use unmanned convenience stores TBSS over time. Longitudinal research will be needed to improve this area.

References

Adapa, S., Fazal-e-Hasan, S. M., Makam, S. B., Azeem, M. M., & Mortimer, G. (2020). Examining the Antecedents and Consequences of Perceived Shopping Value Through Smart Retail Technology, *Journal of Retailing Consumer Services*. 52:101–901.

Anderson, J. C. & Gerbing, D. W. (1988). Structural Modeling in Practice: A Review and Recommended Two-Step Approach, *Psychological Bulletin*. 103(3):411–423.

Bansal, H. S., & Taylor, S. F. (2002). Investigating Interactive Effects in the Theory of Planned Behavior in a Service-Provider Switching Context, *Psychology & Marketing*. 19(5):407–425.

Bansal, H. S., Taylor, S. F., & James, Y. S. (2005). Migrating to New Service Providers: Toward a Unifying Framework of Consumers' Switching Behaviors, *Journal of the Academy of Marketing Science*. 33(1):96–115.

Chang, H. H., Wong, K. H., & Li, S. Y. (2017). Applying push-pull-mooring to investigate channel switching behaviors: M-shopping self-efficacy and switching costs as moderators. *Electronic Commerce Research and Applications, 24*, 50–67.

Cheon, H. M. (2018). The Impact of Unattended Store Service Characteristics on Intelligent Service Value: Focusing on the Moderating Effects of Unattended Store Spreading Expectation, *Journal of Distribution and Management Research*. 21(6):99–107.

Cherian, J. &and Jacob, J. (2012). Green Marketing: a Study of Consumers' Attitude Towards Environment Friendly Products, *Asían Social Science*. 8(12):117–26.

Chiu, C. L., Ho, H. C., Yu, T., Liu, Y., & Mo, Y. (2021). Exploring Information Technology Success of Augmented Reality Retail Applications in Retail Food Chain, *Journal of Retailing and Consumer Services*, 61(1):102561.

Chung, B.-G. & Choi, Y.-A. (2019). Factors Affecting Intention to Experience of 6th Industry—Including Gender Differences—, *Korean Corporation Management Review*. 87:119–140.

Curran, J. M., Meuter, M. L., & Surprenant, C. F. (2003). Intentions to Use Self-Service Technologies: a Confluence Of Multiple Attitudes, *Journal of Service Research*. 5(3):209–224.

Dabholkar, R. A. (1994). Incorporating Choice into an Attitudinal Framework: Analyzing Models of Mental Comparison Processes, *Journal of Consumer Research*. 21(1):100–118.

Dabholkar, R. A. & Bagozzi, R. P. (2002). An Attitudinal Model of Technology-Based Self-Service-Moderating Effects of Consumer Traits and Situational Factors, *Journal of the Academy of Marketing Science*. 30:184–201.

Davis, F. D. (1989). Perceived Usefulness, Perceived Ease of Use, and User Acceptance of Information Technology, *MIS Quarterly*. 13(3):319–340.

Electronic newspaper (2021). *As Unmanned Stores Spread, The New Retail Ecosystem Grows*. Seoul, Korea.

Engel, J. F., Blackwell, R. D., & Miniard, P. W. (2001). *Consumer Behavior*. NY: Harcourt College Publishers.

Fishbein, M. & Ajzen, I. (1975). *Belief, Attitude, Intention, and Behavior: An Introduction to Theory and Research. Reading*. MA: Addison-Wesley.

Fornell, C. & Larcker, D. (1981). Evaluating Structural Equation Models with Unobservable Variables and Measurement Error, *Journal of Marketing Research*. 18(1):39–50.

Gefen, D. (1997). *Building users' trust in freeware providers and the effects of this trust on users' perceptions of usefulness, ease of use and intended use*. Unpublished Doctoral Dissertation, Georgia State University.

Gefen, D. (2003). TAM or Just Plain Habit: a Look at Experienced Online Shoppers, *Journal of Organizational and End User Computing*. 15(3):1–13.

Gelbrich, K. & Sattler, B. (2014). Anxiety, Crowding, and Time Pressure in Public Self-Service Technology Acceptance, *Journal of Services Marketing*. 28(1):82–94.

Ha, J. (2012). The Effects of Dining Atmospherics on Behavioral Intentions Through Quality Perception, *Journal of Services Marketing*. 26(3):204–215.

Hair, J. F., Anderson, R. E., Tatham, R. L. and Black, W. C. (1998). *Multivariate Data Analysis*, 5th Ed., Prentice Hall, Upper Saddle River, NJ.

Handarkho, Y. D. & Harjoseputro, Y. (2019). Intention to Adopt Mobile Payment in Physical Stores: Individual Switching Behavior Perspective Based on Push–Pull–Mooring (PPM) Theory, *Journal of Enterprise Information Management*. 33(2):285–308.

Hilken, T., Keeling, D. I., de Ruyter, K., Mahr, D., & Chylinski, M. (2020). Seeing Eye to Eye: Social Augmented Reality and Shared Decision Making in the Marketplace, *Journal of Academy of Marketing Science*. 48(2):143–164.

Hui, M. K. & Bateson, J. E. G. (1991). Perceived Control and the Effects of Crowding and Consumer Choice on the Service Experience, *Journal of Consumer Research*. 18(2):174–184.

Jeong, S. W. & Park, J.-S. (2020). Impacts of Technology Anxiety and Perceived Productivity on Attitude toward Self-Service Technology—The Moderating Role of Need For Interaction—, *The Research Journal of the Costume Culture*. 28(4):480–491.

Jeon, W., Lee, J. S., Jeon, G., & Choi, J. I. (2023). A study on the switching intention to open source DBMS service. *Journal of Korea Service Management Society, 24*(3), 24–46.

Jung, S. G. & Cha, K. C. (2020). The Relationship among Show-Rooming Usage Attributes, Attitudes and Continuance Show-Rooming Intention of Single-Person Household, *Korean Journal of Marketing*. 35(August):69–89.

Jusoh, Z. M. & Ling, G. H. (2012). Factors Influencing Consumer's Attitude Towards E-Commerce Purchases through Online Shopping, *International Journal of Humanities and Social Science*. 2(4):223–30.

Karahanna, E. & Straub, D. W. & Norman, Chervany, L. (1999). Information Technology Adoption Across Time: a Cross-Sectional Comparison of Pre-Adoption and Post-Adoption Beliefs, *MIS Quarterly*. 23(2):183–213.

Khoa, B. T. (2023). The Role of Self-Efficacy and Firm Size in the Online Advertising Services Continuous Adoption Intention: Theory of Planned Behavior Approach, *Journal of Open Innovation: Technology, Market, and Complexity*. 9(1):100025.

Kim, S. E. (2021). Self-Service Technology: Ease of Use, Usefulness, Need for Interaction, Risk, Anxiety Towards Attitude, *Journal of the Korea Society of Information Technology Policy & Management*. 13(2):2387–2394.

Kim, J. & Jung, Y. (2021). The Influence of the Environmental Characteristics of Unmanned Convenience Stores and the Personal Characteristics of Customers on Emotional Experience, Affectively Based Satisfaction, and Loyalty, *Journal of Channel and Retailing*. 26(3):83–113.

Kim, J. H. & Kim, S. H. (2023). A Study on Attitudes Towards Technology-Based Self-Service (TbSS) in Unmanned Stores: Focusing On The Moderating Effect Of Technology Anxiety and Social Anxiety, *Journal of Marketing Science*. 31(2):73–91.

Kim, K.-M. & Kim, N.-J. (2019). Analysis of Food Consumers of Usage Attitude and Usage Intention Towards Technology-Based Self-Service (TBSS): Focused on TRAM (Integrated Technology Readiness and Acceptance Model), *Journal of Tourism and Leisure Research*. 31(3):237–257.

Kotler, P. & Keller, K. L. (2016). *Marketing management* 15ed. Pearson, New York.

Lacap, J. P. G., Plaza, M. N., Caballero, J., & Cruz, M. D. (2023). Factors Affecting Consumer Attitude and Loyalty: Evidence from a Philippine Chain of Fast-Food Restaurants' Smart Factors Affecting Consumer Attitude and Loyalty Retailing Technology, *Journal of Science and Technology Policy Management*. https://doi.org/10.1108/JSTPM-09-2022-0159.

Lee, N. K. & Park, H. (2021). Key Successful Factors for Unmanned Convenience Stores in the Fourth Industrial Revolution: Case of E-Mart24 Self-Store, *Journal of the Korea Industrial Information System Research.* 26(2):73–94.

Lee, O.-J., Kim, H.-Y., & Lee, S.-B. (2019). The Influence of Relational Benefits of Kiosk on Perceived Usefulness, Confirmation, Attitude and Continuance Usage Intention, *Korean Journal of Hospitality and Tourism.* 28(5):73–88.

Lee, S. M. (2019). *Distribution logistics management 4.0 in the era of the 4th Industrial Revolution.* Dooyangsa, Seoul.

Lisana, L. (2023). Factors Affecting University Students Switching Intention to Mobile Learning: a Push-Pull-Mooring Theory Perspective, *Education and Information Technologies*, 28:5341–5361.

Meuter, M. L., Ostrom, A. L., Roundtree, R., & Bitner, M. J. (2000). Self-Service Technologies: Understanding Consumer Satisfaction with Technology-Based Service Encounters, *Journal of Marketing.* 64(3):50–64.

Meuter, M. L., Ostrom, A. L., Bitner, M. J., & Roundtree, R. (2003). The Influence of Technology Anxiety on Consumer Use and Experience with Self-Service Technologies, *Journal of Business Research.* 56:899–906.

Meuter, M. L., Bitner, M. J., Ostrom, A. L., & Brown, S. W. (2005). Choosing Among Alternative Service Delivery Modes: an Investigation of Customer Trial of Self-Service Technologies, *Journal of Marketing.* 69:61–83.

Meng, F., Park, K. S., & Dh, S. W. (2017). The Moderating Effects of Technology Readiness, User Traits and Situational Factors on Usage Attitude and Intention to Technology-Based Self-Service, *Journal of Korea Service Management Society.* 18(3):69–104.

Min, B. K. & Park, J. Y. (2010). Determinants of Users Acceptance of Technology-Based Self-Service, *Journal of Korea Technology Innovation Society.* 13(1):204–230.

Molina, R. & Saura, G. I. (2008). Perceived Value, Customer Attitude and Loyalty in Retailing, *Retail Leisure Property.* 7:305–314.

Moon, B. (1995). Paradigms in Migration Research: Exploring 'Moorings' as a Schema, *Progress in Human Geography.* 19(4):504–524.

Morosan, C. and DeFranco, A. (2014). When Tradition Meets the New Technology: an Examination of the Antecedents of Attitudes and Intentions to Use Mobile Devices in Private Clubs, *International Journal of Hospitality Management.* 42:126–136.

Mothersbaugh, D., & Hawkins, D. I. (2016). *Consumer behavior: Building marketing strategy.* McGraw-Hill, NY.

Nugroho, A. & Wang, W.-T. (2023). Consumer Switching Behavior to an Augmented Reality (AR) Beauty Product Application: Push-pull Mooring Theory Framework, *Computers in Human Behavior.* 142(May):107646.

Nunnally, I. C. & Bernstein, I. H. (1994). *Psychometric theory* (3rd ed.). NY: McGraw Hill.

Oyman, M., Bal, D., Ozer, S. (2022). Extending the Technology Acceptance Model to Explain How Perceived Augmented Reality Affects Consumers' Perceptions, *Computers in Human Behavior.* 128(12):107127.

Park, Y. B, Jeon, O. S., & Park, S. K. (2008). A study on Relationships between Service Quality and Loyalty to Enhance Profitability of Bank-based the Moderating Role of Technophobia-, *Productive Research: An International Interdisciplinary Journal.* 22(2):25–50.

Park, H. S., & Kim, S. H. (2018). Switching intention of smart appliance: A perspective of the push-pull-mooring framework. *Journal of Digital Convergence, 16*(2), 127–137.

Park, H. J. & Zhang, Y. (2022). Technology Readiness and Technology Paradox of Unmanned Convenience Store Users, *Journal of Retailing and Consumer Services.* 60:102523.

Parthasarathy, M. & Bhattacherjee, A. (1998). Understanding Post-adoption Behavior in the Context of Online Services, *Information System Research.* 9(4):362–379.

Qin, H., Osatuyi, B., Xu, L. (2021a). How Mobile Augmented Reality Applications Affect Continuous Use and Purchase Intentions: a Cognition-affect-conation Perspective, *Journal of Retailing and Consumer Services.* 63(7):102680.

Qin, H., Peak, D.A., Prybutok, V. (2021b). A Virtual Market in your Pocket: How Does Mobile Augmented Reality (MAR) Influence Consumer Decision Making? *Journal of Retailing and Consumer Services*. 58(10):102337.

Shi, T., Tian, R.G., Tu, C.Z., & Lim, C. L. (2022). Affective Factors Influencing Responses to International Brand Alliances, *Marketing Intelligence & Planning*. 40(5):656–670.

Shim, H. S. & Han, S. L. (2012). Effects of TR and Consumer Readiness on SST Usage Motivation, Attitude and Intention, *Asia Marketing Journal*. 14(1):25–51.

Solomon, M. R. (2020). *Consumer behavior: Buying, Having, and Being* 13ed. NY: Pearson.

Son, J., Jin B., & George, B. (2013). Consumers' Purchase Intention Toward Foreign Brand Goods, *Management Decision*. 51(2):434–50.

Troisi, O., Fenza, G., Grimaldi, M. & Loia, F. (2022). Covid-19 Sentiments in Smart Cities: the Role of Technology Anxiety before and during the Pandemic, *Computers in Human Behavior*. 126:1–16.

Van den Berg, H., Manstead, A. SR, van der Pligt, J., & Wigboldus, D. HJ (2006). The Impact of Affective and Cognitive Focus on Attitude Formation, *Journal of Experimental Social Psychology*. 42(3):373–79.

Xu, H., Wang, J., Tai, Z., & Lin, H.-C. (2021). Empirical Study on the Factors Affecting User Witching Behavior of online Learning Platform Based on Push-pull-Mooring Theory, *Sustainability*. 13:7087.

Yun, J.-W., Kim, D.-H., & Park, J.-K. (2022). A Study on the Effect of China Internet Primary Bank Simple Payment Service on Consumer's Attitudes and Continuous Use Intentions, *Journal of Product Research*. 40(4):79–87.

Are We Attractive to You? A Study on Metaverse Recruitment and Organisational Attractiveness

David Jiwon Hong

Abstract The study explores the impact of the "metaverse" on organisational attractiveness in recruitment. It investigates how the use of a metaverse technology influences candidates' perceptions and application decisions. Data from 108 respondents, collected through a questionnaire distributed online, were analysed using R, SPSS, and Excel. The results indicate that organisational attractiveness in metaverse recruitment is influenced by perceived ethics, fairness, and candidates' metaverse experience. Furthermore, gender and socio-professional category also have an indirect effect on candidates' views. Qualitative analysis highlights concern about discrimination and environmental, data protection, and health issues. However, the study acknowledges limitations in sample size and regression model quality. In conclusion, the study emphasises the necessity of investigating the long-term implications of metaverse technology for HRM strategies and recruitment, while also underscoring the importance of further research on long-term effects and ethical considerations.

Keywords Metaverse · Recruitment · Organisational attractiveness · Ethical perception · Fairness perception

1 Introduction

The term "metaverse" has recently caught the attention from both the public and organisations. Some of these entities have already begun integrating virtual worlds as extensions of their physical offices. In 2018, the company Dare. Win conducted job interviews on the game Fortnite (Rabinovich, 2018). Few years later, Carrefour and VR Académie created a metaverse specific to the company for a recruitment session for students (Hooi, 2022). In April 2023, it was Auchan's turn to do the same (Auffray, 2023). Havas also created a virtual world called *Metaverse by* Havas. The

D. J. Hong (✉)
Ecole Doctorale de Management Panthéon Sorbonne – Laboratoire PRISM, Paris 1 Panthéon-Sorbonne University, Paris, France
e-mail: david.hong@univ-paris1.fr

T. Jung et al. (eds.), *XR and Metaverse*, Springer Proceedings in Business and Economics, https://doi.org/10.1007/978-3-031-77975-6_21

objective is to conduct job interviews in a building constructed by the company on a plot of land purchased for €120,000 in the Sandbox (Bonilla, 2022).

The concept of recruiting via a metaverse is derived from remote job interviews conducted on Zoom or Microsoft Teams. The difference between videoconferencing meetings and this proposed method lies in the fact that both parties will be present in the same virtual world, in which each can create an avatar, move around and even take a virtual tour of the company's building. It may even be possible to evaluate a candidate's skills (safety gestures, spotting anomalies in a factory, etc.). However, it is necessary to consider whether this method of recruitment is considered attractive by candidates.

2 Literature Review

2.1 Human Resources Management 4.0

We can distinguish four levels/versions of HRM (Geuze, 2020):

- HRM 1.0: is the first level and is therefore limited to traditional and basic human resources management.
- HRM 2.0: HR is positioned between employees, management, and governance. Collaboration is key.
- HRM 3.0: HR conducts a detailed analysis (modelling, simulation) of the situation, taking other factors into account when making decisions.
- HRM 4.0: It is a combination of the previous three levels and the use of recent technologies such as AI and metaverse.

The concept of HRM 4.0 was born of the introduction of new technologies (such as artificial intelligence and big data) in industry (Galindo et al., 2019). Industry 4.0 is based on automation, digitalisation, real-time information exchange, efficiency and the creation of new opportunities (Verma et al., 2020).

2.2 Current Issues in Traditional Recruitment Sessions

Our study focuses on one aspect of the HR function in particular: recruitment. Recruitment is defined as an essential HRM function that consists of finding the ideal talent (Sinha & Thaly, 2013). In other words, it is the process of finding and hiring the people the organisation needs (Armstrong & Taylor, 2023).

During the last pandemic, organisations had to move from face-to-face job interviews to remote job interviews. Since then, remote interviewing has become the norm in the recruitment process. While this allows candidates to stay at home instead of dealing with traffics and wasting time, it does not address all the concerns from a candidate's point of view. One of the most worrying issues for many job applicants is discrimination: against women, foreigners, French people of foreign origin and older people. As our study focuses on the French population, we can say that these types of discrimination are common in France (Petit et al., 2013). They occur to varying degrees depending on the reputation of the organisation, the job, the traditional dominance of a particular gender, etc. For example, a man will be discriminated against in a job as a waiter in a low-ranking restaurant or in a traditionally female job. Women, on the other hand, will be discriminated against for a position as a waiter in a high class restaurant, or for traditionally male jobs (Petit et al., 2013). Through the metaverse, socio-demographic characteristics can be masked, by choosing an avatar, with a personalised voice, a different skin colour, younger or older facial features, ... (Marabelli & Lirio, 2024).

Another concern associated with remote job interviews is the phenomenon of "Zoom fatigue". A number of studies have indicated that participation in online meetings may result in a specific type of fatigue. This phenomenon has been given the name "Zoom fatigue", which is derived from the name of the videoconferencing software used globally (Luebstorf et al., 2023). This fatigue is caused by repeated and prolonged online meetings, which result in the human brain adapting to a non-natural way of interacting with other humans. For instance, we are not accustomed to seeing faces in front of us simultaneously and with unrealistic sizes. Furthermore, during an online meeting, as we cannot show our entire body, people tend to exaggerate their facial expressions to communicate easily (Webb, 2021). Following their attendance at an online meeting, numerous users have reported feelings of stress, a desire to be alone, and even a desire of cessation of human interaction for a period of times (Fauville et al., 2021). These experiences are indicative of the phenomenon of Zoom fatigue. Luckily, using a metaverse to conduct an online meeting could replace those issues.

Finally, from organisations' perspective, the use of a metaverse is aligned with the evolution of the digital landscape. Next generations of workers are already using different types of metaverses and are therefore familiar with them. In order to attract talents, the construction of a building within a virtual world could be a smart first step.

2.3 Organisational Attractiveness

Organisational attractiveness can be defined as a variable composed of general attractiveness, intention to apply and the prestige of working for the organisation (Highhouse et al., 2003). For our study, we will focus on general attractiveness and intention to apply. General attractiveness reflects an individual's attitude, before making the decision to apply to an organisation (Guillot-Soulez & Roussillon Soyer, 2022). On the other hand, intention reflects a future action and therefore goes beyond attraction, which is simply passive (Highhouse et al., 2003). These two variables are complementary, because a person who is attracted to a company will not necessarily follow it up and apply for a job. They may even be attracted to several companies at the same time, without applying to all of them. However, it is true that the attractiveness of an organisation influences the intention to apply (Collins, 2002; Van Birgelen et al., 2008).

Organisational attractiveness also depends on the age, the gender, educational background and each individual's experience (Reis & Braga, 2016; Roque Gomes & Gonçalves Neves, 2010; Thomas & Wise, 1999; Yalenios, 2016). And these influence the ethical perception of that organisation (da Motta Veiga et al., 2023). Added to this is the fairness perception of a recruitment method. Depending on the method chosen by the recruiter, potential candidates will not have the same view of the attractiveness of that organisation (Maertz et al., 2004). Finally, a person who is familiar with certain tools (such as those based on AI) is likely to be more inclined to use them (Horowitz et al., 2023). For our study, this means that a person who already has experience with the metaverse will be more attracted to this type of tool.

All this leads us to our research question, which is as follows: How does metaverse recruitment influence the attractiveness of an organisation from a candidate's perspective? Based on the literature, we propose the following hypothesis: Metaverse recruiting positively influences the candidate's opinion of the organisation's attractiveness. This hypothesis can be broken down into several sub-hypotheses also based on the literature:

- H1: Age influences the main hypothesis.
- H2: Gender influences the main hypothesis.
- H3: Socio-professional category influences the main hypothesis.
- H4: Recruitment experience influences the main hypothesis.
- H4a: More specifically if the person has already conducted a traditional recruitment session.
- H4b: More precisely if the person has already conducted a metaverse recruitment session.
- H4c: More precisely if the person has already been a candidate in a metaverse recruitment session.
- H5: Experience with metaverses influences the main hypothesis.
- H5a: More precisely if the person has already used a metaverse.
- H5b: More precisely, depending on the number of metaverses used.
- H6: The perception of ethics influences the main hypothesis.
- H7: Fairness perception affects the main hypothesis.

3 Methods

3.1 Sample and Procedure

The questionnaire was developed using Microsoft Form and distributed in groups on social media such as Facebook and on the Survey Circle website from July 24, 2023, to August 16, 2023. Knowledge about metaverse was not a prerequisite, as the main information was available in the questionnaire. The questionnaire had five parts. The first part was used to collect basic information about the respondents: age, gender, and socio-professional category. Previous use of metaverses was also asked to differentiate the profiles. The second part allowed us to focus on our sample's experience of traditional and metaverse recruitment. The third part focused on general attractiveness. This part consisted of four statements to be rated on a five-point Likert scale ("strongly disagree" to "strongly agree"). The fourth part was about the intention to apply and consisted of two statements to be rated on a five-point Likert scale. In the fifth section, participants were asked to rate and, if possible, explain their perception of the ethics and fairness of this recruitment method. The statements in parts three and four were taken from the van Birgelen et al. (2008) study. We used R and SPSS to analyse the results. Specifically, R was used to perform ANOVA, chi-square, and correlation tests while SPSS was used to perform factorial analysis.

Table 1 shows the statements from parts three and four. We managed to collect 108 responses in total. Table 2 summarises the composition of our sample. Note that the socio-professional categories are the ones used by the National Institute of Statistics and Economic Studies of France.

Table 1 Statements from parts 3 and 4 of the questionnaire and their acronyms

Items	Statements
EMA	An organisation is more attractive if it offers a job interview in a metaverse
BON	The fact that an organisation conducts job interviews in a metaverse makes me think that it is a good place to work
DR	Except as a last resort, I would not be interested in an organisation that conducts job interviews in a metaverse
CUR	An organisation offering interviews in a metaverse would make me curious about it
EAC	I would accept if a company offered me a job interview in a metaverse
TAC	I would accept to work for a company that offered job interviews in a metaverse

Table 2 Demographics and characteristics

		Frequency analysis	Percentage (%)
Gender	Male	50	47
	Female	58	53
Age (years)	−18	6	5.56
	18–24	50	46.30
	25–30	36	33.33
	31–35	6	5.56
	36–40	2	1.85
	40+	8	7.41
Socio-professional category	Craftsmen/ entrepreneurs	2	1.85
	Executives and higher intellectual professions	13	12.04
	Employee	10	9.26
	No professional activity	7	6.48
	Intermediate occupations	2	1.85
	Students	47	43.52
	Apprentices	27	25.00
Prior use of a metaverse	At least one	49	45.39
	None	59	54.61
Job interview in a metaverse	As a candidate	3	2.77
	As a recruiter	1	0.93

4 Results

We started our analysis with a factorial analysis using SPSS. Table 3 presents the KMO and Bartlett's tests. As explained in the literature, a KMO value over 0.8 is considered meritorious (Kaiser & Rice, 1974). This means that correlations are of good quality and that this study will have a small number of factors. The Bartlett's test of sphericity is significant ($p < 0.05$) which means that the matrix of correlations will not be an identity matrix, allowing us to conduct a factorial analysis.

Table 3 KMO and Bartlett's test

Test		
KMO		0.837
Bartlett's test of sphericity	Approx. Chi-Square	373.539
	df	15
	Sig	0.001

Table 4 Rotated factor loadings and Cronbach's alpha

	Organisational attractiveness
EMA	0.796
BON	0.784
DR	0.712
CUR	0.862
EAC	0.843
TAC	0.850
Cronbach's alpha	0.874

Next, we drew a scree plot on SPSS, and it showed that only one factor could explain most of the variables. Table 4 presents rotated factor loadings and Cronbach's alpha. The latter is considered "good" as is it between 0.81 and 0.90.

We conducted statistical tests such as ANOVA and Chi^2. Results showed that only three hypotheses had a significant result (p-value < 0.05). We did other statistical analysis to check for other relation between the variables.

Organisational attractiveness is influenced by the fact that a given organisation will proceed in a metaverse recruitment. This relation is moderated by the number of metaverse used by the candidate (p-value = 0.008; $\eta^2 = 0.079$) and the ethical (p-value = 4.10^{-5}; $\eta^2 = 0.155$) and fairness (p-value = 5.10^{-4}; $\eta^2 = 0.150$) perceptions of this method by the candidate. Furthermore, the gender of a candidate seems to have an influence on the number of metaverses used in the past (p-value = 2.10^{-4}) and logically the existence of a prior use of a metaverse (p-value = 2.10^{-4}). The socio-professional category of a candidate has an impact on a potential prior use of a metaverse (p-value = 0.02) and on the fairness perception of this recruitment method (p-value = 0.012).

A qualitative analysis was also conducted for the last part of the questionnaire. "Discrimination" was one of the most repeated key words. Some insisted on the importance of "human warmth". Finally, issues regarding the use of a metaverse were discussed. For instance, on the environmental aspects, data protection and physical health.

5 Discussion and Conclusion

5.1 General Discussion

The use of a metaverse for recruitment still needs to be studied deeply before it can be considered an effective response to an HRM 4.0 strategy. Our hypothesis cannot be definitively validated as our results are not all significant. However, we can conclude that organisational attractiveness is influenced by the perception of the ethics and fairness of this method, in cases where recruitment is conducted

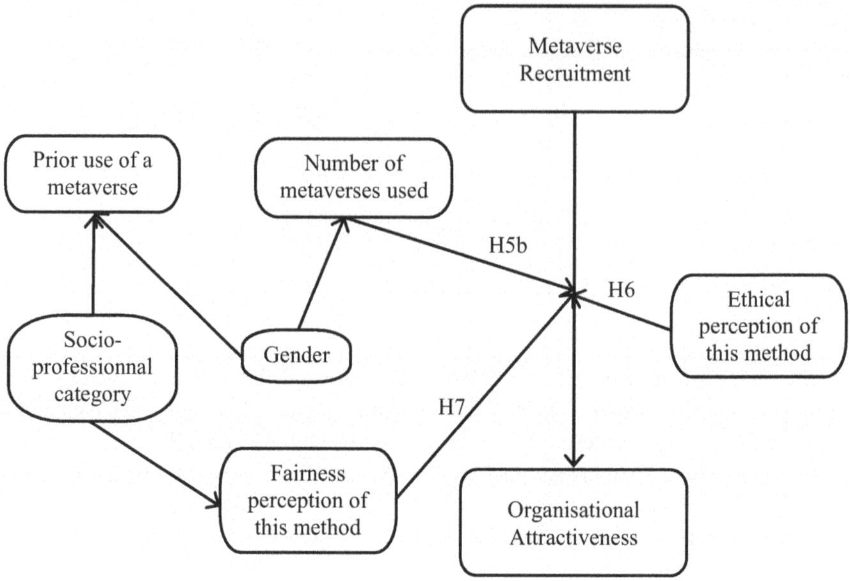

Fig. 1 Research model

using metaverse. Individual characteristics do not appear to be a significant factor. Furthermore, the results were not influenced by whether the participants have already conducted a traditional or metaverse interviews, or whether the participants own a VR/AR/XR headset. Against all odds, ethical and fairness perceptions seemed to be major factors influencing organisational attractiveness when a metaverse is used. Participants explained that discrimination could be avoided thanks to avatars, but others warned against false identity. While the ecological consequences of using a metaverse are currently unknown, it is possible that this technology could encourage people to remain at home instead of driving to attend job interviews. Some have also expressed concern that this method of recruitment lacks human warmth. Figure 1 presents our final research model, which incorporates all the statistical results. We have excluded elements from the qualitative parts of the questionnaire as all the participants did not answer. However, it is important to note that these elements are relevant to the ethical and fairness perceptions.

5.2 Theoretical Contributions

This study has two main theoretical interests. Firstly, it provides an opportunity to examine a brand-new and under-researched field in management science: the metaverse. Until now, "recruitment" has been widely explored, from the point of view of both candidates and organisations and more recently using AI. However, here, we have chosen to focus on a specific and innovative recruitment method. Secondly, organisational attractiveness was also a field of study that was attracting the attention of management science researchers. However, it was unclear how the use of a metaverse would influence the organisational attractiveness. Our findings indicated that ethical and fairness perceptions must be considered more deeply when it comes to studying this topic.

5.3 Managerial Implications

As with all research work, our study has several managerial implications. First, an increasing number of companies are exploring the metaverse, particularly in the context of recruitment. Therefore, the fact that we have conducted a study from candidates' point of view, enables organisations to identify how they can use this recruitment method to attract talents. Secondly, our study indicates that it is still too early to draw any definitive conclusions regarding the impact of this recruitment technique on organisational attractiveness. It is therefore necessary to wait a few years, to allow consumers time to purchase VR/AR/XR headsets and/or become familiar with the metaverse. It can be assumed that younger generations will be the most suitable for this recruitment process, as they have grown up with new technologies.

5.4 Limitations and Future Research

Our study has some limitations. First, the sample size of 108 participants is relatively small for a quantitative study. Furthermore, if we look at the sample, we noticed that half of the participants were under the age of 30. Consequently, it is recommended that future research should aim for a larger sample size and focus on individuals under the age of 30. In contrast to the existing literature, no significant influence of individual characteristics such as the age could be identified. This was probably due to the size of our sample. It is possible that different results may be obtained if the sample were composed solely of individuals under the age of 30.

Second, most respondents indicated that they had never participated in a recruitment session within a metaverse. Although we did not aim for people who already know how this method of recruitment is conducted, conducting this study on people who have experienced it may have resulted in other conclusions. Furthermore, some respondents indicated that they had never used a metaverse. Future studies should provide more detailed information about what a metaverse is and how a recruitment session can be conducted in this environment. For instance, including a video showing a hiring session in a metaverse at the beginning of the questionnaire could be beneficial.

Third, in terms of the analytical approach, our regression model, although statistically significant, cannot be considered to be of an optimal quality. The factorial analysis revealed that only one factor explained most of the variability in the data, while we thought two factors would explain it (general attractiveness and intention to apply). This was maybe because we used four items for the general attractiveness and only two items for the intention to apply. Future research should use more items to differentiate general attractiveness and intention to apply. This limitation is related to another one. In the literature, organisational attractiveness is composed of general attractiveness and intention to apply, and these two variables are complementary. However, in our study, we had to merge these two variables as the factorial analysis only showed one factor. Although this can be interpreted as organisational attractiveness, we could not differentiate the general attractiveness on one hand and the intention to apply on the other. Future studies should analyse these two variables separately.

As we found that the ethical and fairness perceptions were important here, further research should focus on them. We also suggest that further studies adopt another point of view and study the acceptance of this method by recruiters. This could be achieved by using the Unified Theory of Acceptance and Use of Technology 1 for example (Theres & Strohmeier, 2023; Venkatesh et al., 2003).

References

Armstrong, M., & Taylor, S. (2023). *Armstrong's Handbook of Human Resource Management Practice: A Guide to the Theory and Practice of People Management*. Kogan Page Publishers.

Auffray, C. (2023, April 7). Auchan s'essaie au metaverse pour le recrutement. *Coins.fr*. Retrieved June 8, 2023, from https://coins.fr/auchan-essaie-metaverse-recrutement/

Bonilla, B. (2022). How 7 agencies are building metaverse offices: Ad Age took a look at shops using platforms including Havas, Media.Monks, IW Group, R/GA, Virtue and others: Ad Age. *Ad Age*, *93*(6), 16–16. Crain Communications Inc. (MI).

Collins, C. J. (2002). The Effects of Company Recruitment Practices on Job Seekers' Perceived Employment Brand Equity and Intentions to Pursue Job Opportunities. *Academy of Management Proceedings*, *2002*(1), A1–A6.

Fauville, G., Luo, M., Queiroz, A. C. M., Bailenson, J. N., & Hancock, J. (2021). Zoom Exhaustion & Fatigue Scale. *Computers in Human Behavior Reports*, *4*, 100119.

Galindo, G., Garbe, E., & Vignal, J. (2019). Des idéaux à la réalité de l'accompagnement de la GRH dans la digitalisation: Le cas d'une entreprise industrielle. *@GRH*, *30*(1), 11–46. Association de Gestion des Ressources Humaines.

Geuze, F. (2020). Chapitre 4. IA et RH, quels usages? - L'IA pour augmenter la fonction RH ? *L'IA au service des RH : Pour une expérience collaborateur augmentée* (pp. 59–62). Dunod.

Guillot-Soulez, C., & Roussillon Soyer, C. (2022). Capital de marque employeur et attractivité organisationnelle des Big Four. *Revue de gestion des ressources humaines*, *124*(2), 58–79. Paris: ESKA.

Highhouse, S., Lievens, F., & Sinar, E. (2003). Measuring Attraction to Organizations. *Educational and Psychological Measurement*, *63*, 986–1001.

Hooi, M. (2022, May 20). Supermarket Carrefour Is Now Holding Job Interviews In The Metaverse. *The Mediaverse*. Retrieved May 28, 2024, from https://themediaverse.com/supermarket-carrefour-is-now-holding-job-interviews-in-the-metaverse/

Horowitz, M. C., Kahn, L., Macdonald, J., & Schneider, J. (2023). Adopting AI: How familiarity breeds both trust and contempt. *AI & SOCIETY*.

Kaiser, H. F., & Rice, J. (1974). Little Jiffy, Mark Iv. *Educational and Psychological Measurement*, *34*(1), 111–117. SAGE Publications Inc.

Luebstorf, S., Allen, J. A., Eden, E., Kramer, W. S., Reiter-Palmon, R., & Lehmann-Willenbrock, N. (2023). Digging into "Zoom Fatigue": A Qualitative Exploration of Remote Work Challenges and Virtual Meeting Stressors. *Merits*, *3*(1), 151–166. Multidisciplinary Digital Publishing Institute.

Maertz Jr, C. P., Mosley Jr., D. C., Bauer, T. N., Posthuma, R. A., & Campion, M. A. (2004). Do Procedural Justice Perceptions in a Selection Testing Context Predict Applicant Attraction and Intention Toward the Organization? *Journal of Applied Social Psychology*, *34*(1), 125–145.

Marabelli, M., & Lirio, P. (2024). AI and the metaverse in the workplace: DEI opportunities and challenges. *Personnel Review*, *ahead-of-print* (ahead-of-print).

da Motta Veiga, S. P., Figueroa-Armijos, M., & Clark, B. B. (2023). Seeming Ethical Makes You Attractive: Unraveling How Ethical Perceptions of AI in Hiring Impacts Organizational Innovativeness and Attractiveness. *Journal of Business Ethics*, *186*(1), 199–216.

Petit, P., Duguet, E., L'horty, Y., du Parquet, L., & Sari, F. (2013). Discrimination à l'embauche: Les effets du genre et de l'origine se cumulent-ils systématiquement ? *Economie et Statistique*, *464*(1), 141–153. Persée - Portail des revues scientifiques en SHS.

Rabinovich, B. (2018, August 10). Dare Win job interview takes place on Fortnite. *Mail Online*. Retrieved May 28, 2024, from http://www.dailymail.co.uk/sport/esports/article-6047979/Dare-Win-job-interview-takes-place-Fortnite.html

Reis, G. G., & Braga, B. M. (2016). Employer attractiveness from a generational perspective: Implications for employer branding. *Revista de Administração (São Paulo)*, *51*, 103–116. Departamento de Administração da Faculdade de Economia, Administração e Contabilidade da Universidade de São Paulo.

Roque Gomes, D., & Gonçalves Neves, J. (2010). Do applicants' prior experiences influence organizational attractiveness prediction? *Management Research: Journal of the Iberoamerican Academy of Management*, *8*(3), 203–220. Emerald Group Publishing Limited.

Sinha, V., & Thaly, P. (2013). A review on changing trend of recruitment practice to enhance the quality of hiring in global organizations. *Management*, *18*(2), 141–156.

Theres, C., & Strohmeier, S. (2023). Consolidating the theoretical foundations of digital human resource management acceptance and use research: A meta-analytic validation of UTAUT. *Management Review Quarterly*.

Thomas, K. M., & Wise, P. G. (1999). Organizational Attractiveness and Individual Differences: Are Diverse Applicants Attracted by Different Factors? *Journal of Business and Psychology*, *13*(3), 375–390.

Van Birgelen, M. J. H., Wetzels, M. G. M., & Van Dolen, W. M. (2008). Effectiveness of corporate employment web sites: How content and form influence intentions to apply. *International Journal of Manpower*, *29*(8), 731–751.

Venkatesh, V., Morris, M. G., Davis, G. B., & Davis, F. D. (2003). User Acceptance of Information Technology: Toward a Unified View. *MIS Quarterly*, *27*(3), 425–478. Management Information Systems Research Center, University of Minnesota.

Verma, A., Bansal, M., & Verma, J. (2020). Industry 4.0: Reshaping the future of HR. *Strategic Direction*, *ahead-of-print*.

Webb, M. (2021). Zoom Fatigue and How to Prevent It. *Journal of Registry Management*, *48*(4), 181. National Cancer Registrars Association.

Yalenios, J. (2016). Les facteurs d'attractivité d'une organisation dépend-elle du genre ou bien du cursus de formation? Étude auprès d'étudiants hommes et femmes en fin de cursus de formation. *Revue internationale de psychosociologie et de gestion des comportements organisationnels*, *XXII*(54), 171–185. Paris: ESKA.

Comparison of South Korea and China on Customers' Repurchase Intention of Mobile Content Service Based on Motivation Theory

Rui Zhang and Taesoo Moon

Abstract This study is aiming to empirically investigate the consumers' psychological comparison of China and South Korea, including customers' attitudes and repurchase intentions of mobile contents service, based on motivation theory. From April 2023 to September 2023, this study collected valid questionnaires from 300 Chinese and 300 Korean customers using mobile content services and analysed the data using AMOS and Smart PLS4.0. The findings demonstrate that for both countries, mobile content services have a positive impact on perceived usefulness and perceived enjoyment, and it is recognized that these two factors have a positive influence on customers' satisfaction and repurchase intention. Additionally, customers' satisfaction also has significant positive effect on repurchase intentions of mobile contents service. However, in the case of Korean customers, only perceived enjoyment influences repurchase intention, whereas Chinese customers' perceived usefulness and satisfaction positively influence repurchase intentions respectively.

Keywords Mobile content service · Motivation theory · Perceived usefulness · Perceived enjoyment · Repurchase intention

1 Introduction

The mobile content industry is experiencing unprecedented vitality due to the rapid advancements in communication technology, especially the development and application of 5G technology. Currently, mobile devices such as cell phones or smartphones have become indispensable necessities in people's daily lives. Various mobile content services not only provide news, sports, and entertainment information but

R. Zhang
PhD Student in MIS, Dongguk University, Gyeongju, South Korea
e-mail: tianjinghuizi2016@outlook.com

T. Moon (✉)
Professor in MIS, Dongguk University, Gyeongju, South Korea
e-mail: tsmoon@dongguk.ac.kr

T. Jung et al. (eds.), *XR and Metaverse*, Springer Proceedings in Business and Economics, https://doi.org/10.1007/978-3-031-77975-6_22

also help in enhancing people's daily routines. According to Statista (2024), the global volume of mobile content service downloads was 25.5 billion in 2022, an increase of 2.5 billion from 2021. There were 2.69 million apps on Google Play and 810,000 apps on the App Store. The rapid growth of the mobile contents retail market is evident due to increased demand (Meena & Sarabhai, 2023).

Mobile content services possess characteristics such as mobility, portability, and versatility. Although they are generally not constrained by space or geographical limitations in usage, users' perspectives and preferences are influenced by social and cultural factors (Park et al., 2023). In cross-cultural comparative studies, China and South Korea often emerge as contrasting subjects. Despite both belonging to the East Asian cultural sphere with similar geopolitical and cultural features, they exhibit significant differences in their social environments. Additionally, due to constraints imposed by mobile providers, many mobile content services widely used in South Korea are inaccessible in China. Instead, alternative products with similar functionalities but more aligned with the social and cultural environment and user habits have taken their place. As a result, the two countries now have entirely different mobile service ecosystems.

Research on mobile content services is abundant, but there are still various shortcomings and limitations in existing studies. First, the global shift in societal and lifestyle patterns due to the novel COVID-19 pandemic has led to changes in perceptions of mobile content services, especially in China. However, more investigation is needed to determine whether these cognitive changes have a tangible impact on the mobile content market. Second, foundational research tends to focus on specific mobile applications providing content services, lacking comprehensive discussions on mobile content services as a research topic. These limitations may hinder a holistic understanding of the overall mobile content service market. Third, foundational studies primarily build new research models with user intent to use mobile content services as the dependent variable, failing to explain the real phenomena where users, even those who have received basic technical services, may discontinue, or not repurchase. Exploring such phenomena in-depth is necessary to better understand users' long-term behaviour and attitude change toward mobile content services.

Therefore, starting from this background, this study aims to propose research questions to provide mobile services more tailored to consumers in China and South Korea. The research questions are as follows:

1. What are motivational factors to influence customer's usage of mobile content service?
2. What factors motivate customer' repurchase behaviour of mobile content service?
3. Does it exist some difference between South Korean and Chinese customers?

To find answers to the research questions, this study conducted empirical studies in China and Korea, mainly consisting of three parts: Study 1 analyzed surveys targeting to Chinese customers, Study 2 analyzed surveys targeting to Korean customers with the same questions, and Study 3 analyzed pooled data from both countries.

2 Literature Review

2.1 Motivation Theory and Mobile Content Services

This study is based on the technology acceptance model (TAM) of Davis (1989) and the motivation theory of Heijden (2004). Davis (1989) developed the TAM model to explain the process of adopting new information technology. This model elucidates the factors influencing users' acceptance of information technology. Building upon the TAM model, Heijden (2004) conducted a research on the differences in user acceptance models for utilitarian-centric and hedonic-centric information systems. Through cross-sectional empirical research, he demonstrated that for utilitarian systems, external motivations such as perceived usefulness aimed at enhancing user performance are the most influential factors determining user acceptance. Conversely, for hedonic systems, intrinsic motivations such as perceived enjoyment, contributing to enjoyable interactions between users and systems, are the most powerful factors determining user acceptance.

In essence, the hedonic nature of information systems is a crucial boundary condition for the validity of technology acceptance models. Mobile content services, encompassing various service types such as news, music, games, videos, and chat accessible through mobile devices, provide both utilitarian and hedonic purposes. Qing and Haiying (2021) studied factors influencing the continuous usage of brand apps from the perspective of consumer brand engagement. Their results indicate that utilitarian and hedonic motivations indirectly impact continuous usage intention through consumer brand engagement. Akdim et al. (2022) analyzed key factors affecting the continuous usage intention of social mobile apps, considering two practical variables (perceived usefulness, perceived ease of use) and one hedonic variable (perceived enjoyment). They found that practical variables generally have a larger impact on practical apps, while perceived enjoyment has a larger impact on hedonic apps. These findings align closely with the fundamental logic of motivation theory.

2.2 Perceived Usefulness and Perceived Enjoyment

Perceived usefulness, a crucial factor in the TAM, is defined as "the degree to which a person believes that using a particular system will enhance their job performance" (Davis, 1989). Perceived ease of use, as another TAM element, is defined as "the degree to which a person believes that using a particular system will be free of effort." Perceived usefulness and perceived ease of use focus more on external motivations, indicating objective factors such as task performance improvement through interaction with the system using functionality (Davis, 1989; Heijden, 2004). Discovering that users can easily obtain desired information and interact with applications through mobile content services, which provide various types of services like news, music, games, videos, and chatting, is expected to lead to a positive attitude towards technology and, consequently, repurchase intentions (Lin & Lu, 2015).

Perceived enjoyment is defined as "the degree to which engaging in the activity of using a specific technology is perceived as enjoyable, apart from any performance consequences" (Venkatesh & Davis, 2000). The definition of perceived enjoyment emphasizes intrinsic motivation, focusing on the degree of pleasure obtained from using the system (Heijden, 2004). Services offering various mobile content, driven by the entertainment business, are evolving to provide more enjoyment to users, similar to gaming experiences. As the usage brings joy, it is anticipated to enhance consumers' continuous usage intentions and repurchase intentions (So et al., 2021).

2.3 User Attitude and Repurchase Intention

User attitude is defined as an emotional factor that transcends satisfaction and represents relatively persistent emotional elements beyond previous experiences (Oliver, 1993). According to previous research, attitude is the emotional experience during product or service usage, such as pleasure and joy. Venkatesh and Davis (2000) indicated that user attitudes influence their behavioural intentions and are superior to other factors like satisfaction and involvement in predicting user system usage. After a certain period of using mobile content services, users' positive or negative emotions towards the service manifest as attitude. Users with a positive attitude are more likely to continue using and repurchasing (Bhattacherjee, 2001). In this study, repurchase intention is defined as "the intention to purchase the same product or service in the future based on the experience with a product or service that the consumer has purchased" (Jones et al., 2000). Considering repurchase intention as an outcome variable is in line with the Theory of Reasoned Action proposed by Ajzen and Fishbein. Intentions are considered the most appropriate intermediate factor between attitudes and behaviour, making them suitable for verifying consumer behaviour (Wen et al., 2011). Users repurchase intentions for mobile content services are influenced by their experiences with the service. Reliable service quality, transaction behaviour, and benefits help increase user satisfaction and induce the intention to repurchase.

3 Research Methodology

3.1 Research Model

Based on self-determination theory of Deci and Ryan (1987), TAM of Davis (1989), and the motivation model proposed by Heijden (2004), this study established a research model with the characteristics of mobile content as antecedent factors. The model incorporates perceived usefulness, perceived enjoyment, user attitude, and

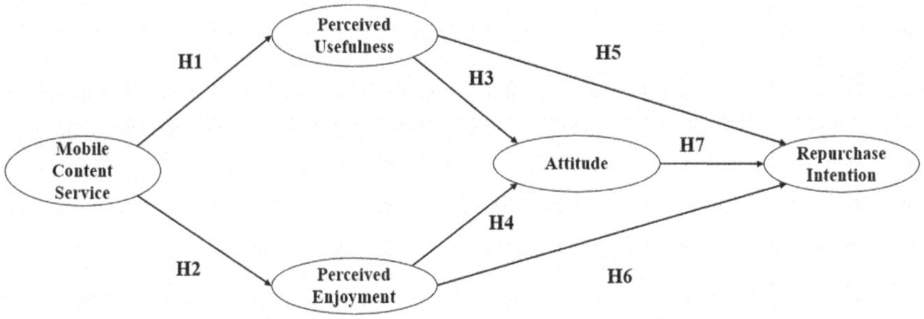

Fig. 1 Research model

repurchase intention as mediator and dependent variables. The developed research model is illustrated in Fig. 1.

3.2 Research Hypotheses

Mobile Content Service. In this study, measurement items for mobile content services mainly consider diversity, loyalty, and support range. Previous research in mobile learning content indicated that the characteristics of content positively influence users' perceived usefulness (Kim et al., 2019; Almaiah et al., 2019). Recent studies on mobile servicescape suggest that characteristics such as aesthetic appeal, financial security, and layout and functionality are positively related to utilitarian and hedonic value (Zhani et al., 2022). A study on mobile online shopping content suggested that characteristics such as diversity and recommendations positively influenced users' perceived enjoyment (Zhou et al., 2007). Additionally, the characteristics of online educational content affect students' perceived enjoyment, influencing their intention to continue using it (Zhou et al., 2017). Therefore, based on these studies, the following hypotheses are proposed:

H1: Mobile content services positively influence users' perceived usefulness.
H2: Mobile content services positively influence users' perceived enjoyment.

Perceived Usefulness and Perceived Enjoyment. In this study, perceived usefulness is measured by factors such as effectively delivering information, accuracy, providing useful information, and providing desired information. Perceived enjoyment is measured by factors like providing enjoyable experiences, creating dedication, satisfying curiosity, and whether it is enjoyable each time used. Davis (1989) demonstrated that perceived usefulness in information systems positively influences user attitudes and behavioural intentions. Many studies have shown that users' perceived usefulness consistently has a positive impact on their attitudes and intentions to continue using various mobile content services (Islamoglu et al., 2021; Suki et al., 2023; Ateş & Garzón, 2023). Entertainment-focused services offering diverse mobile content are shifting towards providing a more enjoyable experience for users, leading to improved user attitudes and increased intentions to continue using (Talwar et al., 2020; So et al., 2021). Researchers studying AR content services and hotel content services have found that users' perceived enjoyment plays a crucial role and has a positive impact on user attitudes (Arghashi & Arsun Yuksel, 2023). Therefore, based on previous research, the following hypotheses are proposed:

H3: Perceived usefulness of mobile content services positively influences user attitude.
H4: Perceived enjoyment of mobile content services positively influences user attitude.

Repurchase Intention. In this study, user attitudes are considered in terms of the usefulness of use, positivity, satisfaction each time used, and satisfaction with fees. Repurchase intention is measured in terms of positive evaluations of usefulness, positive evaluations of use, positive evaluations of fees, and other intentions to track love. Research in mobile learning content indicated that perceived usefulness is the most crucial factor influencing repurchase intentions (Almaiah et al., 2019). A study on mobile shopping by Avcilar and Demirgünes (2017) found that dimensions such as perceived enjoyment have a positive impact on repurchase intentions. Additionally, many studies have demonstrated that user attitudes toward mobile services significantly influence repurchase intentions (Anshu et al., 2022; Asti et al., 2021; Liu et al., 2023; Amoroso & Ackaradejruangsri, 2017). Therefore, based on previous research, the following hypotheses are proposed:

H5: Perceived usefulness of mobile content services positively influences repurchase intention.
H6: Perceived enjoyment of mobile content services positively influences repurchase intention.
H7: User attitude toward mobile content services positively influences repurchase intention.

3.3 Research Methodology

In this study, we referred to factors and measurement items proven in previous research on mobile content services to explore research objectives. This study conducted a survey targeting Korean consumers who used mobile content services from April 2023 to June 2023. The questionnaire was distributed and collected through random sampling. Out of the collected 350 surveys, invalid responses were excluded, and 300 valid responses were used for analysis. Similarly, a survey targeting Chinese mobile content service consumers were conducted from July 2023 to September 2023. The questionnaires were collected through the "Tencent Survey" platform, and out of the 384 collected surveys, invalid responses were excluded, and 300 valid responses were used. Valid questionnaires were analyzed using AMOS and Smart PLS 4.0 for empirical analysis.

4 Data Analysis

4.1 Study 1: China

The valid statistical overview of Chinese mobile content consumers is presented. From the results, among 300 Chinese consumers, the age group of teenagers to twenties combined accounted for 61%, indicating that the main age group for mobile content usage is primarily distributed among teenagers and those in their twenties. Chinese consumers who mainly use mobile content also use both pleasurable content such as music and movies, as well as practical content such as mobile banking and transportation/maps. Additionally, due to the advancement of mobile communication technology, mobile chat content services not only provide pleasurable functions like leisure activities but also have practical functions such as social communication and business performance enhancement.

Validity and Reliability. Validity verification of the research involves measuring the unique characteristics of each survey item to derive each variable. In this study, construct validity was confirmed, and factor analysis was conducted with criteria such as Average Variance Extracted (AVE) above 0.45 and factor loading values above 0.5. Additionally, Cronbach's alpha values were used to evaluate the reliability of the data. Table 1 shows the results of the validity and reliability analysis of the research variables. The validity verification results of this study showed that the five factors were valid, and all of them had Cronbach's alpha coefficients of 0.75 or higher, indicating high validity and reliability. Furthermore, upon examining the correlation coefficients between the variables, it was observed that all variables exhibit positive correlations. Moreover, the square root of the Average Variance Extracted (AVE) values of each measurement item exceeds the correlation values between the variables. This indicates that each variable is sufficiently distinct from one another, thereby confirming the discriminant validity of the model.

Hypothesis Testing. The results of the path analysis, using AMOS18 in this study, revealed the relationship between the influencing factors of mobile content services and repurchase intention, as shown in Fig. 2. Based on the hypothesis testing results, it can be observed that the hypotheses regarding each dependent variable have explanatory power ranging from 57.1% to 87.2%. It was demonstrated that mobile content services have a positive (+) influence on perceived usefulness (0.756***) and perceived enjoyment (0.816***), and that perceived usefulness (0.370***) and perceived enjoyment (0.659***) positively affect user attitude when using mobile content services. Therefore, hypotheses H1-4 are accepted. However, regarding the hypothesis about the influence of user attitude towards repurchase intention, while perceived usefulness (0.305, $P < 0.031$) has a positive impact on repurchase intention, users' attitude (0.519, $P < 0.098$) or perceived enjoyment (−0.026, $P < 0.909$) does not significantly influence repurchase intention. Thus, both hypotheses 5 and 6 are rejected. The summarized results related to the hypothesis settings can be seen in Fig. 2.

Table 1 Validity and reliability of Chinese data

Measurement items	Factor loading	C.R	AVE	Cronbach-α
MCC1	0.611		0.47	0.773
MCC2	0.631	8.66		
MCC3	0.786	10.122		
MCC4	0.7	9.281		
PU1	0.765		0.46	0.763
PU2	0.52	8.455		
PU3	0.712	11.573		
PU4	0.693	10.838		
MUA1	0.741		0.50	0.723
MUA2	0.77	12.997		
MUA3	0.603	9.666		
PE1	0.756		0.49	0.793
PE2	0.664	11.12		
PE3	0.718	11.92		
PE4	0.671	10.96		
MRI1	0.749		0.59	0.812
MRI2	0.793	12.4		
MRI3	0.763	12.01		

CMIN/DF = 2.187, RMR = 0.039, GFI = 0.905, CFI = 0.940, RMSEA = 0.063

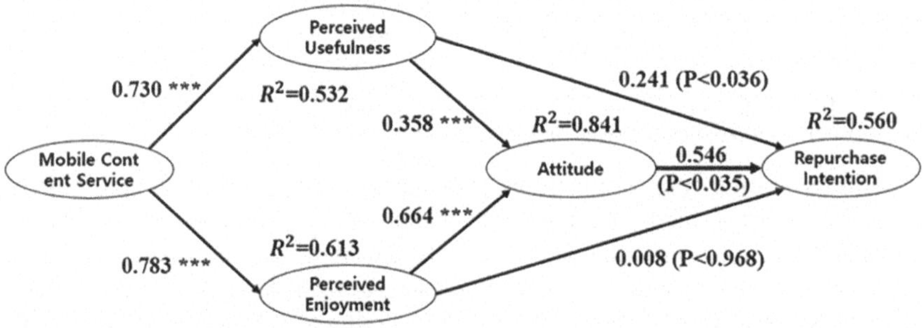

Fig. 2 The results of path analysis (N = 300, China)

4.2 Study 2: South Korea

The general statistical overview of Korean mobile content consumers is presented in Table 2. From the results, similar with the Chinese consumer sample, the teenager's group of Korean (up to twenties) combined accounted for 84.33%, indicating that the main age group for mobile content usage is primarily distributed among teenagers and those in their twenties. Additionally, due to the advancement of mobile communication technology, mobile chat content services not only provide pleasurable functions like leisure activities but also have practical functions such as social communication and business performance enhancement.

Validity and Reliability. Validity verification of this study involves measuring the unique characteristics of each survey item to derive each variable. In this study, construct validity was confirmed, and factor analysis was conducted with criteria such as Average Variance Extracted (AVE) above 0.45 and factor loading values above 0.6. Additionally, Cronbach's alpha values were used to evaluate the reliability of the data. Table 2 shows the results of the validity and reliability analysis of the research variables. The validity verification results of this study showed that the five factors were valid, and all of them had Cronbach's alpha coefficients of 0.75 or higher, indicating high validity and reliability. And this study indicates that each variable is sufficiently distinct from one another, thereby confirming the discriminant validity of the model.

Hypothesis Testing. The results of the path analysis, using AMOS18 in this study, revealed the relationship between the influencing factors of mobile content services and repurchase intention, as shown in Fig. 3. Based on the hypothesis testing results,

Table 2 Validity and reliability of South Korean data

Measurement items	Factor loading	C.R	AVE	Cronbach-α
MCC1	0.752		0.55	0.83
MCC2	0.7	11.515		
MCC3	0.743	11.986		
MCC4	0.774	12.133		
PU1	0.769		0.50	0.796
PU2	0.632	10.467		
PU3	0.699	10.975		
PU4	0.718	11.162		
MUA1	0.734		0.56	0.782
MUA2	0.799	12.591		
MUA3	0.703	10.027		
PE1	0.763		0.61	0.864
PE2	0.733	12.56		
PE3	0.833	13.96		
PE4	0.796	13.85		
MRI1	0.851		0.69	0.865
MRI2	0.873	16.39		
MRI3	0.754	13.96		

CMIN/DF = 2.097, RMR = 0.046, GFI = 0.913, CFI = 0.950, RMSEA = 0.061

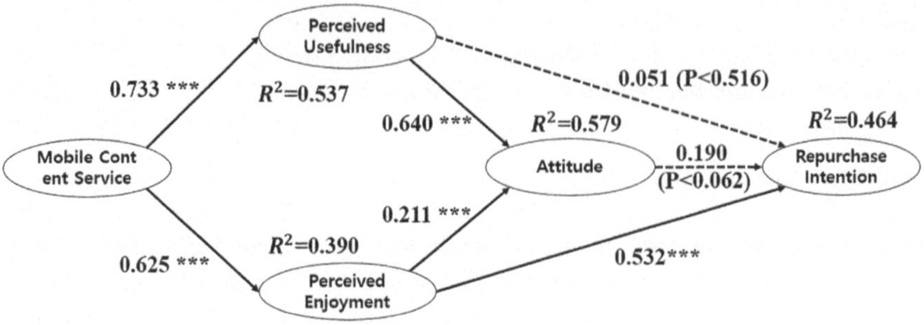

Fig. 3 The results of path analysis (N = 300, South Korea)

it can be observed that the hypotheses regarding each dependent variable have explanatory power ranging from 39% to 57.9%. It was demonstrated that mobile content services have a positive (+) influence on perceived usefulness (0.733***) and perceived enjoyment (0.625***), and that perceived usefulness (0.640***) and perceived enjoyment (0.211***) positively affect user attitude when using mobile content services. Therefore, hypotheses H1-4 are accepted. However, regarding the hypothesis about the influence of user attitude towards repurchase intention, while perceived enjoyment (0.532***) has a positive impact on repurchase intention, either perceived usefulness (0.051, $P < 0.606$) or users' attitude (0.190, $P < 0.062$) has significantly influence repurchase intention. Thus, hypothesis 6 is rejected. The summarized results related to the hypothesis settings can be seen in Fig. 3.

4.3 Study 3: Pooled Data (N = 600, China 300 + Korea 300)

The results of path analysis conducted on a total of 600 samples from Chinese and Korean consumers combined are presented, as shown in Fig. 4. It can be observed that the hypotheses regarding, each dependent variable has explanatory power ranging from 55% to 76.3%. It was demonstrated that mobile content services have a positive (+) influence on perceived usefulness (0.741***) and perceived enjoyment (0.765***), and that perceived usefulness (0.504***) and perceived enjoyment (0.439***) positively affect user attitude when using mobile content services. Furthermore, regarding the hypothesis about the influence of user attitude towards repurchase intention, all the three variances, perceived usefulness (0.169, $P < 0.031$), perceived enjoyment (0.457***), users' attitude (0.198, $P < 0.045$), have a positive impact on repurchase intention. Therefore, hypotheses H1-7 are all accepted. The summarized results related to the hypothesis settings can be seen in Fig. 4.

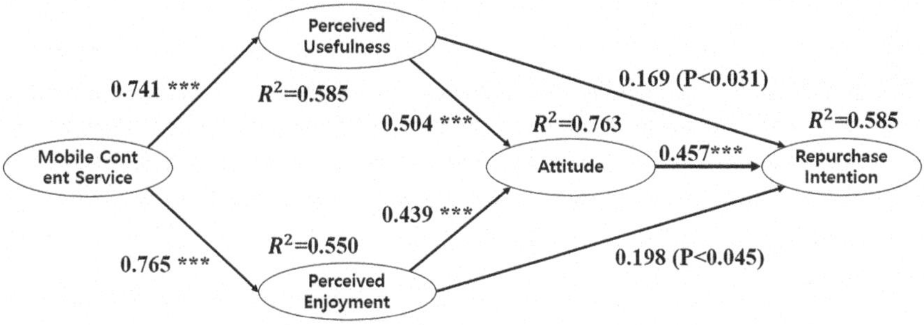

Fig. 4 The results of path analysis (N = 600, pooled data)

5 Conclusion

The study aimed to explore consumer attitudes and repurchase intentions, as well as consumer psychology, based on the motivation theory to enhance mobile content services provided to Chinese and Korean consumers. Empirical analysis was conducted on 600 valid survey data collected through surveys, revealing some similarities and significant differences in the usage patterns between Chinese and Korean consumers of mobile content services.

First, through the analysis of sample data from 600 consumers in China and South Korea, we have demonstrated a high degree of fit in the model, proving that the theoretical model proposed in this paper accurately reflects reality and possesses a certain level of credibility and predictive power. From the analysis results, we can see that in terms of usage experience and satisfaction, mobile content services have a positive impact on perceived usefulness and perceived enjoyment, and it is recognized that these two factors have a positive influence on attitudes. This indicates that perceived usefulness and enjoyment are important mediating factors influencing user attitudes. Additionally, perceived usefulness, perceived enjoyment, and user attitudes also have significant positive effects on repurchase intentions of mobile contents, with user attitudes playing an important mediating role.

Second, in terms of repurchase intention of mobile content, customer perceptions in Korea and China were found to be different. In the case of Chinese customers, it was found that perceived usefulness and attitude had a positive effect on repurchase intention, and perceived enjoyment did not affect repurchase intention. On the other hand, in the case of Korean customers, it was found that perceived usefulness and attitude did not affect repurchase intention, but perceived enjoyment influenced repurchase intention. Chinese customers prefer repurchase based on a positive attitude toward the utilitarian perspective of the service. However, it was analyzed that Korean customers repurchase based on the hedonic perspective of the service, and the mobile content market has a different purpose and direction.

Third, it is about the strategy and direction of mobile content service market in Korea and China. Currently, in Korea and China, mobile content is becoming more entertainment-oriented. Considering the conclusions of this study, it can be inferred that the current mobile content service market in China may not meet the utilitarian needs of users. In addition, even in the case of Korea, providing contents from too practical perspective can lead to user rejection. Of course, the perceived enjoyment factor can induce repurchase intentions with a good mediating effect in inducing a positive attitude of users, but it does not induce direct repurchase behaviour in itself. The results of this study suggest that the content industry needs to readjust its business model and strategy in the production and distribution of content to better meet the needs of actual users.

There are several limitations in this study. First, a significant portion of the samples collected in this study consist of adolescents between the ages of 10 and 20, so the hypothesis testing results may be biased towards the opinions of this age group. Future research endeavours in this area will strive to conduct focused investigations targeting different age groups to explore the differences in perspectives on mobile content services held by various age demographics, thereby providing strategic recommendations useful for market segmentation across different age groups. Second, further research is needed by expanding the sample size or employing other methods and research variables to confirm the differences between consumer perception and repurchase intentions identified in this study. Third, this study found significant differences between Chinese and Korean customers in the usage of mobile application services. Further in-depth research is needed to explore whether these differences are related to variations in perceived usefulness and perceived enjoyment among customers between two countries.

This study builds upon existing research and theories to explore the intrinsic attributes of mobile content service consumers in China and Korea, developing practical models for both markets and expanding and advancing existing theories. According to the research findings, consumers in both countries are influenced by perceived usefulness and attitudes towards mobile content services during initial experiences, but their interests diverge significantly when it comes to repurchase intentions. These differences have significant implications for companies in formulating marketing strategies and enhancing user retention rates by tailoring strategies to meet the preferences and behavioural patterns of consumers in different countries more effectively.

References

Akdim, K., Casaló, L. V. & Flavián, C. (2022). The role of utilitarian and hedonic aspects in the continuance intention to use social mobile apps. *Journal of Retailing and Consumer Services*. 6: 102888.

Almaiah, M. A., Alamri, M. M. & Al-Rahmi, W. (2019). Applying the UTAUT model to explain the students' acceptance of mobile learning system in higher education. *IEEE Access*.7: 174673–174686.

Amoroso, D. & Ackaradejruangsri, P. (2017). How consumer attitudes improve repurchase intention. *International Journal of E-Services and Mobile Applications (IJESMA)*. 9(3): 38–61.

Anshu, K., Gaur, L. & Singh, G. (2022). Impact of customer experience on attitude and repurchase intention in online grocery retailing: A moderation mechanism of value Co-creation. *Journal of Retailing and Consumer Services.* 64: 102798.

Arghashi, V. & Arsun Yuksel, C. (2023). Customer brand engagement behaviors: the role of cognitive values, intrinsic and extrinsic motivations and self-brand connection. *Journal of Marketing Theory and Practice.* 31(2): 146–172.

Asti, W. P., Handayani, P. W. & Azzahro, F. (2021). Influence of trust, perceived value, and attitude on customers' repurchase intention for e-grocery. *Journal of Food Products Marketing.* 27(3): 157–171.

Ateş, H. & Garzón, J. (2023). An integrated model for examining teachers' intentions to use augmented reality in science courses. *Education and Information Technologies.* 28(2): 1299–1321.

Avcilar, M. Y. & Demirgünes, B. K. (2017). Developing perceived greenwash index and its effect on green brand equity: A research on gas station companies in Turkey. *International Business Research.* 10(1): 222–239.

Bhattacherjee, A. (2001). Understanding information systems continuance: An expectation-confirmation model. *MIS Quarterly.* 25(3): 351–370.

Davis, F. D. (1989). Perceived usefulness, perceived ease of use, and user acceptance of information technology. *MIS Quarterly.* 13(3): 319–340.

Deci, E. L. & Ryan, R.M. (1987), "The support of autonomy and the control of behaviour." Journal of Personality and Social Psychology, 53(6): 1024–1037.

Heijden, H. V. D. (2004). User acceptance of hedonic information systems. *MIS Quarterly.* 28(4): 695–704.

Islamoglu, H., Kabakci Yurdakul, I. & Ursavas, O. F. (2021). Pre-service teachers' acceptance of mobile-technology-supported learning activities. Educational Technology Research and Development, 69(2): 1025–1054.

Jo, H. & Park, D. H. (2023). Affordance, usefulness, enjoyment, and aesthetics in sustaining virtual reality engagement. *Scientific Reports.* 13(1): 15097.

Jones, M. A., Mothersbaugh, D. L. & Beatty, S. E. (2000). Switching barriers and repurchase intentions in services. *Journal of Retailing.* 76(2): 259–274.

Kim, B. G., Kim, K. W. & Seo, H. I. (2019). Effects of mobile app service characteristics on user satisfaction and continuance usage intention. *Journal of Information Technology Applications and Management.* 26(3): 99–120.

Lin, K. Y. & Lu, H. P. (2015). Predicting mobile social network acceptance based on mobile value and social influence. *Internet Research.* 25(1): 107–130.

Liu, Y., Sun, J. C. Y. & Chen, S. K. (2023). Comparing technology acceptance of AR-based and 3D map-based mobile library applications: a multigroup SEM analysis. *Interactive Learning Environments.* 31(7): 4156–4170.

Meena, R. & Sarabhai, S. (2023). Extrinsic and intrinsic motivators for usage continuance of hedonic mobile apps. *Journal of Retailing and Consumer Services.* 71: 103228.

Oliver, R. L. (1993). Cognitive, affective, and attribute bases of the satisfaction response. *Journal of Consumer Research.* 20(3): 418–430.

Park, K., Kim, H. J. & Kim, J. M. (2023). The effect of mobile device usage on creating text reviews. *Asia Pacific Journal of Marketing and Logistics, 35*(4): 1011–1029.

Qing, T. & Haiying, D. (2021). How to achieve consumer continuance intention toward branded apps—from the consumer–brand engagement perspective. *Journal of Retailing and Consumer Services.* 60: 102486.

So, K. K. F., Kim, H. & Oh, H. (2021). What makes Airbnb experiences enjoyable? The effects of environmental stimuli on perceived enjoyment and repurchase intention. *Journal of Travel Research.* 60(5): 1018–1038.

Statista. (2024). Mobile app usage—Statistics & Facts. Retrieved from https://www.statista.com/topics/1002/mobile-app-usage.

Suki, N. M., En, Y. J., Suki, N. M., et al. (2023). Smartphones Online Marketing: A Bibliometric and Visualized Analysis. *International Journal of Interactive Mobile Technologies*. 17(8): 4–22.
Talwar, S., Dhir, A., Khalil, A., et al. (2020). Point of adoption and beyond. Initial trust and mobile-payment continuation intention. *Journal of Retailing and Consumer Services*. 55: 102086.
Venkatesh, V. & Davis, F.D. (2000). A Theoretical Extension of the Technology Acceptance Model: Four Longitudinal Field Studies. *Management Science, 46*(2): 186–204.
Wen, C., Prybutok, V. R. & Xu, C. (2011). An integrated model for customer online repurchase intention. *Journal of Computer Information Systems*. 52(1): 14–23.
Zhani, N. Mouri, N. & Ahmed, T. (2022), The Role of Mobile Value and Trust as Drivers of Purchase Intentions in M-Servicescape, *Journal of Retailing and Consumer Services*. 68: 103060.
Zhou, L., Dai, L. & Zhang, D. (2007). Online shopping acceptance model—A critical survey of consumer factors in online shopping. *Journal of Electronic Commerce Research*. 8(1): 41–62.
Zhou, M., Zhao, Q. & Chen, Y. (2017). Mobile internet and technology for optical teaching reform in higher education. *Education and Training in Optics and Photonics*. 104525K.

The Impact of WOM Information Characteristics of e-Commerce Platform on Reuse Intention Through Customer Trust and Satisfaction

Geukjoo Kang and Wonjong Kim

Abstract This study examines the relationships among word-of-mouth information characteristics, customer trust, customer satisfaction, and reuse intention with a focus on users of e-commerce platforms. Despite the importance, studies exploring the word-of-mouth information characteristics of e-commerce platforms and their impact on customer attitudes and behavioural intentions have been relatively overlooked. Therefore, this research aims to contribute to the understanding of the field by highlighting and deeply examining the causal relationship between word-of-mouth information characteristics and reuse intention on e-commerce platforms. Additionally, it is significant that the study focuses on small lodging businesses, such as pensions, which have seen rapid growth since the recent COVID-19 pandemic. Empirical analysis results show that among the word-of-mouth information characteristics, consensus and vividness have a significant positive relationship with customer trust, while recency and playfulness do not have a significant impact. Customer satisfaction has an indirect effect on the relationship between customer trust and reuse intention. The findings of this study provide important theoretical contributions and practical implications regarding the word-of-mouth information characteristics of e-commerce platforms and customer attitudes and behavioural intentions.

Keywords e-Commerce platform · Word-of-mouth information characteristics · Customer trust · Customer satisfaction · Reuse intention

---

G. Kang · W. Kim (✉)
Department of Industrial Management, Gyeongsang National University, Jinju, Republic of Korea
e-mail: wj.kim@gnu.ac.kr

G. Kang
e-mail: kjkang6804@gnu.ac.kr

T. Jung et al. (eds.), *XR and Metaverse*, Springer Proceedings in Business and Economics, https://doi.org/10.1007/978-3-031-77975-6_23

1 Introduction

The tourism industry has achieved continuous growth due to the full implementation of the five-day workweek. The number of trips has increased, and there has been an increase in accommodations offering various experiential programs (Lee & Oh, 2017). However, the COVID-19 pandemic has led to a decrease in outdoor activities and an increase in the proportion of online product purchases. Although the pension industry had a high proportion of online sales, its revenue declined. There were several reasons for this, but the high expenditure on online advertising significantly impacted sales. The revenue of social commerce companies is generated through marketing activities targeting a large number of subscribers. Small pension operators can join social commerce companies as sellers to conduct effective promotions at low costs and generate high sales. However, the decision to join social commerce companies should consider the cost factors, brand factors, and the economic and psychological risks perceived before joining (Jeong & Cho, 2020).

Small pension operators who join social commerce companies face the following issues. First, there is a significant burden related to fees. For example, fees are incurred based on the accommodation price, and additional fees are incurred for top advertising exposure on the social commerce platform. Additionally, excluding external factors such as labor costs and various operating expenses, the actual remaining profit is relatively small. Second, buyers on social commerce platforms tend to focus on popular accommodation products. As a result, pension operators who do not actively reflect accommodation trends face difficulties in increasing sales. Third, there are issues related to the payment methods. Except for some social commerce companies, the payment method involves delayed disbursement over several weeks, causing operational difficulties for the pension operators.

The social commerce industry is gradually shifting towards the e-commerce platform industry. The online commerce market has evolved through the eras of commerce 1.0, commerce 2.0, commerce 3.0, and commerce 4.0. A representative company of the commerce 4.0 era is Naver. Naver attracts consumers by combining fourth industrial revolution technologies with shopping on its existing platform, generating revenue from advertising, and receiving sales commissions from sellers (Jeong & Kim, 2019). Naver Shopping is differentiated from social commerce companies in terms of fees, additional services, and payment methods. Pension operators who have joined Naver Shopping generally show high satisfaction and transaction intentions (Jeong & Kim, 2019). This study distinguishes itself from previous research by focusing on the pension industry. Prior studies related to pensions have examined pension usage satisfaction, pension website quality, attributes of pension selection, pension website images, pension service scape, and attributes of social commerce membership (Kang & Jeong, 2015; In et al., 2018; Jeong & Cho, 2020; Han, 2008; Han & Hyun, 2010). Research that verified the influence relationships of pension products centered on e-commerce platforms has been very limited. Despite the increasing importance of utilizing e-commerce platforms, studies in this field have been relatively insufficient. Therefore, this study focuses on pension products, whose interest has significantly increased during and after the COVID-19 pandemic.

E-commerce platforms provide a more convenient distribution channel for pension operators compared to social commerce, and by applying a low-fee structure, they are emerging as an effective sales channel for pension operators. In fact, among e-commerce platforms, Naver Shopping offers the optimal e-commerce platform for small business owners entering online shopping, and it has been reported that the enrollment rate of new entrepreneurs is higher than that of internet shopping malls (Yoo et al., 2023).

The purpose of this study is to understand the relationship between e-commerce platform word-of-mouth information and the satisfaction, trust, and reuse intention of customers purchasing pension products. Through this, the study aims to identify factors affecting the utilization of e-commerce platforms and product composition, thereby proposing foundational data on marketing strategies for selling pension products via e-commerce platforms.

2 Theoretical Background and Hypotheses

2.1 The Relationship Between WOM Information Characteristics of e-Commerce Platform and Customer Trust

In the information age, there is a plethora of information and data available, and consumers are required to have the ability to select high-quality information. This ability involves not only information about products and services but also the capability to search for valuable information. The domestic e-commerce industry has grown rapidly with the increase in the use of the internet and mobile devices. The e-commerce industry is categorized according to changes over time. The era of commerce 1.0 was centered around online shopping malls, the era of commerce 2.0 involved open markets where transactions occur between sellers and buyers, the era of commerce 3.0 featured group buying via social media, and currently, we have entered the era of commerce 4.0, based on core technologies of the fourth industrial revolution (Jung & Kim, 2019).

E-commerce platform operators are entering various distribution industries by applying the core technologies of the fourth industrial revolution to PCs and mobile devices. Representative e-commerce platform companies include Naver, Kakao, and Google. The characteristic of these companies is that they possess IT technology and have adopted a method that provides product search, payment, and delivery all at once based on their platforms. The paper must be written in the third person and in British English (i.e. colour rather than color or organisation rather than organization). Authors should use straightforward declarative sentences, making every effort to help readers understand the concepts presented. Please explain any acronyms or abbreviations clearly.

Recently, consumers have mainly been using e-commerce platforms to obtain various information as part of the process of searching for products to purchase. Word-of-mouth information provided by e-commerce platforms offers vivid personal reviews of products or services and significantly influences the purchasing decisions of customers (Gao & Koufaris, 2006). Additionally, word-of-mouth information about products helps make the shopping process for consumers more efficient and effective (Yuan et al., 2018). Online purchases on e-commerce platforms differ from offline purchasing methods. Consumers cannot directly check the products and services; they rely on information, images, and word-of-mouth information provided by the website to make purchasing decisions (Song, 2016).

Based on domestic and international prior research, the representative variables measuring word-of-mouth information include consensus, vividness, recency, and playfulness. Consensus refers to the degree to which two or more individuals agree on the performance of a product (Chiou & Cheng, 2003). It also plays an important role in the purchase decision-making process (Song, 2016). The reliability of online word-of-mouth information is judged based on how many consumers agree with the information (Elliott, 2002). Specifically, online comments, views, and recommendations are important sources of information that can confirm the consensus of other consumers (Cheon & Lee, 2012). The study by Kim and Jeong (2007) confirmed that the higher the consensus of word-of-mouth information, the higher its reliability. In e-commerce, the consensus of word-of-mouth indicates the tendency of many consumers to align with a specific target. High-consensus word-of-mouth information reinforces the credibility of the recipients (Im & Jo, 2011).

Vividness is the feeling of having experienced something first hand through online word-of-mouth information (Jo & Jo, 2010) and significantly influences customer behavior (Hanna & Wozniak, 2001). Vividness, in particular, enhances realism and concreteness through various multimedia such as photos, videos, and emojis (Schindler & Bickart, 2005). The study by Kim and Kim (2014) verified that consumers who purchased dining products through an application trust vivid and relatable word-of-mouth information more.

Recency refers to the extent to which the latest product information is quickly delivered to consumers upon product release (Lee & Jeong, 2016). Word-of-mouth information should be prompt, vivid, lively, and reflect recency (Hanna & Wozniak, 2001). Consumers want information to be supplied quickly when needed. Information about a new product that is outdated is difficult to attract customer interest. Information not provided promptly loses its value as information. In particular, in the e-commerce environment, the value of information lies in its quick provision at the desired time (Kim & Kim, 2010). The study by Shin and Jo (2016) verified that the recency of word-of-mouth information on social commerce positively affects customer trust.

Playfulness refers to the degree to which users perceive enjoyment, fun, and interest (Jang et al., 2005). Oh and Kim (2014) emphasized that playfulness is an important variable in forming a positive attitude among consumers and identified it as a key variable that can enhance customer trust. According to the study by Lee (2017), customers experience various playful experiences through shopping on e-commerce platforms.

Trust is a key element in maintaining long-term relationships and building close relationships between customers and companies (Bowen & Shoemaker, 2003). Research on trust has been conducted in various fields, and particularly in e-commerce, trust is the most important factor in the relationship between service providers and customers (Han, 2018). E-commerce in the online environment is conducted between individuals in a non-face-to-face manner and is based on trust. Transactions are made with limited information, and to maintain ongoing relationships, it is essential to reduce uncertainties in e-commerce and establish a favorable trust relationship between sellers and customers (Jang, 2016). Based on the above discussion, the following hypotheses is proposed.

H1: *The word-of-mouth information characteristics of e-commerce platforms will have a positive (+) relationship with customer trust.*

2.2 The Relationship Between Customer Trust and Reuse Intention

Trust is the belief customers have in a company that has delivered positive outcomes in their relationship, creating an expectation that they can rely on the service provider. Trust exists when customers have confidence in the reliability and integrity of the company (Alrubaiee & Alkaa'ida, 2011).Trust is situated between the formation of relationships between buyers and sellers and customer loyalty. It is considered an important variable in forming and developing relationships with customers (Reynolds & Arnold, 2000; Ahn, 2011). Reuse intention refers to the intention of a person who has used a specific product or service more than once to continue using it (Kuo et al., 2009). It is a key concept for maintaining and sustaining the relationship between users and companies (Dorsch et al., 2000).

In terms of the importance of maintaining repeat customers, loyal customers are less price-sensitive than new customers and incur less time and cost to retain. Therefore, companies spare no effort to capture market share by targeting customers who demonstrate reuse intention within the industry (Reichheld, 1996; Song, 2016). Kim and Lee (2017) found that trust in e-commerce platform service providers positively affects reuse intention. Additionally, Song (2016) verified that customer trust in the characteristics of O2O (Online-to-Offline) positively impacts reuse intention. Based on the above discussion, the following hypothesis is proposed.

H2: *Customer trust will have a positive (+) relationship with reuse intention.*

2.3 The Relationship Between Customer Trust and Customer Satisfaction

Trust is a concept that represents the evaluation, feelings, and attitudes towards the other party. It is a core concept of relationship marketing along with satisfaction, but it is a higher level of comprehensive evaluation that serves as an important factor for achieving satisfaction (Kwon et al., 2003).

Customer satisfaction refers to the positive feelings a consumer has towards a transaction or transaction party when their desires are met beyond their expectations through the purchase and consumption of goods and services (Lee, 2019). In (2012) study on the characteristics of social commerce, it was confirmed that trust in social commerce has a significant impact on customer satisfaction. Based on the above discussion, the following hypothesis is proposed.

H3: *Customer trust will have a positive (+) relationship with customer satisfaction.*

2.4 The Relationship Between Customer Satisfaction and Reuse Intention

Customer satisfaction refers to the positive feelings a consumer has towards a transaction or transaction party when their expectations are exceeded through the purchase of goods or services (Lee, 2019). Customer satisfaction creates repeat purchases and favorable word-of-mouth effects, forming a highly loyal customer base that continuously enhances the profitability of the company (DeLone & McLean, 1992; Jeon, 2019).

Reuse intention is an important factor in predicting the actual behavior of customers and plays a crucial role in customer behavior based on **expectations** formed from past experiences (Seol, 2019). Customer satisfaction is a frequently used factor to explain new information technologies and has been proven in prior studies to have a causal relationship with reuse intention (Lee, 2019). In Seol's (2019) study, satisfaction with hair treatment product platform services was found to have a positive impact on reuse intention. Similarly, in Shin's (2019) study, the higher the satisfaction with Starbucks Siren Order, the higher the reuse intention for Siren Order. Based on the above discussion, the following hypothesis is proposed.

H4: *Customer satisfaction will have a positive (+) relationship with reuse intention.*

3 Research Methodology

3.1 Research Model

This study examines the impact of e-commerce platform word-of-mouth information characteristics on reuse intention through customer trust and customer satisfaction. A survey was conducted with e-commerce platform users aged 20 and above who have experience purchasing pension products on an e-commerce platform. The survey was conducted over approximately 30 days, from May 1 to May 30, 2021. A total of 250 questionnaires were collected, and after excluding insincere responses, the data from 194 respondents were used for analysis. Based on prior research, the causal relationships between each factor were reviewed, and the influence relationships between the factors were presented.

3.2 Measurement of Variables

The measurements for WOM information characteristics of e-commerce platform, including consensus, vividness, recency and playfulness, have been hired from studies of Shin and cho (2019). The questionnaire items were modified to fit the intent of this study. An example of a measurement item is "The latest pension information has a high number of views." The responses were measured on a 5-point Likert scale, ranging from 'strongly disagree' to 'strongly agree.'

Customer trust in e-commerce platforms was measured using three items based on the study by Choi et al. (2018). The questionnaire items were modified to fit the intent of this study. An example of a measurement item is "I trust the information provided by the e-commerce platform." The responses were measured on a 5-point Likert scale, ranging from 'strongly disagree' to 'strongly agree.'

Customer satisfaction with e-commerce platforms was measured using three items based on the study by Choi et al. (2018). The questionnaire items were modified to fit the intent of this study. An example of a measurement item is "I am satisfied with the information provided by the e-commerce platform." The responses were measured on a 5-point Likert scale, ranging from 'strongly disagree' to 'strongly agree.'

The reuse intention of e-commerce platforms was measured using three items based on the studies of Ahn (2011) and Oliver (1981). The questionnaire items were modified to fit the intent of this study. An example of a measurement item is "I will continue to use the e-commerce platform." The responses were measured on a 5-point Likert scale, ranging from 'strongly disagree' to 'strongly agree.'

4 Results

4.1 Sample Characteristics

The characteristics of the sample in this study are shown in Table 1. First, in response to the question "Which e-commerce platform did you recently visit to purchase pension products?" all respondents indicated they used Naver Shopping. To the question "How long does it take you to search and purchase pension products on an e-commerce platform?" 76 respondents (41.3%) answered 30–60 min, 37 respondents (20.1%) answered 60–90 min, and 34 respondents (18.5%) answered less than 30 min. Regarding gender, 105 respondents (57.1%) were female and 79 respondents (42.9%) were male. The age distribution showed that respondents in their 20 s comprised the highest number at 167 (90.8%). In terms of marital status, single respondents were the most prevalent at 169 (91.8%). For the question "How many times per year do you use pensions?" 70 respondents (38.0%) answered twice, and 57 respondents (31.0%) answered once. For the question "Who do you usually use pensions with?" 113 respondents (61.4%) answered with friends.

4.2 Confirmatory Factor Analysis

The results of the confirmatory factor analysis are shown in Table 2. The model fit indices were CMIN = 329.308, DF = 210, $p = 0.000$, CMIN/DF = 1.568, GFI = 0.865, AGFI = 0.823, NFI = 0.851, IFI = 0.940, TLI = 0.926, CFI = 0.939, RMR = 0.027, RMSEA = 0.056, indicating that all indices were appropriate. The standardized coefficient values ranged from 0.614 to 0.841, which were appropriate, and the construct reliability values were all above 0.7, and AVE values were all above 0.5. The items vividness 1 and recency 3, which did not exceed the standardized coefficient value of 0.5, were deleted.

4.3 Discriminant Validity Analysis

The results of the discriminant validity analysis are shown in Table 3. Since the AVE values were greater than the squared correlation coefficients, discriminant validity was established.

Table 1 Sample characteristics

Question	Response	Frequency	Ratio
Which e-commerce platforms did you recently visit to purchase pension products?	Naver shopping	184	100.0
	Daum shopping	–	–
	Nate shopping	–	–
	Others	–	–
How long does it take you to search and purchase pension products on e-commerce platforms?	Less than 30 min	34	18.5
	30–60 min	76	41.3
	60–90 min	37	20.1
	90–120 min	13	7.1
	More than 2 h	24	13.0
What is your gender?	Male	79	42.9
	Female	105	57.1
What is your age?	20s	167	90.8
	30s	7	3.8
	40s	3	1.6
	50s and above	7	3.8
What is your marital status?	Single	169	91.8
	Married	15	8.2
How many times per year do you use pensions?	Once	57	31.0
	Twice	70	38.0
	Three times	30	16.3
	Four times or more	27	14.7
Who do you usually use pensions with?	Family	46	25.0
	Partner	23	12.5
	Partner	113	61.4
	Colleagues	2	1.1
Total		184	100.0

4.4 Hypothesis Testing

Path analysis was conducted to test the hypotheses of the study. The model fit indices were CMIN = 328.912, DF = 215, $p = 0.000$, CMIN/DF = 1.530, GFI = 0.867, AGFI = 0.829, NFI = 0.851, IFI = 0.943, TLI = 0.931, CFI = 0.942, RMR =

Table 2 Confirmatory factor analysis

	Estimate	S.E.	C.R.	CR	AVE
Consensus 1	0.678			0.811	0.520
Consensus 2	0.798	0.133	8.849		
Consensus 3	0.780	0.128	8.723		
Consensus 4	0.614	0.122	7.193		
Vividness 1	0.730			0.750	0.501
Vividness 2	0.701	0.215	5.774		
Vividness 3	0.693	0.203	6.133		
Recency 1	0.644			0.767	0.526
Recency 2	0.780	0.154	7.846		
Recency 3	0.745	0.146	7.687		
Playfulness 1	0.652			0.873	0.635
Playfulness 2	0.841	0.143	9.493		
Playfulness 3	0.838	0.134	9.468		
Playfulness 4	0.842	0.138	9.502		
Customer trust 1	0.732			0.808	0.585
Customer trust 2	0.775	0.128	9.488		
Customer trust 3	0.787	0.130	9.604		
Reuse intention 1	0.807			0.776	0.538
Reuse intention 2	0.730	0.101	9.594		
Reuse intention 3	0.657	0.111	8.595		
Satisfaction 1	0.813			0.834	0.627
Satisfaction 2	0.749	0.082	10.621		
Satisfaction 3	0.812	0.081	11.642		

Note CMIN = 329.308, DF = 210, $p = 0.000$, CMIN/DF = 1.568, GFI = 0.865, AGFI = 0.823, NFI = 0.851, IFI = 0.940, TLI = 0.926, CFI = 0.939, RMR = 0.027, RMSEA = 0.056

Table 3 Discriminant validity analysis

	1	2	3	4	5	6	7
1. Consensus	0.520						
2. Vividness	0.294	0.501					
3. Recency	0.227	0.285	0.526				
4. Playfulness	0.322	0.427	0.461	0.635			
5. Customer trust	0.228	0.378	0.214	0.273	0.585		
6. Satisfaction	0.319	0.243	0.251	0.327	0.521	0.538	
7. Reuse intention	0.286	0.305	0.316	0.418	0.564	0.530	0.627

Note AVE values are on the diagonal and squared correlation coefficients are below the diagonal

Table 4 The results of hypotheses testing

Hypothesis		Estimate	S.E.	C.R.	P	Result
H1-1	Consensus → Customer trust	0.204	0.105	2.049	0.040	Accepted
H1-2	Vividness → Customer trust	0.312	0.151	2.280	0.023	Accepted
H1-3	Recency → Customer trust	0.155	0.117	1.356	0.175	Rejected
H1-4	Playfulness → Customer trust	0.191	0.122	1.449	0.147	Rejected
H2	Customer trust → Reuse intention	0.818	0.113	8.558	***	Accepted
H3	Customer trust → Satisfaction	0.440	0.174	2.790	0.005	Accepted
H4	Satisfaction → Reuse intention	0.417	0.144	2.689	0.007	Accepted

Note CMIN = 328.912, DF = 215, $p = 0.000$, CMIN/DF = 1.530, GFI = 0.867, AGFI = 0.829, NFI = 0.851, IFI = 0.943, TLI = 0.931, CFI = 0.942, RMR = 0.031, RMSEA = 0.054

0.031, RMSEA = 0.054. The summary of the results of hypotheses testing is as follow. H1-1 and H1-2 have been accepted while H1-3 and H1-4 have been rejected. Moreover H2, H3 and H4 are shown positive association. The results are shown in Table 4.

5 Conclusion

5.1 Summary and Implications

This study focused on pension users who utilize e-commerce platforms, adopting the online word-of-mouth information characteristics of consensus, vividness, recency, and playfulness as independent variables, and customer trust, customer satisfaction, and reuse intention as dependent variables to examine the hypotheses.

The analysis results showed that consensus and vividness had significant impacts on trust, while recency and playfulness did not significantly affect customer trust. These results suggest that among the online word-of-mouth information characteristics of pension products on e-commerce platforms, consensus based on the number of recommendations and vividly described comments have a high impact on the trust of e-commerce platform users. On the other hand, recency and playfulness did not significantly affect customer trust, indicating that users focus on the reliability of the information itself to determine its trustworthiness. Specifically, trust was found to affect both reuse intention and satisfaction, indicating that to increase reuse intention, it is necessary to focus on managing the word-of-mouth information characteristics of consensus and vividness.

Based on these results, the following research implications were derived. When promoting pension products on e-commerce platforms, consensus (agreement among users) and vividness (specific and lively expression of information) are important factors in enhancing user trust. This indicates that reviews aligning with other users' positive experiences play a crucial role in increasing trust when purchasing or reserving pension products. Therefore, pension operators and e-commerce platform providers should emphasize positive reviews that users can relate to and encourage detailed reviews that capture vivid experiences. Recency (the latest updates of information) and playfulness (the fun elements of information) did not significantly impact customer trust. This suggests that users prioritize the reliability and characteristics of the information itself over the latest information or fun elements. Therefore, it is important to seek ways to present consistent recommendations and detailed information rather than focusing on fun elements.

Customer trust directly impacts reuse intention and customer satisfaction, and satisfaction has a significant indirect effect between trust and reuse intention. This indicates that higher customer trust leads to higher customer satisfaction, which in turn is likely to lead to higher reuse intention. Therefore, e-commerce platforms and pension operators should develop strategies to increase customer trust, thereby enhancing customer satisfaction and inducing long-term reuse intention. For example, they can encourage users to write reviews with high consensus and vividness through review management strategies. Examples include requiring specific experiences when writing reviews, encouraging the inclusion of relatable content, and offering reward programs for positive reviews to motivate users to write reviews voluntarily. Additionally, it is important to provide special experiences during pension use so that users can share vivid experiences in their reviews. For instance, offering special events or services can help users reflect these experiences in their reviews, contributing to higher consensus and vividness.

5.2 *Limitations*

Based on the limitations of this study, the following suggestions for future research are proposed. First, this study used cross-sectional data collected over a specific period, and considering the sample size, it is somewhat difficult to generalize the analysis results. Future research should design longitudinal studies to more clearly examine the causal relationships between variables, and collect larger and more diverse samples. Second, previous research related to the characteristics of word-of-mouth information, which this study focused on, has attempted to approach information from a multidimensional perspective. Future research should consider including other word-of-mouth related variables in the research model, beyond the characteristics examined in this study—consensus, vividness, recency, and playfulness. This could yield valuable insights for practitioners. Finally, consumer interest and use of e-commerce platforms are increasing day by day. To enhance their trust and satisfaction and increase their reuse intention, it is necessary to explore and attempt various strategies that can maximize the effectiveness of information delivery online from multiple angles.

References

Ahn, k. H. (2011). The Structural Relationships among Customer Trust, Satisfaction, and Loyalty inSocial Commerce Context: Focusing onTrust Transfer. SeJong University Ph.D thesis

Alrubaiee, L., & Alkaa'ida, F. (2011). The mediating effect of patient satisfaction in the patients' perceptions of healthcare quality-patient trust relationship, International Journal of Marketing Studies. 3(1):103

Bowen, J. T., & Shoemaker, S. (2003). Loyalty: A strategic commitment. Cornell hotel and restaurant administration quarterly, 44(5–6):31–46.

Cheon, D. H., & Lee, H. J. (2012). A Study of effect on trust, acceptance and spread of word-of-mouth and purchase intention by characteristics of electronic word-of-mouth on travel industry. The Academy of Customer Satisfaction Management, 14(1): 83–100

Chiou, J. S., & Cheng, C. (2003). Should a company have message boards on its web sites?. Journal of interactive marketing, 17(3):50–61

Cho, M. S., & Cho, W. S. (2010). The structural relationship between on-line word of mouth, trust, acceptance of word of mouth and intention of family restaurant visit on the Family Restaurant. Journal of Tourism Management Research, 43: 181–199

Choi, D. O., Lim, D. S., and Yoon, C. H. (2018). A Study on the Impact of Store Characteristics on Customer Impulse Purchase Types in Online Shopping. The e-Business Studies, 19(2), 25–42

DeLone. W.H. & McLean E.R. (1992). Information Systems Success: The Quest for the Dependent Variable, Information Systems Research, 3(1):60–95

Dorsch, M. J., Grove, S. J., & Darden, W. R. (2000). Consumer intentions to use a service category. Journal of Services Marketing, 14(2): 92–117

Elliott, K. M., (2002). Understanding consumer-to- consumer influence on the web, Duke University Ph.D thesis

Gao, Y., & Koufaris, M. (2006). Perceptual antecedents of user attitude in electronic commerce. ACM SIGMIS Database: the database for Advances in Information Systems, 37(2–3):42–50

Han, C. W. (2018). Influence of the usage characteristics of the O2O food delivery platform service on the trust, satisfaction, and continuous use intention according to food-related lifestyle. Master's Thesis, Yonsei University

Han, S. I. (2008). The Effects of Pension Experiences on Intention to Revisit and to Recommend. A case study of Gyungju. Korean Journal of Tourism Research, 23(2): 23–37

Han, S. I., & Hyun, Y. H. (2010). An examination of the role of a decision-making variable between pension Website quality and post-visit behaviors: Focusing on mediating Vs moderating effect. Korean Journal of Tourism Research, 24(6): 271–289

Hanna, N., & Wozniak, R. (2001). Consumer Behavior: An Applied Approach. Upper Saddle River, NJ: Prentice-Hall.

Im, S. T., & Jo, W. S. (2011). The Effects of Business Blog Information Characteristics Influencing on Electronic Word-of-Mouth In the Food Service Industry: Emphasis on Trust Transference. Korean Journal of Hospitality and Tourism, 20(5): 165–180

In, S. H., & Ji, K. Y. (2018). A study on internal marketing factors upon organizational trust and organizational citizenship behavior in service firms: Focused on travel agency employees. International Journal of Tourism and Hospitality Research, 32(3): 171–182

Jang, J. S., Jo, H. J., Park, S. H., & Park, S. M. (2005). Entertainment Marketing Cases : Using Movie Contents on On-Line Media. CERI Entertainment Review, 3: 171–194

Jang, P. (2016). Study on the Effects of O2O Commerce Characteristics and Consumer Characteristics on Trust, Desire and Behavioral Intention in China, Chungnam National University Ph.D thesis

Jeon, P. H. (2019). A Study on the Influence of the Perceived of Service Quality on the Customer Satisfaction and Intention to Rebuy in O2O Commerce and the Moderating Effect of Uncertainty Avoidance Tendency. InHa University Ph.D thesis

Jeong, D. Y., & Cho, M. H. (2020). The effect of social commerce joining factor on perceived risk, joining intention, and joining behavior of pension operators: Entrepreneurship as moderation effect. Korean Journal of Hospitality & Tourism, 29(2): 1–20

Jo, W. S., & Jo, M. S. (2010). The structural relationship between on-line word of mouth, trust, acceptance of word of mouth and intention of family restaurant visit on the Family Restaurant. Journal of Tourism Management Research, 43: 181–199

Jung, Y. S., & Kim, H. J. (2019). Analysis of Typology and Competition of Domestic Online Shopping—Focused on Naver shopping. Korea Research Academy of Distribution and Management Review, 22(1): 35–46

Kang, G, J., & Jung, K. H. (2015). The Effect of Website Image on Customer Performance—Focused on the Lodging Business of Pension—. The Journal of Internet Electronic Commerce Research, 15(6): 295–310

Kim Y. C., & Jeong, H. M. (2007). The Relationship Analysis among Influential Factors to the Effectiveness of Online WOM at Service Industry. The Korean Journal of Advertising, 18(4): 167–183

Kim, H. J., & Kim, Y. I. (2014). The Influence of Building Trust by Characteristics of e-WOM Based on Application of Food Information Service on on Behavior Intention. Korean Journal of Hospitality & Tourism, 23(1): 45–64

Kim, M. J., & Lee, S. B. (2017). The effect of the innovativeness of delivery application users on perceived traits, satisfaction, and continuous usage intention: Using the extended technology acceptance model (ETAM). International Journal of Tourism and Hospitality Research, 31(1): 199–214

Kim, N. E. & Kim, M. H. (2010). The Effects of Word-of-Mouth Information Quality on Word-of-Mouth Effects in Online Tourism Context. Korean Journal of Hotel Administration, 19(4): 59–79

Kuo, Y. F., Wu, C. M., & Deng, W. J. (2009). The relationships among service quality, perceived value, customer satisfaction, and post-purchase intention in mobile value-added services. Computers in Human Behavior, 25(4): 887–896

Kwon, S. H., Kim, T. U., & Lee, Y. K. (2003). The roles of customer's perceived value, satisfaction, trust and their relationship with loyalty in Internet shopping environment. Korean Management Science Review, 20(1): 149–163

Lee, O. (2019). A Study on the Effect of O2O Service Quality on Perceived Value, Satisfaction, and Continuous Intention to Use. Dong-Eui University Ph.D thesis

Lee, E. M. (2017). The Moderating Effects of Critical Incidents on the Relationship Between Affect-Valence and Information Processing in Internet Shopping. The Journal of Internet Electronic Commerce Research. 17(1): 215–234

Lee, S, H., & Jeong, Y, G. (2016). The effects of eWOM Characteristics on Credibility, eWOM Acceptance and Purchase Intentions. Journal of the Korea Contents Association, 16(9): 545–559

Lee, S. H., & Oh, M. J. (2017). Effect relationship between tourism experience, visiting value, satisfaction and behavioral intention of traditional Korean village-Focused on Jeonju Hanok Village. International Journal of Tourism and Hospitality Research, 31(9): 33–46

Lim, S. T., & Cho, W. S. (2011). The Effects of Business Blog Information Characteristics Influencing on Electronic Word-of-Mouth in the Food Service Industry: Emphasis on Trust Transference. Korean Journal of Hotel Administration, 20(5): 165–180

Oh, M. H., & Kim, I. (2014). The Effect of Consumer Attitude toward Fashion Products on SNS's Characteristics to Purchase Intention and On-line Word of Mouth. Journal of the Korean Society of Fashion Design, 14(1): 101–120

Oliver, R. L. (1981). Measurement and evaluation of satisfaction processes in retail settings. Journal of Retailing

Reichheld, F. F. (1996). Learning from customer defections. Harvard Business Review, 74(2): 56–67

Reynolds, K. E., & Arnold, M. J. (2000). Customer loyalty to the salesperson and the store: examining relationship customers in an upscale retail context. Journal of personal selling & sales management, 20(2): 89–98

Schindler, R. M., & Bickart, B. (2005). Published word of mouth: Referable, consumer-generated information on the Internet. Online consumer psychology: Understanding and influencing consumer behavior in the virtual world, 32(1), 35–61.

Seol, N. R. (2019). Use of O2O platform service A Study on the Effects of Hair Treatment on Satisfaction and Persistence. [Master's Thesis, Kyonggi University]

Shin, E. J., & Cho, W. J. (2016). The Effect of Hotel Employees' Humor Style on Their Self-Efficacy and Job Satisfaction. Korean Journal of Tourism Research, 31(3): 157–175

Shin, E. J., & Cho. W. J. (2019). The effects of Word-of-mouth information and characteristics of social commerce hotel products on the customer's satisfaction, trust and use intention. International Journal of Tourism Management and Sciences. 34(2): 217–236

Song, J. H. (2016). A study on the effect of users acceptance attitude of hotel products sales social commerce to trust and usage intention: use of extended technology acceptance model. Doctoral Dissertation, Sejong University

Yoo, B, J., Jung, Y, S., Lee, J, J., & Oh, Y, L. (2023). Analyzing the Economic and Social Effects of M&A Strategies of Digital Platform Companies—Focusing on the Case of Kakao Entertainment. Korea Business Review, 27(1): 77–95

Yuan, S., Feng, L., Wang, K., Pang, J., Bosch, M., Lollar, C., … & Zhou, H. C. (2018). Stable metal–organic frameworks: design, synthesis, and applications. Advanced Materials, 30(37): 1704303

Social Implications of XR Adoption

Decoding Public Sentiments: A Topic Modeling Analysis of the Metaverse Using Reddit Discourse

Lekhika Sharma, Neeraj Kaushik, and Tanvi Sharma

Abstract This paper examines the public perception of the metaverse through a comprehensive analysis of discussions on social media platforms. Utilising data from Reddit, we employed topic modeling, and sentiment analysis to uncover the current state, topics, sentiment orientation, and public concerns regarding the metaverse. Our findings indicate that while there is a general positive sentiment towards the metaverse, there are also concerns about its potential negative implications. Additionally, we observed a significant interest in the metaverse's potential to transform the lives of individuals with disabilities. Our study provides valuable insights into how the public perceives the metaverse, which can help businesses, government entities, and other stakeholders in developing policies and products that align with public sentiment and address concerns.

Keywords Metaverse · Reddit · Text analysis · Topic modelling · Sentiment analysis

1 Introduction

The term "Metaverse" has become extremely popular in recent years. Ever since Facebook's founder Mark Zuckerberg changed the name of his company to "Meta," with a vision to create a "Metaverse", a three-dimensional virtual reality world, the researchers, developers, and the business community have been interested in

L. Sharma (✉)
Department of Business Administration, National Institute of Technology, Kurukshetra, India
e-mail: 62210027@nitkkr.ac.in

N. Kaushik
Faculty, Department of Business Administration, National Institute of Technology, Kurukshetra, India
e-mail: neeraj.kaushik@nitkkr.ac.in

T. Sharma
Government Medical College & Hospital, Chandigarh, India
e-mail: tanvi12698@gmail.com

T. Jung et al. (eds.), *XR and Metaverse*, Springer Proceedings in Business and Economics, https://doi.org/10.1007/978-3-031-77975-6_24

learning more about this new phenomenon and its implications (Dwivedi et al., 2023; Hollensen et al., 2023). The Metaverse is a rich virtual world where users can create *avatars* to interact with other users and own virtual assets (Cheah & Shimul, 2023; Gao et al., 2023; Park & Kim, 2022; Ritterbusch & Teichmann, 2023). It utilises immersive technologies such as mixed reality (MR), augmented reality (AR), virtual reality (VR), and soon-to-be extended reality (XR), which is a catch-all term for MR, VR, and AR (Choi & Kim, 2017; Kim, 2021; Park & Kim, 2022; Rauschnabel et al., 2022; Arya et al., 2023). It is frequently viewed as the next advancement in online technology, permitting people to interact and engage in activities in real-time across geographical, temporal, and other boundaries (Gauttier et al., 2022; Barrera & Shah, 2023; Golf-Papez et al., 2022).

According to Statista, the Metaverse market is expected to grow at a CAGR of 38% in 2024 (Statista, 2023). Likewise, Markets and Markets (2023) predicts that the Metaverse market will increase to $1304 billion by 2030. Its quick development will probably benefit all facets of society, including civic and social life, gaming and entertainment, education, healthcare, and the arts. Although given all the possible opportunities that the metaverse holds, Experts are divided on whether, by 2040, over half a billion people worldwide will find themselves utilising the metaverse as a much more sophisticated and immersive part of daily life or if it's just a hype that will fade out (Atske, 2022).

Existing studies on the metaverse have utilised empirical and survey-based approaches such as measuring the impact of brands on consumer engagement and satisfaction (Bousba & Arya, 2022; Afkar et al., 2022), the intention of the students to use metaverse learning platforms (Ahmad Samed Al-Adwan et al., 2023; Alfaisal et al., 2022; Kaur et al., 2023), satisfaction towards metaverse e-commerce platforms (Mohamed Jahir Hussain & Bee Hwa, 2023; Toraman & Geçit, 2023) but there is a paucity of research directed towards entailing the perspectives of the general audience for the same, clearly leading to a significant knowledge gap. Adamopoulos et al. (2018) emphasised that social media platforms present a unique opportunity to gain deeper insights into users' perceptions of new technologies, which can either amplify or diminish their adoption and usage. Furthermore, observational data from social media platforms eliminates the possibility of biases inherent in traditional survey-based research, such as the Hawthorne effect. It describes the phenomena in which individuals change their performance or behaviour in response to being observed, examined, or the focus of attention (Cook, 1962).

Given its real-world implications, and the potential to impact society as a whole, it is imperative to understand how the common public perceives and comprehends this concept. Therefore, the present study aims to highlight the importance of gauging public perceptions of the metaverse and thereby obtain clarity on the future it holds.

In the era of the digital revolution, consumers' assessments of metaverse technology value are significantly influenced by social media platforms, with public opinion playing a pivotal role in shaping user's decision-making behaviours. Based on all of the aforementioned gaps, the present study employs a novel application of topic modeling and sentiment analysis using *Reddit*. Topic modeling, such as LDA, reveals the topics of public interest within a large collection of texts (Onan et al., 2016), While sentiment analysis offers perceptions into people's attitudes toward specific incidents, goods, and technological advancements (Medhat et al., 2014). Reddit is an anonymous social media network that focuses on subreddits, or communities with shared interests. Collectively, the adopted methodology will lead to findings that will help researchers understand the nuances of public perception and sentiment surrounding the metaverse.

Specifically, the following research questions are addressed by this study:

RQ1: Can integrating analyses from online forums provide a more thorough comprehension of how the general public perceives the metaverse, and what insights (here, topics) can be extracted about the Metaverse?

RQ2: What are the various sentiments and emotions that individuals associate with the Metaverse?

Unlike other studies in the literature currently in publication, our study's broad sample size provides an inclusive viewpoint on the Metaverse. This paper addresses these questions by focusing on public opinion associated with user predictions, expectations, and desires regarding the metaverse. By understanding these dynamics, businesses, government entities, and other stakeholders can gain insights into the public's sentiments about this emerging technology trend, identifying both opportunities and concerns.

The remainder of the paper is organized as follows: Sect. 2 is devoted to the literature review. The research methodology and data collection process employed in this study are outlined in Sect. 3. Section 4 offers a more thorough analysis and discussion of the findings. Section 5 presents the Discussions and Conclusions, along with implications, constraints, and future directions for research.

2 Literature Review

The term "*Metaverse*" was coined by a Sci-fi novelist in his book Snow Crash in 1992, a place where people engage in a range of social activities to create value between the real and virtual worlds (Stephenson, 1992). Ball (2022) defined it as "a massively scaled and interoperable network of real-time rendered 3D virtual world that can be experienced synchronously and persistently by an almost infinite number of users with continuity of data, such as identity, history, entitlements, objects, communications, and payments, and with an individual sense of presence". Despite being a concept for many years, the Metaverse is now more likely to become a reality, thanks to recent technological developments. The development of the Metaverse, a virtual environment where digital and real-world elements coexist, has been made possible by the smooth integration of Internet and web technologies (Lee et al., 2021). Virtual reality (VR) and augmented reality (AR), two technologies that allow for multisensory interactions with virtual environments, digital objects, and people, are combined to create the metaverse (Mystakidis, 2022; Singh, 2023). In summary, Metaverse is an immersive virtual environment where individuals can possess virtual assets and create their own digital identities called "*Avatars*". Avatars are digital representations of individuals within the virtual world, serving as their digital twins (Dwivedi et al., 2022). It has persistent multiuser platforms and is a socially connected, immersive environment. Enabling users to participate in real-world activities together while overcoming time, space, and physical limitations, The Metaverse is regarded as the next stage of the internet's development. Users will be able to engage with life in ways that aren't practical in the actual world.

Many empirical studies have utilised a variety of theories, revealing the complex interplay of factors influencing metaverse acceptance and adoption. Classical theories, like the Theory of Planned Behaviour (TPB) (Albayati et al., 2023; Gupta et al., 2023), the Technology Acceptance Model (TAM) (Van et al., 2022; Alfaisal et al., 2022; Hwang & Koo, 2023), the Unified Theory of Acceptance and Use of Technology (UTAUT) (Lee & Kim, 2022; Teng et al., 2022; Yang et al., 2022) and the Diffusion of Innovation Theory (DOI) (Farhi et al., 2023), which act as foundational pillars and offer valuable insights into the multifaceted dimensions of this virtual world. At the same time, the newer dimensions of cutting-edge technologies like immersive technology, digital twins, and avatars necessitate inputs from the users. Their voice can be heard on social platforms like Reddit, Twitter, etc. where all users openly and vociferously share their experiences and reviews. Hence, this study attempts to fill the existing gap and provide a more holistic understanding of public sentiments. We have utilised data from Reddit following the trends set by numerous studies that have used the platform for qualitative analysis (De Choudhury et al., 2017; Foufi et al., 2019; Ha et al., 2017; Low et al., 2020). It is a well-known social media site with a varied user base and a vast array of subjects covered—the current study endeavours to bridge the existing gap and offer a more holistic understanding of public sentiments.

3 Research Methodology

3.1 Data Source

The corpus was sourced from Reddit (http://www.reddit.com), a widely utilised platform for social networking, online gatherings, and the exchange of news and information. The most recent statistics show that 50 million people use Reddit daily across the globe (Lin, 2023). Since the site's 2005 launch, Reddit has grown significantly in user base, with 52 million daily active users in 2023 compared to 36 million in 2020 (Dean, 2023).

In December 2023, we curated top subreddits with comments surpassing 11,000 from January 2021 to December 2023, focusing on discussions where the keyword "*Metaverse*" was mentioned. We utilised various methods to construct a comprehensive dataset. Our strategy began with downloading 'top' rated posts of all time to systematically capture the most relevant topics based on collective opinions.

We complemented this dataset with 'hot' and recent top-rated posts to encompass emerging topics. To guarantee data accuracy, the removal of duplicate posts from the compilation was carried out. In the concluding phase, our manual curation resulted in a final tally of 10,988 subreddits and their comments. The text was cleaned further using the Quanteda package, and the LDA package was employed for topic modeling. Topic extraction was done using topic modeling, and then topic significance ranking. Additionally, underlying emotions in the comments were calculated through emotion-based sentiment analysis, and the overall outcomes were visualised.

3.2 Topic Modeling

Topic modeling is a statistical technique used to identify patterns in word usage and organise a large corpus into groups, known as topics, that share a common focus (Vayansky & Kumar, 2020). In this study, we employed Latent Dirichlet Allocation (LDA), proposed by Blei et al. (2003), a prominent topic modeling technique. It identifies topics within large collections of texts. It simplifies each document by representing it as a "bag of words," creating a term vocabulary based on word frequency. Based on the probability distribution of words, the algorithm then classifies topics and allocates documents to them according to likelihood.

3.3 Sentiment Analysis

Sentiment analysis (SA) is a computational approach to understanding the opinions, sentiments, and subjectivity expressed in text (Taboada, 2016). It is an effective tool for monitoring attitudes, sentiments, and beliefs about locations, goods, or services that people have expressed on a variety of online platforms. This study used the NRC Lexicon, which was created by Mohammad and Turney (2010), for sentiment analysis. This lexicon divides the text into two sentiments (positive and negative) and eight emotions (anger, fear, anticipation, trust, surprise, sadness, joy, and disgust). Compared to other lexicons, it was selected for the breadth of its word coverage as well as the categories of feelings and emotions it covered.

4 Findings

4.1 Topic Analysis

In our study, LDA is employed to model topics and reveal patterns in public opinions efficiently. In particular, we used perplexity—a technique for figuring out how many topics to have, comparing priors, and assessing the effectiveness of various modeling approaches—to build a 3-topic LDA model (Table 1). It calculates the change in the likelihood of the held-out words as a function of the trained model (Jones, 2019).

Topic 1: **Metaverse Dynamics**: This topic encapsulates the core dynamics and components of the metaverse, highlighting the role of data, virtual experiences, blockchain technology, real-world integration, and human interaction. In addition to the economic aspects of NFTs, money transactions, and market dynamics, it delves into the creation, space, and time dimensions within this dynamic digital ecosystem. Incorporating user-centric elements, inventive concepts, and firsthand accounts enhances the discourse on the complex nature of the metaverse. This is apparent in the community's statements, exemplified by:

> We have a member in our social group who keeps shilling about NFTs, Metaverse and Crypto. Anyways, this guy has been buying NFTs thinking the Metaverse will be so relevant that if you don't get in now, it'll be too late.

This reflects that the individuals are enthusiastic and overly invested in emerging technologies like NFTs (Non-Fungible Tokens), the Metaverse, and cryptocurrencies. This suggests a common belief among some enthusiasts that the Metaverse will be a significant part of the future digital landscape, and investing early will yield significant returns.

Topic 2: **Virtual Lifestyle and Gaming Culture**: This topic delves into the fusion of virtual and real-life elements, covering both technology development and gaming

Table 1 Topics extracted from LDA model

Topic Id	Terms	Label
Topic 1	Metaverse, people, world, real, blockchain, virtual, technology, crypto, digital, internet, data, platform, web, create, space, time, nft, system, money, sell, user, idea, person, nfts, experience, public, single, market, based	Metaverse dynamics
Topic 2	Life, game, people, tech, metaverse, world, lot, games, companies, virtual, time, content, cool, avatar, ready, stuff, build, lol, player, user, love, experience, pretty, avatars, Roblox, happen, fortnite, live	Virtual lifestyle and gaming culture
Topic 3	Facebook, meta, people, metaverse, money, social, don, time, ar, company, headset, idea, mark, Zuckerberg, internet, reality, verse, future, day, media, headsets, bad, oculus, quest, vr, chat, buy, real	Facebook's Metaverse influence

culture. It revolves around the dynamic realm of gaming and virtual encounters. This also highlights the term "avatars," which is a key distinguishing feature of the metaverse. The social and interactive elements of virtual experiences are highlighted by the inclusion of platforms such as Roblox, Fortnite, and Minecraft as illustrated by comments like:

> The "real" metaverses, or the closest thing to them, are existing, large-scale games that have existed for years, and you can make the case that places like Minecraft, Roblox, Fortnite.

Topic 3: **Facebook's Metaverse Influence**: This topic exclusively focuses on Facebook's pivotal role within the metaverse landscape. It explores how the business affects social dynamics, finances, and virtual reality (VR). The conversation covers the company's influence on media, Mark Zuckerberg's innovative ideas, and its significant contribution to the creation of VR headsets such as Quest and Oculus. It thoroughly examines how Facebook affects user engagement, future developments, and user engagement within the metaverse. This is clear from community opinions like:

> The idea of the metaverse has been around for a long time, but it has gained renewed interest in recent days due to the bold vision set out by Mark Zuckerberg (hate on him as much as you like)

4.2 Sentiment Analysis

We utilized the R-package **syuzhet** to conduct sentiment analysis, attributing either "positive" or "negative" valence and further categorizing them into eight different emotions such as "anger," "anticipation," "disgust," "fear," "joy," "sadness," "surprise," and "trust" to each word. It is noteworthy that users hold a positive outlook towards the metaverse platforms which is depicted in the Fig. 1 wherein the positive sentiments amounts to 70.41%. Among the various emotions expressed, "Anticipation" and "Trust" are the most frequently noted, accounting for 20.32% and 24.96% of the sentiments, respectively. This indicates a strong sense of excitement and confidence in the potential of the metaverse. Words like "hype," "hope," "larger," "expect," "finally," and "happen" depict Anticipation, while "content," "true," "unity," "system," and "real" show trust in the metaverse. Additionally, there is a notable sense of "Surprise" and "Joy" that users often exhibit excitement or curiosity about the new platforms and their developments.

While negative (29.59%) emotions like "Anger," "Fear," "Sadness," and "Disgust" are present, they are less prevalent, suggesting that overall negativity in discussions about the metaverse is relatively uncommon. For example, users expressed these negative emotions by using words like "hate," "hell," "terrible," "difficult," "failure," "criticism," "impossible," "criminal," "garbage," "greed," and "sick."

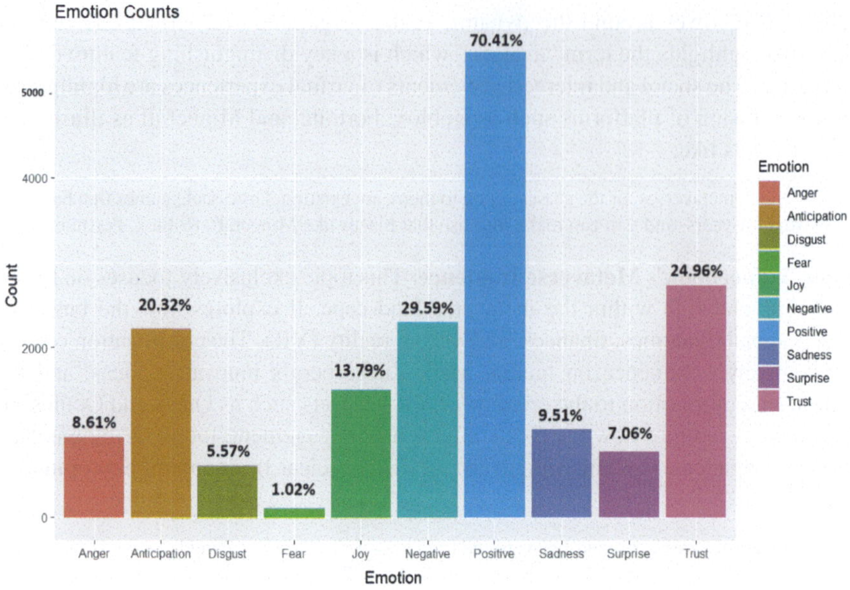

Fig. 1 Sentiment analysis plot

5 Discussion and Conclusion

Through text mining, topic modeling, and sentiment analysis, this study examined the current state, topics, sentiment orientation, and public concerns surrounding the metaverse using data from the social media platform Reddit. Topic 1 reveals that the public possesses a conceptual understanding of the metaverse and its associated components, such as NFTs and blockchain. However, the concern lies in Topic 2, where the metaverse is predominantly perceived as a platform for MMORPG (Massively Multiplayer Online Playing Game). This perception may be influenced by brands like Nike, Gucci, and Hyundai, among others, that are replicating the metaverse within existing gaming platforms such as Roblox, Fortnite, and Decentraland. Through these platforms, they are utilising gamification activities to engage and attract users. Topic 3 sheds light on Facebook's significant influence within the metaverse landscape, particularly through its innovative ideas and contributions to VR headsets like Quest and Oculus. These insights underscore the complexity and diversity of public opinion and perspectives surrounding the metaverse.

Furthermore, the overwhelmingly positive sentiments suggest that people are open to this technology, indicating that developers should take this as a cue to commence crafting products and policies accordingly.

A noteworthy observation has come to light regarding the profound impact the metaverse can have, especially for individuals with disabilities.

> As a disabled man, I want this badly. I want to participate in life, without the function and ability to. When you're stuck and confined to a chair or other apparatus that limits your physical ability; all of what you named doesn't exist. That isolation really damages you over time, if you let it.

The statement underscores the transformative potential of the metaverse for individuals with disabilities, suggesting that it could offer a virtual space where physical limitations are no longer a barrier to engagement and participation. It highlights the need for considering accessibility and inclusivity in the design and implementation of metaverse technologies, ensuring they are accessible to all individuals, regardless of physical limitations. This could lead to the development of innovative solutions and experiences that enhance the quality of life for individuals with disabilities, enabling them to participate more fully in social, educational, and recreational activities.

5.1 Theoretical and Practical Implications

Our research offers theoretic and practical implications. Firstly, it contributes to the theoretical understanding of topic modeling by applying it to a novel context, i.e., the metaverse discourse on Reddit. It demonstrates the use of topic modeling to identify subtle sentiments and discussion patterns in online forums. By examining Reddit discussions, this research offers valuable perspectives on the public's perception of the metaverse. This knowledge can contribute to the larger body of research on sentiment analysis and public opinion as well as theoretical models of technology adoption and diffusion.

Practically, businesses may modify their marketing strategies and product offerings to better suit the needs and preferences of the general public by using the topics and sentiments that have been identified. Policymakers can use the findings of this study to inform regulations and policies related to the metaverse. For example, understanding public concerns and sentiments can help policymakers address potential ethical, privacy, and security issues associated with metaverse technologies. Developers can use the insights from this study to guide the development of metaverse technologies. For instance, understanding the public's perceptions of different metaverse components can help developers prioritise features and functionalities that are most important to users.

5.2 Limitations and Future Research Directions

Our study sheds light on the metaverse's transformative potential and societal implications by providing an innovative investigation into how the general public views it. Like any study, though, it has some limitations that should be taken into account for upcoming research. One possible limitation of the study is its reliance on Reddit data, which confines the opinions of the general public to only a single social media platform. Subsequent investigations may examine alternative social media platforms such as Instagram and Twitter, or conduct a comparative analysis of these platforms. Furthermore, the analysis is restricted to a limited number of subreddits and a particular time period, which may have limited the range of viewpoints that are included. Future researchers can take a larger time frame. Furthermore, because the study is done in English, perspectives from non-English speaking communities may be excluded. Multilevel languages may be used by researchers in the future.

References

Adamopoulos, P., Ghose, A., & Todri, V. (2018). The impact of user personality traits on word of mouth: Text-mining social media platforms. *Information Systems Research, 29*(3), 612–640.

Afkar, E., Hamsal, M., Kartono, R., & Furinto, A. (2022). Prediction of Perceived Consumer Experience, Perceived Brand Engagement, and Gamification towards the Intention to Use Metaverse: An Extended TAM Approach. *Proceeding—6th International Conference on Information Technology, Information Systems and Electrical Engineering: Applying Data Sciences and Artificial Intelligence Technologies for Environmental Sustainability, ICITISEE 2022*, 239–244. https://doi.org/10.1109/ICITISEE57756.2022.10057740

Ahmad Samed Al-Adwan, Na Li, Amer Al-Adwan, Ghazanfar Ali Abbasi, Nour Awni Albelbisi, & Akhmad Habibi. (2023). Extending the Technology Acceptance Model (TAM) to Predict University Students' Intentions to Use Metaverse-Based Learning Platforms. *Education and Information Technologies.*

Albayati, H., Alistarbadi, N., & Rho, J. J. (2023). Assessing engagement decisions in NFT Metaverse based on the Theory of Planned Behaviour (TPB). *Telematics and Informatics Reports, 10*, 100045. https://doi.org/10.1016/J.TELER.2023.100045

Alfaisal, R. M., Zare, A., Alfaisal, A. M., Aljanada, R., & Abukhalil, G. W. (2022). The acceptance of metaverse system: a hybrid SEM-ML approach. *International Journal of Advances in Applied Computational Intelligence (IJAACI), 01*(01), 34–44. https://doi.org/10.54216/IJAACI.010103

Arya, V., Sambyal, R., Sharma, A., & Dwivedi, Y. K. (2023). Brands are calling your AVATAR in Metaverse–A study to explore XR-based gamification marketing activities & consumer-based brand equity in virtual world. *Journal of Consumer Behaviour*. https://doi.org/10.1002/cb.2214

Atske, S. (2022). The metaverse in 2040. *Pew Research Center: Internet, Science & Tech.*

Ball, M. (2022). *The metaverse: and how it will revolutionize everything*. Liveright Publishing.

Barrera, K. G., & Shah, D. (2023). Marketing in the Metaverse: Conceptual understanding, framework, and research agenda. *Journal of Business Research, 155*, 113420.

Blei DM, Ng AY, Jordan MI (2003). Latent Dirichlet allocation. *Journal of Machine Learning Research*, 3(4–5), 993–1022.

Bousba, Y., & Arya, V. (2022). Let's connect in metaverse. Brand's new destination to increase consumers' affective brand engagement & their satisfaction and advocacy. *Journal of content, community and communication, 15*(8), 276–293. https://doi.org/10.31620/jccc.06.22/19

Cheah, I., & Shimul, A. S. (2023). Marketing in the metaverse: Moving forward–What's next? *Journal of Global Scholars of Marketing Science: Bridging Asia and the World, 33*(1), 1–10. https://doi.org/10.1080/21639159.2022.2163908

Choi, H., & Kim, S. (2017). A content service deployment plan for metaverse museum exhibitions—Centering on the combination of beacons and HMDs. *International Journal of Information Management, 37*(1), 1519–1527. https://doi.org/10.1016/j.ijinfomgt.2016.04.017

Cook, D. L. (1962). The Hawthorne effect in educational research. *The Phi Delta Kappan, 44*(3), 116–122.

De Choudhury, M., Sharma, S. S., Logar, T., Eekhout, W., & Nielsen, R. C. (2017). Gender and cross-cultural differences in social media disclosures of mental illness. *Proceedings of the ACM Conference on Computer Supported Cooperative Work, CSCW*, 353–369. https://doi.org/10.1145/2998181.2998220

Dean, B. (2023, March 27). *Reddit user and growth stats (Updated March 2023)*. Backlinko. https://backlinko.com/reddit-users

Dwivedi, Y. K., Hughes, L., Baabdullah, A. M., Ribeiro-Navarrete, S., Giannakis, M., Al-Debei, M. M., Dennehy, D., Metri, B. A., Buhalis, D., Cheung, C. M. K., Conboy, K., Doyle, R., Dubey, R., Dutot, V., Felix, R., Goyal, D., Gustafsson, A., Hinsch, C., Jebabli, I., . . . Wamba, S. F. (2022). Metaverse beyond the hype: Multidisciplinary perspectives on emerging challenges, opportunities, and agenda for research, practice and policy. *International Journal of Information Management*, *66*, 102542. https://doi.org/10.1016/j.ijinfomgt.2022.102542

Dwivedi, Y. K., Hughes, L., Wang, Y., Alalwan, A. A., Ahn, S. J., Balakrishnan, J., Barta, S., Belk, R., Buhalis, D., Dutot, V., Felix, R., Filieri, R., Flavián, C., Gustafsson, A., Hinsch, C., Hollensen, S., Jain, V., Kim, J., Krishen, A. S., … Wirtz, J. (2023). Metaverse marketing: How the metaverse will shape the future of consumer research and practice. *Psychology and Marketing*, *40*(4), 750–776. https://doi.org/10.1002/mar.21767

Farhi, F., Jeljeli, R., Zamoum, K., Boudhane, Y., & Lagha, F. Ben. (2023). Metaverse Technology in Communication Practices: A Case Study of IT Products Retailers in the UAE. *Emerging Science Journal*, *7*(3), 928–942. https://doi.org/10.28991/ESJ-2023-07-03-019

Foufi, V., Timakum, T., Gaudet-Blavignac, C., Lovis, C., & Song, M. (2019). Mining of textual health information from Reddit: Analysis of chronic diseases with extracted entities and their relations. *Journal of Medical Internet Research*, *21*(6). https://doi.org/10.2196/12876

Gao, H., Chong, A. Y. L., & Bao, H. (2023). Metaverse: Literature Review, Synthesis and Future Research Agenda. *Journal of Computer Information Systems*. https://doi.org/10.1080/08874417.2023.2233455

Gauttier, S., Simouri, W., & Milliat, A. (2022). When to enter the metaverse: business leaders offer perspectives. *Journal of Business Strategy*, *45*(1), 2–9.

Golf-Papez, M., Heller, J., Hilken, T., Chylinski, M., de Ruyter, K., Keeling, D. I., & Mahr, D. (2022). Embracing falsity through the metaverse: The case of synthetic customer experiences. *Business Horizons*, *65*(6), 739–749.

Gupta, M. (2023, January 12). Metaverse Applications in the Real World. *Forbes*. https://www.forbes.com/sites/forbestechcouncil/2023/01/12/metaverse-applications-in-the-real-world/?sh=1d00008e48a2

Ha, T., Beijnon, B., Kim, S., Lee, S., & Kim, J. H. (2017). Examining user perceptions of smartwatch through dynamic topic modeling. *Telematics and Informatics*, *34*(7), 1262–1273. https://doi.org/10.1016/j.tele.2017.05.011

Hollensen, S., Kotler, P., & Opresnik, M. O. (2023). Metaverse—the new marketing universe. *Journal of Business Strategy*, *44*(3), 119–125. https://doi.org/10.1108/JBS-01-2022-0014

Hwang, S., & Koo, G. W. (2023). Art marketing in the metaverse world: Evidence from South Korea. *Cogent Social Sciences*, *9*(1). https://doi.org/10.1080/23311886.2023.2175429

Jones, T. (2019). A coefficient of determination for probabilistic topic models. arXiv:1911.11061.

Kaur, N., Singh, V., Mahajan, N., & Garg, N. (2023). Game Based Learning—Immersive teaching and Learning platform through Metaverse. *Proceedings of 2023 3rd International Conference on Innovative Practices in Technology and Management, ICIPTM 2023*. https://doi.org/10.1109/ICIPTM57143.2023.10118239

Kim, J. (2021). Advertising in the Metaverse: Research agenda. *Journal of Interactive Advertising*, *21*(3), 141–144. https://doi.org/10.1080/15252019.2021.2001273

Lee, L. H., Braud, T., Zhou, P., Wang, L., Xu, D., Lin, Z., ... & Hui, P. (2021). All one needs to know about metaverse: A complete survey on technological singularity, virtual ecosystem, and research agenda. arXiv preprint arXiv:2110.05352.

Lee, U. K., & Kim, H. (2022). UTAUT in Metaverse: An "Ifland" Case. *Journal of Theoretical and Applied Electronic Commerce Research, 17*(2), 613–635. https://doi.org/10.3390/jtaer17020032

Lin, Y. (2023, December 11). 10 Reddit Statistics You Should Know in 2024 [Infographic]. *Reddit*. Retrieved January 5, 2024, from https://www.oberlo.com/blog/reddit-statistics

Low, D. M., Rumker, L., Talkar, T., Torous, J., Cecchi, G., & Ghosh, S. S. (2020). Natural language processing reveals vulnerable mental health support groups and heightened health anxiety on Reddit during COVID-19: Observational study. *Journal of Medical Internet Research, 22*(10). https://doi.org/10.2196/22635

Markets and Markets (2023). *Metaverse Market Share, Forecast | Growth Analysis & Trends [2031].* (MarketsandMarkets. https://www.marketsandmarkets.com/Market-Reports/metaverse-market-166893905.html)

Medhat, W., Hassan, A., & Korashy, H. (2014). Sentiment analysis algorithms and applications: A survey. *Ain Shams Engineering Journal, 5*(4), 1093–1113.

Mohamed Jahir Hussain, M. S. F. B., & Bee Hwa, E. T. (2023). Customer e-satisfaction towards online grocery sites in the metaverse world. In *Strategies and Opportunities for Technology in the Metaverse World* (pp. 294–320). IGI Global. https://doi.org/10.4018/978-1-6684-5732-0.ch016

Mohammad, S. M., & Turney, P. D. (2010). Crowdsourcing a word–emotion association lexicon. *Computational Intelligence, 29*(3), 436–465.

Mystakidis, S. (2022). Metaverse. *Encyclopedia, 2*(1), 486–497.

Onan, A., Korukoglu, S., & Bulut, H. (2016). LDA-based topic modelling in text sentiment classification: An empirical analysis. *Int. J. Comput. Linguistics Appl., 7*(1), 101–119.

Park, S. M., & Kim, Y. G. (2022). A Metaverse: Taxonomy, Components, Applications, and Open Challenges. *IEEE Access, 10*, 4209–4251. https://doi.org/10.1109/ACCESS.2021.3140175

Rauschnabel, P. A., Babin, B. J., tom Dieck, M. C., Krey, N., & Jung, T. (2022). What is augmented reality marketing? Its definition, complexity, and future. *Journal of Business Research,* 142, 1140–1150. https://doi.org/10.1016/j.jbusres.2021.12.084

Ritterbusch, G. D., & Teichmann, M. R. (2023). Defining the Metaverse: A Systematic Literature Review. *IEEE Access, 11*, 12368–12377. https://doi.org/10.1109/ACCESS.2023.3241809

Singh, K. (2023). Evaluation planning for artificial intelligence-based industry 6.0 Metaverse integration. Intelligent Human Systems Integration (IHSI 2023): Integrating People and Intelligent Systems. 69(69).

Statista. (2023) *Metaverse—Worldwide | Statista market forecast*. https://www.statista.com/outlook/amo/metaverse/worldwide

Stephenson, N. (1992). Snow Crash, New York, NY, USA: Bantam Books.

Taboada, M. (2016). Sentiment analysis: An overview from linguistics. *Annual Review of Linguistics, 2*, 325–347.

Teng, Z., Cai, Y., Gao, Y., Zhang, X., & Li, X. (2022). Factors Affecting Learners' Adoption of an Educational Metaverse Platform: An Empirical Study Based on an Extended UTAUT Model. *Mobile Information Systems, 2022*. https://doi.org/10.1155/2022/5479215

Toraman, Y., & Geçit, B. B. (2023). User Acceptance of Metaverse: An Analysis for e-Commerce in the Framework of Technology Acceptance Model (TAM). *Sosyoekonomi, 31*(55). https://doi.org/10.17233/sosyoekonomi.2023.01.05

Van, H. T., Si, T. N., Quynh, A. V. T., Kieu, T. N. T., & Vo, T. T. T. (2022). A Conceptual Framework for Determining Metaverse Adoption in Vietnam IT Enterprises. *Proceedings—2022 IEEE/ACIS 7th International Conference on Big Data, Cloud Computing, and Data Science, BCD 2022*, 14–17. https://doi.org/10.1109/BCD54882.2022.9900871

Vayansky, I., & Kumar, S. A. (2020). A review of topic modeling methods. *Information Systems, 94*, 101582.

Yang, F., Ren, L., & Gu, C. (2022). A study of college students' intention to use metaverse technology for basketball learning based on UTAUT2. *Heliyon, 8*(9). https://doi.org/10.1016/j.heliyon.2022.e10562

The Adoption of Virtual Reality (VR) in Equity, Diversity, and Inclusion (EDI) Practices: An Empirical Study

Pietro Paolo Frigenti

Abstract Virtual reality (VR) technology has experienced significant advancements, leading to increased acceptance and use by the scientific community. The technological prowess of VR lies in its high level of intensity, interactivity, and ability to imitate reality for users, making it a viable tool for various applications. The growing commercial interest in VR resulted in increased accessibility and affordability of VR headsets. This article provides an empirical study on how organisations might effectively promote equity, inclusion, and diversity (EDI) using VR education. This study adopts a qualitative methodology through participant observation and semi-structured interviews, exploring their perceptions towards the use of VR for EDI practices. The findings reveal that the use of VR can evoke an emotional response in users, ultimately improving their recognition of EDI misconduct and fostering active involvement in EDI-conscious behaviours. Furthermore, enhanced awareness towards diversity in the workplace appears likely to improve confidence and self-perceived employability.

Keywords Virtual reality · Simulation · EDI · Higher education · Organizational studies · Employability

1 Introduction

Virtual reality (VR) technology has had significant advancements in recent years, leading to increased acceptance and use by the scientific community. VR is a revolutionary change in the way humans engage with digital surroundings. It provides immersive experiences that bridge the gap between the actual and virtual realms. This technology, referred to as a three-dimensional (3D), computer-generated platform that replicates real or imagined settings, has progressed from an innovative idea to an essential tool in multiple industries (Boyd & Koles 2019; Manis & Choi 2019). The technological prowess of VR resides in its high level of intensity, interactivity,

P. P. Frigenti (✉)
Alliance Manchester Business School, University of Manchester, Manchester, UK
e-mail: pietropaolo.frigenti@manchester.ac.uk

T. Jung et al. (eds.), *XR and Metaverse*, Springer Proceedings in Business and Economics, https://doi.org/10.1007/978-3-031-77975-6_25

and ability to imitate reality for users, making it a viable tool for various applications. The potential of VR led to scholars investigating different areas of application of the new technology, to uncover opportunities and best practices. For example, the challenges posed by COVID-19, which limited national and international mobility, drove interest in the fields of tourism marketing and destination branding (Frigenti, 2025), with VR technologies seen as a means to virtually visit the intended destination. In the past ten years there has been a significant increase in research and public interest in VR, due to its expanding use in several fields such as education, marketing, medical, and engineering (Burke 2018; Freina & Ott 2015; Griffin et al. 2017; Pillai & Mathew 2019; Wang et al. 2018). The interest in VR streamed in different directions, focusing, for example, on social presence in cultural settings (tom Dieck et al. 2024), mental well-being considerations (Taylor et al. 2024), and broader reflection on implications for service industries (Jung et al. 2023). Abbas et al. (2023), observe that VR is used in various fields such as recreation, health, work, and education, with this study providing further insights into its relevance for the last two fields. Seen the abundance of opportunities, a significant portion of scientific investigation has focused on recreating realistic and interactive virtual environments, developing increasingly intricate VR systems. However, the utilisation of these systems has not been relatively limited due to the need to adopt specialised VR equipment, which was previously challenging for consumers and organisations to acquire. Nevertheless, the growing commercial interest in the capabilities of VR has now made it possible for this technology to be widely adopted, with headsets increasingly affordable by consumers and easily accessible for most organisations' budgets. The release of one of the most popular headsets called Oculus Quest 2 (Richard 2022), later rebranded as Meta Quest 2, lowered the cost barrier and resulted in a significant volume of sales, marking the beginning of an era of relatively affordable VR devices. Seeing the increased accessibility and affordability of VR headsets, a better understanding of how organisations can leverage these tools to support their agenda appears desirable and relevant. This article provides an empirical study on how organisations might effectively promote equity, inclusion, and diversity (EDI) through VR education. Previous literature suggests that standard EDI training and activities may have limited success in improving organisations' inclusion (Kalev et al. 2006), particularly due to challenges in actually getting involved with EDI initiatives. However, the findings of the current study reveal that the use of virtual embodiment (Gaudiosi 2015) can tackle such challenges, and lead to emotional responses in VR adopters, resulting in users' effectively experiencing situations leading to better recognition and support of the principles of EDI.

2 Benefits and Limitations of VR Adoption

The discourse surrounding the adoption of VR technology is multifaceted, acknowledging both its transformative potential and the obstacles hindering its acceptance. Scholars such as Abbas et al. (2023) and Burke (2018) highlight VR's ability to revolutionise various industries by creating immersive learning environments, enhancing training and offering unique entertainment experiences. However, the literature also addresses challenges such as the digital divide, as noted by Dilanchian (2019), which includes disparities in technology access, digital literacy, socioeconomic status, and cultural factors, potentially exacerbating existing inequalities. Furthermore, studies heightened concerns about the importance of user experience and interface design (e.g., Dibbern et al. 2018; Pirker & Dengel 2021; Zender et al. 2019) for VR adoption, particularly in fields like education and healthcare. Additionally, issues regarding the physical and psychological effects of VR, such as motion sickness and distress (e.g., Chang et al. 2020; Lavoie et al. 2021), pose significant challenges to broader acceptance. In response, there is a growing call for research and innovation to enhance the accessibility and inclusivity of VR technology. Scholars like Dilanchian (2019) and Mott et al. (2019) advocate for developing user-oriented VR experiences that consider factors like cost-effectiveness, user-friendliness, cultural appropriateness, and educational value, aiming to bridge the digital divide and promote social inclusivity. In management studies, research focuses on understanding the factors influencing VR adoption, exploring consumer experiences, and assessing the long-term effects of VR use (e.g., Anderson & Laverie 2022; Tan et al. 2022; Kang et al. 2021; Kim et al. 2022; Kwok et al. 2021). The need to tailor VR experiences to users' preferences appears essential (Dijk 2020), to foster social integration, narrow the gap in technology access, and maximise VR's potential as a widely accessible and transformative technology (Dilanchian, 2019).

2.1 Virtual Reality in Education

Individuals can utilise VR to engage with a simulated visual-based environment through an interactive device, making VR environments ideal to train and educate about specific scenarios without needing to experience them directly. This becomes particularly relevant in scenarios exhibiting non-ideal practices in the workplace (e.g., microaggressions, discrimination, gender bias, etc.) as it allows users to experience the situation without directly hurting anyone. Indeed, for this to happen, it is important to comprehend the factors contributing to the adoption of VR technology (Sagnier et al. 2020; Shahab et al. 2021; Taufik et al. 2021). VR can provide consumers with the opportunity to access events that would be otherwise difficult or impossible to access in the physical world (Bogicevic et al. 2021; Jung et al. 2021; Oriti et al. 2021; Ozdemir 2021). Such opportunities can then lead to improved consumer well-being by facilitating remote social connection, reducing stress, and enhancing social skills, as supported by studies conducted in recent years (e.g., Abdullah et al. 2021; Vaquero-Blasco et al. 2021; Wang et al. 2021). However, despite the advantages of VR for consumers and society, its adoption by consumers and organisations has been limited due to previously discussed obstacles related to accessibility and issues more directly related to the experiential use of the technology. Obstacles include inadequate technological performance that falls short of consumer expectations, high cost, low perceived enjoyment, and limited perceived benefits (Huang 2023; Laurell et al. 2019; Lee et al. 2019). Indeed, for a technology to be accepted and embraced, providing a seamless experience appears essential. Previous studies emphasise that the creation of realistic and relevant content is vital in reducing barriers and fostering acceptance of technology (Cidral et al. 2018; Cobo et al. 2014; Elia et al. 2016; Flavián et al. 2019). Content can be divided into three distinct categories: experience, feature, and function (An & Lee 2023). The concept of "experience" can be examined via the lens of user experience and experiential learning theories (Bulu 2012; Shin et al. 2013). On the other hand, the aspects of "feature" and "function" can be examined by directing attention to the information system success model, educational qualities, and learner attributes (An & Lee 2023). The dimension of experience in the metaverse can be further categorised into three domains: immersion, satisfaction, and achievement (Yang & Heh, 2007). Immersion in the metaverse provides a more engaging and dynamic experience compared to conventional techniques, allowing learners to vividly explore subjects (An & Lee 2023). Satisfaction in virtual environments is directly linked to the user's happiness, which, if maintained, may lead to a more regular and continuous utilisation of these technologies (Mikropoulos 2006). Finally, achievement can result in improvement of both performance and problem-solving abilities (An & Lee 2023).

2.2 *Virtual Reality in EDI*

The utilisation of VR to enhance EDI education is a subject that appears relevant and significant. Literature suggests that VR can revolutionise simulation-based education by enhancing EDI practices (Shirani 2021). Studies have demonstrated that VR technology has potential in education, with the potential to improve learners' motivation and performance, problem-solving abilities, educational fairness, and multimodal learning in educational settings (Kabanda et al. 2022; Kim & Im 2022). Others (e.g., Philippakos et al. 2022) noted that VR can create simulated and regulated scenarios to enhance student performance and motivation, tackling issues of fairness in education. Furthermore, through VR users can fully engage with various cultural environments, resulting in an immersive experience that can augment comprehension and empathy towards different cultures (Mills et al. 2020). Such elements appear extremely important for EDI initiatives, with the application of VR looking particularly relevant to efforts in affecting users' behaviour towards desired outcomes. In EDI education, VR can have a pivotal impact in establishing all-encompassing learning experiences; by producing resources that improve or substitute conventional classroom teaching with a high level of authenticity, VR can promote the participation of underrepresented minorities in diverse fields (Gallardo-Williams & Dunnagan 2021). Moreover, VR can serve as a platform to bring to life theoretical concepts, enhancing students' motivation in their educational pursuits, and potentially fostering a more comprehensive and inclusive learning environment (Sukmawati et al. 2022). The potential of VR to promote EDI in education appears clear, and is further reinforced by the fact that academic libraries have offered support and education on VR through different programmes and curriculum integrations across various disciplines. Such an endeavour suggests that VR has the capacity to reach a broad spectrum of students and foster inclusivity (Hurrell & Baker 2020). Moreover, VR has been employed in educational settings using digital media to promote inclusive education, especially in response to the COVID-19 pandemic. This has underscored its capacity to tackle issues of fairness and aid students in virtual environments (Soman et al. 2023). Ultimately, existing literature suggests that VR holds the potential to augment EDI education, showcasing the capacity of VR technology to revolutionise educational encounters, foster inclusiveness, and tackle issues related to fairness. Through the establishment of immersive and inclusive learning environments, VR appears capable of enabling improved comprehension of different cultures and the support of students in virtual settings, thereby establishing fertile ground for the progress of EDI education.

2.3 *Insight from the VR EDI Landscape*

Within the vast marketplace of apps and providers currently offering training and skill development solutions, some appear to have reserved a key focus for EDI education. Examples include 'Equal Reality', 'Talespin', 'a Mile in My Shoes', and 'BodySwaps', the platform used for the current study. *Equal Reality* is a VR platform focused on diversity and inclusion training in the workplace, offering immersive experiences to raise awareness about bias and discrimination (Equal Reality, n.d.). Currently, Equal Reality's platform is utilised by various organisations globally, including Amazon and PWC, for their diversity and inclusion training programs, suggesting the high potential of the platform. *Talespin* provides VR training simulations for soft skills development, including diversity training and leadership (Talespin, n.d.), enhancing EDI training. Organisations like Accenture (Accenture 2022), Meta, Lenovo and Deloitte (Talespin, n.d.), have partnered up with Talespin for training purposes, highlighting the relevance of the platform in supporting workplace initiatives. Further to adopting existing VR solutions, some organisations started developing their own skill and training development platforms. Such is the case for *A Mile in My Shoes,* a VR experience developed by Michigan State University, a platform that immerses users in the daily lives of individuals from diverse backgrounds, fostering empathy and understanding (Bonsall, 2021). Arguably, such VR experience takes a very interesting angle to support EDI training, providing first-hand experiences of diverse perspectives, and enhancing empathy and cultural understanding. The last of the providers discussed is *BodySwaps*, a VR platform for soft skills training, including diversity and inclusion, offering immersive simulations (BodySwaps, n.d.). BodySwaps' VR simulations provide realistic scenarios for practising inclusive behaviours and understanding diverse perspectives, complementing EDI training. The platform potential has been recognised in the marketplace, with educational institutions such as the University of Liverpool, King's College London and Columbia University utilising BodySwaps for soft skills training, including EDI initiatives. Due to its strong relevance to academic institutions, BodySwaps was the platform used for the current study involving university students.

2.4 Research Aim and Objectives

The primary aim of this research is to explore the implications of VR for EDI education and training. To achieve the research aim, the set research objectives were: (a) To explore users' perception towards the adoption of VR in EDI; (b) To evaluate the impact of VR on individuals' attitudes and behaviours towards EDI; (c) To identify challenges and opportunities associated with the integration of VR in EDI practices.

3 Methodology

The study adopted an exploratory qualitative methodology, which allowed an in-depth exploration of participants' experiences and perceptions towards the incorporation of VR in EDI practices. A total of 10 mixed-gender students took part in the study, which consisted of two stages. Firstly, the students were asked to engage in VR simulations around EDI practices using a VR headset and the BodySwaps application. The virtual sessions focused on microaggressions and non-inclusive behaviour in the workplace, and gender inclusion, requiring the participants to engage with scenarios and interact with virtual avatars. The types of activity undertaken ranged from spotting and identifying inappropriate actions and words using the VR controller to providing actual verbal feedback to the avatars. The platform AI would then analyse the words of the participants and provide constructive feedback on the strengths and weaknesses of their speech. The participants' behaviour during the activity was observed and monitored by the researcher. Secondly, the students were interviewed to gather in-depth information about their perception towards the simulations. The questions investigated their key takeaways, their immediate experience with the virtual environment, and more practical elements, such as the suitability of the VR headset from a well-being point of view. The adoption of two data-gathering techniques–semi-structured interviews and participant observation–strengthened the reliability and thoroughness of the qualitative data. By conducting semi-structured interviews, the participants' perception was investigated facilitating a comprehensive exploration of their experiences with VR-based EDI sessions. This approach adheres to the qualitative interview standards outlined by Kvale and Brinkmann (2009), which prioritises adaptability in questioning to encompass a wide range of viewpoints. Conducting participant observation involved observing individuals as they interacted with VR-based EDI simulations in their authentic environments, yielding significant contextual information. This approach, influenced by the principles of ethnographic research (Spradley 1980), was useful considering the immersive character of VR experiences, enabling the researcher to record immediate responses and activities. The gathered data was then subjected to thematic analysis, utilising the six-phase procedure delineated by Braun and Clarke (2006). The analysis employed an inductive approach to explore patterns and topics pertaining to the efficacy of VR in EDI practices. The methodology allowed a thorough and sophisticated analysis of the data, in line with established standards in qualitative research (Fereday & Muir-Cochrane 2006). Recognising inherent constraints, such as the subjective character of qualitative research and the potential for social desirability bias in participants was a key step of the process to ensure truthful and introspective analysis of the results (Silverman 2016). Similarly, researcher reflexivity was prioritised in this study to ensure transparency and acknowledge the potential impact of the researchers' backgrounds, experiences, and prejudices on the research process (Finlay 2002). The chosen approach allowed the researcher to collect in-depth data and contribute a robust study to the existing literature, where limited academic evidence is available around VR and EDI for training and education.

4 Results and Discussion

The exploration into the use of VR headsets in EDI sessions brought forth different themes, which have been organised in three main groups: (a) Outcome-oriented Themes, focusing on the immediate achievement of EDI-related themes; (b) Experience-oriented themes, focusing on the experience of the participants and effects on their behaviour, following the experience; (c) Practice-oriented themes, focusing on the physical practicalities of using VR in EDI practices. A visual representation of the themes is provided (Fig. 1), with an explanation of each theme included afterwards.

4.1 Outcome-Oriented Themes

The identification of micro-aggressive Behaviour: The interviews revealed that engaging in VR sessions allowed participants to identify micro-aggressive behaviours in a controlled yet authentic environment. The immersive nature of the experience facilitated the recognition of subtle discriminatory actions and remarks that may often be overlooked. By confronting and addressing microaggressions, participants gained insights into the complexities of fostering an inclusive workplace.

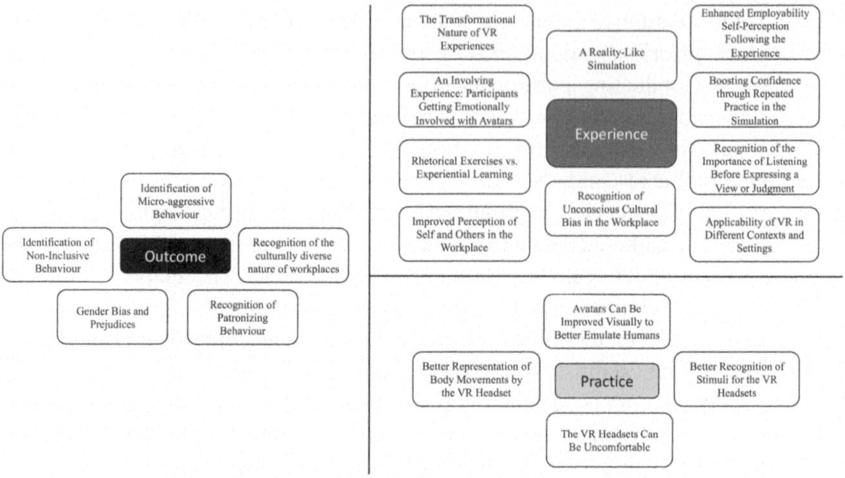

Fig. 1 Thematic mapping of the discussion

Identification of Non-Inclusive Behaviour: VR provided a platform for participants to immerse themselves in scenarios that highlighted non-inclusive behaviours. The opinions of participants suggest that the interactive nature of the sessions allowed individuals to actively identify and experience actions or situations that contribute to an exclusionary environment. This theme underscores the significance of experiential learning in recognising and addressing what is not inclusive.

Recognition of the Culturally Diverse Nature of Workplaces: VR facilitated the integration of individuals with diverse cultures and backgrounds into workplace scenarios. Participants noted that the experience of a diverse working environment allowed them to ponder on themes not usually considered, allowing reflection and increased awareness. The technology provided a space for participants to navigate and understand the impact of cultural diversity on workplace dynamics.

Gender Bias and Prejudices: The VR sessions specifically addressed gender bias, prejudices, and gender-focused patronising behaviours in the workplace. Participants were immersed in scenarios that allowed them to recognise and confront biases related to gender. Interestingly, an emotional response was noted in both male and female participants, who strongly reacted to the intentionally unprofessional approach showcased in the simulation. This theme highlights the potential of VR as a tool for addressing gender-based challenges and promoting awareness and sensitivity.

Recognition of Patronising Behaviour: The VR experience exposed participants to scenarios involving patronising behaviour, allowing them to directly engage with them and understand the impact of such acts. Participants reported an increased awareness as a result of the simulation, in particular towards those little things that often went unnoticed in their daily life.

4.2 Experience-Related Themes

A Reality-Like Simulation: The simulations mirrored real-world workplace scenarios, enhancing participants' ability to engage authentically with the content. Participants appreciated the way in which the sessions were delivered, recognising the sessions' capacity to actively involve them.

The Transformational Nature of VR Experiences: According to the participants, the VR sessions provided an eye-opening experience, challenging their perspectives on workplace dynamics. The participants noted that they felt different after the sessions, more open-minded and, in their opinion, more responsive to future EDI bad practices.

An Involving Experience: Participants Getting Emotionally Involved with Avatars: The emotional involvement of participants with avatars in the VR environment created a more engaging and impactful learning experience. Participants experienced feelings of disappointment towards inappropriate behaviours and even anger towards discussions they found unacceptable. This theme may arguably be the most important, as it highlights the potential of VR to evoke empathy and emotional responses, contributing to a deeper understanding of the impact of certain behaviours on individuals and fostering a sense of connection with virtual counterparts.

Rhetorical Exercises vs. Experiential Learning: A comparison between tick-boxing exercises and VR-based experiential learning was made by the participants, who emphasised the inadequacy of traditional methods in addressing EDI challenges. The interviewees reported that VR offers a more profound learning experience by allowing participants to actively engage with and experience situations, moving beyond superficial compliance.

Improved Perception of Self and Others in the Workplace: According to participants, VR contributed to an improved perception of self and others in the workplace. The immersive nature of the experience allowed participants to reflect on their own behaviours and biases, fostering a deeper understanding of their role in creating an inclusive environment. Arguably, this takeaway is crucial for promoting self-awareness and promoting positive interactions in the workplace.

Recognition of Unconscious Cultural Bias in the Workplace: Participants recognised that unconscious biases may exist in the workplace, particularly the tendency to assume one's cultural views apply universally. The VR sessions brought attention to the diverse perspectives that individuals bring to the workplace, fostering awareness about the need to recognise and challenge assumptions based on cultural backgrounds.

Enhanced Employability Self-Perception Following the Experience: The VR experience positively influenced participants' perceptions of employability. Participants reported increased perceived self-employability in diverse and inclusive workplaces as a result of taking part in the simulations, which were seen as useful in enhancing interpersonal skills and cultural competence. This takeaway provides insight into the potential career development benefits of VR-based EDI training.

Boosting Confidence through Repeated Practice in the Simulation: VR tasks required participants to repeat activities with continuous improvement, which contributed to a boost in their confidence. The participants liked the possibility of answering questions, recording their answers, listening to themselves, reflecting on their answers, and then re-recording with better awareness. This theme highlights the role of VR in providing a safe space for individuals to practise and refine their interpersonal skills, ultimately contributing to increased confidence towards workplace challenges.

Recognition of the Importance of Listening Before Expressing a View or Judgement: The VR sessions emphasised the importance of active listening. Participants recognised that the sessions helped them realise that effective communication involves listening before expressing a view or judgment. This recognition underscores the significance of fostering effective communication skills, particularly in addressing EDI challenges in the workplace.

Applicability of VR in Different Contexts and Settings: The takeaway regarding the applicability of VR in different contexts and settings suggests the versatility of VR technology. Participants acknowledged the potential for VR to address EDI challenges across various industries and scenarios, highlighting its adaptability as a tool for promoting inclusivity in diverse settings.

4.3 Practice-Oriented Themes on the Suitability of VR

Avatars Can Be Improved Visually to Better Emulate Humans: Participants recognised that avatars could have been more realistic in visually emulating the humans they were representing. The practical consideration of improving avatars visually aligns with the need for realism in the VR environment. Enhancing the visual representation of avatars can contribute to a more authentic and relatable experience, improving the overall effectiveness of VR-based EDI interventions.

Better Recognition of Stimuli for the VR Headsets: Participants also noted that often their actions were not correctly recognised and recorded by the VR interface. The practical consideration of better recognition of stimuli is crucial for refining the content presented in VR scenarios. Improving the recognition of stimuli ensures that participants can fully engage with and respond to the content, maximising the impact of the VR experience.

Better Representation of Body Movements by the VR Headset: Similarly, participants noted that the avatars' replication of their movements was somewhat artificial and not fully realistic. Arguably, the representation of accurate body movements in the VR environment is vital for creating realistic and immersive scenarios. Improving the representation of body movements enhances the authenticity of interactions, contributing to a more effective simulation of workplace dynamics.

VR Headsets Can Be Uncomfortable: Participants noted that extensive use of VR headsets could cause light strains on the eyes or neck. Recognising the discomfort associated with the VR headset is an important practical consideration. Addressing user comfort is crucial for ensuring a positive and inclusive learning experience. It can be argued that, as VR technology evolves, efforts should be made to minimise discomfort and enhance the overall user experience.

5 Conclusion

This study aim was to explore the implications of VR for EDI education and training, and three main objectives were defined to achieve the overarching aim. The three objectives are now presented.

5.1 Objective 1: To Explore Users' Perception Towards the Adoption of VR in EDI

The literature acknowledges VR's significant advancements and its potential to revolutionise various fields through immersive and interactive experiences (Boyd & Koles 2019; Manis & Choi 2019). This study's findings, particularly the experience-oriented themes, align with these observations by highlighting users' positive perceptions of VR's realism and immersive nature in EDI initiatives. Participants appreciated the authentic engagement provided by VR simulations, mirroring real-world scenarios. This is consistent with the literature's emphasis on VR's capacity to provide immersive experiences that bridge the gap between actual and virtual realms (Burke 2018; Freina & Ott 2015; Griffin et al. 2017; Pillai & Mathew 2019; Wang et al. 2018).

However, this study also highlighted practical challenges, such as the need for improved visual realism of avatars and better recognition of stimuli by VR headsets, which slightly contrasts with the literature's general enthusiasm. These practical issues are akin to the user experience and interface design challenges discussed by scholars like Dibbern et al. (2018) and Zender et al. (2019). Furthermore, the slight discomfort reported by participants aligns with concerns about the physical and psychological effects of VR resonating with Chang et al. (2020) and Lavoie et al. (2021).

5.2 *Objective 2: To Evaluate the Impact of VR on Individuals' Attitudes and Behaviours Towards EDI*

The outcome-oriented themes from the study demonstrate VR's impact on participants' attitudes and behaviours, showing that VR can foster greater awareness and sensitivity to EDI issues. This supports the findings of Shirani (2021) and Mills et al. (2020), who argue that VR can enhance understanding and empathy towards different cultures and social dynamics. The recognition of microaggressions, non-inclusive behaviours, and cultural diversity through VR reflects its potential to provide transformative learning experiences, which align with the literature suggesting VR's capacity to improve motivation, performance, and problem-solving abilities in educational settings (Kabanda et al. 2022; Kim & Im 2022).

The emotional responses elicited during VR sessions in the study, which led to increased awareness and empathy, further support Gaudiosi's (2015) concept of virtual embodiment. This contrasts with traditional EDI training's limited success as noted by Kalev et al. (2006). The findings suggest that VR can overcome engagement barriers, a key challenge identified in prior research, opening new paths for EDI training.

5.3 *Objective 3: To Identify Challenges and Opportunities Associated with the Integration of VR in EDI Practices*

The study's practice-oriented themes highlight both challenges and opportunities, echoing the literature's multifaceted view of VR adoption. Linking back to the first research objective, the need for more realistic avatars and better stimuli recognition underscores the importance of user experience and interface design, as discussed by Dibbern et al. (2018) and Pirker & Dengel (2021). The discomfort associated with VR headsets aligns with the physical and psychological issues highlighted by Chang et al. (2020) and Lavoie et al. (2021).

Conversely, the opportunities identified in the study, such as VR's applicability across various contexts and its potential to enhance employability and confidence, align with the literature's optimistic perspective. Scholars like Dilanchian (2019) and Mott et al. (2019) advocate for user-oriented VR experiences that are cost-effective and culturally appropriate, aiming to bridge the digital divide and promote inclusivity. The findings support the notion that VR can be a versatile and adaptive tool for promoting EDI in diverse settings, as suggested by Gallardo-Williams and Dunnagan (2021) and Sukmawati et al. (2022).

5.4 Key Takeaways and Future Directions

This study offers significant insights into the adoption and impact of VR in enhancing EDI training. The findings reveal that VR's immersive and interactive nature can substantially improve participants' ability to recognise and address microaggressions, non-inclusive behaviours, and cultural diversity in the workplace, leading to heightened awareness and empathy. These findings align with existing literature on VR's potential to transform educational experiences by fostering deep engagement and emotional responses. Furthermore, the study demonstrates VR's role as a catalyst for real-time introspection and corrective actions by authentically mirroring workplace dynamics, incorporating diverse cultural experiences, and addressing gender biases. Shifting focus from rhetoric to experiential learning fosters emotional engagement, maximising the impact of VR in promoting a deep understanding of EDI challenges. However, the study also highlights practical challenges, such as the need for more realistic avatars, better stimuli recognition, and addressing physical discomfort associated with VR headsets. The author argues that collaborative efforts to refine these features are essential for ensuring an authentic and comfortable learning experience. Overall, VR's outcomes offer a pathway to identify and address workplace challenges, emphasising transformative and engaging learning experiences while highlighting the need for continual refinement for optimal effectiveness. Together, these dimensions form a comprehensive guide for practitioners in leveraging VR to create inclusive and transformative EDI training environments, representing key areas of improvement for practitioners and potential areas of investigation for future research.

References

Abbas, J. R., O'Connor, A., Ganapathy, E., Isba, R., Payton, T., MgGrath, B., Tolley, N., & Bruce, I. (2023). What is virtual reality? A healthcare focused systematic review of definitions. *Health Policy and Technology*, 12(2), 100741.

Abdullah, A., Kolkmeier, J., Lo, V., & Neff, M. (2021). Videoconference and embodied VR: Communication patterns across task and medium. *Proceedings of the ACM on Human-Computer Interaction, 5*, 1–29.

Accenture. (2022, February 17). Accenture Invests in XR-based Immersive Learning Startup Talespin. Retrieved May 11, 2024 from https://newsroom.accenture.com/news/2022/accenture-invests-in-immersive-learning-startup-talespin

An, K., & Lee, Y. C. (2023, June). Metaverse Educational technology Development: Key Factors and AHP Insights from Educators, Developers, and Learners. In *International XR Conference* (pp. 99–110). Cham: Springer Nature Switzerland.

Anderson, K. C., & Laverie, D. A. (2022). In the consumers' eye: A mixed method approach to understanding how VR-content influences unbranded product quality perceptions. *Journal of Retailing and Consumer Services, 67*, 102977.

BodySwaps. (n.d.). Retrieved May 10, 2024, from https://bodyswaps.co/

Bogicevic, V., Liu, S. Q., Seo, S., Kandampully, J., & Rudd, N. A. (2021). Virtual reality is so cool! How technology innovativeness shapes consumer responses to service preview modes. *International Journal of Hospitality Management, 93*, 102806.

Bonsall, B. (2021, March 31). MSU to launch virtual reality application supporting diversity, equity and inclusion. Michigan State University College of Agriculture and Natural Resources. Retrieved May 11, 2024, from https://www.canr.msu.edu/news/msu-to-launch-virtual-reality-application-supporting-diversity-equity-and-inclusion?utm_source=www.canr.msu.edu&utm_medium=referral&utm_campaign=canr-callouts

Boyd, D. E., & Koles, B. (2019). An introduction to the special issue "virtual reality in marketing": Definition, theory and practice. *Journal of Business Research, 100*, 441–444.

Braun, V., & Clarke, V. (2006). Using thematic analysis in psychology. *Qualitative Research in Psychology, 3*(2), 77–101.

Bulu, S.T. (2012). Place presence, social presence, co-presence, and satisfaction in virtual worlds. *Comput. Educ. 58*(1), 154–161

Burke, R. R. (2018). Virtual reality for marketing research. In L. Mountinho & M. Sokele (Eds.), *Innovative research methodologies in management* (pp. 63–82). Palgrave Macmillan

Chang, E., Kim, H. T., & Yoo, B. (2020). Virtual reality sickness: A review of causes and measurements. *International Journal of Human–Computer Interaction, 36*(17), 1658–1682.

Cidral,W.A., Oliveira, T., Di Felice, M., & Aparicio, M. (2018). E-learning success determinants: Brazilian empirical study. *Comput. Educ. 122*, 273–290

Cobo, A., Rocha, R., & Rodríguez-Hoyos, C. (2014). Evaluation of the interactivity of students in virtual learning environments using a multicriteria approach and datamining. *Behav. Inform. Technol. 33*(10), 1000–1012

Dibbern, C., Uhr, M., Krupke, D., & Steinicke, F. (2018). *Can WebVR further the adoption of virtual reality?* University of Hamburg.

Dijk, J. V. (2020). *The digital divide.* John Wiley & Sons.

Dilanchian, A. T. (2019). Virtual reality and the digital divide. http://purl.flvc.org/fsu/fd/FSU_libsubv1_scholarship_submission_1556133089_b1c0e18c

Elia, V., Gnoni, M.G., & Lanzilotto, A. (2016). Evaluating the application of augmented reality devices in manufacturing from a process point of view: an AHP-based model. Exp. Syst. Appl. 63, 187–197

Equal Reality. (n.d.). Retrieved May 10, 2024, from https://equalreality.com/

Fereday, J., & Muir-Cochrane, E. (2006). Demonstrating rigor using thematic analysis: A hybrid approach of inductive and deductive coding and theme development. *International Journal of Qualitative Methods, 5*(1), 80–92.

Finlay, L. (2002). Negotiating the swamp: The opportunity and challenge of reflexivity in research practice. *Qualitative Research, 2*(2), 209–230.

Flavián, C., Ibáñez-Sánchez, S., & Orús, C. (2019). The impact of virtual, augmented and mixed reality technologies on the customer experience. *Journal of Business Research, 100*, 547–560.

Freina, L., and Ott, M. (2015). A literature review on immersive virtual reality in education: State of the art and perspectives. In The international scientific conference elearning and software for education (Vol. 1, No.133, pp. 10–1007).

Frigenti, P. P. (2025). Maximizing tourism benefits from social media. In B. Sousa, P. B. Pires, & J. D. Santos (eds.), Leveraging digital marketing for tourism: exploring strategies and applications in contemporary tourism markets. Springer.

Gallardo-Williams, M. and Dunnagan, C. (2021). Designing diverse virtual reality laboratories as a vehicle for inclusion of underrepresented minorities in organic chemistry. *Journal of Chemical Education, 99*(1), 500-503. https://doi.org/10.1021/acs.jchemed.1c00321

Gaudiosi, J. (2015). *Here's why hospitals are using virtual reality to train staff.* Fortune. Retrieved January 13, 2024, from http://fortune.com/2015/08/17/virtual-reality-hospitals/

Griffin, T., Giberson, J., Lee, S. H. M., Guttentag, D., Kandaurova, M., Sergueeva, K., & Dimanche, F. (2017). Virtual reality and implications for destination marketing. Travel and Tourism

Research Association: Advancing Tourism Research Globally. https://core.ac.uk/download/pdf/84289283.pdf

Huang, Y. C. (2023). Integrated concepts of the UTAUT and TPB in virtual reality behavioral intention. *Journal of Retailing and Consumer Services, 70*, 103127.

Hurrell, C. and Baker, J. (2020). Immersive learning: applications of virtual reality for undergraduate education. *College & Undergraduate Libraries, 27*(2-4), 197-209. https://doi.org/10.1080/10691316.2020.1796879

Jung, J., Yu, J., Seo, Y., & Ko, E. (2021). Consumer experiences of virtual reality: Insights from VR luxury brand fashion shows. *Journal of Business Research, 130*, 517–524.

Jung, T., Cho, J., Han, D.I.D., Ahn, S.J.G., Gupta, M., Gopal, D., Heo, C.Y., Loureiro, S.M.C., Sigala, M., Trunfio, M., Taylor, A., tom Dieck, M.C. (2023). Metaverse for service industries: Future applications, opportunities, challenges and research directions. Computers in Human Behavior, pp. 108039–108039.

Kabanda, G., Chipfumbu, C., & Chingoriwo, T. (2022). A cybersecurity model for a roblox-based metaverse architecture framework. *British Journal of Multidisciplinary and Advanced Studies, 3*(2), 105–141. https://doi.org/10.37745/bjmas.2022.0048

Kalev, A., Dobbin, F., & Kelly, E. (2006). Best practices or best guesses? Assessing the efficacy of corporate affirmative action and diversity policies. *American Sociological Review, 71*, 589–617.

Kang, S., Dove, S., Ebright, H., Morales, S., & Kim, H. (2021). Does virtual reality affect behavioral intention? Testing engagement processes in a K-Pop video on YouTube. *Computers in Human Behavior, 123*, 106875.

Kim, D. and Im, T. (2022). A systematic review of virtual reality-based education research using latent dirichlet allocation: focus on topic modeling technique. *Mobile Information Systems*, 2022, 1-17. https://doi.org/10.1155/2022/1201852

Kim, G., Jin, B., & Shin, D. C. (2022). Virtual reality as a promotion tool for small independent stores. *Journal of Retailing and Consumer Services, 64*, 102822.

Kvale, S., & Brinkmann, S. (2009). InterViews: Learning the craft of qualitative research interviewing (2nd ed.). Sage Publications.

Kwok, P. K., Yan, M., Qu, T., & Lau, H. Y. (2021). User acceptance of virtual reality technology for practicing digital twin-based crisis management. *International Journal of Computer Integrated Manufacturing, 34*(7-8), 874–887.

Laurell, C., Sandström, C., Berthold, A., & Larsson, D. (2019). Exploring barriers to adoption of virtual reality through social media analytics and machine learning–An assessment of technology, network, price and trialability. *Journal of Business Research, 100*, 469–474.

Lavoie, R., Main, K., King, C., & King, D. (2021). Virtual experience, real consequences: The potential negative emotional consequences of virtual reality gameplay. *Virtual Reality, 25*, 69–81.

Lee, J., Kim, J., & Choi, J. Y. (2019). The adoption of virtual reality devices: The technology acceptance model integrating enjoyment, social interaction, and strength of the social ties. *Telematics and Informatics, 39*, 37–48.

Manis, K. T., & Choi, D. (2019). The virtual reality hardware acceptance model (VR-HAM): Extending and individuating the technology acceptance model (TAM) for virtual reality hardware. *Journal of Business Research, 100*, 503–513.

Mikropoulos, T.A. (2006). Presence: a unique characteristic in educational virtual environments. *Virtual Reality 10*(3–4), 197–206

Mills, N., Courtney, M., Dede, C., Dressen, A., & Gant, R. (2020). Culture and vision in virtual reality narratives. *Foreign Language Annals, 53*(4), 733-760. https://doi.org/10.1111/flan.12494

Mott, M., Cutrell, E., Franco, M. G., Holz, C., Ofek, E., Stoakley, R., & Morris, M. R. (2019). Accessible by design: An opportunity for virtual reality. In 2019 IEEE international symposium on mixed and augmented reality adjunct (ISMAR-adjunct) (pp. 451–454).

Oriti, D., Manuri, F., Pace, F. D., & Sanna, A. (2021). Harmonize: A shared environment for extended immersive entertainment. *Virtual Reality, 27* (4), 1–14.

Ozdemir, M. A. (2021). Virtual reality (VR) and augmented reality (AR) technologies for accessibility and marketing in the tourism industry. In C. Eusébio, L. Teixeira, & M. J. Carneiro (Eds.), *ICT tools and applications for accessible tourism* (pp. 277–301). IGI Global.

Philippakos, Z., Rocconi, L., Blake, K., & Summers, J. (2022). Teachers' practices during covid-19: practices and perspectives in elementary and secondary settings. *Social Sciences & Humanities Open, 6*(1), 100324. https://doi.org/10.1016/j.ssaho.2022.100324

Pillai, A. S., & Mathew, P. S. (2019). Impact of virtual reality in healthcare: A review. *Virtual and Augmented Reality in Mental Health Treatment* (pp. 17–31). IGI Global.

Pirker, J., & Dengel, A. (2021). The potential of 360 virtual reality videos and real VR for education—A literature review. *IEEE Computer Graphics and Applications, 41*(4), 76–89.

Richard, I. (2022, March 21). Meta's Oculus Quest 2 is the Top Selling VR Headset of 2021; XR Market Growth Skyrockets. Retrieved January 13, 2024, from https://www.techtimes.com/articles/273303/20220321/meta-s-oculus-quest-2-top-selling-vr-headset-2021.htm

Sagnier, C., Loup-Escande, E., Lourdeaux, D., Thouvenin, I., & Valléry, G. (2020). User acceptance of virtual reality: An extended technology acceptance model. *International Journal of Human–Computer Interaction, 36*(11), 993–1007.

Shahab, M. H., Ghazali, E., & Mohtar, M. (2021). The role of elaboration likelihood model in consumer behaviour research and its extension to new technologies: A review and future research agenda. *International Journal of Consumer Studies, 45*(4), 664–689.

Shin, D.H., Biocca, F., & Choo, H. (2013). Exploring the user experience of three-dimensional virtual learning environments. *Behav. Inform. Technol. 32*(2), 203–214

Shirani, F. (2021). Integrating diversity in simulation-based education: potential role of virtual reality. *Aem Education and Training, 5*(3). https://doi.org/10.1002/aet2.10608

Silverman, D. (2016). *Interpreting qualitative data (5th ed.).* Sage Publications.

Soman, K., Srinivasan, P., Prasad, A., & Menon, V. (2023). Teaching through digital media: acceptance and use of technology among the high school teachers for inclusive education in kerala during the covid-19 pandemic. *Indian Journal of Science and Technology, 16*(8), 583–589. https://doi.org/10.17485/ijst/v16i8.2007

Spradley, J. P. (1980). *Participant observation.* Wadsworth.

Sukmawati, F., Santosa, E., Rejekiningsih, T., Suharno, S., & Qodr, T. (2022). Virtual reality as a media for learn animal diversity for students. *Jurnal Edutech Undiksha, 10*(2), 290–301. https://doi.org/10.23887/jeu.v10i2.50557

Talespin. (n.d.). Retrieved May 10, 2024, from https://talespin.com/

Tan, K. L., Hii, I. S., Zhu, W., Leong, C. M., & Lin, E. (2022). The borders are re-opening! Has virtual reality been a friend or a foe to the tourism industry so far? *Asia Pacific Journal of Marketing and Logistics, 35*, 1639–1662.

Taufik, D., Kunz, M. C., & Onwezen, M. C. (2021). Changing consumer behaviour in virtual reality: A systematic literature review. *Computers in Human Behavior Reports, 3*, 100093.

Taylor, A., tom Dieck, M. C., Jung, T., Cho, J., & Kwon, O. (2024). XR and mental wellbeing: state of the art and future research directions for the Metaverse. Frontiers in Psychology, 15, 1360260.

tom Dieck, M.C., Jung, T., Lee, H., & Chung, N. (2024). Social presence and experience economy: the effects of augmented and virtual reality in museums. International Journal of Mobile Communications, 23(1), 85–109.

Vaquero-Blasco, M. A., Perez-Valero, E., Morillas, C., & Lopez-Gordo, M. A. (2021). Virtual reality customized 360-degree experiences for stress relief. *Sensors, 21*(6), 2219.

Wang, P., Wu, P., Wang, J., Chi, H. L., & Wang, X. (2018). A critical review of the use of virtual reality in construction engineering education and training. *International Journal of Environmental Research and Public Health, 15*(6), 1204.

Wang, X., Young, G. W., Mc Guckin, C., & Smolic, A. (2021). A systematic review of virtual reality interventions for children with social skills deficits. In 2021 IEEE international conference on engineering, technology & education (TALE) (pp. 436–443).
Zender, R., Knoth, A. H., Fischer, M. H., & Lucke, U. (2019). Potentials of virtual reality as an instrument for research and education. *i-com, 18*(1), 3–15.

The Role of Immersive Virtual Spaces in Enhancing Civic Participation and Its Narrative: An Explorative Study in the District of San Giovanni a Teduccio (Naples)

Daniela La Foresta and Ilaria Bruner

Abstract Participatory approaches are increasingly employed to engage citizens in the decision-making process, enabling them to actively articulate their opinions and suggestions. However, nowadays these attempts often come up against a feeling of general disillusionment among the population, especially in some territories, due to the low perception of the positive changes that have taken place and the lack of trust in the institutions, which are often considered too distant and closed in their ivory palace. The new technologies and, specifically, the metaverse with its virtual immersive environments (IVEs) can play a fundamental role in this context, facilitating the meeting between decision-makers and end-users, strengthening the narrative of the territories and their local identity, and representing a place for citizens to put forward their demands by overcoming a variety of territorial and social limits. This paper explores the issue, attempting to lay the groundwork for a future improvement of immersive and virtual co-design processes.

Keywords Immersive virtual environment · Civic participation · Immersive narrative · Metaverse

1 Introduction

In today's world, characterised by an unprecedented pace of development and an increasing connectivity that exacerbates local and global challenges, active civic participation is of fundamental value in creating more resilient societies. Indeed, it is conducive to strengthening democratic and decision-making processes, generating positive impacts on social cohesion and promoting greater collaboration between civil society, governments and NGOs in tackling the contemporary complicated issues. Participation in civic life, being a multi-dimensional concept, has been studied

D. La Foresta (✉) · I. Bruner
Department of Political Science, University of Naples Federico II, San Giovanni a Teduccio, Italy
e-mail: daniela.laforesta@unina.it

T. Jung et al. (eds.), *XR and Metaverse*, Springer Proceedings in Business and Economics, https://doi.org/10.1007/978-3-031-77975-6_26

through the lenses of several disciplines and can be defined, using the words of Campagna et al. (2020), as "*the behaviours and attitudes through which people express their willingness of interacting within the community and contributing to its well-being* [...]".

The topic of active civic participation appears to be closely linked to the practices of design, planning and transformation of urban territories. Indeed, the so-called participatory planning represents an approach capable of actively involving citizens, communities, and stakeholders in the definition of policies, projects and decisions related to the territorial areas experienced (Steen 2013). It is based on several fundamental assumptions that underline its necessity and effectiveness: people–and in this case citizens–are among the first advocates of change and, if change itself is initiated by social groups, it is more lasting than transformations implemented with a top-down approach, since participatory decisions tend to be more accepted and legitimised by the community. Through participatory planning practices, moreover, citizen empowerment is greatly increased: the role of governments evolves from administrator to collaborator and citizens from residents to co-creators (Foth 2017). In other words, active civic participation is an enabling factor to realise the transformative potential of new citizenship in processes of inclusion, involvement and co-responsibility in new spaces of relationship and engagement that can become concrete places of encounter and common action (Urton & Murray 2021; Ferdiani & Boana 2012; Toukola & Ahola 2022).

Modern challenges have surged dramatically in a rapidly evolving global landscape, driven by a complex array of factors, including technological advancements, hyper-connectivity, severe environmental problems, widening inequalities, social marginalization, and educational deprivation. These dynamics profoundly influence society, both negatively and positively: to amplify the positive aspects while simultaneously reducing the negative ones, informed and collective responses from society are essential. Indeed, civic participation, by enabling greater representation of diverse community voices and thus promoting more inclusive decision-making, contributes to enhancing society's resilience and its capacity to adapt to ongoing changes.

However, a worrying decline in civic participation and citizen involvement in urban transformation processes has been noticed, with negative effects on sustainability, democracy, and the quality of urban life (Winthrop 2020; Bronnikov 2020; Davis & Zhang 2023; Banaji & Buckingham 2010). This also reverberates in the construction of an ever-higher barrier between decision-makers and land users, i.e. between governance and citizens: it is therefore no coincidence that territory-governance is still exercised with a dualistic logic that, on the one hand sees agreements between strong powers and stakeholders, and on the other citizens who often confuse participation with opposition.

In this framework, digital means can be a valuable ally and a valuable tool for promoting participatory processes (Steinbach et al. 2019): particularly after the pandemic period, when traditional forms of participation such as rallies, assemblies and face-to-face meetings were suddenly discontinued, the demand for such tools saw a rapid growth, representing the only possible opportunities for citizens to actively take part in public decision-making processes. In particular, digital participation can play a key role in breaking down barriers between government and citizens (Gilman & Peixoto 2019). For the key role played by digital participation in breaking down barriers between government and citizens to unfold to its full effect, it needs to be implemented correctly in the different fields of participation itself, starting with political consultation and ending with territorial design (OECD 2020).

Till now, the spatial planning process "[…] *has been, arguably, slow to adapt and adopt new technologies: it is perhaps only now that it is starting to move into a more digitally focused era*" (Hudson-Smith 2022). And in this context, the real key to the digital shift is the "*emerging metaverse*". Indeed, its immersive technologies allow citizens to visualise and interact with the territory in an enhanced way, being able to visualise development proposals in real time and providing immediate feedback, thus making decision-making processes more tangible and understandable (Birbi & Allam 2022; Allam et al. 2022). These technologies have changed how environmental processes are communicated and perceived (Birenboim et al. 2021; Erhardt & Freitag 2021; Merlo & Lavoratti 2024). A similar positive effect would occur in improving awareness of the territory, its identity and the transformations that have characterised it, resulting in a more aware, informed and involved community. Indeed, it has been argued that as participants are more engaged with the environment provided in IVE, it activates their perception and emotions, improving, therefore, their connection to the identity of the territory (Chowdhury & Hanegraaf 2022; Mokas et al. 2021; Fegert 2023).

The project hereby described builds upon a wider, more comprehensive research initiative. The overarching goal is to explore practical and collaborative approaches to fostering citizen engagement in the social revitalization of San Giovanni a Teduccio, through the establishment of a co-design workshop. This first explorative study, therefore, proposes itself as a first phase, a pilot study, as it starts from the valorisation of the main elements of the districts–tangible and intangible–that make up the local cultural heritage and the community identity through digital and immersive narratives and perception actions involving different local actors–students, citizens, local cultural associations, stakeholders and institutional referents.

The scope of the explorative study was twofold: on one side, it aimed at understanding if and, in case of a positive answer, how the urban transformation of the San Giovanni a Teduccio district, in Naples, is perceived by its community; on the other side, the study proposed to understand whether a more immersive environment corresponds to a greater involvement and understanding of the changes that took place in the neighbourhood. From this twofold scope stream the two research questions that guided the project, with them being consequently one another.

- RQ1: Is the urban transformation of the San Giovanni a Teduccio district perceived by the community? If so, how?
- RQ2: Do immersive virtual environments generate greater involvement and understanding of territorial changes?

For the purpose of this article, a narrow focus will be adopted in the results section, specifically addressing the second scope and research question (RQ2), as these are more pertinent to the topics discussed in this volume.

2 San Giovanni a Teduccio (Naples)

The eastern area of the city of Naples, the capital city of the Campania region located in southern Italy, represents a "*territorial hinge*" (Giarrusso 2011) between the city centre and the Vesuvius coastline, with the latter extending for about 20 km with Mount Vesuvius standing on one side and the sea on the other.

In particular, the district of San Giovanni a Teduccio is part of the Sixth Municipality, together with Barra and Ponticelli, and has a land area of approximately 2.35 km2 with 23,839 inhabitants. It is precisely the Sixth Municipality that represents one of the areas mainly targeted by the Italian government, where the problem of urban suburbs has become a major issue in the political debate. To respond to this need for greater attention to the peripheral areas, an attempt is being made to intervene in this context, eliminating the strong opposition between the centre and the periphery and the negative connotation that often characterises the latter, transforming them instead into "*laboratories of the city of the future*" (Pinto 2007).

San Giovanni a Teduccio is characterised by a twofold dimension: it represents a significant and organic portion of the city's territorial, urban and industrial system, while at the same time constituting a directrix of city expansion. Since the second half of the second century, the district has been closely associated with a strong working-class identity, due to the various factories located there, such as the Cirio food factory and the former Corradini factory. Following the gradual and complete industrial decommissioning, San Giovanni a Teduccio went through a regressive phase in which urban decay and disorder often found fertile ground. Moreover, former industrial buildings, now disused, neglected and abandoned, continue to be present in the area, representing in some cases some of its best-known features. These traits, however, coexist with initiatives related to urban regeneration and collective participation, with some local associations particularly engaged in society through cultural and artistic activities (Procentese & Gatti 2023).

It is precisely to boost urban development strategies that administrations–both central and local–are focusing on plans and programmes for the reconversion of old industrial areas through direct and indirect interventions. In particular, first with the Plan for the Suburbs (1980) and later with the Variant to the Regulatory Plan (2004), the aim is to achieve a reconfiguration of peripheral contexts by focusing on local identity and on the territory's potential–expressed and unexpressed. A fundamental theme of the reconfiguration of the landscape is the redevelopment of the coastal strip, with the redefinition of the waterfront and the creation of integrated services for tourism and the harbour. It is indeed the issue of access to the sea that is strongly felt by the population, which takes a very critical attitude towards the railway break between the village of S. Giovanni and the coastline. Another fundamental element of the past and current transformation processes is the role taken on by the University of Naples Federico II, which, due to the financial contribution of the European Union, has launched an urban regeneration project with the creation of a new headquarters and a real technological hub, attracting the attention and interest of leading international innovation players such as Apple, Cisco, Capgemini and Deloitte. In other words, the intention is also to focus on the so-called 'knowledge economy' in order to strengthen the positive influence within the urban and social fabric of San Giovanni, while at the same time trying to preserve the productive vocation of the place (Addie et al. 2018).

The twofold soul of the area, characterised by degradation and innovation, is also reflected in its community, where disillusionment and hope coexist concerning urban transformations. If, indeed, the efforts of the institutions are not always perceived and appreciated, especially about the interventions implemented–or lack thereof–in the area of the coast or the so-called 'Bronx', it is equally true that the investments related to the university hub and the surrounding areas have had a positive impact on the population and, above all, on the merchants who have benefited directly from them.

3 Methods

The explorative study followed a structured and composite method, involving both on-desk and on-field phases (as shown in Fig. 1). A preliminary on-desk information collection phase was followed by an on-field data collection phase where, through a visit to the neighbourhood of San Giovanni a Teduccio, the first approach to local actors to be involved–such as citizens, cultural associations, and stakeholders–was made and photo-video graphic materials were collected. Then, in order to understand the perception of the urban transformations taking place in the neighbourhood as well as the narrative of San Giovanni and its perceived local identity, open interviews were carried out. The questionnaire delved into these main themes: (a) identity of the territory, (b) level of satisfaction with the transformations, (c) participatory processes implemented by local institutions, (d) impact of international firms on the territory, (e) impact of the university hub on the territory.

Leveraging the insights gleaned from data collection and analysis, the materials collected were systematised in an immersive virtual environment (IVE), named "*A night (of geography) in Naples*" (Fig. 1), created through the online 3D scene editor Spoke by Mozilla, exported as binary glTF (.glb) and uploaded on the Spatial platform. Users can view the immersive environment through a Meta Quest Headset, through the web page or the application on their phone, having the possibility to switch from a third person view to a first-person view. The Immersive Virtual Environment, named "*Una notte (della Geografia) a Napoli*" in Italian can be accessed through the Spatial website via the following link: https://www.spatial.io/s/Una-notte-della-geografia-a-Napoli-660b0914cf44d806eef6b709?share=2061182659442519453

Fig. 1 Visualization of the room via Spatial website

A total of thirty people participated, including university students and academics, local cultural associations as well as stakeholders from politics and industry. The pilot study began with the introduction of the theme and the purpose. Before starting, participants were given a thorough and consistent briefing on operating the VR headset. They were also made aware of potential side effects of using the technology, such as fatigue and dizziness. The study continued by giving them time to freely explore the immersive environment.

After the visualisation in IVE, a second questionnaire was submitted to the participants in order to assess the possible increased understanding and engagement with urban transformations through IVE, as well as to evaluate the experience and receive feedback. The study was concluded with a plenary discussion on the potential of the tool and suggested improvements on the IVE for further development of the project (Fig. 2).

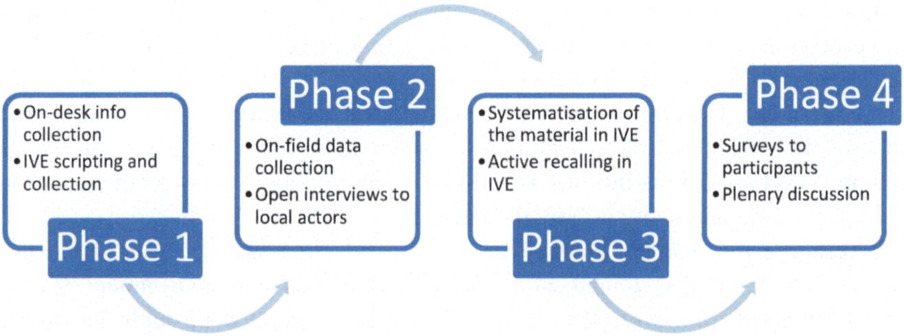

Fig. 2 Structure model of the study

4 Results

As abovementioned, focusing only on the second research question, the results of the third and fourth phases will be described carefully. In detail, three diverse levels were measured: the level of readiness for technology, the level of immersiveness and the level of change in perception.

4.1 The Level of Readiness for Technology

The participants' prior experience with IVE techniques ranged from beginners to experienced users, with most of them being first-time users. Nonetheless, the degree of readiness to use the technologies was rather high, with 87% of the participants preferring the use of hand-held visors–in our case Meta Quest 2–over the use of websites or apps. Four dissimilar categories of technology users were identified (Fig. 3), with innovators and early adopters–those willing to adopt a new technology despite the risks involved–representing the majority.

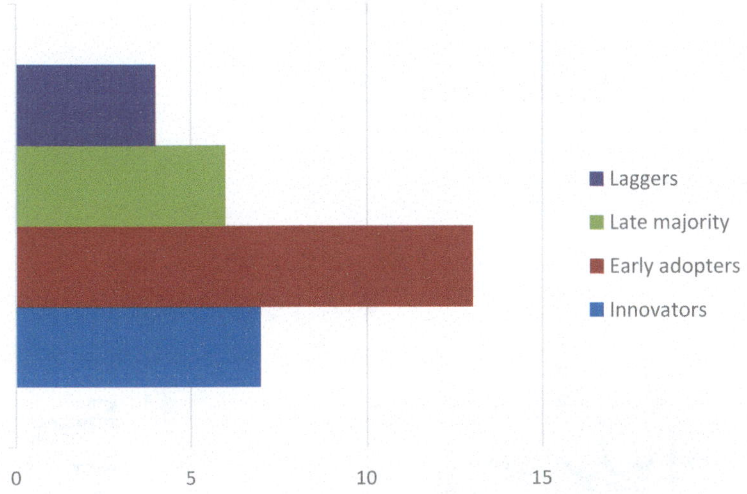

Fig. 3 Categories of technology adopters

4.2 The Level of Immersiveness

The overall feelings of participants (97%) on the IVE were positive. Figure 4 visualizes the most used word to describe the experience, while Fig. 5 shows the interactions of participants with the IVE.

The interface proved user-friendly for the vast majority of participants, with very few encountering technical issues or requiring assistance. The few problems encountered by some of them included the challenging use of the controllers and difficulties in operating certain buttons.

In the pilot study, nearly all participants (94%) reported a sense of immersion within the virtual environment: when asked to rate the level of immersiveness of the IVE from 1 (min.) to 5 (max.) the majority answered between 4 and 5, as illustrated in Fig. 6.

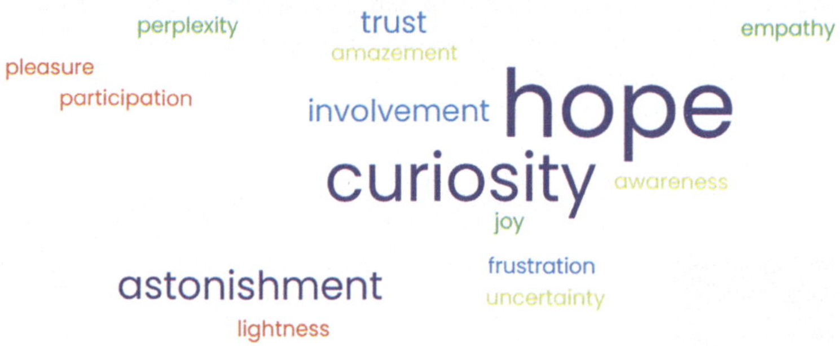

Fig. 4 Word cloud

Fig. 5 Participants reacting with the VR headsets

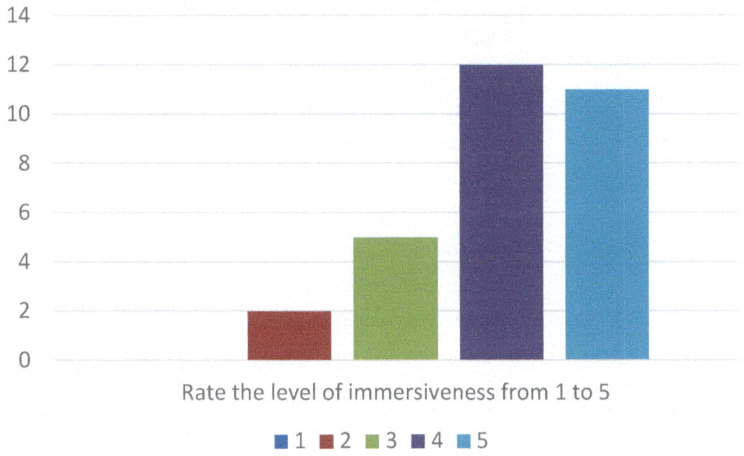

Fig. 6 Level of immersiveness

4.3 The Level of Change in the Perception

In order to evaluate the actual effectiveness of IVE in participatory planning processes, it was crucial to assess the increase in perception and awareness of changes after the use of the environment. Once again, the responses were overwhelmingly positive, with 69.5% of participants stating that they experienced a "substantial increase" in awareness, and 21% a "remarkable increase". A correlation was then made between these results and the findings related to the level of readiness for technology, observing the existence of a positive link (57.4%) between the so-called 'innovators', i.e. those who adopt a technology despite the risks it may generate, and the greater levels of change in perception.

4.4 Discussion and Future Work

Participants unanimously viewed the pilot project as a potential driver for increased civic engagement. The study's findings suggest promise for VR applications in narrative communication and collaborative decision-making. However, in order to be more effective and to be adopted for future co-design actions, the environment should be able to incorporate some additional prompts. Based on Evers et al. (2023), Table 1 lists the suggestions provided, which are ranked according to importance, based on the plenary discussion and the number of participants who made the same or similar proposals.

Table 1 List of suggestions

Suggested improvements	Frequency/Importance
Addition of initial guidelines	2
Moving directions in the IVE	4
Addition of a narrative voice/audio	3
Addition of 3D models	2
Enable tracking techniques	4
Addition of materials and textures	1
Enable screen mirroring on VR	3
Improve animated features	2

5 Conclusions

Urban redevelopment processes are at the centre of the local administration's political agenda in the eastern part of the city of Naples. In particular, the area of San Giovanni a Teduccio figures as a strategic direction for urban development and is for this reason attentively addressed with urban redevelopment plans and programmes. In this context, there is not always a clear understanding of the processes activated, due to a widespread feeling of disillusionment that characterises the relationship between government and citizens. The project presented was aimed precisely at understanding whether innovative technologies and immersive environments can contribute to diminishing this feeling, increasing the perception of transformations and at the same time reinforcing positive feelings, which are also present among the population, albeit to a more limited extent.

The study's findings strongly suggest that participants view the project's potential favourably. User responses confirmed that implementing this method can effectively engage citizens in territorial decision-making. This approach can enhance citizen understanding of ongoing and past transformations, serving as a valuable complement to traditional tools, not a replacement.

Furthermore, well-designed immersive virtual environments (IVE) could facilitate communication between citizens and local authorities during the design process. This would create a novel platform for co-creation, where both experts and non-experts can learn about the spatial and non-spatial implications of projects.

In conclusion, continued research in this area holds immense promise for transforming urban design processes, citizen engagement, and the relationship between residents and local institutions. Immersive spaces and the metaverse have the potential to significantly impact civic life by empowering citizens with greater decision-making influence and fostering a more collaborative environment.

References

Addie, J. P. D., Angrisani, M., & De Falco, S. (2018). University-led innovation in and for peripheral urban areas: new approaches in Naples, Italy and Newark, NJ, US. European Planning Studies, 26(6), 1181-1201.

Allam, Z., Sharifi, A., Bibri, S. E., Jones, D. S., & Krogstie, J. (2022). The metaverse as a virtual form of smart cities: Opportunities and challenges for environmental, economic, and social sustainability in urban futures. Smart Cities, 5(3), 771-801.

Banaji, S. & Buckingham, D. (2010) Young people, the Internet, and civic participation: an overview of key findings from the CivicWeb Project. International Journal of Learning and Media, 2 (1). pp. 15–24. ISSN 1943–6068

Bibri, S. E., & Allam, Z. (2022). The Metaverse as a virtual form of data-driven smart urbanism: On post-pandemic governance through the prism of the logic of surveillance capitalism. Smart Cities, 5(2).

Birenboim, A., Ben-Nun Bloom, P., Levit, H., and Omer, I. (2021) The Study of Walking, Walkability and Wellbeing in Immersive Virtual Environments, International Journal of Environmental Research and Public Health, 18:2, 364, https://doi.org/10.3390/ijerph18020364.

Bronnikov, I.A. (2020). Self-organization of Citizens in the Age of Digital Communications, Outlines of global transformations: politics, economics, law, Center for Crisis Society Studies, vol. 13(2).

Campagna, D., Caperna, G. & Montalto, V. (2020). Does Culture Make a Better Citizen? Exploring the Relationship Between Cultural and Civic Participation in Italy. Soc Indic Res 149, 657–686. https://doi.org/10.1007/s11205-020-02265-3

Chowdhury, S. and Hanegraaf, J. (2022) Co-presence in remote VR co-design, in: Proceedings of the 27th International Conference of the Association for Computer Aided Architectural Design Research in Asia (CAADRIA), 2, 465–474, https://doi.org./https://doi.org/10.52842/conf.caadria.2022.2.465.

Davis, A. P., & Zhang, Y. (2023). Civil Society and Democracy under Pressure: Does Authoritarian Mobilization and Party Incapacity Diminish the Positive Effect of Civil Society? The Sociological Quarterly, 1–21.

Erhardt, J., & Freitag, M. (2021). The Janus-Face of Digitalization: The Relation Between Internet Use and Civic Engagement Reconsidered. Social Science Computer Review, 39(3), 315-334. https://doi.org/10.1177/0894439319861966

Evers S.; Dane G. Z.; van den Berg P., Klippel A., Verduijn T., Arentze, T. (2023) Designing healthy public spaces: a participatory approach through immersive virtual reality.

Fegert, J. (2023) Virtual realities, real participation. Challenges and opportunities of public participation in the metaverse.

Foth, M. (2017) Participation, Co-Creation, and Public Space. The Journal of Public Space2, 4, 21–36, https://doi.org/10.5204/jps.v2i4.139.

Frediani, A. A., and Boano, C. (2012) Processes for Just Products: The Capability Space of Participatory Design, in: The Capability Approach, Technology and Design, edited by Oosterlaken, I. and van den Hoven, J., Springer: London, 203–222, https://doi.org/ https://doi.org/10.1007/978-94-007-3879-9_12.

Giarrusso, R (2011). La città tra terra e mare: il ruolo del waterfront urbano di S. Giovanni a Teduccio nella città di Napoli. URL: http://retedigital.com/wp-content/themes/rete/pdfs/portus_plus/1_2011/Tem%C3%A1ticas/La_recalificaci%C3%B3n_de_los_waterfront/07_RobertoGiarrusso.pdf

Gilman, H. R. & Peixoto, T. C. (2019). Digital participation. In S. Elstub & O. Escobar (Eds.), Handbook of Democratic Innovation and Governance. Edward Elgar Publishing

Hudson-Smith, A. (2022). Incoming metaverses: Digital mirrors for urban planning. Urban planning, 7(2), 343-354.

Merlo, A., & Lavoratti, G. (2024). Documenting Urban Morphology: From 2D Representations to Metaverse. Land, 13(2), 136.

Mokas, I., Lizin, S., Brijs, T., Witters, N., and Malina, R. (2021) Can immersive virtual reality increase respondents' certainty in discrete choice experiments? A comparison with traditional presentation formats, Journal of Environmental Economics and Management, 109, 102509, https://doi.org/10.1016/j.jeem.2021.102509.

OECD (2020), Digital Transformation and the Futures of Civic Space to 2030, Development Policy Paper, OECD-Publishing, Paris.

Pinto, F. (2007). Riqualificazione delle periferie e governo del territorio: politiche e strumenti nell'area metropolitana milanese. The Journal of Urbanism

Procentese, F., & Gatti, F. (2023). Valorizing Community Identity and Social Places to Implement Participatory Processes in San Giovanni a Teduccio (Naples, Italy). Sustainability, 15(19), 14216.

Steen, M. (2013) Co-Design as a Process of Joint Inquiry and Imagination. Design Issues, 29:2, 16–28, https://doi.org/10.1162/DESI_a_00207.

Steinbach, M., Sieweke, J., & Süß, S. (2019). The diffusion of e-participation in public administrations: A systematic literature review. Journal of Organizational Computing and Electronic Commerce, 29(2), 61–95. https://doi.org/ https://doi.org/10.1080/10919392.2019.1552749

Toukola, S., and Ahola, T. (2022) Digital tools for stakeholder participation in urban development projects, Project Leadership and Society, 3, 100053, https://doi.org/10.1016/j.plas.2022.100053.

Urton, D., and Murray, D. (2021) Project manager's perspectives on enhancing collaboration in multidisciplinary environmental management projects, Project Leadership and Society, 2, 100008, https://doi.org/10.1016/j.plas.2021.100008.

Winthrop, R. (2020). The need for civic education in 21st-century schools. Brookings Institute, June.

XR for Industry and Construction

Smart-BuildSite-OD: A Safety Monitoring System for Construction Sites Using Objects Detection

Seungyoub Ssin and Woontack Woo

Abstract The Smart-BuildSite-OD system integrates advanced object detection (OD), augmented reality (AR), and virtual reality (VR) to significantly enhance construction site safety. Utilizing devices such as HoloLens 2, the system captures high-resolution RGB-D images and head pose data for real-time monitoring and spatial mapping. By integrating 3D CAD models and scene graphs, it offers precise visualization of the site, enabling better hazard detection and management. Despite challenges like data accuracy and system complexity, the system improves safety through enhanced communication, real-time hazard detection, and comprehensive data visualization. Continuous advancements are expected to further enhance site safety and efficiency.

Keywords Smart Monitoring System · Object detection · Construction site safety · Machine learning · Computer vision · Risk assessment

1 Introduction

The construction industry occupies a pivotal position amidst rapid societal changes and technological advancements. However, these developments also bring forth various safety challenges (Jacobs & Forst, 2017). Working at heights, operating a multitude of heavy machinery, and handling large volumes of materials characterize construction sites as high-risk environments. Consequently, these sites pose

S. Ssin · W. Woo (✉)
KAIST Post Metaverse Research Center, Daejeon, South Korea
e-mail: wwoo@kaist.ac.kr

KAIST KI-ICT Augmented Reality Research Center, Daejeon, South Korea

S. Ssin
e-mail: youb1649@kaist.ac.kr

W. Woo
KAIST UVR Lab, Daejeon, South Korea

T. Jung et al. (eds.), *XR and Metaverse*, Springer Proceedings in Business and Economics, https://doi.org/10.1007/978-3-031-77975-6_27

significant risks to workers, often resulting in serious accidents and health hazards, leading to human casualties and economic losses (Khorrami Shad et al. 2022).

Effective safety management remains a critical issue in the construction industry, demanding continuous attention and efforts from all stakeholders involved. Traditional safety management methods primarily rely on surveillance through CCTV and security personnel, supplemented by periodic inspections. However, these methods have limitations in promptly detecting and effectively responding to potential hazards in real-time, especially in ambiguous situations, which may restrict subsequent accident mitigation measures (Nnaji & Karakhan 2020; Okonkwo et al. 2023).

Recent advancements in computer vision and machine learning technologies have brought about transformative changes across industries (Liu et al. 2020). Particularly, object detection technology has undergone remarkable evolution, enabling real-time environmental analysis and decision-making capabilities (Amjoud & Amrouch 2023). This technology is used to detect and classify specific objects in images or videos, finding applications ranging from autonomous vehicles to retail analytics.

This paper introduces a system designed to enhance safety at construction sites by leveraging object detection technology to identify various potential hazards. The research aims to design and implement an advanced system that ensures worker safety through innovative application of object detection technology in the construction industry. The goal is to contribute to raising the level of safety management in construction by opening new avenues for industry safety through the innovative application of object detection technology.

1.1 Background

The modern construction industry, advancing alongside urbanization and technological progress, provides increasingly complex and diversified work environments. While these advancements enhance productivity, they also introduce higher safety risks due to the use of advanced technologies. Addressing these challenges requires a rapid and accurate hazard detection system based on object detection technology (Khorrami Shad et al. 2022).

1.2 Research Objectives

This study explores methods to identify and manage safety risks at construction sites using object detection technology. Specifically, it aims to overcome the limitations of existing safety management systems by providing enhanced real-time monitoring capabilities, thereby enhancing worker safety and preventing accidents more effectively. The research establishes a foundation for improving accident prevention and response capabilities in the construction industry.

1.3 Significance of the Study

By proposing a novel approach to safety management through object detection technology, this study aims to surpass the limitations of traditional construction site management methods (Lee & Lee 2023). It is expected to enhance safety levels in the construction industry, providing workers with safer working environments (Murthy et al. 2020). Furthermore, the innovative application of object detection technology is anticipated to unlock various potential applications within the industry (Kim et al. 2023).

This paper proceeds as follows: first, it provides an overview of object detection technology and its applicability in construction sites. Second, it details the design and implementation of the proposed object detection-based construction site safety management system. Third, it validates the system's performance and effectiveness through experimental results and analysis. Finally, the conclusion summarizes the findings of this study and proposes directions for future research.

2 Literature Review

2.1 Construction Site Safety Management

Construction sites are complex environments with numerous hazards. Working at heights, operating heavy machinery, and handling various construction materials consistently expose workers to risks of accidents and injuries. These hazardous conditions pose significant threats to the health and safety of workers, contributing to high accident rates in construction sites (Lee & Lee 2023). As such, the need for effective safety management systems is emphasized. Traditional safety management methods mainly rely on surveillance through CCTV and security personnel, supplemented by periodic inspections. However, these methods have limitations in promptly detecting and effectively responding to potential hazards in real-time (Nath & Behzadan 2020).

The limitations of traditional safety management methods result in significant constraints on proactive hazard prevention. For instance, while CCTV systems can monitor construction sites in real-time, they are limited by the human factor, where quick-changing situations might not be promptly addressed. Additionally, surveillance by security personnel can be compromised by human fatigue and reduced attention spans, leading to missed potential hazards (Mostafa & Hegazy 2021). These constraints highlight the necessity for more efficient and reliable safety management systems.

Against this backdrop, technological advancements have paved the way for more advanced safety management approaches. Modern technologies such as Augmented Reality (AR) have the potential to revolutionize safety management on construction sites. AR technology combines virtual information with the real environment, providing workers with real-time critical information that helps them easily identify hazards and implement safe working practices. For instance, AR can display virtual safety signs or danger zones in real-time on-site, allowing workers to recognize and avoid hazards immediately (Kim et al. 2023).

Additionally, the development of machine learning and computer vision technologies offers significant opportunities to enhance safety management on construction sites. Object detection technology, for example, can be used to detect and identify various objects in real-time on construction sites, enabling the rapid identification of potential hazards. This capability allows for proactive risk management and significantly improves worker safety by ensuring hazards are identified and mitigated promptly (Nnaji & Karakhan 2020). Recent studies have shown that these technologies can significantly improve the safety of construction sites, offering new opportunities to reduce accident rates (Murthy et al. 2020).

The integration of modern technologies such as sensors, AR, and machine learning further strengthens safety management on construction sites. Combining these technologies allows for real-time data analysis and hazard detection, contributing to creating a safer working environment even in complex construction settings. These technologies enable the swift identification of workers' positions, machinery movements, and potential hazards, allowing for timely responses and enhancing overall site safety (Nnaji & Karakhan 2020).

2.2 *Current Technology Integration for Construction Site Safety Monitoring*

The integration of advanced technologies in construction site safety management has revolutionized traditional safety approaches. The Smart-BuildSite-OD system represents a significant advancement in this field by leveraging cutting-edge technologies to enhance safety monitoring on construction sites.

One of the core technologies used in the Smart-BuildSite-OD system is HoloLens 2's sensor streaming. This technology captures high-resolution 3D images of various construction site conditions in real-time, allowing for detailed analysis and monitoring. By using HoloLens 2, the system can quickly identify the positions of workers, the movements of equipment, and potential hazards, enabling prompt responses to any detected risks (Lee & Lee 2023). This capability is crucial in a dynamic environment like a construction site where conditions can change rapidly.

Additionally, the integration of ScanToCAD technology further enhances the system's capabilities by converting scanned 3D data into CAD models. This process creates a digital twin of the construction site, which can be used for accurate simulations and planning. The digital twin allows for the pre-identification of potential issues during the planning and execution phases, thereby reducing the likelihood of accidents (Cheung et al. 2018).

Moreover, the system incorporates advanced object detection technologies such as Omni3D and Cube R-CNN. These technologies excel in accurately detecting and analyzing objects within the complex environment of a construction site. By identifying and assessing various objects in real-time, the system can foresee high-risk situations and provide immediate warnings to workers, thus ensuring their safety (Lee & Lee 2023).

Recent studies highlight the effectiveness of these integrated technologies in modernizing safety management practices on construction sites. For instance, research on wireless sensor networks (WSNs) combined with Building Information Modeling (BIM) demonstrates how these technologies can enhance real-time monitoring and management of safety hazards, including hazardous gas detection (Gupta & Nair 2023). Another study focuses on the use of computer vision and deep learning to improve construction site safety by developing object recognition models that monitor workers' presence, assess fall risks, and ensure the correct use of personal protective equipment (PPE) (Nath & Behzadan 2020).

The use of these technologies represents a paradigm shift in construction site safety management. By integrating real-time data analysis, high-resolution imaging, and advanced object detection, the Smart-BuildSite-OD system significantly improves the ability to manage and mitigate safety risks on construction sites. This integration sets a new standard for safety protocols in the construction industry and provides a robust framework for future technological advancements.

2.3 Object Detection for Construction Site Safety Management

The application of object detection (OD) technology in construction site safety management has brought revolutionary changes to traditional safety practices. OD integrates the real-world environment of construction sites with virtual information, providing workers with real-time crucial data. This technology enables workers to easily identify hazards and implement safe working practices. For instance, OD can display virtual safety signs or danger zones on-site in real-time, helping workers to immediately recognize and avoid hazards (Lee & Lee 2023).

In the planning and simulation stages of construction projects, OD proves to be highly useful. Architects and engineers can use OD to convert blueprints into 3D models, visualizing how actual structures will interact on the construction site. These visual tools enhance the accuracy of project planning and help detect potential design errors in advance. Recent studies demonstrate that OD technology significantly improves construction site safety by detecting hazards in real-time and implementing warning systems (Alateeq et al. 2023; Shrigandhi & Gengaje 2022). For example, a study on OD applications in construction sites showcases methods for using OD to identify safety risks and deploy timely warnings.

The integration of OD with augmented reality (AR) further enhances its effectiveness. AR overlays virtual information on the real-world view, providing an intuitive interface for workers to understand safety measures. By combining OD with

AR, construction sites can benefit from a system that not only detects hazards but also visually communicates them to workers in a comprehensible manner (Nath & Behzadan 2020). Additionally, OD technology can be employed in construction project planning and simulation phases to improve safety outcomes by visualizing potential interactions between construction elements and identifying risks before they materialize on-site (Liu et al. 2022).

Recent advancements in deep learning have further improved the capabilities of OD systems in construction safety management. These systems can now detect a wide range of objects and conditions under various visual scenarios, enhancing the accuracy and reliability of safety monitoring. For example, research on deep convolutional networks has shown significant improvements in detecting construction objects, such as equipment and workers, even in challenging visual conditions (Gupta & Nair 2023). Furthermore, studies have utilized OD to enhance the detection of personal protective equipment (PPE) compliance, ensuring that workers are following safety protocols (Nath et al. 2020).

By integrating OD technology with other advanced systems like sensors and machine learning algorithms, construction sites can achieve a comprehensive safety management approach. This integration allows for real-time data analysis and hazard detection, which is crucial in dynamically changing construction environments. The combination of these technologies enables the swift identification of workers' positions, equipment movements, and potential hazards, ensuring timely responses to mitigate risks (Son & Kim 2021).

3 System Design

The proposed ScanToOXR system integrates advanced object detection (OD) and augmented reality (AR) technologies to create accurate and immersive virtual reality (VR) environments for construction site safety management. Using HoloLens 2 for real-time high-resolution 3D scanning, the system captures and analyzes the construction site's dynamic conditions. The ScanToCAD technology converts this data into CAD models, forming a digital twin of the site. This enables precise simulation and planning, identifying potential hazards. Omni3D and Cube R-CNN technologies enhance this by detecting and analyzing objects in real-time, providing immediate safety warnings. This integration modernizes safety protocols, ensuring a safer construction environment through advanced visualization and hazard detection capabilities (Ainetter et al. 2023; Avetisyan et al. 2019; Brazil et al. 2023) (Fig. 1).

The diagram illustrates an overview of the entire system, depicted in layers. However, it would be more appropriate to describe this as a step-by-step process executed by various teams during the system's development. From start to finish, the system begins with inspectors or workers and ends with the supervisor. We envision an interaction system where these two parties can exchange information and communicate effectively.

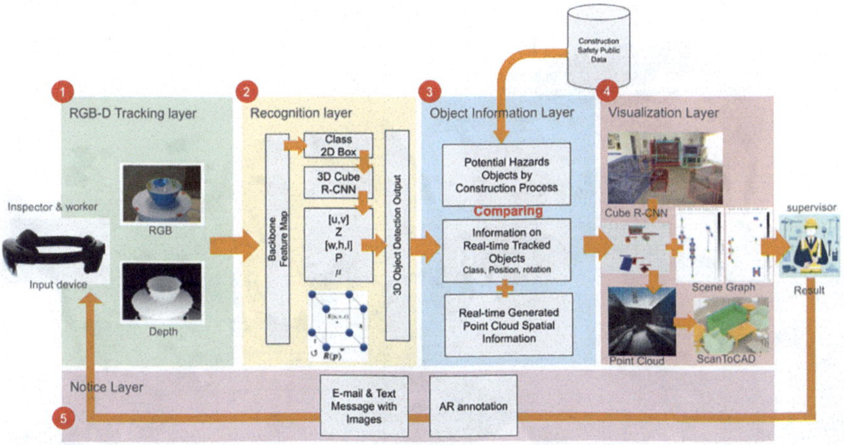

Fig. 1 Comprehensive flowchart of the smart-buildSite-OD system

3.1 Tracking Layer

The first layer, the Tracking Layer, monitors the internal space of the construction site using RGB tracking. This layer extracts and tracks various objects within the construction site in real-time. By continuously monitoring the site's interior, the system ensures accurate tracking of all activities and objects, providing a detailed and up-to-date map of the construction site. This real-time monitoring is crucial for maintaining safety and efficiency on the site.

3.2 Recognition Layer

The second layer is the Recognition Layer. This layer classifies and categorizes the various objects extracted from the scene. Using 3D Cube R-CNN technology, the system places these 2D-tracked objects into the 3D space, accurately determining their positions and relationships (Ainetter et al. 2023; Avetisyan et al. 2019; Brazil et al. 2023). This detailed classification and spatial arrangement allow for a more comprehensive understanding of the site's dynamics, which is essential for effective safety management.

3.3 3D Object Placement

The Smart-BuildSite-OD system's process involves capturing detailed 3D spatial data from construction sites using devices like HoloLens 2 and Meta Quest 2. These

Fig. 2 Objects models aligned on the scanned point cloud

devices gather RGB-D images and head pose data to monitor the environment accurately. The captured data is then processed through a scanning device that generates a spatial map, which forms the foundation for creating a digital twin of the construction site using ScanToCAD technology (Avetisyan et al. 2019) (Fig. 2).

This digital twin is further enhanced by integrating 3D CAD models, which are aligned with the real-world environment through a scene graph generator. The scene graph accurately maps static and dynamic objects within the construction site, ensuring precise spatial relationships and interactions are maintained (Jung et al. 2020).

3.3.1 Data Storage and Visualization

The processed data, including 3D object placements, is stored in JSON format. JSON's structured data format allows for efficient storage and retrieval, making it easy to integrate with other system components. This setup facilitates real-time data updates and seamless data flow across the system, ensuring that all relevant information is accessible for analysis and decision-making (Hou et al. 2023).

3.3.2 Object Detection and Alignment

Advanced object detection technologies, such as Omni3D and Cube R-CNN, are employed to accurately identify and analyze objects within the construction site's complex environment. These technologies ensure that both static and dynamic objects are correctly aligned and tracked, providing a comprehensive overview of the site's conditions (Azhar 2017).

3.4 Visualization Layer

The fourth layer, the Visualization Layer, visualizes real-time point cloud images in 3D. By overlaying CAD models or OBJ files on the point cloud, the system presents a scene graph that shows the relationships and potential hazards to the supervisor. This visual representation allows the supervisor to visually identify risks and make informed decisions quickly. The ability to see a real-time, 3D visualization of the construction site significantly enhances situational awareness and response times (Fig. 3).

Currently, the development stage is halfway through the third stage, with the fourth stage being handled by another team responsible for the scene graph. A simple demo will be created for testing, and the final completed parts will be included in the paper with captured images. This ongoing development ensures that the system is rigorously tested and refined before full implementation, guaranteeing reliability and effectiveness.

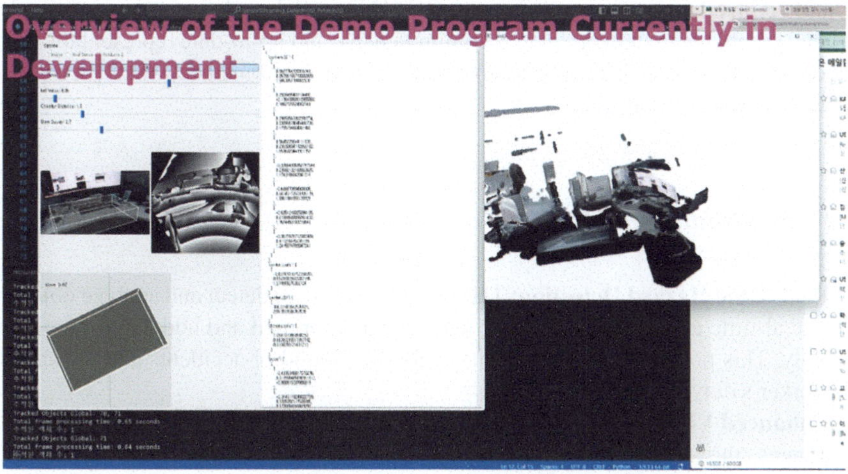

Fig. 3 The process of generating a point cloud while simultaneously performing object detection

This system will significantly enhance the safety of construction sites by enabling effective information delivery and communication between outdoor workers and supervisors. In the future, AR technology can be integrated to visualize risk factors in real-time, further enhancing safety management. The combination of real-time monitoring, advanced object detection, and comprehensive data visualization ensures that all stakeholders have the information they need to maintain a safe and efficient construction site.

4 Discussion and Analysis

The Smart-BuildSite-OD system represents a significant advancement in construction site safety management by integrating advanced object detection (OD) technologies with augmented reality (AR) and virtual reality (VR) environments. This section discusses the system's effectiveness, potential benefits, limitations, and future improvements, emphasizing how it enhances real-time hazard detection and overall site safety.

4.1 Effectiveness of the Smart-BuildSite-OD System

The Smart-BuildSite-OD system effectively monitors construction sites by utilizing HoloLens 2 and Meta Quest 2 to capture detailed RGB-D images and head pose data. This real-time data capture is crucial for accurate spatial mapping and hazard detection. By converting the captured data into 3D CAD models and visualizing it through a scene graph, the system provides a comprehensive and up-to-date representation of the construction site. This enables supervisors to make informed decisions promptly, significantly improving site safety.

4.2 Potential Benefits

- **Real-Time Hazard Detection**: The system's ability to detect and analyze objects in real-time ensures that potential hazards are identified and addressed immediately. This proactive approach reduces the likelihood of accidents and enhances worker safety.
- **Enhanced Visualization**: By overlaying CAD models onto real-time point cloud images, the system provides a detailed visual representation of the site. This helps supervisors understand the spatial relationships and potential hazards better, facilitating more effective safety management.

- **Improved Communication**: The interaction system between inspectors, workers, and supervisors ensures that critical safety information is communicated effectively. This collaborative approach enhances overall site safety and efficiency.
- **Data Integration and Accessibility**: Storing data in JSON format allows for seamless integration with other system components. This structured data format ensures that all relevant information is readily accessible for analysis and decision-making.

4.3 Limitations

- **Data Accuracy and Reliability**: The accuracy of the system's hazard detection relies on the quality of the captured data. Factors such as lighting conditions, sensor accuracy, and environmental changes can affect the reliability of the data.
- **System Complexity**: Integrating multiple advanced technologies (OD, AR, VR) increases the system's complexity. This may require significant technical expertise for installation, maintenance, and troubleshooting.
- **Real-Time Processing Requirements**: Real-time data processing and visualization demand high computational power and efficient algorithms. Ensuring that the system meets these requirements without latency is crucial for its effectiveness.
- **User Training and Adoption**: Workers and supervisors need adequate training to use the system effectively. Resistance to adopting new technologies and the learning curve associated with them can be potential barriers.

4.4 Future Improvements

- **Enhanced Data Capture**: Improving the accuracy and reliability of data capture devices (e.g., advanced sensors, higher resolution cameras) can enhance the system's overall effectiveness.
- **Advanced Analytics**: Incorporating machine learning algorithms for predictive analytics can further improve hazard detection and safety management. Predictive models can identify potential risks before they occur, allowing for preventive measures.
- **User Interface Improvements**: Developing a more intuitive and user-friendly interface can facilitate easier adoption and use of the system. Providing comprehensive training and support resources can also help in this regard.
- **Integration with Other Systems**: Integrating the Smart-BuildSite-OD system with other construction management systems (e.g., project management, resource allocation) can provide a more holistic approach to site management and safety.
- **Scalability and Customization**: Ensuring that the system is scalable to different types and sizes of construction projects and customizable to specific site requirements can enhance its applicability and usefulness.

5 Conclusion

One of the standout features of the Smart-BuildSite-OD system is its enhanced real-time hazard detection capability. By leveraging devices such as HoloLens 2 and Meta Quest 2, the system captures high-resolution RGB-D images and head pose data, facilitating real-time monitoring and spatial mapping of the construction site. This capability allows for the prompt identification and addressing of potential hazards, thereby reducing the risk of accidents and significantly improving worker safety.

Another crucial aspect of the system is its ability to provide accurate 3D visualization. The integration of 3D CAD models with real-time point cloud data, combined with the use of scene graphs, enables precise visualization of the construction site. This detailed visualization helps supervisors and workers to better understand spatial relationships and potential hazards, leading to more effective safety management.

The system also enhances communication between inspectors, workers, and supervisors. By offering a platform for real-time information exchange, it ensures that critical safety information is efficiently communicated, thereby improving overall site safety and operational efficiency.

In terms of data management, the system stores information in JSON format. This structured approach ensures that all object information is easily accessible and can be seamlessly integrated with other system components, supporting real-time data updates and facilitating comprehensive analysis and decision-making.

Despite its numerous benefits, the Smart-BuildSite-OD system does face several limitations. The accuracy of hazard detection is highly dependent on the quality of the captured data, which can be affected by environmental factors and sensor limitations. Additionally, the integration of advanced technologies increases the system's complexity, requiring significant technical expertise for effective implementation and maintenance.

Real-time processing and visualization demand substantial computational resources, posing challenges in ensuring system responsiveness without latency. Furthermore, adequate training is essential for users to effectively operate the system. The learning curve associated with new technology and resistance to its adoption can also present significant hurdles.

To enhance the effectiveness and applicability of the Smart-BuildSite-OD system further, several improvements are suggested. Investing in advanced sensors and higher resolution cameras can improve data accuracy and reliability. Incorporating machine learning algorithms for predictive analytics can enhance hazard detection capabilities, allowing for preventive measures.

Developing a more intuitive user interface and providing comprehensive training resources can facilitate easier adoption and use. Integrating the system with other construction management tools can offer a more holistic approach to site management. Ensuring that the system is scalable and customizable to different project types and sizes can enhance its utility across various construction environments.

The Smart-BuildSite-OD system exemplifies the transformative potential of integrating advanced technologies into construction site safety management. While challenges remain, ongoing improvements and innovations are expected to overcome these hurdles, making the system an indispensable tool for modern construction safety practices. By providing real-time monitoring, accurate hazard detection, and comprehensive data visualization, the system significantly contributes to creating safer and more efficient construction environments, ultimately protecting the lives and well-being of workers.

Acknowledgements This work was supported by the National Research Council of Science & Technology (NST) grant by the Korea government (MSIT) (**No. CRC21012**).

References

Ainetter, S., Stekovic, S., Fraundorfer, F., & Lepetit, V. (2023). Automatically Annotating Indoor Images with CAD Models via RGB-D Scans. Proceedings of the IEEE/CVF Winter Conference on Applications of Computer Vision,

Alateeq, M. M., PP, F. R., & Ali, M. A. (2023). Construction site hazards identification using deep learning and computer vision. *Sustainability, 15*(3), 2358.

Amjoud, A. B., & Amrouch, M. (2023). Object detection using deep learning, CNNs and vision transformers: A review. *IEEE Access, 11*, 35479-35516.

Avetisyan, A., Dahnert, M., Dai, A., Savva, M., Chang, A. X., & Nießner, M. (2019). Scan2cad: Learning cad model alignment in rgb-d scans. Proceedings of the IEEE/CVF Conference on computer vision and pattern recognition,

Azhar, S. (2017). Role of visualization technologies in safety planning and management at construction jobsites. *Procedia engineering, 171*, 215-226.

Brazil, G., Kumar, A., Straub, J., Ravi, N., Johnson, J., & Gkioxari, G. (2023). Omni3d: A large benchmark and model for 3d object detection in the wild. Proceedings of the IEEE/CVF conference on computer vision and pattern recognition,

Cheung, W.-F., Lin, T.-H., & Lin, Y.-C. (2018). A real-time construction safety monitoring system for hazardous gas integrating wireless sensor network and building information modeling technologies. *Sensors, 18*(2), 436.

Gupta, S., & Nair, S. (2023). A review of the emerging role of UAVs in construction site safety monitoring. *Materials Today: Proceedings.*

Hou, X., Li, C., & Fang, Q. (2023). Computer vision-based safety risk computing and visualization on construction sites. *Automation in Construction, 156*, 105129.

Jacobs, D. E., & Forst, L. (2017). Occupational safety and health and healthy housing: a review of opportunities and challenges. *Journal of public health management and practice, 23*(6), e36-e45.

Jung, S., Cha, H. S., & Jiang, S. (2020). Developing a building fire information management system based on 3D object visualization. *Applied Sciences, 10*(3), 772.

Khorrami Shad, H., Tak Wing Yiu, K., Lovreglio, R., & Feng, Z. (2022). State-of-the-art analysis of the integration of augmented reality with construction technologies to improve construction safety. *Smart and Sustainable Built Environment.*

Kim, K., Kim, K., & Jeong, S. (2023). Application of YOLO v5 and v8 for Recognition of Safety Risk Factors at Construction Sites. *Sustainability, 15*(20), 15179.

Lee, J., & Lee, S. (2023). Construction site safety management: a computer vision and deep learning approach. *Sensors, 23*(2), 944.

Liu, C., ME Sepasgozar, S., Shirowzhan, S., & Mohammadi, G. (2022). Applications of object detection in modular construction based on a comparative evaluation of deep learning algorithms. *Construction Innovation, 22*(1), 141-159.

Liu, L., Ouyang, W., Wang, X., Fieguth, P., Chen, J., Liu, X., & Pietikäinen, M. (2020). Deep learning for generic object detection: A survey. *International journal of computer vision, 128*, 261-318.

Mostafa, K., & Hegazy, T. (2021). Review of image-based analysis and applications in construction. *Automation in Construction, 122*, 103516.

Murthy, C. B., Hashmi, M. F., Bokde, N. D., & Geem, Z. W. (2020). Investigations of object detection in images/videos using various deep learning techniques and embedded platforms—A comprehensive review. *Applied Sciences, 10*(9), 3280.

Nath, N. D., & Behzadan, A. H. (2020). Deep convolutional networks for construction object detection under different visual conditions. *Frontiers in Built Environment, 6*, 97.

Nath, N. D., Behzadan, A. H., & Paal, S. G. (2020). Deep learning for site safety: Real-time detection of personal protective equipment. *Automation in Construction, 112*, 103085.

Nnaji, C., & Karakhan, A. A. (2020). Technologies for safety and health management in construction: Current use, implementation benefits and limitations, and adoption barriers. *Journal of Building Engineering, 29*, 101212.

Okonkwo, C., Okpala, I., Awolusi, I., & Nnaji, C. (2023). Overcoming barriers to smart safety management system implementation in the construction industry. *Results in Engineering, 20*, 101503.

Shrigandhi, M., & Gengaje, S. (2022). Systematic Literature Review on Object Detection Methods at Construction Sites. International Conference on Expert Clouds and Applications,

Son, H., & Kim, C. (2021). Integrated worker detection and tracking for the safe operation of construction machinery. *Automation in Construction, 126*, 103670.

Extended Reality for Sustainable Key Performance Indicators: Creation of a Virtual Environment Fidelity Index Matrix

R. S. Johnston, J. D. Mondol, B. Coyle, and A. Wiberg

Abstract The technologies such as Virtual Reality (VR), Augmented Reality (AR), and Mixed Reality (MR) developed under the umbrella term eXtend Reality(XR) is adopted for industrial applications such as training and potentially sustainable KPI communication. It is important to understand the fidelity required for specific use cases and how they differ both from each other within serious gaming technology, but also from the entertainment gaming technology from which the hardware was originally developed. As fidelity is not a solved problem within XR and an agreed standard per use case does not exist, this paper proposes a matrix-based approach to gauge the appropriate XR fidelity for different industry use cases, focusing on the Arcitecture Engeering Construction sector (AEC). A well as to support the literature review of previous XR studies based on commonly available information in order to better understand the direction of initial development work for prototyping.

Keywords Virtual Reality (VR) · Augmented Reality (AR) · Fidelity · Virtual Environments (VE) · Building Information Modelling (BIM) · Stakeholder communication

1 Introduction

Since the launch of high-performance consumer-grade Virtual Reality (VR) Head Mounted Displays (HMDs) in 2016, such as Oculus Rift CV1 and HTC Vive, Extended Reality (XR) technology has seen significant advances. Over the past

---

R. S. Johnston (✉) · J. D. Mondol · B. Coyle
Faculty of Computing, Engineering and the Built Environment/Belfast School of Architecture and the Built Environment, Ulster University, Belfast, UK
e-mail: Johnston-R54@ulster.ac.uk

A. Wiberg
Faculty of Engineering and Design/Department of Architecture and Civil Engineering, University of Bath, Bath, UK

T. Jung et al. (eds.), *XR and Metaverse*, Springer Proceedings in Business and Economics, https://doi.org/10.1007/978-3-031-77975-6_28

eight years, improvements in VR hardware have enabled higher resolution, wireless processing, and the adoption of inside-out tracking HMDs (Al-Jundi & Tanbour 2022). These advancements have facilitated the creation of more immersive user experiences, including mixed reality environments exemplified by the Oculus Quest 3 (Li et al. 2018; Wen and Gheisari 2020; Stals and Caldas 2022). XR applications are predominantly seen in two areas: gaming and entertainment, a sector driving R&D for enhanced leisure experiences, and serious games or industrial applications, which are often crucial for visualization, communication, simulation, training, and decision-making reflective of real-world scenarios (Muller et al. 2006; Gao 2021; Alejandro Huerta-Torruco et al. 2022).

In particular, the Architecture, Engineering, and Construction (AEC) sector utilizes XR to address its urgent decarbonization needs by 2050 (Wiberg et al. 2019), necessitating robust communication across all levels of decision-making (Stals and Caldas 2022). Globally, buildings are responsible for about 37% of energy-related greenhouse gas emissions (UNEP 2009; Birgisdottir et al. 2017). With emissions rising post-pandemic, reaching net-zero by 2050 will require significant shifts, underscored by the increasing emissions recorded in 2022 (United Nations 2022).

XR technology, as a core component of the fourth industrial revolution (Industry 4.0), is pivotal in enhancing physical goods and services through digital technologies, yet its adoption remains in the early stages, primarily utilized by large consultancies involved in major infrastructure projects (Brazina et al. 2022).

Research supports the adoption of sustainable materials throughout the life cycle of a building (Sturgis 2017), which could significantly reduce emissions and increase energy efficiency. Visualizing this data effectively has proven to enhance decision-making (Birgisdottir et al. 2017; Hollberg et al. 2021). XR technologies such as AR, VR, and Mixed Reality (MR) could accelerate the adoption of sustainable building practices by providing a more comprehensive understanding of data through immersive 3D visualization. This helps stakeholders view key performance indicators within a VR context, fostering better engagement (Li et al. 2018).

However, determining the appropriate level of visual fidelity in XR as a Decision Support System (DSS) poses challenges (Al-Jundi and Tanbour 2022; Sermet and Demir 2022). The optimal level of realism varies across applications—from video games to medical training to community planning tools—in order to maximize engagement, integration, and understanding. The sustainability community, in particular, requires careful consideration of how LCA data is visualized to effectively engage both expert and non-expert stakeholders (Hollberg et al. 2021; Stals and Caldas 2022).

In the AEC sector, the accuracy of data and its depiction is crucial, especially in early design phases where overly detailed models might stifle creativity rather than enhance feedback. Therefore, realism must be balanced with performance and development time constraints. Visualization of additional metadata such as cost, time, energy, and embodied carbon is also vital for sustainability decision-making (Zhang et al. 2020; Imottesjo and Kain 2022).

This paper proposes a matrix-based approach to gauge the appropriate XR fidelity for different industry use cases, focusing on the AEC sector. This methodology could potentially be adapted for other industries, aiming to establish standardized visual fidelity levels suitable for serious gaming and other practical applications.

2 Literature

Fidelity and visual fidelity is understood to be an important aspect of XR yet simultaneously poorly standardized (Muller et al. 2006). There is a significant gap in understanding how virtual content is communicated and perceived by stakeholders for a variety of use cases (Kini and Ganeshrao 2023). This underscores the need for more refined measurement and analysis methods to better align virtual experiences with user perceptions and effectiveness.

Visual fidelity significantly influences users' sense of stability and presence within an environment. (Menzies et al. 2016) found that higher fidelity enhances balance compared to having eyes closed, though individual differences, like the ability to learn spatial information, can play a larger role in how well users understand and interact with virtual environments (VEs), as suggested by (Waller, Knapp and Hunt 2001). Further, (Krüger et al. 2022) observed that individuals with better mental rotation abilities benefit more from augmented reality (AR), and their research confirmed that 3D visualization is superior to 2D for enhancing learning across all users. This contrasts with (Bölek et al. 2021), who reported no link between natural spatial abilities and knowledge acquisition. Waller et al.'s findings from 2001 indicate that high realism isn't essential for effective VE training systems, suggesting that even low fidelity, such as wireframe models, can be effective. However, it's important to note that what is considered low fidelity today is far more advanced than in 2001, reflecting significant technological advances over time.

Interaction fidelity extends beyond the physical to influence the psychological motivation of users to engage with content, as noted by (Kini and Ganeshrao 2023). This is particularly relevant when engaging AEC stakeholders with complex data on embodied carbon emissions from construction projects. Motivating stakeholders to utilize tools for sustainable decision-making is crucial, with XR technology offering significant advantages over traditional methods. The impact of this technology on user perception can vary, enhancing or detracting from the experience. Utilizing immersive gamification to foster empathy, immersion, and a shared understanding among stakeholders is a key goal (Wiberg et al. 2019). This raises an important question for visualization researchers: What is the appropriate level of fidelity in the virtual environment to achieve these outcomes?

In 2021, high fidelity in virtual environments (VE) was linked to longer adoption times (Flavián et al. 2021), a finding supported in 2023 by (Kini and Ganeshrao 2023). This connection is primarily due to how immersed users feel, influencing their natural interactions within the VE, as detailed by (Kini and Ganeshrao 2023). For instance, using hand controllers enhances the sense of body ownership, making the VE experience more intuitive. Research also indicates that in collaborative VEs, where multiple users interact, generic partial avatars are less effective compared to full-body or customizable avatars, which improve representation and interaction, as found by (Weidner et al. 2023).

VE fidelity can be considered both separate from and integral to system fidelity (Muller et al. 2006). (Luo et al. 2023) treated VE details as distinct, evaluating the level of detail (LOD) as either high or low, and focusing on how it impacts user interaction and immersion. Their research indicated that interaction fidelity, such as using a keyboard versus more immersive technologies, showed minimal difference in user engagement. However, visual LOD significantly influenced how quickly 120 participants could complete tasks. While realistic VEs are essential for training scenarios, overly realistic environments might increase cognitive load without adding value, suggesting a need for moderation in realism, especially when conveying complex metadata like embodied carbon in non-training contexts. Lower realism could lessen cognitive strain and enhance VR's role in facilitating communication and creative problem-solving. Furthermore, (Moser and Lewalter 2024) study on AR supports that tailored learning strategies enhance long-term retention when aligned with visual content, emphasizing the importance of appropriate fidelity levels in educational AR applications.

Previous efforts to measure fidelity have varied widely, from specific techniques like eye-tracking by (Pastel et al. 2021), to more comprehensive system fidelity evaluations by (Muller et al. 2006). However, these methods often lack a standard for comparative scoring, and when available, they require detailed operational metrics like frame rates or audio quality. For instance, (Al-Jundi and Tanbour 2022) developed a fidelity framework that assesses multiple aspects contributing to user presence, yet it depends on detailed system information.

In VR, frame rate is crucial as complex models like those used in construction (BIM models) demand significant processing power, which can reduce frame rates, disorient users, and induce motion sickness (Al-Jundi and Tanbour 2022). Yet, details such as frame rate, application size, and model optimization are rarely disclosed in AEC XR studies, complicating fidelity comparisons (Stals and Caldas 2022). Game industry optimization techniques, like texturing, enable more detailed and realistic environments without increasing geometry complexity, rendering traditional metrics like triangle count less relevant for comparing visual fidelity outside of XR environments (Walmsley and Kersten 2019). This paper introduces a flexible approach using commonly available information or subjective in-application visuals evaluated against a matrix to facilitate comparisons and promote a standardized scoring system.

3 Methodology

The VE fidelity index matrix provides a method to better understand the role of fidelity in communication, by comparing VE's across immersive studies. The matrix system as shown in Table 1 is based on an accumulative top score of 10, across five categories. (1) Textures, (2) Characters, (3) Lighting, (4) Modelling, and (5) Details. Total scores range from a minimum of 0 indicating a very low fidelity virtual environment to a maximum of 10 indicating a virtual environment with a much higher level of fidelity. Where a scoring measure has not changed from the previous level an * asterisk has been used, this indicates that the same scoring measure for that criteria applies—but also that there may be scope to rise the scoring criteria for that category higher in future iterations of the matrix.

Texture scores range on complexity from wireframes to photorealistic, providing a maximum of 3. Textures also currently have the highest scoring potential of any category to help weight the results on the visuals of the Virtual Environment.

Characters while not a part of the fixed environment are key to engaging with it and others if they are present, currently this is scored between 0 and 2, but there is potential to increase to 3 should trends of lip-sync and next gen immersive avatars become more widely available.

Lighting plays a role in the realism of a scene this has been included with a core determining factor if shadows are present or not, with a maximum score of 2. Added detail such as real-time ray tracing vs baked textures etc.is not considered. But this may play a role in future as such technology becomes more widely adopted and described within the literature for XR applications.

Modelling mainly considered if environments were simple block constructs or complex environments more fully representative of a real building or place such as an adapted BIM model. However, as a complex model does not necessity a suitable frame rate for the experience, this has currently been capped at 2. As publications share more detailed information on models or if a need requires differentiation of models between planned and as built this could be increased to 3. The combined score of modelling and texturing helps to keep the VE the focus of the matrix results, without a bias towards unnecessary complexity. For example, a VE using simple block modelling with photorealistic textures can already achieve a score of 4 out of 5 across those two categories.

Detail was added to capture subjective novel consideration of fine details, such as decals or User Interface (UI) styling that adds to the experience but may be difficult to typically quantify. As this score is the more subjective it is also the lowest with a maximum of 1. It is not expected that the goal should always be for higher scoring

Table 1 Virtual environment fidelity index matrix

Score	0	1	2	3
Textures	None/Wireframe outline only	Basic colour	Use of textured images	Use of photorealistic textures
Characters	None	Included	High Quality	*
Lighting	None	Basic	Shadows	*
Modelling	None	Basic 3D outline	Complex model	*
Details	No novel details	Novel details included	*	*
Max score	0	5	9	10

fidelity environments, instead to provide a means of comparison that can be in turn linked more finely to specific XR use cases to inform future development.

4 Results

The VE Fidelity Matrix was deployed as a part of a systematic review that identified an initial 862 papers, that were subsequently filtered through various criteria to 17 papers that represented original studies utilising VEs, VR, and or AR. Table 2 shows the results from the use of the matrix on these 17 papers, approximately 41% were classified by the matrix as high fidelity, 41% as low fidelity, and 18% as medium. End users were found to be Architecture, Engineering Construction (AEC), Architects only (A), Manufacturing only (M), Facilities management (FM), or Specialists (S).

No tools developed by these papers selected for review were intended for public consultation use, supporting previous findings of (Stals and Caldas 2022) that indicated a general lack of XR tools for AEC public engagement. AEC end users had an average fidelity score of 6.3 across six papers, while Architect only tools had an average score of 4.1 also across six papers.

Three papers with a specialist end user provided an average score of 2. A single Manufacturing, and Facilities Management user paper both scored 7. Studies where Key Performance Indicators (KPIs) played a key role in the study had an average score of 4.1 (or 4.5 for VR exclusive KPIs studies). Where scenarios were used within the studies, to provide a narrative to the XR technology being tested. Five VR only studies with scenarios had an average score of 5.8, opposed to six VR only studies without scenarios with an average score of 5.2.

5 Discussion

Previous studies such as Muller et al. (2006), Menzies et al. (2016), and Luo et al. (2023) suggested that there would be differences in fidelities across studies. The Virtual Environment Fidelity Matrix has confirmed this to be true and provides a consistent scoring mechanism which is different from previous works such as Muller et al. (2006), Al-Jundi and Tanbour (2022). Stals and Caldas (2022) indicated that studies are often tailored towards industry professionals, and while the sample size of the study here is small it supports these findings. One of the most closely align primary studies in Table 2 to the use of sustainable KPIs in XR was (Wiberg et al. 2019), which scored 2 in the fidelity Index Matrix.

While more work is certainly needed with stakeholder feedback, it might suggest that when the focus is KPI communication, the Fidelity of the Environment is less important as suggested by Waller et al. (2001), Luo et al. (2023) might argue that it is important when the focus is the data, the VE should be a low fidelity preventing excessive cognitive load and keeping stakeholder attention focused. Findings from

Table 2 Papers ranked by fidelity index matrix

Reference	Purpose				Technology			Fidelity index matrix score					
	End User	KPI	Scenario	Tested	DDS	Wireless	BIM	Textures	Characters	Lighting	Modelling	Details	Fidelity score
Paravizo (2019)	AEC	✕	✓	✓	PC	✕	✓	3	2	2	2	0	***9***
Nasrazadani et al. (2020)	A	✕	✕	✕	VR	✕	✓	3	0	2	2	1	***8***
Du et al. (2016)	AEC	✕	✕	✕	VR	✕	✓	2	2	1	2	0	***7***
Shi et al. (2016)	FM	✓	✓	✕	VR	✕	✓	2	2	1	2	0	***7***
Du et al. (2018a)	AEC	✕	✓	✓	VR	✕	✓	1	2	2	2	0	***7***
Du et al. (2018b)	A	✕	✓	✓	VR	✓	✓	2	2	1	2	0	***7***
Alejandro Huerta-Torruco et al. (2022)	M	✓	✓	✓	VR	✕	✕	2	1	1	2	1	***7***
Balali et al. (2018)	AEC	✓	✕	✕	VR	✓	✓	2	0	2	2	0	***6***
Ma et al. (2020)	AEC	✕	✕	✓	VR	✕	✓	1	2	2	1	0	***6***
Balali, Zalavadia and Heydarian (2020)	A	✓	✓	✓	VR	✕	✓	2	0	1	2	0	***5***
Miyake et al. (2017)	AEC	✕	✕	✕	AR	✓	✓	2	0	0	1	0	***3***
Sermet and Demir (2022)	S	✓	✓	✕	VR	✕	✕	1	0	0	1	1	***3***

(continued)

Table 2 (continued)

Reference	Purpose				Technology			Fidelity index matrix score					
	End User	KPI	Scenario	Tested	DDS	Wireless	BIM	Textures	Characters	Lighting	Modelling	Details	Fidelity score
Sait et al. (2019)	A	✓	×	×	VR	×	×	1	0	0	1	0	***2***
Wiberg et al. (2019)	A	✓	×	✓	VR	×	✓	1	0	0	1	0	***2***
Imottesjo and Kain (2022)	S	×	✓	✓	XR	✓	×	1	0	0	1	0	***2***
Ding et al. (2016)	A	✓	×	×	AR	✓	✓	1	0	0	0	0	***1***
Min et al. (2019)	S	×	✓	✓	AR	✓	×	0	0	0	0	0	***1***

Luo et al. (2023) might also explain why this study found that papers focused on AEC case studies had higher average fidelity scores and also had scenarios focused more around training. Since higher-fidelity environments have been linked to faster task completion time, for training applications (Luo et al. 2023).

It is interesting when considering the use case of VE's in relation to their score, for example it may be that realism plays an important role in training and equates to a higher fedility score for some of the AEC related studies. While some of the lower scores realte to papers that look at larger scale and more abstract concepts such as early design or city planning. If this is a consistent theme in the wider literature it could be that low fidely VE's are better suited to sustianble KPI communication as it may keep the VE abstact while placing the focus on the data its self. However as technology, software and VE creation methods advantage what is considered high fidelity today is likely to change.

6 Conclusions

The authors propose the creation of a Virtual Environment Fidelity Index Matrix(VEFIM), based on the identifiable gap in quantifying the often-subjective differences between Virtual Environments. Based on commonly shared data from studies, or from discernible information from typical in application screenshots. The Matrix has been designed to cover the main influencing factors within an environment, but its recognised as an early attempt and is open to further development and improvement. The Virtual Environment Fidelity Index Matrix was found to identify in a quantifiable manner variations and trends across a series primary study that utilised VE, AR, or VR technologies. From information that has been commonly shared across AEC XR studies, suggesting it may provide a robust method to support future literature-based work, as well as support the initial direction of early stage XR research in terms of what level of fidelity might be appropriate for their use case.

In conclusion the VEFIM can be considered as a possible methodology for researchers to help compare the results between studies of similar and varying levels of fidelity that has been shown through many previous studies to play a significant role in the experiences and perspectives of users within virtual environments. Understanding the level of detail required to optimally enable stakeholders to make informed decisions about real world scenarios such as climate change and urban infrastructure. While be vital to ensure VE are adequate without excessive development costs, to support adoption of these emerging technologies in the most supportive manner possible. Use of VEFIM across more studies would help better identify existing fidelity trends in relation to KPI communication and specific industrial use cases. Industrial feedback on the Matrix would also better help understand how this method can grow towards a supportive standard.

Acknowledgements Authors would like to thank the Northern Ireland Department for the Economy and Ulster University for funding and supporting this research. And to Spatial Simulations Ltd for their additional dissemination funding.

References

Alejandro Huerta-Torruco, V. *et al.* (2022) 'Effectiveness of virtual reality in discrete event simulation models for manufacturing systems', *Computers & Industrial Engineering*, 168, p. 108079. Available at: https://doi.org/10.1016/j.cie.2022.108079.

Al-Jundi, H.A. and Tanbour, E.Y. (2022) 'A framework for fidelity evaluation of immersive virtual reality systems', *Virtual Reality*, 26(3), pp. 1103–1122. Available at: https://doi.org/10.1007/s10055-021-00618-y.

Balali, V. *et al.* (2018) 'Improved Stakeholder Communication and Visualizations: Real-Time Interaction and Cost Estimation within Immersive Virtual Environments', in *Construction Research Congress 2018. Construction Research Congress 2018*, New Orleans, Louisiana: American Society of Civil Engineers, pp. 522–530. Available at: https://doi.org/10.1061/9780784481264.051.

Balali, V., Zalavadia, A. and Heydarian, A. (2020) 'Real-Time Interaction and Cost Estimating within Immersive Virtual Environments', *Journal of Construction Engineering and Management*, 146(2), p. 04019098. Available at: https://doi.org/10.1061/(ASCE)CO.1943-7862.0001752.

Birgisdottir, H. *et al.* (2017) 'IEA EBC annex 57 "evaluation of embodied energy and CO 2eq for building construction"', *Energy and Buildings*, 154, pp. 72–80. Available at: https://doi.org/10.1016/j.enbuild.2017.08.030.

Bölek, K.A., De Jong, G. and Henssen, D. (2021) 'The effectiveness of the use of augmented reality in anatomy education: a systematic review and meta-analysis', *Scientific Reports*, 11(1), p. 15292. Available at: https://doi.org/10.1038/s41598-021-94721-4.

Brazina, J. *et al.* (2022) 'Application of Industry 4.0 trends in the teaching process', in *2022 20th International Conference on Mechatronics - Mechatronika (ME). 2022 20th International Conference on Mechatronics - Mechatronika (ME)*, Pilsen, Czech Republic: IEEE, pp. 1–6. Available at: https://doi.org/10.1109/ME54704.2022.9983243.

Ding, Y. *et al.* (2016) 'Automatic Measurement System of Visible Greenery Ratio Using Augmented Reality', in. *CAADRIA 2016: Living Systems and Micro-Utopias - Towards Continuous Designing*, Melbourne, Australia, pp. 703–712. Available at: https://doi.org/10.52842/conf.caadria.2016.703.

Du, J. *et al.* (2016) 'Communication by Interaction: A Multiplayer VR Environment for Building Walkthroughs', in *Construction Research Congress 2016. Construction Research Congress 2016*, San Juan, Puerto Rico: American Society of Civil Engineers, pp. 2281–2290. Available at: https://doi.org/10.1061/9780784479827.227.

Du, J., Shi, Y., *et al.* (2018) 'CoVR: Cloud-Based Multiuser Virtual Reality Headset System for Project Communication of Remote Users', *Journal of Construction Engineering and Management*, 144(2), p. 04017109. Available at: https://doi.org/10.1061/(ASCE)CO.1943-7862.0001426.

Du, J., Zou, Z., *et al.* (2018) 'Zero latency: Real-time synchronization of BIM data in virtual reality for collaborative decision-making', *Automation in Construction*, 85, pp. 51–64. Available at: https://doi.org/10.1016/j.autcon.2017.10.009.

Flavián, C., Ibáñez-Sánchez, S. and Orús, C. (2021) 'Impacts of technological embodiment through virtual reality on potential guests' emotions and engagement', *Journal of Hospitality Marketing & Management*, 30(1), pp. 1–20. Available at: https://doi.org/10.1080/19368623.2020.1770146.

Gao, S. (2021) 'Commercial Application of XR and Digital Twin Technology in Smart City', in *2021 3rd International Symposium on Smart and Healthy Cities (ISHC). 2021 3rd International Symposium on Smart and Healthy Cities (ISHC)*, Toronto, ON, Canada: IEEE, pp. 84–89. Available at: https://doi.org/10.1109/ISHC54333.2021.00024.

Hollberg, A. *et al.* (2021) 'Review of visualising LCA results in the design process of buildings', *Building and Environment*, 190, p. 107530. Available at: https://doi.org/10.1016/j.buildenv.2020.107530.

Imottesjo, H. and Kain, J.-H. (2022) 'The Urban CoCreation Lab—An Integrated Platform for Remote and Simultaneous Collaborative Urban Planning and Design through Web-Based Desktop 3D Modeling, Head-Mounted Virtual Reality and Mobile Augmented Reality: Prototyping a Minimum Viable Product and Developing Specifications for a Minimum Marketable Product', *Applied Sciences*, 12(2), p. 797. Available at: https://doi.org/10.3390/app12020797.

Kini, V.G., C, S.P. and Ganeshrao, S.B. (2023) 'Distance Validation and Role of High Fidelity VR Environments on Embodiment and Enjoyment', in *2023 International Conference on Computational Intelligence and Knowledge Economy (ICCIKE). 2023 International Conference on Computational Intelligence and Knowledge Economy (ICCIKE)*, Dubai, United Arab Emirates: IEEE, pp. 215–220. Available at: https://doi.org/10.1109/ICCIKE58312.2023.10131855.

Krüger, J.M., Palzer, K. and Bodemer, D. (2022) 'Learning with augmented reality: Impact of dimensionality and spatial abilities', *Computers and Education Open*, 3, p. 100065. Available at: https://doi.org/10.1016/j.caeo.2021.100065.

Li, X. *et al.* (2018) 'A critical review of virtual and augmented reality (VR/AR) applications in construction safety', *Automation in Construction*, 86, pp. 150–162. Available at: https://doi.org/10.1016/j.autcon.2017.11.003.

Luo, Y. *et al.* (2023) 'Investigating the impact of scenario and interaction fidelity on training experience when designing immersive virtual reality-based construction safety training', *Developments in the Built Environment*, 16, p. 100223. Available at: https://doi.org/10.1016/j.dibe.2023.100223.

Ma, Y. *et al.* (2020) 'Seeing the invisible: From imagined to virtual urban landscapes', *Cities*, 98, p. 102559. Available at: https://doi.org/10.1016/j.cities.2019.102559.

Menzies, R.J. *et al.* (2016) 'An objective measure for the visual fidelity of virtual reality and the risks of falls in a virtual environment', *Virtual Reality*, 20(3), pp. 173–181. Available at: https://doi.org/10.1007/s10055-016-0288-6.

Min, X. *et al.* (2019) 'VPModel: High-Fidelity Product Simulation in a Virtual-Physical Environment', *IEEE Transactions on Visualization and Computer Graphics*, 25(11), pp. 3083–3093. Available at: https://doi.org/10.1109/TVCG.2019.2932276.

Miyake, M. *et al.* (2017) 'OUTDOOR MARKERLESS AUGMENTED REALITY', p. 10.

Moser, S. and Lewalter, D. (2024) 'The impact of instructional support via generative learning strategies on the perception of visual authenticity, learning outcomes, and satisfaction in AR-based learning', *European Journal of Psychology of Education* [Preprint]. Available at: https://doi.org/10.1007/s10212-024-00813-w.

Muller, P., Cohn, L.J. and Schmorrow, C.D. (2006) 'The Fidelity Matrix: Mapping System Fidelity to Training Outcome', p. 11.

Nasrazadani, H. *et al.* (2020) 'Implementation of Building Information Modeling on Construction Site: Addressing the Technology Gap', *Construction Research Congress*, p. 10.

Paravizo, E. (2019) 'Using a game engine for simulation in ergonomics analysis, design and education_ An exploratory study', *Applied Ergonomics*, p. 7.

Pastel, S. *et al.* (2021) 'Comparison of gaze accuracy and precision in real-world and virtual reality', *Virtual Reality*, 25(1), pp. 175–189. Available at: https://doi.org/10.1007/s10055-020-00449-3.

Sait, U. *et al.* (2019) 'A framework outlining a daylight responsive model for smart buildings', *Journal of Physics: Conference Series*, 1343(1), p. 012166. Available at: https://doi.org/10.1088/1742-6596/1343/1/012166.

Sermet, Y. and Demir, I. (2022) 'GeospatialVR: A web-based virtual reality framework for collaborative environmental simulations', *Computers & Geosciences*, 159, p. 105010. Available at: https://doi.org/10.1016/j.cageo.2021.105010.

Shi, Y. *et al.* (2016) 'A Multiuser Shared Virtual Environment for Facility Management', *Procedia Engineering*, 145, pp. 120–127. Available at: https://doi.org/10.1016/j.proeng.2016.04.029.

Stals, A. and Caldas, L. (2022) 'State of XR research in architecture with focus on professional practice – a systematic literature review', *Architectural Science Review*, 65(2), pp. 138–146. Available at: https://doi.org/10.1080/00038628.2020.1838258.

Sturgis, S. (2017) *Embodied and whole life carbon assessment for architects.* London, UK: RIBA, pp. 10–16.

UNEP (2009) *Buildings and Climate Change: A Summary for Decision-Makers. United Nations Environmental Programme.* Paris, pp. 1–62.

United Nations (2022) 'For a livable climate: Net-zero commitments must be backed by credible action'. Available at: https://www.un.org/en/climatechange/net-zero-coalition.

Waller, D., Knapp, D. and Hunt, E. (2001) 'Spatial Representations of Virtual Mazes: The Role of Visual Fidelity and Individual Differences', *Human Factors: The Journal of the Human Factors and Ergonomics Society*, 43(1), pp. 147–158. Available at: https://doi.org/10.1518/001872001775992561.

Walmsley, A. and Kersten, T.P. (2019) 'LOW-COST DEVELOPMENT OF AN INTERACTIVE, IMMERSIVE VIRTUAL REALITY EXPERIENCE OF THE HISTORIC CITY MODEL STADE 1620', *The International Archives of the Photogrammetry, Remote Sensing and Spatial Information Sciences*, XLII-2/W17, pp. 405–411. Available at: https://doi.org/10.5194/isprs-archives-XLII-2-W17-405-2019.

Weidner, F. *et al.* (2023) 'A Systematic Review on the Visualization of Avatars and Agents in AR & VR displayed using Head-Mounted Displays', *IEEE Transactions on Visualization and Computer Graphics*, 29(5), pp. 2596–2606. Available at: https://doi.org/10.1109/TVCG.2023.3247072.

Wen, J. and Gheisari, M. (2020) 'Using virtual reality to facilitate communication in the AEC domain: a systematic review', *Construction Innovation*, 20(3), pp. 509–542. Available at: https://doi.org/10.1108/CI-11-2019-0122.

Wiberg, A.H. *et al.* (2019) 'Visualisation of KPIs in zero emission neighbourhoods for improved stakeholder participation using Virtual Reality', *IOP Conference Series: Earth and Environmental Science*, 323(1), p. 012074. Available at: https://doi.org/10.1088/1755-1315/323/1/012074.

Zhang, Y. *et al.* (2020) 'Virtual reality applications for the built environment: Research trends and opportunities', *Automation in Construction*, 118, p. 103311. Available at: https://doi.org/10.1016/j.autcon.2020.103311.

Study on Development and Application of Smart Factory Digital Twin System

Jae Sung Kim, Dae Kyung Kim, and Seok Chan Jeong

Abstract The digital twin system enhances productivity in smart factories by facilitating real-time monitoring and control of manufacturing facilities and processes. This study introduces a novel digital twin model, along with its implementation results, for smart factory applications. We implemented a digital twin testbed system for a USB packaging facility and an industrial robot designed for assembly operations, based on this new model. Both applications employed 3D digital models that replicated actual facilities and processes with high fidelity, a novel approach developed to enable interoperability and control through the OPC UA protocol. The system supports the real-time monitoring and management of information pertaining to facilities and processes across multiple devices.

Keywords Digital twin · Smart factory · Digital twin model · OPC UA · Extended reality

1 Introduction

Digital twin technology in smart factories enables real-time monitoring, analysis and control of on-site facilities and manufacturing processes. Additionally, the simulation and visualization of manufacturing data significantly reduce both the cost and time required for production. Recognized as a foundational technology for the development of smart factories, digital twin technology plays a critical role in

J. S. Kim
Department of Industrial Management Engineering, Hanbat National University, Daejeon, South Korea
e-mail: jaesungkim@hanbat.ac.kr

D. K. Kim
ICT Group, Mugungwha Information Technology, Seoul, South Korea
e-mail: dkkim@m-it.co.kr

S. C. Jeong (✉)
Department of e-Business, Dong-Eui University, Busan, South Korea
e-mail: scjeong@deu.ac.kr

T. Jung et al. (eds.), *XR and Metaverse*, Springer Proceedings in Business and Economics, https://doi.org/10.1007/978-3-031-77975-6_29

supporting decision-making by simulating and optimizing the monitoring of manufacturing facilities, predictive maintenance, and the design, construction, and operation of production lines within a digital environment (Lee et al. 2021). Within such a framework, the digital counterpart of an actual factory is connected in real-time through a network, facilitating the monitoring and diagnosis of the factory's condition. Predictions of future conditions and responses are generated using simulation technology. Furthermore, extended reality (XR) technology is employed to visualize and manage various manufacturing data, thereby enhancing decision-making and operational control in the field.

To effectively implement a smart factory system, systematic collection and exchange of data from field devices such as actuators and sensors are crucial, along with the integration of various facilities and systems comprising the actual factory. The open platform communications unified architecture (OPC UA) protocol is instrumental in achieving interoperability and connectivity across heterogeneous platforms. Despite its advantages, research and implementation cases utilizing OPC UA in smart factories remain scarce. Furthermore, although digital twin technology offers numerous benefits in manufacturing, there is a noticeable deficiency in technical discussions on the design and construction of models for digital twins. Consequently, it is imperative to develop a model design and implementation method that considers the available information on the physical object and the required level of digital fidelity (Park et al. 2021).

This study presents the results of implementing an XR-based digital twin model and testbed system for smart factories. Utilizing the proposed digital twin model, the actual facility module, programmable logic controller (PLC), and digital models for each process were monitored in real-time using the OPC UA protocol, enabling the implementation of a digital twin system that supports bidirectional interlocking control.

2 Literature Review

Digital twins are an advanced technology that create digital replicas of physical entities, allowing for the prediction and management of changes and behaviors through various simulations and analyses throughout their lifecycles. This integration of physical and virtual systems ensures comprehensive synchronization of information at all stages of manufacturing. From initial design to production and ongoing management, digital twins accurately reflect the real-world manufacturing environment and its operational dynamics, thereby enhancing simulation and optimization processes. Moreover, they streamline production operations by enabling the pre-verification of factory designs, monitoring operations, and detecting and forecasting anomalies not observable on the physical manufacturing floor (Lin et al. 2020).

2.1 Digital Twin

Digital twins facilitate the creation of detailed digital replicas of physical objects, predicting and managing how these objects' properties change over time through diverse simulations and analyses. To implement a robust digital twin system, it is essential to integrate a variety of dynamic and static models, including property information, process models for objects, analysis and simulation models, virtualized control systems, and communication network models. These models must be closely interconnected and capable of simulating and modeling in three dimensions with a degree of realism comparable to the physical objects. The digital twin connects to physical objects through sensor data, reflecting the current state, predicting future scenarios through simulation, and supporting optimal responses. Digital twins extend beyond merely replicating physical systems into virtual environments; they continuously update to mirror the performance, maintenance, and status data of the physical system, achieving real-time data linkage and movement replication (Madni et al. 2019).

A digital twin integrates physical and virtual systems to synchronize information across the entire lifecycle of manufacturing activities, from factory and product design to production and management. This technology accurately mirrors the actual manufacturing environment, including operational and functional elements, facilitating the simulation and optimization of manufacturing processes. Such integration streamlines production operations through pre-verification of factory designs, monitoring of operations, and the detection and prediction of anomalies that are otherwise undetectable at the physical manufacturing site (Negri et al. 2017).

2.2 OPC-UA

The OPC UA, established by the OPC Foundation in 2008, is a machine-to-machine (M2M) communication protocol that has become a standard in various industries owing to its high interoperability across heterogeneous platforms, and the stability and reliability of its data exchange. To implement a smart factory effectively, it is crucial to interconnect various facilities and systems within the factory and collect and exchange data efficiently from field devices. Despite the diversity of facilities and devices used at production sites, achieving interoperability among them remains challenging. For systematic data transmission, reception, and bidirectional control in such varied operating environments, the application of the OPC UA protocol is essential. Current research focuses on designing a cyber physical production system (CPPS) architecture using standardized methods for data processing as prescribed by the OPC UA (Jo et al. 2019, Liu et al. 2019). Additionally, methodologies are being proposed for system design and implementation that involve the collection and monitoring of data from equipment and sensors using the OPC UA and the Asset Administration Shell (AAS) (Lee et al. 2021).

Interoperability between heterogeneous systems via the OPC UA is primarily facilitated through the interfaces between the PLCs. PLCs receive data, such as temperature, current, and vibration, from field devices like IoT sensors. They process this data sequentially according to the programmed logic and then deliver the resulting output to an actuator to control the facility. The OPC UA supports bidirectional communication by providing a unified and standardized interface for communication protocols from different PLC vendors. Furthermore, the OPC UA enables PLCs to securely exchange plant floor data with higher-level systems such as SCADA, MES, and ERP, which are essential for the operation of smart factories.

3 Design of Digital Twin Model

The proposed digital twin model is depicted in Fig. 1. In this model, each facility process is modularized, with each module operating within a server-client structure that exchanges data through the OPC UA protocol, alongside a module manager that integrates and manages the status and control data for each module. This structural design ensures real-time synchronization of the status and process data for each module with both the 3D digital model and the virtual/augmented reality model of the actual equipment corresponding to each module. Consequently, the movement of the actual equipment and its status/process data can be visualized and observed in various environments.

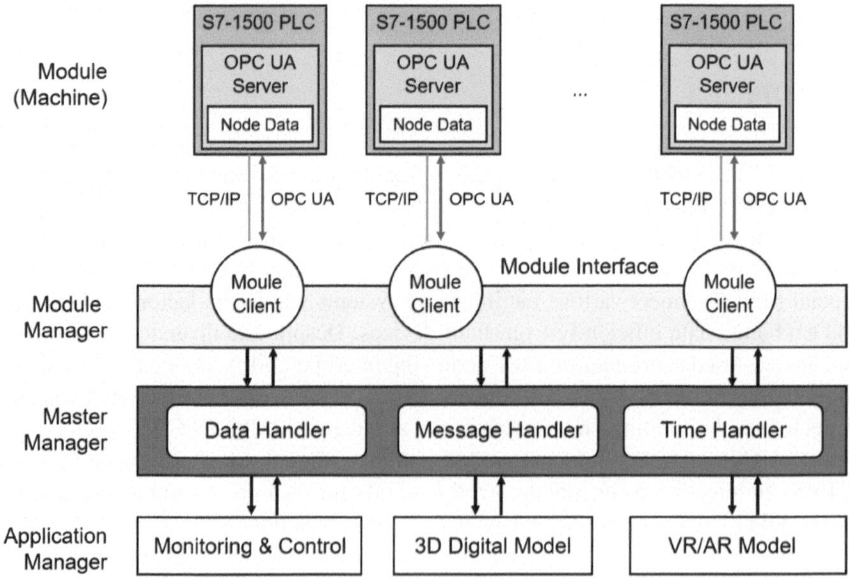

Fig. 1 Proposed digital twin model

The module manager oversees the network functions necessary for data exchange with each module (equipment) and manages the module clients that act as node clients for autonomous data exchange with various external systems. Additionally, the module manager distributes the data exchange messages received from the overarching master manager to each client or forwards the sensor data collected by each module client to the master manager.

The master manager processes and organizes various data collected from each module, liaising between the module manager and the application manager, and subsequently delivers this data to the application manager. The data handler is responsible for defining and managing the metadata related to the sensors, input/output (I/O), and events of each module. Concurrently, the message handler manages the flow of sensor and event messages to and from the module manager. The time handler is tasked with processing and managing time and event data to ensure synchronization. The application manager handles the essential functions of the top-level applications vital for the operation of the digital twins. This includes monitoring and controlling the equipment and processes using the status/process data, sensor/event messages, and synchronized time data obtained through the master manager. Moreover, the 3D digital model and extended reality model are linked in real -time to facilitate the synchronization and visualization of data.

4 Implementation of Digital Twin System and Applications

A digital twin system was developed to evaluate the performance of the proposed model by applying it to smart -factory facilities and processes. Specifically, a digital twin model was implemented in USB packaging facilities and with industrial robots to establish a smart -factory digital twin system.

4.1 Smart Factory Testbed Systems

4.1.1 USB Packaging Facilities and Processes

The USB packaging facility encompasses six detailed processes: input, inspection, marking, additional inspection, covering, and loading. Figure 2 presents a physical model of the USB packaging equipment (Fig. 2a) and a corresponding 3D CAD model (Fig. 2b).

In this facility, a portable storage device featuring two types of engraved logos was packaged and then placed into simple storage after undergoing the six detailed processes. The main functions of each step are listed in Table 1. These include feeding the lower box for USB packaging via the transfer conveyor belt, inspecting the color, height, and material of the USB, and loading the USB into the lower box. After laser marking a user-specified logo on the USB surface, a 6-axis robot assembles the USB

Fig. 2 Smart factory testbed for USB packaging

(a) USB packaging facility

(b) CAD model for USB packaging facility

upper cover. Subsequently, the packaged product was loaded into simple storage, and the pallet was collected. Each process was interconnected via a conveyor belt and controlled by a SIEMENS S7-1500 PLC.

Table 1 Geometry simplification in the smart factory testbed for USB packaging

Stage	Before			After		
	Vertices	Edges	Polygons	Vertices	Edges	Polygons
1. Feeding	315,787	910,561	593,432	70,961	201,107	130,536
2. Checking	323,582	929,124	604,258	80,057	228,243	148,481
3. Marking	293,758	834,888	539,962	54,996	153,894	99,195
4. Inspection	359,415	1,022,695	661,991	52,056	131,015	79,470
5. Assembly	334,606	941,458	625,611	44,536	121,146	76,973
6. Storage	365,395	1,031,931	664,948	57,522	146,970	105,842
Total	1,992,543	5,670,657	3,690,202	360,128	982,375	640,497

4.1.2 Industrial Robot for Assembly

The second application of the digital twin model involves Kawasaki's BX165L robot, an industrial robot designed for assembly operations. The Kawasaki BX165L is exceptionally versatile, well-suited for use in automotive, aerospace, and electronics manufacturing. Figure 3 displays the actual robot and its CAD model.

The BX165L is a 6-axis robot that offers a high degree of flexibility and precision in movement. This robot can handle payloads up to 165 kg and has a maximum reach of 2597 mm. It includes a unit process that picks up and assembles components located on a designated workbench, controlled by a Kawasaki PLC.

4.2 Development of 3D Digital Model

The development of a digital model that accurately represents a real model in virtual space is crucial for realizing a digital twin. In this study, 3D CAD data from an actual facility and process were utilized to create a digital model, ensuring high fidelity in its representation. Unnecessary geometric data were removed and converted using 3D Max and Maya software to produce a 3D digital model optimized for real-time visualization and monitoring. This involved simplifying overly detailed geometric elements in the 3D CAD by repositioning detailed parts of existing models, creating boundary boxes, making multi-cuts, and applying normal mapping. We significantly

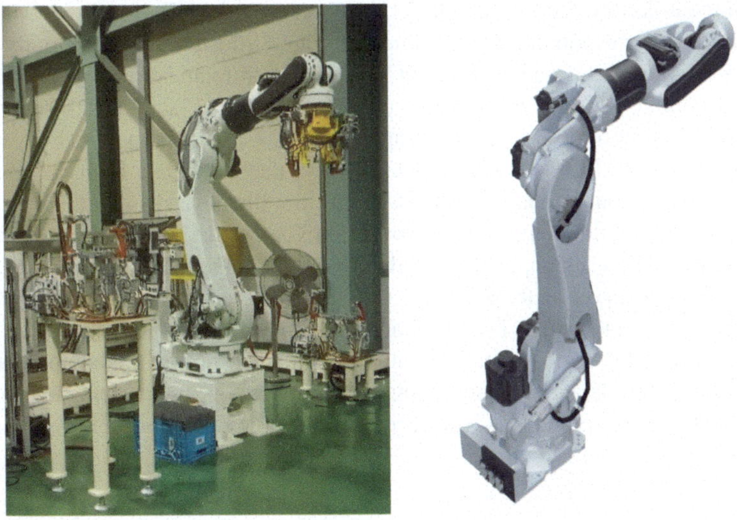

(a) Robot testbed for assembly (b) CAD model for robot

Fig. 3 Industrial robot testbed for assembly

Table 2 Geometry simplification in the industrial robot testbed for assembly

Before			After		
Vertices	Edges	Polygons	Vertices	Edges	Polygons
76,353	454,632	151,544	19,926	114,234	38,078

optimized the number of unnecessary polygons, which dramatically improved real-time rendering speeds. This process maintained the visibility of the digital model while reducing the number of polygons by more than 70% compared to the original 3D CAD model (Table 2).

To establish a real-time connection between the movement of components operating in a physical facility and their digital counterparts, kinematic modeling of the digital components is required. For this purpose, the sequence and movement of the detailed subprocesses within the facility were analyzed, leading to the development of a sub-process model, as shown in Fig. 4a. Based on this subprocess model for each facility, the Born structure was applied to the moving parts through the rigging operation, as illustrated in Fig. 4b. Motion timing and range were then calculated and implemented using the kinematic information from the actual components.

4.3 OPC UA Data Communication

The proposed digital twin system is structured such that sensor data from each piece of equipment is acquired via the OPC UA server on the PLC of each module and relayed to the corresponding module client. Figure 3 illustrates the communication structure of the module client for OPC UA data communication with a detailed process (module). Within each module, the OPC UA server facilitates the transmission and reception of process data through the OPC UA Client and OPC UA of the module client. The PLC of each module conveys the status data from the sensors, solenoids, and actuators via an OPC UA. The raw files that display the operating status of each module are parsed and converted via the PLC data interface into the format required by each application, and then forwarded to the master manager.

The OPC UA server on the PLC directs the I/O data related to each input (sensor, OPC input data) and output (solenoid and actuator, OPC output data) to the PLC data interface, which subsequently monitors and synchronizes the equipment and processes. Control data transmitted through the application and master managers are relayed to the PLC via the PLC interface to control the operation of the equipment (Fig. 5).

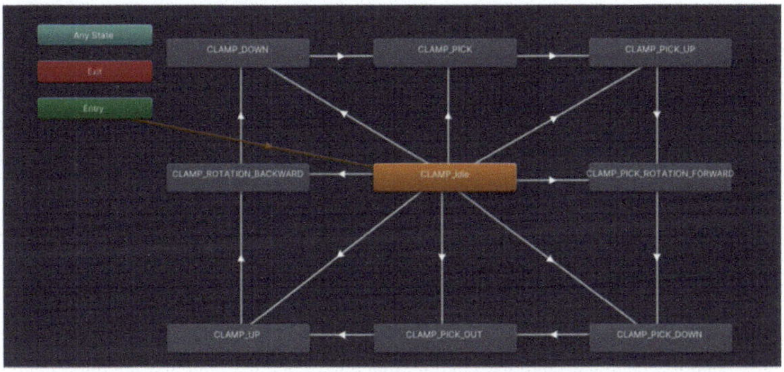

(a) Example of sub process model

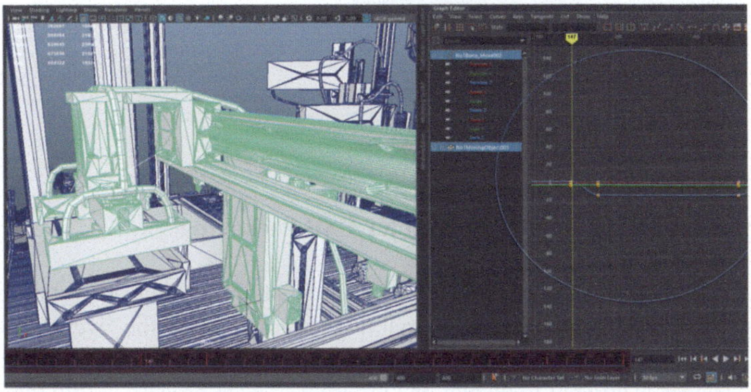

(b) Example of kinematic modelling

Fig. 4 Example of subprocess model and kinematic modeling

4.4 Process Monitoring and Visualization

After transforming the detailed 3D CAD physical model into a 3D digital model optimized for real-time visualization, it was configured to enable interoperability and bidirectional control between the digital and physical models via OPC UA communication. This system transmits and receives status information regarding detailed processes and facilities from the PLC of each module, and visualizes them in real time alongside the 3D digital model. The progress of each process was monitored and managed using a dashboard. Additionally, fundamental control functions, such as starting, stopping, and emergency stopping of the actual process, were executed in the digital model through bidirectional communication based on the OPC UA.

Fig. 5 Module client for OPC UA data communication

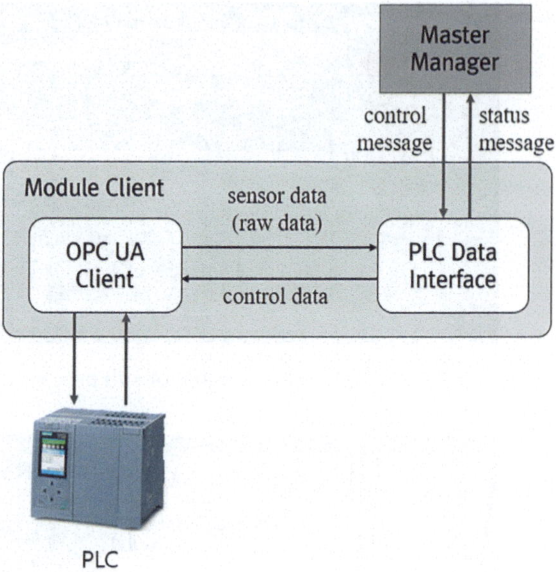

4.4.1 Smart Factory Testbed System for USB Packaging

The I/O data received via the OPC UA communication are relayed to the master manager through the module client, enabling monitoring of the overall process progress as well as individual processes (Fig. 6). The data transmitted from each module manager is utilized to display the progress of each process within the smart factory and industrial robots through an intuitive graphical user interface (GUI). The data collected from the sensors are used to compile essential process metrics, such as the number of tasks progressed or completed for each process, the duration of each process, and the average time required. These metrics aid in future process analysis. When a specific process is selected, the I/O status and progress of each process can be verified.

The status information from the main sensors or solenoids of each process can be visualized in a time-series chart (Fig. 6b) to facilitate a detailed understanding of the progress. Commands to start and emergency stop processes can be issued via buttons located in the upper -right corner of each process interface to control the actual physical equipment. By synchronizing the process I/O status data with the 3D digital model in real time, the status of the actual facility's processes can be visualized and monitored in a digital space. Additionally, process start, stop, and emergency stop commands can be executed directly from the digital model using buttons for each module, similar to those on the dashboard.

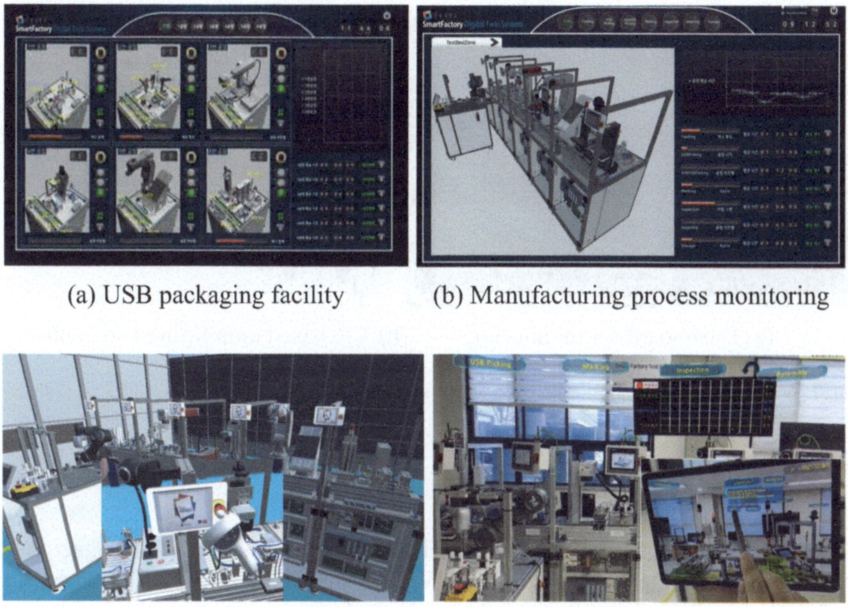

(a) USB packaging facility (b) Manufacturing process monitoring

(c) VR-based monitoring and control (d) AR-based monitoring and control

Fig. 6 Visualization and monitoring for USB packaging

4.4.2 Industrial Robot Testbed System for Assembly

Figure 7 illustrates the results of visualization through a dashboard and virtual reality for the real-time monitoring of the operating status of an industrial robot testbed. Status data such as the speed and position of the robot arm, and the revolutions per minute (RPM) of each axis motor, are collected and monitored in real time using sensors and control PLCs. This collected data is utilized in a predictive maintenance system to diagnose abnormalities and failures in the robots.

Simultaneously, the status data of the robot are transmitted to the VR/AR application manager, who can monitor and observe the robot's status in real time within a virtual reality environment. In this system, commands to start and emergency stop the robot can be executed directly within the virtual reality environment.

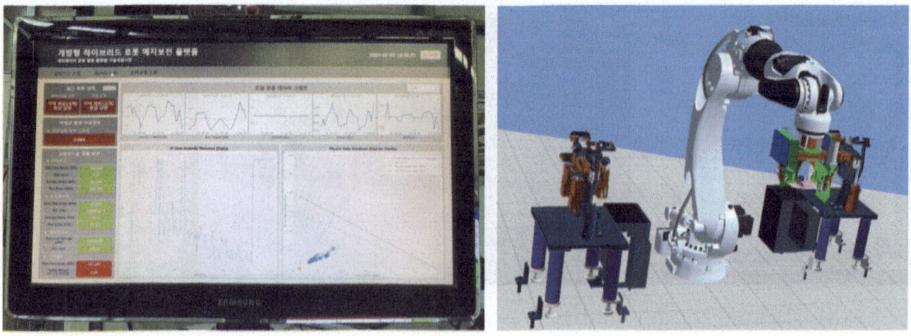

(a) Dashboard for monitoring (b) VR-based monitoring and control

Fig. 7 Visualization and monitoring for assembly robot

5 Conclusion

This study introduced a digital twin model specifically designed for smart factories and explored its practical applications. We implemented a digital twin system in facilities specializing in USB packaging and in industrial robots for assembly operations. Both applications employed 3D digital models that replicated actual facilities and processes with high fidelity, a novel approach developed to enable interoperability and control through the OPC UA protocol. Through the module manager assigned to each process, I/O status information was transmitted and received from the PLC, facilitating the control of the digital model by sending start and emergency stop commands to the PLC. Furthermore, the integration of dashboard, 3D digital, and XR models enabled real-time monitoring of both overall and detailed process progress.

While this study focused on the design and implementation of a digital twin model for smart factory facilities, it identified limitations in the accumulation, analysis, and simulation of big data from actual processes. Future research will aim to collect a more diverse array of process data and enhance data analysis capabilities to improve productivity analysis and process optimization based on actual process improvements.

Acknowledgements This study was financially supported by Hanbat National University Financial Accounting Research Fund in 2024.

Bibliography

Jo, G., Jang, S.H. and Jeong, J. (2019) A Study on CPPS Architecture Integrated with Centralized OPC UA Server, *The Journal of The Institute of Internet, Broadcasting and Communication*, 19: 73-82

Lee, Y. and Jeong, J. (2021) Design and Implementation of Facility Monitoring System based on AAS and OPC UA for Smart Manufacturing, *The Journal of The Institute of Internet, Broadcasting and Communication*,12: 41-47.

Lee, D., Song, S., Lee, C., Noh, S.D., Yun, S. and Lee, H. (2021) Development and Application of Digital Twin for the Design Verification and Operation Management of Automated Material Handling Systems, *Korean Journal of Computational Design and Engineering*, 26:313-323.

Lin, W.D. and Low, M.Y.H. (2020). Concept Design of a System Architecture for a Manufacturing Cyber-physical Digital Twin System, *2020 IEEE International Conference on Industrial Engineering and Engineering Management*, pp. 1320–1324.

Liu, C., Vengayil, H., Lu, Y. and Xu, X. (2019) A Cyber-Physical Machine Tools Platform using OPC UA and MTConnect, *Journal of Manufacturing Systems*, 51: 61-74.

Madni, A.M., Madni, C.C. and Lucero, S.D. (2019) Leveraging Digital Twin Technology in Model-Based Systems Engineering, *Systems*, 7:1-13.

Negri, E., Fumagalli, L. and Macchi, M. (2017) A Review of the Roles of Digital Twin in CPS-Based Produ ction Systems, *Procedia manufacturing*, 11: 939-948

Park, K.T., Son, Y.H., Ko, S.W. and Noh, S.D. (2021) Digital Twin and Reinforcement Learning-Based Resilient Production Control for Micro Smart Factory, *Applied Sciences*, 11: 1-20.

Development of ICT-IoT-VR Ocean Healing Platform Using Wearable Device Linkage Application

Jin Hyeok Park, Yun Seo Choi, and Hak Soo Lim

Abstract The rapid advancement of ICT technologies, including IoT and VR, has enabled innovative healthcare applications. This study proposes an ICT-IoT-VR ocean healing platform utilizing wearable devices for comprehensive health management. Previous research demonstrates the efficacy of wearable devices for continuous monitoring and real-time data collection, as well as VR's potential in psychological therapy and stress relief. This platform integrates wearable devices to monitor biometric data during ocean healing activities, providing personalized health management programs through real-time data collection. VR content simulating ocean environments enhances the therapeutic experience. Smartwatches measure physical activity, heart rate, and steps. This comprehensive approach leverages advanced ICT technologies for personalized health services. Future research will validate the platform's effectiveness through extensive user testing and refine the system for broader healthcare applications.

Keywords ICT convergence · Ocean healing · Healing content · Wearable devices · Health management

1 Introduction

Nowadays, due to various factors such as medical advances, improved living conditions, and balanced nutrient intake, life expectancy has increased and the aging population has increased accordingly. It is no longer the goal for people to live long,

J. H. Park · Y. S. Choi · H. S. Lim (✉)
Marine Natural Disaster Research Department, Korea Institute of Ocean and Technology, Busan, South Korea
e-mail: hslim@kiost.ac.kr

J. H. Park
e-mail: jhpark@kiost.ac.kr

Y. S. Choi
e-mail: dbstj69@kiost.ac.kr

T. Jung et al. (eds.), *XR and Metaverse*, Springer Proceedings in Business and Economics, https://doi.org/10.1007/978-3-031-77975-6_30

but people have become interested in living well. The most important factor in living well is health (Kos & Umek 2018), and the number of individuals seeking to manage their health has increased, which has naturally led to an overall trend in society. However, the existing health management system began to be unable to keep up with the increasing demand because it was a system in which specialized groups and experts managed consumers (Chen et al. 2023). Accordingly, the need arose for individuals to directly manage their health, and in response to this need, health management devices have also developed in a direction to increase convenience for general users. In particular, with the advent of smartphones and smartwatches and the development of IT technologies such as 5G and Wi-Fi, healthcare services that can be easily used by individuals have emerged. Related researchers are paying attention to the potential of wearable devices in healthcare (Kos & Umek 2018), and are expanding the scope of use (Pourbemany et al. 2023) beyond simply health management using wearable devices to providing content or programs necessary for health management. With the advancement of IT technology, the development of platforms for personalized health services, which measure biometric changes in real-time during health activities and programs, is becoming increasingly prevalent. In South Korea, due to its geographical characteristics surrounded by the sea on three sides, numerous studies have been conducted to actively utilize ocean resources. Recently, under the leadership of the government, there have been continuous efforts to develop and applicate ocean resources (Shim et al. 2023; Winarto et al. 2023) and to complete or promote the construction of ocean healing centers that offer health management programs through physical activities in seawater. To verify the effects and efficacy of ocean resources, research has primarily focused on analyzing components based on chemical and biological knowledge and conducting clinical trials (Kwak et al. 2023; Shin et al. 2023a, b). Studies demonstrating the improvement of physical capabilities and body enhancements through specific activities have mainly employed methods of measuring and analyzing biometric information before and after the experience (Shin et al. 2023a, b). The method involves using a smartwatch to measure biometric information, making it accessible for the general public to wear and capable of measuring data even during high-intensity physical activities like underwater exercise and running (Shin et al. 2024; Shin et al. 2023a, b). In addition to direct utilization of ocean resources and geographical characteristics for health promotion, research has also recently been conducted to utilize ocean landscapes as resources to relieve stress (Hong et al. 2024). These studies involve shooting videos with special cameras to create VR content, which is then provided to users using special devices such as Head Mounted Displays (HMDs) to induce psychological calmness and alleviate stress. Hong et al. produced VR content featuring the scenery of Myeongsasimni Beach in Wando, South Korea, and conducted experiments with a small group to test the stress-relief effects of the VR content (Hong et al. 2024). This study is significant as it attempts to demonstrate the effects of VR content through preliminary experiments, although further validation is required for the experimental groups and methods. The second chapter categorizes existing studies on the core technical elements of the proposed method, such as wearable devices, VR content, and platforms, and explains the significance of each study to aid understanding of the technical elements and their connections. The third chapter explains the overall proposed technology and the implementation and results of each element. The presented "Development of ICT-IoT-VR ocean healing platform using wearable device linkage application" is in the intermediate research stage and continuously incorporates improvement measures, with some aspects introduced from an idea perspective. Particularly, the completion of the platform and the recommendation of ocean healing programs will be implemented in the "Living Lab" experiment scheduled for the end of 2024. The effectiveness of VR content for stress relief and the usability of the platform will be verified through additional research. The fourth chapter concludes by summarizing the current status and future research plans of the proposed method, emphasizing its necessity and importance. This will provide significant insights into the potential development of ocean healing methods by integrating IT technology with traditional health management, particularly in ocean healing.

2 Related Works

2.1 Wearable Devices

With the rapid advancement of medicine, patients are now able to receive personalized medical services in hospitals. However, precision medicine applications are mostly available only when patients are hospitalized (Wu et al. 2022). Since patients do not stay in hospitals for extended periods, their lifestyle and environment after discharge can significantly impact disease management and prevention. Therefore, the concept of precision health management focusing on disease prevention has been proposed and is continually evolving (Wu et al. 2022). As the demand for remote health monitoring and treatment increases, there has been a surge in the development of miniaturized smart health devices (Nag et al. 2017). These devices generate real-time data on biometric signals, aiding physicians in formulating treatment plans. Despite their small size, wearable devices are expected to continuously detect, collect, and upload various physiological data, thus enhancing the quality of life (Seneviratne et al. 2017). These devices support cost-effective, patient-centered healthcare models that are more accessible, flexible, and proactive (Vakhter et al. 2023). The continuous advancement of wearable technology expands its application possibilities in various fields such as healthcare, fitness, and entertainment. Specifically, the combination of wearable devices with AI and big data analytics holds potential for personalized health management and predictive analytics. This enables users to monitor their health status in real-time, effectively contributing to disease prevention (Seneviratne et al. 2017). The rapid development of medical technologies has enabled patients to receive personalized healthcare services even when they are not hospitalized. Wearable devices, in particular, offer continuous monitoring and data collection capabilities that enhance disease prevention and management. These devices support a shift towards more accessible, flexible, and proactive healthcare models, integrating real-time monitoring, AI, and big data analytics (Wu et al. 2022). This integration is expected to significantly improve the quality of healthcare services and patient outcomes.

2.2 VR Contents

VR content can be customized to create specific experiences tailored to the purpose and the user. Due to the improved quality of recent VR content, numerous studies have been conducted in the healthcare field (Ahilan et al. 2023; Rizzo et al. 2017, 2021; Rizzo & Koenig 2017; Rizzo & Shilling 2017; Vlake et al. 2023; Yeh et al. 2020). Ahilan et al. proposed a VR-based IoT embedded system for stress diagnosis (Ahilan et al. 2023). This system measures physiological parameters such as electromyography (EMG), galvanic skin response (GSR), oxygen saturation level, and heart rate to detect stress early. The collected data is transmitted through a cloud platform, and MATLAB is used for statistical analysis of the stress state. The study found that VR technology, combined with pleasant music or videos, significantly reduces stress levels. Albert "Skip" Rizzo has conducted extensive research on using VR technology for psychological treatments, including PTSD therapy, ADHD diagnosis, and stress management (Rizzo et al., 2017, 2021; Rizzo & Koenig 2017; Rizzo & Shilling 2017; Vlake et al. 2023; Yeh et al. 2020). These studies highlight four critical points when planning healthcare programs using VR: patient-centered design, the relationship between immersion and treatment engagement, technological advancement and clinical application, and the integration of psychological theories. VR allows for experiences that are as close to reality as possible or the creation of specialized environments or conditions, enabling more in-depth psychological treatment. In conclusion, VR technology is establishing itself as an innovative tool in healthcare, particularly in mental health treatment. The advancement of this technology plays a crucial role in providing personalized and effective treatment methods. Future research and clinical applications are expected to expand its potential further. The integration of VR technology is poised to enhance the quality of medical services and significantly improve patients' quality of life.

2.3 Platform

The rapid advancement in technology has led to significant progress in healthcare and platform development. This section reviews existing studies on integrating advanced technologies such as IoT, and wearable devices into healthcare systems, explaining how platforms can be applied in health management and their key features. The development of IoT platforms enables remote health monitoring by providing real-time data on patients' physiological parameters. These platforms support continuous monitoring of vital signs, allowing healthcare providers to intervene timely.

Bublitz et al. (2019) proposed a wearable device integration system for healthcare delivery in developing countries. This study highlights the potential of wearable devices to collect data on various physiological parameters and upload it to a central system, aiding in early disease detection and management (Bublitz et al. 2019). Mobile health (mHealth) technologies have shown potential in improving healthcare access and quality, especially in remote and underserved areas. Khan et al. (2019) discussed the potential of mobile technologies in transforming healthcare systems in developing countries. mHealth applications enable remote consultations, health monitoring, and patient education, thereby reducing the burden on traditional healthcare facilities and improving patient outcomes (Karageorgos et al. 2018). Examining the key features of these platforms and their application in health management, we find that, platforms are designed to handle increasing data and user demands. For example, Wang et al. (2022) described an intelligent decision support platform using Hadoop architecture, which allows for vertical and horizontal scaling, enabling the platform to grow and adapt to user needs (Wang et al. 2022). In summary, integrating advanced technologies such as blockchain, IoT, and wearable devices into healthcare systems holds significant potential for improving data security, patient monitoring, and overall healthcare delivery. The platforms discussed in the reviewed studies provide a robust foundation for developing secure, efficient, and scalable healthcare solutions. Continued research and development in these areas will further enhance the capabilities of healthcare systems, leading to better patient outcomes and more efficient healthcare delivery.

3 Proposed Method

The ICT-IoT-VR ocean healing platform using wearable device linkage application proposed in this paper is a system expected to be utilized in ocean healing centers that are either completed or under construction near the sea across the country under government leadership, as stated in Chap. 1. The proposed technology consists of three main components: wearable devices, VR content, and an integrated platform. Before starting the full-scale research, a preliminary preparation stage was conducted to analyze the characteristics of the applicable ocean healing centers and to set up pilot ocean healing programs that match these characteristics. This was to shorten the time required for the actual operation of the ocean healing programs and the practical application of the system, and to select wearable devices suitable for measuring biometric data during ocean healing activities. After the preliminary preparation stage, biometric data were collected and analyzed using wearable devices and other biometric measurement instruments. This was to verify the effectiveness of the underwater ocean healing program on daily life and physical health, and to verify the effects of ocean healing programs based on underwater activities (Table 1).

After setting up the pilot ocean healing programs and planning experiments to verify the effectiveness of these programs, wearable devices that can be integrated with the platform to be developed were selected. Among several wearable devices,

Table 1 Initial set of features used for the experimentation collected biometric data for ocean healing program (underwater exercise)

No	List	Content	Data collection method
1	Physical activity	Number of steps, distance traveled, heart rate, etc	Wearable devices
2	Body composition	Weight, body fat mass, skeletal muscle mass, body fat percentage, BMI, etc	InBody measurement device
3	Balance ability	Double-leg stance, single-leg stance	K-Force plate
4	Muscle function	Maximum lower limb strength	Biodex system 3
5	SFT (Senior Fitness Test)	Upper limb strength, lower limb strength, upper limb flexibility, lower limb flexibility, dynamic balance, overall endurance	Muscle strength measurement device
6	Daily living	Ability to perform daily activities, health-related quality of life	Surveys
7	Sleep	Sleep patterns	Wearable devices, questionnaires
8	Gait pattern	Lower limb movement, lower limb muscle activation, etc	Motion analysis and electromyography sensors

including Fitbit, the Samsung Galaxy Watch was chosen based on criteria such as ease of use by the general public without expert assistance, the ability to measure biometric data during various physical activities, including underwater activities, and developer-friendliness during system development. The proposed technology results from research conducted on health management methods utilizing ocean resources. As mentioned in Chap. 1, ocean resources include not only specific substances obtainable from seawater but also all usable elements of the sea and beaches. This includes visual and auditory factors such as beach and underwater landscapes and the sounds of the sea. These resources are used to create VR content that can be utilized for psychological therapy, such as enhancing exercise capacity, improving physical abilities, and alleviating stress. This paper introduces the VR content and production methods created using special filming equipment at domestic and international tourist sites, including Myeongsasimni Beach in Wando and various locations in Micronesia. Lastly, it presents the overall structure and development methods of the platform, which is based on the functionality of storing and analyzing the measured biometric data and providing visual information, including graphs. This chapter provides a more detailed explanation of the development methods and features of the proposed technology introduced above.

3.1 Wearable Devices

To measure the biometric information of participants experiencing ocean healing programs at ocean healing centers utilizing ocean healing resources, it is essential to employ body-attached wearable devices that are either simple in their configuration or easy to attach and use. Since the participants of ocean healing programs are a diverse group with unspecified gender and age, devices requiring expert-level operation are impractical; hence, simple operation is necessary. In addition to simplicity, the devices must be capable of measuring various biometric data and allow for easy storage and upload of collected data to a separate system during the development phase. Samsung's Galaxy Watch was selected for the proposed method due to its capability of acquiring user data via the Samsung Health SDK and its simpler operation compared to other wearable devices. To integrate the biometric data measured by the Galaxy Watch with the self-developed platform, a proprietary application was developed to run on the Galaxy Watch. This application transmits biometric data via SAP communication. In the proposed method, heart rate and step count were considered the primary biometric data to be measured. These data points serve as fundamental data for analyzing the exercise effects during underwater activities in the verification phase of the ocean healing program. Figure 1 provides a brief explanation of the data communication between the Galaxy Watch and the developed application prototype, while Fig. 2 shows the actual measurement of biometric data using the Galaxy Watch running the developed application.

Fig. 1 Communication between wearable devices and applications using SAP communication

Fig. 2 Wearable device and application testing

In the proposed method, the performance of biometric data measurement by the wearable device and the data acquisition performance of the application were verified by measuring heart rate using a custom-developed application for the wearable device and an electrocardiogram (ECG)-based heart rate monitor. The heart rate was measured through an exercise stress test that increased to the maximum heart rate, and the regression determination coefficient was calculated using a regression estimation model. The results are shown in Fig. 3. In three trials, the lowest agreement rate between the developed wearable device and the ECG-based heart rate monitor was 65%, and the highest was 92%. The inconsistency and variability in measurement performance indicate areas that need improvement. Currently, additional enhancement work is ongoing, and future studies are expected to present improved heart rate measurement performance. This paper not only verifies the heart rate measurement performance but also analyzes the effectiveness of the ocean healing program by collecting biometric data through various methods, including the developed wearable device. The experiment was conducted over a total of 10 weeks, and the effectiveness of the ocean healing program was validated by observing significant reductions in weight, body fat percentage, and BMI, along with improvements in sleep quality, as measured through body composition analysis.

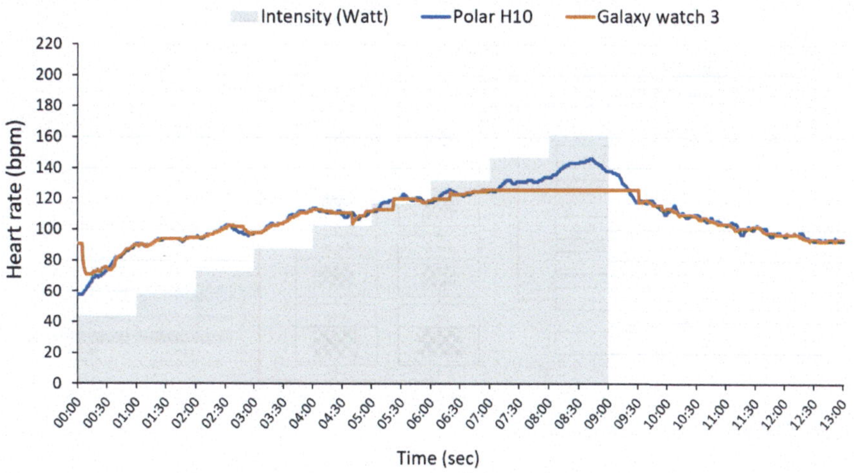

Fig. 3 Results of heart rate measurement using a wearable device

3.2 VR Contents

This paper not only verifies the effectiveness of an ocean healing program using wearable devices but also explores the potential for developing a new healing program utilizing ocean resources. It provides an immersive experience by simulating the ocean environment with VR content. The main goal is to achieve psychological stability and reduce stress by providing an immersive experience that simulates the marine environment with VR content. The development of this VR content goes through several stages. In this study, special filming was conducted using the Insta 360 camera at Myeongsasimni Beach in Wando and beaches in Micronesia. The video was produced in 8 k VR s3D (8192 × 4096 Top/Bottom) 30p, and Fig. 4 illustrates the VR video production process.

The Insta 360 is a specialized camera equipped with eight lenses. During the VR content production process, images captured by each lens are edited using stereo matching and synchronization to create the VR content. When the produced VR content is viewed through a Head Mounted Display (HMD), the user can experience vivid ocean scenery. This paper does not present the results of an experiment verifying the stress-relieving effects of the VR ocean healing content, as such an experiment was not conducted. However, in future research, we plan to conduct verification experiments involving visitors to various ocean healing centers and present the results to validate the effects.

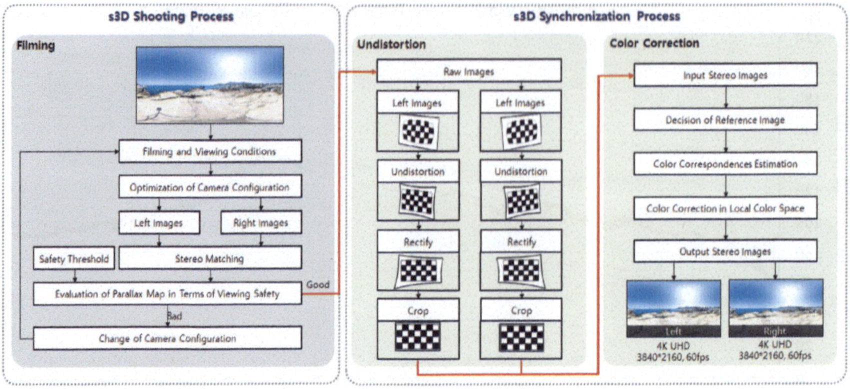

Fig. 4 The VR video production process

3.3 Platform

The ICT-IoT-VR ocean healing platform using a wearable device linkage application aims to measure biometric information using wearable devices. The collected data is then stored and analyzed on an integrated platform to provide personalized ocean healing services. Figure 5 illustrates the configuration of the wearable devices and the integrated platform. As shown in Fig. 6, the platform can directly receive and store data in a Web DB when communication with wearable devices is possible. If communication is not available, the biometric data measured by the device is stored locally and can be transmitted to the platform whenever a connection is established. At this time, as shown in Fig. 6, the Web DB stores the basic biometric information of participants in the ocean healing program, which is entered through a developed linkage application. During the program, biometric data measured by wearable devices are also stored. The platform offers different pages for the ocean healing center operators, platform administrators, and visitors. Administrators can use a dedicated page to analyze the participants' biometric data, recommend suitable ocean healing programs, and adjust schedules. Figure 7 briefly illustrates the process of using the wearable device linkage platform for both participants and administrators.

The data integration process between the database and the server is executed as shown in Fig. 8, and the resulting screen is depicted in Fig. 9. The platform recognizes the user's email address as their ID and displays information about the participant's experience program, along with data measured by wearable devices, including the average heart rate.

As shown in Fig. 9, ocean healing program instructors can use the platform's data analysis features to view analysis results presented in graphs. Based on these analyses, they can recommend personalized programs and manage ocean healing schedules, enabling efficient operation.

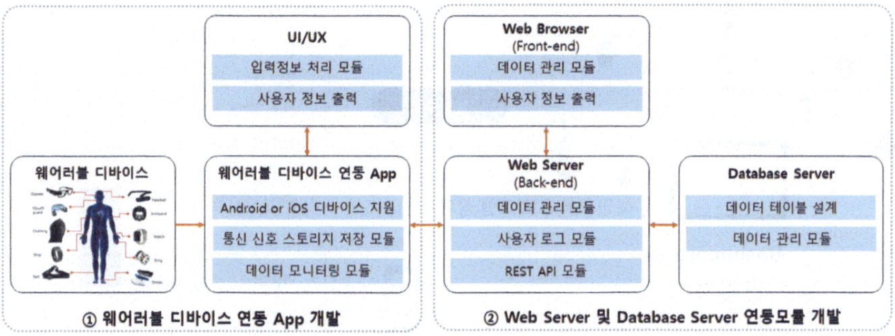

Fig. 5 Configuration between wearable device linkage application and DB and server

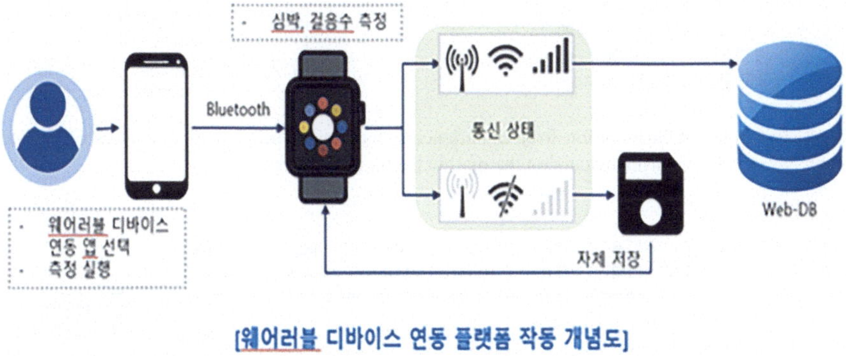

Fig. 6 Method of storing data according to communication with wearable device linkage application

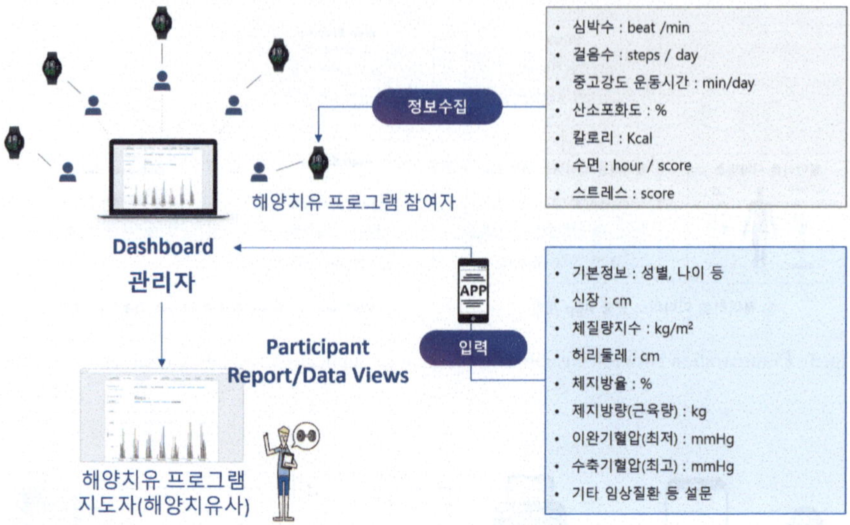

Fig. 7 Examples of information from experiencers that can be utilized by managers of marine healing centers and marine healers on the marine healing platform

이름	Email	센터	프로그램	평균 Heart	평균 Step	평균 Calorie	날짜	
		[illegible]	체험 1	89	2	0	2022-08-16 15시 08분 00초	Excel 다운로드
		[illegible]	체험 2	95	7	0	2022-08-16 13시 39분 30초	Excel 다운로드
		[illegible]	체험 4	97	7	0	2022-08-16 13시 38분 55초	Excel 다운로드
[illegible]	[illegible]	[illegible]	체험 5	89	1	1	2022-08-16 11시 19분 38초	Excel 다운로드
[illegible]	[illegible].com	[illegible]	체험 3	101	9	0	2022-08-16 08시 45분 54초	Excel 다운로드

Fig. 8 Storage of biometric data measured during the marine healing program experience

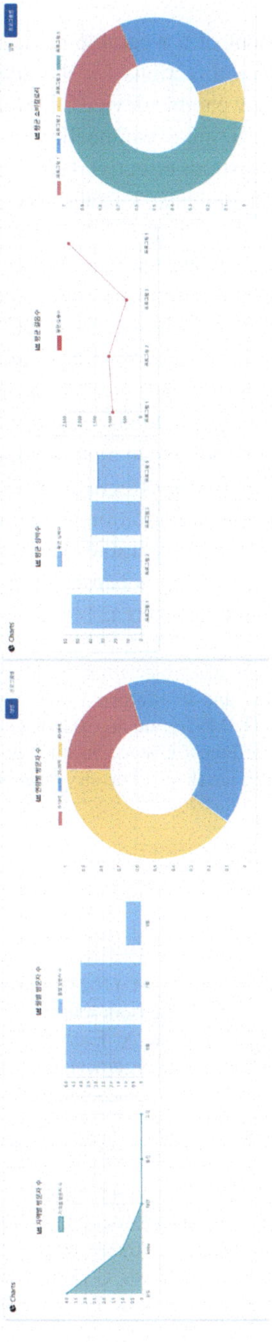

Fig. 9 Example of data analysis function of ocean healing platform

4 Conclusion

This paper presents the development of a wearable device platform based on ICT and IoT technologies, and proposes directions for the advancement of healthcare utilizing IT technologies, including wearable devices. Through this research, we aim to develop a healthcare program utilizing ocean healing resources, verify the effectiveness of the program, and establish an effective healthcare management system to offer personalized programs for patients. Furthermore, to expand the scope of available ocean healing resources, including ocean landscapes, we have developed ocean healing VR content. This VR content requires further development in terms of content composition and the addition of auditory stimuli, such as sounds with stress-relieving effects, and the validation of these effects needs to be addressed. Future research should focus on adding measurable biometric information through wearable devices, improving data processing methods based on communication status, and developing additional functions and database features for the wearable device integration platform. In subsequent studies, we aim to achieve overall performance improvements and provide validation for the effectiveness of ocean healing programs and the system, including those requiring additional verification. Additionally, we plan to actively introduce the developed wearable devices and platform as a new healthcare service, to be utilized across the ocean healing industry, including new ocean healing centers being established in Korea.

Acknowledgements This research was part of a project titled "Efficacy/standardization technology development of marine healing resources and its life cycle safety management", funded by the Ministry of Oceans and Fisheries, Korea (KIMST grant no. 20220027). And This study was carried out with the support of R&D Program for Forest Science Technology (Project No. 2021410 B10-2125-0101) provided by Korea Forest Service (Korea Forestry Promotion Institute).

References

Ahilan, A., Rejula, M. A., Kumar, S., & Kumar, B. M. (2023). Virtual Reality Sensor Based IoT Embedded System for Stress Diagnosis. IEEE Sensors Journal.

M. Bublitz, F., Oetomo, A., S. Sahu, K., Kuang, A., X. Fadrique, L., E. Velmovitsky, P., . . . P. Morita, P. (2019). Disruptive technologies for environment and health research: an overview of artificial intelligence, blockchain, and internet of things. International journal of environmental research and public health, 16(20), 3847.

Chen, C., Ding, S., & Wang, J. (2023). Digital health for aging populations. Nature medicine, 29(7), 1623-1630.

Hong, S., Lim, H. S., Kim, C. G., Park, J. H., Kim, M. G., Chae, G. Y., . . . Kwon, O. J. (2024). Evaluation Method of Ocean Healing Content on Stress Relieve Effects by Using Smart Watch and Questionnaire. Journal of Coastal Research, 116(SI), 493–497.

Karageorgos, G., Andreadis, I., Psychas, K., Mourkousis, G., Kiourti, A., Lazzi, G., & Nikita, K. S. (2018). The promise of mobile technologies for the health care system in the developing world: a systematic review. IEEE reviews in biomedical engineering, 12, 100-122.

Kos, A., & Umek, A. (2018). Wearable sensor devices for prevention and rehabilitation in healthcare: Swimming exercise with real-time therapist feedback. IEEE internet of things journal, 6(2), 1331-1341.

Kwak, J., Hong, G., Lee, K. J., Kim, C.-G., & Shin, D. (2023). Effect of the interaction between seaweed intake and LPL polymorphisms on metabolic syndrome in middle-aged Korean adults. Nutrients, 15(9), 2066.

Nag, A., Mukhopadhyay, S. C., & Kosel, J. (2017). Wearable flexible sensors: A review. IEEE Sensors Journal, 17(13), 3949-3960.

Pourbemany, J., Zhu, Y., & Bettati, R. (2023). A survey of wearable devices pairing based on biometric signals. IEEE Access, 11, 26070-26085.

Rizzo, A., & Koenig, S. T. (2017). Is clinical virtual reality ready for primetime? Neuropsychology, 31(8), 877.

Rizzo, A. S., & Shilling, R. (2017). Clinical virtual reality tools to advance the prevention, assessment, and treatment of PTSD. European journal of psychotraumatology, 8(sup5), 1414560.

Rizzo, A., Goodwin, G. J., De Vito, A. N., & Bell, J. D. (2021). Recent advances in virtual reality and psychology: Introduction to the special issue. Translational Issues in Psychological Science, 7(3), 213.

Rizzo, A., Roy, M. J., Hartholt, A., Costanzo, M., Highland, K. B., Jovanovic, T., . . . Difede, J. (2017). Virtual reality applications for the assessment and treatment of PTSD. Handbook of military psychology: Clinical and organizational practice, 453–471.

Seneviratne, S., Hu, Y., Nguyen, T., Lan, G., Khalifa, S., Thilakarathna, K., . . . Seneviratne, A. (2017). A survey of wearable devices and challenges. IEEE Communications Surveys & Tutorials, 19(4), 2573-2620.

Shim, S. R., Shin, D., Kim, S.-J., Kim, Y. K., & Lee, K. J. (2023). Unveiling the Therapeutic Potential and Healthcare Applications of Marine Therapy: A Systematic Review with Meta-Analysis and Meta-Regression. Marine Drugs, 21(12), 604.

Shin, D., Shim, S. R., Wu, Y., Hong, G., Jeon, H., Kim, C.-G., & Lee, K. J. (2023a). How do Brown seaweeds work on biomarkers of dyslipidemia? A systematic review with Meta-analysis and Meta-regression. Marine Drugs, 21(4), 220.

Shin, S. W., Kim, H., Kang, Y. H., & Kim, J. (2023b). Accelerometer-derived physical activity and sedentary behavior patterns among Korean adults. Physical Activity and Nutrition, 27(2), 25.

Shin, S., Choi, Y., Kang, Y., & Kim, J. (2024). Associations of meeting 24-h movement guidelines and metabolic syndrome in Korean adults during the COVID-19 pandemic. Public Health, 227, 187-193.

Vakhter, V., Kahraman, B., Bu, G., Foroozan, F., & Guler, U. (2023). A prototype wearable device for noninvasive monitoring of transcutaneous oxygen. IEEE Transactions on Biomedical Circuits and Systems, 17(2), 323-335.

Vlake, J. H., van Bommel, J., Riva, G., Wiederhold, B. K., Cipresso, P., Rizzo, A. S., . . . Geerts, B. (2023). Reporting the early stage clinical evaluation of virtual-reality-based intervention trials: RATE-VR. Nature medicine, 29(1), 12-13.

Wang, Z., Sun, Z., Liu, P., Wang, S., & Zhang, Z. (2022). Intelligent decision support platform of new energy vehicles. Journal of Systems Engineering and Electronics, 33(4), 785-791.

Winarto, J., Song, D.-G., & Pan, C.-H. (2023). The role of fucoxanthin in non-alcoholic fatty liver disease. International Journal of Molecular Sciences, 24(9), 8203.

Wu, C.-T., Wang, S.-M., Su, Y.-E., Hsieh, T.-T., Chen, P.-C., Cheng, Y.-C., . . . Kuo, L.-C. (2022). A precision health service for chronic diseases: development and cohort study using wearable device, machine learning, and deep learning. IEEE journal of translational engineering in health and medicine, 10, 1-14.

Yeh, S.-C., Lin, S.-Y., Wu, E. H.-K., Zhang, K.-F., Xiu, X., Rizzo, A., & Chung, C.-R. (2020). A virtual-reality system integrated with neuro-behavior sensing for attention-deficit/hyperactivity disorder intelligent assessment. IEEE Transactions on Neural Systems and Rehabilitation Engineering, 28(9), 1899-1907.

XR & Visual Communication Survey of Sustainable Built Environment KPIs: Including Both AEC and Non-AEC Industry Professionals

R. S. Johnston, J. D. Mondol, A. Wiberg, and B. Coyle

Abstract Climate change is of growing concern and clear understanding and communication between key stakeholder groups is required to make informed decisions. A major sector of focus is the built environment that contributes 40% of global emissions, the need for innovation in this sector will be vital to current national and international targets for 2023 and 2050 as outlined by the IPCC. XR represents a novel system to immerse stakeholders within 3D data and support faster learning, understanding, and decision making. However alternative non-immersive technologies may also offer a viable alternative. This study gathers insight from 47 stakeholders from the Architecture, Engineering, and Construction (AEC) sector as well as other professional disciplines to understand what the current attitudes are towards these technologies, what barriers exist, and where future opportunities may lay.

Keywords Virtual reality (VR) · Augmented reality (AR) · Key performance indicator (KPI) · Stakeholder communication · Digital twin

1 Introduction

Global carbon emissions have continued to rise, reaching 36 $GtCO_2$ in 2016, despite the known dangers of climate change (Giesekam et al., 2018). In 2015, 195 nations adopted the Paris Agreement to limit global warming below 2 °C (Giesekam et al., 2018). However, without stronger actions, temperatures could increase by 2.6–3.1 °C by 2100. In response, several countries declared a climate emergency in 2019, and

R. S. Johnston (✉) · J. D. Mondol · B. Coyle
Faculty of Computing, Engineering and the Built Environment/Department of Architecture and the Built Environment, Ulster University, Belfast, UK
e-mail: Johnston-R54@ulster.ac.uk

A. Wiberg
Faculty of Engineering and Design/Department of Architecture and Civil Engineering, University of Bath, Bath, UK

T. Jung et al. (eds.), *XR and Metaverse*, Springer Proceedings in Business and Economics, https://doi.org/10.1007/978-3-031-77975-6_31

in 2020, the UN Secretary-General urged all nations to do the same (United Nations, 2022).

To combat this, two main emission reduction targets have been set for 2030 and 2050. The 2030 target aims for significant cuts from 1990 levels, with the European Union seeking a 55% reduction under its Fit for 55 agenda (Giesekam et al., 2018). The 2050 goal is to achieve climate neutrality, requiring major innovations across all sectors. Countries like the USA, South Korea, Japan, and the EU have committed to net-zero targets. The 2030 milestone serves as a stepping stone toward the 2050 goal, helping to prevent missing the ultimate target and to foster efficient innovation pathways (Masson-Delmotte et al., 2022; Satola et al., 2022).

Climate modelling considers three scenarios: a "business as usual" approach leading to temperature increases above 2 °C; a Moderate Transition with effective current policies resulting in a 2.5–3 °C rise; and net-zero scenarios aiming to limit warming to 1.5 °C through significant decarbonization and renewable energy innovations. Achieving the net-zero scenario presents an immense stakeholder communication challenge, requiring unprecedented coordination across nations and sectors over several decades (Edenhofer et al., 2014; Masson-Delmotte et al., 2022).

The construction industry significantly impacts global emissions, accounting for 33% (Iacovidou and Purnell, 2016) to 40% (Satola et al., 2022) of energy use and associated emissions, and consuming half of global resources. The Architecture, Engineering, and Construction (AEC) sector is thus critical for climate mitigation efforts. Research initiatives like Zero Emission Neighbourhoods (ZEN) and Zero Emission Buildings (ZEB) in Norway, along with Positive Energy Buildings and Districts elsewhere, focus on decarbonization by targeting operational energy emissions. However, a full Life Cycle Assessment (LCA) offers a more holistic view than considering energy consumption alone (Wiik et al., 2022).

Understanding and harmonizing various emission reduction approaches and standards is crucial ongoing work (Satola et al., 2022). Achieving these goals requires changes in standard practices and significant imagination among stakeholder groups. Historically, humanity's ability to imagine and simulate ideas that don't yet exist has enabled societies to form shared visions, leading to monumental achievements like Stonehenge and the pyramids (Harari, 2015). Effective communication aligns individuals' mental images, bringing a shared vision of "what could or should be" closer to reality. In this context, Extended Reality (XR) technologies have the potential to enhance stakeholders' ability to visualize "what if" scenarios (Hollberg et al., 2021; Stals and Caldas, 2022).

Visualization plays a vital role in modern engineering practices, ensuring a shared vision and securing stakeholder buy-in, while supporting training, cost reduction, and marketing (Khan et al., 2021; Wiik et al., 2022). Building Information Models (BIM) facilitate communication among clients, engineers, and architects, often through specialized software on 2D screens or as printouts (Brazina et al., 2022). Similarly, Geographic Information Systems (GIS) integrate layers of digital information—such as infrastructure and environmental data—into maps viewed on screens or dashboards. These visual technologies foster a common understanding among stakeholders, enabling them to better visualize potential outcomes and make informed decisions (Hanifah et al., 2023).

This paper aims to understand current industry attitudes toward XR as a means of communicating sustainable Key Performance Indicator (KPI) data within a Decision Support System (DSS). It analyzes feedback from 47 respondents to an open survey targeting individuals within and adjacent to the AEC industry, focusing on XR and visual dashboards as tools for sustainable KPI communication. The findings are intended to support future research and highlight the potential of XR as a visual communication platform to enhance sustainable decision-making.

2 Theory

Extended Reality (XR) technologies enhance visualization and enable stakeholders to collaborate across distances through improved verbal and non-verbal communication (Du et al., 2018). Properly designed VR offers new ways to learn and retain information, motivating stakeholders by deepening their understanding of the impact of their decisions (Li et al., 2018; Lindvig and Mathiasen, 2020; Hamdan et al., 2021). In the Architecture, Engineering, and Construction (AEC) sector, XR is primarily used for design visualization, project management, safety training, equipment education, client presentations, and analysing human behaviour (Moore and Gheisari, 2019; Zhang et al., 2020).

While effective for 3D communication, XR's potential to convey Life Cycle Assessment (LCA) data related to low carbon emissions—a fourth dimension—is less explored but promising (Hollberg et al., 2021). Studies have shown that integrating LCA data within Zero Emission Building (ZEB) and Zero Emission Neighbourhood (ZEN) contexts is feasible (Wiberg et al., 2019; Wiik et al., 2022). Adopting a multidisciplinary approach that includes all stakeholders is necessary, as previous work often focused on specific groups, potentially missing opportunities for broader collaboration (Ortega et al., 2019; Badamasi et al., 2021; Grepon and Martinez, 2021).

3 Methodology

A double diamond design methodology led to a survey assessing whether Architecture, Engineering, and Construction (AEC) stakeholders are interested in Extended Reality (XR), dashboards, or if existing tools suffice. The aim was to shift from a technology-led to a solution-led approach, as XR studies often compare XR technologies in isolation rather than against non-immersive communication tools (Woodman et al., 2019; Wang et al., 2020; Badamasi et al., 2021).

To maximize response rates and data quality, the survey employed a 5-point Likert scale in most of its 26 unique questions, with up to 30 questions possible due to follow-up prompts for "Other" responses. This method is well-established in XR and GIS dashboard studies. Most questions had a neutral midpoint and ranged from plus or minus two to gauge positive or negative trends (Wu and Leung, 2017; Woodman et al., 2019; Moscoso et al., 2021; Vedin, 2022).

The survey sought an unbiased understanding of attitudes toward VR, AR, and dashboards as communication tools, especially in the context of sustainable Key Performance Indicator (KPI) communication like Life Cycle Assessment (LCA) embodied carbon data. Recognizing that XR originates from gaming and entertainment, respondents from that sector might have solutions but not fully understand AEC communication challenges. Conversely, data science or GIS professionals might be familiar with dashboards but less aware of AEC KPI demands. AEC participants likely understand communication challenges but may be less familiar with XR technologies. Therefore, the survey targeted a diverse range of industry sectors, hypothesizing that one sector might offer solutions to another's communication challenges.

The survey was created using the Jisc web platform and distributed to stakeholders at Ulster University, Bath University, and via professional networks on LinkedIn. Non-responses to Likert questions were assigned a neutral value. An initial page included ethical information, stating that participation was voluntary, with no reward, and that responses would be anonymized.

4 Results

The survey garnered 47 responses (13 female, 33 male) from eight countries, predominantly the United Kingdom (77%—47% from England and 30% from Northern Ireland). Other respondents hailed from China, the Netherlands, Sweden, the UAE, and the USA. The age distribution was mainly between 25 and 64 years, with minimal participation from those aged 18–24 and 65+. Notably, female respondents were absent in the 35–44 and 65+ age brackets.

Participants identified their professional sectors and areas of specialization. Nearly half (47%) were from the built environment sector, with architecture being the most common specialty. The transport sector had six respondents, while academia accounted for five, as shown in Fig. 1.

Meta/Oculus emerged as the most widely used brand Fig. 2, mentioned 65 times across various devices—even when participants used multiple products from the brand. HTC/Vive was the second most referenced with 33 mentions, and other brands like Pico and HoloLens were cited 48 times collectively. The Oculus Rift and phone-based VR experiences led with 19 mentions each, followed by the HTC Vive and Oculus Quest with 15 each.

Fig. 1 Sunburst chart of stakeholder sectors and specialisms

Communication challenges were universal among participants, irrespective of their industry or academic background. Four primary themes emerged: (1) People—difficulties in communicating with clients, professionals, or contractors; (2) Data—issues with integrating data from multiple sources and aligning it with sustainability targets; (3) Time—a persistent lack of time; and (4) Technology—the need for better tools and challenges in understanding 3D information.

When comparing built environment professionals' Fig. 3 (49% of respondents) with those from other sectors (51%), both groups shared concerns about data communication and time constraints. However, built environment professionals more frequently cited challenges in understanding 3D information and client communication.

Participants rated the effectiveness of various visualization tools in Fig. 4. Infographics were deemed most useful, followed by CAD and photographs. Immersive technologies like VR and AR scored higher than dashboards, with VR being rated

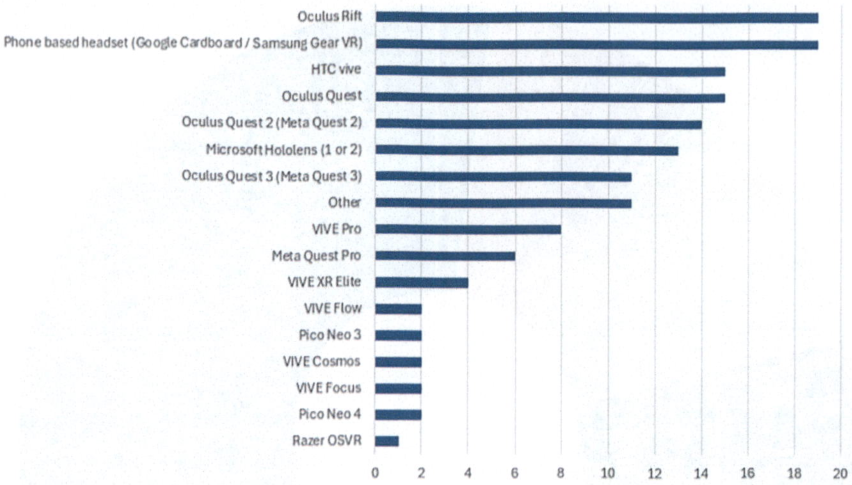

Fig. 2 Count of respondent's use of HMD's

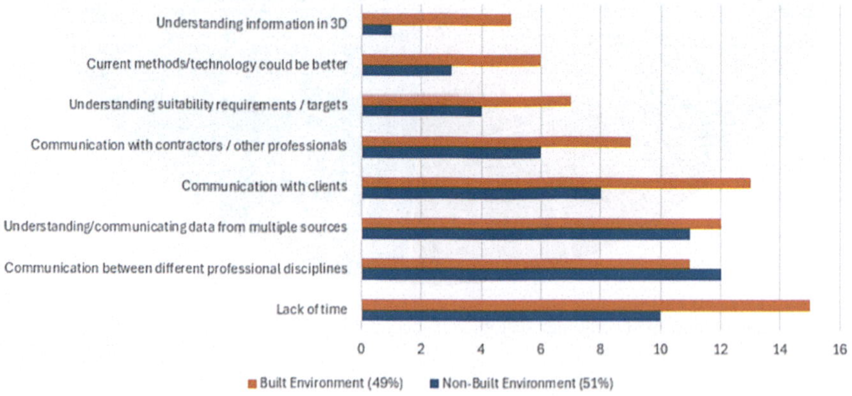

Fig. 3 Built and non built environment stakeholder challenges

slightly more "very useful" than AR. Despite this, both VR and AR had similar levels of uncertainty regarding their potential as communication tools and received comparable negative ratings to Excel and videos.

Stakeholders identified several barriers to VR adoption in professional practice within Fig. 5. The leading challenge was a lack of technical expertise (85% agreed or strongly agreed), followed by the cost of implementation (72%). Other barriers were acknowledged by 51–57% of respondents, indicating widespread concerns.

Finally Fig. 6, stakeholders concurred that dashboards, VR, and AR support communication in the Life Cycle Assessment stages of EN 15978:2011 (Bre, 2018). Dashboards were preferred during the Product (A1–A3) and End of Life (C1–C4) stages, while VR and AR were favoured during the Construction (A4–A5) stage. VR

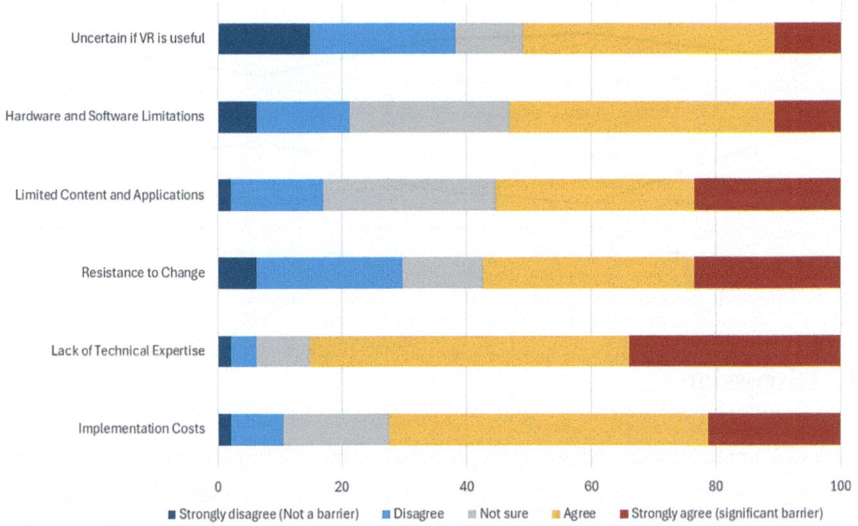

Fig. 4 Communication tool effectiveness as percentage

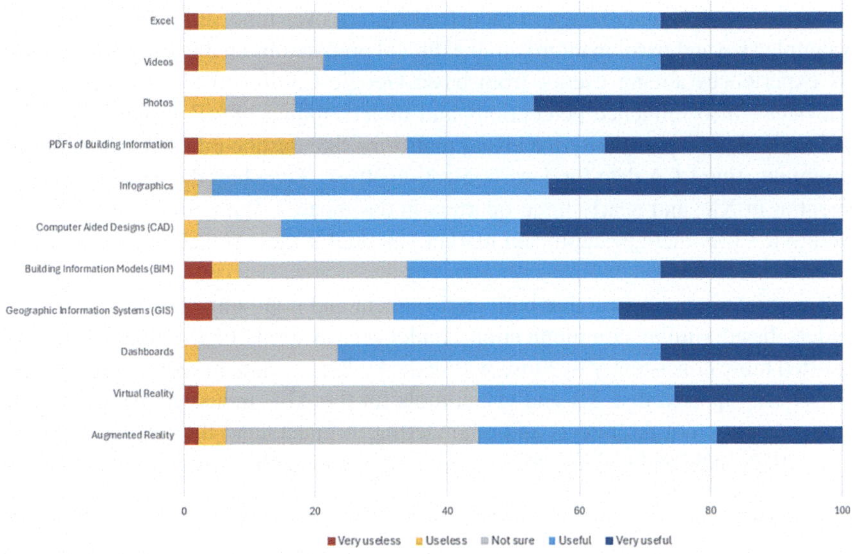

Fig. 5 Perceived barriers to VR adoption as a percentage

generally rated higher than AR across stages A1–B7, except at End of Life. Perceptions of technology implementation varied across different levels of professional experience.

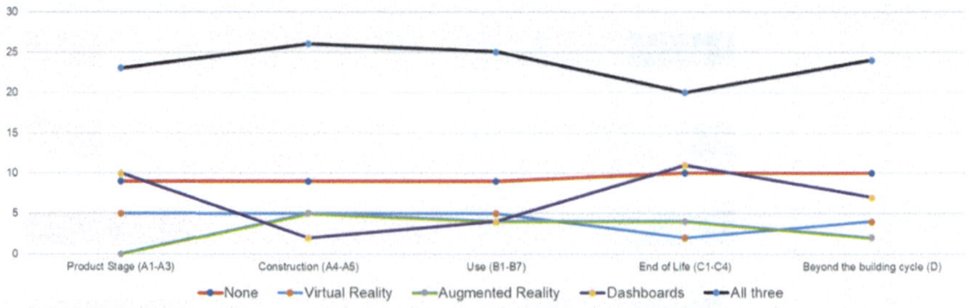

Fig. 6 Life cycle assessment stage opportunities for visual technologies

5 Discussion

Lack of knowledge or expertise is the primary barrier to XR, particularly VR, implementation, with 85% of respondents identifying it as such. Similarly, Badamasi et al. (2021) found that 93% of 123 UK AEC stakeholders saw lack of expertise as a barrier to VR adoption (Badamasi et al., 2021). While cost ranked second in this study, it was third in Badamasi et al.'s research, following cultural change, similar findings from the US was found by Stals and Caldas 2022 (Stals and Caldas, 2022). This shift may indicate a gradual change in industrial culture over time, although differences in sample size and participant mix make direct comparisons challenging. The varied VR experiences among users—from basic Google Cardboard to advanced Quest 3 devices—also influence perceptions and understanding of VR technology. This study reveals an opportunity for visual platforms like dashboards and XR to aid in communicating LCA data for decarbonization efforts. Over half the respondents see potential in XR, and nearly three-quarters in dashboards. With almost 40% unsure about XR's use, there is significant market potential if these stakeholders adopt XR in the future.

It was interesting to see that built environment and non-built environment stakeholders faced similar communication challenges, in terms of the trend. But was reported more consistently by those within the built environment sector. It has previously been reported that XR and visual tools for the AEC industry have been built without input from Architects and engineering to understand their needs (Schiavi et al., 2022; Stals and Caldas, 2022)—possibly the tools they use is consider not to be good enough. Presenting future opportunities to better design in this space (Wiik et al., 2022).

6 Conclusions

In conclusion, XR technologies like VR and AR remain promising communication tools within the stakeholder communication and data visualization arsenal, especially for addressing climate concerns outlined by the IPCC and UN. However, significant uncertainty persists among stakeholders, with common barriers such as lack of expertise and high costs hindering full adoption. Existing visualization technologies, such as dashboards, also offer potential for conveying 3D data without the need for immersive experiences. Stakeholders consistently rated the combined use of immersive technologies and dashboards higher than any single technology for Life Cycle Assessment (LCA) data.

This suggests that cloud-based platforms capable of disseminating urban data could act as a single source of truth, accessible via multiple devices like VR, AR, and dashboards—making the technology choice dependent on the specific use case rather than being technology-driven. Further understanding and testing of XR and dashboards would help to understand these potential use cases to address stakeholder needs.

Acknowledgements Authors would like to thank the Northern Ireland Department for the Economy and Ulster University for funding and supporting this research. And to Spatial Simulations Ltd for their additional dissemination funding.

Appendix

Survey used

(1) Please select your gender
(2) Please select your age range
(3) Location of work
(4) Company staff count
(5) What sector do you currently work in?
(6) Please select your rea of interest/study/profession
(7) Please select the stakeholder group you identify with
(8) Please select your years of experience in the industry
(9) Please select your experience levels with LCA concepts
(10) How important are various forms of collaboration in your role
(11) What are your biggest communication challenges?
(12) What are your top three communication priorities?
(13) What are the top three challenges you see built environment stakeholders facing in the next 10 years?
(14) Do you believe current communication tools are adequate for KPI communication?
(15) How do you view the following statement—Virtual Reality can play a positive role in communicating the following concepts?
(16) How do you view the following statement—Augmented Reality can play a positive role in communicating the following concepts?
(17) How do you view the following statement—Information Dashboards can play a positive role in communicating the following concepts?

(18) The following KPIs are essential for me to understand/communicate with others?
(19) To what extent are the following barriers preventing the use of VR for communication in your organization?
(20) What construction projects are you commonly involved in?
(21) What is your opinion on the following statements? [Statements related to impact of miscommunication]
(22) How useful are the following for communication in your role? [Lists visual technologies]
(23) How aware are you of the following software solutions? [Lists development platforms]
(24) Which headset have you used before [lists HMDs]
(25) Do you engage with system boundary data? [lists five LCA boundaries]
(26) Which of the following technologies could be beneficial to support communication at the described system boundary states? [lists five LCA boundaries]

References

Badamasi, A.A. et al. (2021) 'Drivers and barriers of virtual reality adoption in UK AEC industry', *Engineering, Construction and Architectural Management* [Preprint]. Available at: https://doi.org/10.1108/ECAM-09-2020-0685.

Brazina, J. et al. (2022) 'Application of Industry 4.0 trends in the teaching process', in *2022 20th International Conference on Mechatronics - Mechatronika (ME). 2022 20th International Conference on Mechatronics - Mechatronika (ME)*, Pilsen, Czech Republic: IEEE, pp. 1–6. Available at: https://doi.org/10.1109/ME54704.2022.9983243.

Bre (2018) *BRE Global Methodology For The Environmental Assessment Of Buildings Using EN 15978:2011*. Available at: https://www.greenbooklive.com/filelibrary/EN_15804/PN326-BRE-EN-15978-Methodology.pdf.

Du, J. et al. (2018) 'CoVR: Cloud-Based Multiuser Virtual Reality Headset System for Project Communication of Remote Users', *Journal of Construction Engineering and Management*, 144(2), p. 04017109. Available at: https://doi.org/10.1061/(ASCE)CO.1943-7862.0001426.

Edenhofer, O. et al. (2014) *IPCC, Climate Change 2014: Mitigation of Climate Change. Contribution of Working Group III to the Fifth Assessment Report of the Intergovernmental Panel on Climate Change*. IPCC. United Kingdom and New York: Cambridge University Press Cambridge.

Giesekam, J., Tingley, D.D. and Cotton, I. (2018) 'Aligning carbon targets for construction with (inter)national climate change mitigation commitments', *Energy and Buildings*, 165, pp. 106–117. Available at: https://doi.org/10.1016/j.enbuild.2018.01.023.

Grepon, B.G.S. and Martinez, A.L.M. (2021) 'Architectural Visualization Using Virtual Reality: A User Experience in Simulating Buildings of a Community College in Bukidnon, Philippines'.

Hamdan, H.A.M., Andersen, P.H. and de Boer, L. (2021) 'Stakeholder collaboration in sustainable neighborhood projects—A review and research agenda', *Sustainable Cities and Society*, 68, p. 102776. Available at: https://doi.org/10.1016/j.scs.2021.102776.

Hanifah, A., Aditya, B.R. and Mulyawan, M. (2023) 'Implementation of Double Diamond Design Model for User Interface of Bandung City Dashboard', in *2023 8th International Conference on Information Technology and Digital Applications (ICITDA). 2023 8th International Conference*

on Information Technology and Digital Applications (ICITDA), Yogyakarta, Indonesia: IEEE, pp. 1–6. Available at: https://doi.org/10.1109/ICITDA60835.2023.10427040.
Harari, Y.N. (2015) 'Sapiens : a Brief History of Humankind', in. New York: Harvill Secker.
Hollberg, A. et al. (2021) 'Review of visualising LCA results in the design process of buildings', *Building and Environment*, 190, p. 107530. Available at: https://doi.org/10.1016/j.buildenv.2020.107530.
Iacovidou, E. and Purnell, P. (2016) 'Mining the physical infrastructure: Opportunities, barriers and interventions in promoting structural components reuse', *Science of The Total Environment*, 557–558, pp. 791–807. Available at: https://doi.org/10.1016/j.scitotenv.2016.03.098.
Khan, A. et al. (2021) 'Integration of BIM and Immersive Technologies for AEC: A Scientometric-SWOT Analysis and Critical Content Review', *Buildings*, 11(3), p. 126. Available at: https://doi.org/10.3390/buildings11030126.
Li, X. et al. (2018) 'A critical review of virtual and augmented reality (VR/AR) applications in construction safety', *Automation in Construction*, 86, pp. 150–162. Available at: https://doi.org/10.1016/j.autcon.2017.11.003.
Lindvig, K. and Mathiasen, H. (2020) 'Translating the Learning Factory model to a Danish Vocational Education Setting', *Procedia Manufacturing*, 45, pp. 90–95. Available at: https://doi.org/10.1016/j.promfg.2020.04.077.
Masson-Delmotte et al. (2022) *Global Warming of 1.5°C: IPCC Special Report on impacts of global warming of 1.5°C above pre-industrial levels in context of strengthening response to climate change, sustainable development, and efforts to eradicate poverty.* 1st edn. Cambridge University Press. Available at: https://doi.org/10.1017/9781009157940.
Moore, H.F. and Gheisari, M. (2019) 'A Review of Virtual and Mixed Reality Applications in Construction Safety Literature', *Safety*, 5(3), p. 51. Available at: https://doi.org/10.3390/safety5030051.
Moscoso, C. et al. (2021) 'Window Size Effects on Subjective Impressions of Daylit Spaces: Indoor Studies at High Latitudes Using Virtual Reality', *LEUKOS*, 17(3), pp. 242–264. Available at: https://doi.org/10.1080/15502724.2020.1726183.
Ortega, S. et al. (2019) 'Making the Invisible Visible—Strategies for Visualizing Underground Infrastructures in Immersive Environments', *ISPRS International Journal of Geo-Information*, 8(3), p. 152. Available at: https://doi.org/10.3390/ijgi8030152.
Satola, D. et al. (2022) 'Comparative review of international approaches to net-zero buildings: Knowledge-sharing initiative to develop design strategies for greenhouse gas emissions reduction', *Energy for Sustainable Development*, 71, pp. 291–306. Available at: https://doi.org/10.1016/j.esd.2022.10.005.
Schiavi, B. et al. (2022) 'BIM data flow architecture with AR/VR technologies: Use cases in architecture, engineering and construction', *Automation in Construction*, 134, p. 104054. Available at: https://doi.org/10.1016/j.autcon.2021.104054.
Stals, A. and Caldas, L. (2022) 'State of XR research in architecture with focus on professional practice—a systematic literature review', *Architectural Science Review*, 65(2), pp. 138–146. Available at: https://doi.org/10.1080/00038628.2020.1838258.
United Nations (2022) 'For a livable climate: Net-zero commitments must be backed by credible action'. Available at: https://www.un.org/en/climatechange/net-zero-coalition.
Vedin, E. (2022) 'Promoting User Engagement through Dashboard Design in an Energy Monitoring Platform'.
Wang, M. et al. (2020) 'A Systematic Review of Digital Technology Adoption in Off-Site Construction: Current Status and Future Direction towards Industry 4.0', *Buildings*, 10(11), p. 204. Available at: https://doi.org/10.3390/buildings10110204.
Wiberg, A.H. et al. (2019) 'Visualisation of KPIs in zero emission neighbourhoods for improved stakeholder participation using Virtual Reality', *IOP Conference Series: Earth and Environmental Science*, 323(1), p. 012074. Available at: https://doi.org/10.1088/1755-1315/323/1/012074.

Wiik, M. et al. (2022) *Zero Emission Neighbourhoods in Smart Cities - Definition, Key Performance Indicators and Assessment Criteria.* Bilingual version Version 3.0. FME ZEN: The Research Centre on Zero Emission Neighbourhoods in Smart Cities, p. 56.

Woodman, R. et al. (2019) 'Gap acceptance study of pedestrians crossing between platooning autonomous vehicles in a virtual environment', *Transportation Research Part F: Traffic Psychology and Behaviour*, 67, pp. 1–14. Available at: https://doi.org/10.1016/j.trf.2019.09.017.

Wu, H. and Leung, S.-O. (2017) 'Can Likert Scales be Treated as Interval Scales?—A Simulation Study', *Journal of Social Service Research*, 43(4), pp. 527–532. Available at: https://doi.org/10.1080/01488376.2017.1329775.

Zhang, Y. et al. (2020) 'Virtual reality applications for the built environment: Research trends and opportunities', *Automation in Construction*, 118, p. 103311. Available at: https://doi.org/10.1016/j.autcon.2020.103311.

XR for Health and Wellbeing

Scope of Virtual Reality Training in Trauma and Orthopaedic Surgery: An Experimental Study and Review of the Literature

Ketan Kantamaneni, Suresh Kondi, Alastair Konarski, and Bibhas Roy

Abstract The integration of Virtual Reality (VR) into orthopaedic surgery training is a rapidly growing trend and is poised to significantly influence the education of orthopaedic residents. This paper presents a study that examines the effectiveness of VR training in orthopaedic surgery, specifically focusing on its inclusivity. The research involved an experimental VR training session that utilised the Occulus Meta Quest 2 device and VR training software, with participants encompassing medical students, doctors, and consultants. These participants engaged in various practice modules, and their post-session feedback indicated that the majority found the 3D immersive orientation of surgical procedures to be advantageous. Additionally, they expressed a strong preference for practising techniques in VR that they had not encountered in the operating room. Furthermore, this study includes an extensive review of existing literature on VR training in orthopaedic surgery, covering a wide array of sub-specialities and techniques. This comprehensive analysis provides valuable insights into the perceptions and experiences of surgical trainees pertaining to VR training in orthopaedic surgery.

Keywords Virtual reality · Trauma · Orthopaedics · Surgery · Training · Simulator

K. Kantamaneni (✉) · A. Konarski · B. Roy
Department of Trauma and Orthopaedics, Manchester University NHS Foundation Trust, Manchester, UK
e-mail: kantamnenikethan@gmail.com

S. Kondi
Department of Trauma and Orthopaedics, Portsmouth Hospitals University NHS Trust, Portsmouth, UK

T. Jung et al. (eds.), *XR and Metaverse*, Springer Proceedings in Business and Economics, https://doi.org/10.1007/978-3-031-77975-6_32

1 Introduction

Virtual Reality (VR) represents ground breaking technology that has transcended its initial entertainment and gaming applications to become significant tools in the medical field, particularly in trauma and orthopaedic surgery (Gupta & Ambade, 2022). The application of virtual technology to orthopaedic surgery training and practice aims to increase procedures' safety and accuracy and reduce complications and costs (Longo et al., 2021). VR immerses surgeons in a completely virtual environment, detaching them from the physical world and creating a virtual operating room where surgeons can practice complex procedures on simulated patients or rehearse specific surgical steps before entering the real operating theatre (Bayona et al., 2003; Khor et al., 2019).

While the concept of VR dates to the 1930s, with the invention of the Sensorama, its practical application in medicine emerged in the 1990s. The first documented use of VR in shoulder surgery dates to 2003, when it was employed for preoperative planning and simulation (Pensieri & Pennacchini, 2014). The spectrum of potential applications for VR in orthopaedic surgery is vast and ever-expanding. It has significantly increased in popularity in the area where it provides real-time feedback and guidance to the surgeon (Lohre et al., 2020), such as displaying the optimal cutting plane, screw trajectory, or implant position and orientation (Combalia et al., 2024). Some significant challenges must be solved before these methods become regular parts of training programs. These early simulators did not have enough realism to mimic human tissue fully and may not have all haptic feedback elements (Lee et al., 2021; Shafarenko et al., 2022). User problems with hardware like the Microsoft HoloLens, which is often used in AR, have been reported by many studies, such as the device's weight (590 g) and sickness and dizziness with long-term use (Moro et al., 2017). However, these negative impacts on users are more common with VR applications (McKnight et al., 2020). Despite some problems and difficulties, the future of VR and AR systems is promising for their further use in trauma and orthopaedic practice. These technologies can help save money, improve training, and save time in trauma and orthopaedics (Ugwoke et al., 2023).

We aimed to assess surgical trainees' experience of a VR training session in orthopaedic surgery and analyse their perceptions of its utility.

2 Methods

For our experimental study, a VR training session was conducted at Wythenshawe Hospital and Manchester Royal Infirmary, as shown in Fig. 1, using Occulus Meta Quest 2 device and a trial version of Precision OS software (commercially available provider of virtual reality surgical training solutions for the medical industry, based in Vancouver, Canada). Eighteen participants, including medical students, foundation year doctors, junior clinical fellows, senior clinical fellows, and consultants, participated. Participants had the opportunity to use practice modules, including shoulder arthroplasty (joint replacement), revision knee replacement, robotic knee manipulation, femur intramedullary nailing (insertion of a nail in the femur), hip arthroscopy (insertion of instruments and camera into the hip through small incisions) as shown in Fig. 2 and spinal injections. Each participant was given an induction to VR headset use and was allocated 20 min of practice. A post-session feedback questionnaire consisting of 17 questions, shown in Figs. 3 and 4 was collected, and the data were analysed.

Our literature review was conducted diligently, encompassing a comprehensive search for relevant published reports in the PubMed and Google Scholar databases. Searches within these databases were performed using specific combinations of medical subject headings (MeSH) terms, including 'virtual reality', AND 'Orthopaedics', AND 'Training'. Publications meeting the criteria of being freely accessible and relevant to the application of VR in orthopaedic training within the past decade were included. Exclusion criteria encompassed non-English literature, studies unrelated to orthopaedic surgery or virtual reality, mixed and augmented reality investigations, as well as duplicate publications.

3 Findings

In our trial with the Precision OS VR trainer, we received feedback from all 18 participants. We found that shoulder arthroplasty was the most utilised training module by 83% of candidates, followed by antegrade femoral nail and revision knee modules used by 44% of the candidates. At least a 20% improvement in knowledge about the procedure was observed in 44% of the participants. 83% of the participants preferred to practise a procedure in VR that they had not had the opportunity to experience in the operating room (OR). 78% of participants felt that the 3D immersive orientation of surgical steps benefitted them the most during the VR training. 33% of the participants felt that it is essential to have a VR orthopaedic trainer in the hospital, and a further 61% of the participants felt that it is beneficial to have one. 78% of participants felt that the cost of the VR software is a limitation of VR training. 88% of the participants were willing to take part in a randomised control trial that compares VR training with other modes of simulation training, highlighting the potential of VR in revolutionising orthopaedic education.

Our literature search found 72 articles; after excluding the duplicates and other exclusion criteria, 18 were considered for this study.

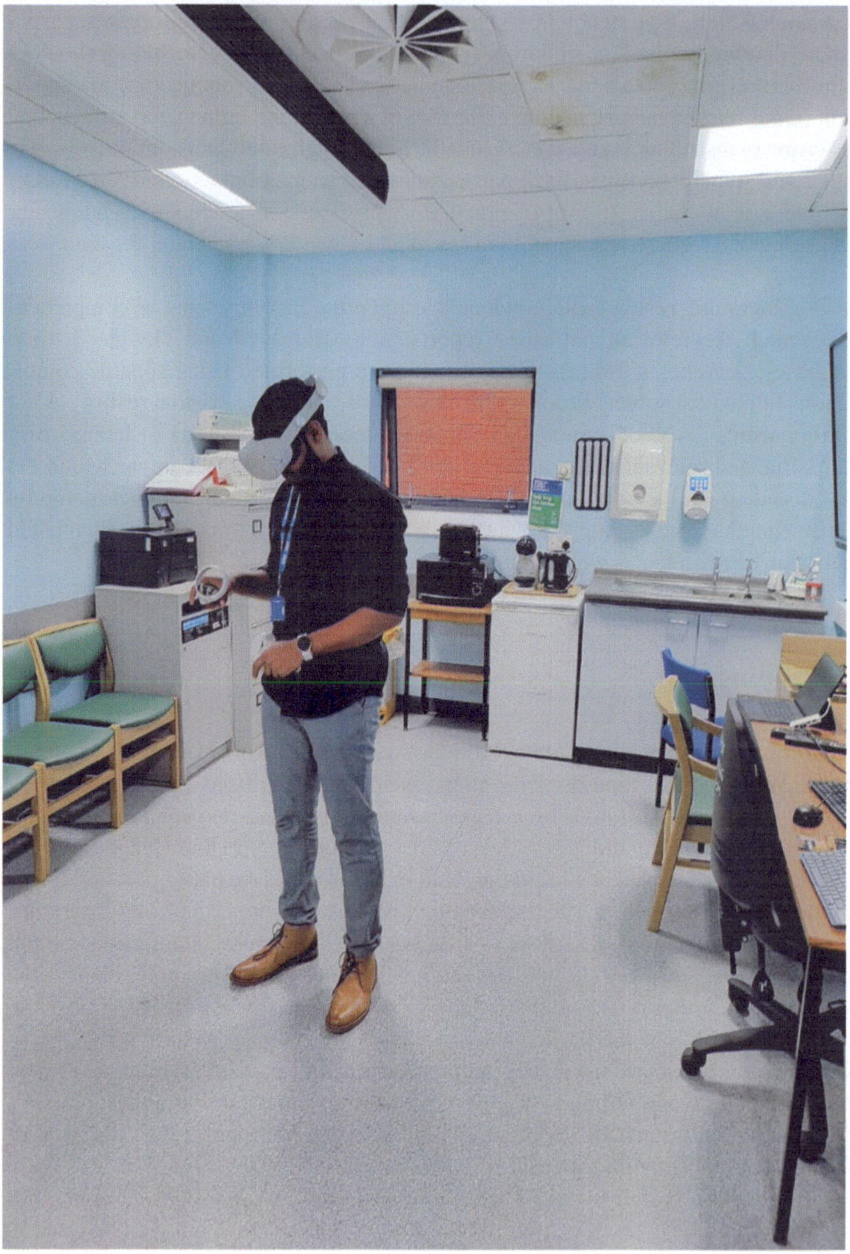

Fig. 1 VR practise session

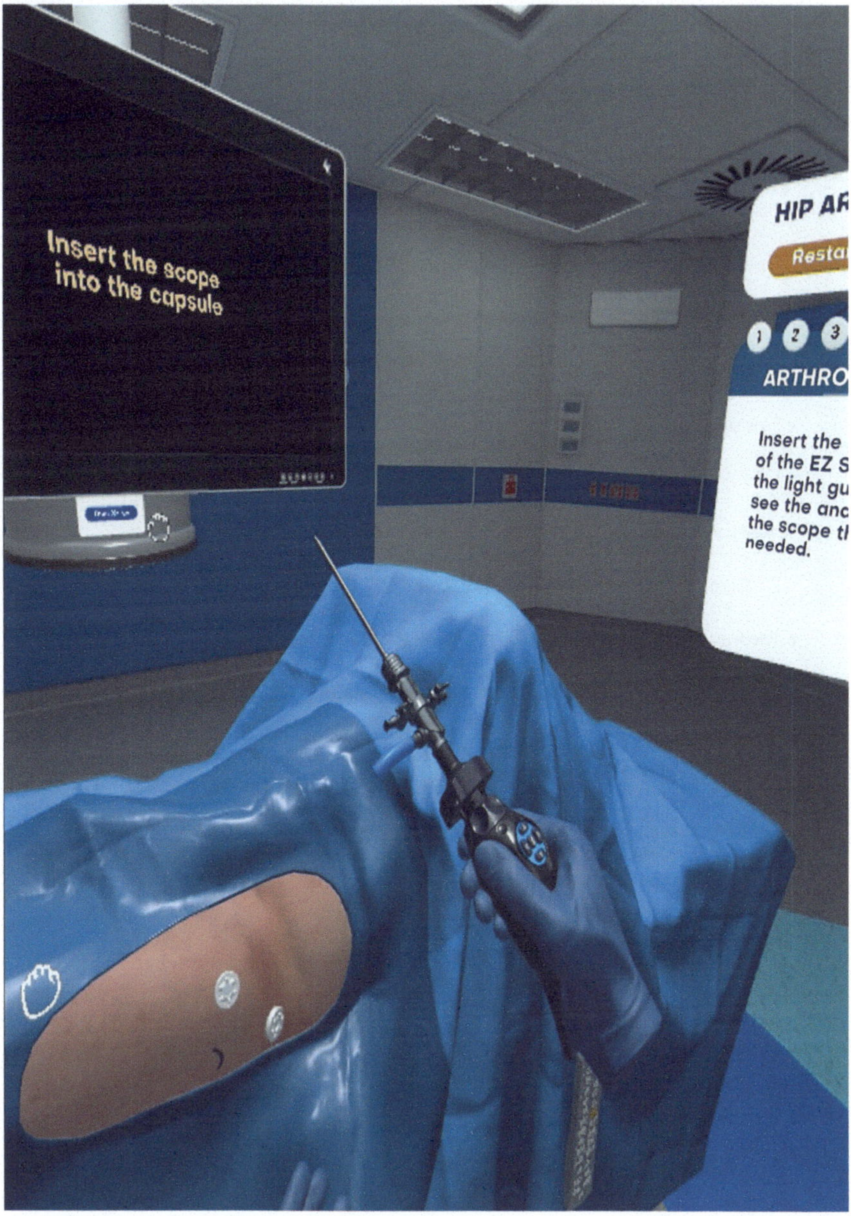

Fig. 2 VR hip arthroscopy module

VIRTUAL REALITY ORTHOPAEDIC SURGERY TRAINING SESSION QUESTIONNAIRE

1. At What level are you currently working in Orthopaedics?

☐ Junior Clinical Fellow/F1 ☐ Senior Clincial Fellow ☐ Post CCT Fellow ☐ Consultant

2. How do you best describe the VR training session ? (Please select all that apply)

☐pleasant ☐Exciting ☐Engaging ☐Informative ☐Motivating ☐Unpleasant ☐Exhausting

3. To what extent do you know the surgical procedure before the VR training session?

☐ 0-20% ☐20-40% ☐40-60% ☐60-80% ☐80- 100%

4. To what extent do you know the surgical procedure after the VR training session?

☐ 0-20% ☐20-40% ☐40-60% ☐60-80% ☐80- 100%

5. What is the average time you feel that you can spend on VR training per session?

☐< 15min ☐15 - 30 min ☐30-45min ☐45 -60min

6. Which module interested you the most? (select all that apply)

☐Hip arthroscopy ☐Shoulder Arthroplasty module ☐Robotic knee module snippet ☐Revision knee module ☐Antegrade femoral nail module ☐L4 -L5 Steroid injection module

7. Which module did you practice in VR today? (select all that apply)

☐Hip arthroscopy ☐Shoulder Arthroplasty module ☐Robotic knee module snippet ☐Revision knee module ☐Antegrade femoral nail module ☐L4 -L5 Steroid injection module

8. What would you rather prefer?

☐ Practicing the surgical procedure in VR that you have already done prior in OR to fine tune the skills
☐ Practicing a new surgical procedure in VR which you didn't get chance to do in the OR

9. How often do you think Orthopaedic surgeons need VR training?

☐Once a day ☐Twice a week ☐Once a week ☐Once a month ☐VR training not necessary

Fig. 3 Post VR session questionnaire

4 Discussion and Literature Review

Our study has found that VR is well-accepted and can be used as an effective alternative training tool. With the advancement of technology, training methods should also evolve beyond traditional classroom and cadaveric teaching. We have gathered sufficient evidence to support the effectiveness of VR technology in orthopaedic training

10. How do you think VR training benefits you the most? (select all that apply)

☐ Felxible training timings ☐ Chance to practice surgical procedures that usually get referred to other trusts for expertise (Eg - Spine) ☐ Repeated practice at own pace ☐ 3D immersive orientation of surgical steps as compared to 2D surgical videos ☐ Improves confidence in OR ☐ No benefit of VR

11. What is your opinion regarding the need of VR Orthopaedic training in your trust?

☐ It is very essential ☐ It will be beneficial to have one ☐ It Makes no much difference with or without it ☐ VR training is just a digital gimmick, other modes of training are much more useful

12. Who do you think will benefit the most from VR training?

☐ Junior Clinical Fellows/F1s ☐Middle Grades ☐ Consultants ☐ All of them

13. What do you think are the downsides of VR training?

☐ Cost of VR Headset ☐ Cost of the training software ☐ Other modes of training are on par with VR training and provide same results ☐ Lack of Senior guidance during VR training session ☐Unique fracture patterns that vary from case to case ☐Cyber Sickness (Nausea while using VR Headset)

14. Would you like to participate in a Randomized Control Trial comparing VR training Vs Other modes of training (Eg - Sawbone training and cadaver training) ?

☐ Yes ☐ No

15. On a scale of 1 - 10, How much would you rate the guidance provided in using the software during your training session?

----

16. Any Suggestions for the improvement of this session for future ?

____

____

17. Any Other Comments?

____

____

Fig. 4 Post VR session questionnaire continued

and surgeries, with several studies demonstrating its positive impact on various areas of orthopaedic training.

Bajuri (Bajuri et al., n.d.) conducted the first study in this field and identified 73 Critical Success Factors (CSFs) for VR integration in orthopaedic training. These CSFs are grouped into six categories: feature factors, usability factors, learning outcome factors, student characteristic factors, control and active learning factors, and limitation factors. This framework can be used to develop and evaluate VR training tools using the design science research methodology.

In addition, other studies have evaluated the use of VR in orthopaedic surgery, particularly in training and education. For example, Barlett et al. assessed the face validity of a virtual reality hip arthroscopy simulator and found that participants enjoyed the experience and felt it provided a non-threatening environment for practice (Bartlett et al., 2019).

Similarly, Le (Le et al., 2023) collected qualitative data from participants who completed a total hip arthroplasty module using a VR trainer and found that 88% of participants would recommend the module to a colleague and found it very enjoyable.

Feeley (Feeley et al., 2021) assessed the content, face, and construct validity of a portable hip arthroscopy simulator and found satisfactory levels of face and content validity for the Precision OS Cam Lesion hip arthroscopy procedure, but the construct validity was incomplete. These studies demonstrate the potential of VR technology in improving orthopaedic training and education.

Similar to the knowledge improvement in the participants of our study, a study conducted by Lamb (Lamb et al., n.d.) compared the skill improvement pre- and post-VR training. In both VR and saw bone hip models, VR groups showed greater improvements in implant placement accuracy through a significant reduction in errors in femoral osteotomy height, angle, inclination, and anteversion.

As shoulder arthroplasty interested most of the candidates, similar studies were found in our literature review—Ahmed (Ahmed et al., n.d.) discussed the use of immersive virtual reality (iVR) as a form of simulation for shoulder arthroplasty education. They highlighted that iVR, which incorporates three-dimensional (3D) virtual worlds, provides an effective learning strategy to offset real-world training. The authors noted that the incidence of shoulder arthroplasty is continuously increasing, with estimates reaching up to 350,558 yearly procedures by 2025. In the context of shoulder arthroplasty, iVR has shown consistent improvements in both technical skill and knowledge acquisition relative to traditional learning formats for trainees.

Handal (Handal et al., 2023) also reported on using VR training for reverse shoulder arthroplasty. They found that VR simulators demonstrated content, face, and construct validity, meaning that the software accurately represents the procedure, realistically simulates an operating room environment, and can differentiate between different skill levels. The study concluded that patients who underwent surgery after the VR training conducted by a resident had a positive prognosis with a good range of movements and functional scores during follow-up.

Other studies have also investigated the use of VR training for implanting femoral nails, a technique used to stabilise fractures of the femur. Sharma (Sharma et al., 2023) investigated the utility of virtual reality (VR) simulators for complex procedures and techniques like the Trochanteric Femoral Nail Advanced (TFNA) procedure. All participants were randomly assigned and provided a study pack comprising an application manual and instructional video for the TFNA procedure. The VR group underwent additional training for TFNA. All surgeons were then observed applying the TFNA in a Sawbones model and assessed by a blinded senior consultant using three metrics: time to completion, 22-item procedure checklist and 5-point global assessment scale. The study concluded that the VR group, on average, outperformed the control group on all three metrics. They completed the TFNA procedure faster, performed a more significant percentage of steps correctly and scored a higher percentage on the global assessment scale.

There are several other areas of orthopaedics where VR training has been studied in the literature. Sugand (Sugand et al., 2015) investigated the training effect of VR haptics by randomising 52 surgical trainees with no prior experience in Dynamic Hip Screw procedures (a technique using a plate and screws to fix a fracture of the femur) were divided into a training group and a control group. The study found that the training group was quicker, took fewer radiographs, had fewer retries at guide-wire insertion, achieved an improved position of the guide-wire, had a lower probability of cut-out of the implant, and obtained a higher global score. The participants agreed that the simulator provided a realistic learning environment and recognised the need for the simulator in formal training where patient safety is not compromised.

In a study conducted by Boudissa (Boudissa et al., 2018), the effectiveness of a patient-specific biomechanical model (PSBM) in pre-operative planning for acetabular surgery was evaluated. The PSBM was utilised in custom software to simulate the biomechanics of the surgery in terms of reduction sequences. The study concluded that pre-operative planning in acetabular surgery based on a PSBM leads to a shorter operative time and reduces blood loss during surgery.

Logishetty (Logishetty et al., 2019) conducted a randomised controlled trial with 24 naive surgical trainees to evaluate the effectiveness of VR training in improving the performance of trainees in performing anterior approach in total hip arthroplasty (THA). Twelve trainees completed a six-week VR training programme in a simulation laboratory, while the other twelve received only conventional preparatory materials for learning THA. All trainees then performed a cadaveric THA, assessed independently by two hip surgeons. The results showed that VR-trained surgeons performed at a higher level than controls, with a median Procedure Based Assessment (PBA) of Level 3a (procedure performed with minimal guidance or intervention) versus Level 2a (guidance required for most/all of the procedure or part performed). VR-trained surgeons completed 33% more critical steps than controls, were 12° more accurate in component orientation, and were 18% faster. The study concluded that procedural knowledge and psychomotor skills for THA learned in VR were transferred to cadaveric performance. VR could augment traditional surgical training to improve how surgeons learn complex open procedures.

In paediatric orthopaedic surgery, a study conducted by Cevallos (Cevallos et al., 2022) assigned surgical trainees to a study guide (SG group) and a VR group. All participants were provided with a technique video and SG; the VR group additionally trained via an Osso VR surgical trainer (ossovr.com) with real-time feedback and coaching from an attending paediatric orthopaedic surgeon. Then, all the participants performed an SCFE (Slipped capital femoral epiphysis) guide-wire placement on a sawbones model embedded in a soft-tissue envelope. Time taken for pinning, pin in and out, articular surface penetrations, distance from pin tip to subchondral bone, and average angle deviation between pin and line perpendicular to the physics were significantly lower in the VR group compared to that of the SG group.

A study conducted by Jiangang (Shi et al., 2018) randomly assigned ten inexperienced residents into a simulation training group (ST group) trained on a virtual surgical training system and a control group who were trained with an introductory teaching session. Each group performed the insertion of a screw into the spine of cadaver specimens. The authors found that the screw penetration rates and screw penetration distance were significantly lower in the ST group compared to the control group. This study proves that virtual reality training can improve the accuracy of pedicle screw placement.

Many studies have assessed the use of VR training in orthopaedics, and several have compared this to traditional methods of training. Crockett (Crockatt et al., 2023) in their study, randomised 14 junior residents to VR training or cadaveric training. They found no significant difference in total Objective Structured Assessment of Technical Skill score, Global Rating Scale score, or time to completion in cadaveric glenoid baseplate implantation between the two groups. The average cost of iVR hardware and a 1-year software license was $4,900, but it can be shared among multiple users at a single training program, thus lowering the cost per resident. The cost of a single cadaver laboratory training was $1,268.20 per resident.

Lohre (Lohre et al., 2023) performed a randomised, intervention-controlled clinical trial of surgical residents to assess the effectiveness of VR training in complex surgical skill acquisition. The iVR training group received training in Precision OS on reverse shoulder arthroplasty for rotator cuff arthropathy. The control group received training using a surgical video for the same procedure. The iVR group were significantly quicker and had higher scores on technical aspects of the surgery.

Despite the several advantages of VR training, the disadvantages include the cost of VR equipment and sophisticated hardware, which may be prone to malfunction and can be a significant barrier to its widespread adoption. This includes not only the cost of the hardware but also the software and maintenance costs. However, powerful yet user-friendly development software such as "Unity®" has made programming applications significantly more accessible than previously, and this will only improve with the recent advances in AI (Combalia et al., 2024). Cybersickness can be an occasional problem triggered by a disconnect between the visual and vestibular systems, leading to symptoms such as nausea, dizziness, headaches, and general discomfort. With continuing improvements and graded exposure with frequent breaks will be of benefit, as will focusing on a stable object away from the screen or the horizon (Fulvio et al., 2019).

There are several legal implications related to data privacy. VR users may generate personal data, such as biometric, health, and location data, which have the potential to be accessed or misused by third parties without their knowledge or consent. The use of this data in VR simulations needs to be addressed.

5 Limitations of the Study

We haven't found any studies in the last ten years comparing Virtual reality training to saw bone training, which is a cost-effective simulation technique. Further studies are needed to assess the performance of candidates after VR and saw bone training on cadaveric models/saw bone models. Designing a VR training structure catering to the needs of orthopaedic residents is the need of the hour. Integrating AI techniques to create personalised experiences can benefit VR training. Future research should explore the synergies between VR and AI and address the gaps in the current state of VR in orthopaedics. Using features such as eye tracking and facial expression recognition, algorithms can adjust exercises in real time.

6 Conclusion

Despite the advances in VR training in orthopaedic surgery, this was the first time that any of the participants in our study had used VR training in surgery. Our experimental study revealed that VR training is a promising tool for orthopaedic surgery education, as it can provide realistic and immersive simulations that enhance skills and confidence. Our survey results confirmed that most orthopaedic trainees are interested in VR training and perceive it as useful. They are also willing to participate in a randomised control trial to compare VR training with other forms of simulation. Furthermore, our literature review provided valuable insights regarding the extensive use of VR in trauma and orthopaedics in recent times. Therefore, we recommend developing a formal and structured VR training programme in orthopaedic training hospitals with the resources to implement this technology.

Acknowledgements The Authors did not receive any monetary funding for this study from the institution or Precision OS company.

References

Ahmed, A., Goel, D., Lohre, R. (n.d.). *Virtual reality for shoulder arthroplasty education.*

Bajuri, M. Y., Benferdia, Y., & Ahmad, M. N. (n.d.). *Critical success factors for virtual reality applications in orthopaedic surgical training: a systematic literature review.* IEEE Access.

Bartlett, J. D., Lawrence, J. E., & Khanduja, V. (2019). *Virtual reality hip arthroscopy simulator demonstrates sufficient face validity.* Knee Surg Sports Traumatol Arthrosc, 27(10), 3162–3167. https://doi.org/10.1007/s00167-018-5038-8

Bayona, S., Rey, U., Carlos, J., Espadero, J. M., Pastor, L., Fernández-Arroyo, J. (2003). *A low-cost arthroscopy surgery training system.* In: Proceedings of the 2003 ACM SIGGRAPH/Eurographics symposium on Computer animation (pp. 305–306). San Diego, California: Eurographics Association.

Boudissa, M., Oliveri, H., Chabanas, M., Tonetti, J. (2018). *Computer-assisted surgery in acetabular fractures: Virtual reduction of acetabular fracture using the first patient-specific biomechanical model simulator*. Orthop Traumatol Surg Res, 104(3), 359–362.

Cevallos, N., Zukotynski, B., Greig, D., Silva, M., Thompson, R. M. (2022). *The Utility of Virtual Reality in Orthopedic Surgical Training*. J Surg Educ, 79(6), 1516–1525.

Combalia, A., Sanchez-Vives, M. V., & Donegan, T. (2024). Immersive virtual reality in orthopaedics—a narrative review. International Orthopaedics (SICOT), 48, 21–30. https://doi.org/10.1007/s00264-023-05911-w

Crockatt, W. K., Confino, J. E., Kopydlowski, N. J., Jobin, C. M., & Levine, W. N. (2023). *Comparing Skill Acquisition and Validity of Immersive Virtual Reality with Cadaver Laboratory Sessions in Training for Reverse Total Shoulder Arthroplasty*. JB & JS Open Access, 8(3), e22.00141. https://doi.org/10.2106/jbjs.oa.22.00141

Feeley, A., Turley, L., Sheehan, E., Merghani, K., Arden, R. (2021). *A portable hip arthroscopy simulator demonstrates good face and content validity with incomplete construct validity.* Arthrosc Sports Med Rehabil, 3(5), e1287–e1293. https://doi.org/10.1016/j.asmr.2021.05.009.

Fulvio, J. M., Ji, M., & Rokers, B. (2019). *Variability in sensory sensitivity predicts motion sickness in virtual reality*. bioRxiv 488817. https://doi.org/10.1101/488817

Gupta, A., & Ambade, R. (2022). *From diagnosis to therapy: the role of virtual and augmented reality in orthopaedic trauma surgery*. Cureus, 14(9), e29099.

Handal, B., Shine, S., Messmer, M., Dann, A. (2023). *The Use of Virtual Reality Training in Preparation for Reverse Total Shoulder Arthroplasty—A Case Report*. Journal of Orthopaedic Experience & Innovation, March. https://doi.org/10.60118/001c.68117

Khor, W. S., Nguyen, D., Kowalewski, T. M., Haverkamp, F., Alarcón, L., Fürst, D., et al. (2019). *Applications of mixed reality technology in orthopedics surgery: a pilot study*. Front Surg, 6, 60.

Lamb, A., McKinney, B., Frousiakis, P., Diaz, G., Sweet, S. (n.d.). *A comparative study of traditional technique guide versus virtual reality in orthopaedic trauma training*. Adv Med Educ Pract.

Le, A., Lambers, A. P., Fraval, A., Hardidge, A., Balakumar, J. (2023). *Utility assessment of virtual reality technology in orthopaedic surgical training*. ANZ J Surg, 93(9), 2092–2096. https://doi.org/10.1111/ans.18501. Epub 2023 May 2. PMID: 37128774.

Lee, G. K., Moshrefi, S., Fuertes, V., et al. (2021). *What is your reality? Virtual, augmented, and mixed reality in plastic surgery training, education, and practice*. Plast Reconstr Surg, 147, 505–511.

Logishetty, K., Rudran, B., Cobb, J. P. (2019). *Virtual reality training improves trainee performance in total hip arthroplasty: a randomized controlled trial*. Bone Joint J, 101–B(12), 1585–1592. PMID: 31786991.

Lohre, R., Warner, J. J. P., Athwal, G. S., & Goel, D. P. (2020). *The evolution of virtual reality in shoulder and elbow surgery*. JSES Int, 4(2), 215–223. https://doi.org/10.1016/j.jseint.2020.02.005. PMID: 32490405; PMCID: PMC7256885.

Lohre, R., Bois, A. J., Pollock, J. W., Lapner, P., McIlquham, K., Athwal, G. S., ... Goel, D. P.; Canadian Shoulder and Elbow Society (CSES). (2023). *Effectiveness of immersive virtual reality on orthopaedic surgical skills and knowledge acquisition among senior surgical residents: a randomized clinical trial*. JAMA Network Open.

Longo, U. G., De Salvatore, S., Candela, V., Zollo, G., Calabrese, G., Fioravanti, S., et al. (2021). *Augmented reality, virtual reality and artificial intelligence in orthopedic surgery: a systematic review*. Appl Sci, 11(7), 3253.

McKnight, R. R., Pean, C. A., Buck, J. S., Hwang, J. S., Hsu, J. R., Pierrie, S. N. (2020). *Virtual Reality and Augmented Reality-Translating Surgical Training into Surgical Technique*. Curr Rev Musculoskelet Med, 13(6), 663–674.

Moro, C., Štromberga, Z., Raikos, A., & Stirling, A. (2017). *The effectiveness of virtual and augmented reality in health sciences and medical anatomy*. Anat Sci Educ, 10(6), 549–559.

Pensieri, C., & Pennacchini, M. (2014). *Overview: virtual reality in medicine*. J Virtual Worlds Res, 7(1).

Shafarenko, M. S., Catapano, J., Hofer, S. O. P., & Murphy, B. D. (2022). *The Role of Augmented Reality in the Next Phase of Surgical Education.* Plast Reconstr Surg Glob Open, 10(11), e4656. https://doi.org/10.1097/GOX.0000000000004656. PMID: 36348749; PMCID: PMC9633082.

Sharma, M., Khanal, P., Patel, N., Patel, A. (2023). *Validation of a virtual reality simulator for intramedullary femoral nail application during an orthopaedic surgical course.* Orthop Procs, 105–B(SUPP_7), 90–90. https://doi.org/10.1302/1358-992X.2023.7.090.

Shi, J., Hou, Y., Lin, Y., Chen, H., & Yuan, W. (2018). *Role of Visuohaptic Surgical Training Simulator in Resident Education of Orthopedic Surgery.* World Neurosurgery, 111, e98–e104. https://doi.org/10.1016/j.wneu.2017.12.015

Sugand, K., Akhtar, K., Khatri, C., Cobb, J., & Gupte, C. (2015). *Training effect of a virtual reality haptics-enabled dynamic hip screw simulator.* Acta Orthopaedica, 86(6), 695–701. https://doi.org/10.3109/17453674.2015.1071111.

Ugwoke, C. K., Albano, D., Umek, N., Dumić-Čule, I., & Snoj, Ž. (2023). *Application of Virtual Reality Systems in Bone Trauma Procedures.* Medicina (Kaunas), 59(3), 562.

The Development of Augmented and Mixed Reality in Orthopaedic Surgery: A Review of Its Evolving Use in the Healthcare Industry

Alastair Konarski, Ketan Kantamaneni, Suresh Kondi, and Bibhas Roy

Abstract Orthopaedic surgery is one of the largest surgical specialties with a massive global market. Augmented Reality (AR) and Mixed Reality (MR) has slowly been introduced, with an exponential increase in its use in this field in recent years. We performed a systematic review of the literature to investigate how Augmented and Mixed reality is being used within orthopaedic surgery, in several areas including planning, training and performing surgery, and the impact this has had on patient care. We review the potential advantages of these tools, along with the limitations to date, and discuss the potential future directions of new technology in this multi-billion dollar healthcare industry.

Keywords Augmented reality · Mixed reality · Trauma · Orthopaedic · Surgery · Training

1 Introduction

Orthopaedic surgery is a specialty which manages acute injuries and chronic conditions of bones, joints and soft tissues. It is one of the largest surgical specialties, and its global market size is estimated to be around $59 billion per year (Fortune Business Insights 2024). The first reported use of Virtual Reality (VR) in Orthopaedic Surgery was over 25 years ago (Chao et al. 1997). It enables the surgeon to interact with a virtual environment and is well established in planning and training for operations. VR however does not allow the surgeon to interact with the real world. Augmented Reality (AR) allows interaction with the real world and was first reported in relation

A. Konarski (✉) · K. Kantamaneni · B. Roy
Department of Trauma and Orthopaedics, Manchester University NHS Foundation Trust, Manchester, UK
e-mail: ajkonarski@doctors.org.uk

S. Kondi
Department of Trauma and Orthopaedics, Portsmouth Hospitals University NHS Trust, Portsmouth, UK

T. Jung et al. (eds.), *XR and Metaverse*, Springer Proceedings in Business and Economics, https://doi.org/10.1007/978-3-031-77975-6_33

to orthopaedic surgery in 1998 by Blackwell et al. (1998). Once the virtual environment is registered to the real environment, mixed reality allows interaction between the virtual image, often derived from scanning technologies such as CT and MRI scans, and real surfaces. Significant research has taken place on how this technology can benefit the workflow of orthopaedic surgery, from training and pre-operative planning, intra-operative navigation, and postoperative rehabilitation (Longo et al. 2021). We aim to review the scientific literature in the field to determine its current impact and its potential future uses.

2 Methods

The literature search was performed on PubMed, Cochrane, Medline, Embase and CINAHL in February 2024 for the following medical subject headings (MeSH) terms; "augmented reality" OR "mixed reality" AND "orthopaedic" OR "orthopedic" AND "surgery". Titles were screened for original articles in English, reporting on the use of AR in Orthopaedic Surgery. Articles were excluded if they were duplicates, were not in English, conference proceedings, were review articles, did not report on augmented reality or mixed reality or orthopaedic surgery. Full texts were then reviewed by the authors (Fig. 1).

Articles were broadly divided into pre-operative planning and training, or intra-operative use. The intra-operative articles were categorised according to subspecialty such as arthroplasty, spinal surgery, trauma or tumour surgery.

3 Literature Review

Following a literature search as described in the methods, we identified 124 papers on the use of Augmented Reality (AR) in Trauma and Orthopaedic Surgery. We categorised the results into broad fields of pre-operative planning, training, trauma, tumour surgery, spinal surgery, and arthroplasty, and review the key papers from each category.

Pre-operative Planning

Several papers investigated the use of AR in pre-operative planning, allowing pre-operative planning images to be overlayed on the patient using a head mounted display (HMD), such as Microsoft Hololens or Google Glass (Longo et al. 2021). Guo used AR to plan fixation of scapula fractures, to pre-bend plates for fixation and then use intra-operative navigation with HMDs, demonstrating reduced surgical time and blood loss (Guo et al. 2022). Yu et al. (2019) performed a study investigating the use of mixed reality software to pre-operatively plan and train students to perform a spinal operation, demonstrating reduced time and radiation when they performed the surgery on a model. The trainees had high satisfaction of the MR training.

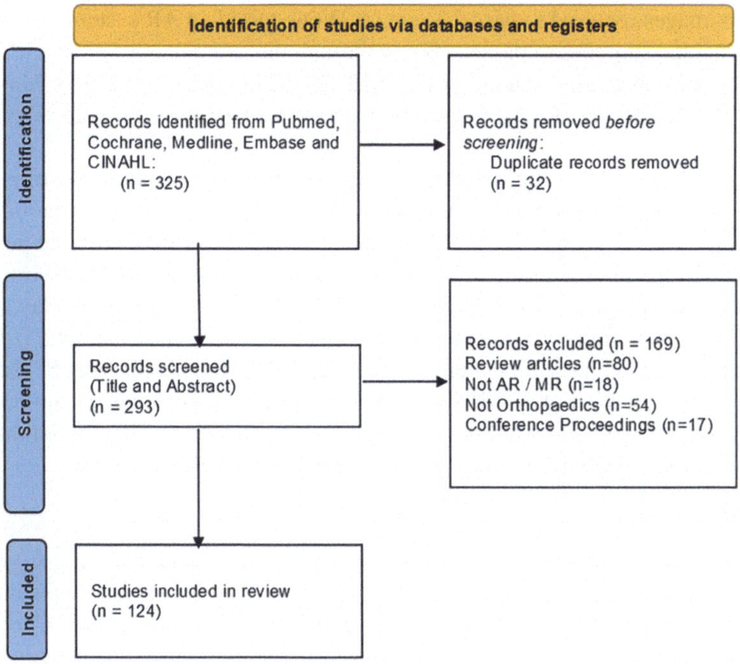

Fig. 1 PRISMA flow diagram of article selection

Training

Studies have demonstrated the use of AR in education for surgical trainees in a variety of settings, including, spinal (Yeo et al. 2011), shoulder (Ponce et al. 2014) and hip fracture surgery (Sugand et al. 2019). It has been used for simulation, including training on cadavers, and remote training, where another surgeon can give real-time feedback during a surgical procedure. Condino et al. (2018) designed a training simulator for performing hip replacement surgery using a 3D hip model in combination with a Hololens HMD, which was found to add realism to the simulation, with positive feedback from trainees. Another study designed a MR training environment to simulate a spinal joint injection using MR rather than fluoroscopy to reduce the radiation, with good accuracy and realism (Stefan et al. 2018).

Trauma

Surgeons rely on 3D orientation to position implants, such as wires, screws or nails, often using fluoroscopy or X-rays which provide 2D information. AR can help overlay 3D imaging onto patients to improve orientation. Diotte and his team were amongst the first to publish on the use of AR to help position a locking screw into a femoral nail. The screw must pass through the skin, fat, muscle and bone, before passing through a 4–6 mm hole in the metal nail and then through the bone on the far side. This has traditionally been done using fluoroscopy, with some studies reporting up to 48 images required to pass the screws. Diotte tested an AR system on a model which enabled surgeons to pass the screw through the nail using only a single X-ray image in a quicker time (Diotte et al. 2012, 2015; Londei et al. 2015). Ma et al. (2018) and Klopfer et al. (2023) have performed similar feasibility studies in tibial nails.

Other studies have been performed to assess the use of AR in positioning a guidewire in the head of the femur. As part of fixation for fractures around the hip, a guidewire is positioned, before inserting a screw over it. Ideally the position should be in the middle of the head and neck. Van Duren et al. (2018) investigated the use of an AR system with orthogonal cameras to create a virtual overlay onto a model, improving training without the radiation exposure. Konda et al. (2023) developed this further with use on patients in a retrospective study comparing 57 patients before the introduction of an AR system to help position a guidewire in hip fracture surgery, with 57 patients after they introduced the technology. They found that the position of the guidewire was statistically improved with the use of AR.

Tumour Surgery

When resecting tumours, it is vital to remove all the malignant tissue, whilst preserving as much surrounding tissue as possible. AR has been tested on pig models to remove simulated lesions from pig legs and pelvis (Cho et al. 2018; Cho et al. 2017) resulting in fewer resection errors when compared to conventional approaches. Moreta-Martinez et al. (2021) combined AR and 3D printing for the management of tumours in orthopaedic surgery. They were able to 3D print models of the tumour and bones for planning and explaining the surgery to the patient. They then 3D printed a custom marker to specifically fit to the patient's anatomy and used a smartphone application to project the tumour onto the patient, allowing accurate resection within 3 mm of plans.

Tigchelaar used AR to navigate the removal of 3 tumours from the spine in their series (Tigchelaar et al. 2022). Pose-Diez-de-la-Lastra evaluated the advances between the Hololens 1 and the Hololens 2 in an AR system designed to navigate the removal of tumours, and found improved accuracy with the Hololens 2, enabling them to use the technology in real operations (Pose-Díez-de-la-Lastra et al. 2022).

Spinal Surgery

Spinal surgery poses a particular challenge, due to the proximity to the spinal cord, with errors in positioning of implants potentially having serious consequences. Articles investigating the use of AR in spinal surgery were the largest category of studies, with over 42 papers included. The first published paper in 2010 investigated the use of 3D MRI models of the spine being projected onto 2D thorascopic images and presenting the possibility of using the technology for discectomy (Bisson et al. 2010). The first reported use of the technology for real patients was in 2013 where Abe (Abe et al. 2013) used AR to plan and guide needle insertion into spinal fractures for vertebroplasty. They reported increased accuracy using the technology.

Several articles have investigated the use of AR in spinal surgery, particularly in positioning of screws or needles in the spine (Elmi-Terander et al. 2019; Wu et al.

2014). Screws or needles are often passed along the pedicles of a vertebra into the body, to allow fixation, or to inject cement to provide support. The pedicles act as a safe corridor to allow passage into the body of the vertebra, and avoid injury to the spinal cord itself, or nerve roots as the exit the spine. Traditionally these screws have been inserted either freehand or using fluoroscopy (X-rays) intra-operatively. Since early feasibility studies on models and cadavers (Elmi-Terander et al. 2016; Wu et al. 2014) showed good accuracy, case series of real patients also demonstrated improved accuracy (Abe et al. 2013; Charles et al. 2021; Hu et al. 2020). Since then, randomised controlled trials have demonstrated equivalent or improved accuracy (Auloge et al. 2020), reduced radiation, and Gu et al. (2020) found improved patient outcome scores in patient where mixed reality had been used.

Other uses of AR in spinal surgery in the literature include case reports of using the technology to help correct spinal deformities (Mozaffari et al. 2022). Von Atzingen investigated the use of AR to help bend rods used for spinal surgery (von Atzigen et al. 2022) and then a custom-built rod bending machine utilising AR reduced the forces transmitted through the pedicle screws (von Atzigen et al. 2024).

Arthroplasty

Arthroplasty, or joint replacement surgery, is one of the largest fields of orthopaedics. It is important to position the implants correctly to fit a patient's anatomy and give the best outcomes for the patient. Many studies have investigated the use of AR in implant positioning in hip, knee, shoulder and elbow arthroplasty (Rossi et al. 2022). These systems typically involve HMDs, and a registration system, to map the patient's anatomy, and correlate this to pre-operative imaging, such as CT or MRI scans. This allows the surgeon to adjust the positioning of implants in real time to match the pre-operative plans. Studies have reported accurate positioning of implants in hips (Ogawa et al. 2018), knee (Tsukada et al. 2021) and shoulder (Kriechling et al. 2023; Schlueter-Brust et al. 2021) replacement trials. The majority of these have been feasibility studies in cadaveric or simulated models, although studies are now being reported in patients (Tsukada et al. 2021).

An early study from 2007 (Atmani et al. 2007) was one of the first to use AR to create 3D models of a shoulder joint, to allow pre-operative planning of the positioning of the implant in the shoulder, and then test the implantation on a model. Since then, many studies have investigated the use of AR in shoulder replacement surgery, using a HMD to enable accurate positioning of the implant in both cadaveric (Kriechling et al. 2023; Rojas et al. 2023) and 3D printed models (Trehin et al. 2023). This commercially available technology is now being used in real patients, although publication of patient outcomes are still awaited.

Over 1 million hip replacements are performed around the world each year (Ferguson et al. 2018). It is one of the most successful operations in terms of patient satisfaction and improving quality of life. Many studies have explored the use of AR to improve the positioning of implants in patients. The position of the acetabular component is important to reduce the risk of dislocation of the hip replacement and reduce the rate of wear of the implant. A randomised study (Logishetty et al. 2019) assessing training of medical students to implant a hip replacement in a model, either taught traditionally by a hip surgeon, or taught using an AR headset, and found equivalent results between the two groups.

Ogawa et al. (2018) were one of the first studies to use an AR system on real patients, where the position of the implant was superimposed onto the surgical field with a smartphone, enabling the surgeons to achieve more accurate positioning than traditional methods. Ogawa et al. (2020) later published the results of a randomised controlled trial comparing their AR system to traditional methods using a mechanical alignment guide, and found no significant differences between the groups. Based on this, they did not feel they could recommend the AR system due to the added costs and time during surgery. The same group again later published another study (Kurosaka et al. 2023) comparing the AR system to the use of an accelerometer in surgery, and again found no significant differences between the groups, again not recommending widespread use of AR in hip replacement surgery. Fujita et al. (2023) compared the same devices using a different technique, with the patient in a different position and again found similar outcomes between the systems, but felt the AR system would be better suited in patients with obesity. Tanino et al. (2024) performed a randomised controlled study using a commercially available AR navigation system for hip implant positioning compared to traditional techniques. Although they found a slightly better positioning with the AR system compared to traditional, they felt this was not likely to be of clinical difference, with no differences in hip outcome scores, but a significantly longer surgical time with AR. They suggested these small differences may make a difference in the long-term outcome of the surgery, but until that was know they did not recommend AR in hip replacement surgery.

Knee replacement surgery is another popular operation within orthopaedics with over 1 million procedures per year worldwide. It has been the subject of several studies using AR, but Pokhrel et al. (2019) felt in 2019 that it was not as successfully implemented due to the errors in cutting. Their study reported on a method that could cut the cutting errors by 1 to 0.40–0.55 mm. Castellarin et al. (2024) were the first to report on the use of an AR tool to guide the bone cuts in a knee replacement in 76 patients, and found they were accurate to within 1° of the planned cut, suggesting excellent accuracy.

Radiography

Many operations in orthopaedics use a portable X-ray machine, or fluoroscopy, to visualise the position of implants within the bone. The limitations of this are that only a 2D image is obtained, for a 3D problem, and there is radiation exposure to the patient and staff. Many studies (Andress et al. 2018; Chen et al. 2014; Fotouhi et al. 2019; Hosseinian et al. 2019; Unberath et al. 2018) have investigated how AR can be used to improve on this technology and reduce the radiation dose. They have tested how different calibration methods work including using multimodal fiducial markers, HMDs and RGB cameras to calibrate X-ray images with the environment, with studies (Andress et al. 2018) finding improved accuracy and reduced radiation with these techniques for positioning guidewires for hip surgery on models.

4 Discussion and Conclusion

We have discussed the major benefits reported from the use of AR in Orthopaedics in the literature review. There are however some limitations we found in the literature. These include registration errors, whereby the registering of anatomic landmarks does not match accurately to the pre-operative imaging, leading to malpositioning. Loss of connection has been an issue, as has poor image resolution, and brightness or contrast limitations. Some users have reported visual discomfort or fatigue, and the weight of the HMD could be an issue, with some users reporting motion sickness. There is a learning curve associated with the use of new technology.

While many studies have shown benefits to AR such as reduced time, reduced radiation, better implant positioning, most literature is in pre-clinical settings or simulation, but now a limited number of studies have demonstrated improved patient outcomes. Some randomised studies such as those investigating the use of AR in positioning hip implants for replacement have shown no significant differences to traditional methods. This may be due to traditional methods becoming accurate over time, where AR tools may only make a small improvement in accuracy that does not result in differences that are clinically felt by patients. There is also a cost implication to consider in the use of AR in surgery.

Our literature search revealed 124 results. Of these, only 26 were prior to 2018. Since then, there has been an exponential rise in the number of articles discussing the use of AR in Orthopaedic surgery (Fig. 2).

The impact of AR on orthopaedic surgery was predicted in 1998, and we are now seeing the evolution from pre-clinical studies to its use on real patients. Given the rapid progression of interest in the use of AR in orthopaedics, with the development of new technology, reducing the concerns from older systems, we predict a significant increase in the use of AR in this field of surgery in the next few years.

It has demonstrated its use in multiple areas of this diverse field of surgery, with many potential advantages, to both the surgeon and the patient. We are still in the early stages of implementing AR systems into real life patient care, but we predict

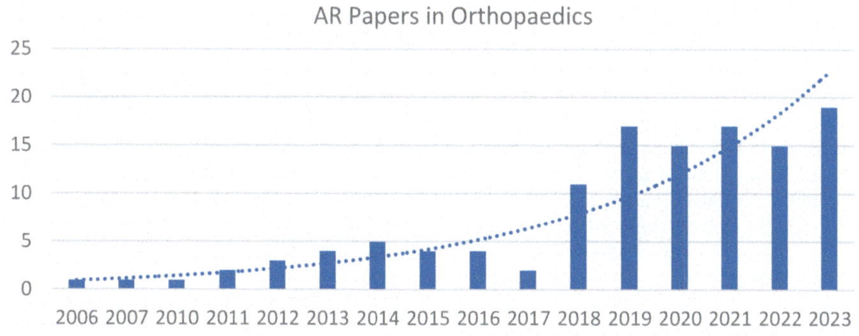

Fig. 2 Trend of number of publications on AR in orthopaedics by year

a promising future for the use of AR in orthopaedic surgery. Further studies should be done to assess the true impact of AR on patient outcomes.

References

Abe, Y., Sato, S., Kato, K., Hyakumachi, T., Yanagibashi, Y., Ito, M., & Abumi, K. (2013). A novel 3D guidance system using augmented reality for percutaneous vertebroplasty. *Journal of Neurosurgery: Spine, 19*(4), 492–501. https://doi.org/10.3171/2013.7.SPINE12917

Andress, S., Johnson, A., Unberath, M., Winkler, A. F., Yu, K., Fotouhi, J., Weidert, S., Osgood, G., & Navab, N. (2018). On-the-fly augmented reality for orthopedic surgery using a multimodal fiducial. *Journal of Medical Imaging, 5*(02), 1. https://doi.org/10.1117/1.JMI.5.2.021209

Atmani, H., Merienne, F., Fofi, D., & Trouilloud, P. (2007). Computer aided surgery system for shoulder prosthesis placement. *Computer Aided Surgery, 12*(1), 60–70. https://doi.org/10.3109/10929080701210832

Auloge, P., Cazzato, R. L., Ramamurthy, N., de Marini, P., Rousseau, C., Garnon, J., Charles, Y. P., Steib, J.-P., & Gangi, A. (2020). Augmented reality and artificial intelligence-based navigation during percutaneous vertebroplasty: a pilot randomised clinical trial. *European Spine Journal, 29*(7), 1580–1589. https://doi.org/10.1007/s00586-019-06054-6

Bisson, M., Cheriet, F., & Parent, S. (2010). 3D visualization tool for minimally invasive discectomy assistance. *Studies in Health Technology and Informatics, 158*, 55–60.

Blackwell, M., Morgan, F., & DiGioia, A. M. (1998). Augmented reality and its future in orthopaedics. *Clinical Orthopaedics and Related Research, 354*, 111–122. https://doi.org/10.1097/00003086-199809000-00014

Castellarin, G., Bori, E., Barbieux, E., Grandjean, V.-P., Jost, G., & Innocenti, B. (2024). Is Total Knee Arthroplasty Surgical Performance Enhanced Using Augmented Reality? A Single-Center Study on 76 Consecutive Patients. *The Journal of Arthroplasty, 39*(2), 332–335. https://doi.org/10.1016/j.arth.2023.08.013

Chao, E. Y., Barrance, P., Genda, E., Iwasaki, N., Kato, S., & Faust, A. (1997). Virtual reality (VR) techniques in orthopaedic research and practice. *Studies in Health Technology and Informatics, 39*, 107–114.

Charles, Y. P., Cazzato, R. L., Nachabe, R., Chatterjea, A., Steib, J.-P., & Gangi, A. (2021). Minimally Invasive Transforaminal Lumbar Interbody Fusion Using Augmented Reality Surgical Navigation for Percutaneous Pedicle Screw Placement. *Clinical Spine Surgery: A Spine Publication, 34*(7), E415–E424. https://doi.org/10.1097/BSD.0000000000001132

Chen, X., Naik, H., Wang, L., Navab, N., & Fallavollita, P. (2014). Video-guided calibration of an augmented reality mobile C-arm. *International Journal of Computer Assisted Radiology and Surgery, 9*(6), 987–996. https://doi.org/10.1007/s11548-014-0995-y

Cho, H. S., Park, M. S., Gupta, S., Han, I., Kim, H. S., Choi, H., & Hong, J. (2018). Can augmented reality be helpful in pelvic bone cancer surgery? An in vitro study. *Clinical Orthopaedics and Related Research, 476*(9), 1719–1725. https://doi.org/10.1007/s11999.0000000000000233

Cho, S., Park, Y. K., Gupta, S., Yoon, C., Han, I., Kim, H-S., Hong, J., Professor, associate, & Park, K. (2017). *Augmented reality in bone tumour resection.* https://doi.org/10.1302/2046-3758.63.BJR

Condino, S., Turini, G., Parchi, P. D., Viglialoro, R. M., Piolanti, N., Gesi, M., Ferrari, M., & Ferrari, V. (2018). How to Build a Patient-Specific Hybrid Simulator for Orthopaedic Open Surgery: Benefits and Limits of Mixed-Reality Using the Microsoft HoloLens. *Journal of Healthcare Engineering, 2018*, 1–12. https://doi.org/10.1155/2018/5435097

Diotte, B., Fallavollita, P., Wang, L., Weidert, S., Euler, E., Thaller, P., & Navab, N. (2015). Multi-Modal Intra-Operative Navigation During Distal Locking of Intramedullary Nails. *IEEE Transactions on Medical Imaging, 34*(2), 487–495. https://doi.org/10.1109/TMI.2014.2361155

Diotte, B., Fallavollita, P., Wang, L., Weidert, S., Thaller, P.-H., Euler, E., & Navab, N. (2012). *Radiation-Free Drill Guidance in Interlocking of Intramedullary Nails* (pp. 18–25). https://doi.org/10.1007/978-3-642-33415-3_3

Elmi-Terander, A., Skulason, H., Söderman, M., Racadio, J., Homan, R., Babic, D., van der Vaart, N., & Nachabe, R. (2016). Surgical Navigation Technology Based on Augmented Reality and Integrated 3D Intraoperative Imaging. *Spine*, *41*(21), E1303–E1311. https://doi.org/10.1097/BRS.0000000000001830

Elmi-Terander, A., Burström, G., Nachabe, R., Skulason, H., Pedersen, K., Fagerlund, M., Ståhl, F., Charalampidis, A., Söderman, M., Holmin, S., Babic, D., Jenniskens, I., Edström, E., & Gerdhem, P. (2019). Pedicle Screw Placement Using Augmented Reality Surgical Navigation With Intraoperative 3D Imaging: A First In-Human Prospective Cohort Study. *Spine*, *44*(7), 517–525. https://doi.org/10.1097/BRS.0000000000002876

Ferguson, R. J., Palmer, A. J., Taylor, A., Porter, M. L., Malchau, H., & Glyn-Jones, S. (2018). Hip replacement. *The Lancet*, *392*(10158), 1662–1671. https://doi.org/10.1016/S0140-6736(18)31777-X

Fortune Business Insights, A. (2024). https://www.fortunebusinessinsights.com/orthopedic-devices-market-102586. https://www.fortunebusinessinsights.com/orthopedic-devices-market-102586

Fotouhi, J., Unberath, M., Song, T., Hajek, J., Lee, S. C., Bier, B., Maier, A., Osgood, G., Armand, M., & Navab, N. (2019). Co-localized augmented human and X-ray observers in collaborative surgical ecosystem. *International Journal of Computer Assisted Radiology and Surgery*, *14*(9), 1553–1563. https://doi.org/10.1007/s11548-019-02035-8

Fujita, M., Hayashi, S., Kuroda, Y., Nakano, N., Maeda, T., Matsushita, T., Matsumoto, T., & Kuroda, R. (2023). Accuracy comparison of cup positioning during total hip arthroplasty using Hip Align and AR-Hip in the supine position. *Archives of Orthopaedic and Trauma Surgery*, *143*(12), 7229–7235. https://doi.org/10.1007/s00402-023-04975-y

Gu, Y., Yao, Q., Xu, Y., Zhang, H., Wei, P., & Wang, L. (2020). A Clinical Application Study of Mixed Reality Technology Assisted Lumbar Pedicle Screws Implantation. *Medical Science Monitor*, *26*. https://doi.org/10.12659/MSM.924982

Guo, Q., Li, X., Tang, Y., Huang, Y., & Luo, L. (2022). Augmented reality and three-dimensional plate library-assisted posterior minimally invasive surgery for scapula fracture. *International Orthopaedics*, *46*(4), 875–882. https://doi.org/10.1007/s00264-022-05303-6

Hosseinian, S., Arefi, H., & Navab, N. (2019). Toward an End-to-End Calibration for Mobile C-Arm in Combination with a Depth Sensor for Surgical Augmented Reality Applications. *Sensors*, *20*(1), 36. https://doi.org/10.3390/s20010036

Hu, M.-H., Chiang, C.-C., Wang, M.-L., Wu, N.-Y., & Lee, P.-Y. (2020). Clinical feasibility of the augmented reality computer-assisted spine surgery system for percutaneous vertebroplasty. *European Spine Journal*, *29*(7), 1590–1596. https://doi.org/10.1007/s00586-020-06417-4

Klopfer, T., Notheisen, T., Baumgartner, H., Schneidmueller, D., Giordmaina, R., Histing, T., & Gonser, C. E. (2023). Next step trauma and orthopaedic surgery: integration of augmented reality for reduction and nail implantation of tibial fractures. *International Orthopaedics*, *47*(2), 495–501. https://doi.org/10.1007/s00264-022-05619-3

Konda, S. R., Solasz, S., Derken, M., Ganta, A., & Egol, K. A. (2023). Improving Cephalad Lag Screw Placement in the Femoral Head During Cephalomedullary Nailing Using a Novel Augmented Reality System. *Journal of Orthopaedic Trauma*, *37*(3), 130–134. https://doi.org/10.1097/BOT.0000000000002504

Kriechling, P., Loucas, R., Loucas, M., Casari, F., Fürnstahl, P., & Wieser, K. (2023). Augmented reality through head-mounted display for navigation of baseplate component placement in reverse total shoulder arthroplasty: a cadaveric study. *Archives of Orthopaedic and Trauma Surgery*, *143*(1), 169–175. https://doi.org/10.1007/s00402-021-04025-5

Kurosaka, K., Ogawa, H., Hirasawa, N., Saito, M., Nakayama, T., & Tsukada, S. (2023). Does Augmented Reality-based Portable Navigation Improve the Accuracy of Cup Placement in THA Compared With Accelerometer-based Portable Navigation? A Randomized Controlled

Trial. *Clinical Orthopaedics & Related Research, 481*(8), 1515–1523. https://doi.org/10.1097/CORR.0000000000002602

Logishetty, K., Western, L., Morgan, R., Iranpour, F., Cobb, J. P., & Auvinet, E. (2019). Can an Augmented Reality Headset Improve Accuracy of Acetabular Cup Orientation in Simulated THA? A Randomized Trial. *Clinical Orthopaedics & Related Research, 477*(5), 1190–1199. https://doi.org/10.1097/CORR.0000000000000542

Londei, R., Esposito, M., Diotte, B., Weidert, S., Euler, E., Thaller, P., Navab, N., & Fallavollita, P. (2015). Intra-operative augmented reality in distal locking. *International Journal of Computer Assisted Radiology and Surgery, 10*(9), 1395–1403. https://doi.org/10.1007/s11548-015-1169-2

Longo, U. G., De Salvatore, S., Candela, V., Zollo, G., Calabrese, G., Fioravanti, S., Giannone, L., Marchetti, A., De Marinis, M. G., & Denaro, V. (2021). Augmented reality, virtual reality and artificial intelligence in orthopedic surgery: A systematic review. *Applied Sciences (Switzerland), 11*(7). https://doi.org/10.3390/app11073253

Ma, L., Zhao, Z., Zhang, B., Jiang, W., Fu, L., Zhang, X., & Liao, H. (2018). Three-dimensional augmented reality surgical navigation with hybrid optical and electromagnetic tracking for distal intramedullary nail interlocking. *The International Journal of Medical Robotics and Computer Assisted Surgery, 14*(4). https://doi.org/10.1002/rcs.1909

Moreta-Martinez, R., Pose-Díez-de-la-Lastra, A., Calvo-Haro, J. A., Mediavilla-Santos, L., Pérez-Mañanes, R., & Pascau, J. (2021). Combining Augmented Reality and 3D Printing to Improve Surgical Workflows in Orthopedic Oncology: Smartphone Application and Clinical Evaluation. *Sensors, 21*(4), 1370. https://doi.org/10.3390/s21041370

Mozaffari, K., Foster, C. H., & Rosner, M. K. (2022). Practical Use of Augmented Reality Modeling to Guide Revision Spine Surgery: An Illustrative Case of Hardware Failure and Overriding Spondyloptosis. *Operative Neurosurgery, 23*(3), 212–216. https://doi.org/10.1227/ons.0000000000000307

Ogawa, H., Hasegawa, S., Tsukada, S., & Matsubara, M. (2018). A Pilot Study of Augmented Reality Technology Applied to the Acetabular Cup Placement During Total Hip Arthroplasty. *The Journal of Arthroplasty, 33*(6), 1833–1837. https://doi.org/10.1016/j.arth.2018.01.067

Ogawa, H., Kurosaka, K., Sato, A., Hirasawa, N., Matsubara, M., & Tsukada, S. (2020). Does An Augmented Reality-based Portable Navigation System Improve the Accuracy of Acetabular Component Orientation During THA? A Randomized Controlled Trial. *Clinical Orthopaedics & Related Research, 478*(5), 935–943. https://doi.org/10.1097/CORR.0000000000001083

Pokhrel, S., Alsadoon, A., Prasad, P. W. C., & Paul, M. (2019). A novel augmented reality (AR) scheme for knee replacement surgery by considering cutting error accuracy. *The International Journal of Medical Robotics and Computer Assisted Surgery, 15*(1). https://doi.org/10.1002/rcs.1958

Ponce, B. A., Menendez, M. E., Oladeji, L. O., Fryberger, C. T., & Dantuluri, P. K. (2014). Emerging technology in surgical education: combining real-time augmented reality and wearable computing devices. *Orthopedics, 37*(11), 751–757. https://doi.org/10.3928/01477447-20141023-05

Pose-Díez-de-la-Lastra, A., Moreta-Martinez, R., García-Sevilla, M., García-Mato, D., Calvo-Haro, J. A., Mediavilla-Santos, L., Pérez-Mañanes, R., von Haxthausen, F., & Pascau, J. (2022). HoloLens 1 vs. HoloLens 2: Improvements in the New Model for Orthopedic Oncological Interventions. *Sensors, 22*(13), 4915. https://doi.org/10.3390/s22134915

Rojas, J. T., Jost, B., Zipeto, C., Budassi, P., & Zumstein, M. A. (2023). Glenoid component placement in reverse shoulder arthroplasty assisted with augmented reality through a head-mounted display leads to low deviation between planned and postoperative parameters. *Journal of Shoulder and Elbow Surgery, 32*(12), e587–e596. https://doi.org/10.1016/j.jse.2023.05.002

Rossi, S. M. P., Mancino, F., Sangaletti, R., Perticarini, L., Lucenti, L., & Benazzo, F. (2022). Augmented Reality in Orthopedic Surgery and Its Application in Total Joint Arthroplasty: A Systematic Review. In *Applied Sciences (Switzerland)* (Vol. 12, Issue 10). MDPI. https://doi.org/10.3390/app12105278

Schlueter-Brust, K., Henckel, J., Katinakis, F., Buken, C., Opt-Eynde, J., Pofahl, T., Rodriguez Y Baena, F., & Tatti, F. (2021). Augmented-reality-assisted K-wire placement for glenoid component positioning in reversed shoulder arthroplasty: A proof-of-concept study. *Journal of Personalized Medicine, 11*(8). https://doi.org/10.3390/jpm11080777

Stefan, P., Habert, S., Winkler, A., Lazarovici, M., Fürmetz, J., Eck, U., & Navab, N. (2018). A radiation-free mixed-reality training environment and assessment concept for C-arm-based surgery. *International Journal of Computer Assisted Radiology and Surgery, 13*(9), 1335–1344. https://doi.org/10.1007/s11548-018-1807-6

Sugand, K., Wescott, R. A., Carrington, R., Hart, A., & van Duren, B. H. (2019). Training and Transfer Effect of FluoroSim, an Augmented Reality Fluoroscopic Simulator for Dynamic Hip Screw Guidewire Insertion: A Single-Blinded Randomized Controlled Trial. *The Journal of Bone and Joint Surgery. American Volume, 101*(17), e88. https://doi.org/10.2106/JBJS.18.00928

Tanino, H., Mitsutake, R., Takagi, K., & Ito, H. (2024). Does a Commercially Available Augmented Reality–based Portable Hip Navigation System Improve Cup Positioning During THA Compared With the Conventional Technique? A Randomized Controlled Study. *Clinical Orthopaedics & Related Research, 482*(3), 458–467. https://doi.org/10.1097/CORR.0000000000002819

Tigchelaar, S. S., Medress, Z. A., Quon, J., Dang, P., Barbery, D., Bobrow, A., Kin, C., Louis, R., & Desai, A. (2022). Augmented Reality Neuronavigation for En Bloc Resection of Spinal Column Lesions. *World Neurosurgery, 167*, 102–110. https://doi.org/10.1016/j.wneu.2022.08.143

Trehin, A., Boas, D., Jouet, V., Zago, B., & Cariou, D. (2023). An accurate scapula registration process in shoulder arthroplasty using mixed reality. *International Journal of Computer Assisted Radiology and Surgery, 18*(7), 1341–1344. https://doi.org/10.1007/s11548-023-02962-7

Tsukada, S., Ogawa, H., Nishino, M., Kurosaka, K., & Hirasawa, N. (2021). Augmented Reality-Assisted Femoral Bone Resection in Total Knee Arthroplasty. *JBJS Open Access, 6*(3). https://doi.org/10.2106/JBJS.OA.21.00001

Unberath, M., Fotouhi, J., Hajek, J., Maier, A., Osgood, G., Taylor, R., Armand, M., & Navab, N. (2018). Augmented reality-based feedback for technician-in-the-loop C-arm repositioning. *Healthcare Technology Letters, 5*(5), 143–147. https://doi.org/10.1049/htl.2018.5066

van Duren, B. H., Sugand, K., Wescott, R., Carrington, R., & Hart, A. (2018). Augmented reality fluoroscopy simulation of the guide-wire insertion in DHS surgery: A proof of concept study. *Medical Engineering & Physics, 55*, 52–59. https://doi.org/10.1016/j.medengphy.2018.02.007

von Atzigen, M., Liebmann, F., Hoch, A., Miguel Spirig, J., Farshad, M., Snedeker, J., & Fürnstahl, P. (2022). Marker-free surgical navigation of rod bending using a stereo neural network and augmented reality in spinal fusion. *Medical Image Analysis, 77*, 102365. https://doi.org/10.1016/j.media.2022.102365

von Atzigen, M., Liebmann, F., Cavalcanti, N. A., Anh Baran, T., Wanivenhaus, F., Spirig, J. M., Rauter, G., Snedeker, J., Farshad, M., & Fürnstahl, P. (2024). Reducing residual forces in spinal fusion using a custom-built rod bending machine. *Computer Methods and Programs in Biomedicine, 247*, 108096. https://doi.org/10.1016/j.cmpb.2024.108096

Wu, J.-R., Wang, M.-L., Liu, K.-C., Hu, M.-H., & Lee, P.-Y. (2014). Real-time advanced spinal surgery via visible patient model and augmented reality system. *Computer Methods and Programs in Biomedicine, 113*(3), 869–881. https://doi.org/10.1016/j.cmpb.2013.12.021

Yeo, C. T., Ungi, T., U-Thainual, P., Lasso, A., McGraw, R. C., & Fichtinger, G. (2011). The effect of augmented reality training on percutaneous needle placement in spinal facet joint injections. *IEEE Transactions on Bio-Medical Engineering, 58*(7), 2031–2037. https://doi.org/10.1109/TBME.2011.2132131

Yu, H., Zhou, Z., Lei, X., Liu, H., Fan, G., & He, S. (2019). Mixed Reality-Based Preoperative Planning for Training of Percutaneous Transforaminal Endoscopic Discectomy: A Feasibility Study. *World Neurosurgery, 129*, e767–e775. https://doi.org/10.1016/j.wneu.2019.06.020

Dementia: Where Reality Meets Imagination—Designing XR Soundscapes and Visuals for Dementia Patients

Bas van der Host, Fabio Campos, and Marnix S. van Gisbergen

Abstract Around 2% of the global population suffers from dementia. Nature-related XR content can improve the quality of life for people with dementia. However, research on dementia raises many challenges around ethical implications, access to the patients and the challenge of capturing their behaviour (due to communication issues). Despite the challenges, a few studies investigated the effect of (nature-based) XR visuals and soundscapes. However, the effect of combining both on patients in advanced stages of dementia has not been investigated. This study investigated the effect of exposure to visuals and the combination of visuals and soundscapes, on the emotions and reactions of the patients. The results indicate that both influence emotion, attention, interest and interaction, but that the combination seems to yield more and longer effects. The results obtained are used to get insights into the potential effects of exposure to nature-related XR media and the observation protocol.

Keywords XR content production · Dementia · XR and quality of life · XR visuals · XR audio

1 Introduction

When designing XR content for the general public our creative freedom comes from a coherence between the reactions and sensations observed in the "real" world and the XR content. In this context measures such as realism, immersion, presence, and interaction make sense precisely for their parallel with our "reality". This paradigm is disrupted when the sense of reality of the target group changes. Imagine, for example how XR content showing a scene of a modern city would be perceived by isolated tribes that never had contact with our "modern reality". Unfortunately, this same reasoning can also be used with our elderlies who suffer from dementia and are more and more being challenged by losing contact with our day-to-day "modern" reality.

B. van der Host · F. Campos (✉) · M. S. van Gisbergen
BUAS - Breda University of Applied Sciences, Breda, The Netherlands
e-mail: ferreira.f@buas.nl

T. Jung et al. (eds.), *XR and Metaverse*, Springer Proceedings in Business and Economics, https://doi.org/10.1007/978-3-031-77975-6_34

This research represents an effort to generate strategies to design XR content for people with dementia, overcoming their self-expression by language challenges, and allowing them to make sense of the "real" world, through visuals and sound. This will not only help people who suffer from dementia but also other groups, like very young children, that deal with similar self-expression through language challenges. In only a few studies this problem is addressed within the domain of XR. As such, in this study, an observation strategy is used around the effect of using nature-related visuals and soundscapes to help people with dementia to make sense of "reality". A meta-study by Cheng and Sabran (2021), reveals that content related to nature can generate positive reactions and a calming and invigorating mood within dementia patients. However, the combination of visuals and sounds (in XR) is missing in previous studies. The few studies available tested visuals only or soundscapes only, but not if there is any value in combining them. To mitigate this gap, this research aims to gain insight into the effects of visuals, and visuals along with soundscapes, on patients with advanced stages of dementia.

2 Literature Review

Dementia is a severe health issue. In the Netherlands alone, there are 290,000 people with dementia, and over 100,000 are likely to have it but without having it diagnosed yet (Alzheimer Nederland 2021). Similar numbers can be found in many countries around the world. Of these 290,000 dementia-diagnosed people, more than 80,000 live in a "care home", a place with specialized care, kept by a professional health organization (Alzheimer Nederland 2021). Dementia can be seen as a "*clinical syndrome characterized by acquired losses of cognitive and emotional abilities severe enough to interfere with daily functioning and the quality of life*" (Geldmacher and Whitehouse 1996, p. 330). It is often observed in people over the age of 65, with the risk increasing the older the people are (Simmons et al. 2011). The dementia "syndrome" can be caused by several different diseases or a combination of them. The most common dementia-causing diseases are Alzheimer's, Vascular dementia, Lewy-body, and the Frontal-Lobe (Geldmacher and Whitehouse 1996; Simmons et al. 2011). All these causes result in loss of cognitive and emotional abilities and interfere with daily functioning and the quality of life of the patients (Geldmacher and Whitehouse 1996).

Dementia is progressive, in the sense that the patient increasingly loses cognitive and emotional skills. People in the early stage of dementia can still live at home with the care of a family or partner. However, when the disease progresses and the patient enters an advanced stage of dementia, this person loses enough of their cognitive and emotional abilities to be able to live independently. This is often the point at which the patient is admitted to a care home where there is special care and attention for their needs (Geldmacher and Whitehouse 1996). People with dementia are confronted with an ever-changing disease, which changes their behaviour and environmental recognition (Geldmacher and Whitehouse 1996). Not recognizing their surroundings, which is often labelled as a 'decrease in recognition', leads to uneasiness among people with dementia. A study by Fleming et al. (2015) looked at the behavioural patterns and disturbances in people with an advanced stage of dementia. This resulted in a list of desirable design features classified into three categories: engagement, calmness, and care. In that study, engagement refers to tasks that focus on the individual's senses, such as sensory perception or stimulating activities. Calmness refers to giving people with dementia a calm and familiar environment that feels homely. And care is related to healthcare as well as to an environment that ensures dignity and privacy. These three categories will be inspirations for the observational strategy used in this study.

However, it is hard to study the effect of VR on dementia, due to the complexity of the medium itself. As such many studies have been conducted, and shown small positive outcomes for people with *mild* cognitive impairment or dementia (Kim et al. 2019). In these studies, different XR tools were used for the intervention, such as a laptop, game controller, VR auditorium, motion sensor, Wii, virtual partner, virtual city, or 3D LCD glasses. Due to the complexity of Dementia, almost none of the studies around VR and dementia made use of new high and immersive VR technologies. For instance, the research of Strong (2020), showed that out of the 25 studies included in the meta-analysis, only three made use of immersive VR, while the other 22 studies had participants view the virtual environment on a (computer or projected) screen.

2.1 XR Media Visuals and Dementia

Research by Ludden et al. (2019) mentions a case study that is called 'Virtual Nature'. The virtual nature case study is about people with dementia interacting with XR media visuals showing nature scenes, based on studies from environmental design. The study is aimed at "*enhancing social engagement amongst residents, thereby also promoting relaxation and reducing restlessness*" (Ludden et al. 2019, p. 15). The results indicate that people with dementia experience positive emotions when engaging with nature. In the present study, the same kind of visuals were used in the XR environment of the research.

2.2 XR Soundscapes and Dementia

Although Ludden et al. (2019) do not specifically address the use of sound in their media installations, other studies provide evidence for the importance of sounds, and soundscapes in particular, in the well-being of people with dementia (Nagahata et al. 2004; Cheng and Sabran 2021; Nagahata et al. (2004) investigated the effect of several kinds of XR sounds on the reactions of people with dementia. Among other things, their results point to some sounds that improve recognition of reality, when the sounds are connected to sounds from the past of the patient, such as kitchen sounds for patients who cooked a lot. The study also indicated more generic sounds that improve recognition by stimulating calmness for patients of any gender and background, such as the nature soundscapes. These results were confirmed in a meta-study conducted by Cheng and Sabran (2021). Due to the lack of research in the area, they only found seven studies regarding soundscape applied to people with dementia (including the study by Nagahata et al. 2004). One of the main findings of the meta-study was that natural soundscapes can make patients feel happy and calm, as well as bring back (lost) memories of dementia patients. Based on these findings, the present investigation aims to generate evidence of the potential added value of the combined use of audio soundscapes and media visuals, in particular, in patients with advanced stages of dementia.

2.3 VR Headsets and Dementia

A review of the studies that used VR headsets in dementia applications shows that they only were tried with patients in earlier stages of the syndrome, that is patients with mild cognitive impairment (MCI). None of the studies found applied VR headsets with advanced stages of Dementia.

In some studies, such as Stargatt et al. (2021), Xie et al. (2023), Balas et al. (2021) and Savundranayagam et al. (2023), the VR headsets were used to train caregivers of dementia patients, and the results showed an increase empathy and understanding of the syndrome.

The studies which used the VR headsets with the MCI patients, focused on cognitive training, Chen et al. (2023), Oliveira et al. (2021), Yun et al. (2020), and Jang et al. (2023), or improving the quality of life and general well-being of the patients, such as Kim et al. (2023) and Huang and Yang (2022). In general, these studies revealed evidence of positive effects, like improvements in overall cognition, attention, memory, and mood, and a decrease in depression and prostration. Nonetheless, we are talking about studies with relatively limited sample sizes, implying that additional research is needed to confirm these positive results.

Additionally, some studies explicitly emphasize some potential obstacles such as the need and strategy to familiarize the patients with the technology (Rose et al. 2019), discomfort with VR headsets for some users (Riaz et al. 2021), the need of involving the patients and caregivers in the design of the experience (Muñoz et al. 2021), and the variability in effectiveness across different age groups and cognitive levels (Xie et al. 2023).

3 Methodology

This research was conducted among patients with advanced stages of dementia, in a closed ward of a dementia care home. This means that all design choices and research procedures were pre-approved based on an ethical and pragmatic point of view, and had to be implemented flexibly in real-time due to the ever-changing nature of dementia and its effects on the day-to-day life of the patients.

3.1 Design

Due to the exploratory nature of the research subject, a qualitative approach was adopted. The investigation was carried out in the form of a quasi-experiment to explore the potential modifications in the perceptions of advanced dementia patients, regarding mainly their reactions and emotions when exposed to visuals and soundscapes. After the organization gave an initial "go" from an ethical and pragmatic point of view, the next step was to discuss the idea with caregivers from the closed dementia ward to assess its feasibility. After some rounds of discussions, some modifications were made in the way of presenting the visuals and other details, and an introductory meeting with the patients was scheduled. The purpose of this introductory meeting was to become more familiar with the patients before the experiment. So, the researcher with the supervision of the caregivers realized this acquaintance strategy and introduced himself to the patients. In this meeting, the idea of the experiment was also introduced. After the caregivers assessed positively the outcome of the introductory meeting and revealed it complied with the ethical, pragmatic and logistic requirements, the green light was given to proceed with the study.

Two conditions were created to gain more insight into the potential added value of sounds. One condition with visuals only and the other condition with visuals plus sounds, each with a duration of 6 min. The patients were confronted with the stimuli in pairs, unless the patient required to be alone, along with a caregiver who also worked as an observer. Half of the patients saw the version with visuals only (condition 1) and half of the patients saw the visuals with soundscapes (condition 2). One patient in the end saw both conditions due to practical circumstances).

3.2 Participants

The study was conducted among people with advanced dementia who live in a closed dementia ward in a care home in the Netherlands. The study (observation) took place in one of the closed dementia wards, taking into account the strict regulations, in which two residential groups live, each with a maximum of eight residents. Information about the patients is limited due to ethical and privacy concerns. The age of the residents is between 62 and 94 years old, they are of Dutch descent and used to live in the province of Noord-Brabant at some point in their life. The residents are all in an advanced stage of dementia. However, even advanced dementia has different levels (Geldmacher and Whitehouse 1996). Some residents are still aware and stimulated by their surroundings, while some are less aware of their surroundings. With the permission of the care home and the help of the care workers, nine patients were selected and agreed to participate in the experiment. However, due to the changing circumstances and health conditions, only seven could in the end participate on the planned days of the study.

3.3 Place

The care home 'De Watersteeg', where the experiment was realized is part of the healthcare organization 'BrabantZorg'. The study and observation took place in the closed ward 'Houtwal Twee-Vier' placing the media with the visuals and soundscapes in the television corners near the window of the closed ward. This section is based on the notion that this is a safe and familiar place the residents usually go to when they are not in their bedrooms.

3.4 Materials

This research used several supporting materials to produce and exhibit the audio and visuals used during the experiment, along with digital recorders to record the experiment and post-experiment interviews. In this section, we will focus on the main materials, such as the soundscapes and visuals. A key decision had to be taken around the use of XR media. As it concerns participants with advanced dementia, the decision was taken not to use VR goggles. The effect of the use of VR goggles has not been thoroughly tested on people with dementia and also would cause confusion and unnatural conditions for the patients involved (Cahill et al. 2007). As such, to mimic the elements, six p's, that create the feeling of presence in VR were included (van Gisbergen 2016). As such a setup was designed to create Proximity and Perspective (a large screen near the window and patients, to create a feeling of being close to the scenes elements in the scene). The use of not only stills but also animations and sounds to create more presence (a feeling of being there) as well as Participation (which for high-stage dementia patients is already high when pointing or interacting with body language to the screen) and Place (to have the experience inside the familiar place where the patients watch outside scenery through the window).

Visual media. The visual content was based on prior research and was mainly based on the 'Virtual Nature' installation study (Ludden et al. 2019). Using Google reverse image search, similar images to the ones used as the first layer of the 'virtual nature' installation were found. The 'Virtual Nature' setup consisted of three different landscapes (see Fig. 1): (1) a park in autumn, which shows a wide park with trees, lawns, and a stream of water. An open cloud field (2) with a blue sky and (3) a coastal dune landscape that shows a visual image of a beach at sunset with coastal dunes in the foreground. The still images (layer one) were added with a second layer of animations: moving elements that create interest and a sense that something is happening (Ludden et al. 2019). For this research, congruent elements were added to the still images described in layer one. The first scene, Autumn Park, has three animated additions: (a) a moving butterfly, (b) an animated tree and (c) a flying bird. The second image, the cloudy sky, has two animated additions: (a) the clouds passing by and (b) birds flying by. The third image, the dune and beach landscape, has three animated additions: (a) birds flying by, (b) seagulls flying by and (c) a kite hovering in the wind.

The animations were created using Adobe Premiere Pro 2020, based on green screen videos and animations from YouTube. All layers are created and rendered as a mp4 file. The images were shown on a mobile screen with a size of 65 inches that was placed in such a way it gives the illusion of looking outside.

Soundscapes. Soundscapes are background sounds that are used as congruent support material for visuals. As mentioned, research revealed that using soundscapes from nature makes an important contribution to the recognisability of the scenes among people with dementia. As such, soundscapes were added to the visual scenes with still images and animations. The first scene, Autumn Park, was enriched with sounds from singing birds and of a nature park. The second scene, blue sky, was

Fig. 1 Visual media. Images on the left were retrieved from Ludden et al. (2019) and images on the right were retrieved from the thesis experiment

added with the sounds of wind and birds chirping as they flew by. The third scene, the beach, was added with sounds from the beach (among others the sound of waves) and the coastal dune landscape (among others the sounds of crickets and seagulls).

3.5 Measures

Research by Geldmacher and Whitehouse (1996) shows that the loss of cognitive and emotional abilities makes it difficult for people with dementia to give reliable answers regarding emotions and reactions to the situation they are in. As it is difficult for people with dementia to express themselves and meaningfully answer questions, it was decided not to actively question the participants but to mainly observe their emotions and reactions towards the nature-based stimuli.

Observation of the emotions and reactions. The advanced dementia patients were randomly exposed to the visuals or visuals with soundscapes. Based on Ludden et al. (2019), decisions were made to, along with free observation, use rating scales to help assess reactions, and involve the caretakers in the evaluation process (once they are "specialists" in the reactions of their patients). The observations were rated on the six basic emotions: anger, disgust, surprise, happiness, fear, and sadness. These basic emotions give a generally representative image, in contrast to other emotions that are more difficult to name (Siedlecka and Denson 2018). In addition to emotions, three reactions were observed and rated based on previous studies that showed that these are common and important reactions for dementia patients (Ludden et al. 2019; Nagahata et al. 2004): (a) calming, (b) stimulating, and (c) engaging.

3.6 Data Analysis Procedure

The free observations, emotions, and reactions were noted in a form, in which one could also assign the level of emotion or reaction observed. The forms were filled out by the researcher and the caregiver during the data collection sessions. The caregiver received instructions about the form and observation strategy. To prevent an observation from being given a preferential position, it was decided to state the researcher's findings and the caregiver's findings separately if they differ from each other. In addition to the form, a follow-up interview with the caregiver was conducted immediately after the experiment to get insights into how the caregiver experienced the observation and the reactions of his patient. The interview was designed using the interview guidelines from Hanington and Martin (2022) and Goodman and Kuniavsky (2012). The filled-out forms were coded and thematic explored using the strategy described by Williams and Moser (2019). Because a preconceived form has been used, there were two predefined themes, emotions and reactions. In addition to these two themes, the data revealed the following ones, related to reactions: (a) attention, (b) interest, and (c) interaction. A codebook was created from which the various sub-themes were analysed and compared between the two designs (with and without soundscapes).

4 Findings

From here on, the observing researcher is named the first observer, and the observing caregiver is named the second observer. Condition 1 is labelled as 'Visuals' and condition 2 is labelled as 'Audio + visuals'.

Emotions. Despite that people with dementia react less intensely, the stimuli evoked various emotions in people with advanced dementia. The emotions of happiness and surprise were most observed. Happiness was often observed by means of participants laughing as well as (spontaneously) telling how they liked certain elements from a scene. Surprise was often observed by means of patients suddenly pointing towards the visuals and showing a surprised look. No clear different patterns were found between the two conditions, although happiness (in combination with disgust) was observed more often in the setup with audio + visuals, while surprise (in combination with happiness and disgust) was more often seen in the setup with visuals only. The observers often both saw the same emotions in the participants, especially when the patients showed a clear expression, such as being scared by a butterfly. However, the first observer more often saw the emotion of happiness during the experiment, while the second observer more often saw the emotion of surprise.

Reactions. The participants showed various reactions during the different setups of the experiment. During the setup with audio + visuals, the observers both saw the reaction of engaging and stimulating in the participants. This is supported by observations such as participants being interested in specific elements of the scenes and the participants starting to talk about the scenes. Some participants even showed signs of recognition, by asking specific questions about the visual media scene and telling stories about how he used to have a house in a place that looked like the scene displayed. The first observer further saw the reaction of calming within the participants as well as tiredness and distraction when the study progressed. When only visuals were used, the patients mainly showed stimulation but also distraction and tiredness. When showing the participants the version of visuals plus soundscapes, this changed, and the majority of the participants only showed engagement and calmness.

Attention. According to both observers, the participants showed the reaction of attention in both conditions. The patients were attentively watching and looking concentrated on the stimuli during the viewing of the scenes. Throughout the viewing, some of the participants also showed signs of distraction, mainly due to things happening in the environment. The lack of attention becomes more apparent in the visuals-only condition, in which the patients show more difficulty maintaining their attention to concentrate and stare at the visual stimuli. The layer two, animations, helped to maintain attention; the focus towards the screen dropped significantly when the animations were not playing in the scenes. This would cause the participants to instantly lose focus and start staring at their surroundings. In addition, the sound helped to attract and maintain attention, and the patients mentioned it was easier to hold it.

Interest. The participants showed a reaction of interest in both conditions (visuals only and audio + visuals). For the setup of audio + visuals, both observers noted most of the participants showing signs of interest towards the experiment. This is supported by the participants mentioning that they like the overall scenes and specific elements of the scenes such as the animals and colours. This was evidenced by several patients starting to ask specific questions about the scenes. Overall, the participants had a more positive interest towards the audio + visuals setup. This is supported by the participants of the just visuals setup having difficulty focussing on the scenes, which is consistent with the results seen in the attention results.

Interaction. Interaction was also observed in both conditions by both observers. The patients showed body responses and started laughing, smiling or interacting with the content, for example, pointing towards elements of the scene they were viewing, and recollecting memories. The latter was observed for instance by a participant who talked about the beach she saw looked a lot like the beach she used to have a house at. The interactions were also present during the visuals-only setup. This is supported by the participants showing interactions during the scene by using body language, such as pointing and smiling. The participants also spoke a few words about the scenes. Another piece of evidence was that some of the participants were mentally absent while viewing the scenes and had less focus during the visuals-only setup.

5 Conclusion

A qualitative experiment was designed and conducted to research the influence of audio-visual media on people with dementia. Despite the strict ethical and pragmatic requirements, the experiment was conducted at a care institution in a closed dementia ward. Regarding the question of what influence visual media have on patients with advanced dementia, the results generated evidence that visual media indeed have an influence. People with dementia have shown various basic emotions during the experiment, predominately the emotions of happiness and surprise. Research by Ludden et al. (2019) mainly showed reactions of calming, stimulating and engaging when testing the 'virtual nature' media visuals, where no audio had been used. While in this study the same results were found, it also showed an increase in the duration and intensity of the emotions due to the inclusion of sounds.

Aside from emotions, the patients also showed other reactions, including calming and stimulating. These findings are supported by similar studies, such Ludden et al. (2019). In addition, this study indicated that animation can hold attention, which is also consistent with the findings of Ludden et al. (2019) who showed that as long as the animations play during the experiment without audio soundscapes, the focus remains on the scenes. However, in this study, it is also indicated that sound only might already attract and maintain a lot of attention as well. One of the reasons for this could be the added recognizability of the audio soundscapes, which Nagahata et al. (2004) also predicted. Regarding the added value of audio (soundscapes) in addition to visuals, the experiment found evidence that audio adds value to the visuals regarding emotions and reactions. The emotion of happiness was predominant in the setup audio + visuals, in line with findings of audio-only experiments, such as Nagahata et al. (2004) and Cheng and Sabran (2021). The addition of soundscapes resulted in more frequent interaction, including recognition, more attention to the experiment, and increased interest. The frequency in which the observed reactions were positive towards the experiment was higher in the setup audio + visuals.

The results evidenced that audio-visual media can positively influence people with advanced stages of dementia and that the addition of audio enhances this process. The emotions most seen in the research are happiness and surprise; and the reactions of interaction, recognition, attention, interest, calming, and engagement. The reactions interaction, attention, and interest can also appear opposite. Therefore, the evidence found suggests that the use of audio-visual media can influence the sensations, and audio can add value to the visuals regarding the valence of the emotions and reactions elicited in patients with advanced dementia.

Being of a qualitative nature, there is no expectation of generalising these results before confirmation from further quantitative research. Nonetheless, the insights elicited by the evidence collected so far are promising and sustain the idea of trying to implement these in more immersive XR media as well. The reactions of the dementia patients seem so promising that this seems to advocate further experiments on the tolerance and acceptance of new immersive VR goggles, for patients that are also in a far stage of Dementia. In the hope that positive results found in this and previous studies will only increase due to a higher feeling of presence inside the VR environment.

References

Alzheimer Nederland. (2021, February). Factsheet cijfers en feiten over dementie. https://www.alzheimer-nederland.nl/factsheet-cijfers-en-feiten-over-dementie

Balas, J. S., Phelps, E., Shaw, C., Washington, E., Glover, C., Ludwig, G. A., Bennett, D. A., Fleischman, D., Volgman, A., & Aggarwal, N. (2021). Leveraging virtual reality to train certified nursing assistants as essential dementia-care personnel in the age of COVID-19. Alzheimer's & Dementia, 17.

Cahill, S., Macijauskiene, J., Nygård, A. M., Faulkner, J. P., & Hagen, I. (2007). Technology in Dementia Care. Technology and Disability, 19(2–3), 53–54. https://doi.org/10.3233/tad-2007-192-301

Chen, R., Wang, S., Xu, X., Wei, L., Sun, Y., & Tong, X. (2023). Design and Evaluation of a VR Therapy for Patients with Mild Cognitive Impairment and Dementia: Perspectives from Patients and Stakeholders. 2023 IEEE Conference on Virtual Reality and 3D User Interfaces Abstracts and Workshops (VRW), 597–598.

Cheng, Z., & Sabran, K. (2021, August). Soundscape Support for People with Dementia: A Systematic Literature Review. Proceedings of the 2nd International Conference on Design Industries &

Creative Culture, DESIGN DECODED 2021, 24–25 August 2021, Kedah, Malaysia, 490–501. https://doi.org/10.4108/eai.24-8-2021.2315262

Fleming, R., Kelly, F., & Stillfried, G. (2015). 'I want to feel at home': establishing what aspects of environmental design are important to people with dementia nearing the end of life. BMC Palliative Care, 14(1). https://doi.org/10.1186/s12904-015-0026-y

Geldmacher, D. S., & Whitehouse, P. J. (1996). Evaluation of Dementia. New England Journal of Medicine, 335(5), 330–336. https://doi.org/10.1056/nejm199608013350507

Goodman, E., & Kuniavsky, M. (2012). Observing the User Experience: A Practitioner's Guide to User Research (2nd ed.). Morgan Kaufmann.

Hanington, B., & Martin, B. (2022). The Pocket Universal Methods of Design, Revised and Expanded: 125 Ways to Research Complex Problems, Develop Innovative Ideas, and Design Effective Solutions. Rockport Publishers.

Huang, L.-C., & Yang, Y.-H. (2022). Can immersive virtual reality reminiscence preserve cognitive decline in people with dementia? Observational study (Preprint).

Jang, S., Choi, S.-W., Son, S., Oh, J., Ha, J., Kim, W. J., Roh, H. W., Kim, K. Y., Lee, S., Jung, E.-J., Cha, W., Chae, H., Kang, S., Kwon, J., Kim, I.-Y., Lee, J.-Y., Shin, H.-K., Ryu, J., Ahn, R.-Y., … Seok, J. (2023). Virtual reality-based monitoring test for MCI: A multicenter feasibility study. Frontiers in Psychiatry, 13.

Kim, O., Pang, Y., & Kim, J. H. (2019). The effectiveness of virtual reality for people with mild cognitive impairment or dementia: a meta-analysis. BMC psychiatry, 19, 1–10.

Kim, J., Kim, Y., Lee, J., Oh, S., & Ory, M. (2023). Efficacy of An Immersive Nature-based Virtual Reality Program on Depression, Emotional Health, and Qualityof-Life among Care Facility Residents with Alzheimer's Disease (AD) and its Related Dementias (ADRD). American Journal of Health Behavior.

Ludden, G. D., van Rompay, T. J., Niedderer, K., & Tournier, I. (2019). Environmental design for dementia care—towards more meaningful experiences through design. Maturitas, 128, 10–16. https://doi.org/10.1016/j.maturitas.2019.06.011

Muñoz, J., Mehrabi, S., Li, Y., Basharat, A., Middleton, L., Cao, S., Barnett-Cowan, M., & Boger, J. (2021). Immersive Virtual Reality Exergames for Persons Living With Dementia: User-Centered Design Study as a Multistakeholder Team During the COVID-19 Pandemic. JMIR Serious Games, 10.

Nagahata K, Fukushima T, Ishibashi N, Takahashi Y, Moriyama M. (2004). A soundscape study: What kinds of sounds can elderly people affected by dementia recollect?. Noise Heal, 6, 63–73.

Oliveira, J., Gamito, P., Souto, T., Conde, R., Ferreira, M., Corotnean, T., Fernandes, A., Silva, H., & Neto, T. (2021). Virtual Reality-Based Cognitive Stimulation on People with Mild to Moderate Dementia due to Alzheimer's Disease: A Pilot Randomized Controlled Trial. International Journal of Environmental Research and Public Health, 18.

Riaz, W., Khan, Z. Y., Jawaid, A., & Shahid, S. (2021). Virtual Reality (VR)-Based Environmental Enrichment in Older Adults with Mild Cognitive Impairment (MCI) and Mild Dementia. Brain Science, 11.

Rose, V., Stewart, I., Jenkins, K., Tabbaa, L., Ang, C., & Matsangidou, M. (2019). Bringing the outside in: The feasibility of virtual reality with people with dementia in an inpatient psychiatric care setting. Dementia, 20, 106–129.

Savundranayagam, M., Chen, A., Norris, G., Schumann, A., Kaur, S., Campos, J., & Orange, J. (2023). Be EPIC-VR: translating an in-person, person-centered communication training program into virtual reality. Innovation in Aging, 7, 316–317.

Siedlecka, E., & Denson, T. F. (2018). Experimental Methods for Inducing Basic Emotions: A Qualitative Review. Emotion Review, 11(1), 87–97. https://doi.org/10.1177/1754073917749016

Simmons, B. B., Hartmann, B., & DeJoseph, D. (2011). Evaluation of Suspected Dementia. American Family Physician, 84(8), 895–902.

Stargatt, J., Bhar, S., Petrovich, T., Bhowmik, J., Sykes, D., & Burns, K. (2021). The Effects of Virtual Reality-Based Education on Empathy and Understanding of the Physical Environment for Dementia Care Workers in Australia: A Controlled Study. Journal of Alzheimer's Disease.

Strong, J. (2020). Immersive virtual reality and persons with dementia: a literature review. Journal of gerontological social work, 63(3), 209–226.

Van Gisbergen, M. S. (2016). Contextual connected media: How rearranging a media puzzle brings virtual reality into being. Breda: NHTV.

Williams, M., & Moser, T. (2019). The art of coding and thematic exploration in qualitative research. International Management Review, 15, 45–55. https://www.semanticscholar.org/paper/The-Art-of-Coding-and-Thematic-Exploration-in-Williams-Moser/c0a0c26ac41cb8beb337834e6c1e2f35b91d071d

Xie, Z., Chen, F., Zou, L., Wang, F., & Yang, L. (2023). Using Virtual Reality in the Care of Older Adults With Dementia: A Randomized Controlled Trial. Journal of Gerontological Nursing, 49 11, 25–32.

Yun, S. J., Kang, M.-G., Yang, D., Choi, Y., Kim, H., Oh, B., & Seo, H. (2020). Cognitive Training Using Fully Immersive, Enriched Environment Virtual Reality for Patients With Mild Cognitive Impairment and Mild Dementia: Feasibility and Usability Study. JMIR Serious Games, 8.

XR Design and Development and Robotics

Study on a LightGBM-Based Model for Detecting Anomaly Operation of Delta Robot

Ji-Yeon Kim, Ki-Hwan Kim, Young-Jin Kang, Young Seok Ock, and Seok Chan Jeong

Abstract With advances in sensors, AI, and robotics, robots are being used in various fields, including industry, healthcare, and the home. These robots provide innovative changes and improved services in each field through several advantages such as productivity improvement, precise work performance, labor reduction, and stability enhancement. Accordingly, the maintenance of robots is becoming increasingly important. In this paper, a model for detecting anomalies in robot operations using LightGBM was built using vacuum pad data of a delta robot performing picking and packing operations in a factory. Data were preprocessed and generated to improve the abnormal motion detection rate, and through this, 82.22% accuracy was obtained.

Keywords Anomaly detection · Robot · LightGBM

J.-Y. Kim
Department of Artificial Intelligence, Dong-Eui University, Busan, Korea
e-mail: jnsp0907@naver.com

K.-H. Kim · Y.-J. Kang
AI Grand ICT Research Center, Dong-Eui University, Busan, Korea
e-mail: 15541@deu.ac.kr

Y.-J. Kang
e-mail: 15073@deu.ac.kr

Y. S. Ock
Graduate School of Management of Technology, Pukyong National University, Busan, Korea
e-mail: ysock@pknu.ac.kr

S. C. Jeong (✉)
Depertment of e-Business and Graduate School of Artificial Intelligence, Dong-Eui University, Busan, Korea
e-mail: scjeong@deu.ac.kr

T. Jung et al. (eds.), *XR and Metaverse*, Springer Proceedings in Business and Economics, https://doi.org/10.1007/978-3-031-77975-6_35

1 Introduction

Robots play a pivotal role in various fields, from industry to healthcare to home, and they are expanding their applicability and effectiveness through various studies. In the industrial field, research is being conducted to improve work efficiency through cooperation between robots and workers. The robot recognized the unstructured work environment and the operator's behavior, and the robot performed autonomous work selection, resulting in improved productivity by shortening the process time (Na et al. 2023). In the medical field, research has been conducted to increase the accuracy and safety of surgery by recognizing various situations that may occur during the surgical process by creating artificial intelligence models using medical data on surgical robots (Zia et al. 2018). In the home sector, there is research on robots integrating full-body remote control interfaces based on mobile to collect data and imitate behaviors to perform housework (Fu et al. 2024). As such, robots in various fields are studied and applied to impact the economic and social dimensions significantly. With these developments, robot's efficient and sustainable operation is becoming increasingly important.

Although robots are used in various industries, their importance is highlighted because the maintenance of robots used in factories is directly related to production efficiency. These robots are put into complex manufacturing processes and perform tasks that require continuous operation and high precision. Robots perform tasks ranging from assembly to inspection and packaging, and each process directly affects the final quality of the product. It is essential to detect abnormal movements of the robot that may occur in this process early and take measures to inspect and replace parts at the appropriate time to ensure continuity of production and maintain the efficiency of work. In response to this, there is a need to develop a technology to detect abnormalities in robot motion.

In this paper, a model was constructed to detect abnormal conditions using vacuum pad data collected from the robot's sensors to effectively detect abnormalities in the operation of delta robots that perform packaging of objects used in the manufacturing. To increase the anomaly detection rate, meaningful information was extracted from the data through data preprocessing and generation and used as training data to improve the model's accuracy.

2 Related Work

Anomaly detection involves identifying abnormal patterns or newly observed patterns within a data set by detecting outliers that deviate from the regular distribution (Miljković 2010). Traditionally, anomaly detection has been performed using statistical methods. There are methods such as Z-score, IQR (Interquartile Range), and Mahalanobis Distance. These methods identify outliers using the data's mean, variance, and quartiles. The Z-score determines outliers by determining how far the data is in standard deviation from the mean. IQR divides the data distribution into quartiles, and considers values outside the range defined by the lower (25%) and upper (75%) quartiles as outliers. Mahalanobis Distance is a distance scale for calculating distance by considering the shape of distribution in multivariate data and detects outliers that deviate from the average. These statistical techniques have the advantage of being able to explain and interpret through the distribution of the data used. However, because they assume the characteristics of the recorded data with a specific distribution, they may have difficulty detecting accurate outliers in the case of complex data (Erhan et al. 2021). Outlier detection research has been actively conducted using machine learning techniques to overcome these limitations. To detect abnormalities caused by cyberattacks occurring in industrial control systems, the characteristics of time series data were explored and identified using the k-means algorithm (Kiss et al. 2014). Chaovalitwongse et al. (2007) used KNN (K-Nearest Neighbors) to classify normal and abnormal activities by comparing EEG records with neighboring data points in a high-dimensional space. In addition, various machine learning techniques, such as SVM (Hornung et al. 2014), DBSCAN (Deng 2020) and others, were used to detect outliers. Techniques using deep learning are also being used for anomaly detection. Wang et al. (2019) performed anomaly detection of UAV sensor data using an LSTM-based prediction model. UAV sensor data, which is time series data, is used as learning data, and the value at the next time point is predicted and compared with the actual value of the data to detect anomalies. When evaluating sensor data from a UAV with point anomalies for anomaly detection, it was shown that LSTM can effectively detect these anomalies. ALMahadin et al. (2023) proposed a GRU-based model for detecting anomalies in VANET (Vehicle Ad-hoc Networks) network traffic. The model demonstrated excellent performance in detecting network anomalies with a lower error rate compared to existing methods. Park et al. (2018) proposed a method to detect abnormalities in multidimensional sensor signals using LSTM-VAE, an LSTM-based variational autoencoder. This method fuses sensor signals and reconstructs the distribution of data to identify anomalies according to a threshold. As a result of the evaluation, a higher AUC (Area Under the Curve) was achieved than existing methods. As such, research is being conducted using deep learning techniques such as CNN (Yu and Zhao 2019), GCN (Pei et al. 2022), and GAN (Li et al. 2019; Lu et al. 2021), as well as models that are particularly strong in processing time series data.

These methods show good performance in anomaly detection, but require high computational resources and memory due to their complex model structure and many parameters. This makes it difficult to apply in robot systems with limited computational resources and memory in general. This is because when a model with a large computational burden is used, it becomes difficult to process data and the response speed may be slow. Considering the need for a lightweight model suitable for the robot system, this study studied the anomaly detection of the robot's vacuum pad operation using LightGBM (Ke et al. 2017) with high computational efficiency and low memory.

3 Methods

3.1 Data Preprocessing

The robot targeted in this study is a robot that performs the work of packaging products and contains information as shown in Table 1, such as data on the robot's condition obtained from a sensor built into the robot controller.

Therefore, a sudden and significant decrease or increase in the vacuum pad's pressure during the pick and pack states, or an increase in pressure when not in the pick and pack states, can have a substantial impact on the process of packaging objects. Accordingly, the vacuum value, according to the pick and pack state information, was considered the target value. To detect it, a state in which the pressure of the vacuum pad unexpectedly changes was regarded as anomaly data. In addition, an explicit criterion for abnormal conditions was established by adding a label column to distinguish between normal and anomaly data and displaying True and False, respectively.

To know the continuous state of the robot's motion, we need to be able to distinguish the motion for picks from the motion for picks from the motion for packs over time, so we sort them in ascending order using the time column. In a dataset sorted based on time, two columns were created and initialized to zero to track whether the current action is in a pick or pack state, allowing for the recording of the cumulative number of action signals by counting the number of pick and packs. In order to track that the current motion is continuous depending on whether the pick and pack states in the data set aligned based on time, two columns were created and initialized to 0 so that the cumulative number of motion signals could be recorded. When 'signal_pick' or 'signal_pack' has a True value, the value of the corresponding column is accumulated and increase by 1 to track continuous motion state of the robot. On the

Table 1 Robot state data collected from sensors

Attribute	Associated explain	Attribute	Associated explain
time	Data collection time	signal_pick	Picking state signal
amp_temp1	1-Axis amp temperature	signal_pack	Packing state signal
amp_temp2	2-Axis amp temperature	speed_1	1-Axis motor speed
amp_temp3	3-Axis amp temperature	speed_2	2-Axis motor speed
amp_temp4	4-Axis amp temperature	speed_3	3-Axis motor speed
cpu_temp	Cpu temperature	speed_4	4-Axis motor speed
interval	Data collection interval	torque_1	1-Axis motor torque
pos_1	1-Axis motor position	torque_2	2-Axis motor torque
pos_2	2-Axis motor position	torque_3	3-Axis motor torque
pos_3	3-Axis motor position	torque_4	4-Axis motor torque
pos_4	4-Axis motor position	vacuum	Vacuum pad pressure

other hand, if it has a False value, it is initialized to 0 to indicate the start of a new motion sequence. Through this, the frequency of repetition was identified so that the robot's motion pattern could be recognized.

In addition, we augmented the data by generating additional anomalous data. This is mainly because the state of normal operation is common at the actual work site, so not only is there a relative scarcity of data on abnormal conditions. Furthermore, intentionally causing malfunctions for the purpose of data collection carries the risk of danger and incurs significant costs. By imitating the abnormal state considered as the above-defined abnormal data, data with a value in which the pressure of the vacuum pad is less than or exceeds a specific value during the pick and pack states were generated. In this way, the problem of unbalanced data was solved by increasing the diversity of data sets.

3.2 *Creation of Detection Model and Results*

The model used in this study to detect abnormal behaviour of the delta robot is LightGBM. LightGBM is a model that improves high memory usage and slow learning speed, which are disadvantages of XGBoost (Chen and Guestrin 2016), and has a fast learning speed. Unlike traditional boosting models, it uses leaf-wise tree splitting to divide leaf nodes in a way that reduces loss without considering the balance of the tree, resulting in faster and more efficient learning. This makes achieving high performance even in complex data structures and good performance even in small data sets is possible (Ke et al. 2017). Considering these features to be well-suited for sensitive and precise tasks, such as robot motion anomaly detection, we used it as our training model. Combined the preprocessed 3.268,273 data with the additional anomaly data that was generated and used it as training data for the LightGBM model. The optimal hyperparameter was derived through repeated learning, and the hyperparameters applied to the learning are shown in Table 2.

The model trained with the defined hyperparameters was evaluated using the confusion matrix and the ROC (Receiver Operating Characteristic) Curve. The left side of Fig. 1 shows a confusion matrix that represents the relationship between the actual values and the model's predicted values from a single evaluation, yielding an

Table 2 Hyperparameters for LightGBM

Parameter	Value
n_estimators	100
num_leaves	31
subsample	1.0
min_child_samples	20
max_depth	−1
learning rate	0.1

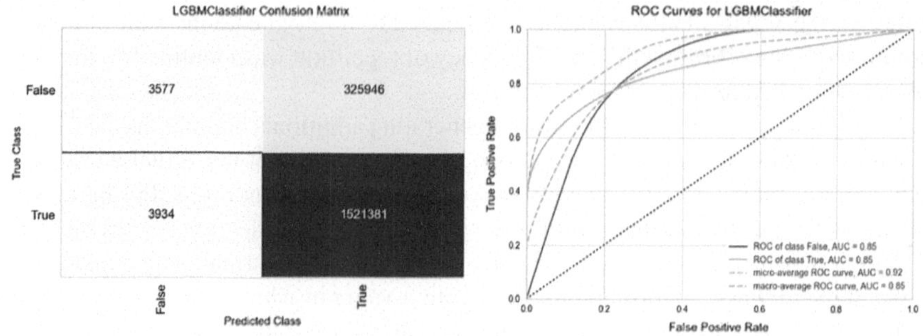

Fig. 1 Performance evaluation of the model. Left: confusion matrix for a single evaluation; right: ROC curve from 10 evaluations

accuracy of about 82.22% and a recall of about 99%. The performance indicators generally showed high values, but it is evident that the number of false positives was also high. This indicates that cases which are actually false are being incorrectly classified as true, which could lower the precision of the predictions. To improve this, it appears necessary to increase the samples from the minority classes. The right side of Fig. 1 presents the ROC Curve based on 10 iterations of the evaluation depicted in the left side of Fig. 1, which is a graph representing the performance of a binary classifier. The x-axis of the ROC Curve represents the False Positive Rate (FPR), and the y-axis represents the True Positive Rate (TPR). As the curve approaches the top left corner, or near 1, the classifier demonstrates better performance by achieving lower false positives and higher true positives. This indicates a more effective classifier, capable of distinguishing between the normal and abnormal data with higher accuracy. According to the graph in Fig. 1, it can be seen that the AUC values for classes 'True' and 'False' are 0.85. This means that the model is showing consistent performance in distinguishing between positive and negative classes.

These results show that the data preprocessing and generation process was effectively performed. It is judged that the method of sorting by time and recording the cumulative count of motion signals provided a basis for clearly recognizing and analysing continuous motion patterns. Through this, it is shown that it was possible to determine whether a specific pattern was followed or if there were any unexpected changes. In addition, the generated abnormal data seems to sufficiently reflect various abnormal conditions that may occur in the field. Through this process, it can be seen that the model acted as an important factor in making it possible to more accurately predict and respond to various situations in the real-world environments.

4 Conclusion

In this paper, we preprocessed and generated the vacuum pad data of the Delta robot and studied the detection of abnormalities in the robot's motion using the LightGBM model. In consideration of the characteristics of the data, additional labels and information were generated to distinguish the state and operation of the robot clearly. Through this, each situation of the dataset was identified in detail so that the model could predict and classify more accurately. In addition, to solve the problem of data imbalance due to difficulty in collecting data for abnormal behavior, an abnormal data generation process was performed, and data diversity was improved through this process to increase the accuracy.

The results and methodology of this study are not only applicable to monitoring systems for detecting anomalies in the operation of actual robots but are also thought to maximize their effectiveness through use in metaverse environments. Modeling the robot in a metaverse environment and applying the data collected to the methodology of this study will allow for more precise analysis and prediction of various robot behaviors and situations. This approach will also allow for early detection of robot behavioural anomalies and potentially save money and time by addressing potential problems in advance. In particular, utilizing the metaverse environment to proactively monitor robot performance in real-time and continuously update detection models based on collected data is expected to increase operational efficiency and reliability in actual use.

In future research, we aim to enhance our ability to detect abnormal patterns by modeling robots in a metaverse environment that mirrors real-world conditions. We will simulate robot behavior under various scenarios to assess anomaly detection performance. By analyzing detailed abnormal patterns from diverse data and virtually reproducing unexpected operating conditions, we expect to significantly improve the precision of our models. This approach will allow robots to undergo experiences that closely resemble real conditions, thereby enhancing their predictive accuracy, stability, and reliability.

Acknowledgements This work was supported by Innovative Human Resource Development for Local Intellectualization program through the Institute of Information and Communications Technology Planning and Evaluation (IITP) grant funded by the Korea government (MSIT) (IITP-2024-RS-2020-II201791).

References

ALMahadin, G., Aoudni, Y., Shabaz, M., Agrawal, A. V., Yasmin, G., Alomari, E. S., ... & Maaliw, R. R. (2023). VANET network traffic anomaly detection using GRU-based deep learning model. *IEEE Transactions on Consumer Electronics*.

Chaovalitwongse, W. A., Fan, Y. J., & Sachdeo, R. C. (2007). On the time series $ k $-nearest neighbor classification of abnormal brain activity. *IEEE Transactions on Systems, Man, and Cybernetics-Part A: Systems and Humans, 37*(6), 1005–1016.

Chen, T., & Guestrin, C. (2016, August). Xgboost: A scalable tree boosting system. In Proceedings of the 22nd ACM SIGKDD international conference on knowledge discovery and data mining (pp. 785–794).

Deng, D. (2020, November). Research on anomaly detection method based on DBSCAN clustering algorithm. In *2020 5th International Conference on Information Science, Computer Technology and Transportation (ISCTT)* (pp. 439–442). IEEE.

Erhan, L., Ndubuaku, M., Di Mauro, M., Song, W., Chen, M., Fortino, G., … & Liotta, A. (2021). Smart anomaly detection in sensor systems: A multi-perspective review. *Information Fusion, 67*, 64–79.

Fu, Z., Zhao, T. Z., & Finn, C. (2024). Mobile aloha: Learning bimanual mobile manipulation with low-cost whole-body teleoperation. arXiv preprint arXiv:2401.02117.

Hornung, R., Urbanek, H., Klodmann, J., Osendorfer, C., & Van Der Smagt, P. (2014, September). Model-free robot anomaly detection. In *2014 IEEE/RSJ International Conference on Intelligent Robots and Systems* (pp. 3676–3683). IEEE.

Ke, G., Meng, Q., Finley, T., Wang, T., Chen, W., Ma, W., ... & Liu, T. Y. (2017). Lightgbm: A highly efficient gradient boosting decision tree. Advances in neural information processing systems, 30.

Kiss, I., Genge, B., Haller, P., & Sebestyén, G. (2014, September). Data clustering-based anomaly detection in industrial control systems. In 2014 IEEE 10th International Conference on Intelligent Computer Communication and Processing (ICCP) (pp. 275-281). IEEE.

Li, D., Chen, D., Jin, B., Shi, L., Goh, J., & Ng, S. K. (2019, September). MAD-GAN: Multivariate anomaly detection for time series data with generative adversarial networks. In *International conference on artificial neural networks* (pp. 703–716). Cham: Springer International Publishing.

Lu, H., Du, M., Qian, K., He, X., & Wang, K. (2021). GAN-based data augmentation strategy for sensor anomaly detection in industrial robots. *IEEE Sensors Journal*, 22(18), 17464-17474.

Miljković, D. (2010, May). Review of novelty detection methods. In *The 33rd International Convention MIPRO* (pp. 593-598). IEEE.

Minwoo Na, Tae Hwa Hong, Junwan Yun, & Jae-Bok Song (2023). Robot-Human Task Sharing System for Assembly Process. The Journal of Korea Robotics Society, 18(4), 419-426, https://doi.org/10.7746/jkros.2023.18.4.419

Park, D., Hoshi, Y., & Kemp, C. C. (2018). A multimodal anomaly detector for robot-assisted feeding using an lstm-based variational autoencoder. *IEEE Robotics and Automation Letters*, 3(3), 1544-1551.

Pei, Y., Huang, T., van Ipenburg, W., & Pechenizkiy, M. (2022). ResGCN: attention-based deep residual modeling for anomaly detection on attributed networks. *Machine Learning*, 111(2), 519-541.

Wang, B., Wang, Z., Liu, L., Liu, D., & Peng, X. (2019, May). Data-driven anomaly detection for UAV sensor data based on deep learning prediction model. In *2019 Prognostics and System Health Management Conference (PHM-Paris)* (pp. 286-290). IEEE.

Yu, W., & Zhao, C. (2019). Broad convolutional neural network based industrial process fault diagnosis with incremental learning capability. *IEEE Transactions on Industrial Electronics*, 67(6), 5081-5091.

Zia, A., Hung, A., Essa, I., & Jarc, A. (2018). Surgical activity recognition in robot-assisted radical prostatectomy using deep learning. In Medical Image Computing and Computer Assisted Intervention–MICCAI 2018: 21st International Conference, Granada, Spain, September 16-20, 2018, Proceedings, Part IV 11 (pp. 273-280). Springer International Publishing.

Intra Prediction Method for Depth Video Coding by Finding Spatial Correlation Using CNN and Attention

Jae-young Lee, Dong-seok Lee, and Soon-kak Kwon

Abstract In this paper, we propose an intra prediction method using CNN and attention mechanism for coding high-resolution depth videos utilized in virtual reality. The proposed method enhances intra prediction performance for depth pictures by predicting spatial correlations between an input block and reference pixels which is adjacent to the block. The proposed network extracts spatial features through CNN layers and predicts the spatial correlations through attention mechanism. Spatial features in vertical and horizontal directions are extracted from top and left adjacent blocks, respectively, and merged to predict the spatial features of pixels in the input block. The attention layers predict correlations between the spatial features of the input block and the reference pixels. Finally, the pixel values are predicted through the predicted correlation. In the simulation results, the intra prediction accuracies are improved up to 3.37% compared with the intra modes of VVC.

Keywords Video coding · Intra prediction · Depth video · Attention mechanism · CNN

1 Introduction

Interest in image and video coding through neural network is increasing. JPEG (Joint Photographic Experts Group) has been promoting the establishment of JPEG-AI, a standard for still image coding, image processing, and computer vision through neural network since 2019 (Ascenso et al., 2020). The goal of JPEG-AI is to provide

J. Lee · S. Kwon (✉)
Department of Computer Software Engineering, Dong-eui University, Busan, Republic of Korea
e-mail: skkwon@deu.ac.kr

J. Lee
e-mail: wodud4143@naver.com

D. Lee
AI Grand ICT Research Center, Dong-eui University, Busan, Republic of Korea
e-mail: 14177@deu.ac.kr

T. Jung et al. (eds.), *XR and Metaverse*, Springer Proceedings in Business and Economics, https://doi.org/10.1007/978-3-031-77975-6_36

a learnable image codec that improve image compression comparing with previous image coding standards such as HEVC (Sullivan et al., 2012) and VVC (Bross et al., 2021). Image compression with neural networks with end-to-end structure has shown significant bit-distortion rate improvement over VVC and HEVC by Huawei and Bytedance. MPEG (Moving Picture Experts Group) concluded that encoders using machine learning, such as artificial neural networks, have improved encoding performance over existing methods in video encoding, and is preparing to establish the MPEG-AI standard from 2023. In the metaverse through VR, the compression and transmission for high-resolution video are especially necessary to provide users with reality.

CNN-based neural networks have been proposed for intra-picture prediction (Li et al., 2018; Schiopu and Munteanu, 2018; Schiopu et al., 2018, 2020), but CNN calculates features of local areas rather than location-based, making it difficult to handle location information. In order to deal with location information, research (Hu et al., 2018, 2019) was also conducted to make predictions within the screen by considering pixels in a specific direction as time series data. Predict spatially consecutive pixels through layers such as RNN and LSTM. However, these network causes gradient vanishing and exploding in training due to their recursive structure (Pascanu et al., 2013). Therefore, RNN has long term dependency problem that the correlation is forget between two elements whose distance are far.

Attention mechanism (Vaswani et al., 2017) can solve this problem. Attention mechanism is originally used in natural language processing (NLP) for finding the correlation between tokens embedding each word. Attention mechanism is also applied to computer vision field. The methods based on attention mechanism has similar or superior performance to the method based on CNNs. Kim et al. (2024) find the spatial correlations between the pixels of a block and adjacent reference pixels through CNN and attention layers.

In this paper, we propose a intra prediction method for video coding by extracting spatial features of reference pixels through a CNN layer and predicting the spatial features of the target block to be coded through attention mechanism. Vertical and horizontal spatial features are extracted through the CNN layer from top and left adjacent blocks, respectively. The features are merged to predict spatial features through correlation with spatial features of the reference pixels through attention mechanism. Finally, the pixels of the target block are reconstructed by decoding the spatial features of the target block through CNN layers. The proposed method improve the intra prediction by select multiple reference pixels for each pixel in the target block through attention mechanism.

2 Related Works

2.1 *Spatial Feature Extraction Through Deep Learning Network*

Pixels in an image can be regarded as time-series data. Therefore, spatial features can be extracted from pixels in a vertical or horizontal direction through RNN. Hu et al. (2018) propose an intra prediction method through RNN layers with various input sizes. The region of reference pixels is scaled to the input sizes. PS-RNN (Hu et al., 2019) predicts the visual features of the reference pixels through CNN layers. The spatial features are extracted through RNN layers guided by visual features. The pixels of the block are predicted by converting the spatial features to pixel domain. However, training the RNN-based network known to be difficult due to a gradient vanishing or exploding caused by its recursive structure (Pascanu et al., 2013).

CNN is also utilized to extract the spatial features. CNN kernels for extracting the spatial features is not square shaped but its height or width is equal to the inputs. The kernels can extract the spatial features in the vertical or horizontal direction. Li et al. (2020) find the spatial features for an electrical impedance tomography to reconstruct its 3D shape.

2.2 *Intra Prediction for Depth Video*

For intra prediction, video coding standards such as H.265/HEVC (Sullivan et al., 2012) and VVC (Bross et al., 2021) provide various intra modes, which predicts pixels in a block through adjacent reference pixels. In color video, pixels with high spatial correlation have similar values, whereas the pixel values in depth video may increase or decrease gradually. Therefore, the existing intra modes may be less accurate for depth video.

Nenci et al. (2014) proposed a intra prediction method for depth video by splitting a depth value with a single channel to multiple channels to reduce the value range. Stankiewicz et al. (2013) transformed the pixel values in depth video through a nonlinear function. However, these methods do not consider the characteristics of depth video. Lee et al. (2021) proposes a intra mode for depth video by estimating plane surface through reference pixels. The plane surface are modelled through the reference pixels and pixels are reconstructed based on the plane surface. However, this method is hard to accurately predict the pixels on other surface type. Lee and Kwon (2022) predicts pixels in depth video by clustering based on spatial correlation of pixels. The spatial features for reference pixels are extracted through CNNs. Cluster areas for the pixels are predicted through the spatial features. The pixels in a cluster are predicted by the average of the reference pixels in the same cluster.

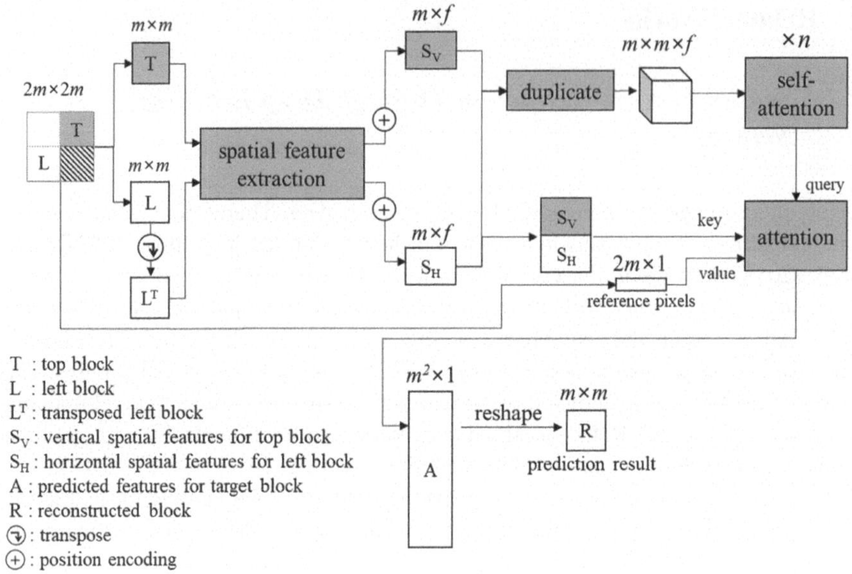

Fig. 1 Flow of the proposed method

3 Intra Prediction for Depth Video Coding Through CNN and Attention

3.1 Network Structure for Proposed Method

We propose a intra prediction method through CNN and attention mechanism. For a $m \times m$ target block, top and left adjacent square regions are utilized to obtain vertical and horizontal spatial features, respectively, through a CNN layer (Kim et al., 2024). Attention mechanism is applied to predict spatial correlations between the target block and the reference pixels. The pixels of the target block are predicted through the feature map for the spatial correlations. Figure 1 shows the flow of the proposed method.

3.2 Extracting Spatial Features Through CNN Layers

Left and top blocks with $m \times m$ sizes adjacent to the target block are designated as reference pixels. Spatial feature maps for the top and left blocks are extracted for predicting the f spatial features of the block. The vertical spatial feature map is obtained through a CNN layer with a size of $m \times 3$ and that is applying only horizontal padding. Figure 2a shows the structure of the CNN layer for extracting the spatial features. For the left block, the block is transposed before inputting to the CNN layer in order to extract the horizontal spatial features. It can reduce the number of the network weights. Figure 2b shows the spatial feature extractions for the top and left blocks.

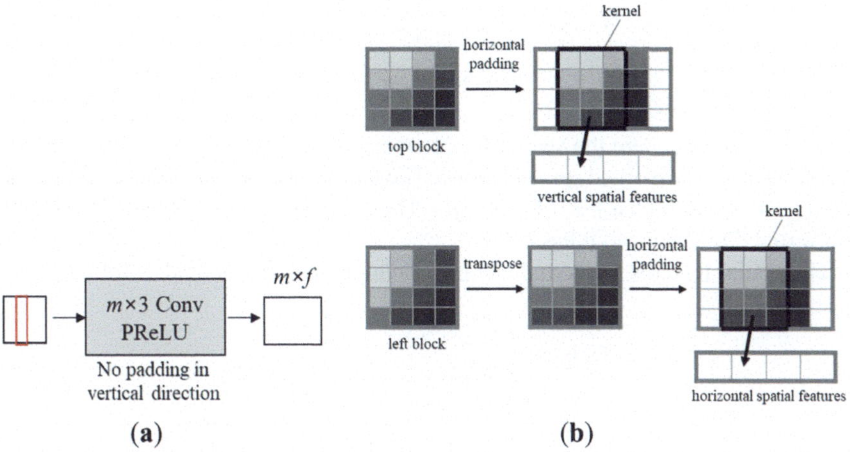

Fig. 2 Spatial feature extraction for reference pixels through CNN layer, **a** structure for spatial feature extraction and **b** spatial feature extractions for top and left blocks

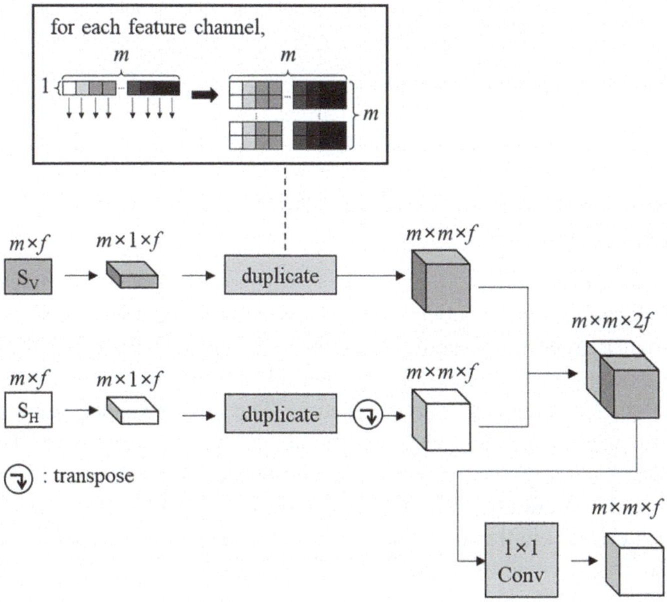

Fig. 3 Merging spatial feature maps of top and left blocks

Before predicting spatial correlations for the target block, the spatial feature maps for the reference pixels are merged as shown in Fig. 3. The spatial feature maps are duplicated at a vertical direction, so the sizes of the feature maps are $m \times m \times f$. Then, the two feature maps are merged in feature dimension as follows:

$$M(i, j, k) = \begin{cases} S_{vert}(j, k), & \text{if } k > f \\ S_{hori}(i, k), & \text{otherwise} \end{cases}$$
$$(0 \leq i, j < m, 0 \leq k < 2f), \tag{1}$$

where S_{vert} and S_{hori} are the spatial feature maps of the top and left blocks, respectively, and M is the merged spatial feature. The feature dimension of the merged map is reduced to f through a 1×1 CNN layer. Then, the feature are flatten in horizontal and vertial dimension, so it has $m^2 \times f$.

The spatial features for vertial and horizontal indices are merged as follows:

$$S_m(i, k) = \begin{cases} S_{vert}(i, k), & \text{if } i < m \\ S_{hori}(i - m, k), & \text{otherwise} \end{cases} \tag{2}$$
$$(0 \leq i < 2m, 0 \leq k < f).$$

The reference pixels adjacent to the block are merged as follows:

$$R(i, 1) = \begin{cases} B(i, -1), & \text{if } i \leq m \\ B(-1, i - m), & \text{if } i > m \end{cases} \tag{3}$$
$$(0 \leq i < 2m),$$

where $B(i, j)$ is a pixel value of the block.

3.3 Predicting Pixels by Finding Spatial Correlation Through Attention

Attention mechanism can selectively focus on various elements of input data, giving more importance to certain elements. Attention mechanism learns which the elements are more important for the input data. Attention has three input data, that are query, key, and value. The query is an input feature. The key and value are a pair of a feature corresponding to the query and the actual value, respectively. The corresponding values are weighted according to similarities between the query and key. Self-attention, that is attention with the same inputs, is utilized to predict correlations between each element in the input data itself. First, the input data for the query, key, and value are transformed by trainable tables as follows:

$$
\begin{aligned}
Q &= X_q \otimes W_q \\
K &= X_k \otimes W_k , \\
V &= X_v \otimes W_v
\end{aligned}
\tag{4}
$$

where X_q, X_k, and X_v are the query, key, and value, respectively, W_q, W_k, and W_v are the trainable tables for the query, key, and value, respectively, and $\otimes$ is a matrix product operator. The correlation between the query and key are found as follows:

$$
D = \mathrm{softmax}\left(\frac{Q \otimes K^{\mathrm{T}}}{\sqrt{f}}\right), \tag{5}
$$

where softmax(·) is a function to convert inputs into a probability distribution. The result of matrix product between Q and transposed K is divided into a square root of f in order to scale it for reducing the effect of the feature amount. Then, the weighted sums of the value are calculated through the probabilities as follows:

$$
FFNN(D \otimes V), \tag{6}
$$

where FFNN(·) is a feed-forward neural network which makes inputs to be non-linear as follows:

$$
\mathrm{FFNN}(X) = \alpha_2 \odot (\sigma(\alpha_1 \odot X + \beta_1)) + \beta_2 \tag{7}
$$

where $\alpha_1, \alpha_2, \beta_1, \beta_2$ are learnable matrices, $\odot$ is an element-wise product operator, and $\sigma(\cdot)$ is an activation function. We use a parametric rectified linear unit (PReLU) as the activation function. We define the series processes in (4)–(7) as $attn(X_Q, X_K, X_V)$.

For the target block, self-attention is applied n times to predict the correlation between pixels in the target block as follows:

$$
\begin{aligned}
A^t &= attn\left(A^{t-1}, A^{t-1}, A^{t-1}\right) \\
&\left(0 < t \le n, A^0 = M\right).
\end{aligned}
\tag{8}
$$

The multiple applications of the self-attention obtain both the global and local correlations of the input block. Therefore, it can process information from different scales and levels of abstraction. Then, the correlations between the reference pixels and the block are found as follows:

$$
Z = attn\left(A^n, S_m, R\right). \tag{9}
$$

The attention result Z is reshaped as $m \times m$ to output the intra predicted result for the block.

Fig. 4 Samples of frames for network training

3.4 Dataset and Network Training

The NYU Depth Dataset (Silberman et al., 2012) is used for training the proposed network. The dataset consists of 1,446 depth frames for different scenes. Figure 4 shows part of the data set. Each screen is divided into blocks of size 2 $m \times 2$ m. We trains the proposed network through approximately 151,000 blocks extracted from 1,157 frames, which is 80% of the whole frames, and the network verification is performed through approximately 51,000 blocks extracted from the remaining frames. Mean square error (MSE) is adopt as a loss function for the network training. A MSE between the predicted and label blocks is calculated as follows:

$$\frac{1}{m^2}\left(\sum_{i=0}^{m-1}\sum_{j=0}^{m-1}(Z(i,j)-B(i,j))^2\right). \quad (8)$$

4 Simulation Results

We measure MSEs for the validation set to measure the performance of the proposed method. The default m, f, and n are 16, 24, and 6, respectively. The number of a batch size, the number of epochs, and a learning rate are 128, 300, and 1×10^{-3}, respectively.

Figure 5 presents the comparison of the intra prediction results by the proposed method and the intra modes for VVC. Square areas with red border in the first row of Fig. 5 are the blocks to be predicted and other pixels are the reference pixels. The

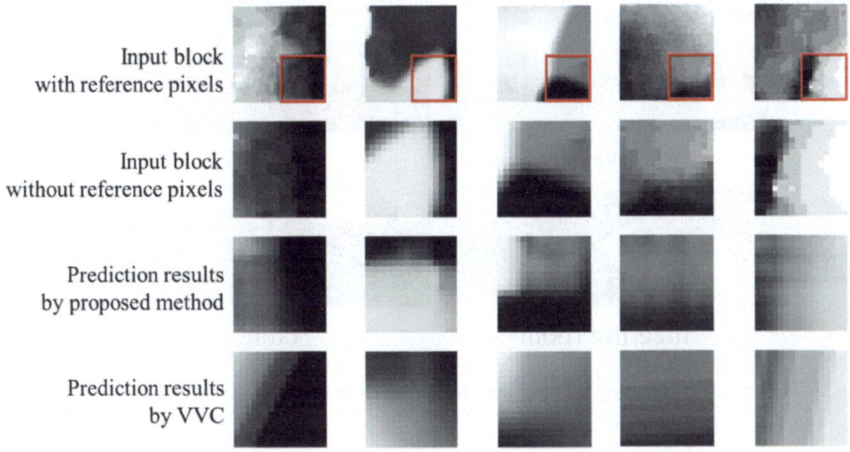

Fig. 5 Comparison of prediction results between the proposed method and VVC

Table 1 Prediction errors by number of features

f	8	16	24
MSE	203.11	198.37	205.12

proposed method predicts the blocks with curve boundaries better than the existing intra modes.

Table 1 shows intra prediction errors by the number of features f. The intra prediction errors are calculated as MSEs between the original and predicted blocks. The intra prediction are more accurate as the features increase. However, the accuracy are reduced if f is greater than 16. If the amount of the feature are too large, the network training become inefficient due to excessive network complexity.

We measure the intra prediction accuracies of the proposed network comparing with the intra modes in VVC. Four depth videos as shown in Fig. 6 are utilized for the comparisons. For each block, MSEs are calculated by selecting best methods among the VVC intra modes and the proposed method. Table 2 shows the comparisons of the intra prediction accuracies between the proposed method and the intra modes. The proposed network reduces the intra prediction errors up to 3.37%. This results show that the proposed method can improve the intra prediction method for the depth video coding.

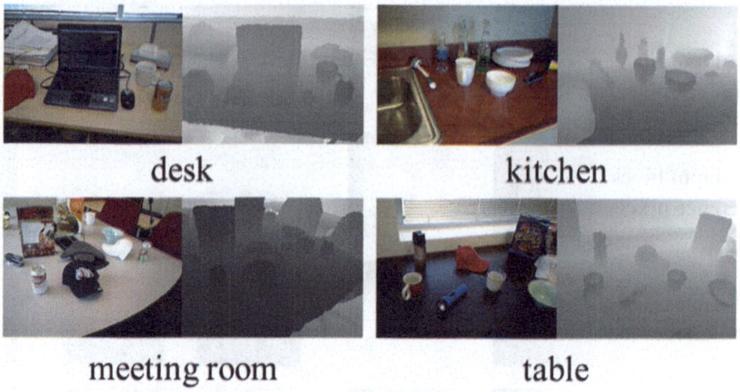

Fig. 6 Depth videos for comparison of intra prediction with VVC

Table 2 Comparison of intra prediction between VVC and the proposed method

Video	MSE		Improved rate (%)
	Intra modes of VVC	Proposed method	
Desk	198.82	194.34	2.25
Kitchen	131.33	126.91	3.37
Meeting room	194.53	190.71	1.96
Table	136.32	132.08	3.11

5 Conclusion

In this paper, we proposed the intra prediction method through CNN and attention mechanism. The spatial features were extracted from the pixels of the top and left adjacent blocks through the CNN. The spatial correlations between the target block and the reference pixels were predicted by attention mechanism. The pixels of the target block were predicted through the CNN layers. The proposed method can find optimal reference pixels for each pixel in the target block. In the future, we will evaluate the proposed network by comparing the intra prediction of the video coding standard such as HEVC and VVC. The proposed method can improve video compression and transmission efficiency by improving coding for high-resolution images. Therefore, it is expected that the proposed method can be applied to metaverse with VR/AR.

Acknowledgements This research was partly supported by Innovative Human Resource Development for Local Intellectualization program through the Institute of Information and Communications Technology Planning and Evaluation (IITP) grant funded by the Korea government (MSIT) (IITP-2024-RS-2020-II201791, 100%) and by the BB21plus funded by Busan Metropolitan City and Busan Techno Park.

References

Ascenso, J., Akyazi, P., Pereira, F., & Ebrahimi, T. (2020). Learning-based image coding: early solutions reviewing and subjective quality evaluation, *Proceedings of the SPIE Photonics Europe—Optics, Photonics and Digital Technologies for Imaging Applications VI*, Article 11353S. https://doi.org/10.1117/12.2555368

Bross, B., Wang, Y., Ye, Y., Liu, S., Chen, J., Sullivan, G. J., & Ohm, J. (2021). Overview of the versatile video coding (VVC) standard and its applications. *IEEE Transactions on Circuits and Systems for Video Technology*, 31(10), 3736–3764. https://doi.org/10.1109/TCSVT.2021.3101953

Hu, Y., Yang, W., Li, M. & Liu, J. (2019). Progressive spatial recurrent neural network for intra prediction. *IEEE Transactions on Multimedia*, 21(12), 3024–3037. https://doi.org/10.1109/TMM.2019.2920603

Hu, Y., Yang, W., Xia, S., & Liu, J. (2018). Optimized spatial recurrent network for intra prediction in video coding. *Proceedings of the Visual Communications and Image Processing*, 1–4. https://doi.org/10.1109/VCIP.2018.8698658

Kim, H. J., Lee, D. S., & Kwon, S. K. (2024). Image Reconstruction Method by Spatial Feature Prediction Using CNN and Attention, *Journal of Multimedia and Information Systems*, 11(1).

Lee, D. S., & Kwon, S. K. (2022). Intra prediction method for depth video coding by block clustering through deep learning, *Sensors*, 22(24), Article 9656. https://doi.org/10.3390/s22249656

Lee, D. S., Kim, B. G., & Kwon, S. K. (2021). Efficient depth data coding method based on plane modeling for intra prediction, *IEEE Access*, 9, 29153–29164. https://doi.org/10.1109/ACCESS.2021.3056687

Li, J., Li, B., Xu, J., Xiong, R., & Gao, W. (2018). Fully connected network-based intra prediction for image coding. *IEEE Transactions on Image Processing*, 27(7), 3236–3247. https://doi.org/10.1109/TIP.2018.2817044

Li, X., Lu, R., Wang, Q., Wang, J., Duan, X., Sun, Y., Li, X., & Zhou, Y. (2020). One-dimensional convolutional neural network (1D-CNN) image reconstruction for electrical impedance tomography. *Review of Scientific Instruments*, 91(12), Article 124704. https://doi.org/10.1063/5.0025881

Nenci, F., Spinello, L., & Stachniss, C. (2014). Effective compression of range data streams for remote robot operations using H.264, *Proceedings of the IEEE/RSJ International Conference on Intelligent Robots and Systems*, 3794–3799. https://doi.org/10.1109/IROS.2014.6943095.

Pascanu, R., Mikolov, T., & Bengio, Y. (2013). On the difficulty of training recurrent neural networks. *Proceedings of the International Conference on Machine Learning*, 28(3), 1310–1318.

Schiopu, I., & Munteanu, A. (2018). Residual-error prediction based on deep learning for lossless image compression. *Electronics Letters*, 54(17), 1032–1034. https://doi.org/10.1049/el.2018.0889

Schiopu, I., Huang, H., & Munteanu, A. (2020). CNN-based intra-prediction for lossless HEVC. *IEEE Transactions on Circuits and Systems for Video Technology*, 30(7), 1816–1828. https://doi.org/10.1109/TCSVT.2019.2940092

Schiopu, I., Liu, Y., & Munteanu, A. (2018). CNN-based prediction for lossless coding of photographic images. *Proceedings of the Picture Coding Symposium*, 16–20. https://doi.org/10.1109/PCS.2018.8456311

Stankiewicz, O., Wegner, K., & Domański, M. (2013). Nonlinear depth representation for 3D video coding, *Proceedings of the IEEE International Conference on Image Processing*, 1752–1756. https://doi.org/10.1109/ICIP.2013.6738361

Sullivan, G. J., Ohm, J. R., Han, W. J., & Wiegand, T. (2012). Overview of the high efficiency video coding (HEVC) standard. *IEEE Transactions on Circuits and Systems for Video Technology*, 22(12), 1649–1668.

Vaswani, A., Shazeer, N., Parmar, N., Uszkoreit, J., Jones, L., Gomez, A. N., Kaiser, Ł., & Polosukhin, I. (2017). Attention is all you need. *Proceedings of the Conference on Neural Information Processing Systems*, 5998–6008.

Presence Drivers: A Unified Approach to User Representation in Spatial Computing Applications

Yevhen Bondarenko, Vladimir Kuts, Simone Pizzagalli, and Tauno Otto

Abstract Spatial Computing (SC) is an emerging paradigm that interlaces virtual 3D environments with physical ones, promising advancements in communication, teleoperation, education, and training. Despite its potential, accessibility of SC experiences across platforms is still a challenge. Virtual environments can be experienced using a diverse array of hardware interfaces, from conventional screens and keyboards to immersive head-mounted displays (HMDs) and full-body tracking suits, and these varying input modalities necessitate extra development efforts to maintain seamless user interaction across different devices and platforms. This paper introduces a concept of "Presence Drivers" (PDs), which offers a unified user representation for SC applications, independent of specific input devices. PDs function as a direct connection layer between the user's body and the SC application, simplifying the development of adaptive, user-friendly spatial software. The article discusses the PD concept within the current technological landscape, outlines its architecture, and proposes a reference implementation using Unity engine.

Keywords Input · Presence · Spatial computing · XR · VR · AR

1 Introduction

Spatial Computing (SC) is becoming a standard term when referring to the functionality of 3D applications which blend the aspects of physical world and virtual environments (VEs). SC holds the potential to improve many fields, including, but not limited to, communication, teleoperation, education, and personnel training. However, accessibility and interactivity of SC applications remains the primary concern when it comes to the adoption of this new computing paradigm.

Modern technology offers an ever growing variety of hardware devices for interacting with VEs, ranging from conventional interfaces such as a computer screen, a

Y. Bondarenko (✉) · V. Kuts · S. Pizzagalli · T. Otto
Department of Mechanical and Industrial Engineering, Tallinn University of Technology (TalTech), Tallinn, Estonia
e-mail: yevhen.bondarenko@taltech.ee

T. Jung et al. (eds.), *XR and Metaverse*, Springer Proceedings in Business and Economics, https://doi.org/10.1007/978-3-031-77975-6_37

keyboard, and a mouse to more immersive solutions such as head-mounted displays (HMDs) with full-body tracking suits. No matter the technological complexity, these devices all serve the same purpose—they provide a way for the user to be "present" in and interact with the VE of an application. However, differences in input modalities dictated by hardware limitations result in extra effort required to develop VEs which can accept users of different input devices without compromising their interaction capabilities.

In this work, we aim to propose a software architecture which can provide a unified representation of the user to a SC application, without being tied to the specifics of the used hardware input device. We call the proposed approach and associated software packages "Presence Drivers" (PDs), which alludes to the concept of device drivers in conventional computing. PDs serve as a direct connection layer between the user's body and intent and the SC application, making it easier to develop software which adapts to the available user representation in the best available way.

This article details the concept of PDs in the context of current state of the art, provides the overview of PD architecture, as well as a reference implementation based on Unity engine, which will be made publicly available at the GitHub organisation page of TalTech IVAR Lab (https://github.com/TalTech-IVAR-Lab [June 6, 2024]).

2 State of the Art

In order to create a reliable representation of the user's body and intent for a SC application to work with, it is important to take into account the capabilities of the input devices used. To get an overview of available interaction and presence features which can be used in SC, let us investigate each of the overarching fields: Virtual Reality (VR), Augmented Reality (AR), and conventional interfaces. Such order lets us progress from technologies that provide the highest level of presence (VR/AR) to the most constrained option that is a conventional desktop computer display, and trace which input modalities are affected throughout this transition.

2.1 XR Input Devices

VR/AR (also known as eXtended Reality (XR)) devices have been historically rich in the number of input modalities they can support, as demonstrated by Thériault et al. (2004). Their modern iterations can estimate user's pose, gaze and facial expressions with relative ease. The most advanced contemporary VR setups provide full-body, face and eye tracking, ensuring the highest immersion for the user and the most accurate user representation for the application.

When it comes to general consumer-level XR devices, the ones providing the highest level of presence are 6-degrees-of-freedom (6-DoF) tracking rigs including a HMD and a pair of handheld controllers (or hand tracking). In such setups, it is still possible to achieve full-body tracking by approximating lower body pose through the use of inverse kinematics (IK), as demonstrated by Jiang et al. (2022). Higher-end consumer headsets also offer facial and eye tracking, which can be useful for attention estimation and social interactions in SC applications.

Although VR and AR originally refer to two distinct approaches of SC (interacting exclusively with virtual scenes vs. virtual elements overlaid onto the real world), modern hardware starts to blur the line between the two approaches and creating a continuous spectrum from AR to VR (as per Arena et al. (2022)). Most of the newer consumer VR headsets utilize inside-out tracking based on cameras and/or LiDARs (https://www.apple.com/newsroom/2023/06/introducing-apple-vision-pro [June 6, 2024]), which allows to get an estimation of the real environment surrounding the user, enabling AR functionality using pass-though rendering. There also exist HMDs focused exclusively on AR content (https://www.microsoft.com/en-us/hololens [June 6, 2024]), but those still provide at least hand tracking for interacting with the digital content.

When talking about AR, it is also important to mention handheld devices. While more limited than HMD-based XR rigs, handheld AR devices are holding a steady place in the industry thanks to their ease-of-use and lower associated costs. Most of the modern smartphones and tablets are capable of reliable external environment tracking though their respective platform's AR Software Development Kits (SDKs) (https://developers.google.com/ar [June 6, 2024], https://developer.apple.com/augmented-reality [June 6, 2024]), allowing to estimate the pose of the device relative to AR content. Certain devices also come with built-in face tracking capabilities (https://developer.apple.com/documentation/arkit/arkit_in_ios/content_anchors/tracking_and_visualizing_faces, [June 6, 2024]), mirroring the functionality found in some XR HMDs. Face tracking also opens the possibility to track user's head pose in AR environment, thus providing user's head representation to any SC applications running on such devices.

2.2 Conventional Input Devices

While XR devices are purpose-built for representing the user's body in VEs, traditional computer interfaces—such as a display with a keyboard and a mouse, or a touch screen—should not be left unaccounted for. Conventional input devices will likely stay dominant in the foreseeable future, and reign supreme now when it comes to affordability and user acceptance. Although not intrinsically equipped with spatial tracking functionality, these devices can be modified to support it without requiring extensive modification or cost investment. For instance, Cheung and Peng (2015) demonstrate how a desktop web camera can be used to track user's gaze and attention. Similarly, facial expressions and head pose can be estimated using camera as shown by Wouterse (2015). On certain mobile devices, face and eye tracking is available though the platform SDKs without requiring AR positioning functionality to be enabled in the application (https://developers.google.

com/ar [June 6, 2024], https://developer.apple.com/documentation/arkit/arkit_in_ios/content_anchors/tracking_and_visualizing_faces, [June 6, 2024]).

2.3 *Unifying User Representation*

Based on the overview above, we conclude that modern XR and conventional input devices provide enough input in order to construct a representation of the user that can be used in a SC application. Having a user body representation can lead to richer interactions and sense of presence in VEs, as demonstrated by Guan and Morris (2022) and Roupé et al. (2014) in their works on body interfaces for XR. We believe that this representation can be used as a unifying factor to develop applications which will allow people to join VEs no matter which device they have available, and still have rich and convenient ways of interacting with other people and objects in the said VE. In fact, several systems that could benefit from such approach are described in the literature. For instance, the studies of Gugenheimer et al. (2017) and Lyu et al. (2022) present systems with VEs which can accommodate both VR and desktop web interface users. The studies indicate increased user engagement and presence stemming from the ability to interact with users of different devices (desktop vs. HMD), showing potential in implementing such multi-user VEs. A study by Cho et al. (2023) presents a single VE implemented in Unity engine, which is accessible though the variety of devices, including a desktop computer, a smartphone, a full-body motion capture system, and a VR HMD rig. The authors specifically mention that due to their goal of supporting so many distinct input devices, development involved a lot of interactions with platform-specific SDKs, and would benefit greatly from a unified library to achieve similar functionality without diving into specifics of each hardware platform. We propose an architectural approach intended to bridge this gap.

3 Presence Drivers

We introduce the concept of Presence Drivers, which are low-level software components bridging hardware input devices with SC applications. The name choice stems from the idea of utilizing user's body as an input device: PDs provide the application with information about the user's pose and attention, while abstracting the physical hardware used to estimate this representation. We believe that such approach makes development of SC applications easier and further decouples the code from hardware, resulting in better support across different platforms with less development effort. PDs also hold the potential to improve the quality of SC applications, as their philosophy shifts developers' attention from the hardware input devices to the user themselves and the ways they interact with the application.

3.1 Architecture

Based on the devices described in the overview section of our work, we define three main hardware categories in the order of increasing tracking capabilities:

1. **Conventional**, which includes desktop and laptop computers using classic mouse-and-keyboard or controller interfaces, as well as touch screen interfaces of common mobile devices such as smartphones and tablets.
2. **Handheld AR**, which encompasses mobile devices capable of tracking their pose in the surrounding environment and visualizing AR content at interactive frame rates.
3. **XR Rig**, which includes HMD-based systems capable of environment and user body tracking and visualizing VR and/or AR content.

PD packages for each hardware category are going to track the features of the user to the extent allowed by the device's sensors, as illustrated in Fig. 1.

Each hardware category has its own PD package, which implements the logic required to translate the state of physical input devices into a virtual representation of a human user. In order to represent the user to the application in as detailed a manner as possible while keeping the architecture of the PD system modular, we also define 8 "tracking features" which can be available to the application based on the currently used hardware interface's capabilities (see Table 1 for detailed platform support info).

Let us explore each of the tracking features, explaining their functionality as well as possible use-cases in SC applications:

1. **Head tracking** provides a 6-degree-of-freedom (6-DoF) pose of the user's head in relation to a tracking origin. Can be utilized to visualize user's head and track their attention when eye tracking is not available.

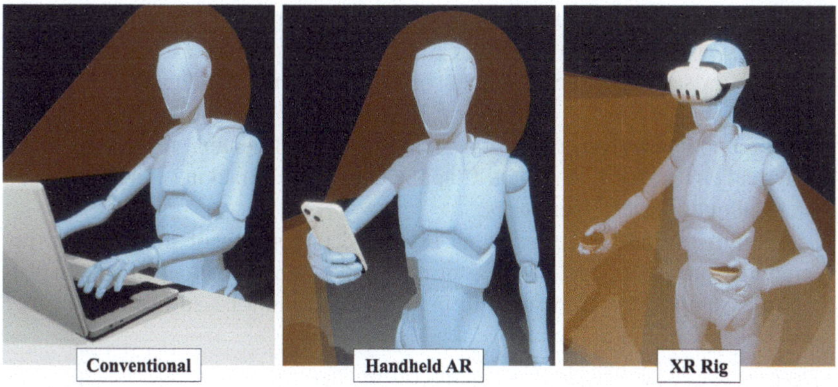

Fig. 1 Three hardware categories in the scope of PDs

Table 1 PD tracking feature support on each hardware platform. Features marked with "(✓)" are not supported out-of-the-box by all devices of the corresponding category, but can be implemented with additional hardware or software extensions

	Conventional	Handheld AR	XR Rig
Head	×	(✓)	✓
Face	(✓)	(✓)	(✓)
Eyes	(✓)	(✓)	(✓)
Hands	×	×	✓
Upper body	×	×	✓
Lower body	×	×	✓
Physical environment	×	✓	✓
Attention	✓	✓	✓

2. **Face tracking** provides an encoded representation of user's facial expression. Can be used to animate user avatar's face and make social SC experiences more engaging.
3. **Eye tracking** provides individual orientation data for each of the user's eyes, as well as combined gaze direction and focal point position. Can be used to track attention and manipulate gaze-based interfaces in VE.
4. **Hand tracking** provides 6-DoF poses of the user's wrists as well as poses and curl values of individual fingers. Can be used to drive virtual hand interactions and implement gesture-based interfaces in VEs.
5. **Upper body tracking** provides 6-DoF poses of user's arms and spine, sampled from hardware trackers or estimated using software IK implementation. Can be used to drive upper body of the virtual avatar without the need to implement a custom IK solution.
6. **Lower body tracking** provides 6-DoF poses of the user's pelvis and legs, sampled from hardware trackers or estimated using software IK implementation. Can be used to drive lower body of the virtual avatar without the need to implement a custom IK solution.
7. **Physical environment tracking** provides a 6-DoF pose of an anchor linked to the physical environment the device is in. Optionally, provides a point cloud or a mesh of the surrounding environment on devices where such data can be obtained (mainly on AR-capable devices and HMDs with inside-out tracking). Can be used for collision and occlusion-aware AR content placement, for sharing user's physical environment in social SC applications, or for tracking synchronization in local multiplayer experiences.
8. **Attention estimation** provides an estimated orientation of the attention ray coming from user's gaze, head, or virtual camera orientation (depending on platform capabilities). Can be used to implement attention-based features for user interfaces and studies.

Each PD package provides a standard API that allows to query whether the specific tracking feature is available at the moment, similar to the approach taken with "extensions" in OpenXR standard (https://registry.khronos.org/OpenXR/specs/1.0/html/xrspec.html#extensions, [June 6, 2024]). Based on this information, a SC application can adapt the user's avatar locomotion and interaction functionality to best match the current platform's capabilities. Harnessing the functionality of PDs, developers can write hardware-independent code that will help them implement SC applications usable for people on different hardware platforms with less development effort. With this, PDs fit into the Hardware Level Packages layer of the XR Framework introduced by Bondarenko et al. (2024).

3.2 *Implementation*

While PD approach is designed to be generic and applicable to any platform for SC application development, we provide a reference implementation of PDs based on Unity engine 1. The engine's license that allows to use it for free for education and research projects, as well as good community support makes it a good starting point for an open-source project such as our PD packages.

Three PD packages (one per each hardware platform) were implemented using the engine's features. Unity provides good support for XR devices with their libraries such as XR Plug-in Framework (https://docs.unity3d.com/2020.1/Documentation/Manual/XRPluginArchitecture.html, [June 6, 2024]) and AR Foundation (https://docs.unity3d.com/Manual/com.unity.xr.arfoundation.html, [June 6, 2024]), which served as a kick-start for implementing Handheld AR and XR Rig PDs. Conventional PD could be implemented using built-in engine functionality, given that it has the least number of tracking features among the platforms. PD for each platform is to be distributed as a package through Unity Package Manager, allowing developers to install it in their project only if they intend to support the specific device type (e.g. Conventional).

The reference implementation repository and packages will be made publicly available at the GitHub organisation page of TalTech IVAR Lab (https://github.com/TalTech-IVAR-Lab [June 6, 2024]).

4 Conclusions

In this work, we introduced the concept of Presence Drivers—software packages which allow to abstract the details of hardware input devices and instead provide a SC application with the direct representation of user's body and attention patterns to be used as inputs. Such approach holds the potential of decreasing the effort required to build asymmetric multi-user VEs, as well as leading to the production of better SC content by allowing developers to focus on the human behind the physical input devices.

Future work includes the development of demo use-case applications which can leverage the benefits provided by PDs, solidifying the definition of PD standard, and its potential expansion to platforms other than Unity engine used for the reference implementation.

References

Arena, F., Collotta, M., Pau, G., & Termine, F. (2022). An overview of augmented reality. *Computers*, *11*(2), 28.

Bondarenko, Y., Kuts, V., Pizzagalli, S., Nutonen, K., Murray, N., & O'Connell, E. (2024). Universal XR framework architecture based on open-source XR tools. In: *Proceedings of the 8th International XR-Metaverse Conference 2023*, Las Vegas, USA (pp. 87–98). Cham: Springer Nature Switzerland.

Cheung, Y., & Peng, Q. (2015). Eye gaze tracking with a web camera in a desktop environment. *IEEE Transactions on Human-machine Systems*, *45*(4), 419–430.

Cho, Y., Park, M., & Kim, J. (2023). XAVE: Cross-Platform based Asymmetric Virtual Environment for immersive content. *IEEE Access*, *11*, 71890–71904.

Guan, J., & Morris, A. (2022). Extended-XRI Body Interfaces for Hyper-Connected Metaverse Environments. *2022 IEEE Games, Entertainment, Media Conference (GEM).*

Gugenheimer, J., Stemasov, E., Frommel, J., & Rukzio, E. (2017). ShareVR. *Proceedings of the 2017 CHI Conference on Human Factors in Computing Systems.*

Jiang, J., Streli, P., Qiu, H., Fender, A., Laich, L., Snape, P., & Holz, C. (2022). AvatarPoser: Articulated Full-Body Pose Tracking from Sparse Motion Sensing. *arXiv (Cornell University).*

Lyu, H., Vachha, C., Chen, Q., Pyrinis, O., Liou, A., Kumaravel, B. T., & Hartmann, B. (2022). WebTransceiVR. *CHI Conference on Human Factors in Computing Systems Extended Abstracts.*

Roupé, M., Bosch-Sijtsema, P., & Johansson, M. (2014). Interactive navigation interface for Virtual Reality using the human body. *Computers, Environment and Urban Systems*, *43*, 42–50.

Thériault, L., Robert, J. M., Baron, L. (2004). Virtual Reality Interfaces for Virtual Environments. *Virtual Reality International Conference.*

Wouterse, P. (2015). Using Facial Feature Recognition and Head Tracking to Control Games. *Utrecht University.*

Dynamic and Autonomous Curbside Management—Design Research in Virtual Reality for Future Adaptive Street Spaces

Markus Holzmair

Abstract The concept of Dynamic and Autonomous Curbside Management represents a significant departure from traditional approaches, integrating autonomous technologies into adaptive urban street spaces. In contrast to the static nature of conventional urban environments, this approach considers how an intelligent street space, comprising autonomous modules, can adapt to meet the evolving needs of stakeholders in real-time. Digital twins in virtual reality are crucial for expediting the evaluation of multiple design prototypes, offering real-time insights into the practicality of proof-of-concepts. The testing of scenarios in virtual reality allows for the instant analysis of eye-tracking data and task completion, providing immediate insights into the acceptability of dynamically moving platforms and objects in the intelligent and adapting street of the future.

Keywords Curbside management · Autonomous · Dynamic · Modular · Virtual reality · Eye tracking · User acceptability · Adaptive architecture

1 Introduction

In the context of the traffic and mobility transition, there is an increasing focus on autonomous vehicles as a potential revolution in urban mobility. This development presents new challenges for city and mobility planners, as public space is limited, and motorized individual transport remains a central issue in the complex challenges of climate, environment, and spatial justice. This research aims to re-utilize technology for autonomous mobility to improve the urban space for all stakeholders and address existing issues in urban environments.

Rather than developing new, futuristic cities and their infrastructure, this approach examines methods for enhancing the streetscape within naturally grown cities with

M. Holzmair (✉)
Institute of Transport and Regional Planning, University of the Bundeswehr Munich, Neubiberg, Germany
e-mail: markus.holzmair@unibw.de

T. Jung et al. (eds.), *XR and Metaverse*, Springer Proceedings in Business and Economics, https://doi.org/10.1007/978-3-031-77975-6_38

Fig. 1 Exemplary adaptive street space design with the autonomous arrangement of modules featuring vegetation, seating areas, and separations for bike lanes (Own representation, 2024)

their space constraints. Through dynamic curbside management, this research aims to enhance the existing urban street design, improve microclimates, reduce noise pollution and hazard zones, and a balanced distribution of the limited road space for all stakeholders.

Virtual reality design research plays a pivotal role in determining sustainable, dynamic, and future-proof urban street space development through design recommendations and planning optimization. The objective of this study is to analyse participants' navigation and safety perception during interaction with autonomous modules in the virtual street space (Fig. 1).

Ultimately, the objective is to develop a prototype and proof-of-concept, which in turn will contribute to creating a design guideline for designers and urban and mobility planners in subsequent phases.

2 Related Work and Research Gap

2.1 Curbside Management

The Smart and digital curbside management concepts (Fogelson, 2021) can be part of integrated mobility planning, and early models show how cities can make limited street space more flexible and dynamic to meet the needs of different stakeholders (Jaller et al., 2020).

Earlier concepts, such as the Flexible Curb Management: Optimizing the Public Curbside model (Flexible Curb Management: Optimizing the Public Curbside, 2023), which is already being implemented in pilot projects, already suggest ways to digitally map space for delivery services or parking spaces for restaurants, thus dynamically reserving space for different stakeholders. However, this flexible concept is largely based on a static infrastructure and does not allow for real-time adaptive adjustment of the entire street space.

2.2 Dynamic Traffic Management and Road Space Allocation Traffic

The "Roadzipper" system is deployed on major roads to dynamically control traffic flow by swiftly adjusting concrete barriers. This opens the middle lane during peak hours, maximizing road capacity in a specific direction (ROAD ZIPPER™, 2017). While not suitable for urban areas, this system inspired prototype modules for our dynamic curbside management concept.

As shown in Fig. 2, a commonly used method for dynamically managing traffic on roads is to alter the direction assigned to the center lanes using overhead signals. However, this approach is only applicable to travel lanes for motorized traffic.

Sidewalk Labs, based in Toronto, has developed a universal concept that uses smart pavement modules with integrated LEDs to dynamically allocate street space for various stakeholders (Aouf, 2018). However, there are limitations to this concept, including its focus on space allocation instead of physical transformations, as well as concerns about economic feasibility and vulnerability to adverse weather events.

Fig. 2 Adaptive travel lane-management with overhead LED signals on the Lions Gate Bridge in Vancouver, Canada (Own photo, taken in 2023)

2.3 Research Gap

Based on current literature and technological advancements, the following research questions remain unanswered:

- How can the entire street space be dynamically adapted in real-time?
- What design principles should be employed for modules to autonomously rearrange in flowing traffic, creating dynamic spaces for pedestrians, cyclists, and various stakeholders such as restaurants or businesses with loading zones?
- How should a module be configured to ensure safe interaction with motorized individual traffic, pedestrians, and cyclists?
- How can the transformation of street space and the rearrangement of modules be conceptualized and sequenced during active pedestrian and cycling activities and is the wayfinding clear and understandable during the transformation phase?

This research contributes significantly to the future design of urban street space, meeting the demands of an evolving mobility landscape.

3 Methodology

3.1 Methodology for Data Collection and Evaluation: Prototype Design Research and VR Test Plan

Insights into the usability, proof-of-concept, and user acceptability of prototype variants will be obtained through eye-tracking and sensor position data. The data will be analyzed in real-time by specialized software (Adhanom et al., 2023) (Fig. 3).

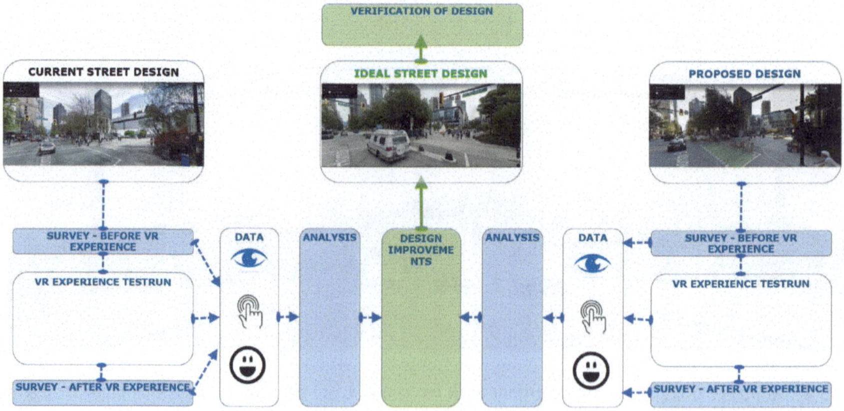

Fig. 3 Test plan for planning optimization through experiments in VR (Own representation, 2023)

This approach allows for immediate conclusions and findings for further optimization processes related to module design and spatial considerations (Clay et al., 2019), including:

- Dynamic and adaptive routing for motorized traffic, cycling, and pedestrians
- Improvements of Urban Spaces
- User Interaction with autonomous modules/robots
- Dynamic allocation of street space
- Intersection configurations and design
- Seating options/restaurant/café/bus stops
- Loading zones, stopping areas, commercial traffic, etc.
- Accessibility.

3.2 Digital Twin for VR-Scenarios

The objective of the research is to evaluate and test the applicability of planning and constructing a virtual street space for various urban environments. The study will be conducted in an exemplary urban settlement in West Vancouver and the Haidhausen district in Munich. Both digital twins be created using SketchUp and Archicad from self-generated images, measurements, and reference plans provided by the respective city authorities. Subsequently, these models will be imported into Unreal Engine 5.3 to create lifelike 3D representations.

4 Findings and Interpretation

4.1 Design Research—Development and Evaluation of a Prototype for Adaptive and Dynamic Curbside Management

The limitations of conventional static approaches for managing urban spaces and infrastructure have become evident during the initial design phase. Therefore, the exploration of dynamic and autonomous street management aims to integrate transformative urban architecture into existing streetscapes, enabling flexible and intelligent adjustments to public spaces and the urban fabric. This concept proposes the idea of streets reorganizing themselves in real-time through autonomous moving modules. This departure from fixed allocations caters to the dynamic mobility needs of various stakeholders and aims to improve the quality of life in the urban realm.

As shown in Fig. 4, during peak hours, additional lanes for motorized traffic can be allocated, while off-peak periods offer opportunities for shading, restaurant seating, bike lanes, or parking. These autonomous, standardized modules can be customized for individual stakeholders, accommodating various purposes such

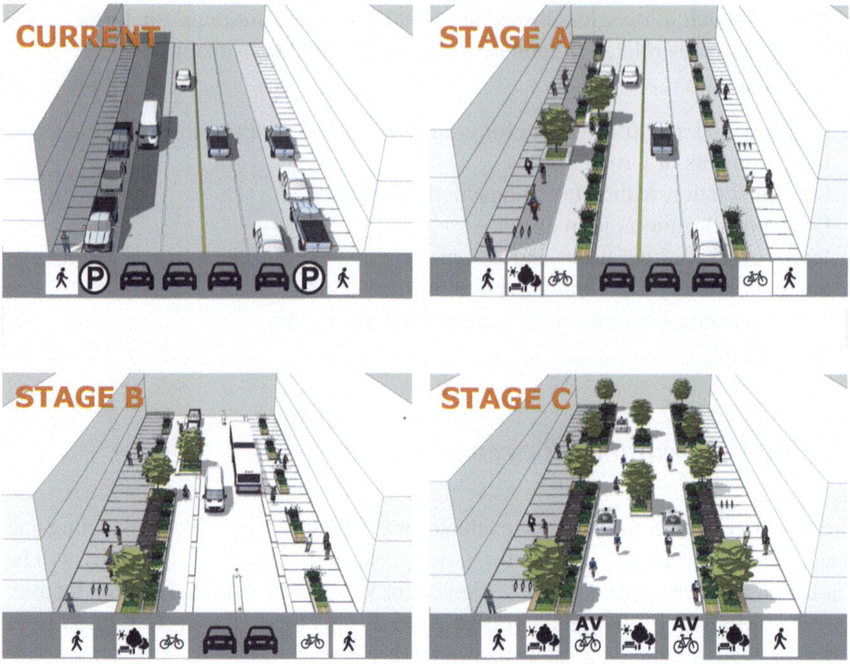

Fig. 4 Dynamic configuration variants of the street space using the example of Marine Drive in West Vancouver, Canada (Own representation, 2024)

as restaurant seating, shading, mobility stations, and movable trees, facilitating a dynamic reconfiguration of street space.

4.2 Evaluating Transformation Sequences in Virtual Reality for a Safe and User-Friendly Operation of an Adaptive Street-Space

For the successful implementation of an adaptive and autonomous rearrangement of street space in flowing traffic, it is crucial to sequence the space-dividing modules precisely. All stakeholders and road users should be involved, and potential conflicts must be minimized in advance.

The restructuring of space, alterations in route guidance, and areas that need to be cleared should be unequivocally evident to all road users, even those without prior knowledge. All movable elements and modules must adhere to accessibility requirements. Signaling techniques should be used to clearly indicate their direction of movement and intention.

It is essential to differentiate whether space-dividing modules actively move autonomously or if they are passively moved by tow-robots.

Nevertheless, it is reasonable to expect, that due to their existing education and experience, vehicle operators will require less time to adapt and navigate these scenarios. It can be reasonably assumed that vehicle operators are more accustomed to dealing with varying traffic conditions and dynamic changes in the road environment.

Consequently, this study focuses primarily on pedestrians and cyclists, operating on the premise that these users typically have no prior knowledge or experience with an adaptive environment that is changing its configuration while it is being used. In contrast to vehicle operators, pedestrians and cyclists often traverse public spaces in a non-linear manner.

The same principle can be applied to the design of virtual reality experiences and scenarios for the participants involved in this study. The preliminary VR test runs indicated that participants should not require prior knowledge or guidance to navigate the virtual environment in order to obtain replicable and comparable data and results.

This approach enhances immersion by eliminating the need for controllers or interfaces and allows participants to make spontaneous decisions that are not influenced by predetermined input choices.

4.3 *Wayfinding and Level of Comfort in Active Adaptive Street Spaces*

To assess the feasibility of integrating adaptive street spaces into existing urban environments and gauge user acceptance, it is imperative to analyze wayfinding strategies and evaluate perceived comfort and trust in the system. Understanding the optimal speeds and configurations of space-dividing modules for clear user comprehension is crucial for developing effective test scenarios. Users must be able to accurately interpret the intended function, direction, and potential consequences of each module—whether to stop, navigate around it, or proceed with caution. Trust in the system's safety is paramount. Multiple VR scenarios are necessary to test these adaptations under controlled conditions (Fig. 5).

4.4 *Universal Autonomous Robots*

A significant challenge in the implementation of adaptive street spaces is the method of module movement. The preliminary virtual reality (VR) testing and prototype development phases revealed that autonomous modules are not a viable solution. The substantial technological burden, including the necessity for advanced battery technology, maintenance infrastructure, and complex control systems, renders this

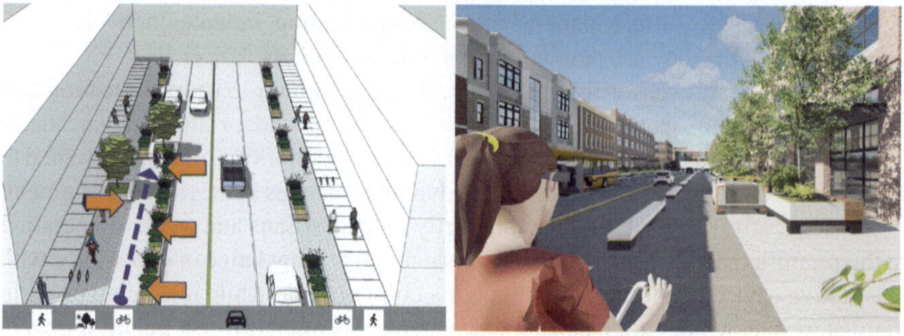

Fig. 5 Wayfinding analysis concept and replication of a VR-users perspective within the virtual scenario (Own representation, 2024)

approach impractical and prohibitively expensive, particularly in light of the large number of modules that would be required for effective adaptive street management.

A more pragmatic solution is presented in the form of a universal robot, as depicted in Fig. 6, which is conceptually similar to industrial autonomous forklifts found in industrial depots. This approach markedly diminishes the financial burden by obviating the necessity for autonomous technology within each module.

The use of standardized pallets allows for a reduction in the complexity of the module design, thereby increasing the overall design freedom. Moreover, the robot's existing capabilities in navigating complex environments and interacting with humans, as developed in industrial settings, can be directly applied to the urban context. To ensure seamless integration and optimal performance, the robot must possess advanced communication capabilities, enabling clear and effective interaction with all road users.

Its functionalities should extend beyond module manipulation to include obstacle removal and potential vehicle relocation. Crucially, the robot's design must harmonize with the urban aesthetic while unmistakably signaling its active role in traffic

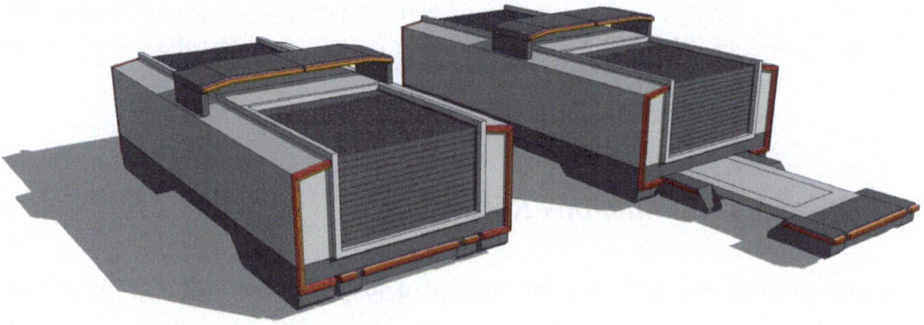

Fig. 6 Design evolution of a universal autonomous robot (UAR) for adaptive street-spaces (Own representation, 2024)

Fig. 7 Examples of modular street furniture and dividers (Own representation, 2024)

management. Furthermore, the design must allow for modularity and standardization of space-dividing modules (Fig. 7).

4.5 Incentives for Municipalities

Similar to flexible curbside management, our system offers cities the opportunity to benefit from a space leasing model and offer space for restaurants or delivery services outside peak hours, for example. With this business model, the financial hurdle for implementing such a system could be lowered considerably. This model is also to become part of the research work in order to be able to prove realistic feasibility for municipalities.

4.6 Virtual Reality for Design Research—Quantitative, Descriptive and Qualitative Analysis

VR headsets generate a substantial volume of data, yet this research prioritizes eye tracking, gaze tracking, and spatial tracking for analysis, as these metrics are most relevant to the intended use case and design research objectives. To facilitate real-time data analysis and dynamic scenario adjustments based on emerging data, the study leveraged data directly from the Unreal Engine 5.3 game engine and its integrated Cognitive 3D plugin (Figs. 8 and 9).

Descriptive Analysis

The VR headset's integrated eye-tracking sensors can be used to precisely determine how a test subject perceives the movements of an autonomous module and to what extent they recognize the specified route. The data obtained is visualized both directly in the engine and in the VR environment using a 3D heat map. However, to gain more in-depth insights into acceptance and feasibility, it has been found that eye tracking

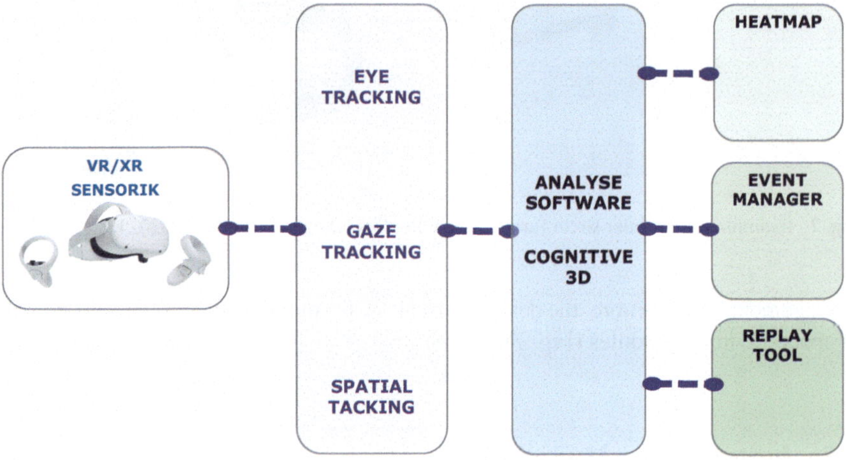

Fig. 8 Data selection for VR analysis (Own representation, 2023)

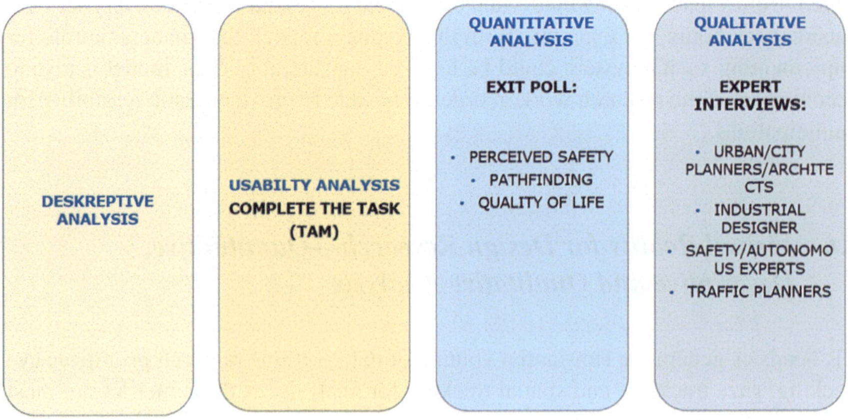

Fig. 9 VR-analysis concept (Own representation, 2024)

data can only provide a meaningful descriptive analysis when used in conjunction with a 'complete the task' analysis.

Usability Analysis

This process is facilitated through an event manager within the eye-tracking analysis software Cognitive 3D. Since this plugin is directly integrated within Unreal Engine 5.3, it allows to track and record all necessary data in the actual 3D space. Therefore, it is possible to evaluate a variety of user interactions in real time, including whether the user has traversed the intended distance within the specified time frame and has accurately recognized and responded to the robot's signals. This comprehensive and methodical evaluation offers invaluable insights into the test subject's behavior, thereby enhancing our understanding of their level of acceptance and engagement with the virtual environment.

Moreover, this functionality is essential for conducting a comprehensive analysis of wayfinding. The event manager determines whether the user has correctly comprehended the intended navigational path. In instances where the path was not understood, the manager analyzes the user's navigation of the transforming space. This detailed analysis allows for the identification and implementation of necessary modifications to the design and process, with the ultimate goal of reducing user conflicts and uncertainties while improving the overall user experience and system efficiency.

Quantitative Analysis

An exit poll, which is conducted immediately after the VR test runs, enables qualitative data to be collected quickly using a questionnaire. This questionnaire relates to the evaluation of the quality of the experience, the user's perception of safety and their personal assessment of the successful completion of the tasks set.

Furthermore, this information serves as an indicator of user comfort and offers valuable insights into whether the transition and adaptive space have undergone improvements in comparison to the current conditions. As the overarching goal of this study is to enhance the environment for all stakeholders, it is essential to evaluate how well the prototype meets this objective.

Consequently, design decisions made during the development of the prototype can be subjected to critical assessment and refinement based on the feedback and perceptions of participants. This evaluation process ensures that the prototype effectively addresses user needs and contributes to the overall improvement of the adaptive space.

Quantitative Analysis

In order to achieve this objective, a series of interviews will be conducted with experts in the fields of autonomous mobility, urban planning and architecture, and curbside management. These specialists have considerable expertise and diverse perspectives, which are vital for evaluating the efficacy and impact of the proposed system.

By integrating both quantitative and qualitative analytical techniques, the objective is to conduct a comprehensive assessment of the user experience. Quantitative methods will furnish empirical data on user interactions, behaviors, and performance metrics, whereas qualitative methods will offer insights into user perceptions, preferences, and overall satisfaction.

This integrated approach allows for a nuanced evaluation of the virtual reality (VR) application, ensuring that both measurable outcomes and subjective experiences are taken into account.

5 Conclusion and Next Steps

In summary, this research aims to establish design guidelines for cities to enhance the quality of life in urban streetscapes through the implementation of a dynamic curbside management concept. The intention is to optimize urban space usage efficiently by strategically leveraging autonomous technology. Virtual reality (VR) is pivotal in conducting this research in a holistic manner, enabling us to anticipate swift results. Achieving a comprehensive understanding of the proposed transformations and their impact on user experience would be challenging without VR.

Further research is required to explore several critical aspects of this system's implementation. First, it is essential to investigate how the system can ensure access for all stakeholders, including users with disabilities. Additionally, the impact of this system on emergency medical services (EMS) and its adaptability to hilly and variable weather environments need to be thoroughly examined. Understanding how temporary systems influence transportation policy and user choices is also crucial, as is assessing their overall effect on traffic patterns.

Furthermore, the impact on microclimates requires further investigation, particularly with regard to the development of temporary shading solutions to combat extreme heat conditions. Furthermore, research should address policy considerations regarding the movement of autonomous vehicles and robots within public spaces, particularly in the event of unforeseen circumstances such as accidents or malfunctions.

Acknowledgements The completion of this research paper would not have been possible without the support and guidance of Prof. Jacoby (University of the Bundeswehr in Munich) and Prof. Sebastian Stadler (Regensburg University of Applied Sciences).

Their dedication and enthusiasm for this research were pivotal in the initiation of this study and research project. Their expertise, particularly in the fields of spatial planning, current mobility challenges, and design research with virtual reality, was invaluable. Their encouragement and insightful feedback played a crucial role in successfully advancing this endeavor.

References

Adhanom, I. B., MacNeilage, P. & Folmer, E. (2023). Eye Tracking in Virtual Reality: a Broad Review of Applications and Challenges. Virtual Reality, 27(2), 1481–1505. https://doi.org/10.1007/s10055-022-00738-z

Aouf, R. S. (20. Juli 2018). Carlo Ratti and Sidewalk Labs collaborate to build reconfigurable Dynamic Street. Dezeen.

Clay, V., König, P. & König, S. (2019). Eye Tracking in Virtual Reality. Journal of eye movement research, 12(1). https://doi.org/10.16910/jemr.12.1.3

Flexible Curb Management: Optimizing the Public Curbside. (2023, 14. Dezember). https://www.curbiq.io/blog/flexible-curb-management-optimizing-the-public-curbside

Fogelson, Y. (2021). Transitioning into new mobility: future curb space design [University of British Columbia]. open.library.ubc.ca. https://open.library.ubc.ca/soa/cIRcle/collections/ubctheses/24/items/1.0396952

Miguel Jaller, Caroline Rodier, Michael Zhang, and Huachao Lin. (2020). Fighting for Curb Space: Parking, Ride-Hailing, Urban Freight Deliveries, and Other Users. https://doi.org/10.7922/G22N50JJ

ROAD ZIPPER^{TM}. (2017). https://doi.org/10.5703/1288284316363

The manufacturer's authorised representative in the EU is Springer Nature Customer Service Centre GmbH, Europaplatz 3, 69115 Heidelberg, Germany. If you have any concerns regarding our products, please contact ProductSafety@springernature.com

Printed and bound by CPI Group (UK) Ltd, Croydon, CR0 4YY
01/10/2026
02225956-0016